D1452901

ASIAN/OCEANIAN HISTORICAL DICTIONARIES
Edited by Jon Woronoff

Asia

1. *Vietnam*, by William J. Duiker. 1989. *Out of print. See No. 27.*
2. *Bangladesh*, 2nd ed., by Craig Baxter and Syedur Rahman. 1996
3. *Pakistan*, by Shahid Javed Burki. 1991
4. *Jordan*, by Peter Gubser. 1991
5. *Afghanistan*, by Ludwig W. Adamec. 1991
6. *Laos*, by Martin Stuart-Fox and Mary Kooyman. 1992
7. *Singapore*, by K. Mulliner and Lian The-Mulliner. 1991
8. *Israel*, by Bernard Reich. 1992
9. *Indonesia*, by Robert Cribb. 1992
10. *Hong Kong and Macau*, by Elfed Vaughan Roberts, Sum Ngai Ling, and Peter Bradshaw. 1992
11. *Korea*, by Andrew C. Nahm. 1993
12. *Taiwan*, by John F. Copper. 1993. *Out of print. See No. 34.*
13. *Malaysia*, by Amarjit Kaur. 1993. *Out of print. See No. 36.*
14. *Saudi Arabia*, by J. E. Peterson. 1993
15. *Myanmar*, by Jan Becka. 1995
16. *Iran*, by John H. Lorentz. 1995
17. *Yemen*, by Robert D. Burrowes. 1995
18. *Thailand*, by May Kyi Win and Harold Smith. 1995
19. *Mongolia*, by Alan J. K. Sanders. 1996. *Out of Print. See No. 41.*
20. *India*, by Surjit Mansingh. 1996
21. *Gulf Arab States*, by Malcolm C. Peck. 1996
22. *Syria*, by David Commins. 1996
23. *Palestine*, by Nafez Y. Nazzal and Laila A. Nazzal. 1997
24. *Philippines*, by Artemio R. Guillermo and May Kyi Win. 1997

Oceania

1. *Australia*, by James C. Docherty. 1992
2. *Polynesia*, by Robert D. Craig. 1993. *Out of print. See No. 39.*
3. *Guam and Micronesia*, by William Wuerch and Dirk Ballendorf. 1994
4. *Papua New Guinea*, by Ann Turner. 1994
5. *New Zealand*, by Keith Jackson and Alan McRobie. 1996

New Combined Series

25. *Brunei Darussalam*, by D. S. Ranjit Singh and Jatswan S. Sidhu. 1997
26. *Sri Lanka*, by S. W. R. de A. Samarasinghe and Vidyamali Samarasinghe. 1998
27. *Vietnam*, 2nd ed., by William J. Duiker. 1998
28. *People's Republic of China: 1949–1997*, by Lawrence R. Sullivan, with the assistance of Nancy Hearst. 1998

Historical Dictionary of Armenia

Rouben Paul Adalian

Asian/Oceanian Historical
Dictionaries, No. 41

The Scarecrow Press, Inc.
Lanham, Maryland, and Oxford
2002

SCARECROW PRESS, INC.

Published in the United States of America
by Scarecrow Press, Inc.
A Member of the Rowman & Littlefield Publishing Group
4720 Boston Way
Lanham, Maryland 20706
www.scarecrowpress.com

PO Box 317
Oxford
OX2 9RU, UK

British Library Cataloguing in Publication Information Available

Library of Congress Cataloging-in-Publication Data

Adalian, Rouben Paul.
    Historical dictionary of Armenia / Rouben Paul Adalian.
        p. cm. — (Asian/Oceanian historical dictionaries ; no. 41)
    ISBN 0-8108-4337-4 (alk. paper)
        1. Armenia—History—Dictionaries. 2. Armenians—History—Dictionaries. 3.
Armenian literature—Dictionaries. I. Title. II. Series.

DS173 .A33 2002
956.6'2003—dc21   2002075844

For
Dvin, Diran
Talar, Haig, Alexandre
Andrew, Alexa,
Matheus and Benyamin

and
To him who recited from the poets

Contents

Editor's Foreword

Eastern Europe has many "new" states that have been reborn with the breakup of the Soviet Union, Yugoslavia, and Czechoslovakia. But none has been reborn quite as often as Armenia, which existed in previous times in various forms until conquered or dominated by the Persians, Romans, Arabs, Mongols, and more recently, the Ottoman Turks and Russians. Not only has it periodically disappeared from the map, when it was reconstituted, it was not always located in the same places. Nor did it include many Armenians who lived first in neighboring countries, and then an increasingly wide diaspora. Present-day Armenia occupies what was formerly the Armenian Soviet Socialist Republic, but also an area long inhabited by Armenians, Nagorno Karabagh, in a loose union that is contested by neighboring Azerbaijan. Today there are still more Armenians living outside of this new formation than within. This is only one of its problems, which proliferate in the political, economic, and social fields.

Nonetheless, Armenia exists again, and this is no small feat. That makes the publication of the *Historical Dictionary of Armenia* particularly welcome, to Armenians in Armenia, to those in the diaspora, and to anyone interested in this amazing and occasionally inspiring state and its many predecessors. As usual, the book includes a large dictionary section, with relatively long entries on crucial persons, places, events, and institutions from earlier times until the present. The smaller sections are no less important, whether the list of acronyms, without which it is hard to decipher much of the literature, or the introduction, which brings together aspects of the country as neatly as possible, or the bibliography, which points toward many other precious sources of information. Perhaps the most useful section, and one where readers might start, is a comprehensive and fairly detailed chronology, which helps us follow the countless twists and turns, the disappearances and reappearances, the successes and failures of yesterday and today.

The author is Rouben Paul Adalian, most of whose career has been focused on Armenia. He has taught the history and politics of Armenia and the Caucasus, first at several universities in California and more recently at George Washington University, Georgetown University, and Johns Hopkins University. He has come much nearer than most to today's Armenia through the Armenian Assembly of America, where he has been director of academic affairs since 1987 and director of the Office of Research and Analysis since 1992. Since 1997 he has been serving as director of the Armenian National Institute in Washington, D.C. These activities include, among many other things, contact with Armenian decision makers visiting the United States, support of American scholars studying Armenia, and the creation of several periodicals on Armenia. To this must be added publications by Dr. Adalian himself, some of them books, and also a steady stream of articles and chapters, and finally, periodic trips to Armenia. Only such close and continuous relations could provide this wealth of knowledge, not only of ancient Armenia, but the even more confusing situation of Armenia at present.

Jon Woronoff
Series Editor

Preface

There was no antecedent model to rely upon and learn from in order to prepare this one volume historical dictionary of Armenia. Virtually all reference works on Armenia are multivolume productions. As a point of comparison, the Armenian encyclopedia consists of 13 volumes. The concise version will be four volumes when complete. Whether in its short or long editions, each volume in the series runs an average of 750 pages in small type. How to compress so much history into a single volume remained the standing challenge from the start to the finish of this project. Various strategies were adopted, all of which will be self-evident to the reader. These strived to capture the Armenian historical experience through representational subjects, figures, events, and places. The dictionary covers the entire span of Armenian history, but does so with the broadest brush strokes for the earlier periods. The 19th and the 20th centuries are covered in more detail, and the recent period is addressed with even closer scrutiny. As a consequence, entries that would be regarded as standard requirements to elucidate ancient or medieval history were sacrificed. Attempts to fill those lacunae would have required a lengthier dedication of time to this book, which took longer to complete than anticipated, not all for reasons that had to do with the project.

Geographical names in historic Armenia are given in their original Armenian: Artashat, Tigranakert, Vagharshapat. Preference was given to using current usage if the spelling of a placename has changed only slightly: Yerevan, instead of Erevan; and Tbilisi, instead of Tiflis. Many placenames have changed completely over the centuries: Gyumri became Alexandropol under the Russians, Leninakan under the Communists, and is Gyumri again. In such instances a placename was used according to its corresponding period. The Soviets changed many placenames. Some of these have reverted to their original Armenian designation since independence. For locations of historic Armenia presently in Turkey, most of whose names have been changed, Turkish toponyms have been provided. Constantinople and Istanbul, however, are used interchangeably though in a manner appropriate for each entry. Some explanation about personal names is also required. The names of kings are of course given by custom according to the tabulation of the monarchial lists. This applies also to catholicoses, or pontiffs, of the Armenian Church, that is to say by first name: Mkrtich I Khrimian; Nerses V Ashtaraketsi; Garegin I Hovsepiants. The latinized version of monarchial names, if applicable, are provided in the entries: Artashes/Artaxias; Levon/Leo; Trdat/Tiridates. To distinguish them and avoid confusion with the catholicoses, patriarchs and prelates are given by their last names: Varzhapetian, Nerses; Ormanian, Maghakia; Srvantztiants, Garegin. Pre-19th century figures are conventionally given by first name: Grigor Narekatsi; Mekhitar Sebastatsi; Davit *Bek*. The use of patronymics did not come into widespread usage among Armenians until the 19th century, except of course in the case of aristocratic, upper class, or learned families: Ardsruni, Bagratuni, or Balian, Chamchian, Patkanian. Even so, persons known by their titular rank are also given according to first name: Nubar *Pasha*; Boghos *Bey* Yusufian.

History is complicated. Armenian history is mercilessly complicated. This dictionary offered a method for unraveling some of those complications. Narrative histories of Armenia either contain too much detail or not enough, depending on the preparation of the reader. A dictionary offered the choice of reading selectively. It risks, however, fragmenting a view of historical development. To compensate for this, the entries of the dictionary were prepared in topical cycles covering the whole span of Armenian history. Accordingly, one may read about cities, royal dynasties, political organizations, national leaders, or prominent figures in the fields of literature or business in a series, and thus benefit by seeing the common threads that bind them across the centuries and, in some instances, across millennia.

The field of Armenian studies is both new and old. While there is much Armenian history recorded, its most recent period, extensively covered in journalistic and periodical literature, is still to be written. Even with the benefit of existing reference works, virtually all of the history covered in this dictionary had to be revisited, in consultation of primary sources to the degree possible, and reverified according to the latest scholarship, not all of which is easily retrieved. All periods of Armenian history are constantly reexamined in light of new discoveries, publications, ideas, and theories. The field remains highly fluid and even some of its most basic facts remain under scrutiny, as better analytical techniques are developed to answer the many outstanding questions. As one example, recent scholarship has renumbered the sovereigns of the Arshakuni royal dynasty, one consequence of which has been that one of its best-known figures, Trdat III, who Christianized Armenia, is now numbered Trdat IV. Only a handful of recent works produced by scholars record this. Most of the historical literature on Armenia continues to reflect the earlier numeration.

Other types of problems abound for the modern period. The school of historical materialism promoted, imposed, in the Soviet period, interpreted a set of facts one way, while other schools of historiography interpreted the same facts in a different way. The selectivity and censorship of the former keeps it suspect, especially for the 20th century, which it viewed in ways in complete contrast, if not at total odds, with non-Soviet historiography. Western academic historiography has not caught up with all aspects of Armenian history and applying its standards of verification meant sifting through variant views and different modes of emphasis and extracting from these a reasonable proposition about the importance of the subject of each entry. Much of the recent history was reconstructed from raw data with all the attendant risks and complications of dealing with imprecise and contradictory information. I earnestly hope that some order has been achieved in this area. Even if complete accuracy was not attained, no effort was spared to reach it. Lastly, many facets of Armenian culture and society are addressed in the dictionary. The main part of it though revolves around political history, which is where the dynamic of the final two decades of the 20th century has relocated public and academic attention.

I need to thank Jon Woronoff, who has skillfully edited the series of historical dictionaries on Asia, for suggesting workable solutions to all my queries, of which there were many. Our correspondence now stretches over eight years, much longer than we planned, but which he patiently tolerated. I also need to acknowledge all my colleagues from whose works I benefited. Their scholarship and learning gave me the confidence that sufficient resources were available to attempt this project. They may not agree with all my views and interpretations, but I hope that the alternative periodizations, and their underlying concepts, proposed across the introduction and various subject entries will be deemed suggestive, if not valuable. The techniques of preparing a dictionary lent themselves to those reconsiderations. In this one respect the conventional periodization of Armenian history applied in most academic works is not reproduced in the dictionary. Throughout an effort was also made to adhere to the intent of a dictionary, a publication with an explicatory objective, and to avoid encyclopedia-style entries that furnish a plethora of detail but at times fail to connect the subject to a proper context or address its significance. If that goal was met then I should be satisfied with the product.

I also need to thank my wife and children for allowing me the time to write this book, time much of which they rightfully could have asked to be devoted to their attention. I live with the hope that in due course they will see themselves in this mirror of their heritage.

Transliteration

With the general reader in mind, a set of conventions was adopted to make this dictionary as easy to use as possible. Some comment on the transliteration system, therefore, is required. As a general rule, all transliteration was done phonetically regardless of language. Throughout the millennia Armenians have come into contact with so many peoples speaking different languages and using different alphabetic systems that any other approach would have been the source of confusion. In the specific case of the Armenian language, transliteration presents serious challenges that specialists have addressed by a number of methods. There is a standard system devised for the use of linguists and philologists known as the Hübschmann-Meillet-Benveniste system. Medievalists and others rely on it, as their discipline requires a dependable consistency in transliteration since the use of original languages is a standard technique in the historical analyses developed by these specialists. Another standard is the Library of Congress system, which is widely used for cataloguing and bibliographic purposes.

Specialists in the modern period rely on a phonetic system as this has the advantage of reproducing Armenian according to adaptations made by Armenians themselves in the spelling of personal names especially. Since the dictionary focuses on the modern period, this dictated the choice of a transliteration system. That, however, did not solve all problems as the Armenian language has two modern standard dialects, a Western and an Eastern. Rather than distort one or the other to fit the rules of a single system, common names with familiar transliteration in the Western dialect were retained. The primary system is based on the Eastern dialect, which was utilized in all instances not impinging on familiar transliterations from the Western dialect.

While these may seem reasonable solutions, they also lead to contrasts that prevent the maintenance of uniformity. For example, the name Gregory is Grigor in Eastern Armenian and Krikor in Western Armenian.

Hence, Krikor Zohrab, the name of a Western Armenian author and national leader, would be spelled Grigor Zohrap according to the Eastern dialect, making it inconsistent with much of the preexisting literature. The result is two variant spellings of the same name and there are many other examples of the like: Petros and Bedros, Babgen and Papken. Modifications in the orthography of the Eastern Armenian language have also resulted in other variant spellings of names.

As for contemporary figures, the spelling of a name in Latin characters according to the preference of the individual has been honored. For example, the first president of Armenia officially signed Levon Ter-Petrossian. A strict transliteration results in Levon Ter-Petrosyan, spelling which is sometimes reproduced in country handbooks that derive all names from the original language. Elsewhere, transliteration per Western Armenian pronunciation results in Levon Der-Bedrossian. Prime Minister Armen Sarkissian, who for many years served as ambassador in London, like Ter-Petrossian, adopted a Westernized spelling for his name, while those with the same last name in Armenian appear in contrast transliterated as Sargsian. Where a conventional Westernized spelling was not adopted by a public figure, the name was transcribed according to the rules of the transliteration table.

A word about the spelling of Armenian patronymics is also needed. The suffix "ian" has come into very wide usage among Armenians. According to native spelling, it is also legitimate to transcribe the suffix as "ean" or "yan" depending on the transliteration system preferred by an author. These variants now appear in bibliographic databases. For this dictionary the popular convention of "ian" was utilized to transliterate all patronymics, historic and contemporary, except where preceded by vowels, in which case "yan" is the common spelling, as in Anastas Mikoyan, or in those cases established otherwise by the bearer of the name, as in Abel Aganbegyan. A couple of other minor details on transliteration: the unwritten "e" in Armenian was not entered in the transliterations, except where absolutely necessary or where convention had already established its usage, as in Mekhitar, and not Mkhitar; also the "u" sound appears in variants forms as "ou" or "oo" again depending on conventional usage, or when appropriate in order to approximate the Armenian more closely.

The one place where none of the above applies is the bibliography where names were reproduced as published. No effort was made to create uniformity as this would only complicate the identification of the source. Some authors have published in several languages in which case variant spellings of their names have come into usage. For example Nicholas Adontz also appears as Nicolas Adonts, not to mention that from the Armenian his name may be transliterated as Nikoghayos Adonts, and Nikolai Adontz from Russian. In the bibliography, publications originally transliterated according to the Hübschmann-Meillet-Benveniste appear according to that system, without diacritics however.

Reprinted with permission: Richard G. Hovannisian, ed. *The Armenian People from Ancient to Modern Times*, 2 vols. New York: St. Martin's Press, 1997.

Acronyms and Abbreviations

AGBU	Armenian General Benevolent Union
AMAA	Armenian Missionary Association of America
ANM	Armenian National Movement
ARF	Armenian Revolutionary Federation
ASALA	Armenian Secret Army for the Liberation of Armenia
ASSR	Armenian Soviet Socialist Republic
BSEC	Black Sea Economic Cooperation
CIS	Commonwealth of Independent States
CSCE	Conference on Security and Cooperation in Europe
CPA	Communist Party of Armenia
CUP	Committee of Union and Progress
DLP	Democratic Liberal Party
EBRD	European Bank for Reconstruction and Development
IMF	International Monetary Fund
NATO	North Atlantic Treaty Organization
NDU	National Democratic Union
NER	Near East Relief
NKAO	Nagorno Karabagh Autonomous Oblast
NKR	Nagorno Karabagh Republic
OSCE	Organization on Security and Cooperation in Europe
PPA	Populist Party of Armenia
RPA	Republican Party of Armenia
RSDWP	Russian Social Democratic Workers Party
SDHP	Social Democratic Hnchakian Party
UAF	United Armenia Fund
UN	United Nations
USD	Union of Self-Determination
USSR	Union of Soviet Socialist Republics

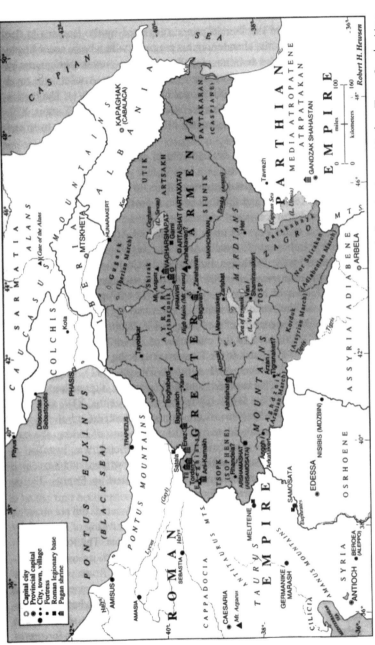

Reproduced with permission: Richard G. Hovannisian, ed. *The Armenian People from Ancient to Modern Times*, 2 vols. New York: St. Martin's Press, 1997.

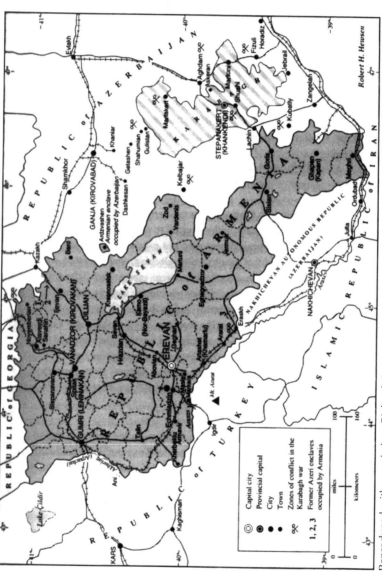

Reproduced with permission: Richard G. Hovannisian, ed. *The Armenian People from Ancient to Modern Times,* 2 vols. New York: St. Martin's Press, 1997.

Chronology

B.C.

ca. 1500–1200 Hayasa-Azzi indigenous tribal confederation on the Armenian plateau. Eponym of the Hay people, as Armenians call themselves.

ca. 1300–1000 Arme-Shupria tribal confederation in Western Armenia. Speakers of the Indo-European Armenian language in the Armenian highlands. Nairi tribal confederation around Lake Van. Country identified as Urartu or Ararat. Speakers of the Urartian language.

ca. 870 Formation of the Urartian state. Arame, first king of Urartu ca. 860–840.

835 Sarduri I, king of Urartu. Rules until 825. Establishes Tushpa, later called Van, as capital city, on shore of Lake Van.

810 Menua, king of Urartu. Rules until 785. Builds 80-kilometer, so-called Shamiram/Semiramis, canal to guarantee regular supply of fresh water to Van.

782 Argishti I, king of Urartu from 786 to 764 B.C., raises the fortress of Erebuni near site of the modern-day capital of Yerevan.

776 Argishti I founds Argishtihinili, later called Armavir, capital of ancient Armenia, in the plain of Ayrarat.

685 Rusa II king of Urartu. Rules until 645. Establishes city of Teishebaini in the plain of Ayrarat.

652 Paruyr Skayordi, legendary first king of Armenians, reigning in land of Arme-Shupria.

590 Fall of the Urartian kingdom under pressure of Scythian invasions. Median suzerainty introduced over the Armenian plateau.

ca. 570 Yervand Sakavakiats, legendary Armenian king. Regarded founder of Yervanduni royal dynasty. Reigns until 560. Successors govern as royal satraps under Persian tutelage.

550 Cyrus II founder of the Achaemenid dynasty in Iran establishes Persian suzerainty over Armenia.

522 Armenians overthrow Persian rule. Darius I restores Achaemenid suzerainty over Armenia.

ca. 520 Darius's inscription of his royal possessions upon the rock at Behistun in Persia makes first written mention of the country of Armena or Armenia.

401 Greek general Xenophon marches through Armenia on the way from Mesopotamia to the Black Sea. Reports reigning Yervanduni to be son-in-law of Artaxerxes I the king of Iran.

336 Darius III Codomannus, former satrap of Armenia, ascends as the last Achaemenid on the Iranian throne.

333 Armenian contingent serving in the Persian army participates in battle of Issus on the Mediterranean between Darius III and Alexander of Macedon. Persian forces defeated. Alexander marches south.

331 Armenians under titular king Yervand serve in Persian army commanded by Darius III in battle of Gaugamela in Mesopotamia against Alexander. Persians defeated. Alexander marches east. Yervand retreats to Armenia as country is formally annexed by Macedonians.

330 Yervand reigning king in Armenia with death of Darius. Armavir made capital of Armenia.

312 Seleucid state formed in Asia by heir to Alexander (d. 323) with claim to Armenia. Yervanduni continue to govern in Armenia under Seleucid tutelage.

ca. 260 Samos, of Yervanduni descent, governs as king of Commagene and Dsopk/Sophene in Western Armenia until 240. Founds city of Shamshat/Samosata.

247 Arsacid dynasty of Parthian origin assumes imperial crown of Iran. Begins recovery of Persian state and lays claim to Armenia.

240   Arsham (Arsamos) king of Commagene and Sophene until 220. Founds cities of Arshamshat/Arsamosata and Arsameia on the river Nymphaios.

ca. 220   Yervand IV, king of Armenia, last of the Yervanduni dynasty, reigns until 201 B.C.

190   Battle of Magnesia. Rome defeats Antiochus the Great in Asia Minor and reduces Seleucid power to Syria.

189   Artashes (Artaxias) I proclaims himself king of Armenia by shedding Seleucid suzerainty. Rules until 160 and founds the Artashesian dynasty that lasts until 1 A.D. Also, Zareh (Zariadris) declares himself king in Dsopk/Sophene, Western Armenia.

176   Founding of Artashat as capital of Armenia by King Artashes I. Established as an administrative center, Artashat becomes the largest city in Armenia and its most important commercial center.

160   Artavazd (Artabastus) I, king of Armenia. Succeeded by Tigran (Tigranes) I who reigns until 95.

95   Tigran (Tigranes) II the Great, king of Armenia. Returns to his homeland after years as a royal hostage in the Parthian court in Iran. Rules until 55.

94   Tigran II unifies Armenia and Dsopk/Sophene into a single state recognized as Armenia Major.

87   Tigran II checks Parthian influence over Armenia by moving his forces on Ecbatana, the Iranian capital. Proceeds to incorporate neighboring smaller states of Atropatene, Adiabene, Gordyene, and Osrhoene as vassal kingdoms.

83   Tigran II overthrows the Seleucids in Syria and occupies Commagene, Cilicia, and Phoenicia. Assumes title of King of Kings. Founds city of Tigranakert as southern capital.

69   Romans under command of general Lucullus enter Armenia and defeat Tigran II's forces at Tigranakert. Tigran retreats into Armenian heartland. Lucullus discontinues advance. Antiochus I of the Yervanduni line, king of Commagene until 34. Raises monumental sculptures of royalty and divinity in syncretistic Hellenistic style of art at Arsameia on Nymphaios and Nemrut Dagh. Exceptional full-length portrait of Armenian regalia depicted.

66 Romans under general Pompey invade Armenia and march on Artashat. Pompey accepts Tigran II's voluntary submission to Rome. Treaty of Artashat signed between Tigran II and Pompey establishes Armenian friendship with Rome and Roman recognition of Armenian sovereignty.

55 Artavazd II, son of Tigran the Great, king of Armenia. Establishes close relations with Parthia. Reigns until 34.

53 Roman triumvir Crassus requires Artavazd II to support his campaign against Iran. Crassus defeated by Parthian king who restores alliance with Armenia.

36 Roman triumvir Mark Antony invades Iran through Armenia and requires Artavazd II to support campaign. Antony defeated.

34 Antony takes Artavazd II captive and removes him to Alexandria, Egypt.

33 Artashes II, king of Armenia, with Parthian support. Reigns until 20.

31 Battle of Actium. Octavian, later Augustus, defeats Antony in last battle of the Roman civil war. Cleopatra, queen of Egypt, orders the execution of Artavazd II.

20 Augustus, Roman emperor, sends Tiberius to Armenia to install Tigran III, son of Artavazd II, as king.

8 Tigran IV, king of Armenia. Placed on the throne by Parthians.

5 Artavazd III, king of Armenia. Placed on the throne by Romans.

2 Tigran IV restored as king with sister Erato as queen. Joint reign until 1 A.D.

A.D.

6 Tigran IV and Erato on the Armenian throne again.

12 Vonon (Vonones) of Parthian origin given kingship of Armenia by Rome. Reigns until 15. First person from the Arsacid dynasty of Iran placed on the Armenian throne.

51 Vologases I becomes king of Iran. Awards Armenian crown to his brother Trdat (Tiridates) I in 52.

54 Trdat enters Armenia as claimant. Conflict with Rome ensues.

58 Roman general Corbulo captures Artashat and subjugates Armenia.

63 Treaty of Rhandia concludes war over Armenia and establishes peace between Rome and Iran. Trdat I formally recognized king of Armenia. Arshakuni (Arsacid) rule introduced in Armenia.

66 Coronation in Rome by emperor Nero of Trdat I as king of Armenia.

88 Sanatruk II, king of Armenia, succeeds his father Trdat I.

114 Trajan, Roman emperor, annexes Armenia to the empire.

117 Hadrian, Roman emperor, relinquishes Roman rule over Armenia and restores Armenian crown to the Arshakuni/Arsacid dynasty. Vagharsh (Vologases) I crowned king of Armenia. Reigns until 140. Founds new royal residence of Vagharshapat. Artashat continues to function as capital until 163.

140 Sohaemos made king of Armenia by Roman emperor Marcus Aurelius. Deposed in 160.

163 Marcus Aurelius sends troops to Armenia to restore Sohaemos to the throne. Sohaemos reigns until 180.

166 Artashat rebuilt after sack by Romans and recognized by treaty between Rome and Iran as one of the official entrepots of the international trade between the two empires. The city flourishes as a center of commerce and industry.

180 Vagharsh (Vologases) II, king of Armenia. Rules until 191.

191 Khosrov (Chosroes) I succeeds his father Vagharsh II to the Armenian throne. Dynastic succession in Armenian Arshakuni/Arsacid line begins. Khosrov I reigns until 217.

217 Trdat (Tiridates) II, son of Khosrov I, king of Armenia. Reigns until 252.

224 Artashir Papakan overthrows Arsacid rule in Iran and introduces Sasanid dynasty. Claims Achaemenid hegemony and ignites conflict with Arshakuni/Arsacid kings of Armenia.

252 Sasanids invade Armenia. The country is divided into Roman and Iranian zones. Sasanids introduce direct rule.

279 Khosrov (Chosroes) II, king in Western Armenia only under Roman protection. Reigns until 293.

298 Trdat (Tiridates) IV raised to the throne of a reunified Armenian monarchy by Roman Emperor Diocletian. Rules until 330.

301 Traditional date of the conversion of Trdat IV to Christianity by Grigor Lusavorich (Gregory the Illuminator). Christianization of Armenia begins.

314 Grigor Lusavorich ordained first bishop of Armenia in Caesarea in the Roman Empire.

325 Aristakes, son of Grigor Lusavorich, bishop of Armenia until 333. Participates in the Council of Nicaea, the first universal gathering of bishops convened by emperor Constantine.

330 Khosrov III Kotak, king of Armenia. Reigns until 338. Founds city of Dvin.

338 Tiran, king of Armenia, deposed by Sasanid king Shapur II in 350.

350 Arshak II, son of Tiran, king of Armenia, deposed by Shapur II in 368.

353 Nerses I the Great, great-great-grandson of Grigor Lusavorich, bishop of Armenia. Presides until 373. Establishes charitable foundations.

354 Council of Ashtishat first church council in Armenia convened by Nerses I.

368 Sasanid forces from Iran ransack Armenian cities. Destruction continues through 369.

370 Queen Parandzem, wife of Arshak II, taken captive and banished to Iran with her husband.

371 Pap raised to the Armenian throne by Romans. Reigns until 374. Pap's conduct condemned by Nerses I.

373 King Pap causes poisoning of Nerses I in conflict between church and state.

379 Mushegh Mamikonian, feudal prince and commander-in-chief of Armenian forces, as regent, raises Pap's children, Arshak III and Vagharshak to the Armenian throne.

387 Formal partition of Armenia between Rome and Iran. Iran acquires eastern two-thirds of the country. Sahak I the Great catholicos until 428. Son of Nerses I the Great. Constructs original cathedral of Edjmiadsin at Vagharshapat. Collaborates with Mesrop Mashtots.

392 Vramshapuh, king of Armenia, reigns until 415. Sponsors Mesrop Mashtots.

405 Mesrop Mashtots invents the Armenian alphabet. Classical Armenian written for the first time. Translation of the Bible into Armenian begun by Mashtots and catholicos Sahak.

422 Artashes IV, son of Vramshapuh, reigns until 428. Last Arshakuni king of Armenia and last person to hold the crown of the ancient Armenian kingdom.

428 Armenian monarchy abolished by Iran and Arshakuni dynasty deposed. Period of government by *marzpans*, viceroys, appointed by Iran begins. Lasts until 650. Catholicos Sahak I removed from patriarchal throne. Catholicosate relocated from Vagharshapat to Dvin.

439 The passing of Sahak I the Great, last descendant of Grigor Lusavorich on the patriarchal throne of Armenia. Hamazasp Mamikonian emerges as the greatest territorial prince in Armenia by his marriage to Sahakanyush, daughter of catholicos Sahak. Parents of Vardan Mamikonian. Vasak Siuni appointed *marzpan* (viceroy) of Armenia by Iranian king Yazdegerd II.

451 Battle of Avarayr. Vardan Mamikonian leads popular resistance to Iranian policy of imposing Mazdaean worship in Christian Armenia. Vardan falls in battle. Iran rescinds policy. Council of Chalcedon held in Roman Empire. Duophysite Christology adopted by bishops. Armenian religious leaders do not participate in the Council because of war in Armenia. They reject duophysitism out of concern over similarities to Zoroastrian dualism and begin separation from Roman church.

482 Armenians under Sahak Bagratuni again resist Iranian religious policies. Sahak falls in battle.

483 Vahan Mamikonian, nephew of Vardan Mamikonian, commissions new cathedral at Edjmiadsin and continues resistance.

485 Vahan Mamikonian appointed *marzpan* (viceroy) of Armenia by Iranian king. Residence of Armenian catholicos relocated to Dvin.

554/5 Council of Dvin confirms Monophysitism of the Armenian Church. Armenia formally separates from Roman church.

591 New partition of Armenia between Byzantium and Iran. Byzantium acquires western two-thirds of the country.

615 Komitas Aghdzetsi catholicos until 628. Commissions construction of church of St. Hripsime at Vagharshapat.

627 Heraklios, Byzantine emperor of Armenian origin, marches through Armenia to subdue Iran and regain control of the eastern Mediterranean territories of the Byzantine empire.

629 Varaz-Tirots II Bagratuni appointed *marzpan* (viceroy) of Armenia by Iranian king.

630 Yezr Parazhnakertatsi catholicos until 641. Commissions construction of church of St. Gayane at Vagharshapat.

640 Arabs capture Dvin and begin conquest of Armenia.

641 Nerses III Ishkhaneti, known as Nerses the Builder, catholicos until 661. Commissions construction of church of Zvartnots near Vagharshapat.

645 Varaz-Tirots II Bagratuni appointed prince of Armenia by Byzantine emperor.

650 Arabs secure permanent occupation of Armenia until 884.

705 Arabs massacre Armenian nakharars in Nakhichevan and impose direct rule. Period of government by Arab *vostikans*, governor-generals, annual governors, instituted by Umayyad caliphate.

732 Ashot III Bagratuni governs as prince of Armenia on behalf of Arabs until 748. Ashot begins consolidation of Bagratuni rule over northern Armenia in alliance with the Arabs.

750 Armenians revolt against Arab rule during civil war between Umayyad and Abbasid for control of the caliphate. Prince Ashot III

Bagratuni blinded by the Mamikonian. Rebellion in Armenia suppressed by the Abbasids upon seizing the caliphate.

761 Smbat VI Bagratuni appointed reigning prince of Armenia by the Abbasids.

774 Armenian rebellion against Arab rule led by Mamikonians and Bagratunis.

775 Battle of Bagrevand. Arabs nearly destroy nakharar presence in Armenia and eliminate Mamikonians from the country. Prince Smbat VI Bagratuni falls in battle. Armenians migrate to Byzantium.

804 Ashot IV *Msaker* (Meateater), grandson of Smbat VI Bagratuni, appointed governing prince of Armenia by the Abbasid caliph Harun al-Rashid. Emergence of the Bagratunis as chief princes of Armenia under Arab rule.

813 Ashot I the Great, grandson of Ashot III the Blind, and prince of the district of Erusheti-Artani in Georgia, appointed prince of Iberia by Arab caliphate.

826 Bagrat II Bagratuni, son of Ashot IV *Msaker*, appointed prince of princes in Armenia by the Arab caliphate.

855 Ashot V, nephew of Bagrat II, assumes leadership of the Bagratuni family in Armenia.

863 Ashot V Bagratuni appointed prince of princes in Armenia by the Arab caliphate. Holds the office until his coronation in 884.

874 Princess Mariam, daughter of Ashot V Bagratuni and wife of Siuni prince Vasak Gabur, commissions building of churches on island in Lake Sevan.

884 Prince Ashot V Bagratuni crowned King Ashot I. Armenian sovereignty recognized by Arab caliphate. Founds Bagratuni royal dynasty of Armenia that rules until 1045.

888 King Ashot I of Armenia crowns Adarnase IV, great-grandson of Ashot I of Iberia, as king of Iberia. Founds Bagratuni royal dynasty of Georgia that lasts until 1800.

890 Smbat I Bagratuni, king of Armenia. Rules until 914.

893/4 Dvin suffers devastating earthquake and is left defenseless. The city is captured by Afshin, the Sadjid emir of Azerbaijan. The capital remains under Muslim control.

900s Middle Armenian spoken and written.

908 Gagik I Ardsruni crowned king of Vaspurakan in southern Armenia with the support of Yusuf, the Sadjid emir of Azerbaijan and representative of the Arab caliphate. Gagik rules until 943.

914 King Smbat I Bagratuni captured and executed by Yusuf, emir of Azerbaijan. Ashot II *Yerkat* (Iron), Bagratuni king of Armenia. Restores the Bagratuni kingdom with Byzantine assistance. Rules until 928.

915 Construction of the church of the Holy Cross on the island Aghtamar in Lake Van. Completed in 921. Commissioned by King Gagik I Ardsruni.

927 Catholicos relocated from Dvin to Aghtamar.

928 Abas I Bagratuni, king of Armenia. Rules until 952.

943 Derenik-Ashot Ardsruni, king of Vaspurakan. Rules until 958.

952 Dvin acquired by Shaddadid family of Kurdish origin. Ashot III *Voghormats* (Merciful), Bagratuni king of Armenia. Rules until 977. Relinquishes effort to obtain Dvin from Arab and Muslim control.

958 Abusahl-Hamazasp, king of Vaspurakan until 968.

961 Ani made capital of Armenian kingdom by Ashot III Bagratuni.

962/3 King Ashot III makes his brother Mushegh king in Kars. Bagratuni kingdom of Kars lasts until 1064.

966 Queen Khosrovanuysh, consort of King Ashot III, founds monastery of Sanahin, new center of learning.

968 Kingdom of Vaspurakan in southern Armenia divided among Abusahl-Hamazasp Ardsruni's three sons.

970 Kingdom of Siunik in Eastern Armenia proclaimed by Siuni prince Smbat II. Rules until 998.

974 Byzantine emperor of Armenian origin John Tzimiskes marches into Armenia. Armenian forces rally around Ashot III Bagratuni. Armenians and Byzantines reach accord.

976 Queen Khosrovanuysh founds monastery of Haghbat.

977 Smbat II Bagratuni, king of Armenia. Rules until 989. Fortifies city of Ani.

982 Smbat II makes his brother Gurgen I king of Lori. Bagratuni kingdom of Lori lasts until 1089.

989 Gagik I Bagratuni, king of Armenia. Rules until 1020.

992 Catholicos relocated to Ani.

998 Vasak VI Siuni king of Siunik. Rules until 1019. Daughter Katranide consort of king Gagik I Bagratuni of Armenia.

1000 Byzantine emperor Basil II annexes northern Armenian province of Tayk.

1001–1003 Grigor Narekatsi writes *Matian voghbergutian* (Book of Lamentations). Work of mystical Christian contemplation esteemed the epitome of medieval Armenian literature.

1008 Georgia unified for the first time into a single kingdom by Bagrat III under the rule of the Georgian Bagratunis.

1020 Hovhannes-Smbat Bagratuni, king of Armenia. Rules until 1041.

1021 Senekerim-Hovhannes Ardsruni, king of Vaspurakan, surrenders his crown to Byzantium under pressure from Seljuk Turk incursions and resettles in Cappadocia with his royal household.

1022 Byzantine emperor Basil II pressures Hovhannes-Smbat Bagratuni into agreeing to surrender the Armenian kingdom upon his death.

1041 Gagik II Bagratuni, king of Armenia. Rules until 1045. Raised to the throne by the *sparapet* (commander-in-chief) Vahram Pahlavuni.

1045 Ani taken by Byzantium. Armenian Bagratuni kingdom abolished.

1047 First full-scale invasion of Armenia by Seljuk Turks.

1054 Tughril Beg begins Seljuk Turk occupation of Armenia.

1064 Ani seized from Byzantines by Seljuk Turk sultan Alp Arslan. Period of Seljuk Turk rule of Armenia begins. Armenians migrate to Cilicia, Syria, and Egypt.

1065 Kars seized by Byzantium.

1071 Battle of Manzikert fought on the northern shore of Lake Van. Alp Arslan defeats Byzantine force and advances into Asia Minor.

1073 Oshin, forebear of the Hetumian dynasty, settles in Cilicia in the service of Byzantium.

1079 Deposed Armenian king Gagik II Bagratuni killed by Byzantines.

1080 Ruben (Rupen), a vassal of Gagik II, takes refuge in the Cilician mountains at Gobidara. Holds fort until his death in 1093/1095 in defiance of Byzantium. Founds Rubenian baronial dynasty in Cilicia.

1091 Constantine I, son of Ruben, seizes fortress of Vahka, creating the basis of a new Armenian state in Cilicia.

1093–1095 Constantine I succeeds Ruben as chief of the nascent principality. Rules until 1100/1102.

1098 The First Crusade passes through Cilicia on way to Jerusalem. Armenians assist Crusaders in capturing Antioch and Edessa/Urfa. Baldwin of Boulogne, new count of Edessa, marries Arda, Constantine's niece.

1099 Crusades capture Jerusalem under Godfrey of Boulogne.

1100–1102 Toros I succeeds his father Constantine I as Armenian prince in Cilicia. Enlarges domain by seizing Bartsrberd and Anazarba and secures Armenian control of the mountains. Rules until 1129.

1100 Baldwin of Boulogne succeeds his brother Godfrey as king of Jerusalem with Armenian wife Arda as queen.

1113 New catholicosate created in Aghtamar.

1129 Levon (Leo) I prince of Cilician Armenia.

1132 Levon I begins expansion of Armenian state into the Cilician plain by seizing from the Byzantines the towns of Mamistra, Adana, and Tarsus on the Mediterranean coast.

1137 John II Komnenos, Byzantine emperor, retakes Cilician towns.

1138 Levon I and sons captured by John II Komnenos and taken prisoner to Constantinople. Levon dies in captivity.

1144 Muslim forces capture Edessa from Crusaders.

1144–1145   Toros II, son of Levon II, escapes and returns to Cilicia.

1148   Toros II begins restoration of Cilician Armenia by retaking Anazarba and Vahka.

1149   Armenian catholicosate settles in fortress of Hromkla on the Euphrates near Cilicia.

1152   Toros II defeats Byzantine force. Makes matrimonial arrangements between Rubenian and pro-Byzantine Hetumian feudal families to improve intra-Armenian relations in Cilicia. Toros's brother Stepane (Stephen) marries Rita. They parent future princes Ruben/Rupen III and Levon/Leo II.

1158   Manuel II Komnenos, Byzantine emperor, enters Cilicia and obtain Toros II's voluntary submission to vassalage.

1170   Mleh, Toros II's renegade brother, rules Cilician Armenia with sponsorship of Zangids of Syria until 1175. Makes Sis capital city.

1174   Armenian and Georgian forces secure control of Ani for the Georgian Bagratuni crown.

1175   Ruben (Rupen) III, prince of Cilician Armenia. Consolidates rule by forging alliances with neighboring Crusader and Seljuk states. Rules until 1186/1187.

1176   Battle of Myriokephalon. Seljuk Turks of Rum defeat Byzantium and sever its link with Cilicia. Nerses Lambronatsi made bishop of Tarsus. Advocates for church union among Armenians, Greeks, and Latins.

1184   Tamar Bagratuni, queen of Georgia. Reigns until 1212. Rise of the Zakarian (Makhargrdzeli) family of Armenian viceroys.

1186–1187   Levon II, ruling prince of Cilician Armenia.

1187   Muslim forces capture Jerusalem from Crusaders. Latin kingdom ended.

1190   Nerses Lambronatsi opens negotiations with German emperor Frederick Barbarossa on the Third Crusade for an Armenian royal crown. Barbarossa dies in Cilicia.

1191 Levon II joins Richard Lionhearted, king of England, and Philip Augustus, king of France, in Third Crusade.

1199 Prince Levon II crowned king Levon I of Cilician Armenia. Founds Rubenian royal dynasty. Rules until 1219.

1201 Queen Tamar gives Ani in fief to the Zakarian family.

1203 Dvin brought under Georgian control. Made part of the Zakarian domain by Queen Tamar.

1219 Zabel, daughter of King Levon I, queen of Cilician Armenia. Reigns until 1252. Constantine the Constable, of the Hetumian family, regent.

1220 Mongols shatter Georgian Bagratuni kingdom and establish rule over Armenia.

1226 Hetum I, son of Constantine the Constable, king of Cilician Armenia. Weds reigning Queen Zabel. Founds Hetumian royal dynasty. Rules until 1269.

1236 Mongols sack Dvin and capture Ani. Extensive destruction in Armenia. Mongols establish rule over Armenia. Armenians migrate to southern Russia, Crimea, and eastern Europe.

1247 Smbat *Sparapet*, King Hetum I's brother, sent on embassy to Mongol court in Karakorum. Secures friendship.

1253 King Hetum I journeys to Karakorum. Negotiates Armenian alliance with Mongols. Receives tax exemptions for Armenian church.

1256 King Hetum I returns to Cilicia through Armenia. Partial economic recovery of Armenia under Mongols.

1266 Mamluks from Egypt led by Baybars invade and devastate cities in Cilician Armenia.

1268 Mamluks capture Antioch from Crusaders. Eastern flank of Cilician Armenia exposed to invasion.

1269 Levon (Leo) II, king of Cilician Armenia. Rules until 1289. Seeks to maintain Armenian alliance with Mongols.

1285 Levon II agrees to annual payment of tribute to Mamluks.

1291   Acre, the last Crusader stronghold, captured by Mamluks.

1292   Hromkla, fortress residence of Armenian catholicos, taken by Mamluks.

1293   Catholicosate relocated to Sis.

1304   Mongol Ilkhans ruling from Baghdad convert to Islam. End of Armenian-Mongol alliance.

1307   Mongols capture and slaughter jointly reigning King Hetum II and King Levon III. Council of Sis convened by Armenian churchmen to consider union with Rome.

1311   Armenian Patriarchate of Jerusalem established.

1316–1317   Council of Adana convened by churchmen to vote for union with Rome. Armenian society divided over proposal for union.

1318   Mamluks renew invasion of Cilician Armenia. Continue raiding for four years.

1319   Ani suffers a major earthquake. The city goes into permanent decline.

1320   Levon (Leo) IV, king of Cilician Armenia. Reigns until 1341. A minor at time of coronation.

1323   Oshin, the regent in Cilician Armenia, travels to Cairo. Negotiates truce with the Mamluks for payment of half the income of the port of Ayas.

1329   Levon IV reaches majority. Orders murder of Oshin. Reverses policy and seeks assistance from West.

1337   Mamluks capture Ayas, Cilician Armenia's main source of external revenue.

1342   Armenian barons remove Levon IV from throne and invite Frenchman Guy de Lusignan of Cyprus to assume Armenian crown. Guy reigns as Constantine II until 1344.

1344   Constantine III of the Hetumian line king in Cilician Armenia. Reigns until 1263. Control of coastline lost with Mamluk capture of Tarsus and Adana.

1374 Leo de Lusignan called from Cyprus. Enthroned as king Levon (Leo) V. Last person to wear Armenian crown.

1375 Mamluks capture Sis and King Levon (Leo) V Lusignan. End of Cilician Armenian sovereignty. State and monarchy abolished.

1387 Leng Timur (Tamerlane) lays waste to Van during plundering expedition through Armenia. Rapid economic decline of Armenia under Turkoman rule.

1393 Levon V dies in Paris after release from imprisonment in Cairo. Buried at St. Denis with French royalty.

1400s Early Modern Armenian spoken and written.

1410 Kara-Koyunlu (Black Sheep) Turks establish rule over Armenia until 1468. Agricultural society in Armenia undermined by increased pastoralism.

1441 Catholicosate restored in Edjmiadsin with the election of Kirakos Khorvirapetsi by the bishops and abbots of Eastern Armenia. Presides until 1443.

1468 Ak-Koyunlu (White Sheep) Turks establish rule over Armenia until 1502.

1461 Putative beginning of the Armenian *Millet* in the Ottoman Empire with the designation of Bishop Hovakim as patriarch of the Armenians in Istanbul by Sultan Mehmet the Conqueror.

1502 Safavids place Armenia under Iranian rule.

1512 First Armenian book printed in Venice.

1514 Battle of Chalderon between Ottomans and Safavids. Ottomans take control of Armenian highland. Delegate local rule to Kurdish chieftains.

1516 Ottomans seize Cilicia and the Middle East from the Mamluks of Egypt. All lands historically inhabited by Armenians incorporated into the Ottoman Empire.

1539 Sinan appointed imperial architect by Ottoman sultan Suleyman the Magnificent. Builds hundreds of structures across the empire in the next 50 years.

1547   Catholicos Stepanos Salmastetsi convenes secret meeting at Edjmiadsin to request Rome's assistance in the liberation of Armenia.

1550   Sinan begins construction of Suleymaniye mosque complex in Istanbul as statement of Ottoman power. Completed in 1557.

1569   Sinan begins construction of Selimiye mosque complex in Edirne. Regarded masterpiece of Ottoman architecture. Completed in 1575.

1582–1583   Ottomans fortify promontory above Zangi/Hrazdan River at Yerevan.

1600s   Modern Armenian in widespread use.

1604   Safavids of Iran capture Yerevan fortress and designate it administrative center of the border province. Shah Abbas deports Armenians from the Arax River valley to Iran. Settles Armenian merchants of Jugha/Julfa near his capital of Isfahan in new neighborhood of Nor Jugha/New Julfa. Armenians migrate to India and southeast Asia.

1648   Van suffers major earthquake.

1653   Renovation of the cathedral of Edjmiadsin begun with addition of central cupola and entrance belfry.

1655   Hakob Jughayetsi catholicos until 1680.

1666   Armenian Bible printed in Amsterdam by Voskan Yerevantsi at behest of Catholicos Hakob Jughayetsi.

1677   Catholicos Hakob Jughayetsi convenes secret meeting in Edjmiadsin to send delegation to the Papacy.

1701   Mekhitar Sebastatsi assembles in Istanbul a new order of Armenian Catholic monks.

1715   Hovhannes Kolot appointed Armenian patriarch of Istanbul. Presides until 1741 turning the patriarchate into the most influential Armenian religious institution of the time.

1717   Mekhitar Sebastatsi and his followers arrive in Venice. The Armenian Catholic order is allotted the island of San Lazzaro by the Venetian Senate.

1720 Naghash Hovnatan paints interior murals of the cathedral of Edjmiadsin.

1722 Davit *Bek* leads first Armenian liberation struggle in modern times. Collapse of the Safavid state in Iran and unrest in Transcaucasia prompts Armenians to resort to self-defense in Zangezur and Karabagh in Eastern Armenia.

1727 Davit *Bek* bestowed right to govern Armenian principality by Shah Tahmasp of Iran. Mekhitar Sebastatsi begins publication in Venice of Armenian grammar books and dictionaries. Fosters cultivation of the Armenian language and sets foundations of modern philological studies.

1728 Mekhitar *Sparapet* assumes leadership of Armenian principality upon Davit Bek's death.

1730 Mekhitar *Sparapet* killed in battle against Ottomans invading Eastern Armenia. Armenian liberation struggle ended.

1763 Simeon Yerevantsi catholicos until 1780. Opens seminary, starts church archives, and orders cadastral survey of the church's landholdings.

1771 Printing press established in Edjmiadsin by Catholicos Simeon Yerevantsi.

1773 Hovsep Arghutian appointed primate of Armenian church in Russia headquartered in Astrakhan. Encourages pro-Russian attitude among Armenians and pro-Armenian policies among Russians. Breakaway group from the Mekhitarian Order in Venice establishes a new center in Trieste.

1776 Mekhitarians establish printing operations. In continuous existence since.

1778 Armenians from Crimea resettle in Nor/New Nakhichevan near Rostov-on-Don in Russia under sponsorship of Russian empress Catherine the Great.

1779 Mikayel Chamchian, Mekhitarian scholar, publishes in Venice the first descriptive grammar of Armenian.

1780 Ghukas Karnetsi catholicos until 1799. Cathedral of Edjmiadsin given its final appearance with construction of additional belfries and restoration of interior murals by Hovnatan Hovnatanian.

1784–1786 Mikayel Chamchian publishes in Venice a comprehensive history of Armenia in three volumes. First work in modern Armenian historical scholarship.

1792 Serovpe Patkanian opens an Armenian school in Pera, suburb of Istanbul. Denounced to Ottoman authorities for educational innovations. Flees to Georgia.

1793 Serovpe Patkanian opens first Armenian school in Tbilisi. Also opens school in Nor-Nakhichevan, Russia.

1810 Serovpe Patkanian opens Armenian school in Astrakhan.

1811 Trieste branch of Mekhitarian Order resettles in new monastery in Vienna. Becomes center for Armenian historical studies.

1813 Treaty of Gulistan signed between Russia and Iran ends First Russo-Persian War and recognizes Russian rule over Georgia, Azerbaijan, and Karabagh.

1814 Nerses Ashtaraketsi appointed prelate in Tbilisi. Leading proponent of Armenian support for Russian intervention in the Caucasus.

1824 Nersisian school opened in Tbilisi. Named for Nerses Ashtaraketsi. School becomes leading Armenian educational institution in the Transcaucasus.

1826 Boghos *Bey* Yusufian appointed minister of commerce in Egypt by Ottoman viceroy Muhammad Ali. Armenians resettle in Egypt.

1827 Russians enter Yerevan. Persian inhabitants depart city.

1828 Russian forces complete occupation of the Persian khanate (principality) of Yerevan. Eastern Armenia brought under Russian control. Treaty of Turkmenchai signed between Russia and Iran formally ends Second Russo-Persian War and establishes the Arax River as the boundary separating the two countries. Iran relinquishes sovereignty over historic East Armenia. Nerses Ashtaraketsi encourages Armenians from Iran to return to Armenia. First effort at reversing eight centuries of dispersion. Provisions made in Treaty of Turkmenchai for repatriation. Armenians resettle across Russia.

1829 Mount Ararat scaled by Frederick Parrot and Khachatur Abovian.

1831 Catholic *Millet* created in the Ottoman Empire.

1832 Yedikule Armenian hospital in Istanbul founded by Kaza Artin *Amira* Bezjian.

1836 Garabed *Bey* Balian appointed imperial architect by Ottoman sultan Abdulmejit. Gabriel Patkanian, son of Serovpe Patkanian, opens school in Nor Nakhichevan. Mikayel Nalbandian is among his students. Russian tsar Nicholas I ratifies *Polozhenie* (Statute) regulating Armenian church in Russia. Primacy of the Holy See in Edjmiadsin codified.

1837 Boghos *Bey* Yusufian appointed minister of commerce and foreign affairs in Egypt by Muhammad Ali. Holds post until his death in 1844. Russians establish military base in Alexandropol/Gyumri.

1839 Beginning of Tanzimat reforms in the Ottoman Empire. Period of modernization of administrative and legal systems until 1876.

1843 Nerses V Ashtaraketsi elected catholicos at age 73. Revitalizes Holy See at Edjmiadsin as leading center of the Armenian church.

1844 Artin *Pasha* Chrakian appointed minister of commerce and foreign affairs in Egypt by Muhammad Ali. Holds post until 1850.

1848 Khachatur Abovian writes in vernacular *Verk Hayastani* (The Wounds of Armenia), first Armenian novel. Abovian disappears in the same year. The work is published in 1858.

1849 Garabed Balian begins construction of the Dolmabahche palace in Istanbul. Completed in 1856.

1850 Gabriel Patkanian made rector of the Nersisian school in Tbilisi.

1855 Rafayel Patkanian, son of Gabriel Patkanian, founds Armenian literary circle at Moscow University. Under collective name of Kamar Katiba, the group issues *Write as You Speak, Speak as You Write*, propounding vernacularism.

1856 Rafayel Patkanian assumes pen-name Kamar Katiba. Publishes poem *Araksi Artasuke* (The Tears of Arax [River]), elegy on the fate of Armenia.

1857 Protestant *Millet* created in the Ottoman Empire.

1858 Mkrtich Khrimian begins publishing *Ardsvi Vaspurakan* (Eagle of Vaspurakan) in Van. First periodical issued in Armenia proper. Publication of the liberal periodical *Hyusisapayl* (Aurora Borealis) started in Moscow by Stepanos Nazariants. First Armenian periodical issued in Russia. Published until 1864.

1860 May 24: So-called Armenian Constitution, or Regulations, of the Armenian *Millet* authorized by the Ottoman government. The Regulations formalize the governance of the *Millet* and include middle-class representation in decision-making councils. Document finalized in 1863.

1861 Daud *Pasha* appointed Ottoman governor of Lebanon. Introduces modern administration. Serves until 1873. Armenians begin settling in Lebanon. Mikayel Nalbandian publishes poems *Azatutiun* (Freedom) and *Mer Hayrenik* (Our Fatherland). First ardent expressions of Armenian nationalism in Russia. *Mer Hayrenik* adapted in the 20th century as the Armenian national anthem.

1862 Mikayel Nalbandian publishes in Paris *Agriculture as the Just Way*, the first political tract issued in modern Armenian. Reflects influence of early Russian socialist thinking. Arrested upon return to Russia and imprisoned. Dies in exile in 1866.

1864 Hagop *Bey* Balian completes construction of the Beylerbey imperial palace for Ottoman Sultan Abdulaziz. Balian brothers begin construction of the Chiraghan imperial palace.

1865 Hagop Baronian writes in Istanbul the first of his satirical plays. None are performed in his lifetime. Nubar receives first appointment to Egyptian cabinet as minister of public works.

1866 Gevorg IV Kerestechian catholicos until 1882. Begins publication of *Ararat* monthly, the official journal of the Holy See in Edjmiadsin.

1869 Mkrtich Khrimian elected Armenian Patriarch of Istanbul. Seeks to create public awareness of plight of Armenians in their homeland and restrain arbitrary rule by local Ottoman officials. Resigns in 1873.

1872 Grigor Ardsruni founds *Mshak* (Laborer) newspaper, the principal voice of Armenian liberalism, published in Tbilisi until 1920. First Armenian political group formed in Van, *Miutiun i Perkutiun* (Union of Salvation) to defend population from unchecked lawlessness in the region. Secret organization has transient existence. Death of 21-year-old Bedros Turian, paragon of Romantic poetry in Armenian.

1873 Nerses Varzhapetian elected Armenian Patriarch of Istanbul. Presides until 1884. Seeks European support for reforms in the Armenian provinces of the Ottoman Empire.

1874 Gevorgian academy, named in honor of presiding catholicos Gevorg IV, opens in Edjmiadsin. Becomes leading school in Eastern Armenia. Garegin Srvantztiants begins publication of series on Armenian folklore and reveals existence of Armenian national epic known as *Sasna dserer* (Daredevils of Sasun) or *Sasuntsi Davit* (David of Sasun).

1875 German linguist Heinrich Hübschmann identifies Armenian as an independent Indo-European language.

1876 Abdul-Hamid/Abdulhamit II assumes the throne in the Ottoman Empire. Adopts then abrogates the Ottoman Constitution and introduces a period of absolute autocracy and tyranny. Rules until 1909.

1877 November 19: Russian forces under Mikayel Loris-Melikov capture Kars from Ottomans.

1878 Second self-defense group formed in Van, *Sev Khach Kazmakerputiun* (Black Cross Society). Nubar *Pasha* serves first term as prime minister of Egypt until 1879. **March:** Mkrtich Khrimian leads Armenian delegation to Europe to draw attention of Great Powers to condition of Armenian population in Turkey. Denied hearing at Congress of Berlin. **March 3:** Treaty of San Stefano concludes 1877–1878 Russo–Turkish War. Includes provision for the introduction of reforms in the Armenian provinces of the Ottoman Empire under Russian supervision. **July 13:** Treaty of Berlin settles 1877–1878 Russo–Turkish War. Russia acquires Kars from Turkey. Ottomans agree to improvements in the administration of the Armenian provinces in the empire. Provision for Russian supervision, however, overturned. The Great Powers addressing the Armenian Question raise expectations of better treatment by Ottoman government. **August:** Khrimian returning from Berlin delivers his *Sermon of the Iron Ladle* in Istanbul raising questions about the value of international promises. Disillusionment settles in quickly among Armenians upon failure of Ottomans to implement reforms.

1880 Maghakia Ormanian appointed dean of the seminary at Armash, near Istanbul. Seminary becomes the principal training ground for the Armenian clergy in Turkey. **February 27:** Count Mikayel Loris-Melikov delegated unconditional powers by Tsar Alexander II to restore order in Russia after period of revolutionary unrest. Introduces liberal reforms and ends emergency. **August:** Loris-Melikov appointed minister of the interior in Russia.

1881 Ghevond Alishan, Mekhitarian scholar, begins publication in Venice of his topographic histories of Armenia. Raffi begins publication in Tbilisi of novels on the themes of political emancipation and national liberation. *Khente* (The Fool) released. **February:** Loris-Melikov presents Tsar Alexander II a program for major administrative reforms in Russia. Alexander signs reform manifesto and is assassinated the same day, March 13. His successor Alexander III dismisses Loris-Melikov and reverts to autocracy.

1882 Raffi publishes *Davit Bek*, a historical novel based on the early 18th century liberation struggle in Zangezur and Karabagh.

1884 Nubar *Pasha* serves second term as prime minister of Egypt until 1889.

1885 Armenanakan party, first Armenian political organization, formed in Van. Quickly suppressed by Ottoman government.

1887 Armenian Social Democratic Hnchakian Party created in Geneva, Switzerland by Russian–Armenians. Issues party organ *Hnchak* (Clarion). Krikor Zohrab, attorney by profession, publishes first collection of short stories introducing the Realist style in Armenian literature.

1888 Andranik joins Armenian revolutionary movement and leads guerrilla activity against Kurdish and Ottoman mistreatment of peasant population.

1890 Mkrtich Khrimian exiled to Jerusalem by Ottoman authorities and denied travel permit. Armenian Revolutionary Federation founded in Tbilisi, in the Russian Empire, by Kirstapor Mikayelian, Stepan Zorian, and Simon Zavarian. Issues party organ *Troshak* (Banner). Hnchaks organize a public demonstration in Istanbul at Kum Kapi in front of the Armenian Patriarchate and present grievances and demands for reforms in the provinces. First instance of protest by a minority in the Ottoman capital.

1891 Dicran *Pasha* d'Abro, Nubar *Pasha*'s son-in-law, foreign minister of Egypt until 1895.

1892 Mkrtich Khrimian elected catholicos. Anointed in Edjmiadsin September 26, 1893. Serves until 1907. Popularly known as Khrimian *Hayrik*, father of the common people.

1893 Komitas *Vardapet* appointed choirmaster of Edjmiadsin. Dedicates life to recording Armenian folk music.

1894 Nubar *Pasha* serves third term as prime minister of Egypt until 1895. Armenians in Sasun resist Kurdish incursion and are subjected to massacre by regular Ottoman army forces. Beginning of the Armenian Massacres in Ottoman Turkey that continue until 1896.

1895 May: Great Powers propose reforms for the Armenian provinces in the Ottoman Empire. Sultan Abdul-Hamid II obstructs the reform plans. **September:** In demonstrations organized by Hnchaks, Armenians in Istanbul protest mistreatment and massacres of the population in the Armenian provinces. Demonstrators and populace massacred by Turkish mobs.

1896 Armenians in Van organize defense against imminent massacre and avert fate of other Armenian-populated cities. Armenians fleeing massacres resettle in Russia, Bulgaria, Romania, and America. Hnchakian party splinters into nationalist and socialist groups in the wake of the Armenian Massacres. Arpiar Arpiarian and others lead in the formation of the liberal Reformed Hnchakian party. Maghakia Ormanian elected Armenian Patriarch of Istanbul. Serves until removal from office upon 1908 Young Turk Revolution. **August 26:** Armenian Revolutionary (ARF) group led by Papken Suni seizes European-owned Ottoman Bank in Istanbul to draw attention of the West to the plight of the Armenians. 5–6,000 Armenians slaughtered in response.

1898 Arshag Chobanian founds the literary journal *Anahit* in Paris. Promotes Armenian writers, literary criticism, and historical scholarship of literature.

1899 Alexandropol/Gyumri linked by rail to Tbilisi. First city in Armenia connected to Russian rail line system. First Marxist group affiliated with Russian Social Democratic Workers Party founded in Armenia by Stepan Shahumian.

1901 Vahan Tekeyan publishes his first of five volumes of poetry.

1902   Yerevan connected by rail to Alexandropol/Gyumri and yonder to Tbilisi, the communications hub of the Russian Transcaucasus.

1903   Tsar Nicholas II of Russia decrees confiscation of Armenian church properties to undermine rising tide of Armenian nationalism. Catholicos Khrimian defies edict. Policy has reverse effect and provokes empire-wide protest from generally pro-Russian Armenian population.

1905   Revolution breaks out in Russia. Turmoil in the Caucasus as Armenians and Azeris clash across the region. Armenians in Baku massacred. 1903 confiscation edict rescinded in Russia. Ottoman sultan deprives Krikor Zohrab, attorney famed for defending cases against the government, of license to practice law.

1906   Armenian General Benevolent Union founded in Cairo, Egypt, under leadership of Boghos Nubar *Pasha*.

1907   Siamanto starts publishing dramatic poetry on Armenian condition in the Ottoman Empire with *Ap me Mokhir*, *Hayreni Tun* (A Handful of Ash Native Home). **June 26:** Armenian Bolshevik revolutionary Kamo stages daytime robbery of state funds in Tbilisi.

1908   Young Turk Revolution restores the Ottoman Constitution and briefly introduces era of liberalism and optimism in the Ottoman Empire. Armenians join in welcoming end of the Hamidian autocracy. Nicholas Adontz publishes in St. Petersburg seminal work in modern Armenian historiography, *Armenia in the Period of Justinian*.

1909   Hrachia Ajarian ushers in modern Armenian linguistic scholarship with his study of the Armenian dialects. Avetik Isahakian publishes his poetic masterpiece *Abu Lala Mahari*. Alexander Khatisian appointed mayor of Tbilisi. Retains post until 1917. Siamanto publishes collection of poems *Bloody News from My Friend* voicing outrage in response to Adana massacre. Taniel Varuzhan publishes first important collection of poetry, *Tseghin Sirde* (The Heart of the Race). Articulates a new nationalism in reaction to the massacres. **April:** Massacre of Armenians of Adana province, medieval Cilician Armenia, in Ottoman Turkey triggered by the Hamidian counter-revolution. Young Turks, also implicated in massacres, depose Abdul-Hamid and exile him under arrest to Thessaloniki. Armenians in Hajen/Hadjin and Chokmarzban/Dortyol resist massacres.

1912   Gabriel Noradoungian appointed Ottoman foreign minister: serves until 1913. Ohannes Guyumjian appointed Ottoman governor of Lebanon: serves until 1915. Calouste Gulbenkian organizes the Turkish Petroleum Company in the Ottoman Empire. Secures 5 percent control upon expansion of company in 1914. Maghakia Ormanian begins publication of *Azgapatum* (National History), a comprehensive chronicle of the Armenian church. Publication completed posthumously in 1927. Taniel Varuzhan publishes second collection of poems, *Hetanos Yerker* (Pagan Songs), invoking pre-Christian ethos as source of national pride.

1913   Committee of Union and Progress (CUP) stages a coup d'etat in Istanbul and installs the Turkish ultra-nationalist triumvirate of Ismail Enver, Ahmed Jemal, and Mehmet Talaat. Armenians oppose Turkification policies. In Paris, Krikor Zohrab, under a pseudonym, publishes his findings on the 1909 Adana Massacres. Implicates Young Turks.

1914 August: World War I breaks out in Europe. CUP government signs secret alliance with Germany. Armenians in Turkey pledge loyalty and are drafted into the Ottoman army. **October:** Ottoman Turkey enters World War I by opening hostilities against Russia. Armenians in Russia volunteer to the front. **December:** Ottomans wage disastrous winter campaign against Russia on the Caucasus front.

1915   Dr. Varastad Kazanjian from the United States pioneers reconstructive surgery in European battlefields. **February:** Ottomans begin disarming and executing Armenian recruits in the armed forces. **April:** Armenians organize self-defense in Van under the leadership of Aram Manukian as Young Turk government begins massacre of Armenian populace in the Ottoman Empire. **April:** Allies land forces on Gallipoli and wage unsuccessful campaign against Ottoman defenses on the peninsula. **April 24:** Beginning of the Armenian Genocide. Leading figures of the Armenian community in Istanbul, including Siamanto, Taniel Varuzhan, and Komitas, are arrested, deported, and most subsequently executed. Krikor Zohrab, Ottoman parliamentary deputy, protests summary actions to Mehmet Talaat, Ottoman minister of the interior and principal organizer of the Armenian Genocide. **Spring and summer:** Armenians across the Ottoman Empire massacred wholesale or deported en masse to Syrian desert. One and a half million Armenians perish in series of mass atrocities lasting into 1923. **May:** Russian forces advance on Van and lift Ottoman siege of Armenian neighborhood of Van. **June 3:** Krikor Zohrab stripped of parliamentary immunity by Talaat. Deported to Diyarbekir and executed. **July 21:** Armenians of Musa Dagh defy deportation edict, retreat to the mountain and resort to self-defense. Withstand siege by regular Ottoman army forces until sighted by Allied naval vessels and rescued September 12, 1915. **July 31:** Russian forces retreat from Van upon Ottoman counter-offensive. Mass exodus of Armenian survivors by long march to Yerevan to flee certain death.

1916 Yeghishe Charents publishes his first major work of poetry, *Danteakan Araspel* (Dante-esque Legend) upon witnessing the Armenian Genocide. July: Young Turk government suspends the Regulations/ Constitution of the Armenian *Millet*, effectively abolishing the institution and exiles the Armenian Patriarch Zaven Der-Yeghiayan of Istanbul to Jerusalem. Sahak II Khapayian Catholicos of Cilicia designated by regime Catholicos-Patriarch in Jerusalem.

1917 Vahan Tekeyan, spared from the Armenian Genocide by chance, publishes the plaint *Pidi Esenk Astudso* (We Shall Say to God). October–November: Bolshevik coup in Russia overthrows democratic government in St. Petersburg. Bolsheviks seek end of war at any price. Transcaucasia left undefended does not recognize Bolshevik authority.

1918 January: Aram Manukian tasked with the defense of Yerevan by the Armenian National Council in Tbilisi as Russian armed forces on the Ottoman front disintegrate after the Russian Revolution. **April 22:** The Transcaucasian Seim (legislature) in Tbilisi declares the secession of the Democratic Federative Republic of Transcaucasia from Russia. Dissolves by May 28 into separate states of Georgia, Azerbaijan, and Armenia. **May:** Armenians defend territory of Yerevan province from Ottoman forces. Battles at Sardarapat, Karakilise, and Bash-Abaran. Ottoman advance halted. **May 28:** Republic of Armenia founded with proclamation of statehood in the former Russian province of Yerevan. City of Yerevan becomes capital of Armenia. Administration run by the directorate of Aram Manukian until arrival of Armenian cabinet from Tbilisi. **June 4:** Treaty of Batumi signed between the Republic of Armenia and the Ottoman Empire ending hostilities. Russian province of Kars claimed by Armenia is occupied by Turkey. **June 30:** First government of the Republic of Armenia formed with Hovhannes Kachaznuni as president-prime minister. **July 19:** Armenian government arrives in

Yerevan from Tbilisi. **August:** Baku Commune under Stepan Shahumian and Russian revolutionaries overthrown. **September:** Ottoman forces reach Baku and install Azeri government. Stepan Shahumian and Bolshevik leaders of commune arrested and executed in Central Asia. Armenians in Baku massacred.

1919 June: Electorate goes to the polls for the first time in the Republic of Armenia. Gives majority of seats in parliament to the ARF. **June:** Alexander Khatisian, prime minister, forms new government in Armenia. Serves until May 1920.

1920 May: First attempt to Sovietize Armenia by local Bolshevik revolutionaries is suppressed. **May:** Hamazasp Ohandjanian, prime minister, forms new government in Armenia. **August 10:** Treaty of Sèvres signed by Avetis Aharonian on behalf of the Republic of Armenia. Armenia extended international recognition. **September:** Turkish Nationalist forces invade and partition the Republic of Armenia. **October:** Eight-month siege of Hajen/Hadjin in Cilicia by Turkish Nationalist forces ends with flight of last survivors to Adana. **November:** Red Army forces enter the Republic of Armenia. **November 24:** Momentary transfer of authority in Armenia to Prime Minister Simon Vratzian. **November 29:** Armenia declared a Soviet republic. Sargis Kasian heads the Communist revolutionary committee. **December 2:** Power formally transferred by treaty from ARF-led government to Bolshevik authorities in Armenia. Treaty terms disregarded by Communists. Repression introduced.

1921 Turkish Nationalist forces massacre refugee Armenians and drive out survivors from southern Turkey and Cilicia. Armenians resettle in Syria, Iraq, Lebanon, Cyprus, France, and Americas. Treaty of Moscow signed between Turkey and Soviet Russia defines the boundary between the two countries. Kars is formally incorporated into Turkey. Nakhichevan is separated from Armenia and assigned to Soviet Azerbaijan. Armenian Democratic Liberal Party formed in Istanbul. **February:** Revolt against Soviet rule in Armenia. Simon Vratzian heads Committee for the Salvation of the Fatherland. Communists briefly driven from Yerevan. Lenin appoints Alexander Miasnikian as head of the Communist Party of Armenia (CPA) to restore Soviet authority.

1922 January 30: First congress of soviets in Armenia adopts a constitution for the Armenian Soviet Socialist Republic (ASSR). **March 12:** Soviet Armenia, Georgia, and Azerbaijan joined into the Federation of Soviet Socialist Republics of Transcaucasia. **September:** Turkish Nationalist forces enter Smyrna/Izmir and burn Armenian and Greek neighborhoods. Greek forces evacuate Asia Minor. Last surviving Armenian community in Anatolia destroyed. Armenians resettle in Greece. **December 10:** Transcaucasian federation further centralized by Stalin into a single Transcaucasian Socialist Federated Soviet Republic. Dissolved into separate republics in 1936. **December 30:** Union of Soviet Socialist Republics (USSR) formed with the Transcaucasian Republic as a constituent state.

1923   Nagorno Karabagh Autonomous Oblast inhabited by majority Armenian population created inside Soviet Azerbaijan. Stepanakert named capital city. Anastas Mikoyan elected full member of the Central Committee of the Communist Party in Moscow. Charents publishes his patriotic novel *Yerkir Nayiri* (Land of Nairi). **July 24:** Treaty of Lausanne extends formal Allied recognition of the Turkish Republic. The Armenian Question closed as a subject of European Great Power diplomacy.

1924   Armenian General Benevolent Union (AGBU) relocates from Cairo, Egypt, to Paris, France. Vosdanik Adoian in the United States begins signing his paintings with the pseudonym Arshile Gorky.

1925   Miasnikian dies in a plane crash. Ashot Hovhannisian succeeds as CPA leader until 1927.

1926   Major earthquake strikes Leninakan/Gyumri.

1927   Gulbenkian's company discovers oil in Kirkuk, Iraq.

1928   Simon Vratzian publishes in Paris *Hayastani Hanrapetutiun*, a record of the first Republic of Armenia. Soon after settles in Lebanon as principal of the Neshan Palanjian academy.

1929   Rouben Mamoulian makes film-directing debut in United States with *Applause*. Alex Manoogian founds Masco auto parts manufacturing company with partners in Detroit, Michigan. Company goes public in 1936.

1930   First of six hydroelectric stations built on Hrazdan River to harness waters of Lake Sevan. Catholicos Sahak II Khapayian and Coadjutor Catholicos Papken Giuleserian relocated the Catholicosate of the Great House of Cilicia to Antelias, Lebanon. **May:** Aghasi Khanjian appointed first secretary of the CPA by Stalin. Holds office until 1936. Oversees collectivization. Personally popular leader in Armenia.

1933 Franz Werfel publishes *Forty Days of Musa Dagh*. The novel is an instant best-seller. Film production in Hollywood suppressed by U.S. Department of State at behest of Turkish Embassy in Washington. Rouben Mamoulian directs Greta Garbo in Hollywood film classic *Queen Christina*, assuring lasting stardom for the actress. Archbishop Ghevond Turian assassinated in New York. Armenian church split over question of authority between the Edjmiadsin catholicosate in Soviet Armenia and of the catholicosate of Cilicia relocated to Antelias, Lebanon.

1934 William Saroyan publishes in the United States *The Daring Young Man on the Flying Trapeze* to critical acclaim.

1935 Anastas Mikoyan elected full member of the Politburo of the Communist Party in Moscow. Rouben Mamoulian stage directs George Gershwin's musical *Porgy and Bess* at Broadway premiere.

1936 Yeghishe Charents, leading poet and writer in Soviet Armenia, jailed in Yerevan. **July 9:** Aghasi Khanjian reported by Lavrenti Beria to have committed suicide. Stalinist purges and Great Terror begin in Armenia.

1937 Yeghishe Charents dies in prison.

1938 Khoren Muratbekian, catholicos in Edjmiadsin since 1932, murdered by Soviet secret police. Catholicosate left vacant until 1945. Religious institutions in Soviet Armenia decimated. Anastas Mikoyan appointed USSR minister of foreign trade. Retains post until 1949.

1939 Viktor Hambartsumian appointed the first professor of astrophysics in the Soviet Union.

1940 Artem Mikoyan leads team in the USSR that constructs the high altitude aerial combat plane named in his honor MIG-1, principal World War II Soviet fighter plane. William Saroyan's play *The Time of Your Life* wins Pulitzer Prize. Also publishes *My Name is Aram*.

1941 Alan Hovhannes receives recognition in the United States for his musical compositions. Yousef Karsh, in Canada, photographs World War II iconic portrait of Winston Churchill. Rouben Mamoulian directs Tyrone

Power and Rita Hayworth in his best-known dramatic film *Blood and Sand*. Nazi Germany invades the Soviet Union. 500,000 Armenians are mobilized into service in Soviet armed forces during World War II.

1942 Aram Khachaturian composes *Gayane* ballet.

1943 Rouben Mamoulian stages Richard Rogers and Oscar Hammerstein's musical *Oklahoma!* at Broadway premiere. William Saroyan publishes *The Human Comedy*. Also made into Hollywood film.

1944 Arshile Gorky begins to produce his major abstract expressionist works. Avetik Isahakian elected permanent president of the writers' union in Soviet Armenia. Serves until 1957. Patronizes young literary talents who revere him as the "master."

1945 Red Army Armenian Division, after a continuous advance from the Caucasus against Nazi forces, takes part in the capture of Berlin. 174,000 Armenians fall in battle by war's end. Garegin I Hovsepiants catholicos of Cilicia until 1952. Attempts unsuccessfully to heal rift in Armenian church.

1946 Anastas Mikoyan appointed first deputy chairman of the USSR Council of Ministers, effective vice-premier of the Soviet Union. Soviet Armenia encourages repatriation of diaspora Armenians until 1948 to make up shortfall in manpower after World War II. Viktor Hambartsumian founds the Byurakan observatory. Provides major impetus to advanced scientific research in astronomy, physics, and computers in Armenia.

1947 Viktor Hambartsumian elected president of the Academy of Sciences in the ASSR. Holds post until his death in 1996.

1952 Anton Kochinian president of the Council of Ministers of the ASSR. Serves as prime minister until his 1966 promotion to first secretary of the CPA.

1953 Suren Tovmasian, a Khrushchev appointee, first secretary of the CPA until 1960. Alex Manoogian, Detroit industrialist and owner of Masco, assumes presidency of AGBU, relocated to New York since 1942.

1954 Masco begins rapid expansion with manufacture of single handle faucet. Becomes billion-dollar corporation by 1960s. Anastas

Mikoyan tests de-Stalinization in Soviet Armenia two years before Nikita Khrushchev's denunciation of Stalin at Communist Party congress in 1956. Yeghishe Charents and others purged are rehabilitated in Armenia by Mikoyan.

1955 Ivan Baghramian, World War II Soviet army commander on the Baltic front and USSR deputy defense minister, promoted to marshal of the Soviet Union. Ivan Isakov, World War II naval commander, promoted to admiral of the Soviet Navy. Vazgen Palchian catholicos in Edjmiadsin until 1994. Begins restoration of the church in Soviet Armenia and travels to the diaspora. Calouste Gulbenkian Foundation created in Lisbon, Portugal, upon decease of the oil magnate.

1959 Soviet census counts 1.5 million Armenians out of a population of 1.7 million in the ASSR and 2.8 million Armenians in the entire USSR, of whom 443,000 live in Georgian SSR and 442,000 live in Azerbaijan SSR.

1960s French popular singer Charles Aznavour at height of popularity. Tigran Petrosian world chess champion.

1960 Zakov Zarobian, a Khrushchev appointee, first secretary of the CPA until 1966.

1961 Gamal Abdel-Nasser introduces nationalization of domestic commerce in Egypt. Armenians begin leaving the Middle East under mounting pressure of Arab nationalism.

1962 Kirk Kerkorian begins building business empire in aviation, Las Vegas hotels, Hollywood movie studios, and eventually Detroit auto manufacturing.

1964 Anastas Mikoyan elected chairman of the Presidium of the USSR Supreme Soviet, titular president of the Soviet Union, until 1965. Sergei Paradjanov makes first individualistic film, *Shadows of Our Forgotten Ancestors*. Regarded breakthrough production in Soviet film-making.

1965 Armenians worldwide commemorate 50th anniversary of the Armenian Genocide. Demonstrations in Yerevan suppressed as illegal expression of nationalism.

1966 Anton Kochinian, a Brezhnev appointee, first secretary of the CPA until 1974.

1969 Sergei Paradjanov films *Nran Guyne* (The Color of Pomegranate). Iconoclastic production based on life of 18th century Armenian minstrel Sayat Nova is subjected to censorship. Film and director receive Western accolades.

1972 Armenian Assembly of America founded. Represents U.S.–Armenian community with federal government in Washington.

1974 Karen Demirchian, a Brezhnev appointee, first secretary of the CPA until 1988. Sergei Paradjanov imprisoned and prevented from film-making again until 1984.

1975 Michael J. Arlen publishes *Passage to Ararat*, groundbreaking memoir on Armenian diaspora identity and best-seller in the United States. Civil war breaks out in Lebanon disrupting the largest Armenian diaspora community based in Beirut. Exodus of Armenians begins. **April:** Armenian Secret Army for the Liberation of Armenia (ASALA), underground organization based in Lebanon promoting political violence against Turkish targets, makes appearance. Remains active for a decade in an avowed campaign of revenge for the Armenian Genocide.

1976 Fadey Sargsian appointed president of ASSR Council of Ministers. Serves as prime minister until 1989.

1979 Iranian revolution topples shah's regime and establishes an Islamic republic. Armenians begin leaving Iran.

1983 George Deukmejian elected governor of the state of California in the United States. Serves two terms until 1991. Karekin II Sarkissian catholicos of Cilicia until 1995. Enlists Armenian church in Christian ecumenical movement. ASALA plants bomb at Orly airport in France. New policy of targeting civilians splinters organization and undermines support.

1985 Gary Kasparov wins world chess championship at age 22. Mikhail Gorbachev elected first secretary of the Communist Party in the USSR. Seeks end of the Cold War.

1987 Gorbachev introduces *perestroika* (restructuring) in the Soviet Union based on the economic theories of Abel Aganbegyan. **September:** Union for National Self-Determination formed in Armenia. Led by Soviet dissident Paruyr Hayrikian. Functions as political party after independence.

1988 February 11: Karabagh Movement begins with public meetings in Stepanakert followed by mass meetings in Yerevan. Demonstrations call for unification of Nagorno Karabagh and Armenia by popular invocation of *perestroika.* **February 28:** Pogroms break out against Armenians in Azerbaijan. **May 18:** Suren Harutiunian, a Gorbachev appointee, first secretary of the CPA until 1990. **December 7:** Earthquake centered in Spitak destroys cities in northern Armenia. Leninakan/Gyumri severely damaged. 25,000 reported dead, 12,000 injured, 500,000 homeless, out of a population of 3.5 million in the country.

1989 May 31: Arrested after the earthquake and jailed in Moscow, Karabagh Committee is released from prison. **June–October:** Armenian National Movement (ANM) organized as a political force growing out of the Karabagh Movement.

1990 Republican Party of Armenia formed. **April:** Vladimir Movsisian, a Gorbachev appointee, first secretary of the CPA. Effectively last party chief in Armenia. Eventually resigns from the organization and cooperates with democratic forces. **August:** Free elections in Armenia. ANM gains control of the Supreme Soviet or parliament. Legislative authority passes from communists to democrats. Vazgen Manukian, an ANM leader, appointed prime minister by the Armenian parliament. Serves until October 1991. First non-Communist government installed in Armenia. **August 4:** Levon Ter-Petrossian elected president of the Armenian parliament. Effectively first non-Communist head of state. **August 23:** Parliament in Armenia issues a declaration on independence charting the course of secession from the Soviet Union. Country formally renamed Republic of Armenia.

1991 June: Armenian parliament enacts legislation creating post of president of the republic. **August:** Democratic Party of Armenia formed by former Communists. **September 2:** Nagorno Karabagh Republic (NKR) established. Local Armenian authorities declare the Nagorno Karabagh Autonomous District a republic, severing relations with Azerbaijan. **September 21:** Referendum held in Armenia. Overwhelming majority votes to secede from the Soviet Union. Referendum results confirmed September 23. Armenia formally independent. **October 16:** First popular presidential elections held in Armenia. Levon Ter-Petrossian wins by large majority of votes. **November:** Gagik Haroutiunian prime minister of Armenia until July 1992. **December 10:** Referendum on independence held in Nagorno Karabagh. **December 28:** Elections held for the first parliament of the Nagorno Karabagh Republic.

1992 Agrarian Democratic Party formed by former Communists. National Democratic Union (NDU) formed under leadership of Vazgen Manukian. **January 6:** The Parliament of the Nagorno Karabagh Republic (NKR) officially declares independence. **May 9:** Armenian forces in NKR take control of Shushi from Azeris. They proceed to open a corridor to Armenia through Lachin by May 18. **July 30:** Khosrov Harutiunian prime minister of Armenia. Serves until February 11, 1993. **August 15:** State Defense Committee formed in NKR to respond to war emergency. Committee in existence until December 1994. **Winter:** State of emergency declared in Armenia due to lack of heating fuel caused by blockade of the country by Azerbaijan and Turkey.

1993 February 16: Prime Minister Hrant Bagratian's first cabinet appointed. Serves until July 26, 1995. **March:** Armenian forces seize Kelbajar region in Azerbaijan and close the breach between Armenia and NKR. **August 21:** Serge Sargsian, commander of the NKR forces, appointed defense minister of Armenia. **October:** Armenian forces establish defense perimeter around NKR. **December 18:** Azeri forces stage last major offensive of the Karabagh war.

1994 May 14: Truce signed by commanders of the Armenian, NKR, and Azeri armies. **December 17:** Hambartsum Galstian, Karabagh Committee leader and former mayor of Yerevan, killed in Yerevan. **December 22:** NKR parliament elects Robert Kocharian president. State Defense Committee dissolved. Civilian government introduced in NKR. Leonard Petrosian appointed prime minister. Serves until 1998. **December 28:** President Ter-Petrossian suspends ARF in Armenia on charges of members' involvement in criminal activities.

1995 April 4: Karekin II Sarkissian, catholicos of Cilicia, elected Supreme Patriarch and Catholicos of All Armenians in first pontifical elections held in over 600 years in an independent Armenia. Anointed as Garegin I in Edjmiadsin. **April 30:** Parliamentary elections held in NKR. Oleg Yesayan appointed chairman of the legislature. **July 5:** Constitution adopted for the Republic of Armenia by popular referendum. Vote confirmed July 7. Coinciding parliamentary elections give majority of seats in the new National Assembly to the ANM. Election results are disputed. **July 27:** Prime Minister Hrant Bagratian's second cabinet appointed. Serves until November 3, 1996.

1996 February 6: Constitutional Court created in Armenia. Gagik Haroutiunian appointed chief justice. **September 22:** Presidential elections held in Armenia. Levon Ter-Petrossian and Vazgen Manukian leading candidates. Ter-Petrossian declared winner in contested vote. Popular unrest breaks out in Yerevan. **November 4:** Prime Minister Armen Sarkissian's cabinet appointed. Serves until March 20, 1997. **November 24:** Robert Kocharian elected president of NKR. Resigns in March 1997 to accept appointment as prime minister of Armenia.

1997 March 20: Prime Minister Robert Kocharian's cabinet appointed. Serves until April 8, 1998. **September 1:** Arkady Ghukasian elected president of NKR. Reappoints Leonard Petrosian prime minister on September 10.

1998 February: Vazgen Sargsian assumes leadership of Republican Party of Armenia (RPA). Combines political party with Union of Volunteer Defenders of the Land, called *Yekrapah*, which he also leads. **February 3:** Ter-Petrossian resigns presidency of Armenia. ANM ministers as well as speaker of the National Assembly Babken Ararktsian resign from the government. **February 4:** Khosrov Harutiunian elected speaker by National Assembly deputies. Holds post until June 15, 1999. **March 16:** Special presidential elections held in Armenia. **March 30:** Run-off presidential elections held between leading candidates Robert Kocharian and Karen Demirchian. Kocharian declared winner. **April 20:** Prime Minister Armen Darbinian's cabinet appointed. Serves until June 14, 1999. **May:** Populist Party of Armenia (PPA) founded by former Communist Party chief Karen Demirchian. **June 13:** Zhirair Poghosian prime minister of NKR. Serves until 1999.

1999 May 30: Parliamentary elections held in Armenia. RPA led by Vazgen Sargsian and PPA led by Karen Demirchian form winning bloc. **June 10:** Karen Demirchian voted speaker of the National Assembly by deputies. **June 15:** Prime Minister Vazgen Sargsian's cabinet appointed. Serves until October 27, 1999. **June 30:** Anushavan Danielian appointed prime minister of NKR. **September 22–23:** Major Armenia-Diaspora conference convened in Yerevan under sponsorship of the president and prime minister. **October 27:** Prime Minister Vazgen Sargsian and National Assembly speaker Karen Demirchian along with other lawmakers gunned down in the chamber of the National Assembly. Garegin II Nersisian, bishop of the diocese of Ararat, in Armenia, elected catholicos in Edjmiadsin. Anointed November 4. **November 3:** Aram Sargsian appointed prime minister. **November 13:** Prime Minister Aram Sargsian's cabinet appointed. **November 17:** President Robert Kocharian travels to Istanbul, Turkey, for Organization for Security and Cooperation in Europe (OSCE) heads of states meeting convened in the Chiraghan palace. President Kocharian meets with President Suleyman Demirel of Turkey. Discuss improving relations between countries. Turkey conditions establishment of diplomatic relations on settlement of Karabagh conflict. **November 18:** President Kocharian addresses OSCE summit and introduces new security proposal for Transcaucasus. Also meets with U.S. President Bill Clinton to discuss ongoing peace talks with Azerbaijan. **November 19:** OSCE issues Istanbul summit declaration. Includes endorsement of direct negotiations between Armenia and Azerbaijan for settlement of Karabagh conflict. President Kocharian and Armenian delegation to OSCE summit pay visit to Armenian Patriarchate of Istanbul. **December 24:** Karen Demirchian, son of the late Stepan Demirchian, elected chairman of the PPA.

2000 January 15: Vladimir Darbinian elected chairman of the Communist Party of Armenia. **February 20:** State funeral led by President Kocharian for the reinterment in Armenia of World War I-era national hero General Andranik. **March 22:** Assassination attempt against NKR President Arkady Ghukasian. Former NKR minister of defense accused of coup plot. **May 8–9:** U.S.-Armenia economic task force, created to improve the efficiency of U.S. economic assistance to Armenia convenes in Yerevan. **May 11:** Alexander Arzoumanian, former foreign minister, elected chairman of the ANM. **May 12:** Andranik Margarian appointed prime minister of Armenia by President Kocharian. **June 18:** Parliamentary elections held in NKR. Oleg Yesayan returned as chairman of the 33-member legislature. **June 27:** President Kocharian meets with President Bill Clinton and Vice-President Al Gore in the White House on a visit to the United States. **November 8:** The Council of Europe votes on conditional admission of Armenia to membership. **November 10:** Pope John Paul II and Catholicos of All Armenians Garegin II meet in the Vatican and issue a joint communiqué on the occasion of the Year 2000 Jubilee and the forthcoming 1700th anniversary of the proclamation of Christianity as the state religion of Armenia. **November 15:** European Parliament adopts resolution on Turkey's membership calling on its government to normalize relations with Armenia and recognize the Armenian Genocide. **December 11–12:** On tour of the region's capitals OSCE Minsk Group delegation visits Stepanakert for a meeting with President Ghukasian.

2001 January 29: France formally recognizes the 1915 Armenian Genocide with the adoption of a law by both chambers of the legislature. **February 4:** Serving cabinet minister Davit Vardanian emerges as contender for NDU party leadership held by former prime minister Vazgen Manukian. NDU splinters into small groups. **March 3–5:** President Kocharian and Azerbaijan President Heidar Aliyev hold meetings in Paris convened by French President Jacques Chirac to discuss resolution of the Karabagh conflict. **April 3–6** President Kocharian and Azerbaijan President Heidar Aliyev hold meetings in Key West, Florida, convened by U.S. Secretary of State Colin Powell to discuss resolution of the Karabagh conflict. **May 10:** World Bank President James Wolfensohn and President Kocharian open in New York an international conference on investment in Armenia. **May 21:** The International Monetary Fund (IMF) announces a new aid program for Armenia to combat poverty and a loan package to encourage foreign investment. **September 2:** NKR celebrates ten years of statehood. **September 21:** Tenth anniversary of Armenian independence celebrated. **September 25–27:** John Paul II makes first papal visit in history to Armenia. The Roman Catholic pontiff celebrates Mass at the Holy See of Edjmiadsin, the Mother Cathedral of the Armenian Apostolic Church and pays tribute to the victims of the Armenian Genocide at the Tzitzernakaberd Memorial.

Introduction

There are two Armenias, the current Republic of Armenia and historic Armenia. The modern state dates from the early 20th century. Historic Armenia was part of the ancient world. It expired in the Middle Ages. Its people, however, survived, and from its residue recreated a new country.

The history of the Armenians is the story of how an ancient people endured into modern times, and how its culture evolved from one conceived under the influence of Mesopotamia, the cradle of human civilization, to one redefined by the civilization of Europe. In this it is as much a story of the spiritual migration of a people as of their physical peregrination across the globe.

The crisscrossing of all these pathways is what places Armenia today at the southeasternmost frontier of Europe, a country straddling one of the great civilizational divides of the world: to the East the great landmass of Asia, its vast estates parceled out among its permanent inhabitants as in Iran, India, and China; and to the West a bevy of peoples, heirs to an intellectual dynamic that has made of Europe the most developed part of the global community in modern times.

Armenia inhabits this intermediate zone between Asian permanence and European change. It is this awareness of location that makes Armenia a constant question of polity more so than a matter of geography. The question remains even at the dawn of the 21st century. Wherein the Armenians are to be self-governing and where not are still contested.

Contest is the other characteristic of Armenia. Every facet of Armenia has been contested: its location, borders, government, religion, culture, language, and people. Nothing has been spared in Armenia: neither its kings nor queens; its bishops nor knights; its castles nor pawns. Armenia has been a chessboard on which great powers have waged virtual combat and actual bloodbaths.

Users of this volume should note that cross-refrences to dictionary entries are printed in boldface type.

Who would have mastery of Armenia has been a question asked more frequently than who would be master in Armenia. The imbalance of power thereby is also another characteristic of Armenia's history, ever confronting its people with the wages of sovereignty, survival, and submission. Lastly, for all the fracturing of their political history, overarching continuities have made of the ancient Armenians a living people of the modern world. In the face of periodic threats of extinction they have retrieved resources and strength to regenerate their society and aspire again to rejoin the community of nations.

GEOGRAPHY AND ENVIRONMENT

The Republic of Armenia is situated in the south Caucasus, or Transcaucasus, at a point of geography where the extreme southeast of Europe intersects the southwestern quadrant of the Asian landmass. Armenia is an ancient country with a long history. Its current **political geography**, however, was shaped in the early 20th century and is the product of modern history. Armenia is bounded on the north by Georgia, the east by Azerbaijan, the south by Iran, and the west by Turkey and the Azerbaijan exclave of Nakhichevan. It lies mostly between longitude 39 and 41.5 north, and latitude 43.5 and 46.5 east. Its total area is 29,800 sq. km. (11,506 sq. mi.) with 28,400 sq. km. of land and 1,400 sq. km. of water, which is mainly **Lake Sevan** (1,200 sq. km.) covering nearly 5 percent of the superficies, and holding 90 percent of the standing water, of the country. Armenia is landlocked, with the total length of its border measured at 1,254 km. (779 mi.), of which 164 km. is with Georgia, 566 km. with Azerbaijan proper, 35 km. with Iran, 221 km. with the Azerbaijan exclave of Nakhichevan, and 268 km. with Turkey. Almost half the length of the border with Turkey is marked by the **Arax River**, while the same river delineates the entire stretch of the border with Iran as well. Armenia is also watered by the Akhurian, Medsamor, Hrazdan, Azat, Arpa, Vorotan, Debed, and Agstev Rivers. Of these, the Hrazdan, which drains from Lake Sevan, produces most of the hydroelectric energy available in the country and supplies the drinking water for the capital city of **Yerevan.**

The most distinctive features of Armenia are its mountains, which cover most of the country, with the alluvial Plain of Ararat (Ararati Dashte) as the country's principal agricultural zone. Only 17 percent of the land is arable and with just 3 percent under irrigation and bearing permanent crops. Because of its elevation and terrain, 24 percent to 30 percent of the land is permanent pastures, and between 12 percent and 15 percent woodlands and forest. The remaining nearly 40 percent of the country is uninhabitable due to the ruggedness of the highlands, the barrenness of the land, and the steepness of its mountain slopes. The highest peak in Armenia is Mount Aragats at 4,090 meters. A better index of the size of this volcanic cone is its circumference measured at 200 km. The higher peak of Mount Ararat, which is visible throughout much of southern Armenia, lies in Turkey. The lowest point in the country is measured at 400 meters, and the average elevation between 1,800 and 2,000 meters. This topographic aspect of Armenia means that none of its rivers are navigable because of their rapid descent from higher elevations. All in all, despite the small size of the country, travel across it is difficult due to the obstruction of steep mountain ranges. The highway system covers 10,500 km. (6,525 mi.) of road, and 840 km. (522 mi.) of railroad, which was integral to the Russian rail system, and therefore of a different gauge than neighboring Turkey and Iran.

The climate of Armenia also ranges widely from the subtropical in the lowlands to the alpine in the highlands. However, the country is arid and receives little precipitation, measured at 33 cm. (13 in.) in Yerevan. Northern Armenia receives more rainfall than the rest of the country as it catches the weather fronts moving over the Black Sea. This also makes the region more forested compared to parts of the south, which are very dry. Winters are cold, with the mean temperature in January at –3 C (27 F). The winter snowfall in higher elevations is considerable. The summers are hot and the mean temperature in August is 25 C (77 F).

The **historical geography** of Armenia covered a much larger area encompassing what is called the Armenian plateau, the elevated terrain from the Kura River on the east to the Euphrates River on the west, with the Pontic and the Anti-Taurus ranges defining the northern and southern boundaries respectively. The mountains in the Republic of Armenia constitute part of the Lesser Caucasus range that runs north from **Nagorno** (Mountainous) **Karabagh** and the Siunik, or Zangezur, branch in the panhandle of southern Armenia all the way to the north of the country and into southern Georgia linking with the Pontic range near the Black Sea. The entire Armenian plateau is earthquake prone and regularly affected by tremors and occasionally by major shifts of the tectonic plates. The most recent severe tremor was the **Spitak Earthquake** of 1988.

POPULATION AND SOCIETY

In the year 2000 the population of Armenia was variously estimated between 3.5 and 3.7 million. At the same time approximately 700,000 were reported to have emigrated, with some estimates placing the figure closer to a million or more. In 1987, prior to the political upheavals that altered the demographic pattern of the entire Caucasus region, the population of Armenia counted at 3,411,900. The birthrate is estimated at 16 percent per 1,000 and the death rate 8 percent, resulting in a natural increase of 8 percent. Living conditions in Armenia, however, fluctuated widely during the decade of the 1990s considerably altering natural demographic progressions, and seriously affecting the most vulnerable age groups, namely the very young and the old, which resulted in the lowering of the natural population growth rate down to as low as 1 percent. Life expectancy in the early 1990s for the total population was 71 years, varying from 68 years for males to 75 years for females. Life expectancy declined in the intervening decade.

The demographic evolution of Armenia in the 20th century took many sharp turns. A population of 1 million in 1913 inhabiting the area of the future Republic of Armenia dropped to 720,000 by 1920 as a consequence of the Ottoman and Turkish invasions of the region in 1918 and 1920. Growth in the early Soviet period was slow. In 1926, the population was at 881,000, which, however, reached 1,320,000 by 1940. Growth was arrested again because of the huge losses during World War II, though in the case of Armenia, which was spared invasion, the male population serving in the armed forces virtually suffered all the casualties. In 1959 the population of Armenia was only 1,763,000. The industrialization of the country thereafter, which led to rapid economic expansion, was reflected in demographic trends as well. In 1970, the population of Armenia had reached 2,491,900, and by 1979 it was 3,030,000. The eastern part of the country being mountainous, the population has always been concentrated in the west, where virtually all the farmland and urban centers are to be found. Average population density in 1992 was measured at 115 per sq. km. (297 per sq. mi.), although, once again, density varies widely between the eastern and western halves of the country.

Along with the growth of the population of Armenia, another noticeable trend was reflected in the demography of the country, namely an increasing degree of ethnic homogeneity. The Armenian republic, formed out of the Erevan/Yerevan and Kars provinces of the Russian Empire in 1918, had begun with an ethnic Armenian majority. Its contraction in 1920 with the attending expulsion of Armenians from occupied territories who then concentrated in the remaining Sovietized portion of the republic gave the country a mostly Armenian population. In 1926, 84 percent of the population of the Armenian Soviet Socialist Republic (ASSR) was Armenian. By 1979, the country was 90 percent Armenian, and in 2000, it was close to 95 percent. There were only three minority ethnic groups in Armenia of any size: Kurds, Russians, and Azeris, numbering, 51,000, 70,000, and 161,000 respectively in 1979. Their numbers dropped in the 1990s, with only Kurds and a small number of Russians remaining as visible minorities. Three other minorities, Greek, Assyrians, and Georgians, each numbering less than 10,000, live scattered across the country.

The ethnic minorities remaining in the Republic of Armenia also happen to be religious minorities, which explains their continuing residence in the country. Christianity has been the dominant **religion** of Armenia since the fourth century. From the viewpoint of the Christian world, Armenia stands at its eastern frontier, surrounded on three sides (Azerbaijan, Iran, and Turkey) by Islamic countries, creating a deep cultural divide between Armenia and most of its neighbors. Georgia to the north, which has a Christian majority, is a religiously fractured society with a substantial Muslim minority. Even though the population lost the habits of religious practice during the Soviet era, the vast majority of Armenians, in the range of 95 percent, nominally still adheres to the **Armenian Apostolic Church**. With independence, the Armenian Catholic and Protestant communities that had gone into hiding slowly assembled new parishes. A small Jewish community numbering between 1,000 and 2,000 resides in the country. The Russian minority, which is concentrated in a number of farming communities, consists mainly of sectarians like the Molokans who were resettled along the periphery of the Russian Empire in the tsarist era. The Kurds of Armenia belong to the Yezidi sect, a faith of ancient origin distinct to a subgroup of the general Kurdish population. The Azeris were the only Islamic minority in the country.

The breakup of the Soviet Union affected the Armenian population in more ways than just those registered in Armenia proper. Of the total 4,627,277 Armenians in the Soviet Union in 1989, only 3,081,920 lived in the ASSR, meaning that well over 1.5 million Armenians lived in other republics of the USSR. They mostly concentrated in the two neighboring countries of Georgia and Azerbaijan, with a substantial number in Russia. In 1959, Armenians constituted 15.9 percent of the population of the two adjacent Soviet republics. While their number registered absolute gains, they declined comparatively as the nationality associated with each nominal republic, as in Armenia, also registered faster growth. In 1979, the 475,000 Armenians of Azerbaijan and 448,000 Armenians of Georgia constituted about 11 percent of the total population of those republics. Another 532,000 ethnic Armenians lived in Russia, with 60,000 in Ukraine, and a respectable number in Central Asia, including 50,000 in Uzbekistan, 31,000 in Turkmenistan, and 19,000 in Kazakhstan. This distribution made for a paradoxical set of facts. Armenia was the most ethnically homogeneous republic of the USSR. At the same time, only two-thirds of the total Armenian population of the USSR resided in Armenia, making Armenians the most widely dispersed nationality of the Soviet Union.

This set of demographic statistics combined with a geography of instability in the late- and post-Soviet period resulted in a population crisis manifested as a widespread refugee problem. In the year 2000, an estimated 240,000 refugees, virtually all Armenians, had sought asylum in Armenia. This population consisted mostly of Armenians from Azerbaijan, with 200,000 from Azerbaijan proper and 30,000 from Nagorno Karabagh, with an additional 10,000 from Abkhazia and Chechnya. Approximately 400,000 Armenians were displaced from Azerbaijan between 1988 and 1992, only about half of whom sought refuge in Armenia, the remainder seeking shelter in Russia, and beyond. Moreover, 60,000 inhabitants from the eastern border districts of Armenia were internally displaced as a result of the conflict with Azerbaijan. During the same timeframe the Azeri population of Armenia was displaced and sought refuge in Azerbaijan.

The profile of the Armenian population of Azerbaijan explains the split decision among the displaced on the option of relocating to Armenia, and that had much to do with their urban character. By the late 1980s both the population of Armenia and the Armenian population of the entire Caucasus was highly urbanized. For example, with an estimated population of 1,278,000 in 1995, Yerevan alone housed a full third of the population of Armenia. During the course of the 20th century the capital city grew more than tenfold. Armenia underwent intensive urbanization in the Soviet period. In 1926 only 19 percent of the population in Armenia lived in urban settings, indication that a large majority of the working people was engaged in agriculture. By 1959, in little over a generation, 50 percent of the population was living in cities. By 1979, but another generation later, 66 percent were in cities, and by 2000 an estimated 79 percent of the population was living in urban areas.

Ancient cities dotted the landscape of historic Armenia. Of these many are located in the Republic of Armenia, but only two have grown into modern cities, Yerevan and **Gyumri**. The other urban centers of Armenia are the result of the modernization of previously small towns and villages. Gyumri, once with a population over a quarter million, remains a city badly scarred by the 1988 earthquake. The towns of Hrazdan, Abovian, and Edjmiadsin each have a population of a little over 50,000. All remaining towns in Armenia have populations below 50,000, including Ghapan, Alaverdi, Hokdemberian, Kamo, Dilijan, Vanatzor, Stepanavan, Artik, Sevan, Jermuk, Goris, Ijevan, Ashtarak, Artashat, Ararat, Spitak, and Charetsavan. Again with the exception of Yerevan and Gyumri, all received municipal status between 1924 and 1985. As a consequence of economic difficulties and population shifts, Armenia may be one of the few countries in the late 20th century to have registered a reversal and undergone some degree of de-urbanization.

HISTORY

Early History

Abundant archaeological evidence indicates that early man inhabited the Armenian plateau and all the changes associated with the Neolithic Revolution can also be traced in the oldest sites uncovered to date. This development was due to the proximity of Armenia to those centers where mankind took the decisive steps that led to the development of civilized existence based on the permanent exploitation of the environment through the domestication of plants and animals. Located to the north of Mesopotamia and to the east of Anatolia, the two main centers of the Neolithic Revolution, Armenia enjoyed the benefit of their discoveries through the rapid diffusion of the use of their tools and methods of cultivation. The less hospitable climate of the highlands and the shorter growing season tempered the pace of progress, and the formation of a complex society lagged until such time as political power was consolidated in the country. Animal husbandry more than matched farming as the primary sector of Armenia's Neolithic economy. Metallurgy too made its appearance as the country's mineral resources began to be exploited and exported. In due course agricultural settlements and towns appeared in the fertile plains and valleys of Armenia. That occurred slowly as the terrain of Armenia initially lent itself more to the engendering of tribal society than the encouragement of urban settlements.

The earliest inhabitants are known by the name of their tribal confederations, such as the Hayasa, Arme-Shupria, and Nairi, that over the course of more than a thousand years of interaction eventually fused into a single people. The form of speech they came to have in common was the **Armenian language**. The Semitic languages never penetrated the highlands despite the fact that they were, and continue to be, widely spoken across the Middle East, and became the fonts of a series of ancient civilizations based in Syria and Mesopotamia, both regions immediately bordering Armenia to the south. Raw materials and goods were regularly exchanged between north and south, and the Tigris and Euphrates Rivers provided access routes through otherwise impassable mountains. The oldest form of speech known to have been spoken in the highlands was Hurrian, a family of languages that expired with the ancient world. The most accomplished representatives of the Hurrian-speaking peoples were the Urartians who left their name on the most recognizable landmark of the Armenian plateau, Mount Ararat. In the second millennium B.C., speakers of Indo-European dialects joined the Hurrians. Speakers of Caucasian dialects inhabited northern parts of the country.

Civilization in Armenia, therefore, deeply influenced by the patterns of culture absorbed from Mesopotamia and the south, nevertheless was formed in contradistinction by peoples who spoke languages other than the dominant ones of the ancient Middle East. Thus the population of the highlands early acquired a distinct identity perceived in relation to more advanced neighboring cultures, absorbing new traits from them as needed and wanted, while maintaining a sense of distance. The topography of Armenia also engendered a political culture at odds with the uniformity and conformity that emerged in the highly urbanized parts of the flatlands of the ancient Middle East. The tribal confederations that constituted the earliest noted forms of political organization in Armenia had banded for the common purpose of defense against the increasingly more powerful neighboring states ruled by Assyrians and Hittites, both distinguished as militaristic and highly organized and hierarchically structured societies. The mountain ranges transecting the plateau impeded the formation of a centralized political order. Rather, the country depended for its defense on the martial spirit of its inhabitants and on their preference for self-government over the services of a bureaucracy and an army.

The Age of Kings

Nairi/Urartu

The Bronze Age in Armenia is told through the story of the first state forged in the highlands, the kingdom of Urartu. That is the name by which the powerful Assyrians called the region. The Urartians called their country Nairi. The difference in nomenclature has to do with the fact that Urartu started as a confederation of lesser monarchies based in the highlands, with its earliest center, dating back to the 11th century B.C., found west of Lake Urmia (presently northern Iran), possibly based around the temple, later used as the main treasury, of Musasir. The Urartian state, however, came to full flowering in the ninth century B.C. when its center of gravity was relocated to the **Lake Van** basin, namely the country of Nairi. The Nairian people of Urartu rapidly developed a highly sophisticated and tightly organized society. The answers to the questions, how they emerged, how they seized hold of the country, and why they resorted to policies of rapid development indicate that the people of the highlands underwent a fundamental transformation in those intervening centuries that lifted them from their age-old tribal patterns and rudimentary economy and launched them on the scene of world history. There did not seem to be sufficient resources or riches worth pursing in Armenia before the Urartians created their state. Until that time no external power bothered to seek acquisition of the wealth of the country. After the Urartians organized the land, from then right down to the present, Armenia has remained the object of external interest and forcible possession.

The rapid consolidation of Urartian political power in the Lake Van basin and its expansion across the entire highlands, effectively unifying the Armenian plateau for the first time into a single administrative unity, and meeting the challenge of Assyrian expansionism, attest to the effective and systematic marshaling of the resources of the country. Both the economy and the population of the highlands must have been prepared by earlier developments, of which little is known, that allowed the Urartians to imagine that a state of the kind they created could be conceived and realized in such difficult terrain. While early confederation also points to the emerging need to band together for greater effectiveness, and very likely in response to Assyrian might, at the end of the day the Urartians unified the country through their own military and administrative skills. The material remains of their civilization are of such dimensions that they are still visible as archaeological landmarks across the Armenian plateau.

The Urartians were the first great builders in Armenia, and the art of building in stone, in an earthquake-prone country, was one of the legacies handed down by them. The great cyclopean fortresses, especially on the Rock of Van and at Erebuni, attest to engineering skills placed at the service of strategic considerations. The selection of those locations, among many others, made permanent settlements of those sites. The beginning of urbanization in the highlands, therefore, dates from this era. The Urartian domestic agenda was not confined to fortresses alone. The great military installations of the Bronze Age were actually the nerve centers of regional economies encouraged by the Urartians, who also introduced the concept of irrigation by constructing the earliest stone-lined canals. Some, amazingly, remained in use right into the 20th century. Both large-scale construction and the cultivation of virgin land required the employment of a sizable labor force, and once again, the height of the Urartian achievement points to the crossing of a demographic threshold in the highlands, which made this labor pool available, be it voluntary or involuntary. Urartians promoted settlement policies in areas selected for development. In so doing they not only enhanced the economic and demographic potential of the country, but also contributed to the breakdown of the ethnic and linguistic differences that the terrain of Armenia had engendered in its many valleys separated by even more numerous mountains. In overcoming the physical barriers of the highlands, and by reducing the ethnic and linguistic differences of the various groups, the Urartians contributed to the ethnic consolidation of the country. What is interesting though about this process was its outcome, for the longer-term beneficiaries turned out to be another of the major groups in the highlands inhabiting the western portion of the plateau, namely the Armenian-speakers.

If the consolidation of political power by the Urartians is explained by their advantage over the rest of the population in the sphere of military and administrative skills, their fall is explained by the gradual loss of that advantage. In unifying the country and creating a single seat of power, the Urartians put themselves at odds against both external and internal competitors. While at their height in the eighth century B.C., the Urartians checked Assyrian power, but by the next century the Assyrians were making inroads. As military struggles sapped their strength and the Assyrians made deeper incursions against the Urartian kingdom, the domestic hold of the Urartian kings weakened as well. In the middle of the seventh century B.C., local forces already contested Urartian rule in the highlands. At the head of that movement stood a figure to whom the Armenian-speakers attributed the rise of their own royal house. According to the Armenian historical narrative the Medes recognized Paruyr Skayordi's claim to royal stature. So it was that Urartu in its final decade in the early sixth century B.C. was surrounded by newly emergent powers, and the entire system of pre-existing states of the ancient Near East collapsed in the face of invasions by Iranian-speaking Medes and Scythians, and the Armenian-speakers who became ascendant in the highlands.

The Armenian State

The **Armenian kingdom** took a form very different from the Urartian political system. The state that the Armenians gradually assembled in the highlands was based on political values and an outlook at considerable variance with the Urartian view of royal hegemony over a stretch of territory. It may even have been constructed to be unlike the Urartian monarchy that they overthrew. The Armenians never sought to create a centralized monarchy that imposed its will through the stationing of troops across the land. Unlike the Urartian conquest of the highlands, the slower growth of the Armenian kingdom took the characteristics of the gathering of the various tribal and territorial principalities without upsetting the domestic institutions and the social basis of the small regional powers. In time that process even assimilated the Urartians. Nor did the Armenian political system ever resort to, or seemingly even show any inclination toward, bureaucratic management. The Armenian political system extended wide latitude toward regionalism and recognized the autonomy of local authority. Some of this was attributable to the Indo-European social system of the Armenians with its aristocracy of warriors who commanded their role by virtue of their military performance and bloodlines. The Urartian political order was a reflection to a considerable degree of the Mesopotamian monarchial system relying on a religious and scribal support base. That was the only political model of their age and had proven tremendously effective when matched with military competence. Babylonia and Assyria, as the embodiments of Mesopotamian civilization, communicated with their success the fundamental formulae for political management.

The Armenians, on the other hand, were more akin to the Medes and Persians, and even the Scythians, all peoples speaking Iranian dialects, for whom royal authority was not based so much on the inheritance of a throne as on the qualities of leadership. Though soon enough any state that stabilized called on the scribal traditions of Mesopotamia, and the Persians who created a vast empire encompassing the whole of Iran and the ancient Near East did not hesitate to draw on the benefit of bureaucratic management. The Urartians had been good record keepers, inscribing much of their deeds in stone. They had borrowed the cuneiform writing system and adapted it to their tongue. The early Persians did the same. Not the Armenians, for whom government remained a less formal affair defined by customs and traditions, by lineages, titles, and relations, and by an unshakable allegiance to local authority that no royal might ever succeeded, not that it tried hard enough, to dilute.

The Armenian kingdom was governed by three successive royal dynasties: **Yervanduni**, **Artashesian**, and **Arshakuni**. All three were closely associated with the imperial dynasties ruling in Iran. The Yervanduni intermarried with the Achaemenid dynasty that created the Persian Empire. The Artashesian intermarried with the succeeding Arsacid dynasty of Parthian Iran. As for the Armenian Arshakuni line, it started as a junior branch of the royal house of the Parthian Arsacids. If Assyria symbolized hegemonic power in the first third of the first millennium B.C., Achaemenid Iran represented the global power of the second third of the millennium. The Armenian state formed in the shadow of this great empire that stretched from the Indus River to the Mediterranean and Aegean Seas. The center of Iranian power, however, was never so close as Nineveh of the Assyrians. The two great capitals of the Persian and Parthian empires were located at Persepolis, in the depth of the Persian plateau, and at Ctesiphon, in the middle of the Mesopotamian plain. Armenia remained peripheral and extended the privilege of autonomy whenever the Iranians secured hegemony over it.

Yervanduni Dynasty

The first recorded mention of the country of Armenia occurs in one of the imperial inscriptions of the Achaemenids dating back to the sixth century B.C., which listed the lands over which they ruled. This leaves the impression that Armenia started as a subordinated entity, and clearly the Armenians paid tribute to the great king, but it does not convey the full story. Imperial inscriptions were meant to project the power and majesty of the sovereigns and to communicate the loftiness of their authority as conveyed by the enumeration of their subordinates. The Armenian-Iranian relationship of the period, however, was more complex, and it accounts for the continuing governance of a domestic royal house. Armenia may have been a client kingdom, but then, as far as Armenia was concerned, Iran was the only imperial power on the face of the earth. No contestants to its might were anywhere in sight, until the Greek resistance around the Aegean Sea was organized by the Macedonians under Alexander, who brought the whole empire crashing down. The Armenians too rebelled whenever Achaemenid power slackened as the imperial dynasty embroiled in conflict over the succession to the throne. That they considered doing so and that the Yervanduni house continued, nevertheless, to be maintained despite reversals is evidence of a fairly stable political order at whose apex stood an Armenian of regal stature.

Few records of this period of Armenian history survive. This very scarcity is the evidence of a style of government that relied on tradition and conventions that did not require announcement and amplification. In this respect it was a period of little innovation and possibly of considerable stability. The Persian Empire effectively protected Armenia from external conflict. Moreover, the level of tribute extracted appears to have been tolerable, for the country continued on a course of economic development, which may have lacked the intensity of Urartian management, but whose progress was measurable by the sizable contingents the Armenians provided the imperial army. Manpower and horses were the two principal Armenian contributions to the Achaemenid order. The occasional appearance of the Yervanduni king at the head of the Armenian troops establishes the nature of the service the Armenian ruler could muster and deliver on command.

The Persians originally divided Armenia into two administrative units, or satrapies, seemingly between the Armenians in the western half and the Urartians in the eastern half, though the population of the entire plateau had become intermixed by that time. By the end of the Achaemenid era this division had disappeared and Armenian speech had spread throughout the country. The emerging internal cohesion may be grasped by the migration of the center of Armenian royal authority from the west toward the middle of the country in the Van basin, where the Yervanduni relocated, and ultimately to the eastern part of the plateau into the great plain watered by the Arax River. When Achaemenid influence over Armenia ended in the wake of Alexander's march across the Persian Empire, the Yervanduni only increased their power in Armenia and created a new royal capital at **Armavir** in the third century B.C. Thereafter the political center of Armenia remained right down to the present within a radius of less than a day's journey on horseback from Armavir. What this points out also is the relocation of Armenia's center of productivity to the plain of Ararat, implying an enrichment of the economy far beyond the original center of agricultural production in the Van basin, which was intensively cultivated since the ninth century B.C.

Artashesian Dynasty

As the Macedonians chased plunder and glory across Asia, the Yervanduni retreated into their mountains and continued to govern Armenia. Their low-key policies kept them out of harm's way. The Achaemenid patrons were gone, and Armenia was cut loose from the new imperial system taking shape under Greek and Macedonian rule. When the Seleucids established their power as Alexander's heirs in Asia, the urban basis of Greek civilization focused the attention of the new administrators on the founding of cities, the encouragement of commerce, the monetarization of the economy, and the introduction of Hellenistic political values that rested on a literate culture of learning and sophistication. These rapid transformations in the central parts of the ancient Near East reduced Armenia to a comparatively under-developed country. The Yervanduni made attempts to integrate Armenia into the new global economy created by the Greeks. The standard coin of exchange, the Greek *drachma*, was likely the first currency widely circulated in Armenia, and its novelty was sufficiently impressive to have left in the Armenian language the very word for money, *dram*. The Yervanduni, heirs of long-standing customs by the third century B.C., however, did not adapt to the dynamic of Hellenistic civilization. Though their court and country's commerce could not avoid exposure to the flow of Greek concepts of governance and exchange, the Yervanduni remained more concerned with the endurance of their monarchy in the face of these profound changes occurring around them, and also remained guarded and uncertain about the integration of their country in the expanding networks of communication spreading out in every direction.

That isolation could not endure. New pressure from the Seleucid Empire transformed the Armenian political order and launched Armenia toward an unexpected and uncharacteristic moment of supremacy in the ancient world. Among the goals of Antiochus the Great, who, early in the second century B.C., aspired to recreate Alexander's realm, was influence over, if not control of, Armenia. With his patronage, a new dynasty ascended the royal throne of Armenia. The seizure of power by **Artashes** and Zareh, who redirected Armenian polity and set it upon completely new tracks, suggests the rise of new political forces in Armenia more closely aligned with the pattern of external developments. While insisting on dynastic continuity, they set the country on a new course. The rise of two crowned heads, dividing the country between east and west, however, still indicated that the economic and political integration of the highlands was not entirely complete. Moreover, the formation of the kingdom of Dsopk, or Sophene, as the western monarchy was known, also attested to an enduring tradition of royal legitimacy based in that portion of the country. The kingdom of Dsopk had one significant advantage. Located on the Euphrates River, it was placed close to the centers of economic activity to the south and west. Its program for development was based on further urbanization and greater integration into the commerce of northern Syria. This was the era of the founding of the cities of Samosata, Arsamosata, and Arsameia. The kingdom of Dsopk, however, also had one shortcoming. It enjoyed little room for expansion, other than in the economic sphere, making it rather a plum for future acquisition.

Whether Artashes and Zareh knew this difference is difficult to say, but one thing is certain, Artashes, who seized the more remote and less developed western region of Armenia, was a man of a different character. With Artashes Armenia had at its helm more than just a crowned head. For the first time a decidedly ambitious and imaginative figure was in charge, remembered in legend as the most beloved of Armenian kings at whose death an entire nation wept. He is the first Armenian whose personality can be sketched, and if any one characteristic stands out, it was a superior quality of leadership that envisioned the state as a resource and government as the formulator of innovative domestic and foreign policy. It was a vision that leaped beyond the responsibility of just good management, maintaining order, meting justice, and protecting the land. His leadership was driven by the goal of securing power that matched the strength of any neighboring state and of guaranteeing the full sovereignty of his realm. The organization he introduced, the economic uplift he encouraged, the territorial expansion and boundary definition that he sought, and his military successes registered with the Armenian people in the acceptance of a powerful monarchy more centralized, more commanding, and more respected than at any other time. Succeeding generations celebrated the reign of Artashes as the most glorious chapter of ancient Armenia's national mythology.

Artashes's achievement reached fulfillment in the first century B.C. with the enthronement of his descendant, **Tigran II**, the greatest of Armenian kings, during whose reign the entire Armenian highlands were peaceably unified into a single and solid monarchy. Tigran's reign coincided with a moment of serious weakness both in the Seleucid state in Syria and the Parthian state in Iran. He did not hesitate to take advantage of both, and for the first time, an Armenian king led his troops beyond the formal boundaries of his country in pursuit of imperial ambition. Artashes's program had yielded greater wealth, greater manpower, and greater organizational efficiency in the Armenian state than anyone else had realized. In the hands of another vigorous ruler, the outlet remaining was the gambit for overlordship. It was not a question of resources and of leadership alone that drove Tigran's vision of his royal authority, but a political imagination that conceived of Armenia as a country capable of such an undertaking in imitation of neighboring societies that had engendered imperial states. The Romans, whose military superiority went unmatched in the ancient world, ultimately restrained Tigran's territorial ventures. His desire to integrate Armenia into the political, economic, and cultural order of the Hellenistic Near East, for both good and bad, endured as his permanent legacy. With Tigran Armenia ceased being peripheral. Thereafter the country was fully exposed to, and buffeted by, all the currents of life, culture, and politics flowing from East and West.

How strongly the currents of the West flowed into Armenia was shown in the reign of Tigran's son, Artavasd II, who, despite his caution, was ensnared by the unbridled schemes of the Roman triumvirs Crassus and Mark Antony, and the latter's consort Cleopatra of Egypt. The Roman drive to the East unsettled Armenian affairs, for the Romans did not yet know the limits of their still unchecked expansion around the Mediterranean. Persia, which the Macedonians once toppled, proved impenetrable to the Romans. Roman power, therefore, crested at the border of Armenia. Which border that would be, whether the eastern or the western frontier of the highlands, meant all the difference for the security and independence of Armenia. The conquering generals thought nothing of wrecking and enslaving whole nations, and in the first century B.C., they had reached Armenia. The Armenians, on the other hand, unlike the peoples of the Mediterranean basin, were not prepared to accept the eventuality of Roman domination. The ensuing resistance ultimately guaranteed that the Roman frontier stopped at the western edge of Armenia and the country remained free of Roman administration and taxation. Thus Armenia came to straddle the unstable zone between East and West. The direction, however, toward which these influences weighted at the time is revealed in the cultural refinement of Artavasd II, Armenia's only philosopher king, for he was schooled in the classics and was credited with the authorship of original works in Greek, which regrettably did not survive the passages of time.

Arshakuni Dynasty

The vibrant dynasty of the Artashesians came to a natural end at the turn of the millennium. The monarchy they shaped lasted for four more centuries. The social order they created endured for a dozen centuries. The tribal chieftaincies of the Yervanduni era were forged by the Artashesians into an aristocratic elite closely identified with the monarchy and ensured rank and status by the potent legitimation of participation in the Artashesian experiment in statecraft. The most enduring concept the Artashesians imparted may have been the very idea of Armenian statehood based on the ethnic content of the highlands, and which, advantageously by the time of their rise to power, had attained country-wide coherence through the use of a common tongue. They bequeathed the Armenians the sense of a common political culture that informed all of their subsequent political calculations. Countless states and monarchies formed and reformed in the lands surrounding Armenia. While each had a cultural, linguistic, or ethnic core to it, in the final analysis, all were territorial formations lacking the kind of durability Armenia exhibited. Some of these states expanded into great empires. Yet, by so enlarging they could not count on the loyalties of their subjects whom at the least they dominated and at worst subjugated. The differentiating characteristic of the Armenian state remained its singular ethnic content, or a majority of such, circumscribed by the bounded geography of a mountainous plateau territorially and culturally fused into a single and solid political entity. This made Armenia compact and kept it small, but also made it sturdy enough to outlast its enemies for the next thousand years.

So it was that when the last Artashesian was no more, the question concerning all around was not whether the Armenian monarchy was in jeopardy, rather, who would be inheriting the Artashesian legacy. Princes resort to combat and drag their countries into civil war to determine the outcome of the contest for a royal crown. When two world empires faced each other over the vacuum of the Armenian throne, that meant the contest would pit great forces in conflict in order to prevent an unfavorable outcome. It took a half-century to sort it out between the Romans and the Parthians, but after their drawn-out struggle, the Armenians came out the winners, for they obtained a new dynasty reigning with the consent of both imperial parties. The acclamation of **Trdat I** as king of Armenia became an event of international significance, so much so that the new sovereign discovered that the journey from Ctesiphon, the Parthian capital, to **Artashat**, the Armenian capital, passed through Rome, the imperial capital.

That the chosen dynasty sprang from the ruling Arsacid imperial family of Parthian Iran announced a turning point in the history of the Armenians. The Romans had alienated the Armenians, who, joining in arms with the Parthians, had made the occupation of Armenia too costly. The emperors Augustus, Nero, Trajan, Marcus Aurelius, and Septimius Severus, each tried and sent their armies marching into Armenia. None of the occupation lasted long enough for the Roman legions to make a home for themselves in the Armenian highlands. Armenia was too remote to hold and the Armenians too resistant to hold down. The Parthian support for Armenia guaranteed that a Roman settlement unacceptable to Armenians and Parthians would never last. The strategic value of Armenia for Parthia's northern defenses was too great to concede the country to the enemy. Armenia's political neutrality, more properly its buffer status, kept the contending powers apart.

The elevation of an **Arshakuni** to the Armenian throne, however, was a concession to the demonstrated cultural proclivity of the Armenians. Armenia and Iran still shared customs of monarchy and aristocracy, and the whole culture surrounding class defined societies. The Roman Empire, like the Mesopotamian empires, was a large administrative machine manned by paid servants of the state, be they uniformed legionnaires or toga-wearing tax farmers who functioned by a legal order that did not necessarily uphold aristocratic privilege and honor lineage. The Roman system ultimately excluded Armenian society and Armenia was spared the removal of its established governing class. At a juncture when Armenia had been opened to Western influences, it abruptly turned its face away from the most threatening manifestation of Western civilization when it made its appearance in the form of the Roman Empire. Armenia turned east toward Iran, welcoming its new Arshakuni kings and absorbing and sharing in the privilege of a common ruling echelon. In the next two centuries Iranian cultural influences, especially as related to the conduct of royal affairs and the accommodation of aristocratic values, permeated Armenia. The Armenian aristocracy had shown its mettle against the Romans, and any king of Armenia was beholden to the nobles to keep him on his throne. This new order held for a century and a half until the unexpected occurred.

In the early third century the Parthian Arsacids were overthrown in Iran and replaced by the Persian Sasanids, a dynasty espousing religious zeal and harkening to an Achaemenid heritage. This new state expanding under the banner of Mazdaism presented a serious challenge to all the countries bordering Iran, among them Rome, but especially Armenia, which harbored its royal dynasty and chose to go to war against the might of Iran, rather than surrender the sovereignty and independence symbolized by its indigenized royalty. The Sasanids would not tolerate either Armenian defiance or an Arshakuni monarchy and proceeded to invade Armenia and subject its cities to a methodic policy of destruction. By the middle of the third century the devastation was sufficiently damaging to see the flight of the Armenian kings. This was also a period of internal disorder in the Roman Empire, which lacked a foreign policy sufficiently forceful to respond to the Sasanid threat. When Diocletian and then Constantine restored the unity and strength of the empire in the fourth century, the tide turned, and at this critical moment in their cultural and spiritual life, the Armenians turned away from Iran by resorting to the option of adopting a wholly new religion and formulating a new and unique culture that would shield the population from external ideologically motivated impositions.

King Trdat IV's decision to adopt Christianity may have been an act of political clairvoyance, if not a stroke of genius. It attested to the fact that at a critical juncture Armenian society was creative enough to tackle a challenge warranting the consideration of a bold and totally new direction in polity and society. He had a partner in realizing the Christianization of Armenia, **Grigor Lusavorich**, Gregory the Illuminator or Enlightener. Christianity was still the religion of the downtrodden in the early fourth century. Governing classes despised it. At best they found it strange. Armenia adopted Christianity as its state religion, not just as a new faith extended tolerance or even privilege as in Rome, but to be promoted as the new cult of the state and intended as part of King Trdat's strategy of restoring and strengthening Armenian society with a feature of faith that others had not yet embraced with similar intent. The policy was a success, so much so that within a century the popular requirements of the new religion propelled Armenians to invent a whole new culture for themselves by first adopting an alphabet for their language. Devised in the early fifth century by a man of acknowledged genius named **Mesrop Mashtots**, the Armenian alphabet was so perfectly tuned to the native tongue that it unleashed the spiritual and cultural creativity of the Armenian people. For all the vicissitudes of the rest of their history, the Armenians never reconsidered parting from either their religion or their language and its alphabet. Neither, however, prevented Armenia from eventually being reduced to a client state and partitioned in 387 between Rome and Iran, and by 428 of having its Armenian monarchy abolished.

The Age of Princes

The Roman invasions and the Persian wars placed Armenia on permanent alert. The constant demands of warfare militarized society as the defense of the state required the concentration of resources in the hands of those delivering the armed forces into the field. The difficulties of the Armenian terrain also required the maintenance of troops on each of the vulnerable frontiers of Armenia. These responsibilities were historically delegated to the native aristocracy all of whom were trained in knightly service. Constant warring gradually tilted political power in Armenia away from the central monarchy and toward the military aristocracy. By the fourth century the king's forces were no longer sufficient to match the enemy, and his dependence on the arrival of the great lords of the land with their mounted warriors exposed the limits of his influence. Increasingly the monarchy relied on the great princes, the **nakharars**, whose distinguished families held vast domains governed as autonomous fiefdoms. Descended from the old tribal constituents of ancient Armenia and rooted in the corresponding regions of the country, the nakharar houses counted on the unqualified loyalties of the local population. At the apex of the nakharar class hovered the chiefs of the large principalities whose own armies could easily exceed 10,000 men in arms.

Numbers alone, however, do not explain the martial capacity of the Armenian nobility. At the very least three other factors contributed to the remarkable military record of the nakharars, who henceforth for a thousand years tirelessly faced invaders of every persuasion. First, the Armenian armed forces consisted of cavalry. The combination of a skilled warrior in full armor and his trained steed appearing by the tens of thousands on the field of battle gave Armenia a fair chance to fight, if not arrest, the advance of an invading force. Even as the country absorbed the initial shock of incursion or invasion, the makeup of the Armenian armed forces reserved a tremendous military potential in the response ability of the mounted warriors whose battle gear, tactics, and esprit de corps delivered a surprising counter-strike in many instances. Despite the wherewithal of the imperial armies sent into Armenia, the Armenian forces were just sufficient in size to satisfy the basic defense needs of the country. At its height the undivided kingdom could expect 100,000 mounted knights to be available at wartime. Second, exceeding in value any benefit derived from numerical parities or comparative advantages in military skills and habits, the leadership qualities of the great princes, all of whom were expected to demonstrate fearless courage, and repeatedly did so, extended the Armenian forces the benefit of morale, pride, and sheer bravura against superior forces. Throughout the centuries one nakharar family after another shaped the character of a great warrior or a superior military commander. Lastly, these wars amounted to much more than a contest among troops of two nations. If anything accounts for the determination of the nakharars, the explanation is found in the fact that all the wars in Armenia were waged in defense of country and liberty. In that struggle, the nakharar warriors counted on the support and services of a population prepared to bear any burden to secure the values of their society. Each and every war was a struggle for freedom and that issue did not require persuasion to make men want to show their courage.

Iranian Rule and the Mamikonian Dynasty

The question remained whether the nakharar order would endure in the absence of a monarchy; whether the two institutions were so interdependent that Armenian feudalism would fail to function without a king at its apex. Certainly the system was exposed to many stresses, the gravest being the choice of political orientation and its implications for national policy. Caught in between two great empires periodically testing the supremacy of the other in the entire region containing Armenia, those responsible for the political destiny of Armenia also struggled with the serious challenge of balancing external reality with internal obligation. The survival of their individual families and principalities hinged on those choices. Inevitably, in murkier moments, opinion was divided, interests conflicted, political orientation leaned in opposite directions. Yet, when the entire system was put to the test, the nakharar order demonstrated unexpected resilience and a willingness to resort to measures of resistance that made imperial masters reconsider their policies.

There were numerous instances when the nakharars as a group were compelled to meet the political challenge of the day. The most celebrated moment, when the majority of the princes united under a single command to defy an imperial injunction designed to undo the spiritual identity of the Armenians, occurred in 451. The Armenian forces led by Vardan **Mamikonian**, a scion of one of the noblest families, descended to the field of Avarayr to meet the grand army of the Persians, horses, elephants, foot soldiers, and all. Outmatched and ultimately defeated, nonetheless the Armenian warriors waged such fierce combat that the Iranian policy of forcibly converting Armenia to Zoroastrianism was abandoned and eventually a modus vivendi was reached between the Persian king of kings and the chief Armenian nakharar, Vahan Mamikonian, Vardan's nephew, when he was formally appointed viceroy, or *marzpan*, of Armenia. Vardan Mamikonian and his paladins had made the ultimate sacrifice and fallen in combat defending faith, country, and liberty. The Armenian Church found in him its glorified defender and sanctified his memory. Vardan Mamikonian, whose forebears included regents and *sparapets* (commanders-in-chief), however, had demonstrated much more than the religious loyalty and dedication of the Armenian people to their Christian faith. At a crucial juncture in the history of the Armenians, when their country was subject to foreign domination, Vardan Mamikonian and those who participated and supported his rebellion put their imperial masters on notice that Armenians expected their sovereigns to honor their cherished domestic liberties. Among them were their freedom of worship, their own ecclesiastical organization not subordinated to a higher religious authority, their traditional and customary laws, and above all, their mode of local self-government embodied in the political autonomy and social liberty of the nakharar system. This formidable institution outlasted Persian domination, Byzantine rule, and even Arab occupation, to yield in the ninth century a new period of political freedom and restored sovereignty and statehood in Armenia.

From the fifth through the ninth century Armenia remained subject to foreign control. In the early seventh century Iranian dominion was broken by the Byzantines under Emperor Heraklios, himself Armenian-born. Heraklios's reign proved fateful by another turn. At the moment of the restoration of Roman imperium over the Christian Near East and the decisive containment of Iran, the Arabs under the green banner of Islam poured out of the southern desert and overwhelmed the Persians, Romans, Armenians, and everyone else they encountered in their unstoppable advance across Western Asia and North Africa. The ancient world was at an end. Mediterranean unity and its Greco-Roman civilization were in retreat. Christianity as a religion met its match, and international politics, as the Armenians had known it since the time of Tigran the Great for well over a half millennium, no longer mattered. By 650 the Arabs established dominion over Armenia and held it firmly for the next two hundred years.

Arab Rule and the Bagratuni Recovery

There were fundamental differences between Iranian and Arab rule in Armenia despite the fact that both were external and mighty imperial powers based in the Middle East. Armenia and Iran had reached an uneasy accommodation. The Persian monarchy absorbed the nakharar order into its system of governance and by so doing extended latitude and autonomy to the Armenian princes. The office of the marzpan ranked as a viceroyalty and the appointment of leading nakharars to the office was a sizable concession to the Armenians, recognition in Ctesiphon, the Iranian capital. The concept was that on balance it was preferable to have Armenia pacified rather having this critical frontier province facing the Roman Empire destabilized by unrest, uprising, and exposure to Roman inducements. Lastly, the common features of their social systems and its associated culture permitted for a level of integration, as aristocratic societies had an interest in maintaining rank, title, and privilege, and these flowed from the stratifications sustained by a royal authority, be it Armenian monarch or Iranian emperor.

The institution of the Arab vostikanate was a departure from the type of indirect rule to which Armenians were accustomed. Introduced in the early eighth century by the Arab caliphate, the office of the vostikan held powers equal to, if not greater than, the marzpan. It encompassed political, military, and financial responsibilities, including defense of the region and taxation of the province. This all-powerful office was controlled by the center, Damascus under the Umayyad dynasty, and Baghdad under the Abbasid dynasty, through an annual rotation of the governor. To make up for the lack of continuity in the region's management and to secure the Armenian border of the Arab Empire against Christian Byzantium, the caliphs also introduced the policy of settling Muslim tribesmen in the Armenian frontierland. This was done at the expense of the nakharars who continued to resist Arab rule in Armenia. In this struggle, the leading nakharar house, the Mamikonian, remained an implacable foe, but its bravery proved no match to the ruthless policies of the Arabs who were unbeholden to any sense of respect toward privileged classes. This type of bloody contest and the crushing defeats inflicted on defiant rebels induced serious differences in attitude and policy among the ranking nakharars.

Under these new circumstances another leading nakharar house, the Bagratuni, proved much more skillful in devising a longer-term strategy of survival through cooperation and gradual elevation by the Arabs as reward for their services, until such time as the caliph himself bestowed upon the heirs of the Bagratuni house the title of prince of Armenia. This honorific office had emerged in the period of Iranian and Byzantine control of Armenia after the abolition of the monarchy and the occupation of the country. Each of the imperial masters had raised a favorite to such exceptional status, and the appointments of designated princes to the governorship of the country had induced the population as well to think of the leading personality of the day as the *Ishkhan Hayots*, Prince of Armenia. In effect a chief executive's office had evolved with tenure contingent on imperial dispensation. The Arabs continued this practice and by regularly assigning it to the Bagratunis, they created a new center of political influence in Armenia. With prudence and perseverance the Bagratunis relied on their sponsors to acknowledge their consolidation of domestic authority. They also used their opportunities to gather the Armenian lands until the second half of the ninth century, when the Arabs, much weakened by then, acknowledged Armenia's separation and extended the reigning Bagratuni the privilege of royal title. When in 884 **Ashot I** Bagratuni assumed the crown of Armenia and formally restored the sovereignty of his country, he already governed the greater part of it as a fully autonomous prince. For all intents and purposes Armenia was again independent and only the tribute payment to the caliph as a sign of allegiance remained. Even this was no longer a financial burden as Armenia's economy recovered quickly once the Arabs relinquished control.

Bagratuni Dynasty

The rapid economic development of Armenia in the Bagratuni period resulted in a series of achievements that left their lasting imprint on Armenian society and civilization. At the heart of these achievements stood the re-urbanization of Armenia. Cities everywhere grew and prospered. This flourishing cosmopolitan culture relocated the focal points of Armenian life. If mountaintop fortresses, the grim business of warfare, and the indomitable personality of the military figures who controlled the situation defined the Armenian scene in an earlier era, the Bagratuni epoch offered a contrast in riches, periods of peace, expanded commercial activity, and new classes of men who made their living not in the countryside, but in the cities that soon dotted the international trade routes crisscrossing Armenia. This new wealth was invested in the fortification and embellishment of the great cities of Armenia. One stood above all the others in importance. The Armenians built many royal capitals over the course of their millennial history beginning with Van, Armavir, Yervandashat, Artashat, **Tigranakert**, **Vagharshapat**, and **Dvin**. Some of these cities were still in existence at the time of the Bagratunis and their important edifices were kept in use. The new capital of **Ani**, however, rapidly outpaced them all with the extent of architectural monuments that were raised within, and even outside, its walls. For the Armenians the building of Ani came to symbolize the acme of their medieval civilization and its artistry and creativity.

The Bagratuni investment in making Ani into a city worthy of international attention was by design. It aimed to provide the Armenian kingdom a new political and economic center. Not just the king, the catholicos too came to reside in Ani. The great princes built residences in the city. Urban monastic complexes were introduced, and schools of learning revitalized Armenian culture. While each of the arts found its sponsor, architecture flourished most notably as evidenced by the rate of construction and the sheer beauty and elegance of the buildings designed during those years. There was one additional characteristic to Ani that assigned it a role unlike the other great cities of Armenia. Ani was the most northern metropolis of the Armenians. This was so because the Bagratuni realm was based in the northern half of Armenia. The Bagratunis had slowly expanded their holdings out of the northernmost recesses of the country. On account of this the Bagratunis also followed events in Georgia to their immediate north, an area where they developed close relations and interests, and where a branch of their family by chance and intelligence assumed the royal crown of a reunified Christian Georgia. This unusual elite network maintained by a set of reigning dynasties all related by intertwining lineages added a new strategic dimension to Caucasian society and created an atmosphere of political and cultural proximity with long-term benefits to both societies. For the first time an important northern orientation appeared in Armenia's international relations.

Remarkable as the accomplishment of the Bagratuni had been in restoring royalty and sovereignty to Armenia after three and a half centuries of foreign rule, there were also notable limitations to the strength and capacity of the Bagratuni monarchy. The centuries of imperial control, and especially Arab policies of colonization, had taken their toll on Armenia and introduced profound alterations in the composition of the country. Western and southern portions of the country had lost their native governing class and the nakharar system had been uprooted leaving the Armenians exposed to direct rule by their foreign masters. Deficient of the native element that the population naturally turned to for leadership, those territories had been alienated from Armenian political life and were exchanged among imperial powers without resistance from the local population. Armenian rule therefore was restricted to the northern and eastern half of the country.

Even so, a sizable stretch of Armenia came under native rule in the 10th century, especially when the **Ardsruni**, another nakharar family, reigning in the Van region of southern Armenia also acquired royal title. The Bagratuni and Ardsruni competed, and on at least one occasion with very serious consequences resulting in the capture and execution of Ashot I's son, King Smbat I, by the emir of Azerbaijan. On the other hand, the sum of the possessions of their two families, in addition to more remote parts of the highlands governed by the indigenous nobility, including the **Siuni**, ushered in an era of near complete recovery from Arab domination. The Islamification of the Middle East obstructed efforts to restore the entire plateau to Armenian rule. New centers of power had emerged in the intervening centuries and Muslim emirates, with or without the support or connivance of Baghdad, constantly tested the borders of the Armenian states and derailed plans to liberate all of the country.

The centrifugal forces, both of internal and external origin, and in combination, were much too great for Armenians alone to withstand, and the Muslims were not the only source of pressure on Armenia. A resurgent Byzantium from the west encroached on Armenia with similar designs. After a century and a half of self-rule, a piece at a time Armenia succumbed to the Byzantine Empire. By the middle of the 11th century Armenia had been almost wholly absorbed. The Greek occupation did not last very long, but it proved so disruptive that it left Armenia vulnerable to further invasion by an opposing power. As it would happen, like the Arabs four centuries earlier, another people made their appearance just at this time. When the Seljuk Turks brought their main forces to Armenia in 1071, appreciating the danger presented by the new invaders, the Byzantine emperor went to meet them with his own army. The battle of Manzikert, fought in the heartland of Armenia, was one of those fateful military conflicts that changed the course of history and the destiny of nations. The defeat was so crushing that Byzantium never recovered. The Seljuks seized Asia Minor and Hellenic culture that had defined life there for well over a thousand years ceased to function. The onetime bastion of Christianity was toppled, and Armenia proper lost its direct link with the West for the next seven hundred years.

The Zakarian and Rubenian-Hetumian Dynasties

Because Asia Minor offered greater spoils and a warmer clime than Armenia, the Seljuk Turks preferred to colonize it and delegated rule in Armenia and surrounding districts to their vassals. The absence of a strong central government in the region presented Armenians opportunities to recover from the Seljuk invasions. Two alternative strategies were explored, both of which yielded considerable success. Georgia had been spared Seljuk occupation and Armenians turned to it for assistance. The readiness of the Armenians to ally themselves with Georgia paved the way for Georgian expansion southward. For the first and only time in its history Georgia reached across the Armenian mountains and challenged the Muslim and Turkish captains governing in Armenia. In their quest the Georgians enlisted the Armenian soldiery that had taken refuge in Georgia and the mountains of northern Armenia. From amongst them rose one family that became the leaders of the Georgian military. By bringing together Georgian and Armenian forces and unifying them under their command, the Zakarians, or Mkhargrdzeli in Georgian, assembled a new war machine in the Caucasus in the service of the remaining Christian sovereignty of the region. That the Georgian monarchs were of Bagratuni lineage did not hurt matters. The Zakarian recovery of northern and Eastern Armenia in the 12th century stretched from Ani to Dvin, which the last of the Armenian Bagratuni had failed to repossess from the Arabs. At the height of their power the Zakarians governed Armenia as viceroys of the Georgian sovereigns and in so doing partially restored self-rule in the country.

The Armeno-Georgian state forged by the Bagratuni and Zakarians might have gone on to stabilize the region where the situation remained fluid with no single power holding it together. All that suddenly changed in the 1220s when the Mongols swept through the Middle East, smashed the Georgian state, and brought Armenia under their control. The period of Zakarian recovery may have been at an end. The economic ruin of Armenia was only beginning. The Seljuks had sacked the Armenian cities in the 11th century. Matters had improved somewhat in the following century. From the 13th century onward the economy of Armenia unraveled, and with it faded the social coherence created by the Armenians on their plateau over the course of the preceding two thousand years.

Despite its political consequences in the Armenian mainland, the expansion of the Mongol empire resulted in one of the most unlikely alliances of all time, and certainly one of the most outstanding accomplishments of Armenian diplomacy. Since the late 11th century Armenians dislodged from their homeland by the Seljuk invasions had migrated into the previously Byzantine province of Cilicia. There, under the agile leadership of the **Rubenian** dynasty, Armenians formed a new state. The last of this line of princes, **Levon I**, had persuaded the

Crusaders, the Papacy, and the Holy Roman Empire, to award him a royal crown. A king once again reigned in the name of the Armenian people, yet the kingdom he ruled over was an entirely new political formation conceived and created by Armenians in territory they had colonized on the Mediterranean Sea. Given the state of affairs in the Middle East they could not have chosen a better location. It positioned the Armenians at the nexus of the two great economic forces of the period: the seafaring Italians of the West who controlled trade in the Mediterranean, and the Mongol horsemen who controlled virtually the entire Asian continent. These two vast zones of commerce converged in Cilicia, the only country on the Mediterranean coast on friendly terms with both parties.

The Armenians of Cilicia most literally owed their fortune to their king **Hetum I**, who married Levon I's daughter and heir, and whose family and dynasty, was called **Hetumian** in his honor. He ushered in a period of great prosperity and good governance as the Armenians had not known for over two hundred years by striking an alliance with the Mongols. A onetime Caucasian people joined the Mediterranean community, sharing in its commerce, culture, social ethos, and religious controversies. The success of the Cilician Armenian state was measured by the virtuosity of its artists, the learning of its theologians, the acumen of its diplomats, the confidence of its statesmen, and the wealth of its merchants. The last also attracted the attention of competitors. When the Mamluks of Egypt checked the Crusaders and the Mongols, they also aimed to control trade in the Mediterranean. They went to war against Cilician Armenia and one at a time reduced the mighty fortresses ringing the country seaside and on land. It took them more than a hundred years to constrict the Armenian kingdom to the capital city of Sis, which they finally seized in 1375.

The Age of Merchants

With the fall of Sis Armenians lost the last vestige of their independence. Statehood and sovereignty ended with the reduction of the Armenian monarchy. Dramatic as the expiration of the long line of Armenian kings might have been, the associated extirpation of the Armenian military aristocracy, that longer-lasting reservoir of Armenian political life and identity, more importantly signified the exhaustion of the Armenian capacity for self-government. Only pockets of the nakharar system remained in places such as Siunik, Artsakh, and Lori, in the mountains of Eastern Armenia. Bands of hardy mountaineers, as in Sasun in southern Armenia and Zeitun in Cilicia, also continued to abide by their customs of self-rule, but their autonomy was as much a function of isolation as of the fierce defense of their way of life. Moreover, the inhabitants of these mountains were not in contact with each other and represented no political concept.

Turkic Rule and the Breakup of Armenia

Only one institution survived the Turco-Mongol-Mamluk occupations of Armenia: the church. As for the social order, only merchants and peasants remained. If the lot of peasants had been difficult as a rule, hereafter it was an ordeal. Their tribulations stemmed less so from the hardships of coping with the vagaries of nature, and the requirement of constant labor to produce the fruit of the land, as much as the struggle for survival in a world where the ruling class did not have the Armenian peasants' interests in mind, and whose laws and practices aimed to subvert the peasants' ownership of his property. The alienation and emigration of the Armenian peasantry from the land over time reduced the Armenian demographic presence in its historic homeland. It also fragmented Armenian society, dissolving the Armenian continuum across the highlands and introducing other ethnic elements, primarily Turks and Kurds. Slowly Armenia was converted into the residence of two wholly unintegrated societies: one was Christian, the other Muslim; the Christian was subordinate, the Muslim dominant; the Muslims were armed, the Christians disarmed. In serious competition over the resources of the country, Armenians endured under circumstances deprived of any legal and political protection.

In this period of disorder and anarchy the leadership of the Armenian people passed to the church and its sole supporting class, the merchants. In effect, with the loss of the upper class, soldiers, nobles, and royals, Armenian community life came under the management of the middle class, whose means of existence was predicated on international trade and local commerce. By no means were they equipped, however, to project any sense of political purpose as their livelihood depended on the tolerance negotiated and afforded by the controlling states holding Armenia in subjugation. Moreover, trade and commerce being driven by the market, with its rules of supply and demand that Armenians did not control, the Armenian merchant class came to acquire the characteristics of a migrant, more accurately, a **diaspora**, society.

The phenomenon of the Armenian diaspora predated the rise of the Armenian merchant class. With the excision of the aristocracy, however, the middle class was all that was left as the substitute element in a position more privileged than the masses that earned their living farming or laboring in the nonagrarian sphere of the economy. The urban character of this class made it highly mobile geographically and adaptable socially and culturally. The Mongols had taxed Armenia heavily and damaged its economy. The breakdown of the Mongol empire only complicated life in Armenia as it also left the country completely exposed to further invasion by other Turkic tribes riding out of Central Asia. The Turkoman onslaught under Tamerlane in the 1380s wiped out the towns and cities that still functioned under Mongol rule. Thereafter Armenia became a place of more interest to herdsmen than merchants and townspeople. The tribes that seized Armenia preferred its pastures to its commerce.

During this bleak period of Armenian history when economic and cultural life seemed at a standstill, if not in full retreat, Armenians concentrated their energies on salvaging their surviving national institutions from possible perdition and on seeking new locales for habitation that offered greater security. Despite its unhappy origins stemming from destruction and dispersion, and its melancholy culture of reminiscence in the midst of foreign lands, the Armenian choice of resorting to the formation of diaspora settlements soon demonstrated its value as a viable alternative to the impossibility of maintaining community in many parts of Armenia. The diaspora took root, endured, expanded, and even flourished to a point where by the 19th century Armenian cultural life had thoroughly relocated to these new centers of Armenian concentration, the two largest being at the time Tiflis (Tbilisi) in Russia and Constantinople (Istanbul) in Turkey.

The Church Reorganized

Before the diaspora emerged as the more dynamic sector of Armenian society, the Armenian Church underwent an elaboration of its organization that came to reflect the prevailing reality of the Armenian condition, namely its segmentation and dispersion. On the one hand it fractured the unity of the church, on the other, it made this key institution more responsive to the needs of a people bereft of political leadership. Increasingly the church assumed and was delegated by the ruling powers the privilege of representing the Armenian people. As an institution devoid of military capacity, it proved a ready and pacific mechanism through which ruler and ruled communicated. The consent of both parties to this instrumentality repositioned the Armenian Church in its relationship with the Armenian people and with state authorities, and entrusted it with responsibilities exceeding spiritual comfort, the regulation of religion, and social services. In the process the Armenian Church became an international organization. All this would not have occurred without the sanction of the state. As Armenians by the 15th century, when the Armenian Church was internationalized, were dispersed across the entire Middle East and the Black Sea basin, they lived as subjects of a number of countries, hence each unit of the church was shaped under the auspices of a different state. Once all the pieces became operational, however, a cross-border network emerged.

The Mamluk capture of Cilicia confined the Armenian catholicos to his residence in Sis. Earlier the Mamluks had promoted the elevation of an Armenian patriarchate in Jerusalem as a competing center of authority and loyalty for Armenians in the Arab world. Geographic distances and the risks of travel through unsafe territory prevented any one center from prevailing over the others. The Armenians of Cilicia preferred to continue honoring the titular head of the church who resided in their country and perpetuated the institution of the 'Catholicos of Cilicia.' In the long run the regionalization of the catholicosate in Sis had less to do with Jerusalem than with developments in Armenia, where in 1441 the prelates, local chieftains, and leading merchants appealed to the Kara Koyunlu warlord governing Armenia to accede to their desire to reconstitute the Armenian catholicosate at its historic birthplace of Edjmiadsin, much closer to their hometowns than distant Sis held under the mastery of a competing power. The restoration of Edjmiadsin proved to be one of those acts of foresight and intelligent strategy that sustained the Armenian people when they were denied every other form of protection. The 'Catholicos of Edjmiadsin' provided the population of Armenia a modicum of religious leadership, and a point of focus for an otherwise powerless and scattered people. This development prompted and facilitated the formation of an additional center of Armenian religious authority when the Ottoman Turks captured Constantinople in 1453, and created of their own will a new branch of the Armenian church organization by designating in 1461 an Armenian patriarch in the imperial city with dignity on par with the ancient Greek patriarchate of Byzantium. Over time the Armenian patriarchate of Constantinople extended its authority over all parts of the Ottoman Empire while respecting the regional jurisdiction of the other anointed leaders of the church. By this same process the **Armenian *Millet*** as the instrument of Ottoman governance took form.

Lastly, in the absence of aristocratic and royal patronage, learning retreated to the confines of an impoverished church. Though conditions gave little impetus to creativity, the church, mostly through its monasteries, salvaged the relics of Armenian civilization. The rudiments of Armenian culture were passed down from churchman to churchman, from one monastery to another. Even so, the losses exceeded what little was saved. Invaders, conquerors, and rulers thought nothing of pillaging ecclesiastical centers and burning their libraries. Over the centuries when everything of value was expropriated, all that remained in the hands of Armenians were books. Thus manuscripts became the most precious possessions of the Armenian people, one of the few tangible testaments to their ancient culture and unique identity.

The Diaspora Emergent

Political sanction was an advantage, but the church at this stage of its existence enjoyed little revenue, and would have remained a skeletal operation but for the benefaction of Armenian merchants. The rise of an Armenian bourgeoisie in diaspora coincided with, and was conditioned by, the expansion of European commerce. Armenians specialized in the role of intermediary between East and West. As a people culturally straddling both worlds they were equipped to render the services provided by middlemen who facilitate the transfer of goods and capital between distant points and between manufacturers and consumers. In short order Armenians could be found from the town square all the way to the international marketplace in countries as distant and separate from each other as Poland, Italy, Egypt, and Iran, and just about everywhere in between. Frequently Armenians were invited into a country precisely because its rulers wanted to introduce economic policies designed to encourage trade, the monetarization of exchange, and the accrual of domestic capital. As a result Armenian communities sprouted across Anatolia, the rest of the Middle East, southern Russia, and eastern Europe.

Governments pursuing economic expansion, seeking domestic entrepreneurs, or skilled merchants to counter foreign competition, and businessmen with capital to provide basic banking services, called on Armenians to settle in designated parts of their country. Some, as in Turkey, Iran and Russia, went so far as to assign them the management of various commercial monopolies, which were important sources of revenue for the state. The one location where Armenian merchant capital played a role larger than elsewhere in the world was the Iranian city of Isfahan. Armenians and Isfahan had not linked up before 1604 when Shah Abbas decided to embellish the new capital of the Safavid state with the wealth and services Armenian merchants could furnish. Thereupon he ordered the resettlement of the entire Armenian community of Jugha/Julfa in southern Armenia, a city that had positioned itself as the gatekeeper of a key entry port on the main trade route crossing from Asia into Armenia and Anatolia. The deportation ruined another part of historic Armenia and deprived it of its resourceful population. Shah Abbas was more interested in the commercial skills of the Armenians and compensated the merchants by arranging for them to mediate with Europe the Iranian silk trade, a state monopoly. The result was the rapid enrichment of the Armenian community of Isfahan, resettled in the suburb of Nor Jugha/New Julfa, and the just as rapid expansion of an Armenian trade network that soon reached India, Russia, Smyrna on the Aegean coast, Amsterdam on the Atlantic, and Venice on the Adriatic. Armenians connected the sea-lanes of European commerce with the land routes of Asia by channeling through the Asian trade. They repeated this pattern time and again right into the 20th century.

The Armenian interaction with Europeans exposed them to changes occurring around the world that inaugurated the process of modernization. More so than any other people originating from the Asian continent, Armenians absorbed Western culture at a rate that soon began to differentiate them from the other peoples living in the East and Middle East and also began to redefine them as a people who evolved from being an indigenous contingent to one whose outlook and interests aligned increasingly with the West. At first it was a question of Western commercial practices and Armenian familiarization with its methods. Concomitantly, the acquaintance with Western manufactured goods, the need for their transport, the development of new markets, and the retailing of these products strengthened the middleman role of the Armenians and more closely realigned the Armenian outlook, giving it a distinct new orientation consistent in its direction and practical in its results. Commerce added a layer of reality to vague and inchoate thoughts of religious proclivity to Europe as the sphere of Christian freedom at a time when most Armenians lived as disenfranchised subjects of Islamic kingdoms. By the early 18th century, the major European powers began to challenge the potentates of the East and the political structure of Europe turned the tide against the realm of Islam along the frontier zones where East and West converged, and wherein Armenians conducted their affairs. The might of the European monarchies became more palpable to Armenians. Louis XIV of France, Peter the Great of Russia, or Maria Theresa of Austria led states with foreign policy objectives capable of influencing events and trends in parts of the world inhabited by Armenians.

Commerce may have improved the economic and social status of many Armenians in the diaspora, but of its own it would not necessarily have altered the outlook and culture of Armenians in the absence of a national framework. The arrival of a sense of connection across the discontinuous space of the diaspora and the fractured history of Armenia depended on the introduction of another European instrument whose uses Armenians grasped early. While swift technological improvements in Europe resulted in the development of an armaments industry that gave the inhabitants of the continent the capacity to physically dominate the rest of mankind through the superiority of their weaponry, and to change the size and shape, if not existence, of the states Armenians inhabited, another area of the technological revolution in Europe that empowered its users with the advantage of education and intellectual persuasion appealed to Armenians even more. Armenians here and there may have purchased muskets. More of them picked up the products of the printing press. Churchmen and merchants together in the 18th century fostered the publication of books in Armenian. Both depended on literacy and the use of the written word to meet their function in society. Their joint interest in books changed the culture and fate of the Armenian people.

The Intellectual Flowering

In the imagery of 19th-century Romanticism, Armenians described the revival of their culture as a flowering. The growing perception of national self-expression as a socially organizing principle reassigned the role of culture in modern life and Armenians were quick to respond to the idea. If any one thought located itself at the core of the new Armenian self-conception, it was the idea of culture in all its meanings. There was no shortage of proponents for the idea, and for them the notion of a distinct Armenian culture was the vehicle for moving the Armenian people from its medieval mindset formed under psychological siege into the liberating exercise of the intellectual generation of new means of communication. For a dispersed people for whom communication was central to obtaining connectivity, the primary mechanism for the articulation and dissemination of culture was literature. All other facets of culture flourished too, but none other penetrated as widely and deeply the physical and mental terrain of the Armenian people as the published word. It was more transportable than other mediums, and Armenians were still a highly mobile population.

This very mobility in many respects was the cause of concern about the future of the Armenian people that had prompted thinking persons in the diaspora to consider the application of the tools of modernity. Indeed it was those from the very periphery of the Armenian diaspora, those most distantly removed from their historic homeland, who first experimented with the printing press. As a fact the earliest Armenian publications appeared in Holland, Poland, Iran, India, and Italy, and more precisely in Amsterdam, Lvov, New Julfa, Madras, and Venice. The experiment in Venice, however, differed from the other efforts in one profoundly significant way. The early presses attempted to transfer the existing manuscript literature of Armenia into print. The churchman **Mekhitar Sebastatsi**, and the group gathered about him in Venice in 1717 that became known as the **Mekhitarian Order**, took a step that went far beyond mere reproduction. They created new works of learning and literature in Armenian. It was a long and arduous process requiring a century of gestation, or germination to stay with the floral analogy.

The 19th-century cultural revival introduced an entire new element in the makeup of Armenian society. As part of the urban middle class of the diaspora, there emerged an intellectual elite who began to command the attention of their community. **Khachatur Abovian, Mikayel Nalbandian, Raffi, Alishan,** and **Grigor Ardsruni** were just some of the more notable members of this group. As writers, publishers, and educators, they reshaped the thinking of Armenian society. While they clashed with the conservatism of the merchants and the churchmen, many also functioned within the very institutions maintained by both, and both actively encouraged the spread of education through the construction of schools. Everywhere Armenians built schools and nothing more symbolized the economic progress and cultural aspirations of the Armenians than the educational institutions paid for by the mercantile class and overseen in many instances by the clerical class. The harbingers of modern Armenian culture had an uphill struggle to wage, but the impediments kept on falling as the benefits of literacy, education, progress, and opportunities for professionalization swept the resistance to change. By the end of the 19th century, literacy was widespread, the vernacular was the common medium of communication, thousands of books were in print, and hundreds of schools were opened. Poets who scaled the heights of Armenian literary creativity were articulating powerfully moving ideas and giving expression to a new range of values from the dignity of the individual to the collective sense of destiny and worth. They molded a national self-consciousness harboring aspirations that were soon contradicted by the prevailing political reality and opposed by the wielders of power and state authority.

The Age of Politics

How the intellectual currents of the Armenian cultural revival and its associated literary flowering reached the point of crisis in the late 19th century is a facet of the political history of the same century. Throughout the 19th century the Armenian Church organization grew stronger. While monasticism was no longer in vogue, the clergy were more numerous than ever before. The role of bishops, prelates, and catholicoses loomed ever larger as Armenian communities themselves grew more numerous and prosperous. In the absence of a national government and state funding for Armenian institutions, the entire ecclesiastical edifice and educational network of the Armenian people was supported by its privileged class engaged in commerce. More and more Armenians moved to the cities and a growing segment of the urban population moved up from its working class origins into the propertied class.

The Armenian social transformation was so rapid that foreign observers who were only acquainted with the Armenians of Constantinople or of Tbilisi, the two largest concentrations, or other cities, were left with the impression that Armenians were a commercial people for whom the ownership of a shop or a business, or the practice of a trade, a craft, or a profession were culturally conditioned. A larger percentage of the Armenian population still lived on the land and consisted of a peasantry whose main source of income remained agriculture. Their plight became a growing concern, and the inability of the clergy and bourgeoisie to be effective in remedying, or even alleviating, the problems of the unprotected people in the Armenian homeland, began to compromise and undermine their leadership role in Armenian life. The increasing secularization of culture also weakened the sense of allegiance to traditional organizations. Lastly, expanded opportunities to obtain more than an elementary education fostered the rise of yet another group of men for whom an examination of the Armenian condition prompted an unsettling appreciation of the political liabilities defining a seemingly advantaged community.

The political activist working in a group to bring about institutional change and advocating for a sense of national purpose, and seeing the Armenian predicament in terms of controlling factors that may be challenged, was a wholly new phenomenon in Armenian life, and long absent from the imagination of the Armenian people. Why Armenian society increasingly looked toward this new type of individual as an alternative to the conventional sources of leadership is the central question of the history of the late 19th and early 20th century. The answer lies in the increasing alienation of the Armenian people from the states governing their destiny, an alienation brought about by the disappointment of expectations expressly denied them through mounting repression and violence.

Partition and Modernization

About the year 1500 three great powers formed just beyond the horizon of Armenia. It would take Muscovite Russia three hundred more years to cross the Caucasus and reach Armenia. Ottoman Turkey and Safavid Iran, however, clashed in 1514 and remained in conflict over Armenia for another century and a half, until each side resorted to scorched-earth policies that left little to fight over. The settlement ultimately reached between the contenders who partitioned the Armenian plateau, and separated into two a much frightened population who now inhabited either side of a war zone. Two thirds of the country was absorbed by the Ottoman Empire. The eastern third was taken over by Iran. In this same period Shiism became the dominant sect of Islam in

Iran. Less tolerant than the larger Sunni sect, Iranian Shiism aggressively sought to convert the entire population of the Safavid state regardless of religion, and the Christian populations of the Caucasus experienced periods of religious persecution. For this and other reasons the Iranian political system never completely stabilized. In contrast, the Iranian border with Turkey proved more durable. Even after the Russians occupied the Caucasus, the same border more or less reproduced itself.

It took the Russians from 1800 to 1828 to occupy all of the Transcaucasus. Despite the initial disruptions of life, Russian rule transformed the region. For one, Iran permanently abandoned its claim to the entire area giving Russia secure control up to the Arax River. With this, Eastern Armenia became part of Russia, and by extension Europe. For the Armenians of the entire Caucasus, the Russian presence wholly altered their long-time status as second class citizens of an Islamic state. Now they were the subjects of a Christian monarchy and that was sufficient to alter the very nature of their relationship with their government, foreign still though it might be. The Russians governed the Caucasus as a colonial power, but the hostility and exploitation associated with Islamic rule was gone. That was salutary in itself, and vastly expanded the freedom of action, movement, and association among Armenians. If the political environment was conducive to the exercise of greater social liberty, the economic opportunities presented by Russian rule were even greater. The Caucasus joined the vast commercial space of the Russian Empire, which in the 19th century itself was undergoing rapid economic development. In brief, the Caucasus registered a very significant expansion in commerce, to a degree that even local agriculture joined the international market with the production of cash crops. The process of urbanization transformed country towns into small cities and Tbilisi, the administrative center of the Caucasus, grew into a virtual cosmopolis with a majority Armenian population engaged in activities ranging from industry to banking. The discovery of oil on the Caspian shore and the rapid growth of the petroleum industry, as well as the construction of rail lines connecting the cities of the Caucasus with Russia proper and with the shipping lanes of the Black Sea, added to the indices of economic and demographic growth.

In this process of creating a modern society built upon new economic foundations governed by the flow of capital the old Caucasian social order was turned upside down. Onetime nearly landless Armenians became the largest property-owning element surpassing the local Georgians and

Azeris whose economic and social structure depended on a landowning gentry. The relocation of social power from the country to the city, the concentration of industry and commerce in the city, the accumulation of capital and the role of banking managed from the city, and the visible investment in educational and cultural institutions also located in cities, altogether catapulted Armenian society across a threshold that fed growing expectations that the sphere of progress would embrace the entire Armenian population and lead to the consolidation of privileges associated with political liberalism and distinct nationhood emancipated of the strictures of colonialism.

Though nowhere near replicating the same scale of social progress, the expansion of the economy in the Ottoman Empire brought about vast changes in the social makeup and outlook of the Armenians there too. Liberal reforms in Turkey also broadened the sphere of social, economic, and cultural activity, while actually strengthening the Armenian *Millet* structure. As in Russia, some Armenians even entered government service. Armenians played a very prominent role in the international commerce of the Ottoman Empire. They led in the introduction of industry. Early on they had played a prominent role in banking, but European interests soon controlled the financial services sector and associated businesses. In the Ottoman Empire too the expansion of the country's economy shifted social influence to new classes and from the country to the city, but the hindrances of religious prejudice and ethnic resentment toward Armenians and minorities obstructed the path of steady progress. When the empire went into decline, these social, economic, and political imbalances in the domestic order became the sources of serious conflict and deepening fissures. The new thresholds established by Armenians in the Ottoman Empire raised concerns in some Turkish quarters and envy and suspicion in other quarters as a minority community of contemptible infidels appeared to grow in privilege and stature, while the majority of the population that labored by the rules of a system laden by the customs and traditions of centuries of Turkish might and Islamic domination did not experience similar levels of improvement in their overall economic standing.

The Armenian Question

A series of developments in rapid succession raised hopes among Armenians and others that legal and political reforms preparing for the introduction of constitutional government in Russia and Turkey were in the offing. Just as rapidly trends reversed and dashed those very hopes setting the stage for a host of political groups to ask questions about the legitimacy of the existing order and resolving that the two systems had become impermeable to needed change. For the Armenians, who in the course of the century had reached a new social and national consensus and new accommodations with their respective governments, these trends portended a difficult period. The coincident emergence of the Armenian Question in the Ottoman Empire only heightened the tensions and risks. The 19th century consensus began to unravel in 1876 when the Russo-Turkish War triggered an international crisis. The Russian victory and Ottoman capitulation disturbed the balance of power in Europe and diplomatic pressure from England and France set about to redress the situation and modify the preponderance of Russian power. The main territorial issues concerned the Balkans where independent states emerged in the wake of the Ottoman retreat from the peninsula. The initial result of the war had raised hopes among Armenians that their cause for improvements in the Armenian-inhabited areas of Turkey would receive attention as well. In the March 1878 Treaty of San Stefano that ended the war, the Ottomans agreed to reforms in the six so-called Armenian provinces with the understanding that Russian forces that had occupied most of those parts of the Ottoman Empire would remain in a supervisory capacity to guarantee implementation of the reforms.

The July 1878 Treaty of Berlin altered these terms to the extent that the Ottomans agreed to reforms while the Russian military was required to withdraw. To many the Treaty of Berlin appeared to provide stronger guarantees than the Treaty of San Stefano. With Britain, France, and Germany as additional parties to the agreement, the Armenian Question had received international attention and elicited Great Power involvement with the deteriorating condition of the Armenian population in the eastern provinces. Yet, within a few brief years changes in government and foreign policy deprived Armenians of any support in seeing the terms of the treaty implemented. Abdul-Hamid II, who had risen to the throne in 1876 with the promulgation of an Ottoman Constitution, quickly suspended the liberties announced by the constitution and squelched the parliamentary system thereby introduced. Instead, he introduced a repressive autocracy that concentrated even more power in the hands of the sultan, and which relied on an army of spies to maintain it. Presumably to contain the situation in the Armenian provinces, he formed the Hamidiye corps named in his honor, armed irregular cavalry units given police powers, manned by Kurds and staffed with Turkish officers, whose primary purpose was to dissuade the Armenian population from engaging in political activity. By so doing the sultan created a system licensing the exploitation of ethnic and religious differences in order to arrest the further development of Armenian society. Tight censorship and a clamping down on the media meant that Armenians living outside the provinces also felt the hand of repression even if spared the coercion of the Hamidiye. In Russia too autocracy and reaction became the norms of government during the reign of Alexander III who assumed the throne upon the assassination of his father by revolutionaries in 1881. Censorship and repression of national minorities in Russia carried the added pressure of Russification measures enforced by closing down Armenian schools.

The international system as a whole began to fail as well in the face of the obdurate autocracies that dismissed all thought of liberal reforms. With their acquisition of the Suez Canal, the British interest in maintaining the Ottoman Empire as a buffer against Russian expansion only increased. Despite differences, the two reached an accord on preserving the status quo. As for Germany, unified by Bismarck in 1870, by playing neutral broker in the drafting of the Berlin treaty eight years later, its new stature invited the renegotiation of alliances. The Ottomans found in Kaiser Wilhelm II a militarist who put greater stock in winning the friendship of the Ottomans than other Europeans critical of the brutality associated with Abdul-Hamid's reign.

For Armenians who began to witness the deterioration of their situation and a reversal of their expectations from the new regional order drawn up by the Treaty of Berlin, the cause of their national emancipation encountered a crisis of unexpected proportions. The emotional and intellectual investment in bourgeois liberalism, constitutionalism, moral and social progressivism, and political and legal reform suddenly encountered barriers on all sides. It appeared as though Europeans signed treaties they had no intention of upholding, governments made promises on reform that they had no intention of honoring, and the cause of emancipation that had seen nations form and secure independence or autonomy in Europe appeared an option that would not be available to Armenians when the heavy hand of autocratic repression planted roadblocks everywhere. Under the influence of Russian revolutionary politics, itself a response to the failure of liberal reform in Russia, Armenians too in the Caucasus began forming political societies to address the Armenian predicament and to challenge the injustices of state authority.

Starting in 1887 an **Armenian revolutionary movement** picked up momentum when the autocracies foreclosed all other political options. Despite the self-representation of the Armenian political activists as revolutionaries in ideological consonance with trends in Russia and Europe, the national aspect of the Armenian movement predominated and motivated participation more than socialism. On the other hand, the demographic diffusion of the Armenians across Anatolia and Transcaucasia was not conducive to separatist objectives. The securing of fundamental rights and national recognition within the framework of the existing states was preferable to many. From the standpoint of officialdom, however, these types of political demands actually sounded even more radical than territorial nationalism as the latter did not appear an imposition on the total system as much as a portional secession. That was the case at least for the Ottoman Empire. Armenian nationalism also sought to find common ground between the interests of an urban bourgeoisie in diaspora and a rural peasantry inhabiting the Armenian homeland. In light of the evident privilege of the urban segment of Armenian society and the comparative security of Russia, the focus of concern was the condition of the Armenian peasantry in the Ottoman Empire for whom self-defense was the last resort against state exploitation and violence. The Ottoman government preferred to construe acts of desperation and defiance even of unlawful demands by officials as insurrection and escalated its response by organizing systematic violence. The **Hamidian Massacres** of the 1890s and the 1909 **Adana Massacre** devastated Armenian society across the entire length of the Ottoman Empire resulting in hundreds of thousands of casualties, enormous property loss, and a profound sense of alienation from a brutal system.

Global War, Mass Murder, and the Death of West Armenia

When the Young Turk extremists seized the reins of power in Constantinople in 1913 they decided that the resolution of the Armenian Question lay in the elimination of the Armenians from the Ottoman Empire. They saw their opportunity arrive sooner than expected when the European Powers declared war in August 1914. The Young Turk regime threw its lot on the side of Germany and invaded Russia. Armenians knew that war spelled disaster as the Russian-Turkish border bisected historic Armenia. Regardless of which direction forces advanced Armenians were in harm's way. Russia being the superior power, however, there were doubts whether the Ottoman army was up to the task. That was proven to the contrary and contributed to the prolongation and expansion of the war. With German logistical support the Turkish forces entered the fray in October and fought until the end of World War I. The Young Turks gambled that Germany would best Russia militarily and calculated that the war was an occasion to restore Ottoman prestige and to carve out a new Pan-Turanian empire at Russia's expense. That objective was delayed when the Russian army at first prevailed on the Caucasus front but advanced slowly as its main forces were committed to the European front. The initial Ottoman defeat in December 1914 at Sarikamish in the east and the April 1915 Allied landing at Gallipoli in the west provided sufficient cover to license the destruction of the Armenian communities all across Asia Minor right up to the Caucasus. This was achieved within the year through deportation, massacre, and starvation.

For all intents and purposes the Armenian presence in all of Anatolia from historic West Armenia all the way to the Aegean shore of Asia Minor was terminated. By 1923 only the Armenians of Constantinople remained, though deprived of their leadership and many of their former institutions. **Krikor Zohrab**, **Taniel Varuzhan**, **Siamanto**, and other prominent figures arrested during the roundup of April 24, 1915, had been summarily executed. **Komitas** had become emotionally unhinged. The finest exponents of the cultural flowering that had so inspired the Armenian people were decimated. The total demographic catastrophe is estimated in the range of a million and half victims who perished in those years. The scale of the genocidal policies of the Young Turk government is better understood in relation to the prewar estimate of the Armenian population in the Ottoman Empire, which was placed at 2.1 to 2.3 million persons. The losses inflicted on the Armenians went beyond the mass murder of human beings. The **Armenian Genocide** also entailed the total plunder and confiscation of Armenian assets depriving even survivors of their rightful property. The program to eradicate the Armenians went so far as to involve the destruction of the physical remains of Armenian civilization. Everything from historic monuments of great antiquity to ordinary tombstones in common graveyards was smashed with the goal of erasing the millennial record of the Armenian presence in that part of the world.

Ideology, Revolution, and the Fate of East Armenia

Militarism, mass slaughter, and the total mobilization of society for global conflict were only part of the larger consequences of igniting World War I. Mobilization assumed a different character in each of the belligerent nations and doing so required the pronouncement of ideological justification. The violence associated with external warfare and the attendant exactions led domestically conditioned populations to the acceptance of ever more radical ideological propositions. The grave dangers of warfare and the prospects, or reality, of defeat unleashed new and powerful social forces that redefined the political order. While this happened at the end of the war in Germany, for instance, it occurred at the beginning of the war in Turkey.

The Young Turks had burst upon the scene in 1908 when they brought Hamidian despotism to an end. The Young Turk Revolution restored the Ottoman Constitution and parliamentary government. By 1913 the democratic and pluralistic phase of the Young Turk era had ended under the stress of the Balkan Wars, and the Committee of Union and Progress (CUP) made up of the most chauvinistic elements of the movement had seized power. When the Great War began in Europe a CUP triumvirate controlled the Ottoman government. The ideals of the revolution were abandoned, while the CUP was driven by its ultra-nationalistic ideology. For a multiconfessional and multiethnic empire, such redefinition of the social content of the state could only be realized through radical and extreme measures. The war offered a perfect opportunity to advance the Young Turk revolution to a new stage by permitting its leaders to implement their covert programs without restraint and with unparalleled violence.

World War I is better known for having fostered conditions that propelled another revolution, the one in Russia. The short-lived democratic phase introduced by the 1917 February/March Revolution also espoused ideals that proved insupportable in the context of ongoing war. The overthrow of the Provisional Government by the Bolsheviks in the 1917 October/November Revolution introduced an ideologically driven self-acclaimed vanguard unrestrained in its application of violent measures justified in the name of creating a new utopian society.

In sum Armenians were suddenly living in two countries run by competing revolutionary regimes, both legitimized by agreements with Imperial Germany. The March 1918 Treaty of Brest-Litovsk that ended the conflict on the eastern front between Germany and Russia was also signed by Turkey. It marked the high point of the Triple Alliance (Germany, Austria-Hungary, Turkey), as it spelled the end of the Triple Entente (France, Russia, Great Britain). The Young Turks shared in the moment of German victory by seeing the formal withdrawal of Russia from the war and by regaining territory in the Caucasus by the terms of the negotiations.

For a people who were not masters of their own destiny and whose fortunes in wartime and peacetime hinged on the decisions of great powers and remote governments, the implications of the Treaty of Brest-Litovsk were just as momentous as the 1878 Treaty of Berlin. Against the background of the long-term disastrous results of that agreement, the consequences of the new settlement were self-evident. Two other processes complicated matters even more. The Bolsheviks enjoyed little legitimacy and Russia began to disintegrate. Without a central government the Caucasus was adrift and its population made the best of attempting to run its own affairs. While that would have been a challenge under normal circumstances, the breakdown of Russia also meant the dissolution of its army. With the defenses of the frontier removed, there was little to stop the Ottoman armies from filling the vacuum. Armenian soldiery made a brave effort to hold the line, but they were no substitute for the Russian forces and their numbers no match to the advancing Turkish divisions. By May 1918 the Russians had departed the scene, the Turks were poised at the Arax River, and Armenians had nowhere left to retreat. The armies of a genocidal regime were on an invasion course of East Armenia as they swept Armenians everywhere they advanced.

The fateful hour had arrived when the very existence of the Armenian people hung in the balance. The ensuing struggle between Armenian volunteer forces and the Ottoman army was fought on a front extending along the entire northern perimeter of East Armenia, from the Plain of Ararat to Alexandropol (Gyumri) and beyond. It is more famously remembered as the Battle of Sardarapat, the point of deepest penetration by Ottoman forces, but an hour from Edjmiadsin. The country was saved when the populace joined in arms and after two weeks of hard fighting the Turks called for a truce. In the final days of the battle, the Transcaucasus fragmented into its ethnic components. Georgia and Azerbaijan declared their independence. The Armenian National Council in Tbilisi, recognizing the significance of the moment, issued its own announcement about the appointment of an Armenian government.

The Independent Republic of Armenia

On May 28, 1918, the Republic of Armenia came into existence, born out of war and the threat of annihilation. Its territory encompassed the former Russian province of Erevan/Yerevan. Its economy was a shambles, half its population destitute. Its resources consisted of not much more than farmlands. Its borders were undefined, its government an improvised administration, and its status unrecognized but by its mortal enemy. From such inauspicious beginnings and unpromising circumstances the Armenian people set about creating for itself a new state. Herein the Armenian revolutionary movement, just when its hopes appeared to have been dashed and its efforts in vain, retrieved from the chaos of war and revolution the crucible of a new nation. In those critical years the **Armenian Revolutionary Federation** (ARF), the one political association with the broadest popular support among the Armenian masses, played the leading role. The ARF pooled the Armenian political leadership within its organization, and men like **Aram Manukian**, **Andranik**, **Avetis Aharonian**, **Alexander Khatisian**, and **Simon Vratzian** brought their contributions to the framing of a new Armenian polity.

World War I continued for another five months and the future of the Armenian state remained uncertain until the Armistice and the surrender of the Turks to the Allies. Armenians breathed a sigh of relief in November 1918, but a merciless winter took a further toll of an exhausted population. By the spring of 1919 the situation in the country had improved. The Allies required the Ottomans to withdraw to their prewar boundaries. The result was the incorporation of the province of Kars into the Armenian republic giving it territory sufficient to create a viable state. Armenians, however, were counting on a more lasting settlement. As a people caught in the fighting of the Great War, their representatives at the Paris Peace Conference hoped for status as belligerents who had contributed to the cause of ending the conflict. The victorious powers, however, were more absorbed by the details of a European settlement where the map of the entire continent was being redrawn. As they delayed making commitments to the Armenians, events in Russia and Turkey soon outpaced the ability of the Allies to impose their will in the Caucasus. The Bolsheviks won the Russian Civil War. In Anatolia former Ottoman forces regrouped under the banner of the Turkish Nationalist Movement. As Armenians counted on the Western Powers to stabilize the Caucasus and waited for them to extend the Armenian republic international support, Mustafa Kemal and Vladimir Illyich Lenin made other plans. What they had in common was their opposition to European colonialism, even as one espoused an exclusive Turkish nationalism and the other professed leadership of international socialism.

The August 1920 Treaty of Sèvres drawn up by the Western Powers was intended to do for the Middle East and the Caucasus what the June 1919 Treaty of Versailles had done for Europe. It was meant to settle all conflicts, appease all significant parties, redraw the map, and extend formal recognition to newborn states. For Armenia the Treaty of Sèvres marked a legal watershed in its status as now it enjoyed de jure recognition by the victorious Allies and a defeated Turkey. Except that two governments by then were in existence in Turkey and the Ottoman signatory was the impotent representative of a fast fading entity being replaced by the Turkish Nationalist Movement. If anything, the Treaty of Sèvres undermined the Ottoman government in Constantinople and emboldened the Turkish Nationalist government in Ankara. By 1923 the former was overthrown, the Ottoman Empire abolished, and the Turkish Nationalist regime under the lifetime presidency of Mustafa Kemal proclaimed the legitimate government of the Republic of Turkey.

Before any of that happened the Turkish Nationalists had removed the Armenian republic from the map of the world. In so doing they were partners with Communist Russia, which also flouted the Treaty of Sèvres. In September 1920 Turkish Nationalist forces advanced on Armenia. With orders to eliminate its existence, the Turkish army captured Kars in October and puts its population to flight and to the sword. By November it had entered Alexandropol again. At the point of collapse against superior forces, the Armenian government handed over power to another military contingent advancing on Armenia from the east: namely the Red Army. Recognizing the futility of such a small country waging war on two fronts and suspecting the ulterior motives of the Turkish army, the Armenian government surrendered to the only alternative that offered some guarantee for the physical survival of the Armenian people.

The Armenian Soviet Socialist Republic

On November 29, 1918 the **Communist Party of Armenia** (CPA), effectively a device of the Russian Communist Party, proclaimed Armenia Sovietized and advised Lenin in Moscow of its voluntary union with Communist Russia. Made up of a handful of Armenian Bolsheviks, the CPA represented no real power so much as a fictive mechanism for the legalization of Armenia's occupation by the Red Army. The entry of the Red Army brought hostilities on the soil of Armenia to an end and the Turkish assault to a stop. The legal instrument for the territorial settlement of the Caucasus between the two powers of the region was signed in Moscow in March 1921. The territory of the former Republic of Armenia was partitioned between Turkey, where no Armenians remained living, and Russia, where the surviving population was concentrated.

The Sovietization of Armenia involved more than the extinguishing of Armenian independence and the reannexation of its territory. Sovietization also delivered the ideological revolution of Communism and its associated class warfare. In the specific instance of the Armenians it meant the destruction of the nationalists who had formed the republic and the bourgeoisie that had all along constituted the core social group of the Armenian population of the Caucasus. With the disempowerment of these two groups, the platform of the Armenian intelligentsia also collapsed. In essence the CUP phase of the Young Turk Revolution, continued by the Kemalist Movement, and the Communist phase of the Russian Revolution both targeted specially the elite elements of Armenian society, and in effect destroyed them. The two revolutions also expropriated property. The abolition of private property and private enterprise in Communist Russia ruined the Armenian mercantile class.

Whether by revolution or by genocide, Armenian society was leveled. All its stratifications were lost. Its entire leadership was vacated. The three new classes or groups, associated with emergence of modern society, each mobilized by a different set of concerns, and yet all related and connected by a cultivated sense of identity and group solidarity, were utterly destroyed: the merchant middle class that constituted the enterprising core of the Armenian diaspora and which voluntarily sustained the Armenian nation through its resources; the intellectual elite and the many exponents of the Armenian cultural revival reflecting its thoughts, from the village grammar school teacher to the big city publisher; the political activists who espoused national aspirations and who furnished leadership under the most trying circumstances. The total result may be said to have amounted to the proletarianization of the Armenian people, so thoroughly was the century-old structure of modern Armenian society eradicated. In 1921 destitute peasantry in war-torn Armenia and stateless and impecunious deportees huddled in refugee camps across the Middle East made up the bulk of the Armenian population in the world.

The wrecking of the preexisting social order was a requisite for the monopolization of political power in the hands of the Communist Party. The first decade of Soviet power in Armenia was dedicated to that end. In the earliest months Sovietization proceeded so rapidly and violently that it provoked a popular rebellion in February 1921; the only occasion when Communist authorities were actually chased from office after having been installed by the Red Army. The Armenian response to the methods of expropriation and political arbitrariness prompted Lenin to remove **Sargis Kasian** from the chairmanship of the party. A more orderly transition to Communist rule was overseen by **Alexander Miasnikian** who refocused the energies of the party and of the population on reconstruction. To facilitate more centralized planning and accelerate the economic development of the region after years of conflict, in March 1922 the three Transcaucasian republics were merged into a federation, which in turn joined the Union of Soviet Socialist Republics (USSR) when it was formally constituted in December 1922. By the 1936 Stalin Constitution the Transcaucasian federation was dissolved and separate republic status restored to Armenia.

The comparative relaxation of political repression and policies of economic control upon the resolution of the federative structure of the Soviet Union brought a period of respite and recovery to the Armenian population. Irrigation schemes, the construction of hydroelectric plants, the introduction of urban planning, the installing of basic infrastructure, and the organizing of a comprehensive educational system slowly set in motion progressive steps toward the development of an egalitarian society. The decade of the 1920s was tolerant enough to see even some very prominent intellectuals consider making Soviet Armenia their home. They assumed responsibility for bridging a politically isolated and ideologically controlled society with its cultural heritage. By their presence, example, and contributions to education, they rescued the record and knowledge of the past and relocated it in the new institutions founded under Communist rule. Among them were the writers **Avetik**

Isahakian and Hovhannes Tumanian, the scholars **Hrachia Ajarian**, Hakob Manandian, and Toros Toramanian, and the artist Martiros Sarian. This gathering was augmented by the great new talent of **Yeghishe Charents**, whose flamboyant poetry reattached the sentiments of Armenian patriotism to the spirit of a revolutionary dawn by reworking the treasury of Armenian literature into a contemporary mythology that began filling the void of the missing identification between people and state. Charents's writings were original and passionate enough to resonate beyond Armenia and reach the forlorn Armenian diaspora. During a period of profound alienation from politics Armenians once again tapped into the fundaments of culture to retrieve from the blight of totalitarianism and obliteration by genocide elements of an identity that relied again upon the circulation of the printed word.

The era of Stalinism suspended the policies of tolerating national differences and reintroduced conformity and Russification. The terror of the 1930s silenced many voices, including that of Charents. The CPA cadre was purged, much as the rest of the Communist Party in Russia. Old Bolsheviks along with young Communists lost their lives, among them the charismatic party leader **Aghasi Khanjian**, who had started as a Stalin protégé. The repression of the voices of leadership constituted part of the process of eliminating resistance to the harsh collectivization measures introduced by Joseph Stalin and to the ruthless concentration of power in the hands of his secret service apparatus. The murderous regime was even unsparing of the life of Catholicos Gevorg V Muratbekian, by then no more than a figurehead confined to the compound at Edjmiadsin. The economy of Armenia, much like the rest of the USSR, regressed in the mid-1930s during the early phases of collectivization, especially as peasants and farmers everywhere resisted the forced measures and preferred killing their livestock to handing it over to the state. For Armenia, whose economy had been badly damaged during World War I, the nationalization of property and the collectivization of the economy impeded the rebuilding process. In the late 1930s Armenia was still mainly an agricultural country far from exhibiting a modern character, let alone delivering on the promise of a utopian system. The country was only to undergo further strain when Nazi Germany invaded the Soviet Union in 1941 and Armenians found themselves at war once again. The territory of Armenia escaped the ravages of invasion this time as the Soviet Army made its stand at Stalingrad. Armenia, however, contributed all of its fighting-age manpower. By the time the conflict ended, and Armenian military units had fought all the way to Berlin, 174,000 men had given their lives. The demographic toll on Armenia was onerous, a country with a population of barely more than a million and a quarter.

For all its costs, World War II changed the relationship between Armenia and the Soviet Union. Armenians had fought bravely, contributed decorated leaders to the Soviet armed forces with men such as Marshal **Ivan Baghramian** and Admiral **Ivan Isakov**, and supported the struggle against Nazism and fascism the world over. As the Soviet Union gained in global stature, Soviet Armenia now was seen as an integral and constitutive element of a larger system successful in war and seemingly vindicated by its ideology. The remoteness of the country, the isolation of its society, and the provincialization of its culture, all were overcome when the USSR emerged from World War II an even more cohesive and centrally commanded unity than before. Armenians more easily assimilated into the Soviet system and sensed the derivation of benefit in being part of a major power enjoying respect around the world. This new-won fame also altered the nature of the relationship between Armenia and the diaspora, and for the first time channels of contact and communication were opened. Tens of thousands were persuaded to emigrate to Armenia under the guise of a repatriation policy. This special dispensation to Armenians by Moscow may have had the ulterior motive of enhancing the much shrunken labor pool in Armenia and their settlement at a peripheral republic did not present a serious problem of ideological contamination by persons who had not grown up under the Soviet system and were unfamiliar with its requirements of political conformity and obedience to party discipline. The proletarian character of the diaspora also ameliorated the repatriation program, but the gulf in values turned out to be wider than anticipated and the repatriates were never fully absorbed into Soviet Armenian society, certainly not its power structure.

Real change in Soviet Armenia occurred in the postwar years. The engine of change was the industrialization of the country. In light of the fact that the industrialization of Armenia occurred within the framework of the Soviet command economy, the process was based on little economic logic because it was not driven by the exploitation of resources or the capacity of the country. Rather, the decision in Moscow to invest so heavily in Armenia, a remote corner of the vast Soviet empire, was an ideological and political calculation. It may have had more to do with the educational level, the skills set, the work ethic, and the political reliability of the Armenian population. As a sizable portion of Soviet industry was geared to building and supplying the huge Soviet military apparatus, many of the plants constructed in Armenia produced advanced military technology. Armenia did not have the mineral ore for heavy industry, but its skilled workers were perfectly suited for the manufacturing of modern technological equipment. Electronics, precision instruments, chemicals, and eventually mainframe computers were some of the stronger sectors of the Armenian economy.

The rapid acquirement of the technical know-how, the scientific knowledge, and the management skills demanded by modern industry and a developing economy was met by an equally rapid expansion of the educational system in Armenia. The postwar years witnessed a veritable explosion in higher education. Tens of thousands were admitted into universities. Research capacity in the country expanded with the proliferation of specialized institutes as part of a vast Academy of Sciences. The gamut of knowledge from philology to physics was promoted. Armenian scientists excelled in mathematics, physics, astrophysics, and related applied disciplines such as electronics, avionics, computers, and programming. No less an expansion of education in the fine arts was registered. Industrialization and the associated social changes also altered the demographic profile of Armenia. The demand for labor encouraged the movement from the countryside. Along with the expansion of the administrative bureaucracy, and the concentration of educational institutions in the city, this trend resulted in the rapid urbanization of Armenia. With the high-rise as the typical Soviet residential complex, the result was high-density living.

Yerevan the Modern Metropolis

Urbanization reintroduced politics in Armenian life. That occurred not just by virtue of numbers. It had as much to do with the emergence of a critical mass capable of questioning the status quo and demonstrating the value of change as social improvement in the face of the ideological patrols manning the entryways of influence and power. That social capacity for change derived from the widening of the better-educated classes. In the case of Soviet Armenia, the economic necessity of encouraging the expansion of education in order to mold the citizenry required by industrialization and urbanization policies also produced new generations more exposed to facets of Armenian culture. Despite the barriers, a strengthening of national identity occurred. This imposed an obligation on the political order, which realized that, if it were to retain legitimacy and preserve its monopoly, repression and censorship were no longer sufficient controls. An accommodation was required and a cooptation of socially popular national concepts and views.

This general trend, however, depended on a locus. Arguably because of the diaspora, the aspiration of the Communist system for international legitimacy advantaged Soviet Armenia by turning its capital city into a showplace of the success, standards of living, and national self-expression achievable under socialism. When the Armenian government first chose Yerevan as the capital city, it had two considerations in mind. It was centrally located and somewhat more defensible than Alexandropol, the other town of any significance in the country. Yerevan had been garrisoned over the centuries because of its strategic position, but Alexandropol, connected by rail to Tbilisi, had outpaced it by the early 20th century. That very reason also made the city a military objective as witnessed in 1918 and 1920. Although an ancient settlement, Yerevan lacked a civic character and in this respect it was well suited for a Soviet experiment in urban planning. Soviet Armenian designers set out to create a wholly modern city, and unlike the sterile spaces and featureless structures that came to inhabit most Soviet towns, they gave Yerevan an urban character based on a plan that fanned out from a center dominated by architecturally harmonized buildings.

Decades later the city of Yerevan raised in a central plaza a statue of Alexander Tamanian of a size competing in height with that reserved for the edified captains of the Communist Party. In that respect Tamanian's importance as the designer of an appreciated urban environment indeed matched the influence of political decision makers. Within the core of the city Tamanian strategically distributed the new institutional landmarks that a national capital would possess. By the 1960s, a thriving city boasted theaters, concert halls, cinemas, an opera house, a state university, museums, publishing houses, hotels, government buildings, sports facilities, and a public life in which artists, musicians, authors, scholars, scientists, architects, academicians, professors, sports figures, and chess masters enjoyed respect and acclaim for their accomplishments. The CPA, which once dominated all aspects of life, invariably conceded space to an intellectual and cultural elite of whom not everyone necessarily was a member of the party. The CPA still controlled the levers of power and the resources of the country. It marched to the tune of Moscow and followed the decisions and commands of the Central Committee, but locally it also shared a city whose populace increasingly gained confidence and achieved consensus in its collective identity.

The first manifestation of the surging role of national identity in a Soviet republic occurred on April 24, 1965, when the Yerevan populace spontaneously gathered in the city center to hold an unauthorized commemoration of the Armenian Genocide. This demonstration alerted the authorities that for all the repression of a totalitarian system and the controls on public life, aspects of historical memory still exercised a prevalent role in national identity. Out of these public demands came concessions that sought to channel these sentiments and harness them to the benefit of the state. Some of the key markers of national history that had been subjected to ideological condemnation or manipulation were revisited and permitted latitude for reconsideration. The most tangible manifestation of the political change brought about by the popular movement for commemoration appeared in the authorized construction of two monumental complexes, one dedicated to the Armenian Genocide, and the other dedicated to the Battle of Sardarapat. The latter was constructed on site an hour by car from Yerevan. The genocide memorial, however, was situated upon a height overlooking the city where in an annual rite hundreds of thousands converged to mark a day that was never adopted on the official Soviet Armenian calendar.

The genocide memorial was a concession with larger implications as it reflected upon the foreign policy of the Soviet Union, and in this respect, irrespective of Turkey whose standing policy was denial and obstruction of any public discussion within official circles anywhere in the world, the signal to the Armenian diaspora was loudly audible and inescapable. Even before these manifestly national monuments were erected, Yerevan had already begun to attract the attention of the Armenian diaspora as the focal point of the Armenian nation as a whole. All of the significant changes in the cultural life of the Armenians had occurred in the post-Stalin era and the so-called "thaw" introduced by Nikita Khrushchev, which marginally softened the Cold War ever so briefly, nevertheless went further in lifting the harshest domestic restrictions on cultural life. The transition from the sanitized folkloristic culture permitted the nationalities under Stalin to a more contemporary civilization occurred in the late 1950s and early 1960s. Despite the reversals of the later Brezhnev era, the broader trends continued. Once again a new generation of poets captured the imagination of the Armenian public. Hovhannes Shiraz, Silva Kaputikian, and Paruyr Sevak tackled the objects of national value in a new sentimental style penned in rhyme that easily lent itself to elocution. Their verse offered a radical departure from monotone paeans to socialism, Leninism, collectivism, and Soviet patriotism that passed for literature under Stalin. Sevak's elegy to Komitas was released in 1966 as a new epic cycle giving expression to the spirit of unadulterated devotion to culture's redeeming triumph over evil as retold through the life of the churchman who rescued the music of historic Armenia before the voices of its singers were silenced by genocide. There remained nothing overtly Soviet about this literature. Its hero, its subject, its historical content, and its richness of language invoked the lofty summit of individual genius.

This reassembling of the Armenian heritage by Paruyr Sevak reflected the larger phenomenon of the gathering of Armenian culture and its centralization in Yerevan. A historical museum and a national gallery displayed the artifacts of Armenian civilization, for instance, but a much more imposing structure at the far end of the widest boulevard of Yerevan was constructed for what would have been regarded elsewhere as the arcane purpose of preserving manuscripts. The Madenataran, the repository of Armenian manuscripts, was designed as a modern temple to Armenian civilization, its entrance guarded by a colossal statue of Mesrop Mashtots and its front wall lined with statues of ancient savants. Whether it had been so intended or not, the Madenataran became the city's most popular tourist attraction, displaying the glowing pages of medieval illuminations and conveying a people's lasting love of books as its most precious possessions. When Stalin's own colossus was removed from the pedestal high above the hill into which the Madenataran was built, in the reported sarcasm of locals an equally sized statue of Mother Armenia was swiftly raised in its stead lest another tyrant desire to occupy it. The visual redefinition of Yerevan made Soviet Armenian society less forbidding to the point where encouragement of tourism to the country's cultural, architectural, and natural landmarks was official policy by the 1970s.

The permission to allow the circulation of diaspora Armenians resulted in further modifications. An officially atheistic society that had banned the practice of religion could not impede visitors' desire for pilgrimage to Edjmiadsin. With their donations the cathedral, residence, and compound of the Catholicosate were gradually restored to standards respectful of the spiritual leader of the Armenian people. Far be it from restoring the Armenian Church that remained virtually nonexistent beyond the walls of the Edjmiadsin monastery, nevertheless the office was elevated in public life. In Catholicos Vazgen I Armenians found an increasingly tactful emissary who by his longevity and avoidance of friction with the authorities restored the image, if not the prestige, of the church as an Armenian institution.

The Karabagh Revolution

If by the 1980s Armenians in the homeland and in the diaspora appeared to have made gains in charting their own course and in asserting their national and other collective objectives, one problem had continued to fester out of sight. The question of **Nagorno Karabagh** was particularly nettlesome, obscured and overlooked, but its population, despite its isolation in Soviet Azerbaijan, had not remained unaffected by the currents of life in Armenia. When in 1987 Mikhail Gorbachev sought to undo the damage of what was termed the stagnation of the late Brezhnev era with policies to restructure the economic system through freer public discourse, Karabagh Armenians perceived an opening to raise their concerns about the status of their autonomous district and its uncertain future. A tentative step that started as little more than a petition to the Central Committee of the Communist Party in Moscow for the reassignment of jurisdiction overnight assumed the dimensions of a mass popular movement in Armenia. It ignited the spark of a revolution that leaped beyond the boundaries of the titular republics in question, and which within four years of its first manifestation saw the dissolution of the Soviet Union.

No other issue in the 20th century so galvanized the Armenian people everywhere as the Karabagh conflict. To them all the struggle carried the nightmarish hallmarks of the agonizing experiences of the first decades of the century. It mobilized Armenians the world over. It radicalized the population in Armenia who grew increasingly defiant of the authorities. It militarized the situation in Karabagh as the center lost its grip and events spun beyond its control. Without the heavy hand of repression it turned out, the Soviet empire would not hold. Without Armenia to its back, without Yerevan where a million strong gathered at Opera Square or at the foot of the Madenataran, without diaspora Armenians clamoring for rectification, the struggle in Karabagh might have been another last stand against larger numbers. The complicated maze of events from February 1988 to December 1991 eventually resulted in a series of changes in the region with global ramifications. Among them were the independence of Armenia and of Karabagh, the waging of a difficult and ultimately successful war, the draining of the economy of the region, demographic upheavals, and an environment of hostility and strategic competition.

The Third Republic

On September 21, 1991, Armenians voted in a referendum and opted by an overwhelming majority for independence. The day marked a triumph for the **Armenian National Movement** (ANM), a popular front type coalition that unified all democratic currents in Armenia into a powerful force that overthrew the Communist system entirely. With strong democratic credentials, despite the surrounding violence of the Karabagh conflict, through peaceful tactics relying on popular pressure, the ANM forced the retreat of the CPA from power. A multiparty democracy was introduced in Armenia and the new government under the presidency of **Levon Ter-Petrossian** quickly received international support. Optimism permeated the moment and fed the belief that with rapid democratization and a clear policy on the right of private ownership the process of revamping of the economy toward the free enterprise system would proceed just as rapidly. Those hopes were undone by the consequences of the Karabagh conflict as Azerbaijan and Turkey jointly placed Armenia under blockade. Cut off from Russia and the rest of the former Soviet Union, upon which it so completely depended, Armenia's economy totally unraveled. The political and social progress registered in the country was undermined by the harsh economic realities imposed by external factors.

Armenia survived its first three years thanks to international aid that just barely kept the population from starving and freezing in the winter months. Conditions slowly improved after 1994 when a cease-fire ended hostilities in Karabagh. By then the political consensus that had been agreed upon had fractured under the pressure of war and its privations. The populace, consumed by the daily struggle for survival, had withdrawn from politics and the arena became filled with parties that could no longer muster voter support sufficient to govern with the types of mandates that had catapulted the ANM to leadership and power. The contested elections for the legislature in 1995 and the presidency in 1996 marked the low points in the political evolution of Armenian society and a retrenchment from its course of democratization. It also marked the beginning of the end for the era of ANM supremacy as the declining popularity of the party drained power from the government and Ter-Petrossian called upon a new figure to salvage the situation. The appointment of **Robert Kocharian** as **prime minister** of Armenia in 1997 ushered in a new era by virtue of the fact that he succeeded as **president** in 1998 with the support of newly configured political forces. It turned out that the man who led the struggle for freedom in Mountainous Karabagh would be the helmsman of the Armenian nation at the crossing into a new millennium striving to forge new consensus for a resolution of Armenia's domestic and international challenges.

The presidents of Armenia registered modest successes on the international scene by conducting a balanced **foreign policy** that took into account the competing interests of the major regional and international powers. While relations with Armenia's immediate neighbors were strained and complicated by suspicion and hostility, relations with Russia and the United States, the two most significant players in the Caucasus, were conducted by a more normal course. The prevailing foreign policy challenge for Armenia remained the terms of the settlement of the Karabagh crisis. While the two presidents steered the military situation such as to secure the defense of Armenia and Karabagh, the refusal of Azerbaijan to reach a compromise agreement obstructed efforts to reduce tensions in the area.

Ter-Petrossian and Kocharian were the most visible figures on the international scene. On the domestic front the prime ministers played an equally critical role. With the presidents preoccupied with Armenia's foreign relations, the prime ministers were delegated the economic management of the country. The overall thrust toward liberalization of the economy imposed responsibilities on the prime ministers, and on the cabinet officers in charge of the ministries of finance and economy, which, in a country with resources as limited as Armenia's, were difficult to meet. In Armenia restructuring of the economy under circumstances of extreme duress actually translated into the dismantling of society as it had functioned for 70 years and recreating afresh mechanisms for the flow of goods and services on the basis of business principles.

The dependence on external sources of energy, materiel, and transportation systems, however, drained whatever capacity remained in the domestic industries. The country's small market, the limited options for newer streamlined production facilities, and the evaporation of the population's purchasing power threatened the working class with unemployment and impoverishment. The diminishing of the country's capital, the reconcentration of wealth in the hands of a new commercial class, and the exhaustion of individual reserves created massive social problems and conflicts that the government could only deal with partially. The population responded with a variety of individual strategies. Some resorted to private initiative, others to emigration, and others came to depend on diaspora support and charities.

Of the 10 persons to head the Armenian cabinet between 1990 and 2001, perhaps the longest serving and the shortest serving were the most influential prime ministers. **Hrant Bagratian** (February 1993 to November 1996) took the early lead in the reform efforts and established working relations with the international financial institutions advising and encouraging the transformation of the post-Soviet republics. The infusion of Western funds for purposes of development proved critical for maintaining a functioning system in Armenia. By the time **Vazgen Sargsian** (June 1999 to October 1999) became prime minister, however, the atmosphere in the country was charged with severe tensions stemming from the widening gulf between the new rich and the majority poor, as well as those controlling the system and those deprived of access to it. Sargsian was perceived in sharply contrasting images. On the one hand he was seen as a strong figure capable of controlling the situation and reining in corruption, and on the other hand as a divisive figure symbolizing by his willful methods the very source of the aggravating problems. His assassination caught on television cameras put the country and its constitution to the test, while also creating a huge vacuum on the political scene. The breach proved difficult to repair, but the survival of the government and avoidance of anarchy helped restore among the citizenry appreciation for the gains made since independence and for the regulated conduct of public affairs as vested in an elected government.

By the end of its first decade of existence the viability of the third Republic of Armenia seemed more assured than at any time earlier. The era of rapid and dramatic changes marked by armed conflict, political upheaval, and plunging economic performance was at an end. Incremental improvements in every facet of life in Armenia were visible and measurable. Enough sustainability had been introduced that the economy began to show signs of life and here and there even changes in lifestyle reflecting the benefits of a free market system.

In the course of the 20th century Armenia was remade three times over. Each experience left behind a layer to build upon. At the start of the 21st century, for all the challenges it faced, Armenia was a country on a course of rebuilding again. Armenia's energy needs were being met year round. Sound monetary policy checked inflation. Food supplies were available in sufficient quantities. Critical points of the country's infrastructure had been repaired. New roads and bridges improved communication and transportation. Much of the country's commercial assets and all its land had been privatized. The free enterprise system had taken hold. Small-scale industrial works were in production. The state improved revenue collection. Even trade relations expanded. Compared to the needs of the population, economic growth was slow, employment opportunities were limited, and income not enough for purchases beyond basic commodities. The country was still a long way from developing the capacity required to satisfy the expectation of normal living standards. Yet a new generation had tasted freedom thanks to the currents of change their parents had called forth. Reversing course no longer an option, it only had reasons for looking ahead.

ECONOMY

By the 1980s Armenia had achieved 100 percent literacy. The Armenian language was used across all disciplines and sciences, even at institutions of higher learning. Russian was the second language of the country and widely used. This combination of high literacy and a high level of bilingualism contributed to the development of a skilled labor force employed across a range of industries. For a country scarce in natural resources, the employment of an educated labor pool created a period of economic wellbeing in the late Soviet era even under the strictures of central planning. As the circumstances of geographic distance and isolation proved after independence, however, the Armenian economy was, if anything, overplanned. In the post-World War II period, Soviet central planning had transformed a peripheral agricultural economy into an integrated industrial society.

With the generous infusion of investment, the planning commissions based in Moscow rapidly expanded the industrial output of Armenia by constructing large factory complexes almost totally supplied from other parts of the Soviet Union. Between 1950 and 1978 Armenia's gross industrial output rose at a rate of 10 percent a year.

The types of industry introduced in Armenia made it wholly dependent on the Soviet command structure. Machine building, electronics, petrochemicals, metallurgy, and manufacturing required the importation of raw materials and the exportation of the finished products. Many plants were part and parcel of the Soviet military industrial complex. Only the mining and the building materials industries were tied to local resources. This made Armenia transport dependent. Even as the expansion of local educational institutions that trained the technical and research staff of the industrial plants in Armenia created added employment and new sources of revenue, little of the manufactured goods were consumable domestically. The distance of Armenia from the center and the ruggedness of its terrain, which made the country not easily accessible by truck transport, meant that virtually the entire flow of goods and materials in and out of Armenia was shipped by rolling stock through the rail hub in Baku, Azerbaijan, whence the rail system connected with Russia to the north. These same conditions also made Armenia energy-dependent requiring the importation of fuel and oil for heating, manufacturing, and processing. Hydrocarbon consumption was augmented with hydroelectricity, and by the 1970s with nuclear energy from the atomic power plant at Metsamor. Disruption in any one of these systems potentially could wreak havoc with Armenia's economy. Simultaneous disruption threatened utter economic disaster. In the winter of 1993 Armenia reached that low ebb.

The economic consequences of the disintegration of the USSR were felt more acutely in Armenia than in any other former Soviet republic. The first sign of a serious breakdown occurred in the transport sector in 1990, when, as a result of the escalating conflict over Nagorno Karabagh, Azerbaijan impeded the rail passage to Armenia. By 1993, as Turkey joined the embargo, landlocked Armenia was under near total blockade. With no connections to Iran at the time, and with regional and domestic unrest in Georgia choking off Armenia's last outlet, economic isolation unraveled the country's most basic linkages with the rest of the former Soviet Union. The embargo's most catastrophic effect was felt not so much by the prevention of the movement of goods as by the blockage of the transit lines delivering oil and gas to Armenia. By the winter of 1993 the economy of Armenia was in full retreat as the energy blockade of the country brought all industry to a standstill and drove the rest of society into a state of frigid hibernation. The introduction in November 1993 of a domestic currency, the *dram*, necessitated by the Russian government's abolition of the *ruble* zone, under such unfavorable circumstances proved a recipe for inflation, wiping out the middle class and raising the early indicators of wide-scale impoverishment. The economic decline led to food shortages that brought underprivileged sectors of the population to the brink of famine.

The country avoided internal chaos for a number of reasons. The population focused on the struggle for survival and understood that these conditions resulted from objective reasons beyond the government's control. The functioning of society facilitated the delivery of international aid and its domestic distribution. Furthermore, under such trying conditions, the government of Armenia adopted reform programs designed to undo the communist system and gradually introduce a free enterprise system. This Armenia coordinated with the International Monetary Fund (IMF), which, with the end of hostilities in the Karabagh conflict in 1994, began an infusion of funds to support the systemic transformation of the country. As early as 1990 Armenia had legalized private property ownership. With this legislation, farmland was denationalized and privatized soon after. Subsequently, home ownership was introduced, as well as the privatization of small businesses. The sale of state assets in medium and large businesses, however, took longer, as the capital necessary for their devolution was unavailable, and with a persistent energy crisis, the incentive for investment was absent. By 1994 the Metsamor nuclear plant, which had been decommissioned five years earlier, was reactivated and began supplying the country's minimum energy needs. Lastly, foreign aid from the United States and Europe supported Armenia's budget as it shifted from emergency and humanitarian assistance to development aid. In 1995 the economy began to turn around. By that point, however, it may well have shrunk by up to 90 percent, and any recovery was going to be a long-term proposition.

Despite all the upheavals Armenia stayed the course of economic reform, creating a central bank, stabilizing its currency through predictable fiscal policies, implementing infrastructural improvements, and with a cease-fire holding, finding outlets for some export and the importation of fuel to restart the country's economy. A decade of hardship, however, had taken it's toll by the year 2000, and the country's losses also began to register beyond economic indices with the steady departure of the working age population in search of employment opportunities in Russia, or through emigration to Europe and America.

The Dictionary

– A –

ABOVIAN, KHACHATUR (1809–1848). Author and educator. Abovian was born in Kanaker, a village in the vicinity of **Yerevan**, at the time the seat of a Persian khanate. He was a student at the **Edjmiadsin** seminary and continued his education at the Nersisian Academy in Tbilisi. Abovian witnessed the conquest of the province of Yerevan by Russian troops in 1828. The following year he was serving as secretary and translator at the Catholicosate of Edjmiadsin, which was how he came to act as guide and interpreter for Professor Friedrich Parrot of the University of Dorpat when the latter made a scientific expedition to the area and scaled the peak of Mount **Ararat** in 1829. Thus Abovian became the first Armenian known to have reached the summit of the "sacred" mountain of the Armenians. Impressed by the young man's abilities, Parrot arranged for Abovian to attend the University of Dorpat, also making him the first Armenian known to have attended a European university, at least in the Russian Empire. Exposed to German and French Enlightenment literature, upon his return to the Caucasus in 1836 Abovian devoted himself to writing and educating. He was not, however, well received by the clergy who were responsible for **education** in the region, and most of his writing never saw light in his lifetime. He vanished in 1848. Speculation of his disappearance has included the suggestion of suicide over his chagrin at the rejection by an Armenian society unprepared to listen to his advocacy of modern education, while another theory advanced the notion of a secret arrest and banishment by tsarist police for espousing seemingly radical ideas at a time of revolutionary ferment elsewhere in Europe.

Abovian wrote pedagogical works and poetry, and prepared translations of Enlightenment writers. He is best remembered, however, as the author of the first Armenian novel. *Verk Hayastani* (The Wounds of Armenia) was written in 1848. It was published in 1858, ten years after his disappearance. *Verk Hayastani* is also regarded as the harbinger of Armenian patriotic literature wherein the virtues of national self-esteem are lauded and the price of submission to foreign rule was critiqued. To convey his ideas and his message directly to fellow Armenians, Abovian also became the first figure in Armenian literature to write most of his oeuvre in the vernacular. With his efforts then begins the cultivation of the Eastern Armenian dialect as a literary language, a matter of considerable historical significance, and not just from the standpoint of cultural modernization. The emergence in the early part of the 20th century of an Armenian state in Eastern Armenia resulted in the formalization of this dialect as the state language of the Armenian Republic. Abovian today is celebrated as a major figure in Armenian culture with schools, streets, a town, and, in the Soviet era, even an entire district of Armenia, named after him. *See also* ARMENIAN LANGUAGE.

ADANA MASSACRE (1909). The second series of large-scale massacres of Armenians to break out in the Ottoman Empire. The atrocities committed in the province of Adana in April 1909 coincided with the counterrevolution staged by supporters of Sultan Abdul-Hamid (Abdulhamit) II (1876–1909) who had been forced to restore the Ottoman Constitution as a result of the 1908 Young Turk Revolution led by the Committee of Union and Progress (CUP). A prosperous region on the Mediterranean coast encompassing the old principality of Cilicia, once an independent Armenian state between the 11th and 14th centuries, the province of Adana had been spared the 1890s massacres. The disturbances were most severe in the city of Adana where a reported 4,437 Armenian dwellings were torched, resulting in the razing of nearly half the town and prompting some to describe the resulting inferno as a "holocaust." The outbreaks spread throughout the district and an estimated 30,000 Armenians were reported killed. While attempts at resistance in Adana proved futile, and Armenians in smaller outlying villages were brutally slaughtered, two towns inhabited mostly by Armenians organized a successful defense. Hadjin (*Hajen* in Armenian) in the Cilician Mountains withstood a siege, while 10,000 Armenians in Dortyol (*Chokmarzban* in Armenian) held off 7,000 Turks who had surrounded the town and cut off its water supply.

The intensity of the carnage prompted the government to open an investigation, but the failure to prosecute dashed Armenian expectations of liberal reforms by the new regime. The reactionary elements of the Ottoman Empire were suspected of instigating the massacres to discredit the CUP, but the Young Turks were also implicated. The Adana Massacre exposed the twin composition of the Young Turk Movement, which consisted of both liberal and radical nationalist elements. It also demonstrated the convergent interests of the nationalists with the reactionary and conservative elements of the Ottoman state in their policies toward a progressive-minded minority. For the Young Turks, the Adana Massacre proved a rehearsal for gauging the depth of Turkish animosity in the Ottoman Empire toward Christian minorities and for testing their skills in marshaling those forces for political ends. Despite the restoration of a constitutional government, the specter of mass violence was reintroduced as a mechanism of state power. *See also* ARMENIAN GENOCIDE; ARMENIAN MASSACRES; HETUMIAN; RUBENIAN.

ADONTZ, NICHOLAS (1871–1942). Historian. Adontz (nee Nikoghayos Ter-Avetikian) is regarded as the founder of Armenian analytic historiography. Born in the village of Brnakot in the Sisian district of Armenia, Adontz received schooling at **Edjmiadsin** and in Tbilisi before entering St. Petersburg University, where he studied under Nicholas Marr. Upon completion of his doctoral research in the department of oriental languages and of history and philology, he received appointment in 1916 as a professor at the university. He left Russia after the revolution and lived in France from 1920 to 1930, when he was invited to join the faculty at the Université Libre de Bruxelles as professor of Armenian studies. Adontz resided in Belgium until his death during the Nazi occupation of the country.

Adontz is the author of the seminal work in Armenian historiography. His *Armenia in the Period of Justinian: The Political Conditions Based on the Nakharar System* (printed in Russian in 1908, translated into English, 1970) represents the first major analytical reconstruction of ancient and medieval Armenian society. Its basic thesis argued on behalf of a specific type of Armenian feudalism, one based on dynastic territoriality, a thesis improved upon only in the details since it was published. Adontz authored dozens of articles on many aspects of medieval Armenian history and culture, including the intellectual influence of Hellenism in Armenia. In the last years of his life he researched the contributions of Armenians in Byzantium, identifying the figures, such as church patriarchs, army generals, emperors and empresses, who had played a prominent role in Byzantine culture and politics.

AGANBEGYAN, ABEL (1932–). Soviet economist. Aganbegyan was born in Tbilisi, Georgia, and received his early education locally before proceeding to Moscow where he attended the State Institute of Economics. Upon graduation in 1955 he went to work for the State Committee of Labor and Wages. In 1961, however, he left to join the new Siberian branch of the Academy of Sciences in Novosibirsk whose Institute of Economics and Industrial Organization was becoming a center of important research on the growing problems of the Soviet command economy. By 1967 he was the director of the Institute. Aganbegyan's ideas for reforming the Soviet economy received serious attention when the new chairman of the Communist Party in 1985, Mikhail Gorbachev, embarked upon a program to restructure both Soviet economy and society, a process that became known as *perestroika*. By 1985 Aganbegyan himself was heading the economics section of the USSR Academy of Sciences in Moscow where he emerged as the principal theoretician of perestroika.

The concepts Aganbegyan proposed involved revamping the administrative apparatus of the Soviet Union in order to make the system more receptive to change, which, in a radical departure from communist doctrine, for the first time since the years of the New Economic Policy (NEP) of the 1920s, proposed experimenting with market forces in order to deal with the problem of chronic shortages and continuing decline in productivity. The process also involved introducing the self-administration of state enterprises that was treated as a step toward political democratization as well. Aganbegyan's program also raised the concept of joint ventures with Western profit-making enterprises as the principal method of injecting capital into Soviet industry and for introducing modern management and production techniques. The reform proposals were received with great interest around the world. As Gorbachev's chief economic advisor, Aganbegyan also became the main spokesman for perestroika to Western business circles. Although conservatives in the Communist Party prevented the complete implementation of the perestroika reforms and ultimately caused the dissolution of the Soviet Union in 1991 by their reactionary policies, Aganbegyan's economic program had already transformed the environment in which the Soviet Union's economic managers conducted business and thereby prepared the way for the free market system.

AGHBALIAN, NIKOL (1875–1947). Political leader and educator. Aghbalian was born in Tbilisi and received his primary education at the local Nersisian Academy. He continued his education at the Gevorgian Seminary at **Edjmiadsin** and went into teaching. For higher education he attended the universities of Moscow, Paris, and Lausanne and returned to Transcaucasia in 1905. From 1909 to 1912 Aghbalian served as the headmaster of the Armenian school in Teheran.

An active member of the **Armenian Revolutionary Federation** (ARF), Aghbalian participated in the fateful eighth congress of the party convened in Erzerum in August 1914 just as war was breaking out in Europe. He soon assumed a leadership position as a member of the Armenian National Council in 1914–15 and helped recruit Armenian volunteer forces for the war effort. During the independent Republic of Armenia he served as a member of parliament in 1918 and was appointed minister of education in **Alexander Khatisian**'s cabinet. During his term of office he organized a center of higher learning in Alexandropol (**Gyumri**). Founded on January 31, 1920, this institution became the nucleus of the university established in **Yerevan** during the Soviet period. Arrested by the Bolshevik authorities after the occupation of Armenia by the Red Army, Aghbalian was released after the February 1921 uprising. He fled to Iranian Azerbaijan upon the restoration of Bolshevik power in Armenia.

In the **diaspora** Aghbalian resumed his career in education and played a major role in organizing new academic and cultural institutions while he remained active in the Dashnak party leadership. Between 1923 and 1928 he was the director of an Armenian school in Alexandria, Egypt. He moved to Lebanon in 1928 where he lived the rest of his life. By founding the Hamazkayin Cultural Association and the Neshan Palanjian Academy, known simply as the Jemaran, he became the teacher and mentor of a new generation of Armenians who grew up in the diaspora and learned the **Armenian language** and literature in his classes at the Jemaran. *See also* VRATZIAN, SIMON.

AGHTAMAR. Island in **Lake Van** and location of one of the most important architectural monuments of medieval Armenia. All that remains of the 10th-century royal palace on the island of Aghtamar is the Church of the Holy Cross (*Surp Khach*). Constructed as the palatine chapel attached to the residence of the Armenian kings of the **Ardsruni** line that ruled over the region of Vaspurakan, the Church of the Holy Cross is the most famous work of Armenian ecclesiastical architecture. Popularly known as the church of Aghtamar, it is distinguished by the sculptured reliefs encircling its exterior.

Commissioned by Gagik Ardsruni, King of Vaspurakan (908–943), it was built by the architect Manuel in the years 915–921. Along with Trdat, the architect of the Cathedral of **Ani**, Manuel ranks among the geniuses of Armenian architecture, men who created a distinctive national style. Aghtamar was designed in the cruciform plan, consisting of a central square with semicircular vaulted apsidal niches on all four sides and smaller cylindrical niches at the four corners. A large dome with a polygonal drum covers the entire central square giving it the appearance of a highly compact and solid edifice. In this regard it echoes the design of the Church of St. Hripsime at **Vagharshapat**. However, Manuel's construction involved a more complex assignment. The royal chapel was designed not just for private service, but for public display, and as such was decorated with bas-reliefs consciously intersecting the lineage and the legitimacy of the Ardsruni monarchy, a new kingdom in Armenia whose crown was worn by one of its oldest feudal dynasties.

The iconography of the sculptural cycles that wrap around the exterior of Aghtamar juxtaposed religious themes with secular subjects resulting in an astonishing ensemble of portraiture spanning historical time as understood by medieval civilization beginning with Adam and Eve and ending with the majesty of the royal house. The famous personages of the Ardsruni family, heroes from the Bible, the central figures of the Christian faith, heraldic symbols, and folkloric imagery, altogether emphasize the importance and the contributions of the new royal house. The centerpieces of the bas-relief cycles are the portraits of Christ and of King Gagik in richly detailed garb, clearly dividing among themselves sacred and profane power. The scenes of Abraham and Isaac, Jonah and the whale, Daniel in the lion's den, and David and Goliath share the common theme of individual struggle and triumph and evoke the role of the sovereign in overturning Arab dominion over Armenia. Portraits of the evangelizers of Armenia, of saints, angels, of Christ, and of the Virgin enthroned, as well as Gagik's antecedents fill the walls. Lastly, scenes of hunting, harvesting, and feasting, complemented with traditional Armenian ornamentation in interlaced designs of vines and grapes, embellish Aghtamar with finely carved detail. It is less well known that the interior of Aghtamar was emblazoned with frescoes, which are rare in Armenia. They completely covered all the wall surfaces with further Biblical narrative and the portraiture of the fathers of the Church.

Aghtamar represents a unique accomplishment in Christian architecture displaying for the first time sculpted imagery on the exterior of a church in such an elaborate profusion. Manuel, the gifted mason of Aghtamar, turned the austere and flat surfaces of the Armenian church, whose architects for long had aspired to create a simple external geometry masking complex internal designs, into a canvas for the narration of the life of the Armenian people under the rule of one of its great dynastic families.

AHARONIAN, AVETIS (1866–1948). Writer, educator, and political figure. Aharonian was born in the town of Igdir, then in **Yerevan** province of the Russian Empire. He received his primary education at the **Edjmiadsin** seminary and became a teacher in his native town before pursuing higher education in Lausanne and Paris. After his return he joined the **Armenian Revolutionary Federation** (ARF) and became associated with its main organ *Droshak* (Banner) while gaining recognition as the author of works of romantic nationalism. He served as headmaster of the Nersisian academy in Tbilisi from 1907 to 1909, then faced arrest, imprisonment, and exile at the hands of the tsarist police. He escaped from prison in 1911 and fled to Switzerland. Returning to the Caucasus in 1916 he became one of the organizers of the Armenian National Congress, which convened in October 1917 to provide representation for the Armenian population in democratic Russia. The Armenian National Congress, dominated by Dashnaks, elected an executive body called the Armenian National Council with Aharonian as its chairman. In the wake of the breakup of the Russian Empire after the Bolshevik Revolution, this same Council, still under the chairmanship of Aharonian, assumed responsibility for the declaration of an independent Armenian state in the area of Yerevan province in May 1918.

Although he had no prior diplomatic experience, trusting his commitment, penmanship, and knowledge of the French language, the Republic of Armenia relied upon Aharonian as its most visible envoy on the international scene. First he led a delegation to Istanbul in June 1918 to negotiate a settlement of the Armenian border with the Ottoman Empire, which had been at war with Russia in the Transcaucasus. The assignment required meeting with the Young Turk government leaders, including then Prime Minister Talaat and Minister of War Enver, both held responsible by Armenians for the deportations and massacres instituted against the Ottoman Armenian population in 1915. In December 1918 the Armenian Parliament named Aharonian as president of the permanent delegation to the Paris Peace Conference. Aharonian arrived in Paris to discover that the Republic of Armenia was denied a seat at the conference. He stayed to sign the Treaty of Sèvres on behalf of the republic in August 1920. The agreement that finally extended international recognition to the Republic of Armenia two years after its formation became a dead letter with the Sovietization of Armenia at the end of November 1920. Aharonian remained in France and continued to represent Armenian interests until such time as the Armenian Question was buried by the 1923 Treaty of Lausanne, which avoided all mention of Armenia. Aharonian spent the rest of his life in Marseilles where he died in 1948. *See also* KACHAZNUNI, HOVHANNES; KHATISIAN, ALEXANDER; VRATZIAN, SIMON.

AJARIAN, HRACHIA (1876–1953). Linguist. Born in Istanbul and educated in Europe, Ajarian traveled widely across the Armenian communities of Turkey, Russia, and Iran to record the multitude of regional dialects spoken by the Armenian people at the time. He studied with the two eminent European specialists of the **Armenian language**, Antoine Meillet in France and Heinrich Hübschmann in Germany, before submitting his doctoral dissertation, *Classifications des dialects arméniens*, at the University of Sorbonne in 1909. After an early career in teaching at various Armenian parochial schools, in 1923 he received appointment to a professorship at **Yerevan** State University in Soviet Armenia, a position he held until the end of his life. Before his arrival in Yerevan he had already published a number of important works on the history and culture of the Armenian people including a history of modern Armenian literature, a history of the

Armenian Question, a history of the Armenian **diaspora**, a history of the invention of the Armenian alphabet, as well as the first of a series of catalogues of Armenian manuscripts.

These many significant contributions, which would have been a life's work for the ordinary scholar, were merely prefatory to the encyclopedic productions that followed and that came to define the field of Armenian linguistics. *Hayeren Armatakan Bararan* (Armenian Etymological Dictionary) traces the root words of the Armenian language. A prodigious display of linguistic knowledge, the etymological dictionary includes 11,000 entries on root words and 5,000 explanatory entries on the roots, each systematically cited with its sources in ancient and medieval Armenian literature, definitions, a critical survey of previous research on the word, dialectal usages and forms, and the borrowings of the word by other languages. The etymological dictionary was first released in seven volumes between 1926 and 1935 as a mimeographed publication in Ajarian's handwriting because the typefaces of all the languages and scripts utilized were not available in Armenia. The printed version was issued by Yerevan State University in four volumes between 1971 and 1979. Ajarian's *Hayots Antznanunneri Bararan* (Dictionary of Armenian Proper Names) in five volumes was issued between 1942 and 1962. His *Hayots Lezvi Patmutiun* (History of the Armenian Language) in two volumes appeared between 1940 and 1951. The subtitle to his final monumental contribution attests to his genius and his incomparable breadth of linguistic knowledge and skill. *Liakatar Kerakanutiun Hayots Lezvi, Hamematutiamb 562 Lezuneri* (Complete Grammar of the Armenian Language, in Comparison with 562 Languages) was issued in six volumes between 1952 and 1971. Ajarian single-handedly prepared the central scientific reference works on the Armenian language and in so doing vastly expanded the modern knowledge and understanding of Armenian civilization through its entire course of development. *See also* ADONTZ, NICHOLAS.

ALISHAN, GHEVOND (1820–1901). Writer and historian. Alishan, baptismal name Kerovbe Alishanian, was born in Istanbul and attended the local Armenian Catholic school before going to Venice to continue his education at the **Mekhitarian** monastery. He joined the Mekhitarian Order in 1838 and later was ordained a priest. Although the author of a number of religious works, Alishan spent his adult years as an instructor in the educational institutions maintained by the Mekhitarians. Early he developed an interest in Armenian folklore and turned to composing poetry. The last third of his life he devoted solely to scholarship.

Alishan gained fame as a prodigious writer of historical works. He published a 22-volume series of Armenian primary sources from the manuscript collection in the Mekhitarian monastery. He also issued a set of folio-sized illustrated volumes on various provinces of historic Armenia, *Shirak* (1881), *Sisvan* (1885), *Ayrarat* (1890), and *Sisakan* (1893) containing therein all the geographical, topographical, historical, architectural, and other information that he culled from ancient and contemporary sources. These volumes provided the basis for developing a strong sense of national identification with Armenia among Armenians in expatriate communities and among younger generations of Armenians who began to perceive of Armenia as a land imbued with history and creativity and not just desolation and oppression. In the last year of his life, on the occasion of the 200th anniversary of the founding of the Mekhitarian order, Alishan issued his culminating worked called *Hayapatum* (Armenian History), in which he arranged in order selections from the works of the ancient and medieval Armenian historians into a comprehensive narrative history.

While most Armenian translators put works from French and German into Armenian, Alishan was one of the rare figures of the 19th century Armenian cultural renaissance who also learned English. He traveled to England in 1852 and published that same year the translation in Armenian of a section of Milton's *Paradise Lost*. Subsequently he issued translations of Byron and Longfellow. In 1867 he published his *Armenian Popular Songs Translated into English*, believed to contain the first English renditions of Armenian poetry. Alishan died in Venice never having seen historic Armenia.

ANDRANIK OZANIAN (also Antranig) (1865–1927). Guerrilla fighter and the leading figure of the Armenian resistance against Ottoman rule. Andranik Ozanian is popularly known as General Andranik (Andranik *Zoravar* in Armenian). He was born in Shabin-Karahisar in central Anatolia. He received only an elementary education and was trained as a carpenter. He became involved in revolutionary activities in 1888 and joined the **Armenian Revolu-**

tionary Federation (ARF) in 1892. Soon after he emerged as the leader of a band of guerrilla fighters involved in the defense of Armenian villages in the region of Sasun and Mush during the 1894–96 massacres instigated against the Armenians in the Ottoman Empire. He gained legendary stature among provincial Armenians after breaking out of the Arakelots Monastery in the Moush area in which he had been trapped by Turkish troops. He retreated with his men into Persia, resigned from the ARF, and thereafter traveled to Europe, where he participated in the First Balkan War in 1912 at the head of a group of Armenian volunteers fighting in the Bulgarian army.

With the outbreak of World War I, Andranik went to Transcaucasia and took command of a contingent of Armenian volunteers supporting the Russian army in the campaigns against the Ottomans. He was promoted to the rank of major general, and eventually placed in charge of a division consisting of Armenian conscripts who were left to defend the front as the Russian army disintegrated in the wake of the Bolshevik Revolution. Forced to retreat against superior Ottoman forces, Andranik had a falling-out with the political leadership of the just-founded Republic of Armenia for submitting to Ottoman terms in the Treaty of Batumi signed on June 4, 1918. Resigning his command, he formed a new brigade consisting of Western Armenians. He took refuge in the Zangezur district of Eastern Armenia where he continued fighting against local Muslim forces and was about to march to relieve the Armenians of Karabagh when a telegram from General Thomson, the British commander in Baku, informed him of the end of the war and ordered him to cease hostilities. The moment proved fateful as the British commander subsequently decided to place Karabagh under Azerbaijani jurisdiction. Forced by the British to disband his troops, Andranik left Transcaucasia in 1919 and traveled to Europe to plead the cause of the Western Armenians deported and dispersed by the Ottomans. He eventually settled in the Armenian community of Fresno, California, where he spent his remaining years. Communist authorities in Armenia denied his remains entry while in transit, thus he was buried at Père Lachaise cemetery in Paris. In February 2000, he was finally reinterred in Armenia and laid to rest at Yerablur, the cemetery reserved for the fallen defenders of **Nagorno Karabagh**. *See also* ARMENIAN REVOLUTIONARY MOVEMENT; MANUKIAN, ARAM.

ANI. Capital of medieval Armenia. The city of Ani started as a fortress constructed above a naturally defensible triangular plateau formed by the bluffs of the Akhurian River (Arpa Chai) and its tributary the Alaja Chai. As far back as the fifth century its strategic importance as the central point of the vast Shirak plain of northern Armenia was appreciated by its original owners, the great feudal family of the Kamsarakan, once closely associated with the royal house of the **Arshakuni**. With their decline during the period of Arab rule, the Kamsarakans sold the district of Shirak to Ashot *Msaker*, whose recognition by the Abbasid caliph in 804 as Prince of Armenia inaugurated the gradual rise of the **Bagratuni** family as the dominant feudal dynasty of northern Armenia. In the mid–10th century, after decades of struggle against the Arab garrisons holding the city of **Dvin**, the capital of Armenia since the fifth century, the Bagratuni abandoned the quest to position themselves in the Armenian heartland. Already in possession of royal title since 884, they took further steps to secure the sovereignty of their state by establishing a new capital. Ashot III, King of Armenia (953–977), formalized the designation of the city as the capital of the Bagratuni kingdom with his ceremonial coronation in Ani by Catholicos Anania Mokatsi (Ananias of Moks) in 961. With the concurrent establishment of the catholicosate in the neighboring town of Argina, the recentralization of Armenian political and ecclesiastical authority was complete.

The Bagratuni spared no expense to transform their city into the medieval metropolis of Armenia. Within a hundred years Ani was dotted by edifices of unparalleled elegance. First, the size of the enclosed area was tripled by new fortifications constructed by King Smbat II. Between 977 and 989 the defenses of the city were strengthened by a system of double walls guarded by massive round towers. Bridges spanning the surrounding gorges connected the city in all directions. Royal residences, baths, and other public buildings followed. More than its secular buildings, Ani was noted for the magnificence of its religious structures, earning it fame as the city of 1001 churches. While the number was an overstatement, the beauty of the churches testified to the esthetic creativity of the architects and masons who build them. Of these, the most famous is the cathedral of Ani, a very large building by standards of Armenian architecture. The Church of the Holy Virgin (*Surp Astvadsadsin*) proper, the cathedral, is famous for its novel design features. While from the exterior the domed basilica with its blind arcades spoke of artistic refinement, the interior, with its pointed arches and clustered piers rising to the ribbed ceiling vaults, included innovations whose parallels would appear in Gothic architecture in western Europe a century later. The cathedral was begun in 988/989 under King Smbat and completed with the sponsorship of Queen Katranide in 1001 during the reign of King Gagik I.

Trdat the architect further demonstrated his unequaled skills with the construction of the Church of St. Gregory the Illuminator (**Grigor Lusavorich**) for King Gagik in the years 1001–1010. He modeled it on the singular jewel of Armenian architecture, the seventh-century round cathedral of Zvartnots. These great symbols of royal authority, ecclesiastical alliance, economic prosperity, and artistic sponsorship were augmented by the chapels constructed under the auspices of the second great family of the city of Ani, the house of the Pahlavuni, the commanders-in-chief of the Armenian military forces. Ani also became a center of learning where new translations of Greek classics were prepared. The revival of cultural activity also witnessed a new school of historical writing. The international character of the city and the height of its cultural development were epitomized by the Pahlavuni prince, Grigor Magistros, who corresponded with Greek and Arab savants as he dealt with the obligations of office and political responsibility.

Despite the efforts of the Pahlavuni lords to resist encroachment and the young King Gagik II to reach an accommodation, Ani succumbed to Byzantine pressure. To spare the city from a siege, in 1045 the Catholicos Petros *Getadarts* delivered it to the emperor, thereby closing the chapter on a period of sovereignty marked by the residence of the Armenian kings in the royal city of Ani. Before the Byzantines had time to consolidate Greek rule over Armenia, the city was captured by an invader whose strength and speed were unsuspected. Under the command of Alp Arslan, the Seljuk Turks stormed Ani and entered it on August 12, 1064, ushering in a period of nearly a century of Islamic rule. Arriving as an adventurer and forager in these parts, Alp Arslan sold the city to his vassals, the Shaddadid, who already governed in Eastern Armenia.

Throughout this period Ani retained its importance as the administrative and commercial center of Armenia. While the spate of building activity may have decreased, trade continued to flow along the great northern route connecting through Ani the seaport of Trebizond on the Black Sea with the overland trade of the Asian continent to the east. The city remained a military objective of the powers contending for dominion over Armenia, with the royal family of Georgia, also descended from the Bagratuni line, laying claim to Ani. Twice its forces entered the city, under King David II the Restorer in 1123 and his grandson King Georgi III in 1161, though more permanent Georgian rule was not secured until after 1174 by which time a stronger alliance had been forged between the Armenians and the Georgians. In 1201 Queen Tamar gave Ani in fief to her viceroys, Zakare and Ivane of the Armenian Zakarian family, known in Georgian as the Mkhargrdzeli. The Zakarians governed Ani not only on behalf of the Georgian monarchs, but retained their royal office for the rest of the century even after the Mongols captured the city in 1236. The period of Zakarian rule was marked again with building activity commissioned by the wealthy merchants of the city. The most famous of the churches to be constructed during the Georgian period is that paid for by the merchant Tigran Honents. Completed in 1215, the Church of Surp Grigor Lusavorich is especially noteworthy for its interior, which is richly decorated with frescoes. The expenditure incurred by this one individual attests to the restored prosperity of the city and to the extent of trade and monetary wealth circulating at the time.

The breakup of the Mongol Empire disrupted the Asian trade routes. Increasingly onerous taxation by later rulers and growing insecurity seriously impaired international commerce. With its economic importance already in retreat, Ani suffered a devastating blow with the great earthquake of 1319. A large portion of the population emigrated and, slowly, the once glorious metropolis was abandoned.

More than any other city, Ani left a profound impression on Armenian historical memory and Armenian artistic appreciation. From the 12th century on, Armenian exile communities throughout southern Russia, the Crimea, and eastern Europe recalled their origins in Ani. The new Armenian princes in Cilicia sought legitimacy by invoking relations with the Bagratuni kingdom of Ani. The 19th century rediscovery of Ani exercised a powerful influence on Armenian Romantic thought. The character and accomplishment of the medieval city were recalled as the zenith of Armenian civilization and the emblem of the historic legitimacy of Armenian self-rule. Until its annexation by Turkey in 1920, Ani was a site frequented by historians and poets, all of whom came seeking connection with its happier past and to write elegies to Armenia's faded glory and tragic destiny. On the very border of Turkey and the Soviet Union, throughout most of the 20th century, Ani remained nearly inaccessible. While some foreign tourists were eventually permitted to visit the site, Ani remained off-limits to the Armenians. Unprotected, the ruins of Ani have suffered damage, and evidence indicates that some of the historic structures associated with the site have been dynamited. Even so, the monuments of Ani continue to attract international attention and remain a continuing source of artistic and architectural inspiration. *See also* AGHTAMAR; ARTASHAT; DVIN.

ARARAT. Highest and largest mountain on the Armenian plateau and the highest peak in western Asia. Mount Ararat, called Masis by the ancient Armenians, consists of two extinct volcanic cones resting on the banks of the **Arax River**. Great Ararat, or *Meds Masis*, is 5,720 meters (16,900 feet) high, while Little Ararat, *Pokr Masis*, is 4,267 meters (14,000 feet) high. The two peaks are separated by a saddle 14 kilometers (seven miles) long at a height of 2,677 meters (8,800 feet). The entire massif covers an area of approximately 1,200 square kilometers. Great Ararat has a permanent ice cap, and in winter time the two peaks retain a snow cover.

Located in the very heartland of the Armenian plateau, Mount Ararat has exercised enormous power over the imagination of the Armenian people. Visible from every point of the great Plain of Ararat, millions have lived within sight of the great mountain. The twin peaks stand alone at the lowest point of the plain, and the unobstructed view allows for a full appreciation of an immense panorama, as well as the massive height of Great Ararat, making it one of the highest peaks clearly visible at all times of the year. While the summer dust and autumn clouds may obscure the sight, the winter snow cover makes for a nature's canvas floating in the sky. The play of sunlight on the mountain during all seasons has made its scenery ever the Armenian artist's subject.

Though the mountains today are devoid of vegetation, until the Middle Ages their spurs were populated with dozens of villages specializing in viticulture and forests were still to be seen. The village of Arguri stood on Great Masis at an altitude of 1,740 meters until 1840, when on June 20, a large earthquake opened a vast fissure on the north slope precipitating an avalanche that completely destroyed Arguri along with its 1,600 inhabitants, as well as the monastery of St. James two kilometers above the village.

The word Ararat preserves the Armenian pronunciation of the name of Urartu, the first kingdom established in the highlands in the beginning of the first millennium B.C. Only in the late Middle Ages did the mountain become associated with the Biblical story of Noah's Ark under the influence of Europeans who imagined the highest mountain in the region to be the logical site for the ark's landing after the Flood. The earliest existing image to depict this association is one of the door panels of Sainte Chapelle, the private Gothic sanctuary of the French kings on the Isle de France, where the ark is shown against the landscape of the mountain complemented by the outline of an Armenian church on the model of Zvartnots. While the mythology associated with the pagan worship of the mountain is now lost to popular belief, Mount Ararat has played a very large role in the political imagination of the Armenian people. In more recent centuries, the mountain has been assigned a central role in determining the boundaries of the states that competed for control over Armenia.

From the 16th to the 18th century, the Ararat range formed part of the frontier between the Ottoman and Safavid Empires. By the 1828 Treaty of Turkmenchai, Great Ararat was designated the convergence point of the Turkish, Persian, and Russian imperial frontiers. The 1921 Treaty of Moscow, which redefined the border between Turkey and Soviet Russia, placed Great Ararat entirely within Turkish territory. The 1932 Turco-Persian agreement, which transferred a sliver of territory from Iran, concluded the incorporation of Little Ararat into Turkey. Though called Aghri Dagh (Mountain of Pain) by the Turks, the mountain remains popularly known around the world as Ararat. Separated by nothing more than the Arax River, Armenia and Ararat now stand apart. This poignant partition has come to symbolize the brutal division of Armenia after World War I, and the great mountain has become invested with the concepts of captivity and liberation. Despite the fact that it does not lie in Armenian territory, nevertheless, Mount Ararat appears on the official insignia of the Republic of Armenia.

There is probably more poetry written about Mount Ararat than any other mountain on earth, and arguably no other mountain has exercised such a hold on the national identity of a people. Armenian legend told that the summit of *Meds Masis* could not be reached as the climber falling asleep at night after a day of scaling up the mountain would awake to find himself magically transported back to the beginning point of his ascent. The physical challenge of coping with the high altitude of the peak aside, the gently rising slopes of the volcanic cone actually make it a comparatively easy climb, and Mount Ararat has been a popular destination for mountain-climbers. The first recorded ascent was made in 1829. Friedrich Parrot, a University of Dorpat professor, reached the summit accompanied by his Armenian guide, the young **Khachatur Abovian**.

ARAX RIVER. The longest river in historic Armenia. Called Yeraskh in classical Armenian, Araxes by the Greeks and Romans, and Aras by the Persians and Turks, in Antiquity the Arax River flowed entirely through the Armenian kingdom. Today its greater part demarcates the boundaries of Armenia and Azerbaijan on the northern banks of the river, and Iran and Turkey on the southern banks. The headwaters of the Arax rise in the Bingol Mountains south of Erzerum, where too springs the northern branch of the Euphrates River, the Arax flowing east and the Euphrates flowing west. The river flows directly east to the current Turkish border with Armenia where it makes a large arc sweeping in a southeasterly direction before resuming its easterly course. A fast-flowing river whose drainage system encompassed Eastern Armenia, taking most of its tributaries on its northern bank, the Arax has changed course over the centuries. Therein lies part of the explanation for the relocation of Armenia's ancient capital cities, and even Roman engineers, as Virgil writes, are said to have recognized the difficulty of throwing a bridge over its swift current and inconstant channel. In ancient times the Arax River flowed directly into the Caspian Sea. It now joins the Kura River in the lower reaches of the Plain of Mughan to travel for another 100 kilometers (60 miles) before reaching the Caspian.

The total length of the Arax is measured at 1,080 kilometers (650 miles) and its drainage areas at 102,000 square kilometers. While its annual runoff, measured at its junction with the Kura, is averaged at 210 cubic meters per second, the climatic difference on the Armenian plateau between the cold winters and hot summers makes for a wide variation in the amount of discharge entering the Arax from its feeder tributaries carrying down the snow-melt from the mountains.

The river is at its height in April and May and at its lowest in August and September, thus making it fordable in late summer.

The Arax Valley, the Yeraskhatsor of the Armenians, formed one of the main arteries of trade, invasion, and emigration through Armenia. Here in the great alluvial plain stretching along its banks was located the royal domain of the Armenian kings. The fertile Plain of Ararat along the middle course of the river between the great peaks of Ararat to the west, Mount Aragats to the north, and the Gegham Mountains to the east, enclosed the Armenian heartland. Intensively cultivated, its orchards were famous for their pomegranate, olive, grape, and indigenous apricot. Densely populated throughout the periods of Armenian self-rule, the economic importance of the great valley is evidenced by the numerous towns and cities it supported throughout history. The most important of these included the capital cities of **Armavir**, Yervandashat, **Artashat**, **Vagharshapat**, and **Dvin**, and the commercial centers of Nakhichevan, Julfa, and Meghri. **Ani** rises on a northern tributary, the Akhurian River. Kars is located on a branch of the Akhurian, and on an eastern tributary, the Hrazdan (Zangi) River, stands modern-day **Yerevan**.

Throughout history, invaders have used the river valley to raid Armenia from the south and the east, while conquerors from the west have relied on the corridor to penetrate northern Iran. Yeraskhatsor made Armenia the crossroads of ancient empires. Persians and Romans battled over it, Arabs and Byzantines fought for it, and Ottomans and Safavids plundered it. The Byzantine emperor Heraklios invaded Persia in 627 by marching his troops directly across from the Caucasus into Iran. The Persians invariably moved their forces into Armenia from its southern opening. The Arabs began their conquest of Armenia in 640 by charging through it, and Seljuks, Mongols, and Turkomans, all came raiding through the wide expanse of the inviting valley. The devastations visited upon the Armenians of the Plain of Ararat culminated in their enforced exodus in 1604 upon the order of Shah Abbas of Persia. They waited until 1828 when the Russians reached the valley to begin returning to their homeland.

By then the Arax River valley had ceased from serving as a trade route and was increasingly relied upon as an international boundary separating Iran and Russia, and Turkey and Russia, and in so doing dividing Armenia through its very core. By the 1813 Treaty of Gulistan, Russia established its boundaries on the Arax River for the first time. When the regions of Yerevan and Nakhichevan were occupied in 1828, the Treaty of Turkmenchai extended the boundary between Russia and Persia up along the course of the river, while the 1829 Treaty of Adrianople fixed the boundary between Turkey and Russia along the upper reaches of the river valley. Though Russian and Ottoman armies would breach the Arax River many times again, for all the bloodshed and ruin of Armenian habitations, the boundary changed little. By the 1921 Treaty of Moscow, Turkey and Soviet Russia once again affixed the international boundary separating them at the Arax River. Today the Arax River marks the international boundary between Armenia and Turkey in the west, and Armenia and Iran in the south.

With the tremendous concentration of historic sites along its banks and the intensity of dramatic events played out in its great plain, the Arax River has come to be viewed by Armenians as the nourisher of their country and the nurturer of their civilization. From the time the mighty cyclopean fortress of Erebuni was raised by the Urartian king Argishti I in 782 B.C., military might was projected out in all directions from here. The royal dynasties built their palaces in the shade of its poplar trees. Whether ruled independently or subjugated to foreign domination, the *Vostan Hayots*, the capital district of Armenia, was almost always located in the Plain of Ararat. Armenian monarch, Persian *marzpan*, and Arab *vostikan* held court in its castles and citadels. **Yervanduni**, **Artashesian,** and **Arshakuni** kings sat upon their throne in sight of Mount Ararat, and the great lords of the land from near and far, the princely **Bagratuni**, **Mamikonian**, Kamsarakan, **Siuni**, Rshtuni, **Ardsruni**, and dozens of others gathered here on ceremonial occasions or to organize the defense of their homeland in case of foreign invasion. The residences of the catholicos were located at Vagharshapat or Dvin, where bishops gathered for important ecclesiastical councils and common folk came on pilgrimages. Dozens of churches, beginning with **Edjmiadsin** and Zvartnots, dotted its landscape. This retrospective contemplation of the cultural importance of the river became the source of its edification as the maternal waters of Armenia, whence arose the frequent literary reference to the river as *Mayr Arax*. *See also* GEOGRAPHY, HISTORICAL.

ARDSRUNI, GRIGOR (1845–1892). Writer and publisher. Ardsruni was born in Moscow and received his early education at the Russian *gymnasium* in Tbilisi. He pursued higher education at the University of Moscow and St. Petersburg and in 1867 entered Heidelberg University in Germany. He graduated two years later with a doctorate in political economy and philosophy. In 1869 and 1870 he studied Armenian with the **Mekhitarians** first in Vienna and then Venice. He returned to Tbilisi in 1870 and became a teacher in the Gayanian school for girls. Between 1865 and 1870 Ardsruni contributed to the periodicals *Meghu Hayastani* (Bee of Armenia) and *Haykakan Ashkharh* (Armenian World). In 1872 he founded the newspaper *Mshak* (Laborer), which he edited until his death. Through *Mshak* Ardsruni emerged as the most outspoken proponent of liberalism in Armenian political and cultural life and influenced an entire generation in their thinking on Armenian issues. *Mshak* was published until 1920. *See also* ARPIARIAN, ARPIAR; RAFFI.

ARDSRUNI. Princely family and royal dynasty in medieval Armenia. A princely family of **Yervanduni** descent, the Ardsruni made their historical appearance during the reign of **Tigran the Great**. In the **Arshakuni** period they became closely associated with the region of Vaspurakan in south central Armenia. Originally lords of the fiefdom of Greater and Lesser Aghbak, districts located southeast of **Lake Van**, the Ardsruni expanded their domain incorporating the large province that comprised the eastern half of the Van basin. Their military obligation during the Arshakuni monarchy was rated at 1,000 knights, a number that would not rank them in the highest tier of the Armenian feudal aristocracy, but their lineage and ascribed service as the *bdeashkh*, or margraves, of Adiabene, the Median Marchland of the Arshakuni kingdom, made them a very important family. The margraves governed as fully empowered viceroys of the Armenian crown. Because of their geographical location, like the **Siuni**, the Ardsruni also tended to espouse a pro-Iranian orientation. At quite a distance from the Roman, and later Byzantine, parts of Armenia, the Ardsruni maintained their policy of casting their destiny with the nearer power. After the Arabs overran Vaspurakan in 653, the Ardsruni continued to subscribe to an accommodationist policy.

Their skill in adaptation, which was balanced by a readiness to act independently, kept the Ardsruni positioned to take advantage of the major political changes affecting the country. When the Arshakuni monarchy was disbanded in 428, the Ardsruni encroached on the neighboring lands of the Mardpetakan, the hereditary domain of the grand chamberlain to the Armenian kings. When Byzantine influence rapidly declined in the second half of the seventh century against the growing Arab presence in Armenia, the fortunes of the competitors of the Ardsruni in the Van area, such as the Rshtuni family, also began to wane. The **nakharar** family that benefited most from Arab patronage, however, was the **Bagratuni**, whose domains were far less exposed to the Arab program of tribal settlement in southern Armenia. Arab emirates sprung up all along the northern shore of Lake Van, a process that prompted the remaining Armenian princes to conduct a more coordinated policy of self-preservation. When in 862 the Bagratuni prince, **Ashot I**, secured the title of prince of princes from the Arabs, a new point of political focus emerged in Armenia, and his subsequent elevation to kingship in 884 ushered in a time of centripetal momentum as the lesser Armenian princes gathered around him. The importance of the Ardsruni was underscored by the marriage of their reigning prince, Grigor-Derenik, to Ashot I's daughter. The naming of Grigor-Derenik's son and successor as Ashot gives a hint of the closeness of the emerging alliance.

The coincidence of impetuosity and tragedy against the background of the constant competition from the local Islamic principalities as Abbasid power in the Caucasus rapidly diminished in the early 10th century ended the period of inter-Armenian cooperation and a new center of power appeared on the Armenian scene. Prince Ashot Ardsruni's son and successor, Gagik-Khachik, proved unwilling to accede to vassalage and challenged the overlordship of King Smbat I Bagratuni (890–914). He found his ally in Yusuf, the Sadjid emir of Azerbaijan. The Sadjid had formed the most powerful Islamic state in the region and openly competed with the Bagratuni. They acknowledged Abbasid suzerainty, but they also governed with a free hand. When Yusuf offered him a crown, Gagik seized upon the intent of the Arabs and declared himself king. The subsequent defeat and demise of King Smbat at the hands of the Sadjid nearly unraveled the Bagratuni state and extended Gagik the occasion to consolidate the new Ardsruni kingdom. The Byzantines too joined the effort to undo the Bagratuni and further elevated the importance of Gagik's crown by recognizing him in 921/922 by the title of *archon ton archonton*, prince of princes, thereby presuming to shift political legitimacy among the Armenians to the Ardsruni. Finally, when **Catholicos**

Hovhannes (John) V abandoned the patriarchal residence in **Dvin**, which remained in Muslim hands, and sought asylum in Vaspurakan in 924, the paramouncy of Gagik Ardsruni among the Armenians was abundantly evident. Church and state were once again reunited in an Armenian kingdom for the first time since the Arshakuni. The catholicosate remained in Vaspurakan until 961.

The Kingdom of Vaspurakan enjoyed a period of exceptional prosperity during the long reign of Gagik Ardsruni (908–943). The king appears to have spared no expense on a building program that ranged from the restoration of fortresses, the expansion of urban settlements, the founding of monasteries, and the embellishment of the royal residences. This spate of construction activity is epitomized in the architectural triumph achieved with the Church of the Holy Cross on the island of **Aghtamar**. Architecture counted only as one area of cultural accomplishment sponsored by the royal house, as Aghtamar also represented the combined expression of sculpture, painting, and historical learning. The private counterpart to the large and public frescoes of Aghtamar was found in the illuminated manuscript of the Gospels commissioned by Gagik's consort, Queen Mlke, one of the rare and certain possessions of Armenian royalty to survive. Further to glorify the new monarchy, Tovma Ardsruni, the scholar of the dynasty, authored the *History of the Ardsruni House* tracing for his sovereign a Biblical heritage all the way back to King Sennecherib of Assyria. Everything about Gagik points to a flamboyance and a determination to obtain the objectives of guaranteeing the political stability of the state, the prosperity of his subjects, and the inheritance of his dynasty. At a time of turbulence in the Near East, Gagik Ardsruni's policies resulted in a century of comparative peace for the Armenian people living in the kingdom of Vaspurakan. He was succeeded by his sons Derenik-Ashot (943–958/9) and Abusahl-Hamazasp (958/9–968/9) during whose reigns the Bagratuni recovered their power in central and north Armenia sidelining the Ardsruni state in the process and reducing it to nominal vassalage.

The steady Byzantine expansion during the 10th century under the emperors of the so-called Macedonian dynasty reached the borders of the independent Armenian states by the first quarter of the 11th century. As the Byzantines encroached in the west, and the eastern parts of Armenia came under mounting pressure from Turkic tribes, the

Ardsruni felt unequipped to confront the looming crisis. Internal strife and the constant strain of defending against attacks by Muslim states exhausted the kingdom of Vaspurakan. A series of raids by Turkic invaders in 1016/1018 persuaded King Senekerim-Hovhannes to negotiate with Emperor Basil II for a voluntary transfer of his state to the Greeks in exchange for territory in a safer part of the Byzantine Empire. In one of the great migrations of the Armenian people, the entire royal household, its retinue, and thousands of dependents abandoned their homeland to resettle in Cappadocia in 1021 thus closing the chapter on the Ardsruni kingdom. Vaspurakan was annexed and made a catepanate, a military district, to remain under Byzantine control until 1065 when the Seljuk Turks overran Armenia and permanently swept the Byzantines from the Armenian highlands in 1071 after the battle of Manzikert, fought along the northern shore of Lake Van.

The Ardsruni themselves, however, were far from finished in Byzantium or Armenia. Appointed strategos, military governor, of Cappadocia in Asia Minor, King Senekerim and his sons rendered loyal service to their new sovereign. For helping suppress the rebellion of Nikephoros Phokas in 1022, Senekerim's son David was rewarded with the governorship of Caesarea and Tzamandos, and when his father died in 1025, he inherited Sebastia/Sivas also. David was succeeded by his own brother Atom-Ashot who joined forces with Gagik Bagratuni of Kars in 1079/1080 in a failed attempt to rescue the deposed King Gagik II Bagratuni of **Ani** from his Greek captors. While the direct royal line came to an end in 1080 with the assassination of Atom by the Greeks, other branches of the Ardsruni family remained in the service of Byzantium. A relative of Senekerim who had emigrated with him, Abelgharib Ardsruni received the governorship of the Cilician towns of Sis, **Adana**, and Tarsus from the Byzantines. His tremendous importance in legitimating the process of implanting Armenian principalities in the area is evidenced by the marriage of his daughters to Davit Bagratuni, the son of Gagik II of Ani, and of another daughter to his liege Oshin, the baron holding for the Byzantine emperor the strategic fortress of Lambron in the Cilician mountains. In this respect the Ardsruni played a critical role in the settlement of the Armenians in Asia Minor and in Cilicia where communities at a safer distance from the troubled frontierland of Armenia flourished in succeeding centuries. Some of the Ardsruni are thought to have joined the Chalcedonian faith and fully integrated into Byzantine society as one family going by the name of Senacherim which is known to have remained in the imperial camp. Another junior branch had earlier joined its fate to the Bagratuni in Armenia and later Georgia. Assigned the fortress of Mahkanaberd on the Georgian border, as the Mankaberdeli family, they rose to prominence between the 12th and 14th centuries and the first important figure from this family, Sadun I, even governed Ani for the Georgians in the mid-12th century. During the Mongol period, another Sadun Mankaberdeli served as regent from 1269 to 1278 for the young King Dmitri III (1269–1289). The scope of Sadun's influence reached beyond his immediate responsibility at court. He held territories directly from the Mongols and even had possession of Kars. His lofty stature in the Armeno-Georgian society of the period is further attested by the fact of his marriage to the daughter of Avag Zakarian, or Avag Mkhargrdzeli, the most prominent Armenian family in the service of the Georgian Bagratuni monarchy, whose estates he administered.

Not all the Ardsruni left Vaspurakan. One minor branch staged a most unusual restoration. Abdelmseh Khedenikian, a descendent of Khedenik, presumed a third son of King Gagik-Khachik, and a titular Byzantine curopalate, struck upon an ingenious method for preserving his family's lands by converting it into church property, a legal condition more tolerable to Muslim overlords. In another stroke of political creativity recurrent in the history of the Ardsruni family, when Catholicos Barsegh I (1105–1113) finally fled the Muslim overlords of Ani and took refuge in Aghtamar, Abdelmseh used the occasion of Barsegh's death to presume to arrange the succession to the Armenian patriarchate by convening a local council to elect his son Davit as catholicos. The contrived election precipitated an administrative schism in the **Armenian Church**, but the supreme patriarchs in direct succession to **Grigor Lusavorich** were in no position to resolve the challenge as they were in exile themselves and did not find a permanent place of settlement until they moved into the fortress of Hromkla near Cilicia in 1149. The long reign of Davit I (1113–c.1165) helped establish the Catholicosate of Aghtamar. Through a grandniece married to another Ardsruni named Sefedin, this regional patriarchate became a hereditary possession of the Sefedinian family. With the instrumentality of the catholicosate, the Sefedinians held sway over the region to the east and south of Lake Van in the guise of ecclesiastical property. The schism was resolved in 1409 after the supreme patriarchate was nestled in Sis and the Armenian kingdom of Cilicia too had fallen. The Catholicosate of Aghtamar, now even more remote, was tolerated and legitimated as a local institution within the Armenian Church hierarchy, and the Sefedinians held it right down to the 16th century. *See also* HETUMIAN.

ARGHUTIANTS, HOVSEP (Iosif Argutinsky) (1743–1801). Religious leader. Arghutiants was born in Sanahin to one of the few remaining families of noble lineage in Eastern Armenia. He received his education at **Edjmiadsin** where he studied under the tutelage of Catholicos **Simeon Yerevantsi** and where he was ordained a celibate priest. Elevated to the rank of bishop in 1769, he was appointed primate of the Armenians of Russia in 1773 and moved to its diocesan headquarters in Astrakhan. In 1780 he was also appointed primate of the Crimean Armenians. He, along with Harutiun Lazarian of Moscow, met with Prince Potemkin and General Suvarov in that year to discuss Russian policy toward the Armenians and the Caucasus whereto Russian forces were advancing. He organized the exodus of the Armenians from the Crimea in 1778 during the Russo-Turkish wars for control of the peninsula and settled them in Nor Nakhichevan, near Rostov-on-Don, in southern Russia, by a charter received from the Empress Catherine II. In 1792 he also undertook the settlement in Grigoriopol of Armenians emigrating from Moldova and Bessarabia. Arghutiants promoted Russian expansion into the Caucasus and encouraged Armenians to assist Russia. In return he enjoyed the favor of Catherine the Great and received in 1789 from the Emperor Paul I a proclamation taking the Armenians under his protection. Arghutiants was elected catholicos in 1800 but passed away in Tbilisi on his way to Edjmiadsin before his formal elevation. *See also* NERSES V ASHTARAKETSI.

ARLEN, MICHAEL J. (1930–). American author. Arlen became the most popular American writer of Armenian background since **William Saroyan**. His *Passage to Ararat* (1975) signaled the rediscovery of heritage and the expression of a new reconciliation by **diaspora**-born and assimilated generations with the legacy of the **Armenian Genocide** and its consequences. Through a personal and conscious search for connection with the past, he framed and articulated the new diaspora identity that fuses multiple sources of experience into its own unique paradigm. The work appealed to wide audiences and became a best-seller. A writer for the prestigious *New Yorker* magazine, Arlen had already attained professional recognition as an astute observer and critic of the mass media. He specialized in the effects of television on society and authored a number of works on the subject, the first of which was the *Living-Room War* (1969). His father was also a writer who published under the pen-name of Michael Arlen (1895–1956). He was born Dikran Kouyoumjian and emigrated from Bulgaria to England, where he became a successful writer in the 1920s before settling in the United States. *The Green Hat* (1924) was his most famous work. *See also* SURMELIAN, LEON Z.

ARMAVIR. Capital of ancient Armenia. Armavir was founded by the Urartian King Argishti I (ca. 786–764 B.C.) on a previously unoccupied hill overlooking the **Arax River** in the Plain of Ayrarat. It lies 40 kilometers east of modern-day **Yerevan**. Originally named Argishtihinili, Argishti's city, the fortified settlement was developed by the Urartians on a scale to make it a second capital of their state and the main administrative center of the northern regions of Armenia brought under their sway. The military and economic investment by the Urartians presaged the eventual migration of the center of political gravity in ancient Armenia from the **Lake Van** basin, where the nucleus of the Urartian state was formed, to the great alluvial plain of the Arax River whose agricultural potential exceeded that of any other part of the Armenian plateau. The late seventh century B.C. incursions by the Scythians from the north weakened the Urartian state and, for a time, undermined the political importance of Armavir. The Scythians raided the city and destroyed the Urartian citadel.

When the conquest of the Persian Empire by Alexander the Great in the late fourth century B.C. resulted in the removal of Iranian dominion over Armenia, the **Yervanduni** family, which governed Armenia as vassals of the Persian King of Kings, and already held royal title, selected Armavir as the site for the new capital of their independent monarchy. Thereafter, all the capital cities of Armenia, until the construction of **Ani**, would lie along this stretch of the Arax River where the plain is widest and where the most important trade routes of the ancient world crossing over Armenia intersected. The Yervanduni rebuilt Armavir as both the political and religious center of Armenia. It served as the royal capital until the end of the third century

B.C., when Yervand IV (ca. 220–201 B.C.), the last of his dynasty, transferred the capital further east to the newly founded city of Yervandashat. Greek inscriptions found in the course of archeological digs indicate that Armavir remained an important place frequented by foreigners and its habitation endured into the Roman period in the first century A.D. *See also* ARTASHAT; ARTASHESIAN; VAN.

ARMENAKAN. *See* ARMENIAN REVOLUTIONARY MOVEMENT; POLITICAL PARTIES; VAN.

ARMENIAN APOSTOLIC CHURCH. The national church of Armenia. The Armenian Church is an autocephalous ecclesiastical institution whose claim to distinctness is based on apostolic origins. That is to say, the Armenian Church traces its beginnings to Christ's own apostles, St. Thaddeus and St. Bartholomew. In the Armenian tradition, the two apostles evangelized among the Armenians thereby introducing Christianity directly into Armenia and dignifying the Armenian Church with the right of self-government. The early entry of Christianity into Armenia is evidenced by the circumstances surrounding the conversion of the Armenian king **Trdat (Tiridates) IV** in 301, which is connected with the story of his persecution of Armenian Christians, presumably in tandem with Rome's religious policies of the time given Roman patronage of his elevation to the throne. The Armenian account attributes the monarch's pangs of conscience and the reconsideration of his moral views to the martyrdom of St. Hripsime and St. Gayane who had been innocent victims of his indefensible command. Moreover, Trdat's release at the urging of his own sister, Khosrovanuysh, of Grigor (Gregory), a high functionary of the court whom the king had earlier cast into prison for his adherence to Christianity, altogether indicate that by the third century the new **religion** was sufficiently widespread to have even penetrated the royal household in Armenia. It remained for King Trdat to adopt Christianity formally as the religion of Armenia, and to enlist Grigor as the country's first bishop in order to organize the church as an instrument of national policy.

The voluntary selection of a religion through the agency of a national monarch and an indigenous evangelizer has long constituted one of the prized values of the Armenian people. The church fused the apostolic, royal, and evangelic heritages surrounding its origins as the foundation of its exceptional and lasting influence as a uniquely Armenian institution. For all the demands pressed upon the Armenian Church through its later centuries of captivity, the traditions it honed about its founding proved a constant buttress for maintaining its integrity and for preserving a separate space for the religious convictions, ecclesiastical customs, and theological positions developed by the Armenians. In so doing, with the erosion and ultimately the absence of the political institutions that had defined Armenia in Antiquity and in the Middle Ages, the consolidation of another national institution centered on spirituality and faith contributed to the preservation of the ethnic identity of the Armenians as adherents of an autochthonous church.

In honor of **Grigor Lusavorich** (Gregory the Illuminator) the Armenian Church is at times called the Armenian Gregorian Church. More frequently it is referred to as the Armenian Orthodox Church, indicating by this designation that it constitutes part of Eastern Christendom separate from Western Catholic Christianity. In the Christian worldview, orthodoxy furnished the index of legitimacy and the Armenian Church avoided heresy and maintained a constant vigil on this matter. The early challenge of Zoroastrianism and Manichean dualism from Iran specially sensitized the Armenian Church to the question of orthodoxy as an expression of unqualified monotheism. The Armenian clergy responded vigorously and developed the theological knowledge and Christological positions necessary to counter these influences. Hence from the start, in Armenia, theology approximated political ideology. While the antiquity of the Armenian Church had much to do with its orthodoxy, political developments also determined the church's decisions on the central tenets of the faith.

The Armenians parted company on doctrinal matters from the church in the Roman Empire as a result of the coincidence of one of the severest conflicts Armenia faced politically and militarily with the timing of the Fourth Ecumenical Council, known as the Council of Chalcedon. Armenian church authorities had participated in the Council of Nicaea, the First Ecumenical Council, convened by Emperor Constantine in 325 to decide on Christian doctrine, and in subsequent councils held in Constantinople and Ephesus. The Armenian Church had adopted the Nicene Creed, which emphasized the divinity of Christ. The Council of Chalcedon in 451, by raising the matter of Christ's humanity and by crafting the doctrine of duophysitism, the existence of two natures, divine and human, in the singular Son of God, unwittingly created a serious predicament for the Armenian Church. The inability of the Armenian clergy to attend the council added another hindrance. The pivotal battle between Christian Armenia and Zoroastrian Iran fought on the field of Avarayr in the same year represented far more than a diversion from intellectual debate. The avoidance of dualisms reminiscent of Manichean beliefs ranked high as a consequence among the concerns of the Armenian clergy, and the Armenian Church inclined therefore to the safer position of monophysitism, which stressed the divine aspect of Christ over his human nature.

These were serious issues that went beyond the interest of theologians alone as doctrine also defined a person's communion with a specific church and his exclusion from others. By 554/5 [551] the Armenian Church had effectively separated from the Imperial Church in Constantinople, latterly known as the Greek Orthodox Church, as opposed to the Roman Catholic Church, which also underwent its own drawn-out process of separation from Constantinople. As Armenians resisted Zoroastrianism on the one hand, on the other hand, Iranian dominion over Armenia provided the political framework for the disengagement of the Armenian Church from conformity with Constantinople, a compromise that partially appeased Iranian concerns over Armenian proclivities toward the Roman Empire. By the mid-sixth century Armenian clergy were convening their own synods and the Armenian Church's independence was legislated in the 554/5 Council of **Dvin**. Traditionally dated 551, the Armenians looked upon the moment less as the closing of a chapter in their ecclesiastical history and much more as a new beginning thereby affixing the start of the Armenian calendar in that year. That conventional date noted one type of separation. The calendrical difference between Eastern and Western Christianity was most notably accentuated by the day of the Nativity of Christ. Rome selected December 25 to replace a popular pagan holiday with Christmas. Eastern Christendom with an earlier custom to which Armenia subscribed retained January 6 as the day to celebrate Christmas.

In the course of the delicate theological negotiations conducted through the thicket of the conflict between Rome and Iran over Armenia, the Armenian Church found the confidence to seek its own destiny thanks to another development of which it had been chief sponsor. The invention of the Armenian alphabet by **Mesrop Mashtots** in 405 had equipped the church with a powerful instrument with which to educate its clergy, preach to its flock, develop its own liturgy, and forge its own identity. The masterful translation of the Bible into Armenian by Mesrop and the **Catholicos** Sahak so impressed their countrymen that they took to calling it *Asdvatsashunch*, "The Breath of God." In the absence of any preceding models, the rendering of the Bible by a clear and accessible literary style that recorded for the first time the Armenian language as written text also affixed the Bible as the foundation of Armenian literature. Armenians now had direct contact with a profoundly thoughtful religion; a religion with an affinity for literary elaboration through commentary, exegesis, sermon, homily, and ritual. Armenians now also had at their disposal a vocabulary and an inventory of expressions that constituted the canonical usage of the Armenian language. In the Mediterranean world the Bible competed with a vast body of literature before gaining ascendancy as the central document of a new faith. In contrast, the Bible entered Armenian life with explosive effect, cleaving Armenian civilization and setting a wholly new trajectory for its development. Everything thereafter for centuries to come would be written against the backdrop of, in reference to, or on the basis of, the Armenian Bible.

If at the beginning, therefore, monarchy joined forces with the church in order to harness a new institution for the purposes of consolidating domestic policy, the church in turn harnessed the instruments of cultural communication and intellectual appeal by promoting the use and instruction of the native tongue in literature. In this regard the church also came to occupy a much larger place in Armenian society than in the rest of Christendom in the early Middle Ages because a native tradition of secular literacy was nonexistent and all writing was done within the framework of Christian thought. Moreover, as governance was the concern of a military caste and was not dependent on a scribal bureaucracy, other or competing centers of learning and writing did not flourish in Armenia. Virtually the whole of medieval Armenian civilization, therefore, was developed under the influence of the church. Even when an alternative ideological outlook emerged in the 19th century, the Christian perspective remained central to the Armenian worldview.

Christian values were infused into every sphere of life by the church. The many facets of Mesrop's educational program already carried the seeds of an intellectual awakening that he trailblazed. Instruction in the use of the Armenian alphabet constituted only the elementary facet of the program. The preparation of books in Armenian constituted the more sophisticated aspect of the enterprise, and it was decided that the effort could be facilitated through the shortcut of translating existing models and authoritative texts of the Christian religion. That option automatically created conditions for the rapid expansion of learning through the acquisition of Greek or Syriac and by developing the methods of linguistically transporting and relocating texts from one neighboring culture or another into the Armenian medium. From the beginning, therefore, the translator as interpreter, implied in the Armenian designation of *targmanich*, played a major role in the shaping of Armenian culture and literature, a practice that since the start has not gone out of fashion regardless of the fact that the audience for the translation would always be a very small number. The desire of transposing valued knowledge in order to incorporate it into the national culture remained a constant even when the vagaries of national life would seem to have militated against such preoccupation. To underline the importance of this cultural transference, the Church went so far as to designate a specific feast day for the commemoration of the Holy Translators (*Srbots Targmanchats*) of the Bible.

The long list of learned churchmen begins, of course, with Mesrop's own students of whom the most gifted began to create original works in Armenian. Appropriately, the first original work authored in Armenian was the life of the great inventor written by his youngest pupil Koriun, who sketched it more in the form of a hagiography than a biography, and in so doing imparted the spiritual motivation and religious inspiration that yielded the keys to the Armenian language. He in turn was followed by the likes of Yeznik Koghbatsi (Yeznik of Koghb), whose *Refutation of the Sects*, registered the introduction of theological writing in Armenian. Agatangeghos (Agathangelos) authored the first historical treatise in Armenian, naturally focusing on the establishment of the church by registering the events surrounding the conversion of Armenia: the story of King Trdat, Grigor Lusavorich, the martyrdom of Hripsime and Gayane, Grigor's securing of their relics and building of their martyriums, which became some of the oldest centers of Christian worship in Armenia, and lastly the founding of **Edjmiadsin** as the episcopal seat of Armenia.

Along with Koriun, Agatangeghos stands at the start of the best-developed literary tradition among the Armenians, the authorship of historiography, which relied on the two as its original anchors and built a continuous record of events in Armenia. The so-called Pavstos Buzand continued Agatangeghos with his narrative of the royal and patriarchal houses of Armenia, a narrative that in a later century was embellished and elaborated upon chronologically back in time to the origins of the Armenian people by **Movses Khorenatsi** (Moses of Khoren). As churchmen shaped the remembered historical profile of the Armenian nation, to an even greater extent other authors cultivated a spirited narrative of heroic struggle first centered on the Battle of Avarayr. Ghazar Parpetsi (Lazarus of Parpi) and, in the next century, Yeghishe (Elijah) created the basis of a new national epic that located the defense of the church and the struggle for freedom of religion as the focal point of the Armenian historical experience. The burst of creativity associated with the fifth century had a great deal to do with the strengthening of the Armenian Church. The effectiveness of the intellectual response in a time of political crisis ensuing the breakdown of the Armenian monarchy went a long way in developing a sense of national purpose against the forces of political diffusion, social disintegration, and religious assimilation.

The Church became the regular harbor of virtually all the men of learning for the next fifteen hundred years. In the 10th century, Armenia's greatest poet, **Grigor Narekatsi**, was a hermit his entire adult life and never lived outside a monastery. In the 12th century, the ecumenist theologian, Nerses Shnorhali, was virtually born for the church. For a century his antecedents occupied the patriarchal throne of Armenia. In the 14th century, the theologian Grigor Tatevatsi, who almost single-handedly led the defense of the Armenian Church against encroaching Catholicism, carried out all his work from the remote monastery of Tatev (short for Tatevos, Thaddeus), for which he is named.

Christian learning came to reside primarily in monasteries and the Armenian Church's cultural legacy is closely associated with the educational institutions, libraries, and scriptoria located in the cloisters that eventually dotted all the major centers of Armenian concentration, even when the Armenians dispersed far and wide after the 11th century. Although Edjmiadsin ultimately commanded center stage in the Armenian monastic network that spanned Western Asia, foci of ecclesiastical activity predate its founding. Grigor Lusavorich headed the Armenian Church from his seat at Ashtishat in Taron in southern Armenia. He did so deliberately in order to transform Armenia's ancient center of pagan worship into the new locus of Christian religiosity. The temples of Ashtishat were replaced by the monastery of St. John the Baptist (*Surb* [*Hovhannu*] *Karapet*) that remained a center of pilgrimage for the next 16 centuries.

The construction of monasteries was widely patronized during the period of **Bagratuni** and **Ardsruni** rule in Armenia in the 10th and 11th centuries. In the northeast the secluded cloisters of Sanahin, Haghpat, and on the island of **Sevan** were matched by the more urban monastic complexes associated with the city of **Ani** and its environs. In subsequent centuries, Klatzor, Tatev, Gandzasar, all in Eastern Armenia, emerged as centers of religious, educational, cultural, and administrative activity. In the south the monasteries of Varag and Narek were both connected to Grigor Narekatsi and his family, and **Aghtamar**, once a royal residence like **Vagharshapat**, became the shelter of another insular monastery. With the settlement of Armenians in Cilicia and Cappadocia, monasteries were formed in those parts as well, as at Skevra, Hromkla, and Sis, and along with the general movement of the population in that direction, so did the monastery of St. James (*Surb Hakob*) in Jerusalem become a permanent establishment and the magnet around which grew the Armenian Quarter of the Old City. Monasteries were even founded in Crimea and other parts of eastern Europe, and when in the early 17th century Armenians were forcibly resettled in Isfahan, in the heartland of Shiite Muslim Iran, there too they founded the All-Savior (*Amenaprkich*) monastery. Toward the end of the same century, the monk named **Mekhitar Sebastatsi** walked out of the monastery of the Holy Cross (*Surb Nshan*) in Sebasteia/Sivas in central Anatolia, joined the Roman Catholic Church, and some years later founded an Armenian Catholic monastery in Venice.

Some monasteries served only the most basic functions of a hermitage. Others were endowed with income-generating property and supported substantial facilities. Still others founded with the patronage of the grandees of Armenia were constructed by the finest architects of the land. The distinctive style of Armenian architecture is almost wholly connected with the visual appearance of Armenian churches. The geometric simplicity of the exterior with its flat surfaces and gabled roof almost always capped by a conical dome masked an endless variety of floor plans usually based on a cruciform interior. Armenians came to associate this ecclesiastical architecture so completely with their sense of national identity that they continued, and do so to this day, to apply its basic elements in the construction of new churches anywhere in the world where local laws and conditions do not restrict them from raising a building with an Armenian dome. They can be found in the major cities of most of the countries where Armenians in the diaspora inhabit.

The church was also the nurturer of one more of the arts that completed the total environment of devotion enclosed within the space of its edifices. The Armenian tradition attributes the earliest music composed to Mesrop Mashtots also, with whom began the singing of the *sharagan*, the Armenian Church hymns. The entire Armenian liturgy is sung during Mass and the populace participates in the choir, closely acquainting it with portions of the service whose melodies count among the cherished markers of Armenian culture. The Lord's Prayer (*Hayr Mer*), sung at the end of Mass, is universally familiar. As for the soulful melodies of the Sanctus (*Surb, Surb*) and the Kyrie Eleison (*Der Voghormia*), they represent for Armenians the essence of worship through music. In the long centuries of foreign domination and dispersion, through the serenity of music, the weekly plaints for divine mercy and consolation helped bind a people to its faith. Even in communities that lost the facility of Armenian speech, the Mass, and especially its choice passages, were memorized phonetically and continuously performed. As late as the 20th century, the greatest Armenian musician still was a clergyman, and the name given him when he entered the priesthood was that of the seventh-century catholicos famed for his musicianship, **Komitas**.

For all of its contributions as the primary crucible of medieval Armenian civilization, in the final analysis, it was the church's ministry that made the real difference. From the beginning the Armenian Church was ascribed a critical leadership role. The official church competed with the feudal order, invested the social system with a new set of values and morals, and articulated concepts appealing to higher national and patriotic ideals to which the ruling class was unaccustomed. When the **Arshakuni** dynasty was removed from the

Armenian throne and the monarchy abolished in 428, the church remained the sole institution enjoying countrywide loyalty. The office of the patriarch assumed greater political responsibilities. Even so, the church could not avoid the stamp of the prevailing political order, and its organization soon reflected the feudalistic apportionments of the territorial princes of Armenia. While in earlier centuries the scions of the military caste led by the **Mamikonian**, Bagratuni, **Siuni**, and other princely families may not have deigned ministry in the Church, by the High Middle Ages the great noble houses of Armenia assigned the bishoprics of their principalities to junior members of the dynasty. Eventually, some aristocratic families, such as the **Ardsruni**, Pahlavuni, and Orbelian became closely linked with various patriarchal seats such as those of **Aghtamar**, Hromkla, and Siunik. In the 18th century the Catholicosate of Cilicia ensconced in the town of Sis became virtually hereditary in the local Adjapahian (Achabahian) family. So had the catholicosate of Aghvank based in Gandzasar become hereditary in the Hasan-Jalalian family. All, of course, had been preceded in this example by the family of Grigor Lusavorich whose male heirs in the fourth and fifth centuries were elevated to the pontifical throne of Armenia.

The ministry of the church, however, was open without distinction of class to all prepared for a life of religious service. In this regard, with the exception of the crafts and commerce, the church remained the only outlet for men of talent, certainly men of intellect. Although the regional bishoprics eventually may have become appointive offices controlled by the feudal lords, the practice of the election of the catholicos, the supreme patriarch, became the established custom once the male line of Grigor Lusavorich expired. As the historical sources testify again and again, the national significance of a new patriarch's election and of the ceremony of his anointment called for the presence and participation of the laity. In the Middle Ages the princes cast their ballots along with the prelates, much as in later centuries the heads of the merchant class and other community leaders assembled with the bishops to choose the next successor to Gregory the Illuminator. Men of great learning have held the office, among them Sahak Partev, the last descendant of Gregory, and Mesrop Mashtots's collaborator in the translation of the Bible, the illustrious catholicoses from the Pahlavuni family, such as Grigor Vkayaser (Gregory the Martyrophile) and Nerses Shnorhali (Nerses the Gracious) in the 11th and 12th centuries, and in modern times, **Simeon Yerevantsi**, Babgen Kiuleserian (Papken Giuleserian), **Garegin I Hovsepiants**, and **Garegin I (Karekin II) Sarkissian**. More so than learning, however, administrative skill, political wisdom, and an ability for leadership were the qualities sought in the choice of catholicos, for the heavy responsibilities of the office required the talent of diplomats and managers to guide the Armenian Church and ipso facto the Armenian nation through difficult political circumstances defined by the absence of statehood.

The office of the supreme patriarch of the Armenian Church now bears the title of Catholicos of All Armenians. The origins of the office are well documented and the line of succession has remained unbroken since the ordination in 314 of Gregory the Illuminator as the first bishop of Armenia and the head of its church. The evolution of the office, however, is another story, as complex as the history of the Armenians, and its fate and migrations a mirror image of the turmoil and tribulations endured by its flock. The highest and holiest office of the Armenian Church did not spare its occupants the risks of captivity, exile, imprisonment, and penury. If anything, the honor came with the knowledge that the head of the church would also bear the grief of a suffering people frequently left unprotected and often ruled by foreigners and out-and-out opponents of Christianity. The challenges of spiritual governance under Islamic rule were many. While the Armenian people experienced periods of religious persecution, and the Sadjids of Azerbaijan and the Mamluks of Egypt were particularly notorious for their mistreatment of the Armenian catholicos, on the whole Islamic governments respected the sacrosanctity of the patriarch. Even as the Safavids of Iran deported the great mass of the Armenian population from the **Arax River** valley, they also recognized and upheld the rights of the catholicosate in Edjmiadsin, though left behind a virtual island in a desert in the early 17th century.

Edjmiadsin might have commanded a place of respect in the religious imagination of the Armenians because of its many associations with the founding of Christianity in Armenia. The fact remained that the office of the patriarch tended to relocate to the political center of the country. When kings no longer resided at Vagharshapat, Dvin became the focal point of administration under Persian and Arab rule. In 485 the residence of the catholicos was transferred to the new capital. When in the post-Arab period the Ardsruni and Bagratuni vied for political dominance and legitimacy, the catholicos too migrated from Dvin, first to Aghtamar in 927 and then in 992 to Ani, the capital of the larger Armenian state ruled by the Bagratuni kings. The catholicos went into exile from Ani and eventually settled in 1149 in the fortress of Hromkla on the Euphrates at a midpoint between historic Armenia and the newly settled land of Cilician Armenia. From Hromkla it removed in 1293 to Sis, the capital of the new Armenian kingdom of the **Rubenian** and **Hetumian** dynasties.

With the fall of the last Armenian kingdom in 1375, the unity of the Armenian Church was seriously undermined. Armenians across Western Asia became stranded in distant pockets as Mamluks and Turkomans divided up the Armenian lands. By then church leaders in different parts of Armenia had resorted to local strategies to preserve some semblance of religious authority among the people. In the process, the Armenian Church became increasingly segmented and vulnerable to abuse and manipulation. By the first half of the 15th century consensus had emerged among the clergy in Armenia that the church should once again be headquartered in the historic heartland of the country. In 1441 the bishops of Eastern Armenia decided the moment had arrived to relocate the catholicosate to Edjmiadsin, nearly a thousand years after its departure. At a time when Armenia was at the point of greatest weakness, its lay and religious leaders exercised an act of such foresight that they could not have imagined all its implications, but whose significance they well appreciated as a necessary restoration for a people who by the 15th century was completely dominated by foreign and Islamic rule.

With the decision to revive the Holy See in the mainland as it were, the Armenian Church's administrative organization became a standing contradiction and a source of conflict and feud, for it brought into existence two lines of catholicoses both of whom were regarded as legitimate successors to the patriarchate of Grigor Lusavorich. By assuming the mantle of the original Holy See of Armenia, the new line of catholicoses enjoyed the loyalty of the Armenians of the East none of whom had any contact or access to the catholicosate in Sis. The bishops of Cilicia, however, chose to perpetuate the catholicosate in exile as it enjoyed the legitimacy of continuity with the original line of succession. Beside the legally pre-eminent catholicoses, regional catholicosates had come into existence even before the revival of Edjmiadsin. In 1113 a catholicosate had been established in Aghtamar with jurisdiction over southern Armenia. In the 14th century another catholicosate appeared in Gandzasar with jurisdiction over Artsakh, or Karabagh, easternmost Armenia. In 1311 the Armenian Patriarchate of Jerusalem came into being. Each was the outgrowth of ancient bishoprics that sought ecclesiastical autonomy to compensate for the lack of control and communication from a central pontificate. A mere 20 years after the inauguration of the Edjmiadsin catholicosate, putatively in 1461 the Armenian Patriarchate of Constantinople was founded. Each pontiff owed allegiance to a different suzerain lord. The Ottoman Turks ruled in Constantinople. The Kara Koyunlu Turks ruled over the Armenian highlands. The Mamluks of Egypt governed Palestine, Syria, and Cilicia.

When the Ottomans of Turkey and the Safavids of Iran finally divided the Middle East between them in the 16th century, the new balance of power also altered the juridical reach and comparative political importance of the Armenian catholicosates and patriarchates. In the east Gandzasar became subordinate to Edjmiadsin. In the west the catholicosate of Cilicia became restricted to a regional episcopate, while the influence of the patriarchate in Jerusalem grew. None, however, matched the reach and responsibility thrust upon the Armenian Patriarchate of Constantinople by virtue of the fact that it resided in the capital of one of the mightiest powers on the face of the earth. By the 19th century the patriarch exercised theoretical jurisdiction over the entire **Armenian *Millet*** in the Ottoman Empire, so designated by the sultanate itself. The episcopal center closest to Europe, the patriarchate of Constantinople occupied a pivotal location, as Armenians were increasingly exposed to Western ideas and influences.

The rapid rise of Edjmiadsin to prominence in the Armenian Church hierarchy came with the 1828 Russian occupation of Eastern Armenia and the recognition by the Romanov dynasty of Edjmiadsin's jurisdiction in all the Russian lands, in effect doubling the geographic reach of the catholicosate as it already enjoyed jurisdiction granted it by the Safavids over the Armenian communities of Iran and further east into India. It was not the size of the territory or the breadth of the church's responsibility that singled out Edjmiadsin over the other pontificates. With the annexation by Russia, Edjmiadsin became the only Armenian religious center located in a Christian state. That totally tipped the balance as more and more Armenians looked toward the pontificate enjoying the greatest freedom of expression with regard to their concerns and troubles to assume spiritual helmsmanship of the nation.

The role and responsibilities of the Armenian Church toward its community and especially the state were formalized by the regulations drawn up in 1836 and 1863 in the Russian Empire and the Turkish Empire respectively. By these regulations customary practices were given a legal framework and the Church's political role was made all the more pronounced as these regulations created the perception that church authorities had means of appeal to the authorities to correct injustices. The predicaments of the church only multiplied. In the course of the 19th century the Armenians underwent a process of modernization in attitudes that altered their sense of themselves from that of a religious minority to that of an ethnic community espousing national ideals. The growing tensions between the Armenians and the ruling systems may be traced in any number of conflicts into which the church was drawn despite its general reluctance to compromise relations with state authorities.

The Statute (Polozhenie) of 1836 issued by Tsar Nicholas I (1825–1855) effectively subordinated the Armenian Church to Russian state control. In granting it exemption from taxes as well as the freedom to oversee instruction in Armenian parochial schools, the state also created conditions for the church to expand its financial capacity and thereby encouraged the spread of education. The rapid improvement of the economic well-being of Armenians in 19th century Russia, matched by the security guaranteed the church's property and landholdings, only increased the role of the church in Armenian society. When in the reign of Alexander III (1881–1894) and Nicholas II (1894–1917) the state resorted to Russification policies as countermeasures to the spread of national sentiment in the growing middle class, the state assumed oversight of the Armenian schools. Policies of the like, however, only alienated loyal Armenians, and when in 1903 the state confiscated the church's properties, the already strained relations between Armenians and the Russian state ruptured. The personal defiance of Catholicos **Mkrtich Khrimian** marked a turning point. The Armenian Church was provoked into taking a political stand in the face of spreading civil unrest and against the threat presented to the catholicosate's leadership role.

Khrimian personified the religious helmsman as national leader. Himself an ardent patriot, nonetheless, he still represented the centrist position as Armenian political organizations had emerged by the late 19th century that pressed upon the church on many issues of national policy and advocated resistance against colonial repression. The Russian government's decision in 1905 to rescind the 1903 edict of confiscation, however, did little to restore the church to earlier prominence. Practical leadership had passed to the political organizations at the forefront of the resistance.

The 1863 Regulations issued in the Ottoman Empire to reform the Turkish state's relations with the Armenian *Millet* also located the Armenian Church at the center of the intensifying dynamic between growing liberal attitudes among middle class elements and the centralizing trend in Ottoman administration. As a matter of fact Khrimian's appreciation of the condition of the Armenian populace under oppressive Islamic rule and his political outlook had been formed by his experiences in the Ottoman Empire, including his brief stint as Armenian Patriarch of Constantinople. The strain placed upon the Armenian Church in the Ottoman Empire during the period of the massacres in the late 1890s and into the 1920s was considerable. Clergymen were singled out for persecution and many suffered veritable martyrdom for their faith during the **Armenian Genocide**. For all intents and purposes the Armenian Church in the Ottoman Empire was destroyed, and with it the numerous and ancient centers of worship dating back to the time of Gregory the Illuminator. Sanctuaries became the site of gruesome deaths. In 1895 thousands perished in the Armenian cathedral of Urfa, ancient Edessa, when it was set ablaze. Similarly, countless numbers were locked in and killed in churches in the city of Adana in 1909. With the decimation of the Armenian population, by the 1920s surviving Armenian ecclesiastical buildings in Turkey had been expropriated and converted to other uses, some even into mosques. Only the Armenian churches of Constantinople remained under the protection of the patriarch, and his office barely survived the depredations of the Young Turk regime.

In July 1916 the Young Turk government, in a move designed to uproot the Armenian Church once and for all, decreed the Catholicosate of Cilicia in Sis, the Catholicosate of Aghtamar, the Patriarchate of Constantinople, and the Patriarchate of Jerusalem combined into a single office, designated the Catholicos Sahak II Khapayian (Sahag Khabayian) of Sis as the Armenian Catholicos-Patriarch, removed him to Jerusalem, and deported the deposed Patriarch Zaven

Der-Yeghiayan of Constantinople to Jerusalem also. By a single stroke the Young Turks demolished the centuries-old structure of the Armenian Church in the Ottoman Empire. Patriarch Zaven and Catholicos Sahak both returned home from exile in 1919 to communities that had become shadows of their former selves. For Catholicos Sahak, the return was short-lived. In 1921, he departed Cilicia a second and final time with Armenians fleeing the Turkish Nationalist takeover of the region from the French occupation army. The Catholicosate remained without an abode until the facilities of a one-time orphanage constructed by the American Near East Relief agency on the outskirts of the town of Beirut, Lebanon, were made available as a residence. The aged Catholicos Sahak and his Coadjutor Catholicos Papken Giuleserian settled in Antelias in 1930 where the Catholicosate of the Great House of Cilicia relocated on a permanent basis, from there to revive the Armenian Church in exile among the survivors of the Armenian Genocide and their descendants now dispersed around the globe. Their efforts were supplemented by the likes of Yeghishe Turian and Torgom Gushakian, the able patriarchs of Jerusalem, where religious life had gone uninterrupted.

The Armenian Church in the homeland fared no better. With the Sovietization of the Republic of Armenia in 1920, the church was deprived of all its assets, properties, educational facilities, and other responsibilities. In short order, little was left of the church organization beyond the catholicosate at Edjmiadsin. That too came in harm's way when Catholicos Khoren Muratbekian (1932–1938) was murdered by Stalin's secret police. The real recovery of the Armenian Church everywhere would have to wait for the end of World War II in 1945. It may be argued that the survival and growth of the Armenian Church in exile created conditions for the maintenance of the Catholicosate of Edjmiadsin by Soviet authorities as an alternative source of religious loyalty for the Armenian people. While on the one hand it fostered divisiveness, on the other it necessitated the perpetuation of the office at Edjmiadsin. Independence in 1991 ended much of the ideologically driven acrimony that created deep rifts within the Armenian Church during the Cold War era. Independence also fostered an environment in which the church began to flourish once again in Armenia. Its most visible manifestation took the form of the restoration of the many church buildings that had fallen into disuse and the formation of new parishes to attend the rededicated sanctuaries. By the dawn of the 21st century, the Armenian Church once again had become the largest nongovernmental institution voluntarily maintained by the Armenian people. Its renewed strength and its revived sense of mission was communicated by the celebrations organized around the world leading up to the year 2001 for the 1700th anniversary of its founding.

ARMENIAN ASSEMBLY OF AMERICA. An organization representing the Armenian-American community's interests and concerns with the federal government of the United States. Formed in 1972 by community activists as a nonpartisan forum to promote participation in the American political process, with the support of business leaders Stephen Mugar and Hirair Hovnanian, the Armenian Assembly emerged as the point of focus in Washington, D.C. to the Armenian communities widely scattered across the United States. The appearance of the Armenian Assembly of America also heralded the relocation of the Armenian **diaspora**'s center of gravity with the rapid growth of the Armenian-American communities and the destabilization of the major Armenian colonies of the Middle East that had provided the centers of leadership in the middle decades of the 20th century. The importance of this new reality was manifest by the late 1980s when the breakup of the Soviet Union prompted the Armenian Assembly to encourage American diplomatic support for the movements for independence and self-determination in Armenia and Karabagh respectively.

The December 7, 1988, **Spitak Earthquake** marked a watershed in this respect. Occurring at a moment of fast-moving improvements in Soviet-American relations, the catastrophe occasioned the sending of vast quantities of U.S. government assistance to then still Soviet Armenia. These developments augmented the Assembly's domestic agenda with the need to advocate for increased aid to meet the humanitarian crisis in Armenia. The deterioration of the political situation in the Caucasus and the escalation of conflict over **Nagorno Karabagh,** which led to an influx of refugees at a time coinciding with the massive destruction caused by the earthquake, by the winter of 1992 resulted in an emergency as Armenia came under a blockade that was only relieved by the delivery of critical U.S. aid. Following the independence of Armenia, the Assembly focused on building close U.S.-Armenian relations and in advocating supportive Congressional legislation to provide annual development aid, while seeking American leadership to bear on resolving the Karabagh conflict, recognizing the **Armenian Genocide**, and improving Armenian-Turkish relations. *See also* SPITAK EARTHQUAKE.

ARMENIAN GENERAL BENEVOLENT UNION (AGBU). Philanthropic organization. The AGBU was founded in 1906 in Cairo, Egypt, by a group of wealthy Armenians led by **Boghos Nubar Pasha** who wanted to create a nonpolitical membership organization, which would therefore be above government suspicion in order to carry out philanthropic work among dispossessed and needy Armenians. The idea for an organization of this type had emerged in the aftermath of the **Armenian Massacres** of 1894–1896 that left hundreds of thousands in straitened conditions throughout the Ottoman Empire. The AGBU sought to aid in the intellectual and moral progress of Armenians and to assist in improving their economic situation. To realize these lofty goals the AGBU established and subsidized schools, libraries, trade schools, workshops, hospitals, dispensaries, orphanages, and other cultural institutions. These efforts were intended to provide immediate assistance in case of natural and other disasters, as well as assist the lot of the great mass of the Armenian peasantry in the homeland by improving agricultural techniques and providing the implements necessary to raise their standards of living.

Soon the AGBU's vision and resources were put to the test by the 1909 **Adana Massacre**. The organization responded quickly and proved its value when tens of thousands were made destitute. The AGBU began to grow and by 1915 had founded some 40 schools and dozens of chapters throughout the Armenian communities when the genocidal policies of the Young Turk regime destroyed much of the organization's membership and infrastructure in Turkey. With its headquarters in Egypt, the organization was spared the loss of leadership. At the end of World War I it responded by hastily forming orphanages, hospitals, and refugee camps in places where Armenians had been deported such as Damascus, Mosul, Beirut, and Baghdad. It also set about rehabilitating communities in the nearer Cilician towns such as Mersin, **Musa Dagh**, Adana, Hadjin, Tarson, Kilis, Iskenderun, Urfa, and Dortyol. No sooner had it succeeded in helping resuscitate some of the devastated communities than new waves of Armenian refugees began to flee from Smyrna and Cilicia. The

AGBU quickly proceeded by setting up shelters in Greece at Saloniki, Piraeus, and Athens, and in Aleppo, Jerusalem, Alexandria, and Cairo. At the same time the AGBU raised funds in the United States and elsewhere for projects in Armenia. The AGBU continued to operate in Soviet Armenia during the 1920s where it built schools and medical facilities. In 1930 the town of Nubarashen, in honor of the founder, was started in Armenia with funds donated by Boghos Nubar Pasha and the Armenian community in America. The building of the town was part of the AGBU's program to find permanent homes for the Armenian refugees scattered across the Middle East and to encourage repatriation to Soviet Armenia.

The AGBU's stature received a major boost when the organization was made the trustee of the largest Armenian bequest made up to that time. The $2.5 million endowment established in 1926 by the Melkonian brothers of Egypt for a coeducational high school in Cyprus elevated the AGBU commitment to education. As a boarding school, the Melkonian Institute attracted students from many countries and became the nurturing ground for new generations of Armenians that reached adulthood in the **diaspora**. Many continued their education in overseas universities and thus formed the core of a growing class of professionals. By the last decade of the 20th century the AGBU network of schools reached North and South America and as far as Australia. In one of his last bequests Boghos Nubar Pasha himself endowed the Marie Nubar Students' Home in memory of his wife for Armenians attending university classes in Paris. Since that time the AGBU has annually awarding hundreds of scholarships for higher education. As for the Melkonian Institute, it became one of the main centers for the training of teachers for other Armenian educational institutions.

In 1924 the AGBU moved its headquarters to Paris where it remained until World War II. With the occupation of the city by the Nazis, the AGBU relocated to New York in 1942. The war necessitated turning attention to relief work again. The general economic depression in the postwar period kept many Armenians on the economic margins of the countries they lived in and precipitated another wave of repatriation to Armenia when it opened its doors to immigrants. Once again the AGBU assisted in the process and over 100,000 Armenians resettled in Armenia. In an ideologically polarized world, these programs kept the AGBU at the center of political controversies despite its nonpartisan policies. Always identified with the liberal wing of Armenian political affairs because of the composition of its Central Board, which consisted of prosperous businessmen, nevertheless AGBU political neutrality and willingness to deal with Soviet Armenian authorities on humanitarian issues complicated Armenian community relations and made it the object of anti-Communist criticism. During the Cold War years it became one of the principal organizations around which elements of the Armenian community opposed to the **Armenian Revolutionary Federation** (ARF) congregated. Even so, the AGBU weathered the risks of politicization, and under **Alex Manoogian**, who served as its president from 1953 to 1989, experienced a period of tremendous growth by accumulating assets of over $100 million.

This new financial strength and good relations with the authorities in Armenia had the AGBU well-positioned to stage a major relief effort when the December 7, 1988 **Spitak Earthquake** in north Armenia destroyed whole towns and villages. The entire organization mobilized to render the survivors assistance by shipping food, medicine, and clothing. With Armenian independence in 1991, the AGBU pledged further assistance to the newborn republic. In a major commitment to improve education and introduce Western know-how, the AGBU founded the American University of Armenia. Before that institution was fully functional, the AGBU confronted an even greater challenge than the earthquake when Armenia was placed under blockade in 1992 by Azerbaijan and Turkey, and the country's food, medicine, and fuel supplies were exhausted. AGBU once again emerged among the lead organizations in the Armenian diaspora to render humanitarian assistance on a scale to meet the needs of 3.5 million people.

The AGBU played a central role in the adjustment of the deported Armenian population of Turkey to its new diaspora status. While rendering shelter and material assistance, it remained dedicated to a central mission of improving the moral well-being of Armenians throughout the world through education. Through its publications and cultural activities, it also became an important contributor to the intellectual recovery of the Armenian community in the postgenocide period. Once it cared for tens of thousands of orphans. When those orphans became adults and assumed positions of responsibility in their communities, they transformed the AGBU into the largest sponsor of education and educational institutions. In the last decade of the 20th century, nearly 7,000 youngsters were attending AGBU-sponsored schools throughout the world and 25,000 members were funding and manning hundreds of undertakings large and small in nearly every Armenian community around the world.

ARMENIAN GENOCIDE (1915–1923). The systematic extermination of the Armenian population of historic Western Armenia and Anatolia. In April 1915 the Ottoman government embarked upon policies designed to bring about the systematic reduction of its civilian Armenian population. The persecutions continued with varying intensity until 1923 when the Ottoman Empire itself went out of existence and was replaced by the Republic of Turkey. The Armenian population of the Ottoman state was reported at about two million in 1914. An estimated one million had perished by 1918, while hundreds of thousands had become homeless and stateless refugees. By 1923 virtually the entire Armenian population of Anatolian Turkey had disappeared.

In its heyday in the 16th century the Ottoman Empire was a powerful state. Its minority populations prospered along with the growth of its economy. By the 19th century, the empire was in serious decline. It had been reduced in size and by 1914 had lost virtually all its lands in Europe and Africa. This decline created enormous internal political and economic pressures that contributed to the intensification of ethnic tensions. Armenian aspirations for representation and participation in government aroused suspicions among the Muslim Turks who had never shared power in their country with any minority and who also saw nationalist movements in the Balkans result in the secession of former Ottoman territories. Demands by Armenian political organizations for administrative reforms in the Armenian-inhabited provinces and better police protection from predatory tribes among the Kurds invited only further repression. The government was determined to avoid resolving the so-called Armenian Question in any way that altered the traditional system of administration. During the reign of the sultan Abdul-Hamid (Abdulhamit) II (1876–1909), a series of massacres throughout the empire meant to dampen Armenian expectations by frightening them cost up to 300,000 lives by some estimates and inflicted enormous material losses on a majority of Armenians.

In response to the crisis in the Ottoman Empire, a new political group called the Young Turks seized power by revolution in 1908. Of the Young Turks, the Committee of Union and Progress (CUP) (*Itti-had ve Terraki*) emerged at the head of the government in a coup staged in 1913. It was led by a triumvirate: Enver, minister of war, Talaat, minister of the interior (later prime minister), and Jemal, minister of the marine. The CUP espoused an ultra-nationalistic ideology that advocated the formation of an exclusively Turkish state. It also subscribed to an ideology of aggrandizement through conquest directed eastward toward other regions inhabited by Turkic peoples living beyond the confines of the Ottoman Empire and at that time subject to the Russian Empire. The CUP also steered Istanbul toward closer diplomatic and military relations with Imperial Germany. When World War I broke out in August 1914, the Ottoman Empire formed part of the Triple Alliance with the other Central Powers, Germany and Austria-Hungary, and it declared war on Russia and its Western allies, Great Britain and France.

The Ottoman armies initially suffered a string of defeats that they made up by a series of easy military victories in 1918 before the Central Powers capitulated later that year. Whether retreating or advancing, the Ottoman army used the occasion of war to wage a collateral campaign against the civilian Armenian population in the regions in which warfare was being conducted. These measures were part of the genocidal program secretly adopted by the CUP and implemented under the cover of war. They coincided with the CUP's larger program to eradicate the Armenians from Turkey and neighboring countries for the purpose of creating a new Pan-Turanian empire. Through the spring and summer of 1915, in all areas outside the war zones, the Armenian population was ordered deported from their homes. Convoys consisting of tens of thousands including men, women, and children were driven hundreds of kilometers toward the Syrian desert.

The deportations were disguised as a resettlement program. The brutal treatment of the deportees made it apparent that the deportations were mainly intended as death marches that surgically removed the Armenians from the rest of society and disposed of great masses of people with little or no destruction of property. The displacement process therefore also bore the features of a major opportunity orchestrated by the CUP for the plundering of the material wealth of the

Armenians and proved an effortless method of expropriating all of their immovable properties.

The genocidal intent of the CUP measures was also evidenced by the mass killings that accompanied the deportations. Earlier, Armenian soldiers in the Ottoman forces had been disarmed and either worked to death in labor battalions or outright executed in small batches. With the elimination of the able-bodied men from the Armenian population, the deportations proceeded with little resistance. The convoys were frequently attacked by bands of killers specifically organized for the purpose of slaughtering the Armenians. As its instrument of extermination, the government had authorized the formation of gangs of butchers, most of whom were convicts released from prisons for the express purpose of enlisting them in the units of the so-called Special Organization, *Tashkilati Mahsusa*. This secret outfit was headed by the most ferocious partisans of the CUP who took it upon themselves to carry out the orders of the central government with the covert instructions of their party leaders. A sizable portion of the deportees, including women and children, were indiscriminately cut down through massacres along the deportation routes. The cruelty characterizing the killing process was heightened by the fact that it was frequently carried out by the sword. The ordeal of witnessing the mass killing of innocent persons constituted one of the more emotionally crushing features of the traumatization suffered by survivors. Many younger women and some orphaned children were also seized and placed in bondage in Turkish and Muslim homes resulting in another type of traumatization characterized by the shock of losing both family and one's sense of identity. They were frequently forbidden to grieve, were employed as unpaid labor, and were required to assimilate the language and religion of their captors.

The government also had made no provisions for the feeding of the deported population. Starvation took an enormous toll much as exhaustion felled the older, the weaker, and the infirmed. Deportees were denied water and food in a deliberate effort to hasten death. The survivors who reached northern Syria were collected at a number of concentration camps whence they were sent farther south to die under the scorching sun of the desert. Through methodically organized deportation, systematic massacre, intentional starvation, deliberate dehydration, and continuous brutalization, the Ottoman government reduced its Armenian population to a frightened mass of famished individuals whose families and communities had been destroyed in a single stroke.

Resistance to the deportations was infrequent. Only in one instance did the entire population of an Armenian settlement manage to evade death. The mountaineers of **Musa Dagh** defended themselves in the heights above their villages until French naval vessels in the eastern Mediterranean detected them and transported them to safety. Inland towns and villages that resisted were reduced to rubble by artillery. The survival of the Armenians in large part is credited not to acts of resistance, but to the humanitarian intervention led by American Ambassador Henry Morgenthau. Although the Allied Powers expressly warned the Ottoman government about its policy of genocide, ultimately it was through Morgenthau's efforts that the plight of the Armenians was publicized in the United States. The U.S. Congress authorized the formation of a relief committee that raised funds to feed "the starving Armenians." Near East Relief, as the committee was eventually known, saved tens of thousands of lives. After the war, it headed a large-scale effort to rehabilitate the survivors who were mostly left to their own devices in their places of deportation. By setting up refugee camps, orphanages, medical clinics, and educational facilities, Near East Relief rescued the surviving Armenian population.

In the postwar period nearly 400 of the key CUP officials implicated in the atrocities committed against the Armenians were arrested. A number of domestic military tribunals were convened that brought charges ranging from the unconstitutional seizure of power and subversion of the legal government, the conduct of a war of aggression, and conspiring the decimation of the Armenian population to more explicit capital crimes including massacre. Some of the accused were found guilty of the charges. Most significantly, the ruling triumvirate was condemned to death. They, however, eluded justice by fleeing abroad. Their escape left the matter of avenging the countless victims to a clandestine group of survivors that tracked down the CUP archconspirators. Talaat, the principal architect of the Armenian Genocide, was killed in 1921 in Berlin where he had gone into hiding. His assassin was arrested and tried in a German court that acquitted him.

The acts of vengeance had no effect on the outcome of the genocide. Most of those implicated in war crimes evaded justice and many joined the new Nationalist Turkish movement led by Mustafa Kemal.

In a series of military campaigns, in 1920 against Russian Armenia, in 1921 against the refugee Armenians who had returned to Cilicia in southern Turkey, and in 1922 against the Greek army that had occupied Izmir, where the last intact Armenian community in Anatolia still existed, the Nationalist forces completed the process of eradicating the Armenians through further expulsions and massacres. When Turkey was declared a republic in 1923 and received international recognition, the Armenian Question and all related matters of resettlement and restitution were swept aside and soon forgotten.

In all, it is estimated that up to a million and a half Armenians perished at the hands of Ottoman and Turkish military and paramilitary forces and through atrocities intentionally inflicted to eliminate the Armenian demographic presence in Anatolia. In the process the population of historic Armenia at the eastern extremity of Anatolian Turkey was wiped off the map. With their disappearance, an ancient people that had inhabited the Armenian highlands for three thousand years lost its historic homeland and was forced into a new **diaspora**. The surviving refugees spread around the world and eventually settled in some two dozen countries on all the continents of the globe. Triumphant in its total annihilation of the Armenians and relieved of any obligations to the victims and survivors, the Turkish Republic adopted a policy of dismissing the charge of genocide and denying that the deportations and atrocities had constituted part of a deliberate plan to exterminate the Armenians. One thing was certain, with the genocide, ancient Armenia ceased to exist. When the Red Army sovietized what remained of Russian Armenia in 1920, the Armenians had been compressed into an area amounting to no more than 10 percent of the territories of their historic homeland. Armenians annually commemorate the genocide on April 24 at the site of memorials raised by the survivors in all their communities around the world. *See also* ADANA MASSACRE; ARMENIAN GENERAL BENEVOLENT UNION; ARMENIAN MASSACRES; ARMENIAN *MILLET*; ARMENIAN REVOLUTIONARY FEDERATION; ARMENIAN REVOLUTIONARY MOVEMENT; KOMITAS; MUSA DAGH; SIAMANTO; SOCIAL DEMOCRATIC HNCHAKIAN PARTY; TEKEYAN, VAHAN; VAN; VARUZIIAN, DANIEL; ZOHRAB, KRIKOR.

ARMENIAN KINGDOM. The ancient and medieval Armenian state. Only the legendary origins of the Armenian kingdom are known.

Even so it can be dated with considerable accuracy in light of the historical context in which the narrative is told. The Armenian tradition recalled Paruyr the son of Skayordi as the first to reign in Armenia and to acquire the status of royalty. This occurred at a time coinciding with the breakdown of the Urartian state under the pressure of invading Scythians and Medes, who, more significantly dealt a final blow to Urartu's rival, Assyria, in 612 B.C. The international recognition of his kingship by the prevailing power of the day distinguished Paruyr above others in Armenia and the alliance he appears to have forged with the Median king Phraortes (655–633 B.C.) against the Assyrian king Sardanapal or Ashurbanipal (668–627 B.C.) secured his title. The novelty of his lineage and, hence, the value of the external acclamation of royalty are underlined by his patronymic that betrays a Scythian ancestry, as it means the son of Saka, or Shaka, as the Armenians and Iranians called the Scythians. That the Medes considered Paruyr for such elevation also indicates that he exercised considerable influence and already commanded forces significant in prowess as to draw their attention.

All these developments point to the establishment of a new political entity emerging from the fusion of the multiethnic complex of the Armenian highlands in the late Urartian period when the central power of the Urartian kings waned and new peoples of the Aryan, or Iranian, branch of the Indo-European speakers, such as the Medes and Scythians, entered the scene. Their convergence with the early Armenians, themselves of Indo-European extraction, and long contesting Urartian rule, occurred at a point in history when the ancient states of the Near East created by Semitic peoples were replaced by a new set of political formations. The beginnings of the ancient Armenian kingdom may therefore be dated at about the middle of the seventh century B.C. and the founding of that state attributed to Paruyr, described as a valiant prince raised to the splendor and title of royalty.

The Armenian tradition attributed Paruyr descent from Hayk, the eponymous patriarch of the Armenians. By the time the Armenians began recording their own history in the fifth century A.D., only the faintest memory remained of men whose names were ranked among the antecedents intervening between the historic Paruyr and the mythic Hayk. Modern archeology and the study of ancient epigraphy have rewritten early Armenian history and reconstructed the outlines of Armenia's remote ethnography, though far be it from retrieving a complete royal genealogy. Much more certain, however, is the fact that kingship in the Armenian highlands had origins older than that recalled even in legend. Paruyr may have secured himself a place in the memory of the Armenians because of the exceptional convergence that his rise to royal dignity indicated. His reign may actually have been the point of renewal of an even more ancient kingdom. To begin with, a long line of Urartian kings already claimed sovereignty over the Armenian highlands from their center in the **Van** basin. They were the dominant figures from the ninth to the sixth century B.C. If it were true that Paruyr's legitimacy as a sovereign was recognized by the Medes, it would have been a political act designed to counterbalance Urartian power and check its strength at its source, for the lands over which Paruyr arguably ruled were parts of southwestern Armenia, while the center of the Urartian state lay to its east.

In the legend of Ara the Handsome and the Assyrian queen Semiramis, Armenians recalled a trace of the Urartian monarchy, and the stories from such a remote past handed down orally across a dozen centuries merged this distinct kingdom with the ancestry of the Armenians. Contemporaries, however, were much more impressed by Urartian might and its kings left a clear record of their accomplishments in cuneiform inscriptions, indecipherable by the time Armenians were writing down the recollections of their royal house. In addition, the Urartian monarchs proclaimed themselves by the epithet 'king of kings,' clearly indicating a hierarchy within their own realm where the Urartian sovereigns lorded over regions whose governors were local claimants of royal stature. The Urartian monarch's imperial title was no idle boast as attested by Assyrian, and even earlier Hittite, records, which from the 13th century B.C., in their military encounters with the inhabitants of the Armenian highlands, spoke of kings governing tribal confederations, one notably being the Arme-Shupria, who, along with the Mushki, are believed to have been Indo-European, and thereby the earliest recorded forebears of the Armenians. That Urartu itself started as a composite state is verified by the appearance of 23 kings in the field of battle when the Assyrian king Tiglath-Pilescr I (1114–1076 B.C.) invaded the land of Nairi as the Urartians called their country. Hence Paruyr was heir to an even more archaic tradition of kingship dating back to the earliest Armenian-speakers in the highlands whose customs of self-governance the

Urartians did not root out. If anything, they appear to have accommodated them, for the Mushki apparently left their name in the city and surrounding region of Mush (pronounced Moosh) at the eastern end of the Van basin. As for the legacy of the Arme, it is self-evident in the name they gave an entire, and still living, people.

The Armenian account also vaguely recalled what appears to have been an even older tradition of royalty in the invocation of descent for Paruyr from Torgom (Torgoma in the genitive form), reproducing interestingly enough probable reference to Beth-togarmah (house of Togarma) in Genesis, the earliest book of the Hebrew Bible. Even more curiously and seemingly hinting at a close historical relationship, the biblical references cite Togarmah and Ashkanaz as brothers, and grandsons of Japheth (Hapet in Armenian), with Ashkanaz being the Hebrew appellation of Scythian, or more properly, Shaka. The association of Togarmah with the self-governing city of Til Garimmu, mentioned by Hittites and Assyrians, just to the west of the Euphrates, and dating back to the second half of the second millennium B.C. gives some credence to the theory of the eastward migration of the proto-Armenians across Asia Minor, as well as the tradition of an archaic kingship.

Kingship and kingdom, however, ought not to be confused. The Armenian tradition, for all of its vaunting of patriarchal ancestors and legendary kings took account of the geopolitical framework in which Armenian kings governed, for it noted as well that these royal figures held their crowns by the sanction of emperors who appointed them as prefects, governors, or satraps. In the long course of ancient history, by retaining a line of indigenous kings the ancient Armenians reserved the potential sovereignty of their country and in between the coming and going of external suzerains gradually expanded their dominion to incorporate the entire Armenian plateau thereby making their state coterminous with the geographic unity of the highlands.

Whether Paruyr reigned independently or not remains an open question. Whether the relationship with the Medes remained that of an ally or became that of a tributary is also open to speculation as Phraortes's successor Cyaxares established an empire stretching westward from Media in northern Iran into the heart of Asia Minor, reaching its limits at the Halys (Kizilirmak) River where the Lydians stopped their further expansion in 585 B.C. Such an empire would have included Armenia. The evidence that Paruyr's heirs or successors continued to wear the crown of Armenia is connected to the reign of another legendary king, namely Yervand Sakavakiats (Orontes the Short-lived) dated in the sixth century, who may have given rise to the first recorded Armenian royal dynasty, that of the **Yervanduni**, also called Orontid from the Orontes of Greek records. By 550 B.C., however, the Persians, under their Achaemenid dynasty that had overrun Media, also absorbed Armenia.

It was in relation to, and under the aegis of, the Achaemenids that the Yervanduni flourished. For one, the legitimacy of their title to royalty appears to have been honored. If anything, their stature may have even become more elevated. Ancient sources mention the Yervanduni as son-in-laws of the Achaemenids. Part of the explanation for the marriage of imperial princesses to the satrap of a remote province of the Persian realm famous for its forbidding climate was likely located in the recognition by the Achaemenids of the titular kingship of the Yervanduni. Descendants of the Yervanduni reigning in the neighboring kingdom of Commagene in the first century B.C. lauded their Achaemenid ancestry as a point of distinction. They upheld the sovereignty of their small state by relying on the presumed legitimacy derived from their Achaemenid heritage in order to compete with **Artashesian**, Seleucid, and Roman power all converging along the Euphrates in Asia Minor.

Second, if anything, this close relationship between the Iranian imperial house and the Armenian royal family appears to have secured the continuity of the Yervanduni dynasty, and, with that, given occasion for the increasing centralization of political power in Armenia. This may have been the case, as Yervanduni authority appears to have gone uncontested. When Achaemenid power waned under the blow of Alexander's armies in the late fourth century B.C., the Yervanduni consolidated the Armenian kingdom in the highlands. The relocation of their center of power from the Van basin to the **Arax River** valley, with the founding of the new capital city of **Armavir,** points to the expansion of the Yervanduni realm and the comparative ease with which they extended their authority. The insistence of **Artashes I** (189–160 B.C.) on his Yervanduni origins underscores the importance of the legitimizing principle of lineage. The seeming intradynastic struggle that preceded Artashes' rise to power stresses the importance of continuity. The account glosses over the usurpation of power by a junior, but more assertive, representative of the royal house from the senior line of succession that reproduced the hallowed royal name of Yervand, which terminates with the rise of Artashes.

If the Yervanduni period with its rudimentary administration, indirect government, absence of bureaucracy, and reliance on local mechanisms of command and control reflected the ideological outlook of the Achaemenid political system that absorbed Armenia as a tributary and a satrapy, the Artashesian period is a reflection of quite the opposite. The entire thrust of the Artashesian political program banked on the exploitation of the economic resources and military potential of the country. This outlook is attributable to the new cultural framework of Hellenism and the values animating a more dynamic political philosophy. If the Achaemenids had come to personify the Near Eastern imperial status quo, Alexander and his Greek and Macedonian heirs represented a wholly new outlook, the notion that the state was not mere inheritance enacted through a series of customs, obligations, and understandings, but a means of governance that could be directed toward larger goals through the strength of visionary leadership. That Artashes I began his career as an appointee of Antiochus the Great (223–187 B.C.), the Seleucid heir of Alexander yearning to recreate the great empire, only to smash his forces and dreams against the steadily advancing wall of Roman imperialism in Asia Minor, is testament to a relationship placing the future Armenian king in direct contact with the achievements and risks of political ambition. With Artashes the concept of the state as an instrument of policy emerges in bold outline. With Artashes, therefore, the customary monarchy of the Yervanduni became the kingdom of Armenia Major and afforded clear legitimacy and complete sovereignty. Whether done knowingly or resulting as a distant byproduct, by delineating the empire of Antiochus, the Romans undermined Seleucid claims to Armenia, itself based on Alexander's claim to the entire Persian realm, although Macedonian armies bypassed Armenia completely on their march to India.

Even so, the fluctuating fortunes of Armenia are revealed by the fact that Artashes's most famous descendent, **Tigran II the Great** (95–55 B.C.), was released from the Parthian court to assume the Armenian crown, the Parthians having earlier re-established Iranian dominion over the Near East and influence over Armenia. The Parthians too recognized the legitimacy of the Armenian kingdom, and their policy of crowning their former hostage and protégé was intended to secure a friendly patron-client arrangement with a smaller but strategic neighbor. Quite evidently the Parthians did not anticipate that they had let loose a lion from his cage. With Tigran's unification of Armenia, the topography of the Armenian kingdom was secured and the permanence of its monarchy guaranteed. Though his expansionist gambit was checked by the Romans, Tigran's lasting legacy rested in the fact that, whether surrounded or divided, the Armenian kingdom endured for nearly another five hundred years. Despite attempts at annexation by Romans, and later Sasanids from Iran, when the two great empires virtually divided the known world betwixt them, reluctantly they continued to agree that Armenia should remain a distinct and separate monarchy. That the Arsacid dynasty of Parthian Iran should aspire to control Armenia by enthroning one of its own after the expiration of the Artashesian dynasty in the first century A.D. is further attestation of continued international recognition of Armenia's formal sovereignty. The indigenization of the Arsacid as the **Arshakuni** dynasty, and its survival in Armenia when the senior Arsacid line occupying the imperial throne of Iran was overthrown by the Sasanid dynasty in 224, also attests to the endurance of the state.

The interminable wars of the Romans and Iranians took their toll on Armenia. Conceding its peripheral regions to imperial control, the Armenian kingdom surrendered territories external to the Armenian plateau and retreated into the interior space of the highlands. Even defending a smaller state, however, proved beyond the resources of the central monarchy alone, and the Arshakuni period witnessed the emergence of the great landed aristocracy of Armenia, known as the **nakharar** class. The compensatory role played by the nakharar order in Armenia's political life more than made up for the deficiencies derived from the eventual abolition of the monarchy and the discontinuation of the Arshakuni line. After two centuries of vigorous and bloody contest the Armenian political system reckoned with the irreconcilable hostility of Sasanid Iran toward Arshakuni rule in Armenia. The long drawn-out conflict also demonstrated the capacity of the native political order, the nakharar system, undergirding the Armenian monarchy, to withstand the cost of constant military vigilance. The Roman-Iranian conflict over Armenia regularly drained the monarchy despite internal and external efforts to buttress it as most explicitly demonstrated in the exceptional reign of **Trdat/Tiridates IV** (298–330) who adopted Christianity as the state religion of

Armenia in the early fourth century. Domestic political power in the process devolved to the sturdy nakharar families whose own dynastic continuity surpassed that of the royal lines. This devolution was very evident in the late Arshakuni period when the **Mamikonian** nakharar house exercised regency in the Armenian kingdom when their services as commanders-in-chief became indispensable to the state, and to the weakening monarchy, by then frequently inherited by minors or younger crowned heads.

When the ancient Armenian kingdom finally expired in 428 with the removal of the last Arshakuni, Artashes VI, from the throne, the Armenian monarchy had been in existence for over a thousand years. In one form or another a line of kings had reigned in Armenia, and with this aspiration for continuity through monarchy, an Armenian state in the form of a kingdom regularly afforded international recognition, even if on occasion reduced to an autonomous client, tributary, or vassal.

By the fifth century the notion of Armenia as a distinct political entity was so thoroughly grounded that the concept of its political statehood was not lost even when the monarchy expired. While the men at the head of the state after 428 were imperial appointees, nevertheless, rarely were they mere officials of a central government. Viceroys, called *marzpan* in the Sasanid era, many of the viceroys being Armenian nakharars, oversaw the country. Whenever the Eastern Roman Empire happened to seize Armenia from the Iranians, an appointee by Constantinople, regularly a nakharar, often went by the title of 'Prince of Armenia.' The Arabs who entered the country in the mid-seventh century negotiated its occupation with the last prince of Armenia appointed by the Byzantines, Theodore Rshtuni, another Armenian nakharar, and who also kept his office after Armenia's initial submission to the Arabs. The title, subsequently raised to a true office by the Arabs in the Abbasid period, and even augmented in dignity by being designated 'Prince of Princes' was assigned to the **Bagratuni** nakharar family, who thereupon, under the command of **Ashot I** (884–890), restored the Armenian monarchy from the substantive residue of the ancient Armenian state.

The Armenian kingdom ruled by the Bagratuni constituted a smaller polity than the Artashesian state. Other Armenian dynasties of nakharar origin, such as the **Ardsruni** and **Siuni**, however, recovered additional territories from Arab rule, and created more Armenian-governed states in the highlands. Altogether the medieval monarchies, with the Bagratuni at their center holding the privilege and title of kings of Armenia, virtually recovered the late Arshakuni kingdom. As disruptive an era as the Arab occupation was, which lasted over two centuries, it did not erase the concept of statehood from the political beliefs of the Armenians. Rather, within the framework of the Arab empire, and within the enduring structure of the Armenian nakharar system, the notion of Armenian statehood persisted until fully restored. Notably the two centuries of Bagratuni ascendancy in Armenia marked the apogee of Armenian cultural creativity as exemplified by the royal capital of **Ani**. The reduction of the Armenian states by the Byzantines and later Seljuk Turks in the 11th century did not extinguish the aspiration for statehood either. The Zakarian nakharar house basically restored the Armenian Bagratuni state as an appanage of the Georgian Bagratuni kingdom in whose service they recovered the Armenian lands and for which they governed Armenia as viceroys. It took the brutality attendant to the Mongol invasions in the early 13th century effectively to undermine the political order across Armenia.

While they did so in the highlands, the Mongols recognized the legitimacy of another Armenian kingdom, the one founded by the **Rubenian** and **Hetumian** nakharar families in Cilicia, and secured by their scion, **Levon/Leo I** (1199–1219). By this extraordinary experiment Armenians transported their statehood, recreating it ex nihilo, on the Mediterranean, and proclaimed it the Armenian kingdom. This entity lasted until 1375. Thereafter none held the crown and title of king of Armenia and was so recognized by the Armenian people.

From the mid-seventh century B.C. until 1375, irrespective of its size or its exact location, an Armenian kingdom existed, or the Armenian people were engaged in a struggle to preserve and restore it whenever the monarchy toppled or Armenia was occupied by an outside power. Regardless of the gradations of its sovereignty, for the Armenians, the kingdom represented the legitimate manifestation of their right of self-governance. Viewed from this perspective, the two thousand-years span of time during which an Armenian kingdom was in existence exhibits exceptional continuity in the political history of a people. This continuity is all the more exceptional when the perpetual contestation of Armenian statehood by imperial powers is taken into account. If the heritage of the Urartian kingdom and the earlier archaic monarchies of the tribal period is also taken into account, the tradition of self-governance in the Armenian highlands may be traced back at least an additional half millennium.

ARMENIAN LANGUAGE. Armenian is an Indo-European language. The Armenians call themselves *Hay* and their language *Hayeren*. Armenian was first written in the early fifth century. With a literature spanning 16 centuries, there is a rich record of the Armenian language and of its complicated history. The Armenian language, however, is at least twice as old as its earliest writing. Proto-Armenian was being spoken in the second millennium B.C. and was introduced in the Armenian highlands by the 12th century B.C. Armenian forms an independent and isolated branch of the Indo-European family of languages. Its closest correlatives are Greek and possibly Phrygian, an ancient language spoken in central Anatolia, of which scant record survives. Despite some common morphological features, the kinship with the Hellenic tongue is actually quite remote. This distance is explained by extensive changes wrought in the Armenian language because of its geographical location.

The phonology and lexical inventory of Armenian have undergone close approximation with languages spoken in neighboring countries. Armenian bears analogies with the Georgian sound system, a language belonging to the unrelated Caucasian family, and has extensively borrowed vocabulary from Iranian, a branch of Indo-European but structurally removed from Armenian. Also, early Armenian was spoken by a tribal population who associated closely with other peoples in the Armenian highlands who themselves spoke unrelated languages. The most important was Urartian. Of the Hurrian language family, which has not survived into modern times, Urartian was spoken by people concentrated around **Lake Van.** Having forged the first formal state on the plateau in the ninth century B.C., the Urartians spread their language northward and eastward. In the process their imprint on the toponymy of the country was lasting. The breakdown of the Urartian state in the sixth century contributed to the easier spreading of Armenian from the western parts of Armenia along the Euphrates to all parts of the uplands. By the second century B.C. Armenian had become the universal language of the population of ancient Armenia, an observation noted by the Roman historian Strabo, at a time coinciding with the political consolidation and unification of the country under the **Artashesian** dynasty. In the post-Urartian era, Iran exercised suzerainty over Armenia. Close political and cultural relations were established between Armenia and Iran, a pattern that more or less prevailed for the next 12 hundred years in varying degrees of intensity. Whatever the nature of the relationship at any specific time between the sixth century B.C. and the seventh century A.D., the Armenian language steadily absorbed and modified a vast vocabulary of Iranian provenance, prevalently from Parthian. Terminology describing the political and social system of ancient Armenia specially reflected this influence, as well as underscored the commonalities of values between the two societies, particularly at the level of governing elites.

The invention of the Armenian alphabet by **Mesrop Mashtots** in 405 led to the rapid spread of literacy and the formation of what became known as Classical Armenian. This language was based on the idiom of the royal court and the speech of the central provinces of Armenia. The alphabet of 36 phonemes, containing 28 consonants and 8 vowels, devised by Mashtots was so well suited to Armenian that it has remained intact since the fifth century, but for the later addition of two letters to record sounds not present in the language during the time of Mashtots. Classical Armenian was a highly inflected language with an elaborate system of declensions that retained all seven Indo-European noun cases: nominative, accusative, genitive, dative, locative, ablative, and instrumental. In this and other respects the grammar of Classical Armenian bears similarities with that of Classical Greek. In the course of its evolution since the fifth century, however, Armenian went through three different stages. Old, or Classical, Armenian was in use from the fifth through the eighth century. During this time of tremendous literary activity, the language developed rapidly with the infusion of vocabulary and phraseology to give expression to the expanding realm of cultural, religious, and intellectual interests and pursuits. The simple elegance of early Classical or Mesropian Armenian that drew heavily on the common oral culture of the fifth century, in the hands of gifted authors writing in the second half of the same century acquired florid eloquence capable of communicating the range of high sentiment. In the following two centuries, intellectual curiosity and a commitment to rigorous and truthful translation engendered numerous efforts to expand the scope of linguistic expression and create the literary flexibility necessary to render into Armenian from Greek Christian theological exegeses,

Neo-Platonist and Aristotelian philosophical treatises, Alexandrine scientific works, or to prepare original compositions on these subjects in Armenian. Some of the translations were done so faithfully according to consistent rules of translation developed by Armenian devotees of Greek philosophical thought that reasonable reproduction of them in the original Classical Greek may be attempted by reverse translation from Armenian to Greek. So extensive was the production of the Hellenophile schools dedicated to translation that some ancient works no longer extant in their original language survive only in Armenian.

While some of the new terminology entered the common vocabulary, by the ninth century the vernacular had evolved away from the Classical tongue, and Middle Armenian increasingly came into use. Political and cultural changes explain the emergence of Middle Armenian. The Arab occupation was the most profound of these changes. It introduced a new governing class speaking a language heretofore not heard in the Armenian highlands and bearing the stamp of the new religion of Islam. Armenian earlier had absorbed vocabulary from neighboring Semitic languages, primarily Syriac, the earliest language through which Christianity had first spread in southern Armenia. Arabic appears to have contributed commercial terms attesting to the importance of international trade at the time.

On the other hand, it was not so much the influence of Arabic as much as the fragmentation of Armenia's political structure during the period of Arab occupation that explains the steady departure from Old Armenian. Equally, the regular emulation of the literary models created in the early classical era also explains the growing differentiation between the literary and the vernacular languages. Medieval Armenian writers and learned society in general continued to look upon Classical Armenian as the proper language of literature, whereas the populace remained unaffected and unexposed to the literature being written and copied in monastic scriptoria and court chancelleries. The literature of the **Bagratuni** era betrayed this growing dichotomy. Middle Armenian, however, attained the status of state language with the formation of the Cilician Armenian kingdom. The separation of Cilicia from Armenia proper also meant that the literature that flourished in this new environment articulated but one variant of a language increasingly tending toward the development of dialects in the absence of an embracing or dominant central state.

Isolated pockets of Middle Armenian survived right down to the 20th century in the recesses of the Cilician Mountains in places such as **Musa Dagh**, Zeitun, and Hajen (Hadjin). Speakers in the latter town simply called their dialect *Hajno lezu*, the language of Hajen, so completely inscrutable it had become to other speakers of rustic Armenian. By the 15th century the earliest forms of Modern Armenian were making their appearance. In the 17th century the modern vernacular was widespread, a form of speech even more variegated than Middle Armenian and eventually spoken in more than a hundred dialects among Armenians living by this time in places far removed from Armenia and Cilicia and from each other, places such as Iran, Russia, Poland, and Turkey. Moreover Modern Armenian had undergone a fundamental transformation in its system of declensions moving from inflection to agglutination, a principle common to Turkish, and conceivably occurring under its widespread usage by the ruling elements in the areas inhabited by Armenians. Modern Armenian, however, came into its own only in the 19th century with the formal adoption of the vernacular as the language of literature and literacy. This process was initiated by the **Mekhitarian** fathers in Venice and Vienna who began the cultivation of the Armenian language in the 18th century with the desire of reviving classical usages unencumbered by centuries of changes and accretions from all surrounding languages. The objective had the opposite effect, for, by restoring Classical Armenian, it became all the more evident that it was a completely dead language that could no longer be easily acquired by pupils whose native speech was the modern vernacular. With the appreciation that the literary, so-called *grabar* in Armenian, stood far apart from the vernacular, the *ashkharhabar* or worldly Armenian, and would not be infused back into modern literary usage, the trend reversed toward cultivating the vernacular and developing it into a consistent and regulated language.

In this effort, beyond the equipment of scholarship, the Mekhitarians had one more instrument of modernization in their arsenal. The first Armenian book was printed in 1512 in Venice. The first printed Armenian Bible was brought to press in 1666 in Amsterdam. These and other attempts in Istanbul and elsewhere were short-lived until the Mekhitarians acquired a press in 1776 and began a publishing enterprise that continues to the present. Very effective in the early decades of the 19th century in promoting literacy, the Mekhitarian program was soon overtaken by more localized publishing ventures situated in the major urban centers of Armenian life.

The rapid increase in literacy with the modernization of Armenian society in the 19th century required the standardization of Modern Armenian. As Armenia was divided between the Russian and Ottoman Empires, two distinct vernacular dialects emerged as the normative language of the Armenians. Even though the two dialects and their variants were spoken in Armenia proper, their literary development occurred in the main beyond Armenia in Tbilisi and Istanbul respectively where the emerging Armenian bourgeoisie was largely concentrated. By the second half of the 19th century Eastern and Western Armenian were established as the two vernaculars. Though mutually intelligible, Eastern Armenian preserved classical phonology while Western Armenian demonstrated sound loss among closely related consonants. An abundance of literature was created in both dialects and soon poets, novelists, and dramatists producing original works ranked among the influential figures of the modern age. They shaped and refined the Armenian language and their growing audiences acquired a common medium of communication and a sense of shared cultural identity to the point where the educated classes came to speak in the vernacular being spread through publication and an inspiring native literature, all this in the absence of a sponsoring state.

It was at this time also that the scientific study of Armenian was introduced. The Mekhitarians beginning with **Mekhitar Sebastatsi** had produced a string of grammar books, dictionaries, and historical studies on the Armenian language. These works of scholarship eventually came to the attention of European philologists. In 1875 the German linguistic Heinrich Hübschmann identified the independent character of Armenian in the Indo-European family of languages. The noted French linguist Antoine Meillet further elaborated on the position of Armenian and clarified its relationship with Iranian. Their student, **Hrachia Ajarian**, analyzed the Armenian dialects and uncovered virtually the entire etymology of the Armenian language.

The destruction of Western Armenia and the exile of the Armenian people during World War I assured the extinction of many dialects and brought about the wide dispersion of the Armenian language. As Western Armenian ceased to be spoken in its original homeland, by the mid–20th century it was flourishing again in new centers such as

Beirut, Cairo, and Paris. At the end of the 20th century Western Armenian was being spoken in communities large and small across the Middle East, Europe, Africa, North and South America, and Australia. Its future was in question, however, in environments dominated by mass media transmitted in local national languages. In contrast, Eastern Armenian was secured state status with the formation of the Republic of Armenia in 1918 and has remained the state language since. Eastern Armenian was subjected to extensive modification and became heavily influenced by Russian especially during the Soviet era. New loan words, mostly technical, others political or ideological, entered through Russian. Furthermore, in the 1920s, in a presumed attempt to simplify spelling as a means for accelerating literacy, Mesropian orthography, adhered to since its introduction in the fifth century, and diligently applied by the Mekhitarians for Modern Armenian, was altered. For the first time different spelling rules were introduced for Eastern Armenian. Western Armenian remained unaffected by this state-imposed modification. This alteration in orthography even introduced a division within the Eastern Armenian dialect. While Soviet Armenian orthography was enforceable across the Soviet Union, Armenians in Iran and farther east who also spoke in the Eastern Armenian vernacular retained the Mesropian orthography to which they were accustomed. Eastern Armenian is spoken in the Republic of Armenia, in **Nagorno Karabagh**, Georgia, Russia, and Iran, and in the second half of the 20th century was introduced to North America, first by persons displaced during World War II who emigrated from the Soviet Union to the United States and later by immigrants from Armenia proper.

Of the three and a half million persons estimated to be living in Armenia in the early 1990s, 97 percent spoke Armenian. Of the million persons of Armenian ancestry in other parts of the former Soviet Union, no more than two-thirds spoke Armenian. Of the half million or more Armenians across the Middle East, most continue to speak Armenian. In Europe and the Americas, where half a million and 1.5 million persons of Armenian ancestry are respectively estimated to reside, less than half know the language and its usage in speech is only occasional. Many Armenians, however, are at the very least bilingual, and Armenian remains a common tongue allowing for communication across a community of speakers who at the end of the 20th century encircled the globe.

ARMENIAN MASSACRES (1894–1896). The first near-genocidal series of atrocities committed against the Armenian population of the Ottoman Empire. Also known as the Hamidian Massacres, they were carried out during the reign of Abdul-Hamid (Abdulhamit) II (1876–1909), the last sultan effectively to rule over the Turkish state. The massacres broke out in the summer of 1894 in the remote region of Sasun in southern Armenia, where the government relied on the excuse of Armenian resistance to Kurdish encroachment into the last recesses of the mountains to order the sacking of the alpine hamlets. The incident resulted in strong Armenian protests against the sultan's brutal policies and European interventions to quell further disturbances by persuading the Ottoman government to adopt reforms for the Armenian-populated provinces. The police responded to a demonstration held in Istanbul in September 1895 by Armenian political organizations, which sought to pressure the government and the European Powers to implement the promised administrative reforms, by letting loose a massacre in the capital city. Thereupon, beginning without provocation in the city of Trebizond on the Black Sea, and in a pattern indicating a premeditated plan, a series of massacres spread south through nearly every major Armenian-inhabited town of the empire. It culminated in the single worst atrocity in those months with the burning of the Armenian cathedral of Urfa (ancient Edessa) within whose walls some 3,000 Armenians had taken refuge during the siege of their neighborhood. To a last desperate attempt by Armenian revolutionaries to draw the attention of the world by seizing in Constantinople the European-owned Ottoman Bank in August 1896, the government responded by unleashing wholesale reprisals during which five to six thousand Armenians were killed in the space of three days within sight of the European embassies.

The massacres marked a new threshold of violence in the Ottoman Empire, especially because they occurred in peacetime with none of the exigencies of war invoked as justification for summary action. Their ferocity reflected the sultan's determination to dissuade the Armenians from entertaining any notions of seeing reforms introduced under Western pressure. They were also designed to strike a severe blow to Armenian efforts to organize politically by undermining their expectations and the sense of self-reliance they hoped to develop in order to cope with the aggravated disorder and misrule in the eastern provinces of the empire. Estimates of the dead run from 100,000 to

300,000. Tens of thousands fled the country. Thousands of others were forcibly converted to Islam. The associated plunder of homes and businesses economically ruined countless families, and the destitute counted in the hundreds of thousands. The conflicting interests of the European states, the steady support of the sultan by Kaiser Wilhelm II of Germany, and the reactionary policies of Tsar Alexander III in Russia, all adduced to neutralize the capacity of the Great Powers to hold in check the brutal autocracy of Abdul-Hamid. Labeled infidels by their Turkish overlords and Muslim neighbors, the Armenians remained second-class citizens expressly denied equal protection of the law. The impunity with which the entire episode of systematic massacres was carried out exposed the serious vulnerability of the Armenian population as the Ottoman Empire went into further decline. It also revealed the absence of resolve among the Western states for any kind of humanitarian intervention sufficient to remedy the problems described at the time as the Armenian Question.

Recalled by the Armenians as the "Great Massacres" and described in the literature of the time as the "Armenian Massacres," the atrocities of the 1890s are now often called the Hamidian Massacres to distinguish them from the greater atrocities associated with the 1915 **Armenian Genocide**. The Hamidian Massacres verified the capacity of the Turkish state to carry out a systematic policy of murder and plunder against a minority population and to provide immunity to all parties associated with the crimes in the face of international protest. In retrospect, it had set a precedent all of whose elements, short of organized deportation, would be reproduced during the Armenian Genocide. *See also* ADANA MASSACRE; ARMENIAN *MILLET*; ARMENIAN REVOLUTIONARY FEDERATION; ARMENIAN REVOLUTIONARY MOVEMENT; PASDERMADJIAN, GAREGIN; PAPKEN SUNI.

ARMENIAN *MILLET*. The institution through which the Ottoman Empire governed the Armenians. *Millet* means community or nation in Turkish. The Armenian millet in the Ottoman Empire was an institution devised by the sultans to govern the Christian population adhering to the Monophysite Churches. The millet system extended internal autonomy in religious and civil matters to the non-Muslim communities while introducing a mechanism for direct administrative responsibility to the state in matters of taxation. The reach of the

Armenian millet expanded and contracted with the changing territorial dimensions of the Ottoman state. Originally the Armenian millet was defined as a broad confessional group rather than narrowly as a denomination re-enforcing ethnic distinction. Not only Armenians of all persuasions, which by the 19th century included Orthodox, Catholic, and Protestant, were treated by the Ottoman government as constituents of the Armenian millet, other Oriental Christian denominations, which were excluded from the Greek millet, also were included in the Armenian millet.

The evolution of parallel Armenian and Greek millets has led to the proposition that the Armenian millet was introduced by the Ottoman government as a way of denying the Greek millet, and its leadership in the form of the Orthodox patriarch of Istanbul, governance over the entire Christian community in the Ottoman state. Although Ottoman political theory divided the populace along the lines of the three principal religions, Islam, Christianity, and Judaism, the Christian community was further divided to differentiate between the two branches of Christianity, monophysite and duophysite, and to foster competition within the sizable Christian population of the empire. From the standpoint of the overall system, the Oriental Christian communities related to the Ottoman regime through the intermediary of the Armenian ecclesiastical leadership in the capital city of Istanbul. In practice direct communication with local Ottoman governors as the intercessors with the central authorities was more common. Nor did the system necessarily encompass the entire Armenian population as its settlements entered the Ottoman Empire during the period of expansion. In the remoter parts of the empire, the reach of the millet system was tenuous, and communities operated on the basis of inter-relations traditional to the region. Only in the 19th century did the purview of the Armenian millet attain influence comprehensive to the Armenian population of the Ottoman Empire. However, by that point the Ottomans had agreed to the further fractionalization of the Armenian millet by extending formal recognition, in 1831 and 1857 respectively, to the Catholic and Protestant millets, both of which were predominantly Armenian.

The history of the Armenian millet as an imperial institution is more properly the history of the Armenian patriarchate of Istanbul. Though in the strictest sense an ecclesiastical office functioning within the framework of the **Armenian Apostolic Church**, the patriarchate was created by the Ottomans and its occupant served at the pleasure of the Sublime Porte. There was no precedent of an Armenian bishopric in Istanbul predating the Ottoman occupation of the city. The early history of the patriarchate is barely known. Armenian tradition attributes its origins to the settlement of the Armenians of Bursa in Istanbul upon the command of Mehmet the Conqueror and of the designation in 1461 of the Armenian bishop of Bursa, named Hovakim, as patriarch of this community by the sultan himself. During the first century and a half of its existence, the importance of the office was restricted to the city and the immediate environs of Istanbul. The rapid turnover of bishops deprived the patriarchate of any political or practical significance to the Armenians at large.

The patriarchate emerged as an agency central to the Armenian millet structure in the 18th century. Three factors appear to have contributed to the consolidation of ecclesiastical and political control by the patriarchate: the growth of the Armenian population in and around Istanbul, which had been an area at some distance from the centers of Armenian demographic concentration in the Ottoman Empire, which was mostly in eastern and central Anatolia and the northern coast of the Black Sea; the strengthening of the economic role of the growing community in local trade, international commerce, and the finances of the government; and finally the appearance of primates who commanded respect and expanded the role of the patriarchate in Armenian communal life. The key figure was Hovhannes Kolot whose tenure lasted from 1715 to 1741. Thereafter the Armenian patriarch of Istanbul was regarded as the most important figure in the Armenian Church despite the fact that within the hierarchy of the church itself other offices, such as that of the catholicos at **Edjmiadsin** in Persian, and subsequently Russian, Armenia, the catholicos at Sis in Cilicia, or the Armenian patriarch of Jerusalem, could claim historical and ecclesiastical seniority.

The commercial success of the Armenians was evidenced by the rise of the so-called amira class in Istanbul. Originally merchants, the amiras gained prominence mostly as *sarrafs*, bankers, who played a critical role in financing the empire's tax-farming system. For their services, the Duzian family, for example, were awarded management of the imperial mint. The **Balian** family held the post of chief architect to the sultan from 1750 until the end of the 19th century and was responsible for the construction of virtually all the imperial residences and palaces dating from this era. These Armenian notables put their stamp on the Armenian community of Istanbul when they also received license from their sovereign to establish educational centers, charitable institutions, hospitals, and churches.

Although their status was defined by their connection with the Ottoman system, the role of the amiras in the Armenian millet was determined by the influence they exercised over the Patriarchate. A conservative oligarchy by nature, nevertheless the amira presence underscored the growth of secular forces in Armenian society which soon derived their importance from their role in the economy of the city independent of the monarchy. Those very forces were further encouraged by the revival of interest in Armenian letters sponsored by the amiras.

The *Tanzimat* reforms from 1839 to 1876 unraveled the system of government on which the amiras depended. It also provided additional impetus to the growth of an Armenian middle class increasingly composed of smaller merchants, called *esnaf*, who demanded a voice in the management of the millet and the election of the patriarch. Soon popular sentiment called for the regulation of the election process and the adoption of a formal document prescribing the function and responsibilities of the patriarchate. A long drawn-out debate among conservative clergy and amiras, liberal-minded esnaf, and the press through the 1850s and 1860s resulted in the drafting of a so-called constitution for the Armenian millet. The compromise document was adopted on May 24, 1860, by an assembly consisting of laymen and churchmen. In effect thereafter, its formal approval by the Ottoman authorities took three more years and further modifications until adopted as the official Regulations of the Armenian millet. The Armenians called it their National Constitution and the rights and responsibilities spelled out in the document became the framework by which Armenians throughout the empire reorganized their communities. Affixing leadership of the millet in the Armenian Church, the National Constitution also guaranteed a role for the lay community and provided specific mechanisms for its participation at all levels of management.

The constitution also elevated the office of the patriarch to that of national leader with immediate responsibility in representing the concerns of the Armenian millet with the Sublime Porte. That proved a heavier burden than intended as the flock in the distant corners of the empire began to appeal more and more to the patriarch for relief from their woes at the hands of corrupt administrators and officials prone to violence. The patriarchate catalogued these problems and appealed to the resident ministers of the Great Powers to plead the Armenian case with the sultan. This problem of enhanced responsibility in the face of increasing unrest in the provinces while powerless to persuade the Sublime Porte in political matters seriously compromised the Patriarchate. Segments of the Armenian millet felt disenfranchised and adherents turned to the Catholic and Protestant millets for better protection. The Sublime Porte, on the other hand, scrutinized elections and appointments all the more closely in order to contain the rising tide of Armenian nationalism.

The millet system remained in place until the end of the empire. So did the patriarchate until its suspension in 1916 by the Young Turk government. Although many of the later patriarchs, such as **Mkrtich Khrimian**, **Nerses Varzhapetian**, Matteos Izmirlian, and **Maghakia Ormanian**, were very important figures, Armenian loyalties were already divided by the late 19th century. Political organizations vied for leadership in the Armenian community and the confessional basis of national organization faced serious competition from these and other sources. The patriarchate was restored in 1918 and its role reconfirmed by the Republic of Turkey. By that time, however, the Armenian bishop presided over a community whose congregates had been seriously reduced in numbers and mostly inhabited the city of Istanbul much as in the beginning centuries when the millet system was first introduced among the Armenians. As for the National Constitution, it remains a living document. Armenian communities throughout the world rely on its principles of mixed representation under ecclesiastical leadership in the organization and management of their now dispersed communities. *See also* ARMENIAN REVOLUTIONARY MOVEMENT.

ARMENIAN NATIONAL MOVEMENT (ANM). *Hayots Hamazkayin Sharzhum* (literally Armenian All-National, or Pan-National, Movement), commonly translated into English usage as the Armenian National Movement (ANM) or Pan-Armenian Movement (PAM). The ANM was formed in 1989 in **Yerevan**, Armenia, after a year of political ferment in the country growing out of the so-called **Karabagh Movement**. The short-term impetus of the ANM came from the arrest of the Karabagh Committee, the informal leadership of the popular movement that swept the country in February 1988, and the need stemming therefrom to consolidate the movement into a political process capable of negotiating with authorities both in **Yerevan** and Moscow. The membership of the Karabagh Committee changed during the course of the movement. Its principal figures were **Levon Ter-Petrossian**, **Vazgen Manukian**, Ashot Manucharian, Hambartsum Galstian, Vano Siradeghian, Babken Ararktsian, Rafayel Ghazarian, Davit Vardanian, and early on Igor Muradian.

The original Karabagh Movement arose spontaneously in support of the appeal of the **Nagorno Karabagh** Armenians to President Mikhail Gorbachev for the transfer of jurisdiction of the Nagorno Karabagh Autonomous Oblast (NKAO) from the Soviet Socialist Republic of Azerbaijan to the Soviet Socialist Republic of Armenia. The reluctance of Moscow authorities to satisfy the Armenian demands and the violent response in Azerbaijan mobilized the population of Armenia. Communist Party Chairman Mikhail Gorbachev ordered the arrest of the leading figures of the Karabagh Committee in the days following the devastating December 7, 1988, **Spitak Earthquake** as the committee attempted to lead the Armenian response to the emergency in view of the paralysis of the government. The incarceration and release some six months later galvanized the activists to form a popular front type organization. The leadership of the movement exclusively derived from the Armenian intelligentsia. Three professions seemed represented most: educators, physicist mathematicians, and philologist historians. Nevertheless, the movement drew on the strong support of the urban working class, and on occasion called up to a million people in demonstrations that were held regularly over the course of the first two years of activity.

The ANM advocated the unification of Armenia and Karabagh, the institution of popular democracy, political pluralism, a free market economy, and state sovereignty. Along with the Lithuanian movement Sajudis, the ANM was at the forefront in pressing the Communist Party to revise Soviet nationality policy and to increase republican authority. The ANM stopped short of advocating secession from the USSR, while capitalizing on the changes brought about with perestroika and glasnost. In the first open elections held for the Soviet Armenian Parliament in the first half of 1990, the Communists were democratically voted out of power and the ANM given a plurality of seats. With the support of other nationalist parties, this proved sufficient to give the ANM control of the government. It quickly embarked upon the process of privatizing the economy in Armenia.

Opposing the new federal treaty proposed by Gorbachev, and scrupulously following law and procedure according to the Soviet Constitution, the government organized the referendum on separate statehood held on September 21, 1991. With over 90 percent of the population voting in favor, the ANM lead the Armenians to independence. In the first post-independence parliamentary elections held in Armenia on July 5, 1995, the ANM secured a majority of seats in the new National Assembly. With the **president**, **prime minister**, and the chairman of the National Assembly members of the party, the ANM dominated the Armenian political scene until 1998. Its decline was rapid, however. As the 1999 parliamentary elections showed, the resignation of President Levon Ter-Petrossian the previous year had seriously weakened the ANM. The party garnered only 1 percent of the vote.

As for the members of the Karabagh Committee: Ter-Petrossian twice was elected president of Armenia; Manukian served a term as prime minister and another as defense minister and, parting company from the ANM, founded the **National Democratic Union** (NDU); Manucharian became Ter-Petrossian's national security advisor during the height of the Karabagh conflict and resigned over serious differences with the president; Galstian became mayor of Yerevan during Ter-Petrossian's first term as president, went into private business and was killed in 1994; Siradeghian became minister of internal affairs and eventually the focus of much controversy over corruption and other illegal activities resulting in his indictment on criminal charges in 1998; Ararktsian became speaker of the National Assembly; Ghazarian served as titular vice-president of Armenia in his capacity as the first non-Communist vice-chairman of the parliament in 1990–1991, then went into the opposition over the issue of the rule of law; Vardanian joined the NDU, was elected to parliament and served in its foreign affairs committee; Muradian remained an activist. *See also* COMMUNIST PARTY OF ARMENIA; ELECTIONS; POLITICAL PARTIES; STEPANAKERT.

ARMENIAN REVOLUTIONARY FEDERATION (ARF or Dashnak Party). *Hay Heghapokhakan Dashnaktsutiun,* popularly known as the *Dashnaktsutiun*, Dashnak Party for short. The ARF was founded in 1890 in Tbilisi, Georgia, then part of the Russian Empire, with the leadership of Kristapor Mikayelian (1859–1905), Stepan Zorian (1867–1919) known as Rostom, and Simon Zavarian (1866–1913). The initial focus of its operations was Western Armenia or so-called Turkish Armenia, the sector of historic Armenia in the Ottoman Empire. In the early 20th century it also began to organize seriously in Eastern Armenia in the Russian Empire, as well as in the Armenian communities across Russia, Turkey, and Iran. Between 1918 and 1920, during the period of the independent Republic of Armenia, its activities were centered in the new country. After Sovietization, the ARF moved abroad, first fleeing to Iran, and eventually settling in Beirut, Lebanon, whence it guided Armenian political life in the Middle East until the Lebanese civil war erupted in 1975.

The ARF was organized to gather and coordinate the efforts of numerous small groups of Armenians in the Caucasus region involved in revolutionary activity. Bringing together a literate elite, local activists, and peasant guerrillas into a single party was one of its principal achievements. With its leadership schooled in the Russian educational system as well as current revolutionary doctrine, nationalist, populist, and socialist, the ARF articulated the goals of the numerous strands of Armenian society into coherent collective national objectives.

With relieving the plight of the Armenians in the Ottoman provinces as its primary goal, the ARF concentrated on arming the population in the countryside to resist the arbitrary rule of Ottoman administrators. Eventually it resolved to oppose despotism at its source by planning to assassinate Abdul-Hamid (Abdulhamit) II (1876–1909). The overthrow of the sultan by the Young Turks and the restoration of the Ottoman Constitution in 1908 seemed to affirm that the struggle against the sultan's regime, despite the increased brutalization of the Armenian population by the army, police, and the Hamidiye corps, had been worth the cost.

Reluctant to divide its energy and its attention, the ARF had chosen to sidestep the problem of autocracy in the Russian Empire. The events leading up to the 1905 Revolution, however, precipitated the decision to oppose the tsar also as a despotic ruler who devised and implemented policies oppressive to the Armenians. Crossing that threshold proved decisive because the consequences of World War I compelled the ARF to reconsider its objectives. With the decimation of the Armenian population in the Ottoman Empire, the ARF goal of seeing a national home built out of the eastern provinces of Turkey was voided. The breakup of the tsarist empire instead provided an opportunity to develop the former Russian province of Yerevan, which was declared an independent republic, into the nucleus of an Armenian state. ARF members virtually ran the entire government of the Armenian republic. This close association had its drawbacks for the Armenian state. Western Powers were unsympathetic toward a government run by a party whose platform advocated socialism at a time when the Russian Revolution had resulted in the formation of the first socialist state in history. Conversely, its nationalist program made it a foe of Bolshevism and hence earned it the enmity of the Soviet regime. Banished from Soviet Armenia, the ARF assumed the mantle of a nationalist government-in-exile. When it reorganized in the **diaspora**, the ARF completely lost its Russian-Armenian character as it found a new basis for its existence among the exile communities in the Middle East mostly composed of the survivors of the former Armenian population of the Ottoman state.

Part of the success of the ARF was explained by the fact that in the period between 1890 and 1920 it attracted a sizable contingent of the Armenian intellectual elite. Whether as party members, advocates, or supporters, they created a huge body of literature. The practice was established by its founders, Kristapor Mikayelian, Stepan Zorian (Rostom), and Simon Zavarian. The party organ, *Droshak* (Banner), was the leading journal of Armenian political thought. During the independent republic many distinguished figures from Russian-Armenian society became associated with the party. **Avetis Aharonian**, famed as a writer, became president of the republic and traveled to Paris to negotiate with the Allies. **Alexander Khatisian**, one-time mayor of Tbilisi, also became president. Others who rose to prominence during this period, such as **Simon Vratzian**, **Nigol Aghbalian**, and Levon Shant, remained central figures in the Armenian diaspora and its endeavors to educate a new generation of Armenians in exile. The ARF also attracted numerous guerrilla leaders and front-line revolutionaries into its ranks. **Papken Suni** led the capture of the Ottoman Bank in 1896 in Istanbul. Men like **Andranik**, **Aram Manukian**, and Drastamard Kanayan, called Dro, led the organized armed defense of Armenian communities and of the Armenian republic. In the diaspora the ARF was less successful in finding the kind of charismatic leadership that once distinguished it as the leading political organization in Armenian society, and the evocation of past leadership became an important element in sustaining the organization's image and role in the diaspora.

From an organizational standpoint the ARF bridged two major chasms in late 19th and early 20th century Armenian society. It created an alliance between Turkish Armenians and Russian Armenians who had become divided by a boundary, and between the rural population and the urban population that inhabited completely separate spaces since the Armenian bourgeoisie lived outside the Armenian heartland. To maintain a network that spanned so widely both socially and geographically, the ARF developed a highly decentralized organization that empowered regional committees with the privilege of deciding policy.

Though based in the urban Armenian communities and deriving support from the lower and middle classes, the ARF program originally addressed principally the condition of the Armenians in the Turkish provinces and of the agrarian population in general. Beyond equal treatment before the law and structural reform in the Ottoman government, the ARF placed great emphasis on improving the lot of the Armenian farmers. An economic program therefore always formed a vital part of its doctrine. With many socialists among its ranks, the party as a whole was still slow to adopt socialism as party platform despite the ideological currency of socialism in Russia. Ideas of the kind seemed remote from Armenian reality in the distant provinces of the Ottoman and Russian provinces. Consequently, despite its urban base, the ARF did not agitate as strongly among industrial workers who tended to be drawn to Social Democratic groups, but rather concentrated on the program of national emancipation.

As a subject minority unequipped to resolve its own problems, in the judgment of the ARF the Armenians depended on the attention of the European Powers. Their sympathetic influence was required to compel the Ottomans to introduce reforms. This policy remained controversial throughout the period as outside powers involved themselves with the Armenian Question on their own timetable of interests and as the Ottoman government in its state of weakness looked upon the strategy with enormous suspicion. The wholesale persecution of the Armenians in the Ottoman Empire during World War I finally aligned the Western Powers on the side of the Armenian Republic. The Western failure to extend enough assistance to make a difference in preserving Armenian statehood, however, raised the question whether the ARF had not misplaced its trust.

The ARF regarded, and continues to regard, itself as a vanguard organization. In its early decades its membership consisted of professional revolutionaries who published its papers, organized its cells, manufactured weapons, led guerrilla operations, and briefly ran a government. Its constituency has not been restricted to any class because it derived its strength from its popular nationalist program. The ARF constituency remains the larger segment of the Armenian diaspora, but it no longer draws the same level of critical support from the professional class as its once did.

With its political mission defused by 1920, the ARF began to devote considerable attention to resurrecting Armenian communal life among the exile settlements. In this regard the ARF became the support system for a range of institutions in the diaspora in order to tend to the needs of newly formed communities. Schools, youth groups, athletic and social service organizations, and even cultural societies emerged from this effort. To name a few, the Armenian Youth Federation (AYF), the Armenian Relief Society (ARS), the Hamazkayin Cultural Association, the Hairenik publishing house founded back in 1899 in Boston, Massachusetts, to circumvent censorship in the home countries, and the once most important educational institution in the diaspora, the Neshan Palanjian Academy in Beirut, Lebanon, among many other schools, were all the products of this undertaking.

The emergence of a new post-Soviet independent Republic of Armenia in 1991 posed special challenges to the ARF that for long had sustained itself in the diaspora with the mythology of national leadership. The rise of a major political movement in Armenia in 1988, the Karabagh Movement that became the **Armenian National Movement** (ANM), sidelined the ARF. These problems arose in the face of earlier difficulties when its principal base of operation was destroyed by the Lebanese civil war in the 1970s and 1980s where the largest and most dynamic diaspora community had provided it with a home in the post-World War II decades. The ARF set up a branch organization in Armenia soon after independence and went into opposition to the ANM. Accused by the Armenian government of clandestine and other illegal activities, in a surprise development the ARF's activities were suspended by a presidential decree issued on December 28, 1994, and an Armenian Supreme Court decision handed down on January 13, 1995. Dozens of alleged members of the ARF in Armenia were taken into custody and brought to trial on a range of criminal charges. The political controversy generated by these acts was diffused by 1998 when the government released most of the accused, but the ARF was left hobbled with organizational difficulties arising from differences among its membership over its future role in Armenia and the diaspora. *See also* ARMENIAN REVOLUTIONARY MOVEMENT; KACHAZNUNI, HOVHANNES; PASDERMADJIAN, GAREGIN; POLITICAL PARTIES.

ARMENIAN REVOLUTIONARY MOVEMENT. In the 1878 Treaty of Berlin the Ottoman government agreed to undertake reforms in the so-called Armenian provinces of the Turkish Empire. Observing a track record of reforms promulgated but seldom implemented, Armenian nationalists disbelieved that any meaningful changes would be forthcoming in the Ottoman administration of the Armenian-populated regions of the Turkish state. Moderate and conservative Armenians, on the other hand, placed much stock in an international treaty signed by the Great Powers (Britain, France, Germany, Austria, Russia) containing an explicit Ottoman commitment to reform. The failure of the Great Powers to hold Abdul-Hamid (Abdulhamit) II (1876–1909) to his promise as they became embroiled in the competition to carve up Africa and Asia, and the sultan's recalcitrance in introducing voluntary reforms, left many Armenians disillusioned with the Ottoman regime. A rising national consciousness obstructed by an increasingly despotic administration under Abdul-Hamid did not take long to prompt a revolutionary movement among Armenians of the Ottoman Empire.

Local self-defense units had already taken to resisting Ottoman authorities. Particularly egregious from the standpoint of rural inhabitants was the government's license and tolerance of Kurdish predation over Armenian towns and villages. In response to this predicament the first formally organized Armenian political society, the Armenakan party, made its appearance in 1885 in the city of **Van**. The group was quickly disbanded by the Ottoman police.

The Armenian revolutionary movement acquired real impetus in the Russian Empire. In an atmosphere of greater freedom, better education, and social advancement, the new intellectual class taking form in the Russian Caucasus spawned a group of political thinkers who began to articulate serious concern with the fate of the Armenians in the Ottoman Empire. Influenced by Russian populism and radicalism, they organized two groups advocating Armenian national goals. The Armenian **Social Democratic Party** first appeared in Geneva amongst Russian-Armenians studying abroad. The husband and wife team of Avetis and Maro Nazarbekian led the group. The party soon was known by the name of its publication, *Hnchak* (Clarion), selected in imitation of the Russian-language publication by the same name issued by the Russian revolutionary Alexander Herzen.

The Hnchakian party subscribed to socialism and called for the restoration of Armenian statehood. It focused its activities on the Ottoman Armenians whom they tried to propagandize and provision with arms. Though it found adherents among Armenians in both the Russian and Ottoman Empires, the Hnchakian party never garnered a large following. Its ideological positions were viewed as too radical and its program infeasible in the face of the overwhelming power of the state and the absence of real political consciousness among the rural masses.

The **Armenian Revolutionary Federation** (ARF) had better success. Organized in Tbilisi in 1890 by a trio of ideologues known as Kristapor, Rostom, Zavarian, the organization became known less by its acronym than by the Armenian word for Federation, *Dashnaktsutiun*. Its members and supporters were thus called *Dashnak*. The ARF gained greater mass appeal as it sought to define a populist platform that was based not so much on ideological propositions as on the objective conditions of the Armenian population. In its early years it advocated reform, autonomy, and self-government, and forsook independent nationhood. The ARF emphasized the need for political organization and support for groups engaged in local struggles that it tried to bring under one umbrella, hence the notion of Federation. The object of their program remained the fate and status of the Armenians in the Ottoman Empire.

After their formative years, three critical developments, the 1894–1896 massacres, and the 1905 and 1917 Russian revolutions, redirected the thrust of the Armenian nationalist movement. The series of massacres inflicted on the Armenian population of the Ottoman Empire between 1894 and 1896 compelled Armenian society to rethink its condition and Armenian political organizations to reassess their course of action. The level of lethal violence unleashed by the Turkish state reached beyond anything experienced by the Armenians up to that point. With hundreds of thousands affected and tens of thousands dead, the revolutionaries were confronted with a very serious dilemma. The sultan's regime used the charge of revolutionary activism against the Armenians in order to justify its wholesale measures. Armenians in the provinces, and in the capital of Istanbul, were openly challenging the state and its representatives. Demonstrations, reprisals against corrupt officials, underground publications, and revolutionary cells, altogether frightened the sultan and were evidence of the emerging nationalism of one more minority in the empire. From the standpoint of the ruling Ottoman class, Russian tolerance of Armenian organizations advocating political change in the Ottoman Empire appeared particularly seditious.

The havoc wreaked in Armenian society by the massacres alienated a large segment of the masses from political involvement. It also destroyed a good part of the Hnchak and Dashnak organizations. Thereafter the distrust between the Ottoman regime and the Armenians was never repaired. The ARF and the Committee of Union and Progress (CUP) of the Young Turks cooperated in their opposition to the sultan Abdul-Hamid, whom even progressive-minded Turks accused of impeding the modernization of the state. After the Young Turk Revolution of 1908, Armenian political organizations were legalized in the Ottoman Empire. The charge of sedition, however, was brought up again by the CUP government during World War I and once again measures were taken against the Armenian population at large. The mass deportations and executions brought an end to the existence of Armenian society in the Ottoman Empire and with that also completely halted Armenian political and revolutionary activity in Turkey.

Events in the Russian Empire took a very different course. The 1905 Revolution witnessed the intensification of radicalism all across society in the empire. Armenians were no less affected. In fact Armenian society already had been galvanized by a measure introduced by the government that had seriously undermined Armenian loyalty to the regime. In 1903 the tsar issued a decree confiscating the properties of the Armenian Church. Designed to undercut the strengthening of Armenian ethnic consciousness by depriving Armenian society of its principal means of support for its educational institutions, the edict energized the moribund revolutionary organizations and helped attract new interest and membership in them. It also impelled them to consider socialism more seriously and finally to oppose tsarism also as a repressive system of government. The igniting of racial animosity and virtual warfare between the Armenians and the Azeris in an effort to distract them from the revolution augmented the prestige of the ARF all the more as it took to the defense of the populace in the absence of Russian policing to contain communal violence. The repression that followed the so-called Armeno-Tatar War once again curbed the activities of Armenian organizations. However, by that point the ARF had gained mass appeal and clearly had emerged as the leading political organization in Armenian society. When the Russian Empire broke up after the 1917 Revolutions, the ARF was in a position to assume charge of the process resulting in the establishment of the Republic of Armenia. From 1918 to 1920 during the entire duration of the independent republic, the ARF was the dominant party in the fledgling state.

Armenian socialists who were members of Russian organizations and opposed to specifically Armenian nationalist parties, soon gained prominence after the Bolshevik Revolution. Though but a narrow strand of the whole Armenian revolutionary movement, the Sovietization of Armenia placed the Armenian Bolsheviks at the helm of Armenian society. Condemning the Dashnaks and others as bourgeois nationalists, the Bolsheviks excluded them from the political process in Soviet Armenia and persecuted them as counter-revolutionaries. By 1921 the momentum of the Armenian revolutionary movement was spent leaving a legacy of catastrophic failure in the Ottoman Empire and of successful nation-building in the Russian state.

ARMENIAN SECRET ARMY FOR THE LIBERATION OF ARMENIA (ASALA). Clandestine terrorist organization. ASALA made its appearance in 1975, in the 60th year after the 1915 genocide of the Armenians in Ottoman Turkey, and remained active into the mid-1980s. The stated mission of the organization was the avenging of the **Armenian Genocide** and the liberation of the so-called occupied Armenian territories in eastern Turkey whence the Armenian population had been deported in 1915. ASALA was an independent organization opposed to the traditional political parties in the Armenian **diaspora**. Based in Lebanon, it had close links with the Palestinian movement.

A similar organization, named the Justice Commandos of the Armenian Genocide (JCAG), was organized soon after the appearance of ASALA. JCAG had the support of the **Armenian Revolutionary Federation** (ARF). Although both ASALA and JCAG carried out propaganda in the Armenian diaspora, in the main their following was drawn from the Middle East. Their principal mode of operation involved the targeting of Turkish government officials for assassination or the selecting of Turkish institutions for bombing. The killing of Turkish ambassadors in Europe and Turkish consular officials in the United States attracted huge media attention in the late 1970s and early 1980s. In 1982 the terrorists even staged a suicidal attack at Ankara airport. However, neither ASALA nor JCAG succeeded in obtaining any concession from the Turkish government or in gaining wide support from Armenians.

As ASALA grew even more violent and began to strike non-Turkish targets, the organization split and went into rapid decline. The bombing of Orly airport in France in 1983 where many civilians were killed proved a turning point. With random violence directed against a non-Turkish target, Armenian terrorism ceased being a problem just for Turks. The incident also resulted in popular revulsion as the campaign of political violence steered wide of its stated objective of dealing punishment to the Turkish government for having prosecuted genocide against the Armenians. Better equipped with information by this point about membership in the terrorist cells, American, European, and Turkish counter-terrorist units eventually defused the movement.

From the age of members who died in terrorist operations, most participants appeared to be persons in their twenties who had been exposed to the radical politics of the Middle East. ASALA members openly expressed their alienation from the political programs of the Armenian diaspora organizations, which they charged with being internationally ineffective in advancing their stated cause of obtaining justice for the Armenian Genocide. Many in the leadership of ASALA and JCAG were reported to be highly educated and multilingual individuals. The most notorious was the shadowy figure of Hagop Hagopian, presumed an alias, who led ASALA during most of its active phase. He, like many of the militants, met a violent death.

One of the very few American-born members of ASALA was Monte Melkonian. He led the splinter movement against Hagopian's wing that was responsible for the Orly terror bombing. Melkonian was probably the most articulate of the participants in the Armenian militant movement. His writings constitute some of the literature central for understanding why the campaign of political violence was embarked upon and how it justified its program as a means to redress the consequences of genocide. Melkonian, along with others, was arrested in France. After the spate of terrorism ebbed, he was released from prison and returned underground. He resurfaced in 1991 in **Nagorno Karabagh** participating in the defense of the local Armenian population during the siege of the region by Azeri forces. He was killed in the battle zone in 1993 at which time he was hailed by local Armenians for having organized and trained the Karabagh men into an effective fighting force that had gone on the offensive earlier in the year. This second career helped change people's views about him. Monte Melkonian was given a hero's burial in **Yerevan**, Armenia.

ARPIARIAN, ARPIAR (1851–1908). Writer, newspaper editor, and political leader. Arpiarian was born in Samsun, Turkey and received his education in Istanbul and the Murad-Rafayelian School in Venice where he studied under **Ghevond Alishan**. He was a contributor to a number of newspapers including *Mshak* (Laborer), published in Tbilisi, for which he wrote for 30 years under the pseudonym of Haykak. He addressed the condition of the Western Armenian population, their economic difficulties and struggle for cultural survival. As a journalist, public speaker, and political activist, he played a major role in spreading liberal ideas, much as he was an advocate of the use of the vernacular Armenian as the language of literature. He was one of the founders of *Arevelk* (Orient) daily, published in Istanbul, in 1884. He also edited *Masis* literary journal and in 1891 became the editor of the periodical *Hayrenik* (Fatherland). Besides being a major promoter of periodical publications and a patron of a circle of younger writers, Arpiarian was also an author in his own right.

Arpiarian was also active in Armenian politics. He was arrested in Istanbul in 1890 on the charge of sedition. He joined the **Social Democratic Hnchakian Party** (SDHP) in 1895 but fled the Ottoman police the following year and went to London. There he edited the journal *Nor Kyank* (New Life) between 1898 and 1901. In 1902 he published *Hay Handes* (Armenian Journal) in Venice. In 1905 he moved to Cairo where he edited *Shirak* and contributed to *Lusaper*

(Beacon). Arpiarian had quit the Hnchakian party in 1901 as the organization had become seriously divided over ideology in the aftermath of the Turkish massacres of Armenians in 1894–1896. A man of liberal persuasion he participated in forming the *Verakazmial* (Reconstructed) Hnchak organization composed of disaffected non-Socialists who like him had left the SDHP. He was assassinated in Cairo by antagonistic Hnchaks.

ARSHAKUNI (ARSACID). Royal dynasty of ancient Armenia. After the **Yervanduni** and the **Artashesian**, the Arshakuni constituted the third dynasty to occupy the throne of Armenia. Unlike the previous two that were of native origin, the Arshakuni house in Armenia represented the junior branch of the Arsacid imperial dynasty ruling over Iran (247 B.C.–224 A.D.). The process of the domestication of the Arshakuni symbolizes one of the most profound cultural transformations registered in Armenia, the end result of which was a country whose social and political system basically reflected an Eastern, specifically Iranian, orientation, hierarchical, tradition-bound, and organized around family and clan, but with a culture that increasingly drew its values and models from the West, specifically from the Greek-speaking world, and its spiritual brainchild, Christianity.

As the Hellenistic monarchies and their royal dynasties of Macedonian origin governing around the eastern Mediterranean declined in the first century B.C. and were successively disinherited by the Romans, only Parthia remained in the East possessing the strength and resources to lay claim to universal monarchy. In view of its geographical position, as well as its own institution of monarchy and aristocracy dating back to the era of the Persian Achaemenids, Armenia gravitated toward the Parthians, themselves heirs of the old Persian Empire. Moreover, the Iranian confederational method of governance contrasted sharply with the annexationist and corporatist policies of the Romans. Iranian forbearance of the political role of an all-powerful aristocracy, for example, manifested in decentralized administrative practices, an organizational model providing considerable assurance to the Armenian feudal class. Lastly, the common practice of marriage among royalty regularly provided occasion to strengthen relations between the two societies where fealty was regarded a matter of personal obligation and responsibility. Armenian-Parthian relations were solidified during the reign of King Artavazd

II (55–34 B.C.) and contact between the Armenian Artashesian and Parthian Arsacid dynasties had become a matter of survival for the later Artashesians as they struggled to preserve the independence of their country under Roman pressure during the Augustan settlement of the imperial borders.

The expiration of the Artashesian line presented a welcome opportunity for the Romans to persist in installing their preferred candidates upon the Armenian throne in an effort to check Parthian dominion over the Caucasus region. Armenian resistance to this policy of encroachment fostered a growing reliance on Parthian support. Yet the Romans alternated between a policy of hostility and friendship with successive rulers of the Arsacid dynasty and themselves were initially responsible for introducing an Arsacid candidate to the Armenian throne. Vonon, or Vonones I, was made titular king of Armenia Major from 12–15 A.D. A series of other nominees also reigned in Armenia, some for shorter and some for longer periods of time. None of the Roman appointees secured dynastic succession.

The situation radically changed with the appearance of a more powerful figure than had previously ruled in Parthia. King Vologases I (51–80 A.D.) strove to make the governing of his empire a true family enterprise. Elevated to the throne with the help of his brothers, Pacorus and Trdat/Tiridates, Vologases handed Media to Pacorus and delegated Armenia to Trdat in 52 A.D. The ensuing conflict with Rome was resolved only in 63 A.D. by the Treaty of Rhandia, by which all parties agreed to the elevation of **Trdat I** to the Armenian throne. The treaty established Roman-Parthian cosuzerainty over Armenia, with the privilege of nomination to the throne extended to the Arsacids, and the right of investiture reserved for the Romans. With this understanding recognized internationally, the Armenians had found themselves a new leader around whom they could rally. The monarchy once again enjoyed a period of consolidation, and King Sanatruk II (88–109) peaceably succeeded his father.

In an age of imperial competition, the Treaty of Rhandia remained an agreement regularly tested, and Parthian assertion of dominion over Armenia on the occasion of the elevation of new members of the Arsacid family elicited Roman response. Twice in the second century Rome directly subjugated Armenia. Emperor Trajan (98–117) annexed Armenia in 114, while Emperor Hadrian (117–138) re-established the Armenian kingdom and restored cosuzerainty with the enthronement of Vagharsh/Vologases I (117–140) as king of Armenia. Emperor Antoninus Pius (138–161) placed his own candidate, King Sohaemos (140–160, 163–180), on the Armenian throne, but Emperor Marcus Aurelius (161–180) had to send troops to occupy the country in 163 to restore the Roman client. At the height of its power during the reign of the Five Good Emperors in the second century A.D., the enforcement of the Pax Romana, except when provoked by Parthian intervention, contributed to maintaining the integrity of Armenia. As a crossing point of the trade from East to West, Armenia also benefited from the great economic engine of the Roman Empire with its insatiable consumption of luxury goods. Once again the revenue of the central administration in Armenia could justify the founding of a new capital, **Vagharshapat**.

The Arshakuni line established dynastic succession from the reign of King Vagharsh/Vologases II (180–191) and his son Khosrov/Chosroes I (191–217) under the protection of Emperor Septimius Severus (193–211), and though Emperor Caracalla (211–217) invaded Armenia in 215, Khosrov's son Trdat/Tiridates II (217–252) was declared king of Armenia upon the emperor's assassination. The anchoring of the Arshakuni as an increasingly indigenous dynasty had long-term consequences, both for the royal house and for Armenia, that could not be anticipated. In 224 Artashir Papakan raised the banner of revolt in Iran, and by 227 had inaugurated the rule of the Sasanids by deposing the Parthians. The Arshakuni in Armenia, as potential legitimate contestants to Sasanid royal supremacy, came under intense pressure and Armenia, as a result, was subjected to repeated invasion and periods of direct occupation. The death of King Trdat II in 252 provided the occasion for the Sasanids to seize the Armenian throne, and the capture of Emperor Valerius (253–260) by the Sasanid Great King Shapur I (241–272) marked the low point of Roman influence in the East. Armenia lay prostrate and divided between, on the one hand, a resurgent Iran ruled by a dynasty styling itself heir to the Achaemenid realm and professing the Mazdaean faith with its Manichaean conception of the world and its practice of the sacred fire worship, and on the other, a Roman Empire undergoing serious internal political and economic troubles in the course of the third century. The Romans continued to sponsor the Armenian Arshakuni, but Khosrov/Chosroes II (279/80–287) ruled only in Western Armenia under Roman protection.

The Arshakuni dynasty staged its recovery during the reign of its most vigorous offspring, **Trdat/Tiridates IV** (298–330). As a protégé of Emperor Diocletian (284–305), Trdat registered a marked reorientation of Armenia's foreign policy. In virtually everything he did he sought to align Armenia closely with the Roman Empire and in so doing distancing it from Sasanid Iran. His decision to adopt Christianity, traditionally dated to 301, also signified more than the change of religions. It fundamentally altered the cultural and political orientation of the Armenian people. In choosing Christianity he remained in step with changes in the Roman Empire where coincidentally Emperor Constantine I (306–337) in 313 legalized Christianity. Lastly, the willingness and capacity to make these decisive changes also attest to his desire and success in strengthening the institution of monarchy in Armenia.

The dependence of the Armenian sovereigns on external support, the numerous interruptions in the dynastic succession of the Ashakuni kings, and the periodic warfare and occupation of the country, all contributed to weakening the institution of monarchy in Armenia. Strong rulers such as Trdat IV strove to restore the prestige and influence of the monarchy in Armenia. By the fourth century, however, it had become an uphill struggle as the power of the local feudal lords was by then solidly implanted on the political landscape of Armenia. More durable than the royal dynasties, the feudal families of Armenia, the so-called *nakharar* houses, thought of their ancestral domains as privileged principalities in their own right. While they served their sovereigns in the administrative capacities assigned to them in what had become hereditary offices, they also jealously guarded their privileges and defied attempts to alter their ranks in the aristocratic hierarchy of the country. Every great lord regarded himself entitled to defend his hereditary rights by appealing to any power that would uphold his rank and ownership of his domain. It made for a difficult system to govern, yet the major nakharar houses also constituted the reliable political and military core of the Armenian state and were ever ready to take to the field of battle, to lead the charge, and to lay down the lives of their finest if the challenge so warranted. A strong monarch could count on the nakharars to uphold the legitimacy of his rule. A weak king was at their mercy.

Trdat IV's successors ruled in the shadow of the long-lived Sasanid King Shapur II (309–379). Their attempts to maintain both external and internal balance ultimately failed and both King Tiran (338–350) and his son King Arshak II (350–368) were captured and deposed by Shapur II. Following the near collapse of Roman power in the East with the defeat of Emperor Julian the Apostate in 363, Armenia was left completely exposed to Iranian encroachment. The nakharars deserted King Arshak and the Sasanids proceeded methodically to ransack Armenia's major cities in 368–369. **Artashat**, Vagharshapat, Yervandashat, Zarehavan, Zarishat, and **Van** were put to the torch and their populations deported to Iran. Queen Parantzem fortified herself in Artagerk castle and held out until 370, when she too was taken prisoner to Persia and, like her husband, banished to the "Castle of Oblivion," where Arshak is said to have committed suicide and Parantzem was executed. Pap, the crown prince and nominally king, managed to flee and take refuge in Byzantium.

Emperor Valens (364–378) supported the restoration of the Arshakuni to the Armenian throne, but conflicts internal to Armenia between competing centers of power and authority continued to undermine the monarchy. The Romans raised King Pap (368–374) to the Armenian throne in 371. His personal conduct invited the condemnations of the Catholicos Nerses the Great (353–373) whom the king caused to be poisoned, and in an effort to restrain the Church he prevented the consecration of the catholicos-elect Husik from taking place in Caesarea. While this action removed the Armenian patriarchate from the jurisdiction of the Imperial Church and introduced the autocephaly of the Armenian Church, it also raised doubts in the minds of the Romans about Pap's allegiance and led to his assassination. Valens then raised Varazdat to the kingship of Armenia. Varazdat's reign (374–378) was also brief as he attempted to overthrow the influence of his principal minister, the *sparapet* or commander-in-chief of the Armenian forces, Mushegh **Mamikonian**. The leading aristocratic family of Armenia, the Mamikonians in the late Arshakuni period virtually rivaled in power the authority of the royal dynasty. As a matter of fact Mushegh's brother, Manuel Mamikonian drove Varazdat from the throne and became regent for the late King Pap's two young sons, Arshak III and Vagharshak (379–384), who were jointly placed on the Armenian throne.

The church and the aristocracy had consolidated sufficient authority and legitimacy by the fourth century to hold their own in Armenian society, and, whether in the name of institutional or national interest, to conduct their affairs directly with external powers. In light of the continuing decline of the monarchy, these were propitious developments. Armenia had de facto been divided between Roman and Iranian spheres of influence since the Sasanid raids under Shapur II. Shapur III (383–387) decided to settle matters with the Romans, which required the formalization of the status quo in Armenia and its de jure partition in 387. By then Arshak III had retired to Roman Armenia where he reigned between 384 and 390. Upon his death Western Armenia was annexed and Armenian self-government brought to an end.

The only king of consequence to rule in Persian Armenia was Vramshapuh (392–415). During his reign, with his authorization and the sponsorship of Catholicos Sahak I (388–428), **Mesrop Mashtots** embarked upon the invention of the Armenian alphabet. Introduced in 405, the alphabet ushered in literacy in the **Armenian language**, a transformation of such momentous importance that it equipped a people soon to be dispossessed of their monarchy with the capacity to form and articulate a culture all its own, equipment of incalculable value when the Armenians no longer governed themselves. It was left to Vramshapuh's son, King Artashes IV (422–428), the ignominy of being deposed by the Sasanid king at the request of his nakharar lords whose confidence in both king and monarchy was reduced to the point where they preferred to govern in their own right under the suzerainty of the Great King. The departure of Artashes IV, the namesake of the first truly sovereign king of Armenia, signaled both the end of a royal dynasty and the abolition of the ancient Armenian monarchy, which by the Armenian epic tradition had been in existence for nearly a thousand years. *See also* DVIN; EDJMIADSIN; GRIGOR LUSAVORICH.

ARTASHAT. Capital of ancient Armenia. Artashat was founded by King **Artashes I** (189–160 B.C.) in 176 B.C. as the capital of his newly proclaimed monarchy. Built at the confluence of the **Arax** and Medsamor Rivers, it was a naturally defensible site surrounded as it was by water on three sides, and guarded on the landside by the citadel later called Khor-Virap. It lies 20 kilometers south of modern-day **Yerevan**. Established in an era of exceptional tranquility and unparalleled prosperity, Artashat rose quickly as a center of power, so much so that later Romans, who called it Artaxata, attributed the selection of its site to their military nemesis, Hannibal, who had gone into exile to the East after the crushing defeat at Carthage in 202 B.C. Artashat, however, was the first city in Armenia laid out on a classical Hellenistic plan. Lying farther south and closer to the trade routes entering Armenia from the east, it was also located at a point more suited to international commerce than the preceding capitals of **Armavir** and Yervandashat. This secured for Artashat both an important political and economic role for centuries thereafter, making it a symbol of Armenian power and the object of possession by rival empires competing for dominion over the region. The effective administration of Armenia for nearly two centuries by the **Artashesian** dynasty and the integration of the country into the world trade network of the Hellenistic era explain the growth of Artashat into the largest urban complex seen in the Plain of Ararat.

A royal residence from the start, Artashat served as the capital of Armenia for over three hundred years. Five times the Romans marched their armies on Artashat. Licinius Lucullus reached its gates in 68 B.C., but had to satisfy himself with the plunder of **Tigranakert**, Armenia's southern capital. Two years later, in 66 B.C., Pompey compelled **Tigran II the Great** to accede to friendship with Rome in a treaty signed at Artashat. It was to Artashat also that in 54 B.C. first news of the defeat and death of Licinius Crassus, another Roman triumvir, was delivered to the Armenian and Parthian kings, when both were in attendance at the performance of a tragedy by Eurepides. The demise of the Artashesian dynasty in the early years of the first century A.D. ignited fierce conflict between the Roman and Parthian empires for dominion over Armenia and control of Artashat. In 58 A.D. Gnaeus Domitius Corbulo, Emperor Nero's fearsome commander, besieged and captured the city. The first **Arshakuni** king of Armenia, **Trdat I** (formally 63–88), helplessly watched as the Romans burned down his capital the following year. When relations improved between Rome and Parthia, in 66 A.D. Trdat was enthroned as king of Armenia in Rome personally by Nero (54–68), and returned to his realm accompanied by Roman architects and craftsmen and a treasury of 200,000 sesterces with the emperor's permission to rebuild Artashat. In 114 Rome once again annexed Armenia under Trajan (98–117), whose governor in Artashat left a large Latin inscription of his sovereign's imperial titles. Roman forces were pulled out only three years later. They returned in 163, during the reign of Emperor

Marcus Aurelius (161–180), under the nominal command of the co-emperor Lucius Verus (161–169), but the actual direction of Avidius Cassius and the consul Statius Priscus who conquered Armenia and again sacked Artashat. With a peace accord reached between Rome and Parthia, the rebuilding of Artashat began in 166, by which time, however, the capital of Armenia had already shifted to **Vagharshapat**.

Despite the changes in political fortune, Artashat remained a very important commercial center. Both Rome and Parthia continued to guarantee by the treaty of 166 Artashat's role as one of the official exchange posts in the international trade between the two great empires. The treaty of 387 renewed this long-standing commercial agreement after the partition of Armenia. A century and half after Arshakuni rule had ended and Armenia had been subordinated, the peace treaty of 562 signed by Byzantium and Sasanid Persia during the reigns of the two indomitable emperors Justinian I (527–565) and Khosrov Anushirvan (531–579) once again reconfirmed the position of Artashat as a designated customs post for the international trade transacted through Armenia.

Even this special status did not prevent the slow decline of Artashat. Along with a number of other important Armenian cities, the Sasanid Persians had wrecked it in 368 during the reign of Shapur II (309–379). Artashat also faced economic competition from the nearby city of **Dvin**, which served as the administrative capital of Armenia under Persian and Arab rule. Yet it continued to function into the 10th century as the center of a prized industry, the extraction of a red dye from the local cochineal, known internationally by the Arabic *kirmiz*, which was used widely in Armenia in the manufacture of carpets, itself a major commodity for the domestic and foreign markets. The final abandonment of the city appears to have resulted from its inundation by the Arax River. By then, Artashat had existed for a thousand years, having once been associated with royal power for a period of 340 years, longer than any other capital city of Armenia.

ARTASHES I (ARTAXIAS I) (189–160 B.C.). King of Armenia and founder of the **Artashesian** dynasty. No monarch in Armenian history left as a great an impression upon his people as Artashes. His reign verily became the stuff of legend, and his life and achievements were celebrated by later generations in epic poetry and song. The defeat of the Seleucid emperor, Antiochus III the Great (223–187 B.C.)

by the Romans at the Battle of Magnesia in 190 B.C. changed the political landscape of the ancient Near East. Codified in the Treaty of Apamea in 188 B.C., Antiochus surrendered Seleucid claims over Asia Minor and withdrew his forces south to Syria. The collapse of the Seleucid Empire freed Armenia. Artashes, Antiochus's protégé in Armenia, discarded all vassalage by what appears to have been an act of self-proclamation as sovereign monarch of Armenia. From his base in the **Ararat** Valley, the central domain of the kingdom, Artashes enlarged his realm in all directions. The expansion toward Iberia in the north was sealed by his marriage to Queen Satenik, an event of such jubilation as to have been preserved in popular memory through the ages in some of the finest epic verse in the Armenian language beginning with the resounding greeting of her future consort by the Alan princess: "I say unto you, brave man Artashes." To the east he seized part of Media Atropatene, the region north of the **Arax River** all the way to the Caspian coast. To the south he incorporated the districts of Phaunitis, Armenian Siunik, and to the west, he took Vaspurakan, the area along the eastern shore of **Lake Van**, the heartland of the old Urartian and **Yervanduni** states.

Artashes paid no less attention to internal affairs. Every one of his policies was designed to increase the authority of the central government and to augment royal privilege over the numerous tribal and regional chieftains governing in the Armenian provinces. One of his most memorable deeds, an innovation at the time, was the erecting of stelae demarcating property boundaries. In so doing he simultaneously extended royal justice and gave evidence of the might of the crown to establish and secure the rights of landholders. This important step in many ways also marked the beginnings of an administrative apparatus for the country, as the royal markers constituted the oldest public records of the ancient Armenian monarchy. That a number of these stelae survive attests to the extent of their application across the country and the near sanctity by which they must have been held. Inscribed in Aramaic script, they would have been legible only to the schooled administrator and their preservation, therefore, was of very high importance to owners of the land, be these fields, villages, or other property. The marker stones also symbolized another change occurring in the makeup of Armenian society. The necessity of recognizing the ownership of real estate and the delimitation of property spoke of an economic transformation. The emergence of a new class of men whose wealth was vested in land is the evidence of the increased cultivation of the soil, a situation much evolved from the Yervanduni era when animal husbandry yielded the greater source of revenue. Artashes's ambitious plans are only explained by the exploitation of this growing prosperity and population of Armenia, whereby the military potential of the country was decisively increased. *See also* TIGRAN II.

ARTASHESIAN (ARTAXIAD). Royal dynasty of ancient Armenia. The Artashesian dynasty ruled continuously from 189 B.C. to 1 A.D., a period of 190 years marking the apogee of the ancient Armenian kingdom. Its energetic monarchs forged a unified country binding together all the Armenian lands under a single crown. With new resources at their disposal, the Artashesians even expanded their domains beyond Armenia proper. For a brief while, as neighboring states lay weak and divided, the Artashesians projected their influence across the borders of their kingdom and made Armenia the most powerful country of the ancient Near East. How a durable state was created in the remote and mountainous country of Armenia is in large measure explained by the vigor, ambition, and astute political judgment of the Artashesians.

Artashes I, the founder of the dynasty, ruled from 189 to 160 B.C. Artashes's rise to power coincides with the waxing and waning of the fortunes of the Seleucid king Antiochus III the Great (223–187 B.C.). As part of his effort to recover the empire of his Macedonian ancestor, Seleucus Nicator, who inherited the Asian provinces of Alexander's realm, Antiochus sought to establish suzerainty over Armenia also and appointed Artashes/Artaxias and Zareh/Zariadris as strategos, or governors, of Greater and Lesser Armenia respectively. The transfer of authority from the **Yervanduni** dynasty, however, appears to have been an internal matter as much as an externally encouraged overthrow of the established order, for as soon as opportunity presented itself, Artashes proclaimed his autonomy and broadcast his own Yervanduni origin, "Arvandakan" as he declared in his inscriptions in Persianate Aramaic, the international court language of the Achaemenids.

Sensing the absence of a suzerain power in the region once the Romans defeated Antiochus III, Artashes and Zareh, who very likely were close relatives, as Artashes himself identified his father as one named Zareh also, in a coordinated strategy quickly consolidated their rule over Armenia. Artashes secured hold of the lands surrounding the central domain of the **Ararat** Valley by incorporating territory from Iberia in the north, Media Atropatene to the east, Phaunitis, or the Armenian Siunik to the south, and Vaspurakan to the west. At the same time, Zareh incorporated the district of Taraunitis, or the Armenian Taron, to the east of his base in Sophene, and annexed lands farther north all the way to Acilisine, or Yekeghiats.

Effectively two unequally sized kingdoms were created on the Armenian plateau, both solidly based upon a single ethnicity already speaking a common tongue from one end of the highlands to the other. These transformations also attest to the emerging contours of a feudal monarchy that consolidated royal power at the apex of a complex social order in which local dynastic houses, numbering up to 120 according to Pliny, distributed domestic political power among themselves. Without doubt the Artashesians forged a tighter system of allegiances by mustering the forces of their vassals for the purposes of territorial conquest, and in winning on the battlefield they gained for themselves the fealty they expected from the indigenous nobility. Artashes's assertion of his Yervanduni ancestry underscored the social values of the Armenian upper class, where lineage by itself assured status and where the claim to royal descent alone provided legitimacy. By invoking that continuity, Artashes also acclaimed the autochthony of his political power derived by lineage, by right, and by a demonstrated capacity for self-government independent of any bestowal of legitimacy by an external suzerain.

The Armenian epic recalls the popular grief and trauma upon the passing of a king as great as Artashes, and his immediate successors remained completely in his shadow. The reigns of Artavazd/Artabastus I and of Tigran/Tigranes I, which span the years 160 to 95 B.C., cannot be properly divided so silent are the historic sources, until the thunderous appearance of **Tigran II** (95–55 B.C.), the mightiest of Armenian kings. Seleucid power in the Near East was fast fading against the rise of a new Persian dynasty. The Parthians under the leadership of their Arsacid kings swept Iran and pressed Armenia enough to require the handing over of the heir to the throne as hostage of the Iranian court. Forty-five years of age at the time of his succession, Tigran is thought to have spent his young adulthood in privileged bondage, for he seized scepter and sword with such ferocity as to wreak vengeance upon the Parthians.

Wherever may lie the source of Tigran's sense of liberation by his enthronement, he must have been extremely well advised of political conditions across Armenia, Parthia, and the rest of the ancient Near East. With a single stroke he unified Armenia by annexing the Kingdom of Dsopk/Sophene in 94 B.C. and casually subordinated its monarch who put up no resistance. Thereafter, until checked by the Romans in 69 B.C., Tigran's reign marked a period of rapid expansion wherein many smaller neighboring kingdoms were attached to Armenia as vassal states. The exposure of the Armenian population to the more developed societies of the surrounding region, especially those to the south and west where some of the centers of advanced Hellenistic culture were to be found, also accelerated cultural change in Armenia. The earlier and strong Iranian cultural influence, impressed upon the Armenians since the days of the Achaemenids, began to give way increasingly to the highly urban character of Hellenism. While Hellenism itself absorbed the court ceremonial of the East, the East absorbed the immense know-how of the Greeks, and even the Persians came under its sway. Philhellenism became the vogue of ruling families, whether of oriental or occidental origin. By establishing a new capital in southern Armenia, Tigran deliberately sought to reposition the center of cultural gravity in his new empire. The choice of building a city on the prevailing Hellenistic model and populating it with the international mix of peoples from the surrounding countries attests to a desire to incline clearly westward. That process was halted when the Roman generals Lucullus and Pompey forced Tigran's retreat to **Artashat**, the capital in the Plain of Ararat, far to the north and east of **Tigranakert**.

Pompey, however, recognized the importance of Tigran as one exercising a tight grip over his kingdom. Though he marched his troops to Artashat, nevertheless, he offered fair terms reserving for the aged monarch the full dignity of his crown and titles. Tigran surrendered his Syrian acquisitions, agreed to the maintenance of friendly relations with Rome, and in return was allowed to continue to style himself king of kings. The Romans secured their empire in the East and imposed an alliance upon a new and important neighbor. Tigran, by an act of wisdom speaking of unflagging courage, salvaged his kingdom intact and kept it free from foreign occupation. Greater Armenia, Armenia Major of the Romans, continued to exist as a single and unified monarchy.

Tigran's son and successor, King Artavazd/Artavazdes (55–34 B.C.), epitomized the Hellenistic attainment in Armenia. A highly educated individual, he had sufficient mastery of the Greek language and evident interest in intellectual pursuits as to author treatises in the lingua franca of the age. As a patron of the arts and an enlightened monarch, Artavazd was at the forefront of the increasing hellenization of Armenian urban and court culture. His political leadership, however, was a different matter, more a delicate and dangerous balancing act. The treaty obligations of Armenia with Rome, placed Artavazd in an especially treacherous predicament. Pompey's settlement was breached by the continuing expansionism promoted by ambitious generals in Rome, a policy that strained Armenia's relations with Parthia, its closer neighbor and competitor for influence in the Caucasus and the Near East.

The balance of power established by Pompey was upset by the third member of the triumvirate of Julius Caesar, Pompey, and Licinius Crassus. In 53 B.C. Crassus came to the East in pursuit of military glory by challenging the Parthians. Crassus demanded support from Artavazd, who grudgingly complied according to treaty obligations cognizant of the undesired conflict it provoked between Armenia and Parthia. Anxious to register a swift victory, Crassus rejected King Artavazd's suggestion of a more cautious advance on Parthia. Crassus seriously underestimated the capacity of his foe. As he overextended his supply line from Armenia by advancing rapidly into Mesopotamia, Crassus was outflanked by the Arsacids. King Orodes II (57–38 B.C.) threatened Armenia, and Artavazd, hastily restoring neutrality, came to terms with the Parthian ruler, who was in the capital of Artashat with King Artavazd, when news was delivered of the crushing defeat dealt to the invading Roman forces along with Crassus's head as proof of the thoroughness of the Parthian triumph. Under the circumstances, Artavazd went so far as to betroth his own sister to Orodes's oldest son, a marriage of the highest political significance for the two greatest contemporary royal dynasties of the ancient Near East.

The rise of Julius Caesar as dictator in Rome and the struggles ensuing his assassination in 44 B.C. kept the Romans absorbed with internal matters until such time as the second triumvirate of Octavius, Lepidus, and Marcus Antonius stabilized the situation. As the senior partner in the triumvirate and styling himself Caesar's military heir,

Marc Antony revived the policy of territorial expansion and aspired to the power that would accrue to him in Rome were he to register an exceptional military triumph on the order of Caesar's victories. With that driving ambition he struck an alliance with Cleopatra, queen of Egypt, to finance his campaigns and renewed conflict with Parthia in 36 B.C. by invading through Armenia and attacking Media Atropatene, Parthia's client to the east. Once again King Ardavazd rendered logistical assistance to the Romans, but was again intercepted by the Parthians, leaving Antony's advance forces insufficiently supported. Unlike Crassus, however, Antony was able to withdraw his forces, and instead overran Armenia in 34 B.C. and captured Ardavazd, whom he held responsible for his earlier failure. Antony presented the Armenian king as a war trophy to his paramour in Egypt. When Antony himself was defeated by Octavian at the Battle of Actium in 31 B.C., marking the end of his ambitions for dominion over Rome, as well as Cleopatra's dreams of joint rule, in a final act of cruelty toward now an easy victim, she ordered the execution of the aged Ardavazd.

The regicide undermined Rome's position in Armenia and complicated Armenian domestic politics as the increasingly violent competition between East and West, Parthia and Rome, over Armenia for the first time led to the appearance of camps leaning in opposite directions. With Parthian support, Artashes II (33–20 B.C.), one of Artavazd's sons who had avoided capture by Antony, became king of Armenia. The unification of the Roman Empire under Octavian, proclaimed Augustus (27 B.C.–14 A.D.), resulted in the restoration of a more formal Roman foreign policy toward Armenia requiring the enthronement of candidates favorable to Rome. Artashes's own despotic conduct may have weakened his rule and his assassination preceded the arrival of Tiberius (later emperor), who was sent by Augustus to settle Roman affairs in Armenia. Tiberius installed another of the surviving sons of King Ardavazd II. Tigran III, who ruled from 20 to 8/6 B.C., had been taken as hostage to Rome from Egypt. He was succeeded by his son Tigran IV, who ruled from 8 to 5 B.C.

Whether the sign of a minority or a weakened dynasty, the crowning of Tigran IV without Roman consultation was construed by Augustus as the signal of a pro-Parthian policy in the Armenian court. He intervened again, this time installing on the Armenian throne Artavazd III (5–2 B.C.), a younger hostage son of King Ardavazd II.

Tigran IV, with his sister Erato as queen, however, was soon restored to the throne, but the death of Tigran IV in 1 A.D. occasioned the Romans to place Median candidates on the Armenian throne. Erato returned to the throne with Roman sponsorship of Tigran V (6–c.12). His death marked the end of the male line in the Artashesian family. Even as the concurrent abdication of Erato brought the reign of the greatest of the Armenian royal dynasties to a close, the Armenian kingdom created and defended by the Artashesians continued to exist as a major state over which Romans and Parthians competed for influence. Its coveted crown would be fought over for another 62 years before another dynasty was espoused as their own by the Armenians.

ARTIN *PASHA* (CHRAKIAN) (1804–1859). Minister of commerce and foreign affairs in Egypt. Artin was born in Istanbul. His father, Sukias Chrakian, managed the commercial affairs of one of the older sons of Muhammad Ali, the *vali* of Egypt. Sukias emigrated to Egypt in 1812 and, two years later, his son followed him there. Artin Chrakian, his brother Khosrov, and a third Armenian, Aristakes Altunian, were allowed to attend school in the palace, where the young prince Abbas, later to inherit the governorship of Egypt, was one of their classmates. Sent to Paris, he studied civil administration. His education completed, Artin returned to Egypt and began working at the war ministry at the mundane chore of translating French military manuals into Turkish. In succeeding years, however, Artin, along with other Armenian colleagues, were entrusted with the responsibility of reorganizing the educational system in the country. In May 1834, he opened the school of engineering at Bulak and in September of the same year, in conjunction with another Armenian, Stepan Demirjian, he opened the school of translation in the citadel of Cairo. In 1836 he was appointed a member of the school council, a body that subsequently became the ministry of education.

By this time Artin was a full-fledged member of the administrative machinery governing Egypt. His appointment as a member of the *Majlis al-Ali*, the state council for civil affairs, brought him in direct contact with the person of the viceroy. From then on his promotion was rapid. Muhammad Ali chose him as his first secretary in 1839 and sent him as an envoy to Paris and London in 1841. Upon the death of **Boghos *Bey* Yusufian** in 1844, Artin succeeded as minister of commerce and foreign affairs. He remained in that post during the reign of Ibrahim. Along with many other Armenians in the employ of the Egyptian government, he fell out of favor after Abbas assumed the post of viceroy. He was removed from office in 1850 and went into exile in Europe. He returned after Said, the succeeding viceroy, invited him back to Egypt. Artin Chrakian was the first Armenian in Egypt bestowed the hereditary title of *Pasha*, the near-equivalent of prince in Turkish titulature. *See also* NUBAR PASHA.

ASHOT I (884–890). King of Armenia and founder of the **Bagratuni** royal dynasty. With their main forces frequently diverted to contain provincial revolts across their vast empire, the Abbasid caliphs continued to tolerate and sponsor Bagratuni administration in northern and central Armenia, and even relied upon the Bagratuni on occasion to restrain the local Arab emirates that were prone to ignore the central government in its moments of serious distraction. This uneasy balance of forces in the highlands, however, kept Armenia within the orbit of Abbasid dominion. The last direct military effort by the Arabs to contain growing Armenian autonomy in the face of the slow weakening of control over the regions by Baghdad occurred in 850. The Bagratuni recovered quickly this time for by then the Arabs already had come to recognize their indisputable paramouncy in Armenia when Ashot *Msaker*'s son Bagrat II Bagratuni, who governed from 826 to 851 as prince of Taron, was conferred by the caliph the title of *batriq al-batariqa*, literally patrician of the patricians, in an Arab terminological borrowing from the Romans, and meaning properly prince of princes. When in 862 the same title was conferred upon Bagrat's nephew, Ashot V, the leading Bagratuni prince since 855, along with the office came the concession of delivering the tribute of Armenia, hence transferring to the Armenians the last critical administrative function of the *vostikan*, the Arab governor, that of collecting the taxes on behalf of the sovereign. The concession canceled the privilege exercised by Arab tax collectors of entering the **nakharar** lands to gather the tribute in person. The political consolidation of the Bagratuni domain was virtually complete.

The only thing remaining to secure the legal sovereignty of Armenia was the restoration of the monarchy and that occurred in 884 when the caliph Al-Mutamid (870–892) extended a crown to Ashot. International recognition followed quickly from Byzantium when the Armenian prince of princes was enthroned as King Ashot I of Armenia. After a four and a half century struggle against three world empires, Sasanid Iran, Rome/Byzantium, and the Arab Caliphate, Armenia was once again an independent kingdom in large measure due to the diplomacy and tenacity of the indefatigable Bagratuni who through the entire length of those centuries did not yield upon the conviction that the Armenian state could be restored and self-government could be regained, and from the time of Ashot the Blind consciously set out to achieve that objective. In the course of his 35 years of leadership as presiding prince and as king, Ashot I restored nearly half of the historic Armenian kingdom and liberated the majority of the Armenian people from foreign rule. From 884 to 1045 nine Bagratuni princes were crowned King of Armenia and during their rule Armenia prospered and flourished. *See also* ANI; ARDSRUNI; DVIN.

AZNAVOUR, CHARLES (1924–). French singer and composer. Aznavour (nee Chahnour Vaghinak Aznavourian) was born in Paris, France, to immigrant parents. A naturally gifted musician, he became a cabaret singer at a young age. Early in his career he was a protégé of the famed French songstress Edith Piaf for whom he wrote a number of songs. She encouraged his singing and helped launch his career in French music, theater, and film. From the 1960s he was among the most popular singers on the French stage and won international fame for his melodic tunes. He toured internationally and added English songs to his repertoire. Aznavour is the composer of hundreds of songs. One his closest compositional collaborators was his own brother-in-law, the Armenian-born Georges Garvarentz, who made a career writing French film music. Aznavour also enjoyed success as a movie actor. He appeared in such films as *La Tête contre les murs* (1958), *Shoot the Piano Player* (1960), *The Adventurers* (1969), *The Games* (1970), *Les Intrus* (1973), *The Tin Drum* (1979), and *Vie la vie* (1984). After the 1988 **Spitak Earthquake** in Armenia, Aznavour established a charitable foundation in France to assist the victims. For his many services on behalf of the people of Armenia, he was named an honorary ambassador by the government of the independent republic.

– B –

BADR AL-JAMALI. *See* DIASPORA, HISTORICAL; RELIGION.

BAGHRAMIAN, IVAN (1897–1982). Soviet general. Baghramian was born in Russian Transcaucasia in the village of Chartakhlu, near Elizavetpol (now Ganja, Azerbaijan). He studied railroad engineering in Tbilisi and volunteered in 1915 for the Russian army on the Caucasus front. He remained a professional soldier for the rest of his life. In 1918 he served in the Armenian cavalry brigade in battles against the Ottoman army including the battle of Sardarapat. After the Sovietization of Armenia in 1920, he served as a squadron leader of the Armenian cavalry brigade of the Red Army. In 1923 he was promoted to commander of the Alexandropol (**Gyumri**) mounted brigade of the Armenian rifle division, in which capacity he served until 1931. He attended the Frunze military academy between 1931 and 1934 and in 1938 graduated from the Red Army Chief of Staff military academy.

In 1940 Baghramian was chief of operations of the Kiev Special Military District when Nazi Germany invaded the Soviet Union and he organized a skillful withdrawal of the Soviet forces in 1941. He was appointed chief of operations of the southeastern front and subsequently served as chief of staff on the same front until 1942. He also participated in the defense of Moscow. In 1942, as general of the 16th Army, he commanded on the Kursk front and organized the retaking of the city of Orlov. In 1943 he was appointed commander of the first Baltic front. His troops operated in Byelorussia and East Prussia and captured Koenigsberg (Kaliningrad) in 1945. Baghramian was awarded the title of Hero of the Soviet Union on July 27, 1944, after winning a major battle against Nazi forces and entering the Baltic countries.

After World War II Baghramian was commander of the Baltic Military District from 1945 to 1954. In 1954 he was appointed USSR deputy minister of defense and in 1955 was promoted to Marshal of the Soviet Union, making him the highest-ranking army officer of Armenian origin to have served in the Soviet armed forces. He was head of the Chief of Operations Military Academy from 1956 to 1958, and continued to serve in the defense ministry in other capacities. Baghramian joined the Communist Party in 1941. He was elected a candidate to the Central Committee in 1952 and was made a full member in 1961. Baghramian was awarded many prizes including the Lenin Medal, the Suvorov Medal, and the Kutuzov Medal. He published his memoirs in 1971 and was also the editor of a number of military textbooks. *See also* ISAKOV, IVAN.

BAGRATIAN, HRANT (1958–). Prime Minister of Armenia. Bagratian was born in **Yerevan**, Armenia. He received his higher education at Yerevan Institute of Economy, graduating in 1979 with a master's degree in economic planning and management. Continuing his studies at the economics institute of the Armenian Academy of Sciences, he completed his doctorate in 1987. An ardent reformist, with the formation of a non-Communist parliament in Armenia in 1990, he was appointed minister of economy on the Council of Ministers still presided over by the Armenian Communist Party Chairman Suren Harutunian, a Gorbachev appointee. At the same time Bagratian served on the executive board of the **Armenian National Movement** (ANM) and was the chief architect of the party's economic strategy for an independent Armenia. With the October 1991 election of **Levon Ter-Petrossian** as **president** of Armenia, Bagratian was given the double portfolio of minister of economy and first deputy prime minister in charge of mapping and implementing the fundamental agenda of the new nationalist government, the transition from a command economy to the free enterprise system. Bagratian quickly established rapport with key international financial institutions, such as the World Bank, the International Monetary Fund, and the European Bank for Reconstruction and Development, and worked out a schedule of reforms to phase out the socialist system of economic management and step by step introduce the instruments, mechanisms, and the financial, budgeting, taxation, and banking structures required for a Western-style liberal economic system. In January 1993, during the harshest winter crisis facing the country as Azerbaijan and Turkey imposed a blockade on landlocked Armenia, Ter-Petrossian named the 35-year-old Bagratian prime minister of Armenia. Bagratian served until the end of 1996, a period of rapid economic decline and serious shortages including winter heating fuel. Despite the hardships and the delays caused in the economic transition, his government stayed the increasingly unpopular path of liberalization. *See also* BAGRATIAN, HRANT FIRST CABINET; BAGRATIAN, HRANT SECOND CABINET.

BAGRATIAN, HRANT FIRST CABINET. Appointed by **President Levon Ter-Petrossian**, the first Bagratian cabinet served from February 16, 1993 to July 26, 1995.

Prime Minister	**Hrant Bagratian**
Deputy Prime Minister	Vigen Chitechian
Agriculture	Ashot Voskanian
Communication	Grigor Poghpatian
Construction	Gagik Martirosian
Culture	Hakob Hakobian
Defense	**Vazgen Manukian** (Acting)
Economy	Armen Yeghiazarian
Education	Hayk Ghazarian
Energy and Fuel	Hirair Hovhannesian
Environmental Protection	Karine Danielian
Finance	Levon Barkhudarian
Food and Provisions	Davit Zadoyan
Foreign Affairs	Vahan Papazian
Health	Ara Babloyan
Higher Education and Science	Vardges Gnuni
Industry	Ashot Safarian
Internal Affairs	Vano Siradeghian
Justice	Vahe Stepanian
Labor and Social Security	Ashot Yesayan
Light Industry	Rudolf Teymurazian
Material Resources	Vahan Melkonian
Trade	Tigran Grigorian
Transportation	Henrik Kochinian

Under the crisis conditions prevailing in Armenia at the time with war in **Nagorna Karabagh** and along Armenia's eastern borders, the near complete blockade of the country, extreme shortages of any sort of fuel, whether for heating or transport, related food shortages, refugees, and the difficulties remaining from the 1988 **Spitak Earthquake**, the cabinet was augmented by six so-called state ministries, which functioned more like super-ministries with coordinating responsibility and authority over the standard ministries.

Humanitarian Assistance	Rafayel Bagoyan
Construction	Gagik Martirosian
Agriculture	Gagik Shahbazian
Energy and Fuel	Sebuh Tashjian
Defense	**Vazgen Sargsian**
Science and Culture	Armenak Ghazarian

Each of the state ministries carried critically important responsibilities under emergency or exceptional conditions. The arrangement for the delivery of international assistance and the distribution of aid to the needy, which was a growing segment of the population, became a major function of the government.

With the collapse of the Soviet social welfare system, the influx of refugees from Azerbaijan and Karabagh, the population without permanent shelter in the earthquake zone, the rapid decline in employment, all contributed to creating a massive humanitarian crisis requiring major intervention by the international community and necessitated urgent state-level coordination. The stalled efforts at reconstruction in the earthquake zone and the pressing need to provide shelter and rebuild the infrastructure of the region required extraordinary effort under circumstances of extreme privation. The rapid privatization of agriculture, one of the more successful reform programs of the government, presented its own challenges as former cooperative workers learned to become independent farmers and required assistance with conversion of the products they grew for the Soviet market to the staples required by the home market, not to mention the difficulties stemming from the allocation of scarce farm equipment as collectives were broken up and an unequal distribution of assets was the result. The import of fuel remained as much a political challenge as an economic one. However, the prime responsibility thrust upon the state minister of energy, an American nuclear physicist, was the upgrading and reactivation of Armenia's atomic power plant at Medsamor, which had been mothballed earlier for fear of radioactivity leakages. As for defense, the formation of an army and the prosecution of the war in Karabagh taxed the limited resources of the country and required an iron will to face the unfavorable odds given the Armenians in the conflict. The convergence of the defense strategy of Armenia and Karabagh was evidenced by the appointment on August

21, 1993, of Serge Sargsian, the commander of the Nagorno Karabagh Republic defense forces, as Vazgen Manukian's replacement. The Bagratian cabinet carried on in an increasingly polarized environment as leading political figures such as Vazgen Manukian and later Ashot Manucharian, the president national security advisor, both previously prominent in the Karabagh Committee, parted company with President Ter-Petrossian over central policy issues. At the same time Deputy Minister for Foreign Affairs, Jirair Libaridian, also an American citizen, assumed growing responsibility as the country's diplomatic troubleshooter and the president's personal emissary for the ongoing international efforts to find a negotiated settlement of the Karabagh conflict. *See also* BAGRATIAN, HRANT SECOND CABINET.

BAGRATIAN, HRANT SECOND CABINET. Appointed by **President Levon Ter-Petrossian**, the second Bagratian cabinet served from July 27, 1995, to November 3, 1996.

Prime Minister	**Hrant Bagratian**
Agriculture and Provisions	Ashot Voskanian
Communication	Grigor Poghpatian
Culture, Youth Affairs, and Sports	Hakob Movses Hakobian
Defense	Vazgen Sargsian
Economy	Vahram Avanesian
Education and Science	Vardges Gnuni
Energy	Gagik Martirosian
Environmental Protection and Natural Resources	Suren Avetisian
Finance	Levon Barkhudarian
Foreign Affairs	Vahan Papazian
Health	Ara Babloyan
Industry	Ashot Safarian
Information	Hrachia Tamrazian
Internal Affairs	Vano Siradeghian
Justice	Marat Alexanian
National Security	Serge Sargsian
Social Welfare, Employment, Population Migration and Refugee Affairs	Rafael Bagoyan

Trade, Services, and Tourism	Vahan Melkonian
Transportation	Henrik Kochinian
Urban Planning	Felix Pirumian

The second Bagratian cabinet was formed after the contested July 1995 parliamentary elections and was dismissed a little over a month after the even more controversial September 1996 presidential elections. Even though the **Armenian National Movement** (ANM) consolidated its influence in parliament, the period marked a low point in the postindependence period as international support flagged in response to the domestic crisis in Armenia. Bagratian held to policies of economic reform, but results were negligible. The growing polarization in society and expressions of discontent elicited the expansion of the internal security apparatus to the point where political repression threatened the democratization process. The disaffection expressed against the policies of the government as manifest in public protest over the results of the 1996 presidential vote spelled the end of the Bagratian premiership. *See also* BAGRATIAN, HRANT FIRST CABINET.

BAGRATUNI (BAGRATID). Princely family of ancient Armenia. The most durable and prolific of ancient Armenia's princely families, the Bagratuni emerged as the most important of medieval Armenia's royal dynasties. Of **Yervanduni** descent, the Bagratuni family was originally domiciled in the district of Bagrevand, in central Armenia, which they held as appanage from the first royal family of Armenia. During the reign of the **Artashesian** dynasty the first known historical figure from the Bagratuni family was appointed viceroy of Syria and Cilicia by **Tigran II the Great**. The offices that the Bagratuni held during the time of the **Arshakuni** royal dynasty attest to the prominence and importance of the family. As *tagadir* or coronant, the Bagratuni prince enjoyed the high honor of affixing the royal diadem during the coronation of the Armenian king. Keepers of the symbol of monarchy, the Bagratuni constituted an important presence at the royal court, a presence reenforced by their second office as *aspet* or master of the cavalry, presumably of the royal household. No other princely family in ancient Armenia concentrated in its hands such notable ceremonial, political, administrative, and military functions.

The increasing feudalization of ancient Armenia under the strain of incessant warfare, however, relocated power and authority to the offices of those holding title as margraves and as *sparapet*, commander-in-chief. The Bagratuni fielded 1,000 knights in battle, not nearly a numerical match for the great warring families that carried the brunt of military responsibility in the face of external threat. While the Bagratuni princes were regular participants in the political life of the country, the **Mamikonian**, **Siuni**, Rshtuni, Kamsarakan, or **Ardsruni** represented effective domestic rivals. In the late Arshakuni period, the Bagratuni were thus partially sidelined. Their domain was confined to the northern district of Sper encompassing the valley of the Jorokh River, centered on the castle of Bayberd, whose name preserved the meaning of "wooden fort," hinting at the remoteness and ruggedness of the terrain. The wealth of Sper, however, did not lie in its woodlands as much as in its silver mines. The ingenuity and durability of the Bagratuni, perhaps, may be explained by their appreciation of the economic value of resources other than land upon which much of the strength of the feudal system in Armenia rested. For the Bagratuni this would have been especially important as their fiefdoms were scattered across the country. Beside Sper in the north, they held Koghovit in central Armenia, and Tmorik in the south.

If anything, the Bagratuni distinguished themselves by turning what might have appeared to their adversaries as political handicap into strategic advantage by adhering to long-term policies. At the root of their policies rested their acceptance of imperial dominion and agreement of cooperation. They schooled themselves in flexibility and political acumen ever preserving their status and regularly receiving reward by appointment to the highest office of state in Armenia. That office came in the form of the presiding prince in the aftermath of the abolition of the Armenian monarchy in 428. Depending upon the calculus of its geographic location on the map of Armenia and its ideological relations with respective suzerain powers, each *nakharar* family developed its own individual political strategy. Forging consensus among the great lords remained a standing challenge for any presiding Armenian prince. The difficulty of finding common ground was compounded by the imperial powers that competed for influence and ultimately control over Armenia. That rivalry that resulted in the partition of the country in 387 placed the Bagratuni domains on two sides of the dividing line. The critical fiefdom of Sper fell under Roman suzerainty. Unlike most of the other princely houses whose condition or aspiration required inclination toward one or the other of the imperial sovereigns, the Bagratuni risked dispossession with partisanship and opted for restraint and prudence, a self-interested balancing act upon the razor's edge separating Rome and Iran, the two greatest military powers of the ancient Near East.

If the Bagratuni chose their moments carefully, they were also driven by a family ambition that kept their reigning princes at the forefront of Armenian political life. If steady cooperation with the court in Constantinople made them dependable cohorts and earned them legitimacy through the bestowal of imperial honors, their political skills made them equally useful to the Persians. When the Mamikonians raised the banner of revolt in 451 against the Sasanid king for imposing Mazdaean worship in Christian Armenia, the Bagratuni sided with the Siuni and avoided direct conflict. Yet in 482 when the nakharars proclaimed Sahak Bagratuni reigning prince, and a similar situation threatened, he joined forces with the Mamikonian. Although Sahak paid with his life, the autonomy of Armenia and the integrity of the nakharar system remained intact throughout the period of Persian rule.

It was in the late sixth and early seventh century though, when two mercurial scions of the Bagratuni family established a personal relationship with the emperor in Constantinople, that the primacy of their dynasty in Armenia became a real possibility. Smbat IV's exceptional talents saw him inducted to the highest ranks of both the Imperial and Sasanid courts. The Emperor Maurice (582–602), in a sign of special favor, adopted him as a son for rendering critical military and other services, yet the restless warrior ended his days in the service of the Great King Chosroes II who elevated him to the third highest rank in the Sasanid realm. Smbat's son, Varaz-Tirots II Bagratuni, who was brought up at court and made cupbearer of the Great King, was appointed *marzpan*, or viceroy, of Armenia in 629. He went over to the Romans as the Sasanids prosecuted their last major campaign to overthrow Roman rule in the Near East. With the restoration of the empire and the occupation of all of Armenia under Heraklios (610–641), Varaz-Tirots was appointed prince of Armenia in 645 and given the title of curopalate, one of the three highest titles bestowed by a Roman emperor.

The crushing defeat of Sasanid Iran by the Romans paved the way for the Arab conquests and by mid-century Armenia too submitted to the forces of Islam. Its nakharar families continued to govern in the country and the Arabs retained the office of the presiding prince as the ready instrument of vassalage during the early decades of rapid expansion. The Bagratuni too continued to rank among the candidates for the office. Arab rule, however, took a turn in the eighth century as first the Umayyad in Damascus sought to impose more direct rule over Armenia and more tribute, and then the Abbasid in Baghdad from 750 onward, through even harsher measures, introduced a policy of tribal settlement in Armenia to oust the nakharar families from their lands and integrate the country with the rest of the Arab empire. The ensuing fierce and bloody struggle ruined Armenia, dislodged many an ancient princely dynasty from its ancestral domains, and wholly reconfigured the balance of internal forces in the highlands. In the absence of any further guarantees for the integrity of the nakharar system, a political environment was created where the princely families realized that not even the survival of the fittest was assured against the overwhelming force and brutal repression of the Arab forces. One turning point came during the reign of the Caliph Abdul-Malik (685–705) when in 705 many a nakharar prince with his family was deceived and slaughtered in Nakhichevan by the Arabs. A war against the Armenian feudal system was declared and the surviving elite faced the challenge of coping with an enemy that did not respect their rank and recognize their privileges. The Mamikonian, the traditional leaders of resistance against foreign incursion, carried on a valiant and costly struggle until dissipated of strength they angrily bowed out of Armenian political life and took refuge in Byzantium. The Bagratuni made peace with the Arabs and offered their services instead as the caliphs introduced direct rule through the new office of the *vostikan*, installed in the capital city of **Dvin** as governor of the province of Arminiya.

If such policy was an admission of weakness, it was tenacity that yielded the rewards. This course of action was epitomized in the career of Ashot III, possibly one of the most politically calculating leaders of the Armenian people. Ashot governed as prince of Armenia on behalf of the Arab caliph from 732 to 748, a tenure long enough to consolidate his base of power both within and without the Bagratuni family by persuading the Umayyad to remove his rivals from the country. The demise of the Umayyad dynasty left Ashot without the protection of his sponsors and the Mamikonian exacted personal revenge by blinding him. It marked the final attempt by the Mamikonian princes to recover their once vaunted position in Armenia. The suppression of the revolt of 750 and the more consequential rebellion of 774–775 witnessed the near destruction of the nakharar system. The Mamikonian were completely dispossessed of their fiefdoms by the Arabs and thus permanently excluded as vital players in the political life of the country.

Upon the reconsolidation of Arab rule in Armenia, the Bagratuni once again were restored to primacy by the Abbasids with the appointment of Ashot the Blind's son, Smbat VII, as the high constable in 761. He, along with the Mamikonian princes into whose family he had married, met his demise at Bagrevand in 775 in the last significant attempt by the Armenian nakharars to restore Armenian autonomy through armed revolt, against the advice of the still-living Ashot the Blind. The latter's bold and vigorous namesake and grandson, Ashot IV *Msaker*, the Meat-eater, returned to his grandfather's more patient and deliberate policy of internal consolidation while assuring obedient vassalage to his sovereigns. Fiercely holding the line against further Arab incursion into the Armenian heartland, he peaceably gathered the self-governing provinces under his control. Through inheritance from the dislodged Mamikonian, he acquired Taron. From the Kamsarakan, he purchased Shirak and Arsharunik. These central provinces and other peripheral districts he unified into the largest territorial unit in Armenia and secured legitimate domain over them with his recognition as prince of Armenia by the Caliph Harun al-Rashid (786–809) in 804. *See also* BAGRATUNI, ROYAL DYNASTY.

BAGRATUNI (BAGRATID). Royal dynasty of medieval Armenia. The political recovery of Armenia under King **Ashot I** (884–890) is in part explained by the increasing power of the Byzantine state, which under the so-called Macedonian dynasty had secured Asia Minor from further Arab incursion and had taken the offensive against the Arabs along the Euphrates from Armenia down to Syria. The stabilization of the Greek-speaking empire had contributed to a new geopolitical balance in the region as well as to the improvement of economic conditions. As a client kingdom Armenia represented a neutral zone, nonthreatening to either the Byzantines or the Arabs. To the contrary, the Bagratuni in particular rendered service to both by buffering the northern reaches of the two empires. The growing security of the country had also contributed to the shifting of trade routes into northern Armenia and the rapid expansion of internal and international commerce. This activity was manifest in the growth of cities across Armenia epitomized in the embellishment of **Ani** by the Bagratuni. Towns and cities everywhere expanded, and the construction of public structures, including numerous churches, monasteries, bridges, and caravansarai, attested to a rapid increase in wealth to justify expenditure beyond the necessities of fortification, armament, military readiness, patronage, and the obligations of delivering tribute to greater potentates.

The Bagratuni estate had truly been a family enterprise. Above and beyond the reliance on their kinsmen as retainers, the reigning princes had long entrusted their brothers with command of their forces in order to meet conflicts and challenges arising at different points of their extended domain. Alongside King Ashot I was always his brother Abas, and the forging of the Armenian monarchy had been a joint venture in the true sense of the words. Their father Smbat the Confessor served as *sparapet*, military commander, of the family in Shirak while his older brother Bagrat II ruled in Taron. Their father Ashot *Msaker* relied upon his own brother Shapuh as the sparapet of the realm. More so than primogeniture, military and political skill had been the deciding factor in the transfer of leadership in the Bagratuni clan. Under the pressure of constant warfare, the ancient **nakharar** tradition of the *nahapetutiun*, the tribal chiefdom, had given way to a process of selection that favored the individual with the strongest leadership skills. Where sweat and blood, the perennial dangers of warfare, and a lifetime of military service defined manhood, the Bagratuni were also riven by the internal tensions that came with a family consisting of strong personalities, ambitious soldiers, and prideful princes. In a family whose hallmark was as much political skill and diplomatic acumen as it was military strategy, striking that balance required the patience born of intellectual gifts in the face of the customary audacity of a military caste prone to action. Sustaining the balance required imposing restraint on the temperamental, the courageous, and the reckless.

Although pronounced among the Bagratuni, these were characteristics not unique to the family. The entire nakharar system functioned on the basis of the theoretical equality of the great princely families and as legitimacy rested in inherited title and patrimonial fiefdom, the elevation of Ashot to the status of monarch did not assure the complete acknowledgment among the princes that royalty was now vested in the primary male line of the Bagratuni family. Abiding tradition, family jealousy, and personal gain undermined the potentiality of the moment, and the Armenian princes almost squandered their opportunity. In staying wedded to feudal customs, the occasion to forge a strong Armenian state passed. For all their remarkable success, the countervailing forces to centralization were simply too strong to be overcome even by the artful Bagratuni.

Upon King Ashot's death many of these forces converged to undo the Bagratuni realm. The troubled reign of King Smbat I (890–914) was inaugurated with an attempt by his uncle Abas Bagratuni to seize the crown. The graver threat came when the Caliphate assigned the *vostikan*, governor, of Azerbaijan the privilege of forwarding the tribute from Armenia. Since the Abbasid had stopped designating vostikans for Armenia, the Sadjid emirs of Azerbaijan invoked this license to impose their will over the region. They did so by directly confronting the Bagratuni king and contesting his territory. Though Smbat I kept the Sadjid Afshin in check, he had less success against his successor, Yusuf, who, as the vostikan (901–919), waged an implacable war against the Armenians. Disaster befell the Armenian king, however, when his vassal, Gagik **Ardsruni** of Vaspurakan, broke rank and joined forces with Yusuf for the promise of a royal crown. Thus in 908 Yusuf succeeded in dividing the Armenian state, and having done so prosecuted the war against the Bagratuni until the capture and execution of King Smbat.

But for the extraordinary son of Smbat the Martyr, Armenia might have disintegrated and the grand Bagratuni experiment in state building brought to an ignominious end. In the tradition of his formidable antecedent whose name he carried, King Ashot II (914–928), with an iron will that gave him his sobriquet, reconstituted his patrimony. By personally appealing to the Emperor Constantine VII Porphyrogenitus (913–959) he secured Byzantine military support and restored the Bagratuni kingdom. The Arabs recognized his achievement and conferred upon him the title *Shahanshah*, king of kings, once again elevating the Bagratuni to primacy among all the Christian kings and princes of the Caucasus. With the Sadjid beaten back, King Ashot *Yerkat*, Ashot the Iron, bequeathed his immediate successors, Abas I (928–952) and Ashot III (952–977), a country more at peace and more secure than ever before.

The reign of King Ashot III marked the apogee of the medieval Armenian kingdom. Shedding all vestiges of a client relationship with its exemption from paying tribute to the Caliphate, the Bagratuni poured their resources into major construction projects. In 961 Ashot III permanently relocated the capital of Armenia to Ani. He also sponsored the relocation of the Armenian catholicosate to the nearby town of Argina. His philanthropy, which earned him the epithet *Voghormats*, the Merciful, was augmented by Queen Khosrovanuysh who founded the monasteries of Sanahin in 966 and Haghbat in 976, which became two of the most important centers of medieval Armenian learning and culture.

In this period of greatest stability and security, the main political trend in Armenia, however, was the administrative splintering of the country among the royal princes. In 962/3 Ashot the Merciful extended his brother Mushegh a royal crown and an estate of his own to govern from the city of Kars, which had long served as one of the main residences of the royal house. The Kingdom of Kars passed down to Mushegh's son Abas (984–1029) and grandson Gagik Abas (1029–1065). In 982, Ashot the Merciful's younger son, Gurgen I, was given a royal crown and the district of Lori as his estate farther north of Kars. The Kingdom of Lori passed down to Gurgen's son Davit (989–1048) and grandson Gurgen II (1048–1089), also called Kiurike. From 970 the Siuni princes deigned themselves king of Siunik in Eastern Armenia, while in southern Armenia, with the passing of King Gagik I Ardsruni's successor, Abusahl-Hamazasp (958–968), the kingdom of Vaspurakan was divided among his three sons, Ashot-Sahak (968–990), Gurgen-Khachik, and Hovhannes-Senekerim.

As Arab influence waned, Byzantine expansion into Armenia slowly proceeded eastward. With the annexation of Taron in 966 during the reign of the Emperor Nikephoros Phokas (963–969), the Byzantines neared the center of the highlands. But when the Emperor John Tzimiskes (969–976) appeared at the head of an army in 974, the Armenian princes in a unified show of force rallied around Ashot III and went into the field to meet the Byzantines. The two monarchs, both Armenian-born, reached an accord assuring Ashot the Merciful's sons and successors, Smbat II (977–989) and Gagik I (989–1020), the security of their kingdom. Smbat built the great outer walls of Ani that stand to this day, and during the reign of Gagik the magnificent cathedral of the capital city was completed by the architect Trdat, who subsequently restored the cupola of the Hagia Sophia in Constantinople after it had been damaged by an earthquake.

The fall of the Bagratuni kingdom came rapidly. A new combination of external forces placed the Armenians in a vise that compelled them to consider the better option between two choices. Both required the surrender of sovereignty. Although an understanding had been reached with John Tzimiskes, Basil II (976–1025), having checked the Bulgarians and restored hegemony over the Balkans, turned his attention to Armenia, and renewed the policy of its piecemeal annexation more through the display of arms than by outright military contest. In the year 1000, he seized the northern province of Tayk, in 1021 negotiated the surrender of the kingdom of Vaspurakan from the Ardsruni, and in 1022 pressured Hovhannes-Smbat (1020–1041) into an agreement to transfer the Bagratuni kingdom of Ani upon his death. After a brief period of resistance during the reign of the young King Gagik II (1041–1045) organized by the sparapet Vahram Pahlavuni, the Byzantines forces entered the city of Ani and extinguished the Bagratuni monarchy. In 1065 the Byzantines completed the occupation of central Armenia with the annexation of the remaining kingdom of Kars.

The Seljuk Turks, however, had entered Ani in 1064 and Byzantine rule over Armenia quickly disintegrated. Byzantine penetration of central Armenia in the first half of the 11th century was facilitated by the increasing frequency of raids by Turkic tribes from the east that staged their first full-scale invasion of Armenia in 1047. By 1054 Tughril Beg had begun the occupation of the country. When in 1071 Alp Arslan led the Seljuks to victory over the grand army of the Emperor Romanos IV Diogenes at the battle of Manzikert, fought along the northern rim of **Lake Van**, the Byzantines were swept from Armenia.

While the Armenian Bagratuni lost their kingdoms and the Byzantines lost Armenia, the Georgian Bagratuni gained in stature. Both branches of the dynasty traced its descent from Ashot the Blind, whose son Vasak had married a Georgian princess. Their offspring Adarnase, as prince of Erusheti-Artani, was heir to a district directly to the north of Armenia and had settled in his new domain. His son, Ashot I the Great, was appointed prince of Iberia (813–830) by the Arabs, and whose great-grandson, Prince Adarnase IV was crowned king in 888 by King Ashot the Great of Armenia. King Adarnase's descendent Bagrat III became the first king of a unified Georgia in

1008. The Bagratuni of Georgia survived the Seljuk incursions, and under David II the Rebuilder (1089–1125) emerged as the most powerful state in the Caucasus. The Armenians rallied around the Georgian Bagratuni forging an alliance with the royal dynasty that reached fulfillment during the reign of Queen Tamar (1184–1212). When the Zakarian family, known as the Mkhargrdzeli among the Georgians, led the forces of the queen into Armenia, they brought vast swaths of its northern and eastern parts under Georgian rule. The Mongol invasion of 1220 shattered the Georgian kingdom, leaving behind the Zakarians to govern briefly in Armenia. The Bagratuni retained title to the Georgian crown through all the succeeding centuries until the annexation of the country by Russia in 1800. A Russified branch of the Georgian family entered the service of the Romanovs, with Prince Bagration distinguishing himself in 1812 at the Battle of Borodino against Napoleon.

The Armenian Bagratuni, however, did not endure. In the aftermath of the defeat at Manzikert, in an act of contempt the Byzantines killed the royal heirs. Gagik II, the former king of Ani, who was removed to Caesarea (Kayseri) was murdered in 1079, and his sons, Hovhannes and Davit, and Davit's son Ashot, were soon after poisoned. In 1080, Gagik, the son of Abas, the last king of Kars, was killed, as well as Atom-Ashot and Abusahl, the sons of Senekerim, the former Ardsruni king. In response to this treacherous treatment of Armenian royalty, one among their courtiers named Ruben/Rupen raised the flag of rebellion against the Byzantines in the mountains of Cilicia. His descendents founded a new Armenian state on the Mediterranean coast. *See also* BAGRATUNI, PRINCELY FAMILY; RUBENIAN.

BALIAN, GARABED (1800–1866). Ottoman architect. Garabed *Amira* Balian, the son of **Krikor Balian**, was the most prolific builder of the family, who in 1836 was conferred all of his father's court privileges. In keeping with the modernization efforts in the Ottoman Empire, Garabed became the architect of new schools, hospitals, barracks, reservoirs, and factories. The factory buildings he designed testify to the program to introduce industrial manufacturing in the Ottoman Empire. The Imperial Textile Mill at Hereke was originally built for the Armenian brothers Ohannes and Boghos Dadian in 1843 before Sultan Abdulmejit (1839–1861) acquired it. A year earlier, in 1842, Garabed had built the broadcloth mill at Izmit for Ohannes *Bey* Dadian, who held the office of director of the state gunpowder factory, and who was one of Turkey's first industrial entrepreneurs. Garabed also built the iron and steel foundry at Zeytinburnu, which Sultan Abdulmejit had instructed Ohannes Dadian to construct. Similarly, Garabed raised the cotton mill at Bakirkoy for Ohannes Dadian in 1850.

While these early factories were first constructed by private Armenian industrialists and later acquired by the state, most of the other structures designed by Garabed were government commissions. The new building of the Imperial War Academy for the training of military officers went up in 1846. That same year the sultan himself inaugurated the opening of the Imperial Medical School, the first modern medical facility in the Ottoman Empire. Abdulmejit also attended the 1849 opening ceremonies of the Gumushsuyu military hospital of the artillery corps. The new Imperial Engineering College for the training of artillery officers was constructed in 1850. Earlier in 1837–1839, at the command of Sultan Abdulmejit, Garabed had rebuilt in stone the Kuleli cavalry barracks, so-called for the spired towers, which stand at the two ends of the building. Garabed also rebuilt in stone the Gumushsuyu imperial barracks, which housed the military music school where the court musicians were trained.

Garabed Balian's greatest architectural achievements, however, were reserved for the imperial family. The mausoleum of Mahmut II, completed in 1840, while Ottoman in form, is wholly European in spirit with its large round arched windows and pilasters topped with Ionic capitals. Like the elegant Dolmabahche Bezmialem Valide Sultan mosque constructed for Abdulmejit's mother in 1852–1854, the mausoleum was an exercise in neoclassical restraint. On the other hand, Garabed's developed style, which was heavily influenced by contemporary French architecture, acquired its grandest expression in the imperial residences he constructed. The first of these was the old Chiraghan palace built between 1835–1843 with a colonnaded facade and a central neoclassical portico. In 1855 Garabed also designed a pair of comparatively modest residences for the Abdulmejit's daughters known as the Jemile Sultan and Munire Sultan Palaces.

These residences of the imperial household pale in comparison to the Dolmabahche Palace, Garabed Bey Balian's architectural triumph. Built between 1849 and 1856 at the command of Sultan Abdulmejit, the Dolmabahche is the grandest structure designed in the Ottoman Empire during the 19th century. Its opulence stood as much as a symbol of Ottoman power and the empire's entry in the Concert of Europe as of the profligacy of the sultan whose extraordinary expenditure on the palace bankrupted the state treasury. Sitting astride the Bosphorus, the main building of the palace consists of a large central structure whose facade is articulated with a flourish of detail and a series of both freestanding columns and pilasters. Extending from both sides are two lower wings whose length is used to advantage by a pattern of recesses alternating with porticoes with windows stretching end to end to capture the light of the sun and the glimmer of the sea. Reflective of the contemporary French Empire style, the ornateness of the palace made it wholly unique.

The real splendor of the palace, however, was to be found in the interior. Its sumptuous halls brought the art of palatial design to an unequaled level of intricate and colorful ornamentation. While the walls and ceilings of numerous reception rooms were given detailed attention, none surpassed the exceeding grandeur of the audience hall. A dome covers the great space of the throne room. Resting upon a set of arches supported by 56 columns arranged in pairs and quadruplets bearing Corinthian capitals, it rises 36 meters from the floor. It was in this hall on December 23, 1876, in the presence of the eminencies of the empire that 34-year-old Sultan Abdul-Hamid (Abdulhamit) II (1876–1909) proclaimed the Ottoman Constitution.

Garabed relied on the services of many Armenians for the construction of the Dolmabahche palace. His son **Nigoghos Balian** worked together with him in the design and construction of the palace. The grand audience hall was Nigoghos's feat. Bedros Nemtse (1830–1913) served as the assistant architect. The iron gates of the fantastic portals that guard the palace grounds were the products of Krikor Malakian. Neshan Tashjian shipped the marble used for the palace from Malta. Bedros Sirabian, known as Monsieur Pierre, did the gilded decorations of the interior. The chief court painter, Haji Megirdich Chrakian, designed the wall paintings. Ohannes Ajemian and David Triantz accomplished the wall and ceiling decorations. Kapriyel Kalfa Megirdichian did the painting of the ceiling of the audience hall.

Garabed was also the architect of a number of Armenian churches, including Surp Sarkis in the Armenian village of Bandirma, Saint

Mary's in Beshiktash, Holy Cross in Kurucheshme, Holy Trinity in Galatasaray, and Saint James in Zeytinburnu, all in an Italianate Baroque style. He was also active in Armenian community affairs. He and his brother-in-law Ohannes *Amira* Serverian, who worked with Garabed as part of the team consisting of his sons, met the expenses of the Jemaran Armenian school, which they established in Uskudar in 1838. In 1854 he opened a school for agricultural technicians beside the Armenian Church of Holy Savior in Yedikule. In 1858 he and Boghos Bey Dadian were instrumental in opening Saint James Monastery and a seminary for the education of priests. He also built and contributed to the financing of the Yedikule Armenian Hospital, which had been established by Kazaz Artin Amira Bezjian in 1832–1834. He also financed the publication of books by several authors and established endowments for churches and an educational foundation.

BALIAN, HAGOP (AGOP) BEY (1837–1875). Ottoman architect. The son of **Garabed Balian**, Hagop studied architecture in Paris, Vienna, and Venice. Like his brother **Nigoghos Balian**, Hagop first worked with his father and continued primarily as a designer of buildings that his third brother, **Sarkis Balian**, constructed. A man of the finest artistic sensibility, Hagop was the architect of possibly the most exquisite of the monumental structures the Balian family ever built. The Beylerbey Palace, completed in 1864, was built on the Asiatic shore of the Bosphorus for the pleasure of Sultan Abdulaziz (1861–1876). With its classical exterior features and its proportional harmony, Beylerbey could pass for a High Renaissance palazzo. Its interior halls, on the other hand, are decorated with brilliant arabesques painted in blue, orange, yellow, and gold colors, which were executed by Migirdich Givanian (1848–1906). Bedros Nemtse served as assistant architect of the project. Among other buildings, Hagop also designed a number of royal pavilions, as well as the Pertevniyal Valide Sultan Mosque and Tomb in Aksaray.

BALIAN, KRIKOR (1764–1831). Ottoman architect. During the entire length of the 19th century, members of the Balian family served as architects of the Ottoman sultan. They designed and constructed virtually all the imperial palaces, residences, and mosques, as well as numerous other structures for the use of the government, including ministry buildings, military barracks and schools. By designing buildings mostly in the contemporary European neoclassical style, some heavily laden with conventional Middle Eastern and Ottoman artistic motifs and decorative patterns, they created a school of architecture unique to the period, to the Ottoman capital, and to their family, a style sometimes called Ottoman Baroque. As buildings of a new age, most were raised along the shores of the Bosphorus beyond the confines of the old city where the Byzantine remains and **Sinan** Pasha's High Ottoman style defined both the skyline and the architecture of Istanbul.

The first member of the Balian family to enter the imperial service was Bali *Kalfa* (d. 1803) of whom little is known other than that he originated from the village of Deverenk in the province of Kayseri and had emigrated to the Ottoman capital. Sultan Selim III (1789–1807) appointed his son Krikor court architect. He retained his post with additional honors and privileges, including the title Amira, bestowed upon him and his family, into the reign of Sultan Mahmut II (1808–1839).

Krikor *Amira* Balian built, repaired, and expanded a number of imperial residences including the Aynalikavak palace, Beshiktash palace (renovations completed in 1815), the Chaghlayan summer palace, and the Defterdarburnu palace, all of which were in a style still akin to traditional Ottoman court architecture. The interiors, however, abandoned their reliance on the Iznik tile works and instead were given to Italianate decorations. Most of these palaces consisted of an entire complex of buildings including the main residence, multiple, and depending on location, waterfront pleasure pavilions, gardens, and fountains.

Krikor was also responsible for the construction of a large number of more functional buildings including military barracks for the new modern Ottoman army that replaced the Janissaries corps upon their destruction in 1826. Virtually all of these structures were massive quadrangles, some with elaborate towers at the four corners, including the Davutpasha barracks (1832) and the Maltepe barracks (1827). The Selimiye barracks built in Uskudar on the Asiatic side of the Bosphorus served as British military headquarters during the Crimean War. A wing of the Selimiye barracks was used as a military hospital, where Florence Nightingale began the medical reforms that introduced the concept of professional nursing of the wounded in war. Krikor also designed the new imperial mint building on the grounds of the Topkapi Saray, the old imperial palace, and the Nusretiye mosque, completed in 1826, whose flowing lines give it an elegance reminiscent of Rococo architecture. Fellow Armenian, *Haji* Megirdich Chrakian (1799–1899), served as assistant architect and chief draftsman of the project. Lastly, Krikor was also the architect of the Armenian cathedral of *Surp Asdvadsadsin*, or St. Mary's, in Kumkapi, which atypically abandoned the millennial Armenian church architecture identified by its geometric central cupola, for the conventional basilica with two rows of fluted columns roofed by a depressed barrel vault. The church became the model of a new Armenian ecclesiastical architecture that closely resembled European, and especially Italian, sanctuaries. *See also* BALIAN, GARABED; BALIAN, HAGOP; BALIAN, NOGOGHOS, BALIAN, SARKIS.

BALIAN, NIGOGHOS *BEY* (1826–1858). Ottoman architect. Nigoghos, the son of **Garabed Balian**, was the first of his family to receive a formal education in architecture in Paris. He worked with his father all his life and was responsible for the design of the great audience hall of the Dolmabahche palace as well as the elaborate portals of the palace that stand as monuments to his fantastic artistic imagination. Nigoghos also built a very ornate modern theater at Dolmabahche in 1858 for the production of operas and other types of performances.

Between 1864 and 1871 Nigoghos's younger brothers **Sarkis Balian** and **Hagop Balian** oversaw the construction of the new Chiraghan palace, which replaced the mostly timber pavilion constructed by their father. Built at the command of the Sultan Abdulaziz (1861–1876), the palace was based on preliminary designs by Nigoghos. While the symmetrical exterior of the longitudinal structure conveyed the sense of a European palace, the interior involved a whole new experiment contrasting widely with the awesome dimensions of the Dolmabahche reception halls. The interior of the new Chiraghan palace was decorated entirely in an Arabian style consciously based on Moorish and other Oriental examples. The carpentry for the palace was placed under the charge of an Armenian cohort, Vortik Kemhajian. In 1909 the New Chiraghan Palace was designated for the use of the Ottoman parliament that reconvened on November 14 for the first time after the Young Turks ended the Hamidian autocracy in 1908.

Nigoghos's architectural heritage suffered the misfortune of two fires that destroyed the Dolmabahche theater and the new Chiraghan palace a mere two months after the Ottoman legislature began holding its sessions in the former imperial residence. The more certain legacy of Nigoghos is best preserved in the gorgeous palatial residences whose construction he personally supervised. These smaller European-style modern mansions, called *kasir* in Turkish, come in two varying styles. The Adile Sultan kasir in Uskudar built in 1853 and the Beykoz kasir, originally commissioned by Muhammad Ali, the viceroy of Egypt from 1805 to 1848, but ultimately presented as a gift by his son Said Pasha, khedive of Egypt from 1854 to 1863, to the Sultan Abdulaziz, were almost wholly neoclassical in appearance both inside and outside. The even smaller Goksu kasir built in 1856 and the Ihamur kasir built between 1848 and 1853, both constructed as resort mansions for Sultan Abdulmejit, have heavily ornamented exteriors replete with outlandish cornucopia carved in high relief.

A similar contrast can be seen between the Kuchuk Mejidiye, or Chiraghan, mosque and the Buyuk Mejidiye, or Ortakoy, mosque. Built in 1854–1855, the Ortakoy mosque represents the acme of the French Empire style so frequently imitated and embellished by the midcentury Balian architectural designs. Its curvilinear walls were spaced by two tiers of fluted columns reaching to four massive arches that span each side of the proportional cube of the structure, which was topped by a large dome covering the entire roof. Situated right on the shore of the Bosphorus, against the dark blue of the water and the light blue of the sky, the edifice evokes a Venetian landscape. Arguably, it is Nigoghos Balian's finest work.

BALIAN, SARKIS *BEY* (1846–1899). Ottoman architect. The son of **Garabed Balian**, and the brother of **Hagop Balian** and **Nigoghos Balian**, with whom he worked as a team during their lifetime, Sarkis's forte was as an engineer and contractor. He was trained in engineering in Paris and was appointed, along with Hagop, imperial architect in 1866 upon the demise of his father. Beyond the construction industry, Sarkis pursued other business interests in railroads and mining. Like his brothers, however, his principal contribution was in architecture. He was primarily responsible for realizing the building plans drawn by them.

All told, Sarkis and his brothers designed and built some fifty structures of artistic, or of some other, significance, including six palaces, fifteen mansions and pavilions, two hunting lodges, three mosques, four barracks, two ministry buildings, and two schools. Like so many of the functional structures constructed by his Balian predecessors, many of the edifices raised by Sarkis are also still in use in Istanbul. The imposing neoclassical quadrangular structure, with a row of Ionic columns at its entrance, once the Mejidiye barracks at Tashkishla (1864) is presently the Istanbul Technical University. The ministry of war building (1864), with its main gate to the grounds a virtual Oriental triumphal arch, is part of Istanbul University. The sturdy naval ministry building (1868), with its Moorish arches framing its windows, is still used by the same service.

Much like that of his brothers and predecessors, Sarkis's architectural legacy has its unique characteristics also. The Ayazaga mansion and the Ayazaga hunting lodge, both for the use of the sultan, relied on tile decorations for the interior reminiscent of an earlier Ottoman style. As for the Yildiz palace, to which the Sultan Abdul-Hamid (Abdulhamit) (1876–1909) retreated, it was more properly a whole complex of buildings reproducing in many ways the enclosed miniature city of the old seraglio. Nearly all were plain neoclassical structures, none approaching the dimensions of the palatial residences commissioned by earlier sultans. Their interiors, however, continued to be lavishly decorated. Of the religious structures raised by Sarkis, the Chaghlayan mosque (1862) echoes the elegant lines of the Ortakoy mosque. The Pertevniyal Valide Sultan mosque at Aksaray and the Hamidiye mosque at Yildiz, on the other hand, represent quite a departure with their neo-Gothic exteriors and strong Arabian motifs for the interior.

Like others in his family, Sarkis Balian was a patron of the arts and a great friend of the Russian-Armenian painter Ivan Aivazovsky who was in Istanbul in 1874. Sarkis introduced Aivazovsky to Sultan Abdulaziz, who commissioned a whole series of tableaux, of which 34 alone hang at the Dolmabahche palace. For his extraordinary skill as an architect and his reputation as an engineering contractor with an ability to move rapidly from the design to the completion of a building, in 1878 Sultan Abdul-Hamid bestowed upon him the title of Chief Architect of the State. The title was never awarded again after Sarkis's death. He was the last of a long line of architects of Armenian origin in the service of the Ottoman sultans, a line stretching all the way back to **Sinan** Pasha, the great architect of Suleyman the Magnificent.

BARONIAN, HAGOP (1843–1891). Playwright. Baronian was born in Edirne, in Turkey. Though he received only a very basic education, Baronian became the founder of the Western Armenian theater to the extent that he authored an important body of plays. None were performed in his lifetime and he earned his living as a writer for Armenian newspapers, as a teacher, and as an accountant. He also served a term as the representative of the Armenian community of Edirne to the Armenian National Assembly in Istanbul. For the absence of sponsorship, he lived and died in dire poverty. He was unable to hold a job for very long mainly due to his biting criticism of the conflicts and contradictions in the life, values, and practices of an emerging upper middle class in Armenian society in the second half of the 19th century. All of his important works are satirical comedies exposing a topsy-turvy world of confused standards and morals, further distorted by deception and connivance, and resulting in tragicomic consequences. His oeuvre includes *Servant of Two Masters* (*Yerku Terov Dsara me*) written in 1865, *The Oriental Dentist* (*Atamnabuyzhn Arevelian*) (1868), *National Bigwigs* (*Azgayin Djodjer*) (1874), and *The Perils of Politeness* (*Kaghakavarutian Vnasnere*) (1886/7). *Brother Balthazar* (*Baghtasar Aghbar*) (1886/7), a hilarious comedy of family morals, and his book *The Honorable Beggars* (*Medsapativ Muratskanner*), which savaged the Armenian nationalist and political activists and their fundraising efforts as the self-serving enterprises of social parasites, are regarded his wittiest pieces. His plays now constitute part of the standard repertoire of the Armenian theater. Their popularity has not diminished and they remain the best of comic entertainment produced in the **Armenian language**.

BOGHOS *BEY* (YUSUFIAN) (1775–1844). Minister of commerce and foreign affairs in Egypt in the 1820s and 1830s. Boghos Yusufian, better known as Boghos *Bey*, was born in Izmir to a family well connected to the city's Armenian merchant class involved in overseas commerce. He made his money in Egypt as a customs official and trader. He was skilled in languages and he served the British as an interpreter in the campaign against the French under Napoleon. He was first hired by the new governor of Egypt, Muhammad Ali, as an interpreter and rapidly progressed to that of personal secretary. With Muhammad Ali's consolidation of his rule in Egypt, the ambitious governor found in Boghos the instrument for pursuing policies independently of his Ottoman sovereigns. Having earned his trust during his service in the palace in Cairo, Boghos *Bey* was made minister of commerce in 1826. He ran his office from Alexandria and proved an adept intermediary between Egyptian economic policy and European commercial interests. In a reorganization of the government in 1837, Muhammad Ali created the joint ministry of commerce and foreign affairs and appointed Boghos as head of the department, leading many foreigners to assume that he served as the "prime minister" of Egypt.

To help modernize the administration of the country and improve its economy, Muhammad Ali patronized the Armenians. With Boghos Bey as its leading figure, the Armenian community in Egypt grew from a few dozen to 2,000. Among them were his relatives whom he brought over from Izmir, including the Nubar(ian) and Abro(yan) families. Arakel *Bey* Nubar (1826–1859) followed in his uncle's footsteps and rose to become minister of commerce. Boghos *Bey*'s more famous nephew, however, was **Nubar** *Pasha* who served three terms as prime minister of Egypt in the last quarter of the 19th century. Dicran *Pasha* d'Abro was minister of foreign affairs in the 1890s.

Among his many assignments Muhammad Ali also entrusted Boghos with the training of new and capable administrators. Charged with sending the most promising to Europe for further education, with the approval of the pasha, Boghos also sponsored the education of the sons of many Armenian merchants in the service of Muhammad Ali. Besides his relatives, among them was also his successor to the ministry of commerce and foreign affairs, **Artin** *Bey* **Chrakian** (1804–1859), whom Muhammad Ali appointed upon Boghos' death.

BOGHOS NUBAR *PASHA* (1851–1930). Political leader and philanthropist. Boghos Nubar was born in Alexandria, Egypt. He was the son of **Nubar** *Pasha*, the 19th century prime minister of Egypt and nephew and protégé of **Boghos** *Bey* **Yusufian**, his son's namesake and the great minister of Muhammad Ali, the founder of modern Egypt. Boghos Nubar received his training as a civil engineer in France and served as a director of the state railways in Egypt.

In 1906 Boghos Nubar, heir to his father's title and family fortune, took the lead, along with a group of wealthy Armenians in Egypt, to found the **Armenian General Benevolent Union** (AGBU) in Cairo, Egypt. Growing out of the concern for the tens of thousands of Armenians made destitute by the Hamidian massacres of 1894–1896, the AGBU hoped to support the recovery of the Armenians from the brutalization suffered at the hands of the Ottoman government. Within three years of its founding, the 1909 **Adana Massacre** of Armenians precipitated the AGBU to focus its resources in building orphanages, hospitals, and shelters for widows and elderly survivors in the region of Cilicia. The 1915 deportations and massacres of Armenians required the AGBU to recommit significant funds to attempt a measure of relief for the entire Ottoman Armenian community now made refugees. The AGBU set up orphanages and clinics all across the Middle East wherever the Armenian refugees concentrated.

In 1918 Boghos Nubar headed the Armenian National Delegation in Paris to represent the disenfranchised Armenians of the Ottoman Empire with the hope of establishing a national home for them. In France Boghos Nubar was also instrumental in getting the French army to approve the formation under its command of the *Legion d'Orient* manned mostly by Armenians who saw fighting in the Allied campaign in Palestine. Though a person of conservative political leanings, with his pedigree Boghos Nubar emerged as the leading spokesman for the Armenians at the Paris Peace Conference. He had little success, however, in obtaining support for his ideas of an expanded Armenian state to serve as a national home for the Armenian refugees dispersed across the Middle East.

Boghos Nubar died in Paris. Before his passing, he had already set the AGBU in a new direction. After the immediate minimum physical needs of the Armenian refugees had been met, he donated funds to the AGBU, and in so doing set an example emulated since by other well-to-do Armenians, for the establishment of educational programs and institutions to begin the moral and intellectual recovery of a generation of Armenians who had known nothing but exile, hunger, and privation. Over the decades the philanthropic organization founded by Boghos Nubar Pasha grew to become the largest in the Armenian **diaspora** with chapters around the world supporting schools, orphanages, clinics, libraries, youth centers, theaters, publications, and a host of other activities designed to sustain Armenian culture and identity in diaspora communities. *See also* ARMENIAN MASSACRES.

– C –

CATHOLIC CHURCH, ARMENIAN. The Armenian Catholic Church is a distinct unit of the Roman Catholic Church, with its own leader, called **catholicos**, as in the **Armenian Apostolic Church**, and its own rites that are performed in the Armenian language, but which are theologically consonant with Roman Catholicism. The population living in Armenia Minor and the districts of Armenia Major under Roman rule were always exposed to Chalcedonian influence and a segment thereof participated in the Imperial Church. The gradual breakdown of ecclesiastical relations between Rome and Constantinople meant that Chalcedonian Armenians became adherents of the Byzantine Church and relations with Rome were nonexistent. Contact was reestablished in the late 11th century. The settlement of Armenians in Cilicia on the Mediterranean coast, the concomitant arrival of the Crusaders, and the **foreign policy** of the new **Armenian kingdom** established by the **Rubenian** and **Hetumian** dynasties in Cilicia, created numerous occasion for Armenians and Latins to interact and in the process exposed Cilician Armenia to the influence of Catholicism. The objective of the reigning dynasties, first to obtain a royal crown, and second to secure political and military support from the West, created a powerful incentive to align the Armenian Church with the Papacy, which in the 12th and 13th centuries was at its height of authority in western Europe and the Mediterranean.

Good relations with the Papacy were central to Cilician Armenia's foreign policy to the degree that differences between Armenians and Latin Crusaders were always a source of friction. The question of **religion** and sectarian attitudes were among the major sources of the problem. King **Levon I** supported the union of the Armenian Church with Rome and the agreement to such appears to have been part of the bargain between him and the Papacy in order to secure its endorsement for the awarding of a royal crown by the Holy Roman Empire. It was also in the strategic interest of the Papacy to bring the Armenians into its fold as a means of buttressing the Crusader states that were surrounded by Islamic countries. While the political and ecclesiastical hierarchy favored union, the Armenian clergy and populace in general were less disposed to give up the liturgy and traditions to which they were accustomed. The many attempts at a union as negotiated in **Adana** in 1316 and 1317, for instance, never materialized in a formal relationship, among its hindrances being the reluctance of the Armenian Church, long accustomed to autocephaly, to subordinate itself to a remote pontiff.

Even so, the Papacy made sufficient inroads in Cilician Armenia that by the 14th century it felt equipped to missionize in Armenia proper. In 1320 the Fratre Unitore, the Friars of Union, was organized as the Armenian branch of the Dominican movement to convert the Orthodox Armenians to Catholicism. The movement registered success in pockets of eastern Armenia where Italian commercial interests had penetrated along the trade routes to the Mongol Empire, the very same path traveled by the Venetian merchant Marco Polo. The spread of Catholicism in Eastern Armenia, part of the country lacking Armenian church leadership, as the Armenian catholicos, in flight from the Turks, had settled in the Cilician mountains, prompted a local movement to revive the Armenian catholicosate at **Edjmiadsin**. The collapse of Cilician Armenia in 1375, even after resorting to the coronation of members of the French Catholic Lusignan dynasty ruling in Cyprus, ended diplomatic relations between Armenia and the Papacy. The reemergence of Edjmiadsin in 1441 as a viable center of Armenian church activity also reversed the influence of Catholicism among Armenians. Even so, ongoing Armenian commercial contact with Italy meant the culture of the West and the vaunting religious leadership of the Papacy against Islam would exercise a continuing influence on the Armenian imagination. By the time of the announcement, however, of a formal union at the 1439 Council of Florence, the mechanisms for the realization of the idea were no longer extant and the Armenian Church was in captivity.

The spread of Catholicism among Armenians picked up momentum with the Counter-Reformation. The initial zealotry of the drive against Protestantism, however, proved disruptive of Armenian communal life as sectarians fell under the label of anathematized schismatics even though the Armenian Apostolic Church and the Papacy as institutions had not come into direct conflict. The most negative effect was registered in the Armenian **diaspora** community in

Poland, where religious conformity became part of state policy. Armenians, who for centuries had been tolerated, even welcomed as productive citizens, allowed communal rights and their own ecclesiastical organization since the 14th century, saw their religious institutions disintegrate as the populace was pressured to convert to Catholicism. Many did, while others preferred to abandon their former homes and seek asylum elsewhere. The most important convert was the Armenian archbishop Nicholas Torosowicz, who by his decision removed his diocese from the jurisdiction of Edjmiadsin and placed it under Rome. The Armenian Catholic archbishopric of southeastern Poland centered in Lvov was in existence from 1635 to 1944, by which time its community of adherents was dwindled and assimilated into the general population. The new Armenian Catholic community in eastern Europe also gravitated toward the expanding Hapsburg Empire where Armenians settled in areas of Hungary seized from the Ottoman Empire. Soon word reached them of a new movement among Armenian Catholics and some of them made the journey further west to join them.

In contrast to developments in Poland, Catholicism among Armenians in Islamic Turkey registered a more formative influence and from the start of the 18th century rapidly evolved toward acquiring an organized and indigenous character. A minor development at the time, which sparked one of the processes of cultural modernization among Armenians, occurred in 1701 in Constantinople when a convert from Armenian Orthodoxy gathered a small monastic order committed to the mission of bringing learning to the benighted Armenians living under Turkish rule. By constituting the **Mekhitarian** fraternity named for him, **Mekhitar Sebastatsi** assured that Catholicism would play a large role in the intellectual revival of the Armenian people, and in so doing gradually alter Armenian perception of Catholicism as a competing and threatening institution. The Armenian Church opposed the appearance of like groups, and the Mekhitarians eventually settled in Venice and Vienna, but the Armenian Church's own spiritual ossification and intellectual paralysis under the suffocating strictures of Islam were among the contributive factors to the search for alternative sources of moral guidance. Over the long haul the Counter-Reformation gave impetus to the Armenian Church to revitalize itself in order to meet the new challenge of missionizing Catholicism in the East.

If the Mekhitarian contributions were to be in the main of an intellectual order, at the popular level, Armenian Catholicism as a formally constituted church with its own hierarchy came into existence in 1742 when Pope Benedict XIV confirmed Abraham Ardzivian (1679–1749) as patriarch of the Armenian Catholics of Cilicia and Syria. Ardzivian took the pontifical name of Abraham Peter. All succeeding leaders thereafter included Peter as part of their pontifical name as an expression of allegiance to the church founded by St. Peter. Ardzivian's background as a former Armenian Apostolic bishop of Aleppo, where the Jesuits and Capuchins had been active since 1626 and 1627 respectively, and his assumption of the title of catholicos directly challenged the authority of the Armenian catholicos of Cilicia, whose condemnation of this development and ensuing reaction prompted Ardzivian to take refuge in Lebanon. In 1771 on a mountaintop overlooking the Mediterranean the Armenian Catholic hierarchy secured a monastery among the Lebanese Maronites at a place called Bzommar to serve as headquarters and seminary. The remoteness of Bzommar restricted the capacity of the Armenian Catholic Church to consolidate its organizational structure and Armenians in other parts of the Ottoman Empire located closer to Constantinople relied on the Latin vicar of the capital city who exercised spiritual authority over the Levantine Catholics of the region.

Through the intercession of France, the Armenian Catholics in the Ottoman Empire received separate status as a *millet*, or religious community, in 1830. Among the conditions of the Ottoman government was the appointment of a patriarch domiciled in Constantinople, as with the **Armenian** [Orthodox] *Millet*. The complication of two Catholic patriarchates was solved by unifying the offices in 1847 with election of the Armenian Catholic prelate of Constantinople as patriarch in succession to the line earlier established at Bzommar. Thereby leadership of the entire Armenian Catholic community of the Ottoman Empire passed to Anthony Peter IX Hassoun, born Anton Hasunian in 1809 in Syria and previously prelate of Cilicia. An energetic promoter of Catholicism, he encouraged conversion from the Armenian Apostolic Church. His activities, however, prompted in the 1850s both a strong reaction from the Orthodox clergy and a split within the ranks of the Armenian Catholic clergy specifically over the national content of the church. The eminent scholar **Maghakia Ormanian**, a strong proponent of Armenian enlightenment, and his followers, withdrew from Catholicism over the debate about the national mission of the church and joined the Orthodox clergy. To expand the reach and services of the Catholic Church, Hassoun oversaw in 1847 the founding in Constantinople of the Armenian Sisters of the Immaculate Conception dedicated to the education of Armenian girls. For his many services Hassoun became the first Armenian raised to the rank of cardinal. The continuing controversy surrounding him, however, eventually persuaded the Papacy to recall him to Rome where he died in 1884. Hassoun had been trained in the so-called Propaganda school, the Sacred Congregation for the Propagation of the Faith, the missionary arm of the Papacy, but the conflict surrounding his views made clear the imperative of developing a curriculum specifically for the education and advanced theological training of Armenians for the priesthood. Accordingly, in 1883, Pope Leo XIII (1878–1903) founded a pontifical college in Rome for that very purpose. Known among Armenians as the Levonian College in honor of the pope, the school continues to operate. In the chapel of the college, Hassoun was laid to rest.

The losses of the Catholic community during the **Armenian Genocide** were such that the Papacy decided to relocate its surviving institutions from Turkey. In 1922 the motherhouse of the Sisters of the Immaculate Conception was moved to Rome, and in 1928 the patriarchal seat was transferred to Beirut, Lebanon, which had become home for the largest Armenian Catholic community in the wake of the persecutions of the Armenians in the Ottoman Empire. In the following decades the Armenian Catholic Church regained its stature in Armenian diaspora life under the astute management of its greatest son, born Ghazaros Aghachanian (1895–1971), but more famously known as Cardinal Grigor/Gregory Agagianian.

Agagianian emanated from the Akhaltskhe, Georgia, and at a young age was sent to receive his education in Rome, where he earned doctorates in philosophy, theology, and Canon Law from the Urbanian University run by the Propaganda office. He returned to Georgia in 1919 to assume pastoral responsibilities in his home country, a tenure cut short by the Sovietization of Georgia in 1921. Back in Rome he was appointed vice-rector of the Pontifical Armenian College and by 1932 rector of the school. Thereafter he served in a succession of increasingly important positions in the Roman Catholic Church starting with his appointment as papal emissary to Lebanon in 1935. Within two years the Armenian Catholic bishops elected him patriarch, an office he held as Gregory Peter XV from 1937 until 1962 when he resigned for reasons of his appointment in 1960 by Pope Pius XII (1939–1958) as prefect of the Congregation for the Propagation of the Faith (since renamed Congregation for Evangelization of Peoples), in which capacity he served until 1970. Earlier Pope Pius had raised him to the rank of cardinal, the youngest at the time in 1946. As head of the Roman Catholic Church's global mission programs, Agagianian traveled widely and earned a highly respected reputation as the papal representative to the rest of the world at a time when the Roman pontiffs traveled less frequently beyond Vatican City. By virtue of his experience, he was a key figure in the Vatican Council II reform efforts and served as a presiding officer. He was held in such esteem in the College of Cardinals that he was considered a candidate for the Papacy after the deaths of Pope Pius XII and Pope John XXIII (1958–1963) were a non-Italian to be elected.

The honor of being elected the first non-Italian pope in modern times went in 1978 to Cardinal Karol Wojtyla of Poland, who as John Paul II in September 2001 became the first Roman pontiff in history to visit Armenia on the occasion of the Armenian Apostolic Church's celebration of the 1,700th anniversary of the adoption of Christianity in Armenia. Ten years earlier, in 1991, he had authorized the reestablishment of the Armenian Catholic Church in Armenia 70 years after its suppression by the Soviets. By the beginning of the 21st century, Armenian Catholic congregations could be found in every major Armenian diaspora community from Iran in the Middle East to France in western Europe, and Canada in North America to Argentina in South America. The fall of Communism also allowed the return to worship of congregations gone into hiding. The worldwide Armenian Catholic community is estimated at 150,000 members.

CATHOLICOS (KATOGHIKOS). Title for the pontiff of the **Armenian Apostolic Church**. Derived from Greek, the title indicates the universal role of the holder of the office as head of the entire body of the Armenian Church, people and clergy alike, nationally and internationally. The full title of *Katoghikos Amenayn Hayots* in the Classical Armenian language would have meant "Catholicos of All Armenias," once again indicating the universal claim of the head of the Church to religious leadership among all parts of Armenia in light of the many partitions of the country over the centuries. Irrespective of the **religion** or sect of Christianity of the imperial states ruling over Armenia, the Armenian Church claimed the allegiance of all Armenians of Christian faith. When the Armenians lost political control of their country and became dispersed across the Islamic empires of Western Asia, the meaning of the title evolved to be understood as the Catholicos of All Armenians, implying religious leadership of a people, as opposed to a country. While Christian hegemonic states, such as Byzantium, restricted the territorial jurisdiction of the Armenian catholicos, Islamic world empires tended to do the opposite, as they tolerated the practice of the Armenian Christian faith regardless of location.

The origins of the title are obscure as the first bishops of Armenia, beginning with **Grigor Lusavorich**, are noted in historic sources by the title *hayrapet*, translated as bishop or head bishop. The borrowed term of patriarch was also used. Since there was but one leader of the Armenian Church, elected to office by laity and clergy, the exact title by which the ecclesiastical leader of Armenia went was less critical than the legitimacy of his ordination. The question of title became important beginning with the dispersion of the Armenian people in the 11th century and the appearance of multiple claimants to the title of catholicos. Eventually there were four offices going by that title, the so-called catholicoses of Aghvank, **Aghtamar**, Sis or Kilikia (Giligia), i.e. Cilicia, and Armenia. The matter of titles and jurisdictions was only sorted out in the 19th century and only due to the fact that Eastern Armenia fell under Russian rule and Western Armenia remained under Ottoman rule.

Two of the catholicoses survived into the 20th century. They are at times thought of as the catholicos of the **diaspora** and the catholicos of Armenia, though such a division would be far from the reality of their jurisdictional reach. The catholicos of Cilicia, sometimes called the catholicos of Sis, as this was the capital of Cilician Armenia where he resided, departed Turkey in 1921 and since 1930 has resided in Antelias, Lebanon. His official title is *Katoghikos Meds i Tann Kilikio*, "Catholicos of the Great House of Cilicia." The catholicos of Armenia, sometimes called the catholicos of **Edjmiadsin**, because of his permanent residence at that site in the Republic of Armenia, enjoys the title of *Tsayrakuyn Patriark yev Katoghikos*

Amenayn Hayots, meaning "Supreme Patriarch and Catholicos of All Armenians."

The Armenian Church in the 20th century became divided into four jurisdictions. The Armenian Patriarchate of Istanbul is a direct continuation of the office created in Constantinople at the time of the Ottoman sultans for the governance of the **Armenian *Millet***. It is formally recognized by the Republic of Turkey as the office holding religious responsibility and leadership of the Armenian community in that country. Its jurisdiction is also legally restricted by the state to Turkey alone. The Armenian Patriarchate of Jerusalem has been in continuous existence since the Middle Ages. Its current jurisdiction is limited to Israel and Jordan. The catholicos of Cilicia exercises administrative jurisdiction over the Armenian communities of the rest of the Middle East, including Iran, and partially in North America. The catholicos of Edjmiadsin exercises administrative jurisdiction over the Armenian Church organization in just about the rest of the world, including a large network in North America.

The overlapping jurisdictions caused by ideological rifts in the American community is traced back to differences over the question of the allegiance owed to the catholicos of Edjmiadsin during the Communist era. Then, nationalists, primarily associated with the **Armenian Revolutionary Federation**, objected to the subordination of the Armenian Church in the diaspora to the administrative oversight of Edjmiadsin as the Holy See was not an independent agency, and if anything, tightly controlled by the Soviet state. These differences, further marred by violence, alienated the two branches of the church and divided communities. The end of Communism did not lead to any immediate resolution of the division. Nonetheless, with the Armenian Church functioning freely in an independent Armenian state since 1991, all office holders came to respect the supremacy of the catholicos of Edjmiadsin, and in regular occasions laden with symbolism, such as the election of a new pontiff, or other high occasions, all four heads of the Armenian Church have gathered in the cathedral founded by Gregory the Illuminator to renew the unity of the church. The divisions of the Armenian Church as such are purely administrative. No theological or sectarian differences distinguish its various parts, and clergy from each branch are recognized as equal servants of the church.

In the absence of national leadership during long centuries of occupation, the catholicos came to fulfill numerous functions as the representative of the Armenian people recognized by the governing state. As such his stature always exceeded that of merely the chief administrator of the Armenian Church. Sovereigns treated and addressed the catholicos as head of the Armenian people. The office retained that aura even into the 20th century as political authority, whether in Soviet Armenia or in the diaspora, did not enjoy universal legitimacy, and the leader of the Armenian Church remained the most acceptable figure standing in for the head of the nation. Such respect did not necessarily translate into influence, but it gave the catholicos access to governments, therein reinforcing the central and unique role of the office. This function of the catholicos receded in the wake of the introduction of democracy in Armenia and the popular election of its president, who is assumed to be carrying the mantle of national leadership acknowledged by Armenians everywhere.

CHAMCHIAN, MIKAYEL (1738–1823). Author and historian. Chamchian was born in Istanbul to an Armenian family of the Roman Catholic faith. He was trained as a jeweler in the employ of the Armenian amira Mikayel Chelebi Diuzian, the imperial jeweler. Abandoning secular life, Chamchian joined his brother in Venice at the monastery of the Armenian Mekhitarian order in 1762. Upon the completion of his education and training, he was sent as a preacher among the Armenians of Aleppo and Basra. In 1774 he was appointed instructor of **Armenian language** and grammar at the monastery, and in 1795 he was assigned to Istanbul as the resident Mekhitarian representative. He died there after a long and productive life.

Chamchian was more than a missionary and an educator. As grammarian, theologian, and historian, he was the intellectual giant of his age. His *Kerakanutiun haykazian lezvi* (Grammar of the Armenian language) (Venice, 1779) is a landmark in Armenian linguistic studies. It was the first descriptive grammar of the Armenian language, though still for Classical Armenian. His theological studies were defenses of Roman Catholicism, which, however, did not pass the censor in Rome for its attempt to reconcile Catholic theology with Armenian Orthodoxy.

Chamchian made his most important contribution, however, as a historian. He authored *Patmutiun Hayots i skzbane ashkharhi minchev tsam diarn 1784* (Armenian History from the Beginning of the World to the Year 1784) (3 vols., Venice 1784–86). Written in the format of a universal history, Chamchian developed a continuous narrative depiction of the Armenian people from the Creation to his own time. Though still grounded in the biblical framework of the origin of mankind and of the nations, nevertheless, Chamchian crossed a number of important thresholds from a medieval worldview and interpretation of events toward more modern practices of historiographic methodology. First, he familiarized himself with current scholarship. Second, he contextualized Armenian history by studying the classical historians. Third, he examined all the extant Armenian historical works. And fourth, he constructed a comprehensive history of the Armenians. As a result, Chamchian's *History* is regarded as the first work in modern Armenian historical scholarship. *See also* ADONTZ, NICHOLAS; ALISHAN, GHEVOND; MEKHITAR SEBASTATSI.

CHARENTS, YEGHISHE (1897–1937). Poet. Born Yeghishe Soghomonian in Kars, then in the Russian Empire, Charents grew up to become the most celebrated poet of the early Soviet period in Armenia. He received his elementary education in Kars. His first poem was published in Tbilisi in 1912. He briefly served with Armenian volunteer units in the beginning of World War I and witnessed the aftermath of the genocidal policies of the Ottomans when he entered **Van** in 1915 with the Russian forces. The calamities of war that he witnessed became the source of his *Danteakan Araspel* (Dante-esque Legend) published in 1916. He went to Moscow that year to continue his education. Caught up in the revolutionary ferment of the time, he joined the Red Army in 1917 and saw combat at Tsaritsyn (later Stalingrad) in November. By Soviet accounts, Charents signed up with the Communist Party in 1918, but he went to **Yerevan** in 1919 to work as a teacher in the new Armenian republic. **Nikol Aghbalian**, who as a literary critic appreciated Charents's early writings, hired him to work in the ministry of culture. In 1919 he also published his *Ambokhnere Khelagarvads* (The Frenzied Masses) invoking the revolutionary fervor of the times and glorifying the struggles waged by the people.

After the Sovietization of Armenia, Charents returned to Moscow in 1921 for further studies. In a manifesto issued in June 1922 known as the "Declaration of the Three," signed by Charents, Gevorg Apov, and Azad Veshtuni, the young authors called for a new revolutionary poetry reflecting the ideals of a Communist society and criticized nationalism and literary romanticism. Charents emerged as a major influence in the nascent Soviet Armenian literary scene. His exuberant confidence was displayed in the autobiographical *Charentsname* (The Book of Charents) recalling in its title the genre of Iranian royal epics and his family's origins in the city of Maku.

Charents's patriotic novel *Yerkir Nayiri* (The Land of Nairi), invoking the ancient Urartian name of Armenia, appeared in 1923. Regarded as a milestone in Armenian literature, *Yerkir Nayiri* rendered the trials of the city of Kars, Charents's birthplace, and its Armenian population as it changed hands from the Russians and the Armenians to the Turks into a symbol of the fates visiting his people. With his fame assured, Charents became the leading spirit of the Armenian Writers' Union formed in Yerevan in 1926 (dissolved in 1932), and as editor of the literature division of the state publishing house between 1928 and 1935, he was able to promote the works of new talents forming in Soviet Armenia.

Charents continued to write in the 1920s on the topic of the revolution in poems such as *Ballad Vladimir Ilyichin, Muzhikin yev mi Zuyk Koshiki Masin* (The Ballad about Vladimir Ilyich [Lenin], the peasant, and a pair of shoes) (1925), *Komunarneri Pate Parizum* (The Wall of the Communards in Paris) (1925) and *Ballad Ksanevetsi Masin* (Ballad of the Twenty-Six) (1928) about the Bolshevik commissars of Baku who were executed by the British. At the same time Charents wrote extensively on literary criticism seeking to establish the new standards and measure of socialist and Armenian literature culminating in *Epikakan Lusabats* (Epical Dawn) published in 1930 wherein he laid claim to the entire Western and Armenian tradition of epic poetry from Homer to Dante, Pushkin and Hovhannes Tumanian.

The last published volume of poems, *Girk Janaparhi* (Book of the Road) (1934), while further developing the national themes Charents had labored over also combine with his disillusionment into a great allegorical contemplation on the centuries-long tribulations of the Armenian people and their struggle for liberation through such poems as *Sasuntsi Davit* (David of Sasun), the mythical hero of the medieval Armenian national epic, *Patmutian Karughinerov* (At the Crossroads of History), and *Mahvan Desil* (Vision of Death). Charents was denounced in 1933 and *Girk Janaparhi* was published only after **Anastas Mikoyan**'s intervention from Moscow. Even so Charents participated in the first convention of the Soviet Writers' Union in 1934 where he met Maxim Gorky and Boris Pasternak. In 1935 he was subjected to further denunciations and persecution during the Stalinist purges. He was finally jailed in 1936 where he died under unexplained circumstances on November 11, 1937.

Charents was rehabilitated in a speech given by Anastas Mikoyan in Yerevan on March 11, 1954, in a presage of the political and cultural thaw that followed the death of Stalin a year earlier and anticipating the Khrushchev speech announcing de-Stalinization a year later. His unpublished and banned writings began to be issued in the 1960s. In 1961 the Armenian town of Lusavan in the **Ararat** Valley was renamed Charentsavan and the state museum of literature and art was named for him also. His most famous poem, which starts with the words *Yes im anush Hayastani arevahar barn yem sirun* (I love the sun-sweet taste of the word Armenia), a lyric ode to his homeland composed in 1920/21, is taught to every schoolchild in Armenia and the Armenian **diaspora**. *See also* COMMUNIST PARTY OF ARMENIA; KHANJIAN, AGHASI; MIASNIKIAN, ALEXANDER.

CHOBANIAN, ARSHAG (also TCHOBANIAN) (1872–1954). Writer and publicist. Though an accomplished author in his own right, Chobanian is remembered as an ardent promoter of appreciation for Armenian literary and artistic culture. Chobanian was born in Istanbul and received his education in his birthplace. He was active in the local Armenian literary and political scene from an early age, but left Istanbul for Paris in 1895 at the height of Hamidian persecutions. Chobanian remained in France for the rest of his life, which he dedicated to publicizing Armenian culture to both Armenian and European audiences. He founded the influential literary journal *Anahit* that was in production between 1898 and 1911 and again from 1929 to 1949.

Chobanian was responsible for drawing the attention of the public and of scholarship to late medieval Armenian poetry by being the first to publish the works of writers like Nahapet Kuchak and Naghash Hovnatan. He also published the collected poems of **Bedros Turian** and Mgrtich Beshigtashlian. Chobanian authored an extensive oeuvre of literary criticism about these writers and about many other modern and medieval Armenian writers, including **Khachatur Abovian**, **Ghevond Alishan**, the satirist **Hagop Baronian**, the dramatist Gabriel Sundukian, **Raffi**, Perj Proshian, Alexander Shirvanzade, Hamastegh, and others. These were collected in his series called *Demker* (Profiles, 1924–1929). He was also the first to recognize the talent of younger poets such as **Vahan Tekeyan**, **Siamanto**, and **Taniel Varuzhan**, who became the authors of the riveting poetry of national embitterment in response to the persecutions of the Armenians under the Ottoman Turks. As a publicist of Armenian culture in Europe, Chobanian was in touch with contemporary French literary figures. For their benefit, and that of a larger audience, Chobanian published Armenian poetry in French translation. In this respect, *La Roserie d'Arménie* marked a watershed by introducing Armenian letters to foreign readers.

Chobanian was also active in the Armenian **Democratic Liberal (Ramkavar) Party**. He was a member of the Armenian National Delegation headed by **Boghos Nubar** at the Paris peace conference in 1919. An early defender of Soviet Armenia, which he visited in 1933, he later became critical of the Communist regime.

COMMUNIST PARTY OF ARMENIA (CPA) (*Hayastani Komunistakan Kusaktsutiun*) (*HKK*). Political party. The CPA was formed in January 1920 in **Yerevan** in anticipation of the Sovietization of Armenia. Originally composed of mostly local Bolsheviks, it was subsequently augmented by members previously in the Russian Communist Party in Moscow once the Red Army installed a Revolutionary Committee (Revkom) in Armenia in December of the same year. Marxist groups affiliated with the Bolshevik wing of the Russian Social Democratic Workers Party appeared as early as 1899 in Armenia under the leadership of **Stepan Shahumian**, later Lenin's representative and party leader in the Caucasus during the Russian Revolution. Shahumian's execution in 1918 deprived the Armenian Marxists of their most prominent and effective leader and the Revkom chairmanship was placed in the hands of **Sargis Kasian** whose extremist policies prompted his removal by Lenin within months of the Sovietization of Armenia. More prominent Communists such as **Anastas Mikoyan** and **Lev Karakhan** were based in Moscow, where from also came the appointment of **Alexander Miasnikian**, the CPA's most important first secretary in the early years of Communism. The May 1920 uprising by the Communists to overthrow the independent Republic of Armenia had been brutally suppressed by the **Armenian Revolutionary Federation** (ARF) government whose latent influence was evident when the Soviet regime was driven out of Yerevan by an ARF-inspired revolt in February 1921, itself a reaction to the violence applied by the CPA with the Sovietization of Armenia.

Miasnikian consolidated Soviet rule in Armenia in 1921 and began the cultivation of local cadres to build up the party whose membership was under 5,000 in a country of about three quarter million people. His death in 1925 cut short a promising career and Ashot Hovhannisian (1925–1927), Hayk Hovsepian (1927–1928), and Haygaz Kostanian (1928–1930) headed the party in quick succession. The rise of **Aghasi Khanjian**, a Stalin protégé, and a dynamic organizer who led the collectivization process in Armenia, reinvigorated the CPA. First secretary of the CPA from 1930 to 1936, his popularity proved his undoing and he was liquidated during the purges. He was not alone in his fate. Kasian, among others, too was liquidated. Hovhannisian, a prominent ideologue, and many other intellectual figures were exiled. When Lavrenti Beria and Mir Jafar Baghirov consolidated their personal control over the local Communist Party apparatus in Georgia and Azerbaijan respectively during the long years of the Stalin regime, Grigor Harutiunian (Arutiunov), a Beria underling sent from Georgia headed the party in Armenia. Despite the absence of popular support for the regime, the CPA was able to undertake the modernization of the country. In this effort, war-weariness, poverty, and the hardships of the refugees were more their allies than ideological persuasion.

The postwar years saw more stable Communist leadership in Armenia. From the time of Joseph Stalin's death until the rise of Mikhail Gorbachev, four men held the post of first secretary of the CPA: Suren Tovmasian (1953–1960), Zakov Zarobian (1960–1966), Anton Kochinian (1966–1974), and **Karen Demirchian** (1974–1988). The party's stature significantly improved with Soviet victory over Nazi Germany. A very large percentage of the male population in Armenia had been inducted into the armed forces. Their integration into the Soviet system and the rapid rise through the ranks of those skilled in the military profession expanded the base of party support. The CPA also capitalized on the new international receptivity afforded the Soviet Union prior to the intensification of the Cold War and waged an overseas campaign to encourage immigration from the Armenian **diaspora** to Soviet Armenia as a device for the rapid increase of the labor pool that had been seriously depleted because of the losses suffered during World War II. Despite the strict controls, this and other measures to enlist a favorable view among diaspora Armenians extended the CPA some leeway from Moscow and even encouraged the center to turn Armenia into a showcase of socialist development.

De-Stalinization was first attempted in Armenia under Mikoyan's guidance and the cultural thaw ushered in by Nikita Khrushchev saw a comparably more liberal lifting of restrictions on expressions of nationalism than in many other Soviet republics. The once-virulent anti-ARF rhetoric, which had been exploited to label and condemn national sentiment, moderated and the co-opting of symbols and pages from history once banned from discussion became part of the new policy. In response to popular demands, a monument complex dedicated to the **Armenian Genocide** was constructed in the second half of the 1960s. This was followed by raising of monuments at the site of the battle of Sardarapat fought in May 1918, a struggle associated with the founding of the independent republic whose legitimacy had been long denied. The official line did not go as far in articulating these changes in critical areas of ideological reinterpretation. The public, however, was permitted its own perception of these and other gestures of increasing moderation and national expression.

Rapid industrialization and urbanization, promoted by the CPA in postwar Armenia, resulted in unforeseen consequences. For one, in less than half a century, these developments shifted the majority of the population from agricultural production to the factory and office floor. The emphasis on machine tools production and its outgrowth in the form of advanced technologies created a large educated middle class, a social phenomenon absent in the earlier decades of Soviet power in Armenia. The generous subsidization of cultural, educational, and technological institutions also contributed to an outpouring of literature, scholarship, and even breakthroughs in scientific research. These achievements fermented a new intellectual outlook and fed expectations that the CPA soon had difficulty in delivering to the populace. The slow pace of economic expansion, the rigidity of the governing system, and habits of party patronage also fostered corruption. With stagnation setting in the economy in the later years of the Leonid Brezhnev era, corruption tarnished the party's reputation and undermined its standing.

The Gorbachev reforms of glasnost and perestroika, openness and restructuring, therefore, enjoyed a particularly receptive audience in Soviet Armenia. By the time Gorbachev dismissed Demirchian and appointed new leadership, the CPA was fast loosing political control under the strains created by the unauthorized popular nationalist movement that swept the country. Suren Harutiunian (1988–1990) and Vladimir Movsisian (1990) led the CPA in the final years of the Soviet Union. In the face of a daring campaign waged by the Karabagh Committee calling for democracy and for sovereignty, and the overwhelming popularity of the **Karabagh Movement**, the CPA yielded power, and from August 1990, with its monopoly ended, it briefly shared authority with the **Armenian National Movement** (ANM) as it continued to administer the institutional levers of control. Democratic forces in Armenia, however, were uncompromising on one issue. Communists were excluded from post-Soviet cabinets. On the other hand, as an able administrator, Movsisian, who abandoned the CPA after peaceably transferring power to the ANM, was appointed to a number of ministerial posts during the **Levon Ter-Petrossian** presidency.

With independence, the CPA was reduced to a minority delegation in the Armenian parliament. With a membership of approximately 50,000 stalwarts, it still registered a political presence. Under the leadership of Albert Sahakian and Sergei Badalian, the CPA participated in the electoral process and garnered sufficient votes to continue to send delegates to the new National Assembly. Adhering to doctrinaire socialism, the CPA still advocates for a command economy. As a result, along the way some of its membership moved on to form variants on the socialist theme while in the main opposing privatization. The Democratic Party of Armenia (DPA) split in August 1991, after the coup attempt in Moscow by the Communist reactionaries. Its leader, Aram Sargsian, was the very last Soviet-era CPA first secretary. The Agrarian Democratic Party (ADP) was formed in 1992 and promotes a social welfare state. The Social Democratic Party of Armenia (SDPA) appeared in 1996 and the United Progressive Communist Party of Armenia (UPCPA) in 1998. None succeeded in attracting a sufficient following to enter the arena of political influence.

The comeback of the old guard occurred with the re-emergence of Karen Demirchian as the candidate of nostalgia who enjoyed a spate of popularity in response to the economic travails of Armenia blamed on the ANM. After a 10-year hiatus from the political scene, Demirchian entered the presidential race in 1998. His 40 percent showing in the elections encouraged the formation of the non-Communist **Populist Party of Armenia** (PPA), which with the 1999 elections for the National Assembly, won a sufficient number of seats to make Demirchian the leading contender for the chairmanship of Armenia's legislative body. Political anarchy in neighboring Georgia and Azerbaijan prompted the restoration to power of former Communist Party bosses Eduard Shevardnadze and Heidar Aliyev. Demirchian's resurgent popularity paralleled that phenomenon only to the extent that he tapped the reservoir of economic discontent, but his restoration testified to the prestige once associated with the office of first secretary of the CPA.

CONSTANTINE THE CONSTABLE. *See* HETUM I; HETUMIAN; LEVON I.

CONSTITUTION. The constitution of the Republic of Armenia was adopted on July 5, 1995, by popular referendum. It describes the country as a sovereign, democratic state with power vested in the people. Authority is divided among executive, legislative, and judicial branches. The constitution provides for the election of all executive and legislative authorities including the **president**, the National Assembly, and local governments. It also formally regulates political pluralism by recognizing a multiparty system. The constitution provides for a presidential system of government. The president exercises wide-ranging authority including the appointment of the **prime minister**. He is vested with responsibility for the functioning of all branches of government, can dissolve the National Assembly and call for special elections. Legislative power is vested in the National Assembly consisting of 131 deputies. In addition to the adoption of laws and the state budget, the National Assembly may cast a vote of no confidence in the government requiring the prime minister to tender the resignation of the government. According to the constitution, executive authority is vested in the government, which properly consists of the prime minister and the other ministers. The president, however, can chair meetings of the government. The president also chairs the Judicial Council that the constitution vests with the authority to appoint judges. The constitution guarantees the supremacy of the law and establishes a Constitutional Court with final authority on questions regarding the conformity of all legal instruments to the constitution. The constitution guarantees civil and political liberties and provides for the protection of human rights and freedoms. The rights of citizens, explicitly provided for in 35 separate articles, include freedom of speech, freedom of movement, choice of employment, privacy, adequate living standard, education, health care, and legal assistance. The Armenian constitution expressly protects the right to private property. The constitution also designates Armenian as the state language, the red, blue, and orange tricolor as the state flag, "Our Fatherland" (*Mer Hayrenik*) as the national anthem, and **Yerevan** as the capital of the republic.

– D –

DARBINIAN, ARMEN (1965–). Prime Minister of Armenia 1998–1999. Born in Leninakan/**Gyumri**, Darbinian studied economics at Lomonosov University in Moscow. Finishing with honors in 1986 he started graduate education and teaching at Lomonosov University. Upon completion of his studies in 1989 he was appointed chief specialist of the economic policy division of Armenia's Permanent Representation in Moscow. He was soon heading the division and serving as Armenia's representative on the Board of Foreign Debt of the former Soviet Union. In the latter capacity he participated in 1992 in the financial negotiations conducted with creditor groups in Paris and London. When the Central Bank of Armenia was formed in January 1994, parliament appointed him vice-chairman of the new institution. By June 1997 **President Levon Ter-Petrossian** had appointed him to the cabinet as minister of finance and economy. With his election to the presidency, **Robert Kocharian** appointed the 33-year-old Darbinian **prime minister** of Armenia in April 1998. Accelerating privatization, improving revenue collection by the state, increasing trade and creating a regulatory environment more conducive to foreign investment headed Darbinian's policy agenda. He served until June 1999. *See also* DARBINIAN, ARMEN CABINET.

DARBINIAN, ARMEN CABINET. Appointed by **President Robert Kocharian** on April 20,1998, the Darbinian cabinet served until June 14, 1999.

Prime Minister	**Armen Darbinian**
Agriculture	Vladimir Movsisian
Culture, Youth Affairs and Sports	Roland Sharoyan
Defense	**Vazgen Sargsian**
Economic and Structural Reform	Vahram Avanesian
Education and Science	Levon Mkrtchian
Energy	Meruzhan Mikayelian
Environmental Protection	Gevorg Vardanian
Finance and Economy	Edvard Sandoyan
Foreign Affairs	Vartan Oskanian
Health	Haik Nikoghosian
Industrial Productions Coordination	Gagik Martirosian
Internal Affairs and National Security	Serge Sargsian
Justice	Davit Harutunian
Post and Communication	Artak Vardanian
Privatization	Pavel Ghaltakhchian
Regional Administration	Davit Zadoyan
Social Welfare	Gagik Yeganian
Statistics, State Register and Analysis	Stepan Mnatsakanian
Trade and Industry	Haik Gevorgian
Transport	Yervand Zakharian

The Council of Ministers formed by Armen Darbinian continued where the **Kocharian cabinet** left off. The Darbinian cabinet sought to foster the economic recovery of Armenia through the privatization of larger industrial enterprises and by permitting their sale to foreign investors. There was no change of personnel in the critical ministries in charge of external and internal security and foreign affairs. Though there was little turnaround in industry, a modest recovery was registered in other sectors of the economy. The program, however, stalled with the downturn in the Russian economy in August 1998, and despite stringent fiscal and monetary policies, the Armenian currency, dram, went from around 400 to about 500 against the U.S. dollar as a result. The Council of Ministers headed by Darbinian also had the character of a national reconciliation cabinet reflecting Kocharian's policy that sought to reduce some of the consequences of the authoritarian aspects of the late period of the **Levon Ter-Petrossian** presidency. For the first time two ministers, Mkrtchian and Sharoyan, associated with the **Armenian Revolutionary Federation** (ARF) were appointed to the government.

DASHNAK, DASHNAKTSAKAN, DASHNAKTSUTIUN. *See* ARMENIAN REVOLUTIONARY FEDERATION (ARF).

DAUD *PASHA*, ARTIN (1816–1873). Ottoman governor of Lebanon. Daud Pasha was born in Istanbul to an Armenian Catholic family. He received his education at a French school. As opportunities for Christian subjects of the Ottoman Empire opened up with the Tanzimat reforms, upon earning a law degree in Berlin, Daud entered the Ottoman civil service. He was first posted as an embassy attaché to Berlin. Then he served as consul general in Vienna. He rose rapidly through the ranks of the state administration and became director of publications and director of the postal and telegraphic services. His authorship of a book on Western jurisprudence, *Histoire de la législation des anciens Germains*, 2 vols. (Berlin, 1845) also earned him in European circles a reputation as a man of erudition. His learning, command of French, diplomatic skills, and successful career in the Ottoman administration made him the favored candidate for the newly created post of *mutesarrif*, or governor-general, of Lebanon. With his new assignment, Daud was bestowed the title of Pasha and raised to the rank of minister, thus making him at the time the highest-ranking Christian dignitary in the Ottoman government.

In the aftermath of the 20-year Maronite-Druze conflict in Mount Lebanon that had resulted in the landing of French troops, the European Powers and the Ottoman government agreed to administrative reforms to quell the internecine warfare. The arrangement, known as the Organic Statute of 1861, established Mount Lebanon as a province separate from Syria, granted it local autonomy, and provided for an administration to be run under European supervision. The Statute also called for the appointment of a Christian Catholic governor designated by and responsible to the Sublime Porte whose appointment was subject to the approval of the European Powers.

As a capable and enlightened official, Daud Pasha used his plenipotentiary powers to establish a modern system of administration that was recognized for its honesty and efficiency. His successful management also introduced an era of calm that helped normalize relations among the sectarian groups in the mountains of Lebanon. Daud Pasha oversaw improvements in all sectors of Lebanese life. With Ottoman troops withdrawn from the mountains, a local militia was trained whose discipline went far in maintaining order in the once war-torn region. Lowered taxes and regulated methods of tax collection contributed to the improvement of the local economy as the region was expected to cover its budgetary expenses through local revenue and was spared tribute payment to Istanbul. The construction of a network of highways further contributed to the growth of local commerce as the isolation of Mount Lebanon was ended by linking it to the cities of Beirut and Damascus, as well as by linking the towns of north and south Lebanon. Educational facilities were built and a justice system organized that introduced equality under the law irrespective of religion. The enactment of progressive laws stimulated more than the economy as the region began to attract Western commercial investment and became fertile ground for European and American educational institutions. These in turn led to the revival of interest in Arabic literature as an Arab intelligentsia slowly formed.

Daud Pasha's tenure ended in 1868 when he resigned under protest as his appeals to join the province to a coastal port went unheeded. Upon his return to Istanbul, he was, however, appointed to the Council of Ministers as the minister of telegraph, post, and public works. Illness forced him to quit his position in 1873 and he passed away in France. The story of modern Lebanon begins with the administration of Daud Pasha who was largely responsible for the proper implementation of the Organic Statute that allowed for the emergence of Lebanon as a distinct country. Of his seven successors as governors-general, the last was another Catholic Armenian, Ohannes Guyumjian Pasha (1858–1933), who was *mutesarrif* between 1912 and 1915.

Ohannes Guyumjian was also born in Istanbul and completed his education in Paris. He entered the Ottoman foreign ministry in 1877 and eventually served some 15 years at the Turkish embassy in Rome. He returned to Istanbul after the Young Turk Revolution in 1908 and was elected a deputy to the Ottoman Parliament. By 1911 he was back at the foreign ministry as a senior counselor. Twice he had declined the offer of the mutesarrifate of Mount Lebanon. With **Gabriel Noradoungian**'s appointment as foreign minister in 1912, he accepted the position. Guyumjian Pasha focused his energies on further improving the Lebanese economy. He established commercial courts and succeeded in opening the port at Juniye, and prevented French interests from monopolizing trade. His tenure was cut short with the outbreak of World War I and the appointment of Jemal Pasha as governor of Syria who abrogated the Organic Statute by stationing Ottoman troops in Lebanon and disarmed the Christian population. Guyumjian was dismissed in 1915 and with him ended the autonomous existence of Mount Lebanon.

Even so, Daud Pasha's and Guyumjian Pasha's legacy to Lebanon outlasted both the Young Turk regime and the Ottoman Empire as the country re-emerged as a distinct multi-confessional state after World War I under French mandate. Though an Armenian presence in the area preceded their governorship, Daud Pasha and Guyumjian Pasha were also instrumental in the growth of the Armenian community of Lebanon. Daud Pasha's administration included a number of Armenians whom he brought with him from the Ottoman capital. Under their patronage, the Armenian **Catholic** community took root in a country where its members had first sought refuge from persecution from their own Apostolic brethren in the late 18th and the early 19th century. The Armenian Catholic Patriarchate was housed at the monastery of Bzommar in the northern range of Mount Lebanon. Daud Pasha and Guyumjian Pasha frequented the site on religious holidays. With the influx of refugees from Cilicia after 1920, one of the largest Armenian **diaspora** settlements took shape in Lebanon. It grew and flourished under Lebanon's comparatively liberal political system until 1975 when the Lebanese civil war revived the many conflicts that had been earlier contained.

DAVIT *BEK* (also DAVID *BEG*) (d. 1728). Leader of the first Armenian liberation movement in modern times. Upon the fall of the Safavid dynasty and the ensuing disorder in Transcaucasia in 1722, the Armenian *meliks*, the traditional feudal lords, of Mountainous Karabagh requested assistance from the Georgian monarch in Tbilisi, who sent them one of his Armenian military officers. Davit Bek assumed command of the Armenian population that had taken up arms in defense of the historic Armenian districts of Siunik and Ghapan, present-day Zangezur in southern Armenia and Karabagh. Expecting aid from the Russians when Peter the Great marched south along the Caspian Sea in the same year, the people in the mountainous areas of Eastern Armenia organized the first liberation struggle among Armenians since the Mongol conquests.

With the support of the Armenian peasantry and the cooperation of the Armenian feudal barons whose governance of the area had long been recognized by the Persian shahs, Davit Bek was able to muster a sufficient number of men to defend the Armenian-inhabited areas from the Muslim tribes competing for influence in the region in the aftermath of the collapse of the Safavid state. In a series of successful campaigns Davit Bek held back local tribal armies until such time as the Ottomans advanced into Transcaucasia. Thereupon, to check the Turks, Shah Tahmasp bestowed upon Davit Bek in 1727 the right to govern the area under his control as a vassal Armenian principality. Davit Bek died the following year as the Ottomans made deeper incursions into the Armenian areas. Command of the region passed to Davit Bek's lieutenant Mekhitar Sparapet who fell to the Ottomans in 1730. Mekhitar's death marked the end of the Armenian struggle. It also marked the beginning of the breakdown of the five Armenian melikdoms of Mountainous Karabagh resulting in the interpenetration of the area with Muslim settlers, mostly derived from the local Turkic tribes. *See also* NAGORNO KARABAGH; RAFFI; STEPANAKART; SIUNI.

DEMIRCHIAN, KAREN (1932–1999). Political leader. Born in **Yerevan**, Demirchian finished studies as a mechanical engineer at the Yerevan state engineering institute in 1954. After a year in Leningrad, he returned to Yerevan in 1955 to work as a senior engineer at the Yerevan electrotechnical plant rising by 1966 to the directorship of the establishment. That same year he was appointed secretary of the Yerevan city committee of the **Communist Party of Armenia** (CPA). Promoted to secretary of the Central Committee of the CPA in 1972, he established close working relations with Leonid Brezhnev, and quickly rose to become first secretary of the Central Committee, a post he held from 1974 to 1988. Mikhail Gorbachev dismissed him when he was unable to quell the **Karabagh Movement**. In 1991 he assumed the directorship of the *HaiElectraMekena* (Armenian Electro-Machinery) operation when it was converted into a limited joint-stock company. He returned to the political arena as a presidential candidate in the March 1998 elections and registered a respectable showing. Thereupon he formed the **Populist Party of Armenia** (PPA). In the May 1999 parliamentary elections he won a seat in the National Assembly and was elected its chairman on June 10. On October 27, 1999, he was gunned down by domestic terrorists in the chamber of the National Assembly.

DEMOCRATIC LIBERAL PARTY (DLP) (*Ramkavar Azatakan Kusaktsutiun*) (*RAK*). Political party. The DLP was organized in 1921 in Istanbul as a liberal alternative to the revolutionary parties that had dominated Armenian political life up to that time. The party was created by bringing together a number of smaller liberal groups and disaffected wings of other political associations. These included the Constitutional Democratic Party (*Sahmanadir Ramkavar Kusaktsutiun*), the Liberal Party (*Azatakan Kusaktsutiun*) of the Reformed Hnchaks, and the Armenian Populist Party (*Hay Zoghovrdakan Kusaktsutiun*) and associates of the old Armenakan Party. From this combination emerged the democratic liberal formula by which the party was known thereafter and its members became known as Ramkavars. With the founding of the DLP the trio of parties that made up the political spectrum in the Armenian **diaspora** for the next 70 years was complete. The main characteristic of the DLP was its distinctly nonsocialist platform expressly defined in reaction to the revolutionary methods of other Armenian organizations. As a Western Armenian political organization the DLP also hoped for a clear ideological line that made its orientation toward the West evident in the belief that the Western Powers withheld support for Armenia because of the socialism espoused by the **Armenian Revolutionary Federation** (ARF).

Regardless of the ideological positions adopted, the DLP came into existence at a time when the Communists controlled Armenia and it opted not to deny the legitimacy of the Soviet state. Since it had not and would not be functioning in the new Soviet republic, the DLP did not represent a serious threat to the Communists and was spared the vitriol of antinationalist propaganda. Ramkavar party centers were organized all across the Armenian diaspora, but with a membership mostly of persons of middle- and upper middle-class backgrounds, the DLP never developed a mass following. Even so, the DLP was effective in the larger or more stable communities where a sufficient stratum existed inclined toward a moderate nationalist identification. These communities were located in Lebanon, Egypt, the United States, and later Canada. On occasion the DLP cooperated with the **Social Democratic Hnchakian Party** (SDHP), more for pragmatic reasons than any meeting of the minds between the two quite different parties. The DLP, however, played a greater role than its size through its influence in the **Armenian General Benevolent Union** (AGBU), the largest Armenian charitable organization in the diaspora. These intra-Armenian community organizational alignments became especially important and pronounced during the Cold War and contributed to serious polarization between groups affiliated with the ARF and those associated with the DLP. The rifts were so deep as to cleave the Armenian Church organization in some communities into opposing camps, a legacy that was institutionalized by the 1950s.

The fall of the **Communist Party of Armenia** (CPA) from power deprived the DLP of its privileged relationship with Soviet Armenian officialdom. Upholding the principle of the legitimacy of the state, the DLP, soon after the **Armenian National Movement** (ANM) took over the government in Armenia, lent its support to the Ter-Petrossian presidency. As the DLP worked to establish a presence in Armenia after 1991, the party became seriously divided internally over the extent of its policy of support for the **Levon Ter-Petrossian** administration. Delegates affiliated with the DLP have served in the post-Soviet Armenian legislature. The party is yet to register a visible role with the Armenian electorate and did not garner sufficient votes to be considered for inclusion in any cabinets during the 1990s. *See also* CHOBANIAN, ARSHAG; TEKEYAN, VAHAN.

DEUKMEJIAN, GEORGE (COURKEN) (1928–). United States governor. Deukmejian was born in Menands, New York, to immigrant parents. He grew up in upstate New York and earned a law degree from St. John's University in New York City in 1952. He moved to California to start his law practice and entered politics as a member of the Republican Party. He was elected to the California Assembly in 1963 and served until 1967, when he was elected to the California State Senate. He was named the Republican floor leader in 1969 and remained in the State Senate until 1979. A conservative Republican, he rose to prominence during the governorship of Ronald

Reagan, later president of the United States. He ran unsuccessfully for the office of state attorney general for the first time in 1970, but won election for the same office in 1978. He was known as a staunch advocate of law and order and of tougher criminal laws. He campaigned for the office of governor of California that he won in the 1982 elections, thus becoming the first American of Armenian descent to occupy the high office of a state governor in the United States. He served two terms from 1983 to 1991. After the end of his term Deukmejian returned to private practice.

The election of George Deukmejian as governor of California marked the most visible threshold in the growth and integration of the Armenian-American community. His successful run for office testified to the new economic and numerical strength of the Armenians in that state. Armenians uniformly supported him, contributed disproportionately to his campaign, and voted en bloc in his favor. As governor, Deukmejian also made a significant contribution in encouraging Armenian-Americans to participate in the political process. He appointed them to his cabinet, to various administrative positions in a number of government agencies, and to judgeships on the California Supreme Court. By serving as the beacon of a formerly quiescent group, he changed the profile of the Armenian-American community and made it into a force to be courted even in U.S. presidential elections. *See also* ARMENIAN ASSEMBLY OF AMERICA.

DIASPORA, HISTORIC. The worldwide community of Armenians living outside historic Armenia from the sixth century to 1915. The divided destiny of the Armenian people can be traced to causes dating back to the time when the world of Antiquity was being reshaped into the medieval civilizations. In the course of events that transformed the cultural pattern of the region containing Armenia, from one defined by Hellenistic and Christian ethos to one dominated by Islam and its two ruling peoples, the Arabs and the Turks, the Armenian diaspora began to form. By that time the Armenian nation had existed for over a thousand years. Thereafter, however, a segment of Armenian society would always live beyond the confines of Armenia. This separation endowed this group of Armenians with a history characterized by developments to a very large extent different from the experience of the greater majority of the Armenian population that continued to live in its historical lands. The absence of the anchor of statehood also meant that the geographic location of these Armenians would be a matter of constant change, each relocation opening a new chapter in the history of the Armenian diaspora.

With the fall of the Western Roman Empire in 476, invasions by barbarian tribes moving in from southern Russia and northern Europe stretched the human resources of the Eastern Roman Empire beyond its limits. Thereupon Roman rulers resorted to forcibly relocating Armenians to the depopulated regions along the European frontiers of the Byzantine state. The emperor Justinian (527–565) went a step further by depriving the districts of Armenia under Roman rule of that stratum of society trained in the martial traditions. He expected to defuse the capacity of Armenian society to resist imperial consolidation and recruit these men for service in his armies, which he directed to distant parts of the Mediterranean in his desire for a restored Roman imperium. One of Justinian's Armenian associates by the name of Narses, the Grand Chamberlain of the imperial court, started as a financial officer and concluded his services as a general of exceptional military skill with his reconquest of Italy from the Ostrogoths. He recovered Rome for the imperial crown in 552 and was rewarded with the governorship of Italy. He administered the peninsula for some 13 years and oversaw its economic recovery after a century of barbarian conquest and misrule.

The Armenian population of Byzantium grew over the decades. Soon entire military units were manned by Armenian soldiers and commanded by Armenian officers. Heraklios, the son of one of these Armenian generals appointed to the governorship of Carthage in Africa, became emperor in 610. He was called upon by the Senate in Constantinople to repel the Persians who had invaded Byzantium from the east and were threatening the capital. Heraklios succeeded in recovering all the territories lost to the Persians, including Asia Minor, Palestine, Syria, and Armenia. But the long years of warfare left him and his men too exhausted to stop the horsemen who came riding out of the Arabian desert in 633 just at the moment of final Roman victory over Iran.

The descendants of Heraklios ruled from Constantinople for another century and led the resistance against the Arabs in Asia Minor. After the demise of the Heraklians a number of Armenian officers aspired for or reached the throne, most notably Leo V The Armenian (813–820). In the ninth century another dynasty fathered by an

Armenian soldier named Basil (867–886) inaugurated a period of recovery for Byzantium and the high point of the Armenian presence in the empire. By the 10th century descendants of Armenian soldiers were so thoroughly integrated into Byzantine society that they occupied some of the highest offices of the state and provincial administration. Men like John Kourkouas continued to command the armies of Byzantium, whereas the likes of Romanos Lekapenos (920–944) and John Tzimiskes (969–976) intermarried with the imperial dynasty and assumed the crown. Some achieved renown as leading intellectuals of the time. Photios, a scholar and erstwhile Patriarch of the Orthodox Church in the ninth century, deigned to draw up a pedigree for Basil that traced the emperor's ancestry to the Armenian **Arshakuni** royal house, by then defunct for four centuries.

The 1071 battle of Manzikert, with the ensuing occupation of Armenia by the Seljuk Turks, and the virtual collapse of Byzantine government in Asia Minor, sharply reduced the Armenian presence in Constantinople. Throughout the cities of Asia Minor, Greeks and Armenians continued living side by side, but in entirely different frameworks thereafter. In the chaos of the late 11th century, Armenians escaping the Seljuk Turks and cut loose from Byzantine hegemony staked out for themselves small principalities in the recesses of the Taurus Range. Directly to the southwest and yet outside the boundaries of historic Armenia, these havens attracted most of those forced out of their homes on the Armenian plateau. The sacking and pillaging of Armenian cities had left tens of thousands searching for new sites to resettle.

In 1080 the prince named Ruben/Rupen, who held a remote mountain fortress, disavowed allegiance to any suzerain, and began carving out a fiefdom for himself. His boldness planted the foundations of a state that would endure for three centuries. From the time he raised his banner over the Cilician Mountains until the coronation of his descendant **Levon**/Leo as King of Armenia in 1199, the **Rubenian** dynasty created a new country on the map of Asia Minor out of the medium of the Armenian diaspora. With the advantage of a population base loyal to its rulers, the Armenian princes of Cilicia forged a state more enduring than the Crusader principalities that were formed almost simultaneously.

Inside or beside their fortresses in Cilicia, Armenians also established monasteries. These institutions, especially their scriptoria, rendered an invaluable service. At a time when libraries were going up in flames in Armenia, scribes in Cilicia dutifully copied as many works as could be rescued from Armenia. The record of medieval Armenian civilization survives because a good portion of its was preserved in the diaspora. Some of the great Armenian manuscript illuminators of the Middle Ages, such as Toros Roslin, were miniaturists working in Cilicia. When Cilician society was disrupted, a considerable portion of its heritage was in turn rescued by being deposited at the Armenian monastery of St. James (*Surb Hakob*) in Jerusalem, today holding the second largest Armenian manuscript collection in the world.

The fall of the Crusader states to the Ayyubid armies of Saladin and the Mamluk slave-soldiers who seized Egypt from Saladin's heirs left Cilician Armenia isolated on the west Asian mainland by the 13th century. Cyprus was the closest Christian state still immune from assault by seafaring Muslim forces. Armenia and Cyprus, ruled by the French Crusader Lusignan family, were practically fused into a single political entity at the time. Ever more beleaguered by the annual invasions staged by the Mamluks, the Armenians appealed for assistance and in return offered the throne to the Lusignans. The struggle ended in 1375 as the capital of Sis fell to the Mamluks and the last Lusignan who had risked assuming the Armenian throne was carried into captivity to languish in Cairo until such time as his relatives in Europe finally ransomed him.

In Egypt, Leo V Lusignan was in the company of Armenians again. The residue of a community much reduced in size and importance, an enclave of Armenian merchants and craftsmen still practiced their faith in the heart of the mightiest Arabian state of the time. Three centuries earlier, their forebears had entered Egypt at the request of its Muslim lord, the caliph al-Mustansir of the Fatimid dynasty, the first successful proponents of the Shiite sect. Racked by civil unrest abetted by competition among various factions of his army, al-Mustansir (1036–1094) secretly turned to his general Badr al-Jamali in Syria to restore order in the realm. Badr, an Armenian convert to Islam, sailed to Egypt with a sizable contingent of Armenian soldiers recruited as his personal retinue. They entered Cairo without raising suspicion and shortly put an end to the factions competing for influence over the caliph. Instead, Badr established his own vizierate and consolidated power in his office. He governed Egypt single-handedly for 21 years (1073–1094) and was succeeded by his own son al-Afdal who held the post for another 27 years. The Jamalid family of viziers restored the government and the economy of the Fatimid state, and for all intents and purposes were the true rulers of Egypt for a half century.

A large Armenian community formed in Egypt under Jamalid patronage. They erected their own edifices and enjoyed such privilege in this far-off land that even the peregrine **Catholicos** Grigor Vkayasar (Gregory the Martyrophile) paid a visit to his countrymen overseas. The Armenian soldiery held the reins of power for almost a hundred years. In 1135, one among them, Bahram al-Armani (Vahram the Armenian), of the princely Pahlavuni dynasty, who had not abjured Christianity, was elevated to the rank of vizier and, surprisingly, bestowed the title *sayf al-islam*, the sword of Islam.

Armenian soldiers in the diaspora were also active in another region of the Middle East. In the wake of the turbulence created by the entry of the Seljuks into the Caucasus region, the Georgian lands to the north of Armenia were unified by David II the Rebuilder (1089–1125). David called upon the displaced Armenians to settle the emptied countryside of Georgia and recruited the surviving Armenian military units to join the ranks of his army. Here, too, the Armenian aristocracy was entrusted with the highest offices of state government, including the chancellery and the supreme command of the army. Indeed, members of the Zakarian family, known as the Mkhargrdzeli in Georgian, who distinguished themselves as the *amirspasalar* (commander-in-chief) of the Georgian army were responsible for the recovery of East Armenia. By driving out the Turkish overlords in that part of the country, the Zakarians regained control of those lands for the emergent Armeno-Georgian monarchy ruled by the Georgian wing of the ancient **Bagratuni** dynasty. By the last year of his reign, David's armies had reached the city of **Ani**. This partial restoration of government by a Christian sovereign over Armenia was in large part the handiwork of Armenians in the service of their neighbors to the north. With the Mongol invasion in the early part of the 13th century, however, everything collapsed. Masses of Armenians were dislodged from historic Armenia once again and Armenians already in the diaspora dispersed further to more distant locations.

Since the 10th century an important commercial and entrepreneurial class had formed in the Armenian cities. It capitalized on the long-distance trade among Oriental merchants who transported Asian goods from the East and European merchants who purchased them for sale in the West. During years of invasion and insecurity, the trade routes transecting Armenia also served as avenues of migration for this particular class of Armenian society. Given that the cosmopolite tradesman was not adept at working the land, rather was the practitioner of a specialized function, it was more likely, in the eventuality of displacement, that he would resettle in another city. Hence, during the High Middle Ages, the merchant emerged on the scene as a noticeable social representative of the Armenian people. However, in his case, as he lacked the legitimizing heritage of noble ancestry, and could not render the obligation of defending with arms, his rise to a position of leadership in the Armenian communities could not recreate the sociopolitical symbiosis of the earlier diaspora settlements. Rather than seek social parity, or political compromise and integration through the force of arms, as the diaspora communities led by the military caste had proceeded to do, the Armenian merchant instead negotiated for a niche in his host society.

With the demise of the Armenian militarized colonies, the individual and collective disabilities of the Armenians became more apparent. It goes with saying that the handler of money was an object of suspicion and resentment in what remained mostly agricultural economies in the East. His personal protection, as well as the safety of his community, had to be purchased through written or verbal agreements that exchanged his contribution to the economy, and part of his earnings, for political sponsorship. Thus, most Armenian commercial communities became dependencies of two variables: the international network for the exchange of goods and services and the local political system.

Armenians in diaspora began to express the trademarks of exile from a homeland and the denial of return. Since the adjustment that territorial attainment can provide, as it appears in the case of the first set of diasporas, namely those of Byzantium, Cilicia, Egypt, and Georgia, was absent in the later diasporas, these Armenians no longer contemplated fixing their settlements as new political structures. Armenians now lived in a *gaghut*, a community of exile. A new vocabulary was invented. The *gaghtakan* was the migrant to the diaspora, connoting in his fate, *gaghtakanutiun*, the dispossessed man in search of an unknown destination. A literature of exile was composed in the verse of lamentations over the loss of home and land. The condition of *ghaributiun*, that of being among strangers (*gharib* in Arabic and

Turkish meaning stranger) underlined even more poignantly the loss of orientation among peoples for whom the Armenian language had not coined a word and selected from the language of the stranger. Its Armenian equivalent was eventually located in the word *odarutiun*. The sureties of belonging to a place and among the community of nations were drastically eroded and the uncertainties of foreign domination were compounded by the unfamiliarity of surroundings. The experience of being reduced to a stateless minority was accompanied by a downslide in self-esteem. The new conditions of life that were absorbed into the mental adjustment of exile and contemplated in the context of the national trauma of defeat, persecution, and dispersion contributed to the universalizing of new Armenian ethos. Though separated by immense distances and spread across continents, the Armenian people in exile developed new instruments of communication through the externalization of a set to new cultural expressions unknown in the homeland. New types and levels of emotive and pensive bonding were devised.

The flight northward from Armenia and Georgia that followed the Mongol conquests set the Armenians in a new continent. Though Armenian settlements had been planted in Thrace, and even Bulgaria, in earlier centuries, these had all been part of the Byzantine state, part of the Eastern world, much as Cilicia and Egypt constituted part of it also. The trek along the Black Sea coast, however, was a venture into unknown lands. Small groups of Armenians entered Kievan Russia in the 11th century. By the 13th century large communities had formed. The greatest concentration was actually in the eastern part of the Crimean peninsula, centered on the town of Caffa (Theodosia), then still under Byzantine suzerainty, but mainly under Genoese control. The selection of a coastal site and the linkage with Italian traders make it sufficiently evident that the Crimean settlement was based on international commerce, another entry point to the vast Mongolian empire stretching from there on to China. The Armenian population was so substantial here that the Genoese even referred to the place as Armenia Maritima.

Through the Crimean chrysalis, the Armenians spread westward into Europe. The event that spurred a flow of Armenian immigrants in that direction was connected to the consolidation of Polish rule in eastern Galicia. Casimir the Great (1333–1370) made a special allowance for the city of Lvov (presently Lviv, Ukraine) in 1356 by granting its inhabitants the privilege of living by their own laws. Poles, Germans, Ruthenians, Jews, Tatars, and Armenians lived side by side in Lvov. Situated at a crossroads of all four points of the compass, Lvov rose quickly as a major trading center in easternmost Europe. The virtual juridical autonomy enjoyed by the Armenian community gave such impetus as to transform Lvov into one of the most important Armenian settlements of the time. The application of traditional Armenian law measurably added to an atmosphere of safety and confidence. Although these legal privileges would be reduced after 1510, the Armenians by then had prospered to a point where they controlled a considerable part of the trade between Poland and the Ottoman Empire that had formed to the south of Poland. The route running from Lvov to Constantinople, one of the main thoroughfares of eastern Europe, was called the "Armenian way." By the 16th century, Armenian settlements had sprouted in nearly all the towns of Moldavia dotting the road from Lvov to the Ottoman capital, and the goods traded frequently passed from the hands of one Armenian merchant to another.

In the meantime, the expansion of the Ottoman state had resulted in major population shifts within the Armenian diaspora. By the first part of the 16th century, with the exception of Poland, the Turkish Empire virtually incorporated all areas in Asia Minor, the Middle East, the Balkans, and the Back Sea coastline where Armenian diaspora communities had been created. By this strange fate, most of the Armenians in the world found themselves living in a single state. Yet, more of them were removed from their homeland than ever before. Despite the fact that much of Armenia also would be absorbed into the Ottoman Empire, it remained a territory contested by more than one foe from the east. The flow of refugees from the Armenian highlands was a continuous stream, sometimes a trickle, sometimes a torrent, but never ceasing. Since no international boundaries had to be crossed, the Armenian population migrated to the safer and better administered provinces of the Ottoman Empire nearer the capital. The cities of Konia, Bursa, and Kutahya in the historic center of the Ottoman state attracted the settlement of sizable Armenian communities engaged in crafts and industries, like tile-making, patronized by the sultans. Additionally, the Ottomans implemented resettlement policies involving the forcible transfer of populations, especially groups noted for their utility. The imperial design of a universal state, as envisioned by Mehmet II the Conqueror (1451–1481), assigned the Armenians certain specific functions in Ottoman society, such as commerce and finance. With the establishment of the Ottoman state as a world power, it was inevitable that an Armenian concentration would grow in Constantinople.

Until such time as the Constantinopolitans gained ascendancy in the diaspora, the more remote communities played a role in Armenian life more influential than the number of their constituents alone would explain. As virtually the only large colony remaining beyond Ottoman borders, Lvov grew in significance as a place where Armenian culture developed unfettered. Lvov Armenians were the first to be exposed to the modernizing currents of European civilization. An Armenian press printed books here, and a theater was established. A literature unique to the community was authored in a language known as Armeno-Kipchak. Works were written in the language spoken by Polish-Armenians, the Turkish dialect of southern Russia that the Armenians had acquired in the Crimea, and which they recorded with the Armenian alphabet. Although a literate society, this colony had already lost use of the Armenian language. The Armenian alphabet, on the other hand, proved a more lasting instrument, as it was adapted to this and other languages by Armenians in various parts of the world.

More significantly, the character of the Armenian communities underwent measurable changes in these centuries. During the pre-eminence of the Italian city-states and their overseas trading colonies, Armenians had found themselves a niche by populating the ports of entry to the Asian continent, whether along the Mediterranean, as in Cilicia, or the Black Sea coast, as in the Crimea. The elimination of the political presence of the Italians permitted the Armenians room for expanding their commercial network. The Ottomans had sought to find among the native populations the merchants who would fill the role of middlemen. Such a policy favored local Greeks, Jews, and Armenians, to the detriment of Italians. As a result, Armenian trade centers expanded their business interests, and began to function more as mercantile operations engaged in a larger array of financial transactions. These communities were all the more defined by mercantile practices and dominated by merchant families since the proscriptions of Islamic law limited the rights of Christians, specifically restricting the bearing of arms. The Armenian colonies of southern Russia and eastern Poland had continued to organize their own military corps and to participate in the defense of their cities. They had fought alongside the Italians at Caffa, for instance, when the Ottomans seized the city in 1475. They organized volunteer corps for the defense of Polish cities under Ottoman attack as at Kamenets-Podolski.

Nonetheless, the spread of Muslim control reduced the status of Armenians even in Europe and defined them more strictly as a community of nonbelievers, or infidels, extended tolerance, but denied a predetermined set of privileges, foremost among them being the right to bear arms. It left the Armenians all the more exposed as their collective existence depended increasingly on commercial activity, which in turn depended on political stability and physical safety, not to mention assurance of property. They were stigmatized by the inability to rely on individual resources for the security of their persons and possessions. The vulnerability of diaspora existence was aggravated by another increment, and that anxiety was exposed by stresses from a most unexpected source. The zeal of the Counter-Reformation shook the confidence of the Armenian-Polish community as it too was targeted for conversion to Catholicism under the charge of sectarianism, even though they were completely unaffected by the rise of Protestantism in the 16th century. The papal program divided and soon diminished the community. Even in Christendom, it turned out, Armenians were not guaranteed refuge.

The community that epitomized the mercantile phase of the Armenian diaspora was not situated in a Western city. Rather, it was to be found deeper in Asia where another Islamic ruler, the Safavid Shah Abbas (1587–1629) of Iran, had decided to embellish his own capital of Isfahan with the wealth that Armenian merchants would bring it. To deny the Ottomans the human and material resources of Armenia, in 1604 Abbas ordered the resettlement of the entire Armenian population of the **Arax River** valley to areas under more secure Safavid control. Specifically, he instructed his troops to arrange for the relocation of the community of merchants from the city of Jugha/Julfa to an outlying neighborhood of his capital city that the Armenian exiles named Nor Jugha/New Julfa.

A new Armenian elite formed in New Julfa whose wealth emanated from the silk trading monopoly extended them by the shah. With the high demand for this luxury item, the Armenian merchants who traded their goods all the way to western Europe, sometimes directly, rapidly accumulated vast wealth. The richer merchants, known as khojas, soon turned to banking. Their venture capital set younger associates to seek their fortune in the four corners of the Old World. Some Armenian colonists from New Julfa traveled to India, and settled in Delhi and Bombay. One amongst them was the negotiator with the suzerain of Bengal for the grant of permission for the English to purchase their first foothold on the subcontinent at Calcutta. They traded mostly in luxury items, especially precious jewels. From these bases other Armenians spread out to Singapore and built in 1834 the first Christian sanctuary on this strategic island. Now preserved as a historic monument by the Singapore government, its Armenian congregation, however, moved on. Armenians in Burma, Java, the Philippines, and Hong Kong all formed part of a network spread across the Asian continent through the sea lanes traversing the Indian Ocean and the South China Sea. Others branched out to the great trading towns of western Europe and could be found contracting their affairs at Cadiz in Spain, at Amsterdam in Holland, at Marseilles in France, and at Livorno in Italy. Still others joined the trade to the West overland and became prominent in Aleppo, and even as far away as Constantinople and Smyrna on the Aegean coast of Turkey.

Perhaps, most significantly, Armenian merchants from New Julfa obtained a further concession in 1667 for the trade between Iran and Russia. The Armenian importation of silk into and through Russia resulted in the formation of a further series of settlements with their center at Astrakhan at the northern shore of the Caspian Sea. As Russian armies were pushing south, Armenian merchants were pushing north. From Astrakhan, Armenians moved to settle in Moscow and St. Petersburg.

The South Asian diaspora, with its nucleus in New Julfa, offered the Armenians an alternative to life under the Ottoman system. Though still subject to Islamic rule in Iran and India, the direct contact made by Armenians with western Europeans began to plant the seeds of a cultural transformation in Armenian life that would confront many Armenians with a process of modernization that set them upon a course of conflict with their Muslim overlords. Before any ideology was fully articulated, the primary investment Armenians made with their newly acquired financial resources was in **education**. Armenians were the first people of Asia actively to promote literacy among their kind by establishing printing presses wherever feasible. The first Armenian book was printed in Venice in 1512. In 1616 Armenians started publishing in Lvov. In 1668 the first major Armenian printing establishment succeeded in issuing the Armenian Bible in Amsterdam. The priests who managed this printing press arrived in the Netherlands from **Edjmiadsin** in Persian Armenia. The selection of Amsterdam doubtless was made on the basis of information Armenian merchants relayed to churchmen back home. Most of the early presses were run by clerics, since they were the only learned persons among Armenians, and because commercial printing was not feasible until such time when a sufficient market of readers would be created to make a publishing venture at least marginally profitable. That would not occur until the 19th century. However, more significant than any of the cultural accomplishments of the Armenians in Iran and India (the first Armenian periodical for instance was published in Madras in 1784 and lasted for two years), the longest lasting contribution of Armenian capital from the East was attained in Venice. In 1717 the brotherhood of **Catholic** Armenian monks headed by **Mekhitar Sebastatsi** founded a monastery dedicated to educating and publishing. They received major financial support from Armenian merchants in India.

When European penetration of Asia turned from mercantilism to territorial colonialism in the early part of the 19th century, the pockets of specialization the Armenians had created eroded quickly, and many an Armenian in the East ended up a British subject. In Iran, with the death of Shah Abbas, Armenians lost their favored status. Once deprived of their monopoly, and even the protection of the state, as religious animosity was at times directly against them, the wealth and status of the Iranian communities diminished also. The combined effect of these two trends meant that Armenian merchants from the East ceased to visit European ports. Just as the Enlightenment was reaching full flowering in Europe, Armenian communication with the West decreased.

It was at this same time, in the 18th century, that the Ottoman-Armenian diaspora attained its importance in Armenian life, and even more fully in the 19th century. In some measure this was due to the economic status of the Armenians in the empire. In relative terms, the Iranian-Indian diaspora enjoyed greater privileges and opportunities and escaped the oppression that marked Armenian life in Turkey. In the economic sphere, the capitulations extended by the Ottoman government to the European trading states, particularly France and England, also meant that the role of the local intermediary would not be as substantial as in further Asia. Armenian commerce did eventually link with western European import-export mostly in the industrial age, and in the coastal towns the nucleus of a new Armenian elite, consisting of businessmen and professionals, began to form. However, the most evident method of capital accumulation in the hands of Armenians, prior to the expansion of trade in machine-manufactured goods, to a considerable extent was based on the Ottoman system of taxation.

The division of the Ottoman population along sectarian lines resulted in the formation of the so-called **Armenian *Millet*** under the leadership of the Armenian Patriarch of Constantinople. His administration of the Armenian community as required by the regulations of the Ottoman state placed in his hands the authority to apportion the collection of the annual *Millet* taxes for the central treasury. Since state revenues were gathered through tax farming, whosoever purchased the right to tax farm stood to keep for himself a share of the profits. In due course, by the 18th century, there emerged the *amira* class in Constantinople. These Armenians of extraordinary wealth gained a special status in the capital city, and for all intents and purposes, seized hold of the patriarchate as their primary source of revenue. Their status was further enhanced by their special relationship with the court. The centuries of decadence in the Ottoman Empire made the purchase of office an accepted custom, and the large sums required for those purchases were advanced in the form of loans from the amiras. With their friends in power, favored amiras stood to receive appointment to head the management of certain state monopolies, including the provisioning of the army or the operation of the mint, which became an inherited position for a single amira family, the Duzians, for over a century. The famous **Balian** family, the imperial architects, built most of the royal palaces and pavilions raised during the 19th century. The political and financial control of the amiras was broken only in the second half of the 19th century as a new Armenian middle class, connected with the penetration of Western capital, emerged to wrest control of communal life and redefine Armenian cultural values.

The expanding social space created by the economic success of the Armenian community of Constantinople fostered an environment in which a rapid cultural revival transported Armenians from their sectarian seclusion toward aspirations of national emancipation. In the conflict between new economic opportunities created by the process of modernization in the Ottoman Empire and the unreformed autocratic regime that governed it, the Armenians increasingly faced the challenge of having to redefine themselves. They did so avidly as they witnessed the entry of European influence in all spheres of life. The resulting cultural revival called the *Zartonk*, the Flowering, took expression in the production of a new literature whose national content and political ideals only enlarged the gulf between Armenians and their rulers. Every facet of Armenian culture was affected, but none attained the refinement of the poetic literature that was produced in Constantinople. It started with the Romantics, Nahapet Rusinian, Medsarentz, and Bedros Turian and ended with the vibrant verse and emotional fury of the Realists, **Siamanto** and **Taniel Varuzhan**. The ranks of journalists, dramatists, novelists, and short story writers included **Arpiar Arpiarian**, **Hagop Baronian**, and **Krikor Zohrab**, and others who started their careers in Constantinople such as **Arshak Chobanian** and **Vahan Tekeyan**. An unparalled number of schools, newspapers, cultural groups, and benevolent associations flourished in the city. With nearly a quarter million in population, their presence and economic dominance made them the object of suspicion and resentment as the political strain between an aspiring community espousing liberalism and an autocracy fearing change led to violent repression. In the truest sense of the word, the Armenian diaspora had acquired an elite, capable of articulating the views and concerns of a subjugated people. Repression alone could not contain the Armenian people any longer as the art and thought of their Constantinopolitan kin was absorbed by communities all across the Ottoman Empire. When in the early 20th century the promise of the Young Turk Revolution went unrealized, the air of apprehension filled the community. Within a year of the start of the World War I, this shining elite was mortally silenced.

Before tragedy struck the Western Armenian diaspora, a new eastern diaspora matured along very similar lines. The decline of the Asian diaspora had resulted in the outmigration of Armenians northward toward Russia. When in 1828 the Russian flag was hoisted in Transcaucasia and the Persian boundary was fixed along the Arax River, the Armenian exodus from Iran accelerated, and the Armenian diaspora in Russia was enlarged by a substantial number of settlers. This new orientation of the Armenian dispersion once again redefined the cultural life of the Armenian people. Armenians were now physically in Europe again.

Here, Armenian merchants, secure in the knowledge that their capital was protected from arbitrary confiscation, seized the initiative in certain sectors of the economy. The Moscow community continued to grow in importance under the guidance of the wealthy Lazarian/Lazarev family, but largely for cultural reasons. Tbilisi (Tiflis), the capital of the Transcaucasus, was the place where Armenians prospered most. Tbilisi owes its modern character to Armenians who transformed the Oriental market town into an industrial city. Russian administration of the region was conducted from Tbilisi thereby concentrating government, commerce, and culture there. More than half the population of the city was Armenian in the 19th century and so were many of its mayors. The native Georgians numbered less than the Russians in Tbilisi.

In Tbilisi a true Armenian bourgeoisie formed, a society based on commercial and new industrial capital as railroads were built and the oil industry in Baku became an ongoing concern. Banking was a major activity. In the safety of this very large community, Armenian culture blossomed as never before. Theater, music, numerous periodicals, schools staffed with distinguished educators, all flourished and absorbed Russian and European culture at a rapid rate. **Khachatur Abovian**, **Grigor Ardsruni**, **Raffi**, **Avetis Aharonian**, **Alexander Khatisian**, and many more leading figures of the Armenian cultural and political revival made Tbilisi their home. As in the Ottoman Empire, Armenian society catapulted to such a pitch of activity that imperial Russia also responded with repressive policies. Russification measures were imposed in the late 19th century by closing Armenian educational institutions and forcing youngsters into state schools. Of greater alarm to state authorities was the response and increase in Armenian political activity as a number of groups, some small, others large, were formed in tandem with the development of underground political organizations in Russia. It was in Tbilisi that the **Armenian Revolutionary Federation** (ARF) was formed in 1890. The revolutionary opposition to tsarism found echo in Armenian society as it began to deal with the effects of Russian colonialism. For modernizing Armenians, here too the limits of progress and liberty had been reached.

The crisis of Armenian society in the early 20th century was the result of a consciousness born of the opposing realities constraining the Armenian people. Politically they were divided into two, between Russia and Turkey, and further divided societally into two, between homeland and diaspora, with the diaspora itself divided into two, and with each part of the diaspora looking in a different direction. The Armenian people had progressed in their development to a stage that presented a challenge to two governments, themselves representing states in mutual conflict. To deal with the Armenian Question, one of the governments opted to physically eliminate the Armenian presence. The Young Turk policy of genocide decimated the Armenian diaspora in the Ottoman Empire, as well as the population of historic Armenia. The by-product of the attendant deportations was the formation of the modern Armenian diaspora by the survivors and their descendants.

DIASPORA, MODERN. The global network of Armenian expatriate communities formed or reconfigured following the **Armenian Genocide** of 1915. With the collapse of the Ottoman Empire in 1918, the Armenians of Anatolia, survivors of a genocide, now reduced to a mass of impecunious refugees stranded and starving in Syria, were once again and overnight in a new diaspora. On this occasion, however, the entire Armenian nation, it appeared, had been dispersed. Certainly most of those originating from the area consolidated in 1923 as the modern state of Turkey were displaced or dead. Tens of thousands of others had sought safety in Russia, and with the defeat in 1922 of the Greek expedition in Asia Minor, remaining Armenians fled to the Balkan countries. By the time the Middle Eastern political and territorial conflicts of the early 20th century were resolved, Armenian refugees were spread across Syria, Iraq, Lebanon, Jordan, Palestine, Egypt, Iran, Cyprus, Greece, Bulgaria, Romania, Russia, and even beyond into France, Italy, the United States, Canada, and South America. In a word, the globalization of the Armenian diaspora had begun.

The movement of Armenians beginning in the second decade of the 20th century took two contrasting courses. As a considerable number of the surviving Ottoman-Armenian population dispersed away from Armenia, a significant portion of the Russian-Armenian population began moving into historic Armenia. The breakup of the

Romanov Empire led to the creation of an Armenian state out of the province of Erevan/**Yerevan** in 1918. Sovietized in 1920, the forms of statehood were preserved, and the Armenian Soviet Socialist Republic (ASSR) was declared a member state of the Soviet Union. With the violent upheavals in the Ottoman and Russian Empires, many Armenians turned to this small and truncated state as a haven. Armenians fleeing Turkish armies took refuge here. Others displaced by massacres and interethnic conflict in Azerbaijan also fled into the former province.

The diaspora played a major role in establishing the Republic of Armenia. In the precipitous and unexpected conditions that led to the emergence of an Armenian state, the Armenian elite capable of dealing with the responsibilities of forming a government, of securing borders, and gaining international recognition for the fledgling country came from abroad. During a period of a few months, in the spring and summer of 1918, Tbilisi surrendered its role as the nerve center of Armenian political activity when the dusty and primitive town of Yerevan was proclaimed the capital of the Armenian republic. In an obvious and exceptional reversal of the trend of past centuries, the diaspora helped restore the political vitality of historic Armenia. In this respect, the currents of political thought and activity that had spawned the **Armenian Revolutionary Federation** (ARF) in Tbilisi in 1890, and turned it into an effective agency of Armenian national aspirations, bore fruit. The necessary talent and commitment required to manage the Armenian state was pooled in the ARF and returned from the diaspora to Armenia.

The entry of the Red Army in Armenia in November 1920 left a sharp ideological divide among the Armenian people. Just at the moment when Armenia and diaspora were merging, and Armenians the world over prayed that the restoration of Armenian statehood would prove lasting, the Turco-Soviet alliance meant the doom of such long-cherished hopes. For much of the remainder of the 20th century, Armenia and diaspora would grow apart.

Once the rudiments for the physical survival of the deported Ottoman-Armenians had been secured, the Armenian people were faced with the question of its long-term existence in exile. Though Armenians dispersed widely, still the bulk of the population was concentrated in the Middle East. In some respects this proved fortuitous in that Armenian communities could be recreated in an environment not unlike that from which they were ejected. The religio-cultural pattern of Arab society, which itself until the end of World War I was part of the Ottoman world, permitted Armenian refugees to reinsert themselves into their new sites of settlement on terms of association with which they were accustomed. Furthermore, the presence of the French and the British as mandatories over the Middle East provided a political framework that guaranteed a peaceful and, in some measure, even a charitable transition from the condition of deportee to that of refugee. The Armenians were assured by their tolerance. American philanthropy made no less a significant contribution at this early stage of adjustment to exile.

The role of the Middle Eastern communities in the modern Armenian diaspora cannot be overemphasized. In large part it is explained by the retention of the Armenian language. The continued usage of Armenian speech made the Middle Eastern settlements the repositories of modern Armenian culture. This proved important in retaining a viable ethnic identity. Because Armenian society had been exposed for some time to a measurable degree of Westernization, and its traits and values had long been shaped in the diaspora, the presence and influence of the French and British permitted for a further acculturation to Western norms. Many Armenians went to French, British, or American schools. French and English became the second language of the educated. Arabic was a distant third. The Armenians thus were added to the ethnic mosaic of the Middle East during an unusually tolerant interlude for them. Four major communities, situated in Syria, Lebanon, Egypt, and Iran, acquired their characteristic features in this period. The size of their populations meant that each had attained demographic stability and could even project steady growth: 40,000 in Egypt, 100,000 and more each in Syria, Lebanon, and Iran, the last including a contingent of refugees from Russian Armenia, and of course, the older communities dating back to the time of Shah Abbas. Smaller communities were located in Iraq, Jordan, Palestine, and Cyprus.

The retreat of the mandatory powers from the Middle East after World War II, and the full independence of the countries of the region changed the status of the Armenians again. With their legal residency translated into citizenship, Armenians faced the very modern challenge of defining their relationship to a new state. The rise of Arab nationalism, its Islamic component, and its anticolonial ideology made for an uneasy situation. Armenians in the Middle East underwent a second readjustment. The new language of government, the new forms of administration, the new ideological struggles, the involvement of the Arab masses in their self-government, as well as the pan-Arab and other nationalist movements, all deeply affected the Armenian communities. Though the economic transition actually proved beneficial to the Armenians in that again they assumed intermediary and entrepreneurial roles, the political transformations, however, exposed their minority condition and highlighted new vulnerabilities as their loyalties were put to the test anew. Once the state structures of the Middle Eastern countries were solidified and the men in power had at their disposal the instruments for shaping national programs, Armenian exclusivity made the Middle Eastern communities enclaves generically resistant to various aspects of public policy. By the 1950s Armenian communal institutions were in place. For instance, a network of schools had been built across the Middle East. Armenian communities appeared to have consolidated some areas that modern governments assumed to be within the scope of their responsibilities. The centralizing and state-building programs aimed at achieving national consensus, combined with the instability of Middle Eastern governments during this era of transition from colonial rule to fully self-governing sovereignties, besieged the Armenian settlements. All the Armenian communities in the Arab countries, one at a time, became the object of specifically restrictive policies or the victims of more general political programs that undermined their economic or institutional foundations.

Every upheaval in the Middle East sent Armenians emigrating, and each Armenian community at one time or another was affected by serious disruptions of civil order, by military conflicts, or by violent turnovers of government. Though individual communities may have been growing and prospering, the overall experience of the Armenians in the Middle East since the 1950s has been that of erosion in communal stability. By the mid-1980s virtually all Middle East communities had lost a significant percentage of their populations. For various reasons the decline of these communities occurred gradually, thereby permitting the remaining population to reconfigure its institutions and adapt to changing circumstances. One community was not so fortunate. Within the space of less than five years the wealthiest Armenian settlement in the Middle East was reduced to a minor enclave. The Armenians of Egypt had escaped both world wars unscathed. The roots of their community dated to the early decades of the 19th century when Muhammad Ali founded modern Egypt. Under the sponsorship of Muhammad Ali's Armenian associates, men such as **Boghos Yusufian**, **Artin Chrakian**, and **Nubar Pasha**, each of whom rose to the rank of prime minister, a prideful and solid community had formed. The **Armenian General Benevolent Union** (AGBU) was organized in Cairo in 1906 by **Boghos Nubar**. The nationalization of foreign-owned firms in the early 1960s suddenly toppled the entire edifice of this 150-year-old community. Whereas the French, British, Italians, Greeks, and others returned to their home countries, for the Armenians, also labeled foreigners though they lacked a home country, the economic ruination of their community meant a whole new dispersal. They headed largely to Canada and Australia, former British colonies like Egypt.

The nationalist fervor and the socialist plank promoted by prominent Arab politicians such as Gamal Abdel-Nasser impacted Armenian communities across the Middle East. In Syria policies akin to those adopted in Egypt stifled political and cultural expression. The Armenian media was virtually banned. The promotion of **education** in Arabic was also imposed on parochial schools. Because the Armenian community in Syria was largely made up of former refugees from Turkey and their descendants, they did not constitute an important element in the Syrian economy, as the Armenians in Egypt did for instance. Therefore, the effect of the socialist program in Syria, rather than destroy the financial basis of that community, placed limits on further economic progress and thereby neutralized possibilities for Armenians to continue to improve their lot. As they were not allowed to emigrate, more and more Armenians from Aleppo and other towns drifted into Lebanon first and from there on to other countries. The civil war in Lebanon, which lasted from 1975 to 1990, initially reversed the flow as many Armenians sought refuge back in Syria. That was a temporary solution. The Syrian economy could not absorb them. The long and bloody sectarian war waged in Lebanon resulted in the diminution of its Armenian settlement to less than half its former size of over 200,000.

Before the civil war, the peculiar constitution of Lebanon, drawn to maintain a fine balance of power in this multisectarian country, had permitted the local Armenian community to develop to its fullest potential.

The commercial experience gained by Armenians in Lebanon was considerable and exceptional. With the economic development of the Arab world, and especially with the income flowing from the sale of oil, the expansion of trade in the Middle East transformed Beirut into a major cosmopolitan city. The laissez-faire economic policies of the Lebanese government invited all sort of investment and made Beirut the financial center of the region. The Armenian success in obtaining the Middle East franchises and dealerships of Western industrial companies positioned them again as a community playing the role of commercial intermediary. The effect of the unrestricted exposure to European and American culture made a considerable imprint upon the Armenian community. The highly tolerant political milieu also permitted for the free exchange of ideas.

For the period from the end of World War II and the beginning of the civil war, Beirut came to symbolize the best hopes of the Armenian diaspora. A veritable beehive of cultural activity, with full-blown programs in music, theater, art, with a strong press, with dozens of schools and cultural associations, the Lebanese Armenians projected upon the rest of the diaspora the fruits of their accomplishments. A diaspora-born intelligentsia visibly played an influential role in Armenian life and consciously engaged the difficult questions of Armenian cultural vitality in the modern era under conditions of exile and dispersion. The impact of the Lebanese civil war on the Armenians of Beirut sent shock waves through the rest of the diaspora and compelled the reconsideration of the premises on which the diaspora had developed. Still, the Armenian settlement in Lebanon often seemed more durable than the country. With Lebanon segmenting, the Armenians grew more united. Aware that their investment in the country was massive, they made every effort to salvage as much of it as possible. Nonetheless, half the Armenians of Lebanon emigrated. A remaining population of about 100,000 became wholly concentrated in Christian East Beirut. Its institutions continued to operate and quickly recovered with the restoration of peace. With the **Catholicos** of the Great House of Cilicia, the **Armenian Apostolic Church** in exile, residing in the Beirut suburb of Antelias, Lebanon remained an important center of Armenian diaspora life. It ceased, however, from being the singular focal point of the diaspora.

The last of this series of stresses on the Armenian communities in the Middle East was caused by the 1979 revolution in Iran. The rise of Islamic fundamentalism, and the consequent increase in intolerance was always a serious concern for Armenians. The success of the movement in establishing a theocratic government in a country that was otherwise modernizing rapidly again underscored the high volatility of the entire region. To Armenians, who associated socially, politically, and economically with the Iranian element promoting Westernization, the regime of the Ayatollah Khomeini reversed many trends and isolated the community. The imposition of Islamic law underscored the distance between the Iranian masses and the minority communities, most of which were inclined to free economic enterprise and progress along Western and secular lines. Another well-to-do community with extensive infrastructure and important economic interests was disrupted. The combined effect of Arab nationalism, religious fundamentalism, military conflicts, repressive regimes, state-managed economies, and sectarian animosities totally altered the environment in which the Armenian communities in the region existed. For most, it meant renegotiating with their governments to preserve their communal structure. In the final analysis the governments that came to power in the second half of the 20th century reconsidered the traditional roles assigned to some Christian and Westernized minorities in the Middle East.

The experience in the rest of the Armenian diaspora was quite different. The forces of assimilation worked more strongly on the Armenian communities of western Europe, North and South America, and of the Soviet Union. The largest concentration of Armenians in Europe is found in France. Besides Cairo, the other city in which the surviving Armenian elite from the Ottoman Empire, and especially the Russian Empire, took refuge was Paris. **Nicholas Adontz**, **Avetis Aharonian**, **Arshag Chobanian**, **Alexander Khatisian**, **Gabriel Noradoungian**, **Boghos Nubar**, and **Simon Vratzian**, among others, resided in France in this period. This gathering of Armenian intellectuals in France gave the community unusual vitality during the interwar years. A considerable corpus of literature was created there. The younger literati of the Paris community first examined the conflicts of diaspora existence. Yet Paris alone did not make up the French-Armenian diaspora. Large settlements of working class families were found in Marseilles, Lyons, and the surrounding towns. They were at a comparative disadvantage.

Educated Armenians from Russia and Turkey brought with them a close acquaintance with French culture. This permitted a stratum of

Armenian society to appreciate the cultural mainstream of the country. It also hastened integration, as well as the confrontation with the probabilities of its outcome. Their offspring who were entirely exposed to French education assimilated quickly. The Armenian community in France did not replicate the network of institutions produced in the Middle East because it did not need to. What Armenian culture and education could offer was no match to one of the most advanced civilizations of the world. Despite this vast gap, the process by which the Armenians integrated into the French, and especially the Parisian, world resulted in an especially dynamic community abounding with creativity in the arts. Musicians, painters, and writers of Armenian extraction, such as **Charles Aznavour**, Carzou, and Henri Troyat, themselves became exponents of the cultural sophistication of French society. This accomplishment made France a magnet for the Middle Eastern elite. The bonds between France and Lebanon, a former French mandate, were particularly strong. In this respect, French-Armenian society radiated its culture beyond the borders of France into the rest of Europe and the Middle East.

Armenians in the United States acquired a dual history on account of the patterns of settlement that occurred in two major waves of migration separated by some 50 years. The immigrants who arrived between 1890 and 1924 entered the country as part of the mass of refugees fleeing the Ottoman Empire. The enormous distance separating them from the rest of their kinsmen in the Middle East and Europe isolated the Armenians in the United States, especially after its government retreated from overseas involvement and, as a general policy, sharply restricted new immigration. Moreover, Armenians settled in different parts of the country at a time before the spread of commercial aviation when crossing the United States meant traversing a continent, usually by train. The size of the country further fractionalized Armenians in the United States. The three main areas of colonization were located in the Northeast and Midwest industrial zones, namely in or nearby the cities of Boston, New York, Chicago, and Detroit, and the central valley of California where Armenians returned to farming the land, in and around Fresno, the birthplace of **William Saroyan** and **Kirk Kerkorian**.

The long separation shaped the character of the Armenian-American community, emphasizing its isolation and distance. Numbering but a few tens of thousands spread across a huge country with a population exceeding 100 million, the early immigrants were confronted with very difficult choices. Impulsively they gathered around the church. In the absence of other reinforcing institutions, the church acquired a greater significance in Armenian-American life than elsewhere in the diaspora. With religious tolerance a prevalent value in American life, and with Christianity practiced in all its diversity, the Armenian Apostolic Church proliferated in the United States. The availability of universal schooling, the need to acquire the dominant language, the desire to shed the onus of a tragic past, and the sheer dynamic of American life tore away at the ancient fabric of Armenian society. Consequently, the Armenian-American community stressed its religious character in accordance with the American habit of defining community on the basis of denomination. Linguistic, cultural, and political traits were quickly diluted. The probability of alienation from such a limited view of the self in a secular, diverse and open society was very high. With the alteration of the economic basis of the Armenian communities, as native-born generations turned to the professions and abandoned the mills and farms, the new workplace obliterated all traces of communal identity. The transition of Armenian life in America from an Old World culture to modern existence occurred outside the framework of Armenian institutions.

When in the 1960s the American understanding of minority identity shifted its emphasis from denomination to ethnic traits, this wider definition created an environment in which new immigrants, who happened to be arriving in the same decade, were able to reconstitute their communal structures swiftly without the pressure for rapid assimilation and the obligation of conformity. At the same time, they exposed the older community to the possibilities of taking up the challenge of reconsidering its own acculturation to American life. The fusion that occurred between the two parts of the Armenian-American community proved a vitalizing experience for both the older and the newer strata. With the successful pattern of integration demonstrated by the new arrivals in the last third of the 20th century, within a generation the lineages separating the two groups became blurred. Significantly, the new immigrants were observant of the experience of the older immigrants and their progeny, and consciously selected choices more conducive to communal stability. Equally consciously, they sought to avoid the confinement to a narrowly defined identity.

The synthesis became evident in the course taken by the Armenian community's involvement in the American political system. Whereas older immigrants assiduously avoided politics and their descendants were not readily motivated as a result to participate in a collective sense, new immigrants expressed little reticence to being active citizens. However, for their desire to acquire reality, a convergence of forces proved necessary. The financial resources available to Armenians from both the older and newer communities first combined. Second, politicians of Armenian extraction were identified whose candidacy was acceptable to a wide spectrum of the electorate. Those candidates emerged from the older more assimilated portion of the community. It was probably less a conscious process than a happy discovery. This phenomenon was epitomized in the 1982 election of **George Deukmejian** as Republican governor of California, the wealthiest and most populous state of the union. It was no coincidence that the largest and most prosperous Armenian diaspora settlement in the world by the 1980s was to be found in the same state. Armenians around the world were uniformly in agreement on the value of seeing their own reach such high office, a validation of their accomplishments and their endurance as a people determined to preserve a sense of worth even in exile.

Armenian-Americans in public service participated beyond the state level and a handful achieved prominence in national politics. Charles Pashayan and Anna Eshoo were elected to Congress from California. Pashayan, a Republican, served six terms from 1979–1991. Eshoo, a Democrat, began serving in 1993 and started her fifth term in 2001. They were preceded in the U.S. House of Representatives by Steven Derounian of New York who served six terms as a Republican from 1953 to 1965. In 1999 John Sweeny joined the New York delegation in the House as a Republican and started his second term in 2001. Others distinguished themselves in the executive branch. Foreign service officer Edward Djerejian, an expert on Russia and the Middle East, who was appointed U.S. ambassador to Syria in 1988, and became Assistant Secretary of State for Near Easten Affairs in 1993, concluded his career as U.S. ambassador to Israel in 1993. Paul Ignatius, having served as Assistant Secretary of Defense from 1964 to 1967, was appointed Secretary of the Navy from 1967 to 1969 by U.S. President Lyndon Johnson.

The reinvigoration of diaspora communities by a new influx occurred elsewhere as the dislocation of thousands of Armenians from the Middle East resulted in their emigration to Canada, Argentina, Uruguay, and Australia, where Armenians had resided since the flight from the genocide. The South American communities shared with the North American ones the problem of distance and isolation. Their adjustment, however, was ameliorated by a number of cultural factors. Armenians fully integrated into Latin culture. Because of this integration Armenians in Montevideo and Buenos Aires did not engage the questions of diaspora life and identity in quite the same fashion and with the same intensity as their kin in the rest of the Western Hemisphere. The nature of the response had much to do with the fact that Latin America was culturally related to the Mediterranean world. Though the Spanish language was unfamiliar to them, nevertheless the value systems and the patterns of social interaction were more akin to those within the Armenians' experience. Hence the early settlement of the South American communities by large numbers of Armenians originating from Cilicia, the affinities with Latin culture, and the absence of sharp social conflicts laid out a pattern of integration and considerable assimilation as well.

The adaptations undergone by the Armenian diasporas in the free world are made clearer when compared with developments in the Armenian diaspora of the USSR. The isolation imposed on Armenians living outside the borders of the Armenian SSR was wholly the result of the Communist program that banned all so-called bourgeois institutions. By a stroke of the pen, the Armenian Church, Armenian schools, clubs, and publications almost ceased to exist outside of Armenia in the Soviet Union. Armenia counted as a constituent member of the USSR, yet Armenians elsewhere in the Soviet Union benefited little from its existence as Soviet ideology gave preference to the institutions of the titular nationalities of the constituent federal republics. Because the Soviet Armenian diaspora was concentrated in Transcaucasia, the formation of national republics dedicated to the promotion of a single ethnic conception doubled the impact of the denial of supportive institutional structures for Armenians in Soviet Georgia and Soviet Azerbaijan, which viewed their large minorities as potentially divisive. Given the size and importance of the Armenian communities in Tbilisi and Baku, the restrictions placed on their capacity for self-expression thwarted the further flourishing of those once-thriving centers of Armenian life. Communities but a train ride removed from Armenia were gradually deprived of the most basic implements for transferring their culture to younger generations. For most Armenians living outside the ASSR, Russian became a first language. For many in Moscow and elsewhere in Russia, the Armenian language disappeared altogether.

Armenians in the Soviet Union faced the very serious challenge of adapting to a controlled society where nationalist expression was an invitation to repression. Virtually all of Armenian society outside of Armenia underwent the same process. Armenians turned from commerce to the professions. They became bureaucrats, engineers, doctors, scientists, analysts, and managers of plants and other state-owned economic enterprises. The high level of education in Soviet Armenia, the comparatively large number of university graduates, and the limited employment opportunities in the smallest republic of the Soviet Union contributed to the outflow of those destined to be technocrats of the planned economy. Many rose to the highest echelons of the Communist Party in Moscow, **Anastas Mikoyan** being the most notable among them. Others rose through the ranks of the military, especially during World War II, as with the examples of Marshal **Ivan Baghramian** and Admiral **Ivan Isakov**. These policies, which also encouraged Russification, changed rapidly in the Gorbachev era as channels of communication were reestablished among Armenians in the Soviet Union. The class of Armenian technocrats and analysts in Moscow also gained new status as the state turned to rationalizing its economic system. In this regard, **Abel Aganbegyan**, the principal economic theorist of *perestroika*, came to embody the Soviet Armenian diaspora attainment.

The collapse of the USSR in 1991 meant the sudden emergence of a whole set of new diaspora settlements. Despite the problems of the USSR, while it still constituted a single entity, regardless of their location, Armenians counted as citizens of the same state. With the emergence of 15 new states, almost as many Armenian diaspora communities appeared all at once. Moreover, with the opening of borders, large numbers of Armenians migrated on a scale not seen before. The conflict with Azerbaijan over **Nagorno Karabagh** sounded the death knell of the Baku community, which was ejected in 1990 and fled to Armenia and Russia. Dire economic circumstances in Armenia set Armenians migrating to southern and central Russia. The existence of Armenian communities in Turkmenistan and elsewhere in Central Asia became known. The movement of employment seekers fed the growth of new communities in eastern Europe. Armenians appeared in places with which they had no historical association, such as the city of Prague in the Czech Republic. Lastly, the migration to the United States introduced one more stratum to the Armenian-American community.

The modern Armenian diaspora, historically forming the third set after the early medieval and the late medieval communities, posed challenges to their constituents that the earlier diasporas never faced. In the modern era, with the absorption of the majority of populations into the urban setting, the relative importance of middleman minorities dropped precipitously. In fact, most minorities no longer represent the core element of the middle class that occupied the comparatively narrow space between the ruling bodies and the mass of the population tied to agricultural labor. Whenever a state began modernizing, the governing class saw Armenians as a social element whose skills could contribute to the realization of certain national economic goals. However, once a middle class formed from the majority nationality who perceived the Armenians, and other minorities, as competition, and who with their increasing political influence could further control the state and economy by excluding weaker collectivities, Armenians were forced out. Both capitalism and communism had the same effect on Armenians. Both destroyed the middle classes that were identified with the older systems of governance. This in part explains why Armenians migrated to the industrialized countries of the West. They represented no threat to the dominant class in those societies. They easily integrated and became productive members of their new communities. Possessing neither the capital nor the experience in acquiring the major sources of wealth in an industrialized society, Armenians in the modern diaspora became entirely defined by what were called "petty bourgeois" values and objectives. In many respects short-term materialist goals raised the greatest difficulties for Armenian cultural cohesiveness and creativity. The opportunities offered by the consumer economy and mass society eroded the obligations of community. Therefore identity in the modern era evolved into a very self-conscious characteristic of an individual's personality. The availability of choice required of each to make decisions throughout the course of life, thus increasing the burden of identity and setting it in serious conflict in a rapidly changing world.

Considering how the modern diasporas started, from a point nearing the total disintegration of Armenian society, when all is added in terms of the challenges that were confronted and regularly overcome, that reorganized collectivities persevere and nurture at times creative milieus, testifies to a society that also overcame the fatalism that might have drowned it when it was cast shipwrecked on the rising tides of the 20th century.

DVIN. Capital of early medieval Armenia. Dvin was the capital of Armenia in the period of Persian (428–650) and Arab (650–884) rule. Its founding is attributed to the son of **Trdat IV**, King Khosrov III Kotak (330–338), who fortified a previously inhabited hilltop at a site used as a royal hunting park. Khosrov's son King Tiran also used the citadel as his royal residence. Dvin is located on the left bank of the Azat, or Garni, River, which flows west into the **Arax River**. It lies just a few kilometers east of **Artashat** and 40 kilometers south of present-day **Yerevan**.

Dvin's growth into a major urban settlement dates to the beginning of the fifth century. In the wake of the partition of Armenia in 387 into Roman and Iranian spheres, the last **Arshakuni** king, Artashes VI, was deposed in 428. Thereupon the Sasanid Persians abolished the Armenian monarchy. To consolidate their hold over Armenia and disassociate the governance of the country from its former royal capital of **Vagharshapat**, the Persians made Dvin the administrative center of their imperial province.

The Sasanids appointed a Persian governor of Armenia, whose title of *marzpan* meant guardian of the frontier, but whose responsibilities extended far beyond his military command over the Iranian forces garrisoned in the country. The marzpan exercised near complete administrative control over Armenia, with authority in matters of taxation, justice, religious affairs, and the regulation of commerce. The office was not restricted to Persians alone, and a number of native lords of the great feudal houses of Armenia were given the assignment.

For medieval Armenia, where a deeply entrenched native feudal aristocracy controlled the land, the powers of the marzpan represented an unusual concentration of authority in a single office. Though controlled by the Persians, Armenia for the time appears to have acquired something of a bureaucracy as the marzpan also maintained the central archives of the country in Dvin, a matter of great importance for the Armenian *nakharars* who jealously guarded their privileges and wanted them renewed by succeeding monarchs. The archives were important for the Sasanid king of kings as well who expected his governor in Armenia to supply him with armed contingents in the numbers required according to the royal lists. Foreign rule thus necessitated the codification of nakharar ranks. In so doing the Persians also perpetuated the established feudal order and continued to rely on the services of the Armenian nobility. One hereditary office from the time of the Armenian monarchy in particular, critical to marshaling the military resources of Armenia, remained in the hands of the **Mamikonian** family, that of the *sparapet*, the commander-in-chief of the Armenian mounted regiments supplied by the nakharar lords. The scions of this nakharar house distinguished themselves as the central figures of the Armenian resistance to Iranian assimilationist policies. They repeatedly opposed practices designed to promote Zoroastrian dualism and fire worship to the detriment of the Christian Church, and they resisted policies intended to undermine the customary feudal order of Armenia. While Vardan Mamikonian led an Armenian rebellion against Iranian rule in 451 and fell in the field of battle, his heir, Vahan Mamikonian, succeeded in obtaining appointment as marzpan in 485 and briefly secured for Armenia a period of considerable autonomy.

Against the background of the struggle for the spiritual allegiance of the country, the city of Dvin played an important role in the religious life of Armenia. Having removed the Armenian king from his throne in 428, the Sasanids also deposed **Catholicos** Sahak I and relocated the catholicosate to Dvin. Even though the Iranian governors conducted their occasional policies of religious persecution from the new capital, and tensions between the **Armenian Apostolic Church** and the Persian clergy under the supervision of a *mogpet* (chief of the magians) were high, nonetheless the catholicosate remained in Dvin for more than 450 years. While the Iranians built fire temples, the Armenians raised a large cathedral in Dvin and constructed a well-organized compound with its own ecclesiastical archives that emerged as the nerve center of the Armenian Church.

The theological choices and direction adopted by the Armenian Church are most readily understood against this background of Iranian rule contested in Dvin. A number of church synods were held in the city. The first Council of Dvin convoked in 505/6 condemned

Nestorianism, which emphasized the human nature of Christ. More significantly, this move was a step in opposition to Chalcedonianism, which recognized both a divine and human nature for Christ, another dualism whose semblance the Armenians hoped to avoid. Nestorianism was more widely spread in lands controlled by Iran, while Chalcedonianism enjoyed imperial sponsorship in Constantinople. The Armenian Church avoided either proclivity and by formally rejecting the theological formula adopted by the Roman Church in the Council of Chalcedon in 451, the second Council of Dvin in 554/5 endorsed Monophysitism, which upheld the divinity of Christ over his human nature. This final break from the Roman Church was treated by the Armenian Church as important enough to make the meeting of the second Council of Dvin the beginning date of the Armenian church calendar.

In the 591 repartition of Armenia between the Byzantines and the Sasanids, Dvin remained in the Persian-controlled sector of the country, but it now lay on the border. The Byzantines in later conflicts twice occupied it. The Emperor Heraklios entered Dvin in 623, and Constantine IV in 652/3, but by then the city had already fallen to the Arabs who had captured it in 640. The Arabs appointed their own governor over Armenia. The so-called *vostikan*, who represented the caliph, continued to reside in Dvin, but his authority was always checked by the Arab tribesmen who settled in the highlands and whose loyalties were more closely held by their own chiefs, or emirs, than the centrally appointed and annually rotated administrator. During the reign of the Abbasid Caliph Harun al-Rashid (785–809), pressure on the Caucasian frontier required the relocation of the vostikan to the more northern city of Partav in 789, thus leaving Dvin as the secondary capital of the province of Arminiya as the Arabs called it.

The bestowal by the caliphs in the early ninth century of the title of prince of princes upon the **Bagratuni** assured their preeminence among the Armenian nakharar houses. The acquisition of Dvin then became an important objective of the new Armenian dynasty, and by the time of **Ashot I** (862–890, king of Armenia from 884), the Bagratuni had come to exercise overlordship of the district of Dvin. The earthquake of 893/4, however, altered the fate of the city. It caused serious damage and resulted in the death of a very large portion of the population, reported in the tens of thousands. The residence of the catholicos was ruined, and Gevorg II Karnetsi (George

II of Karin/Erzerum) was forced to abandon Dvin, but not before he was captured by Afshin, the Sadjid emir of Azerbaijan, who seized the city left exposed by the earthquake's destruction of its defenses. The Sadjids converted Dvin into a military base, founded a separate emirate in the district, and obstructed the reintegration of the city into the new Armenian kingdom. In 951 Dvin passed into the hands of the Shaddadids, a family of Kurdish origin who founded their own emirate in Eastern Armenia. In the first year of his reign, Ashot III (953–977), king of Armenia, made one final attempt to free Dvin, but the defenses of the city had been rebuilt by that time. The proclamation of **Ani** as the new capital of Armenia in 961 also spelled the abandonment of the effort to incorporate Dvin into the **Armenian kingdom**. Shaddadid rule over Dvin did not go uncontested by competing Muslim tribes, and after their entry into Ani in 1045, the Byzantines too advanced upon Dvin but also failed to capture it.

From almost its very beginning Dvin was the most cosmopolitan city in Armenia. It was home to an international community of administrators, manufacturers, merchants, long-distance traders, clergymen of various faiths, and noblemen of sundry backgrounds. Its Armenian population was augmented by a compliment of Persians, Syrians, Jews, and later, Arabs, Kurds, Turks, Georgians, and others. The great East-West trade route linking Byzantium with Iran, India, and China passed through Dvin, and international trade always represented a very significant portion of the economic activity of the capital city as attested by the great number of coins uncovered at the site by archeologists. The diversified economy of the capital district in Armenia assured the long-term prosperity of the city of Dvin. Agricultural production in the surrounding fertile Plain of **Ararat** was supplemented by husbandry, and especially horse breeding, a major source of trade revenue for Armenia since Antiquity. Mining and manufacturing also produced both raw materials and finished goods for export. Like neighboring Artashat, Dvin was another center of the rug weaving and textile industry in Armenia.

Dvin recovered from the devastation of the 893/4 earthquake and prospered during the 10th century. Even though the Bagratuni dedicated great resources to developing Ani as their new capital city and captured a good part of the international commerce conducted across Armenia, the exceptional location of Dvin assured its viability and it remained a major urban center throughout the period. Because of its strategic and economic importance Dvin remained the object of competing powers in the region. While it changed hands with some regularity, the submission of its Muslim overlords to the Seljuk Turks, who occupied the area in the mid-11th century, may have spared it the degree of destruction visited upon other urban centers in Armenia. Dvin was still flourishing when it came under Georgian control in 1203. Ever so briefly the city enjoyed the privilege of hosting Queen Tamar (1184–1212) who selected Dvin as her winter residence. Tamar made Dvin part of the Zakarian domain, and for the first time since the reign of King Ashot I, an Armenian noble family governed the city again. It lasted until the Mongol invasions and the sack of the city in 1236. Dvin never recovered from this blow and its eventual ruin, after nine hundred years of existence, was so complete that not a structure remained standing. *See also* EDJMIADSIN.

– E –

EDJMIADSIN. The spiritual center of the **Armenian Apostolic Church**. The beginnings of Christianity in Armenia are associated with Edjmiadsin. The Cathedral of Edjmiadsin, dedicated to the Mother of God, is the focal point of the Armenian national church. According to tradition, **Grigor Lusavorich** founded the cathedral at a location identified for him by Christ, who, in a vision, descended from heaven to strike the very ground where He wanted the church constructed. The name Edjmiadsin, which means literally "The Only-Begotten-One Descended," comes from this tradition. Lying 20 kilometers west of modern-day **Yerevan**, Edjmiadsin started as the royal capital of **Vagharshapat**. Where once the kings of Armenia held court, today resides the **Catholicos** of All Armenians, the supreme patriarch of the Armenian Apostolic Church.

While the city of Vagharshapat has enjoyed a continuous existence since its founding, its transformation into the spiritual center of Edjmiadsin was a long process with a hiatus of almost eight hundred years in the middle. In the decades after the process of Christianization was started in the beginning of the fourth century, the patriarchal seat was located at Ashtishat, the former center of pagan worship in ancient Armenia, from where Grigor Lusavorich guided his missionary activities. While a chapel for the services of royalty would have existed in Vagharshapat from the time of King **Trdat IV**, the construction of a stone edifice of proportions to match the importance of the Holy See is attributed to Catholicos Sahak (387–428), whose episcopate began in the year of the partition of Armenia between the Romans and the Sasanid Persians. Archeological evidence indicates that the cathedral was raised immediately above a fire altar in a concrete exemplification of the triumph of the Christian Church over the rejected practice of Zoroastrianism and paganism.

The currently existing structure dates from 483 when the great general and defender of the Armenian Church, Vahan **Mamikonian**, the nephew of Vardan the Brave, commissioned a new cathedral. By this act, Vahan Mamikonian perpetuated the existence of Edjmiadsin as a distinctly spiritual center because earlier the Holy See had been removed to the new capital city of **Dvin**, where resided the Persian *marzpan*, the governor-general of Armenia and the personal representative of the Sasanid king of kings. While the political importance of Edjmiadsin declined, its role in the cultural and religious life of Armenia continued to grow. A monastery was organized. Its prior in the late fifth century was a protégé of Vahan Mamikonian, the noted historian Ghazar Parpetsi, who is also credited with starting the monastery's manuscript library.

Edjmiadsin's rise as a pilgrimage destination was strengthened with the building activities sponsored by three seventh-century patriarchs. Catholicos Komitas Aghdzetsi (Komitas of Aghdzk) (615–628) commissioned the exceptionally beautiful church of Saint Hripsime over the mausoleum of the virgin by the same name whose martyrdom was the cause of King Trdat's remorse and decision to convert to Christianity as an act of contrition. Catholicos Yezr Parazhnakertatsi (Ezra of Parazhnakert) (630–641) commissioned in 630 the church of Saint Gayane, another martyr. Catholicos Nerses III Ishkhanetsi (Nerses of Ishkhan) (641–661), also called *Shinarar* (the Builder), commissioned in the 650s the construction of the church of Zvartnots as part of his near-regal patriarchal residence just east of Edjmiadsin. Zvartnots stood until the 10th century when an earthquake pulled it down. Hripsime and Gayane still stand as models of the austere beauty of early Armenian ecclesiastical architecture.

The first period of Edjmiadsin's importance came to a close with the Arab occupation. The catholicoses continued to reside in Dvin, and later when the Bagratuni settled upon **Ani** as the new capital of their kingdom, the patriarchs relocated to nearby Argina. From Ani they went into exile when the Seljuk Turks completely disrupted life in Armenia until they found themselves a more permanent home in the 12th century in the fortress of Hromkla on the Euphrates and then Sis, the capital of Cilician Armenia. Edjmiadsin fell into obscurity and its condition deteriorated so badly that it moved the 13th century poet and archbishop of Siunik, Stepanos Orbelian, to write his *Lamentations on the Holy Cathedral of Vagharshapat.*

Edjmiadsin's slow recovery began with the decision of the bishops of Armenia to restore the catholicosate to Edjmiadsin. The fall of the Cilician Armenian kingdom in 1375 and the isolation of the Catholicosate at Sis under Mamluk rule undermined its capacity to exercise any real influence over ecclesiastical affairs in Armenia proper. The inroads made by **Catholic** missionaries in encouraging the so-called Uniate movement had spread from Cilicia to Armenia, while the church itself was barely holding against the pressure of Islam now that Armenians everywhere had fallen subject to Muslim rule. The monastic movement engendered by Hovhannes Vorotnetsi (John of Vorotan) (1313–1386), Grigor Tatevatsi (Gregory of Tatev) (1346–1409), and Tovma Medsopetsi (Thomas of Medsop) (1378–1446) to revive the church, introduce clerical discipline and doctrinal orthodoxy, fostered the idea of restoring the catholicosate to Edjmiadsin. Though a catholicos still presided in Sis, in 1441 the bishops and abbots of Armenia assembled to elect a successor to the patriarchal throne of Gregory the Illuminator. By anointing Kirakos Khorvirapetsi (Kirakos of Khor-Virap) Catholicos of All Armenians (1441–1443), the bishops and monks gave expression to their long-held goal of retrieving the Armenian Church from captivity and providing the Armenian people a focal point of authority.

Changes in the political fortunes of Eastern Armenia had as much to do with the gradual elevation of Edjmiadsin to ecclesiastical supremacy as did the efforts of clergymen to secure and extend the authority of the revived catholicosate. The reattachment of the catholicosate with its historic center and the absence of worthwhile contact with Sis assured Edjmiadsin the attention of the Armenian people still living in their homeland. Its progress, however, was not guaranteed, and in the 18th century it was overshadowed by the Armenian patriarchate of Istanbul that exercised presumptive authority over the more populous **Armenian *Millet*** in the Ottoman Empire. Even so, the spiritual supremacy of Edjmiadsin went unchallenged.

The Kara Koyunlu Turks ruled Armenia in 1441 when the permission to restore the catholicosate was obtained. The Safavids of Iran who occupied Armenia in 1502 renewed the privileges received by Edjmiadsin both to religious title and to the income generated from the landed properties that it had been granted title as endowment. While the deportation of the Armenians by Shah Abbas in 1604 from the **Arax River** valley left Edjmiadsin stranded in a country denuded of its productive population, the presence of the monastery and its substantial economic privileges secured a beachhead for future demographic recovery. The catholicoses made the best of a difficult situation by continually sending emissaries to the Armenian **diaspora**, whether to distant Poland or the new settlements in southern Iran near the Safavid capital of Isfahan. Donations from near and far helped to rebuild Edjmiadsin. The catholicosate also became the center of political activity as the *meliks*, chieftains of the semiautonomous principalities of easternmost Armenia, conferred in Edjmiadsin over the political future of their country. In 1547 Catholicos Stepanos Salmastetsi (Stephen of Salmast) (1545–1567) convened a secret meeting where the decision was taken to send to Rome a delegation headed by him to plead for the liberation of Armenia with the pope. In 1677 Catholicos Hakob Jughayetsi (James of Julfa) (1655–1680) secretly convened a meeting of the clergy, the *meliks*, and other lay representatives who decided to send a second delegation to the Papacy. The missions to Catholic Rome yielded no results, but another mission to Protestant Amsterdam undertaken alone by Voskan Yerevantsi (Voskan of Yerevan) (1614–1674) was more fruitful. In 1666 he succeeded in printing the Armenian Bible. It would be more than a hundred years before a printing press could be set up in Edjmiadsin, the first in Armenia and in that part of the world.

The turning point in the reemergence of Edjmiadsin as a truly important center of Armenian national affairs may be dated to the primacy of **Simeon Yerevantsi** (Simon of Yerevan) (1763–1780). The introduction of the printing press in 1771 was only part of Yerevantsi's program to make Edjmiadsin a place of learning and an effective headquarter for the administration of the Armenian Church. He founded a seminary, began the church archives, constructed a paper mill to supply the press, the archive, and the seminary, and, perhaps most importantly, he ordered a cadastral survey of Edjmiadsin's endowments in real estate to secure the church's title to its property. It was during the tenure of Yerevantsi's' successor, Ghukas Karnetsi (Luke of Karin/Erzerum) (1780–1799) that the appearance of the cathedral was given its final form. A new central cupola and a three-tier belfry at the front entrance of the church, both lavishly carved in contrast to the plain walls of the older base structure, had been added in 1653–1658. Three belfries were added on the apses in the early 18th century giving the cathedral its uncommon roof with its ensemble of conical domes steeply thrusting skyward. As for the interior walls, they were filled with murals, and the great central dome decorated with persianate Armenian floral patterns, all created by the artist Naghash Hovnatan (1661–1722) in 1720, and restored with elaboration by his grandson, Hovnatan Hovnatanian (c.1730–1801) in 1782–1786.

Simeon Yerevantsi's reforms prepared Edjmiadsin for the great responsibilities that would soon be thrust upon it with the annexation of Eastern Armenia by Russia in 1828. For the first time since the Mongol invasion of 1220, Edjmiadsin was located in a country ruled by a Christian monarch. This new political reality immensely improved the welfare of the Armenian Church as its clergy and flock were permitted to practice their faith undisturbed. The role of the Armenian Church in Russia was regulated in 1836 with the adoption of the Polozhenie (Statute) codifying its governance and formally recognizing the pontificate of the Holy See. Edjmiadsin's stature in the eyes of the Armenian people was also elevated by the fact that the three other primates of the Armenian Church, the Catholicos of the Great House of Cilicia in Sis, the Patriarch of Istanbul, and the Patriarch of Jerusalem, all remained subjects of the Muslim Ottoman Empire. Despite its conservative purpose, and even reactionary priests, Edjmiadsin inevitably became a place of Armenian national life. During the tenure of Gevorg IV Kerestechian (1866–1882), the monthly *Ararat* was inaugurated, which served both as the official publication of the catholicosate and a journal of learning. In 1874 the Gevorgian Academy was opened, which very quickly gained renown as an educational institution. Edjmiadsin became the rallying point of the Armenian emancipation movement of the late 19th and early 20th centuries when Tsar Nicholas II (1894–1917) ordered in 1903 the confiscation of the Armenian Church's properties on the charge that it was promoting nationalism and separatism. Catholicos **Mkrtich Khrimian** (1892–1907), who had been a fervent advocate of self-reliance, in one last gesture in his old age, galvanized the Armenian people by defying Russian autocracy. The insurrection was quelled only after the edict was rescinded in 1905.

Edjmiadsin was caught in the whirlwind of the troubled decades of the early 20th century. The monastic compound was turned into a refugee camp for Armenians fleeing atrocities in the Ottoman Empire during World War I. The repression of religion under Soviet rule left virtually nothing of the larger institution as churches were closed everywhere in Armenia. Lastly, the murder of Catholicos Khoren Muratbekian (1932–1938) by the KGB and Stalin's refusal to allow the election of a new catholicos meant that the patriarchal throne of Armenia for the first time since its founding would remain vacant and Edjmiadsin no longer exercised a role in the religious life of the Armenian people. The ban was lifted in 1945, and with the election of Vazgen Palchian (1955–1994) as catholicos, Edjmiadsin was given a new lease. During his long tenure Catholicos Vazgen patiently reassembled the privileges of the Armenian Church, oversaw the renovation and expansion of the facilities at the monastery, and gradually restored the stature of his office by traveling to the diaspora. By weathering the bitter and divisive community conflicts of the Cold War era, he lived to see Edjmiadsin once again heralded as the universal spiritual home of the Armenian people upon Armenia's declaration of independence. *See also* AGHTAMAR; ARGHUTIANTS, HOVSEP; NERSES V ASHTARAKETSI; GAREGIN I HOVSEPI-ANTS; GAREGIN I SARKISSIAN; HETUMIAN; KOMITAS; MESROP MASHTOTS; GRIGOR NAREKATSI; PATKANIAN; SRVANTZTIANTS, GAREGIN.

EDUCATION. Mesrop Mashtots opened the first school in Armenia. It consisted of his pupils whom he trained in the use of his newly minted alphabet and in the art of translation. Learning in Armenia began with translation, first of the Bible and immediately thereafter of the fathers of the Christian Church. Education in the Middle Ages remained grounded in biblical and theological studies augmented by the examination of a growing corpus of works translated from Greek, primarily the scholarship of Late Antiquity associated with the city of Alexandria, Egypt, the greatest center of learning at the time. For higher education, aspirants invariably traveled abroad to the main centers of Christian learning, to Edessa, Antioch, Jerusalem, and Alexandria, before the Islamic conquests, and to Constantinople thereafter. They returned with copies of the classics, new theological works, and scientific treatises collected from the libraries of the Hellenistic world. In Armenia, schools were located in monasteries and religious training remained the primary objective of education. Not all who studied in the monastic schools were necessarily clerics and literacy in the Middle Ages was not confined to churchmen alone. The aristocracy produced a number of writers who authored historical and legal treatises and literary tracts lauding the achievements of one great feudal dynasty or another.

While new and important monasteries were founded in the **Bagratuni** era, one aristocrat stands out as the intellectual giant of his age and as the emblem of the standard of secular learning achieved in **Ani**. Grigor Magistros Pahlavuni, besides lifelong service in the Armenian and Byzantine governments, revitalized education by training a new school of translators. He himself specialized in interpreting Plato into Armenian. His son who became the catholicos Grigor *Vkayaser*, Gregory the Martyrophile, continued this tradition and passed it down through the Pahlavuni family, which came to possess the patriarchal throne at Hromkla, all the way to Nerses Shnorhali (Nerses the Gracious), the preeminent ecumenist of the **Armenian Apostolic Church** and a man of great learning himself. The acquisition of any sort of an advanced education remained a function of the eminence of a monastic savant around whom gathered a group of acolytes, and the renown of the schools at Varag and Narek in southern Armenia, of Haghpat, Sanahin, Klatzor, and Datev in Eastern Armenia, and many others elsewhere in Armenia and Cilicia, had more to do with the residence of a learned scholar than its institutional attributes. On the other hand, from the 5th to the 18th century, the monastic scriptoria trained the copyists and miniaturists who produced the thousands of manuscripts that survive to this day. Judging from the fact that more than 40,000 Armenian manuscripts are still in existence, the rate of production and the education of the scribes who prepared them must have been a significant and ongoing enterprise, for the historical record is also amply clear of the extensive destruction suffered by monasteries, libraries, and churches at the hands of foreign invaders, and such vast scale destruction of ancient Armenian books continued right down to the 20th century.

Manuscript copying and illuminating disappeared with the introduction of the printing press. It was precisely for purposes of education and edification that early efforts at printing were made by venturesome clerics. With the decline of Armenian learning during the period of Armenia's occupation by various Turkic groups, the shortage of books necessary for the proper conduct of priestly duties and services prompted church leaders to explore the mass production of Armenian books. The potential of publishing to generate movement for a modern education, however, was anticipated by the Armenian **Catholic** and **Protestant** communities. The **Mekhitarians** played a pivotal role in this process, for their two monastic compounds in Venice and Vienna became important educational centers in their own right for training generations of learned scholars and teachers of every stripe. Many among the eminent Mekhitarians, such as **Mikayel Chamchian**, Arsen Bagratuni, **Ghevond Alishan**, Arsen Aytenian, Hovsep Gaterjian, started as teachers before producing their great works. The religious and cultural challenge posed by Catholicism in turn prompted the Armenian Apostolic community's educational efforts to gather momentum. A second challenge in the form of a better financed educational program by western European and especially American missionaries also confronted the Apostolic community with the need to expand its educational activities. By the early 20th century, all Armenian communities large and small everywhere supported schools and the emphasis for a good modern education had resulted in the establishment and growth of high schools and academies that trained the talented youth.

Beginning in the middle of the 18th century the Mekhitarians built schools in Hungary, Italy, France, Turkey, the Caucasus, and Crimea. Though the Murat-Raphaelian school, opened in Venice in 1836, and the Samuel-Muratian school, opened in Paris in 1846, became the two most famous of their institutions, every school represented a critical junction for the infusion of Western knowledge and values into Armenian culture. The Catholic church itself and the European missionary orders, Jesuits and Franciscans, mostly manned by French clerics, added more schools to the network of Catholic educational institutions.

From the middle of the 19th century Protestant missions, founded by American evangelicals, quickly built up an additional network of educational outposts, most of them among Armenians in the Ottoman

Empire. By 1914 their 46 high schools and 369 elementary schools enrolled 4,090 and 19,361 students respectively. More importantly, from 1863 the Protestant colleges introduced a whole new level of learning. Robert College in Istanbul, Euphrates College in Kharpert/Harput, American College in Van, Central Turkey College in Aintab, St. Paul College in Tarsus, and Anatolia College in Marsovan/Merzifon imported Western education to the doorstep of the Armenian communities of the Middle East. Within a generation many among the faculty were Armenian and a new social stratum of a professoriate appeared enjoying the respect of succeeding generations of Armenian pupils to whom they imparted a revived sense of national consciousness through dedication to enlightenment. The Mekhitarians operated along the periphery of the Armenian world and in the preexisting centers of the Armenian Catholic diaspora. The Protestant mission-based schools pursued a vigorous campaign of evangelization that formed out of the previously disenfranchised a new and privileged community distinguished by a higher level of learning and literacy than the general Armenian population, not to mention the gradual expansion of familiarity with the English language as an added characteristic of their instruction.

These Catholic and Protestant schools propelled their gifted students to university education in western Europe and the United States. Many returned with the skills to shape a modern economy and society as doctors, engineers, lawyers, and business managers. Nevertheless, the fact of the matter remains that the Armenian Apostolic community constructed with its own resources a network of schools much larger than either the Catholic or Protestant. Soon after permission was extended in 1789 to the **Armenian *Millet*** to open schools, Istanbul became the hub of Armenian education in the Ottoman Empire where the wealthy began sponsoring private academies for the edification of their own children. With the support of benefactors and benevolent associations these expanded to allow for the education of talented youth from underprivileged families. The Ketronakan, or Central, college and the Berberian college were perhaps the better known of these advanced schools among eventually the more than three dozen that were opened in the capital city and its environs. These schools enrolled students both locally and from the provinces allowing for the regeneration of Armenian national life in the remotest corners of the vast empire. By 1915 all Armenian communities, large and small, boasted a school, and a system for advancement to higher levels of education was in place to assure that the most promising were given opportunity to progress through the ranks. The rapid process of modernization and Westernization among Armenians and the formation of a vital national culture are all explained by the tremendous voluntary investment made in education by the Armenian people. In a century when states already were key sponsors of education and governments allocated funds for the establishment of schools and colleges, the Armenian community worldwide through its own resources launched its youth to embrace the concepts of progress, science, and reason that rested at the foundation of the modern perception of nationhood.

The decimation of most of these institutions in the Ottoman Empire during World War I meant that ultimately the educational system created by the Armenians in the Russian Empire would exercise the longer-term influence upon the intellectual destiny of the Armenian people. Here too the process of building schools started from the center and spread to the provinces. In 1815 the leading Armenian family in Russia founded in Moscow what became one of the most important Armenian cultural institutions of the 19th century. With its publishing, research, and teaching operations, the influence of the Lazarian academy was widespread and it became the conduit for the training of educators who returned to the Caucasus to impart Russian and Western culture to the entire region. When in 1824 the Nersisian academy opened in Tbilisi, the most populous Armenian urban center in that part of the world acquired the status of a center of learning also. From there, Alexandropol/**Gyumri**, Kars, Shushi, and all the other towns, even yonder into northern Iran, such as Tabriz, received their teachers and new generations of educated youths. When the Gevorgian academy opened in 1874 in **Edjmiadsin**, the historic heartland of Armenia acquired a school that trained many distinguished clerics and laymen who gained the sense of generational familiarity and solidarity that transformed the destiny of Eastern Armenia. These schools were also the workplace of many a prominent figure of the Eastern Armenian cultural revival. **Khachatur Abovian**, Gabriel **Patkanian**, his sons Kerovbe and Serovbe, and grandson, Raphael, **Hrachia Ajarian**, and many others were at one time or another employed as teachers. The leaders of the Armenian political movements in Russia were all products of the parochial schools.

Education in the native tongue so vigorously encouraged by the 19th century men of letters had nurtured an articulate national elite capable of exercising leadership and of forming associations that stood apart from the church, the sole surviving traditional institution of the Armenians.

The Bolshevik Revolution arrested the cause of national education. The importance of ideological indoctrination in the Soviet period meant tight state control over education in the Armenian Soviet Socialist Republic (ASSR). This level of conformity also required the exclusion of whole strata of educators who once manned the Armenian schools and whose views supported liberal thought and national feeling. The early years of Sovietization across the former Russian Empire resulted in the degradation of the Armenian community's standards of schooling and education. In fact, the assignation of nationality to each of the new Soviet republics automatically undermined the communitarian basis of the Armenian school network, removed it from Armenian institutional oversight, and inaugurated the process of their closure across the Soviet Union.

The construction of the socialist utopia, however, required the mandatory education of children. Elementary schooling in the ASSR became compulsory in 1923 and was provided for free. Even so, shortages of teachers and school buildings meant that not all school-age children in Soviet Armenia could receive the services offered by the state. Education remained mostly an urban function in the 1920s though the number of pupils attending school grew from 65,000 to 83,000 during the course of the decade. Despite this slow and uneven beginning, and the years of violent repression in the 1930s and World War II, steady progress was made in spreading education countrywide. High school education became mandatory in the ASSR only in 1959, but in the following decades Soviet Armenia achieved the goal of universal schooling and 100 percent literacy. In 1960, 1,219 schools were open in Armenia educating 319,000 pupils. By 1985, the number of schools had grown to 1,479 where 573,000 pupils received instruction from 46,000 teachers.

Preparing new cadres for the **Communist Party of Armenia** (CPA) and managers of the Soviet command economy also required the introduction of institutions of higher learning. **Yerevan** State University formally opened its doors on January 23, 1921, a mere two months after the Red Army takeover of Armenia. With the noted historian Hakob Manandian as its first rector, the faculty initially consisted of two departments: philology and social sciences. By the 1980s the institution was a full-fledged university and had served as the incubator for faculties in the sciences, which in the course of the expansion of the educational system were spun off to form separate universities and institutes. In 1930 the Polytechnic Institute was created. In 1934 a pedagogical institute was started in Leninakan/ **Gyumri**. A conservatory of music, agricultural schools, and an economics institute opened in 1975 complemented these. In 1986, 59,778 students were enrolled in the 13 institutions of higher learning in the ASSR. That same year, 11,465 graduated with degrees in 156 specializations. The explosion in advanced education in the final two decades of the Soviet era was evidenced by the fact that of the 246,564 university students graduated between 1929 and 1986, 155,670 had earned their degrees in the 15 years preceding 1986.

This highly educated elite stood at the forefront of the democratic movement that undermined Soviet authority in Armenia in the late 1980s. In the new political leadership that emerged, philologists, physicists, and mathematicians spearheaded the nationalist agenda. While their skill and learning resulted in coherent policies and effective strategic planning in the early years of independence after 1991, there was little they could do to prevent the rapid decline of Armenia's vaunted educational system in the face of economic collapse. As state employees, teachers suffered a precipitous fall in living standards. Inflation wiped away their income and the government budget for education was reduced to a bare minimum as state coffers went empty. At the height of the energy crisis during the winters of 1992 through 1994, schools were closed and education came to a standstill. Modest increases in funding starting in 1995 began reversing the process. By that time the system was hamstrung with shortages of teachers, inadequate teaching materials, and deteriorated facilities that went for years without upkeep.

Starting in the 1960s Soviet Armenia opened its institutions of higher learning to the Armenian diaspora and the students from less developed countries pursued degrees or training in a host of professions ranging from medicine to music. Most came from the new network of parochial schools constructed across the Armenian diaspora in the years following World War I. The deported and displaced Armenians, who resettled in the Middle East, in eastern Europe, Egypt,

Iran, and many other places, slowly built new schools in their communities. In Lebanon where the largest number of Armenians concentrated prior to the 1975 civil war, 68 schools were founded. No sooner had the refugees reached the country than they began to establish schools. Between 1922 and 1926, the Armenian Apostolic community started 15 schools, the Catholic eight schools, and the Protestant six schools. In Syria more than a hundred schools were opened. In 1935 the Armenians in Egypt supported some 20 schools. In the 1960s community leaders and activists in North and South America concerned over the rate of assimilation began a movement to open private Armenian schools. Dozens of elementary and a few high schools were established in major cities. By the end of the 20th century nearly 230 schools were being voluntarily maintained by the Armenian diaspora worldwide attesting to a people's commitment to education and the preservation of its identity under adverse conditions and in the face of the challenge presented by public education and mass culture.

The interest in education manifested itself also in the demonstrated achievement of Armenians in the field of teaching at institutions of higher learning. The universities of Armenia supported a sizable professoriate in the full range of learning in the sciences and humanities. With the sole exception of **Nicholas Adontz**, nearly all the great scholars of the early 20th century, the historian Hakob Manandian, the linguist **Hrachia Ajarian**, the historian of literature Manuk Abeghian, the historian of architecture Toros Toramanian, and many others, joined the educational establishment of Soviet Armenia despite the hardships and repression. The sciences received their greatest encouragement with the rise of the astrophysicist **Viktor Hambartsumian**. Armenian scholars and scientists also distinguished themselves in institutions of higher learning all around the world in fields ranging from economics to engineering, medicine and sociology. By the late Soviet period, **Abel Aganbegyan** was the leading economist in Russia. Earlier in the century the American physician **Varazdat Kazanjian** had pioneered plastic surgery. The most spectacular career in higher education in the United States was achieved by Vartan Grigorian, who in 1989 rose to the presidency of Brown University, one of the so-called Ivy League schools, the premier universities in America. He went there as the former president of the New York Public Library, the largest such institution in the United

States, and left Brown University to assume in 1997 the presidency of the Carnegie Corporation of New York, one of the leading charitable foundations in the country supporting learning and research.

ELECTIONS. The people of Armenia went to the polls eight times in the 20th century to vote in free elections. The first time was in June 1919 when they cast ballots for the popularly elected parliament of the independent Republic of Armenia and gave the majority of seats to the **Armenian Revolutionary Federation** (ARF). They had to wait until 1990 to exercise again the right to chose their own representatives. With non-Communist candidates allowed to run in open elections, for the first time the people of Soviet Armenia voted in a series of elections running up to August 1990. These elections positioned the **Armenian National Movement** (ANM) at the forefront of the political process in Armenia. On September 21, 1991, the people of Armenia went to the polls again, this time to vote in a referendum on the future of their country and overwhelmingly cast their ballots for independence from the Soviet Union. Less than a month later, on October 16, 1991, **Levon Ter-Petrossian** became the first popularly elected **president** of Armenia. Voters went to the polls again on July 5,1995, to elect a new parliament, renamed the National Assembly, and returned the ANM as the largest faction of the first post-Soviet legislature. That same day they also voted on a referendum for the adoption of a new constitution. The first presidential elections in post-Soviet Armenia were scheduled for September 22, 1996, with the leading candidates being the incumbent and **Vazgen Manukian**. In highly disputed balloting and widespread charges of vote tampering, Levon Ter-Petrossian was declared the winning candidate. His resignation in February 1998 resulted in the early scheduling of the next presidential elections on March 16, 1998, with Prime Minister **Robert Kocharian** and former **Communist Party of Armenia** (CPA) chairman **Karen Demirchian** (running as an independent) as the two popular candidates. In the runoff elections of March 30, 1998, Robert Kocharian was elected president of Armenia. By the May 30, 1999, parliamentary election, a new legislature was installed in accordance with the provisions of the 1995 **Constitution**. With the Unity Alliance as the largest bloc of deputies, the leadership of the government was divided between the constituent parties making up the coalition. Defense Minister **Vazgen Sargsian**, who headed the list of the **Republican Party of Armenia** (RPA), was nominated prime minister. Karen Demirchian, as head of the **Populist Party of Armenia** (PPA), was nominated chairman of the National Assembly. *See also* POLITICAL PARTIES.

– F –

FOREIGN POLICY. To secure sovereignty, Armenia's foreign policy was historically governed by the question of the country's alignment with one or another neighboring major power. The invariables of its geographic location and its modest size, contained in the larger regional framework of the south Caucasus, obligated Armenia to weigh the necessity of political orientation. The hostility of neighboring states and the cultural gulf separating them from Armenia further conditioned the necessities of a foreign policy demonstrating the requirement of an unequal relationship with a larger security provider. Whenever such a relationship, however strained, was negotiated, Armenia preserved its sovereignty and integrity. When such a relationship was unavailable, Armenia was overwhelmed by the greater might of an occupying force. When two such powers competed for dominion over Armenia, it was commonly divided. Features of this historic pattern persisted into the 20th century and the conduct of the foreign policy of the modern-day Armenian states reveals many features that can be explained by this prevailing reality.

Founded in the final year of World War I, the first Republic of Armenia sought status as a belligerent to receive entry into the halls of the Allied Powers as they convened in 1918 to draw up treaties of peace and redraw the boundaries of the defeated states. Despite a legitimate claim to such status by virtue of the armed resistance waged by the Armenian republic against the advancing forces of the Ottoman Empire conquering through the former domains of the Russian Empire in the Caucasus, formal recognition of Armenia was delayed by the victors who concentrated first on resolving matters concerning Europe as finalized in the 1919 Treaty of Versailles. In the immediate postwar environment, the Armenian policy of seeking Allied endorsement and intervention did not differ from the strategy pursued by many other smaller states that sent representatives to France where the Allied negotiators were meeting. The remoteness of Armenia and its then lack of strategic value failed to attract the attention of France or Britain to assume either a mandate or a protectorate over Armenia. When they referred the matter to the United States, the American Congress declined interest and entanglement.

By the time the Allies turned their attention to negotiating the Treaty of Sèvres in 1920 to settle affairs in the Middle East and carved up the Ottoman Empire, the delays and the contradictory policies of France and Britain vis-à-vis Turkey had undermined Armenia's security. Unwilling to commit troops or resources to buttress the secessionist states of the old Russian Empire, even as they opposed Bolshevism, the Allies abandoned Armenia to its own resources. The rise of the Turkish Nationalist movement under Mustafa Kemal and the Red Army victory in the Russian Civil War wholly altered the geopolitical context in which Armenia existed. The success of these two new political forces marked a reversal of the postwar condition in which both countries lay prostrate. Moreover, the newfound alliance of Nationalist Turkey and Communist Russia in opposition to Allied intervention and Western colonialism constricted the space occupied by Armenia. Sandwiched in its own neighborhood by the two resurgent regional powers, Armenia's gamble to secure Allied protection as a pro-Western state yielded no tangible results. To the contrary, it thrust Armenia into a situation where its military capability was no match to the double-pronged advance into its territories by Turkey and Russia. The net result was the collapse of the First Republic at the end of 1920 and the resignation of Armenia from claims of sovereignty.

Armenia as a constituent republic of the USSR conducted no independent foreign policy. That function was centralized in Moscow under whose instructions **Yerevan** waged an anti-nationalist campaign in the Armenian overseas communities. The persistence of Armenian political organization in the **diaspora** that challenged the legitimacy of the Soviet state therefore kept Yerevan involved in matters pertaining to the foreign relations of the Soviet Union. Though it lacked the character of state-to-state relations, it seemingly made inter-Armenian issues a question of international attention. In a century that witnessed the spread of nationalism and the call for independence, Soviet policies vis-à-vis the diaspora divided the ideological loyalties of Armenians. It also placed many communities in some jeopardy as host countries viewed with suspicion the pro-Soviet tendency among a sector of the diaspora. This tendency was cultivated by Yerevan and

Moscow and served a number of purposes in the Cold War context, the most critical of which was the encouragement of anti-Turkish attitudes. In light of the historical experience of the Armenians under the Turks in the late Ottoman period, Russian policy made much of the contrast with the physical survival of the Armenians in the Soviet state, while taking no practical steps to address the legacy of the **Armenian Genocide**. The combination of sentimental patriotism, diaspora nostalgia, proletarian views among impoverished refugees, the constant trope of the successes of the Soviet system, created at worst mixed attitudes and at best genuine belief and support for Communism. Yerevan as a result proved instrumental in keeping a diaspora people potentially at serious odds with the Soviet regime from presenting a unified front and in consolidating its interest in alignment with the West when the two systems waged a struggle for greater dominion.

The foreign relations propaganda from Yerevan displayed at least two broad objectives: to denigrate Armenian nationalism, especially as embodied in the **Armenian Revolutionary Federation** (ARF) and its anti-Bolshevik rhetoric; and to encourage a favorable view of the Soviet state by casting Armenia as the model workers' state. It has been argued that the rapid modernization of Armenia, particularly in the post-Stalin era, was motivated in part by the desire to demonstrate the productive capacities of Communism and the progress registered by the Soviet system to overseas Armenian audiences who represented a constituency predisposed to relating a positive image about their homeland. This relationship was choreographed through an institution unique to Armenia, the so-called "kapi komite" or "spiurk komite" more properly the Committee for Relations with Diaspora Communities, hence the shortened "relations committee" or "diaspora committee." The committee successfully developed contact with at least one sector of the Armenian diaspora, mainly with the **Democratic Liberal Party** (DLP), the moderate nationalists who acknowledged the status of Soviet Armenia as a legitimate state. Despite its only partial success, this tightly controlled mechanism still allowed for mutual exposure primarily through the arts as a safe and noncontroversial zone of the Armenia-diaspora relationship.

These elaborate instruments for programmed communication disintegrated in the wake of the 1988 **Spitak Earthquake**. Both for emergency reasons and for purposes of scoring political dividends internationally, USSR Communist Party chairman Mikhail Gorbachev opened Armenia for the immediate delivery of critical assistance. Overnight an immense human tragedy placed Armenia on the map of international relations as countries from around the world organized a major airlift to deliver vital aid to victims and survivors. The earthquake occurred in the year when the **Karabagh Movement** gripped the population of Armenia. The opening of the country at a time of greater political freedom in the Soviet Union meant the relocation of Armenia under a new light. Circumstances provided that Armenia's relations with other countries would begin to circumvent the total control of the center. While the international system continued to function on the basis of formal state relations with Moscow, Armenia was placed on a path toward developing a separate international identity, and even expounding a foreign policy in terms of the support expected for its democratic movement. The popular campaign for the unification of Karabagh with Armenia, which had drawn international attention, had already shaken the Soviet state and sent the loud signal that the mighty empire was fraying at the edges. The interest in the outcome of the campaign inevitably focused policy attention as Western countries were placed in a position of extending avowed moral endorsement without seeming to trespass the sovereignty of the Soviet state. That difficult and delicate balance unraveled in 1991 as events outpaced policy. The USSR peaceably dissolved and its constituent republics proclaimed their independence.

The foreign policy of the Third Republic reflected the basic ideological redirection that the **Armenian National Movement** (ANM) sought to introduce. Its primary goals were international recognition of Armenia's sovereignty and the securing of its independence. Neither was guaranteed even though the USSR was dissolved. That was the case because history and geography dictated that Armenia's survival depended more upon its external relations than its internal strength. While many of the post-Soviet states, including some of the former East European satellites, had difficulty at this initial stage in conceptualizing an independent foreign policy, Armenia very early articulated clear goals and pursued them vigorously. Early Western hesitation about the security architecture that would replace the Soviet umbrella compelled Armenia to seek a close military and defense alliance with Russia. The leadership of the two countries encouraged the rapid maturation of this relationship. As prominent figures of the democratic front in the Soviet Union, Boris Yeltsin and **Levon Ter-Petrossian**, the presidents of Russia and Armenia respectively, were long-time allies and reached a series of strategic accommodations ranging from security guarantees to energy supplies. Much of this was done within the framework of the Commonwealth of Independent States (CIS), which Armenia joined as a founding member in December 1991. This alignment, however, did not hamper Armenia's other foreign policy objective of establishing multilateral relations with the West. Central to that objective were close ties with the United States of America. Armenia's strong credentials as a democratic country on the path of liberal economic reforms won major support in the U.S. and facilitated the extension of critical financial aid to Armenia. This pro-Western tendency was also manifest in ties cultivated with Europe, particularly France. In proportion to its size and population, Armenia was rewarded with wide-ranging humanitarian aid and development funding that sustained it through the hardships of its transition from the command economy to the free market. By the end of the decade of the 1990s, Armenia had received nearly one billion dollars in U.S. foreign assistance and had been extended loans amounting to $800 million from the World Bank, the International Monetary Fund (IMF), and the European Bank for Reconstruction and Development (EBRD).

Armenia's early foreign policy successes were in large part due to President Ter-Petrossian's role as master strategist. Among his more daring policies was the proposal to normalize relations with Turkey. By the narrow definition of state-to-state relations, Armenia and Turkey had no history to speak of as these were cut off since 1921 with the advent of Sovietization. Historical memory and the polemic of accusation, however, had kept the two countries within each other's sights. The consequence of the 1915 genocide dominated popular attitudes toward Turkey and overcoming this impediment proved a greater hurdle than expected. Ter-Petrossian hoped to start with a clean slate and persuade Turkey that a new opportunity for a different relationship existed. This imaginative policy that the Third Republic offered a fresh start and did not carry the ideological baggage of previous decades had many considerations at its source. Repulsive as the thought was to many Armenians, Ter-Petrossian was prepared to gamble his personal reputation on this policy. It formed part of the delicate balance he sought to create between the continuing and looming influence of Russia and the country nominally representing the West in the Caucasus by virtue of the fact it constituted part of NATO. Turkey's failure to reciprocate and ready support of Azerbaijan by imposing its own blockade of Armenia starting in 1992 only hardened views across the historic divide. An equally complicated relationship was cultivated with neighboring Iran, which under the circumstances of Armenia's blockade by Azerbaijan and Turkey, remained the sole reliable outlet for the country when Georgia virtually disintegrated in 1992.

None of these relations flourished and instead of normalization, highly skewed imbalances systematically reduced Armenia's options and increased its isolation. At the heart of the matter rested the **Nagorno Karabagh** conflict. Rather than diplomacy and foreign policy, a low-intensity conflict that escalated into full-fledged warfare between Armenians and Azeris defined the basic assumptions in the reactions Armenia elicited from its neighbors and putative friends. Apart from the armed conflict, the situation surrounding Karabagh engendered suspicion among surrounding countries, ignited intense competition for alignment, and fed constant speculation about means and ends. The proliferation of such variables straddled Armenia with the tremendous responsibility of aiding the Armenians of Nagorno Karabagh while shouldering the burdening of defending their case in the court of international opinion. That opinion divided between those who argued for the legitimate right of peoples to self-determination and the legal right of states to territorial integrity. Although international norms and institutions favored the latter, the confused state of the Soviet legacy along the periphery of the former empire and the remoteness of Nagorno Karabagh kept the region beyond the pale of conceivable intervention, effectively leaving matters to be resolved on the field of battle.

The settlement of the Nagorno Karabagh question, therefore, dominated the foreign policy objectives of Armenia irrespective of the fact that Armenia assiduously cultivated a program to distinguish between the two Armenian states that appeared on the map with the dissolution of the Soviet Union. The conduct of relations by other states, however, did not necessarily make these fine distinctions. In 1992, in an effort to be constructive partners in the evolution of the post-Soviet states, the Conference on Security and Cooperation in Europe (CSCE) ventured a foray into conflict resolution. This so-called Minsk Group of CSCE members was directed to create conditions for the meeting in the city of Minsk of the parties to the conflict under the guidance of third parties with an interest in the permanent settlement of the Karabagh question. Membership in the Minsk Group evolved over the years and the assemblage never met in Belarus. Even so, it created a mechanism for conducting shuttle diplomacy until such time as the parties began to take tentative steps toward bilateral negotiations.

The fundamental change on the ground dictated by a series of military campaigns that brought the warring parties to the realization that further hostility threatened the viabilities of their respective states marked the turning point. With Armenia's support, Nagorno Karabagh had prevailed in securing itself a defensive zone by capturing the Azeri districts ringing the self-proclaimed republic. In so doing it had defied and reversed expectations of the ultimate outcome of the conflict given the presumed mismatch of resources and manpower between Armenians and Azeris. With the Russian-sponsored 1994 cease-fire in place, diplomacy took center stage and taxed the resources of Armenia's foreign policy specialists to a degree as strenuous as the struggle had been for a military balance in the immediate region.

The enormity of that diplomatic challenge was traceable through two sets of separate developments that redefined the premises of Armenia's foreign policy yet again. The first concerned the normative standards that the international community introduced over the years. The second concerned the deft manipulation of the importance of hydrocarbon resources for the West by Azerbaijan. If anything, Azerbaijan methodically attempted to turn the tide by seeming to wage peace by marketing its natural wealth in a manner designed to maximize the derivation of political dividends intended to neutralize, if not reverse, conditions on the ground.

The international community's changing positions on the resolution of the Nagorno Karabagh question took its clearest expressions at the CSCE, renamed Organization for Security and Cooperation in Europe (OSCE), heads of states meetings. In its 1994 Budapest meeting declaration the OSCE welcomed the cease-fire and recommended combining the two-track negotiating process into a joint settlement forum. In doing so the OSCE recognized Russia's prevalent and necessary role. The chairmanship of the Minsk Group continued to rotate, but a core and decisive group emerged within the assemblage that increasingly sought to balance Russian, American, and European interests while submitting increasingly more elaborated proposals for a settlement. The lack of progress and reversals in Armenia's democratization process came at a heavy cost when the 1996 Lisbon OSCE meeting concluded with an endorsement of the principle of territorial integrity, which Armenia was obliged to veto with its single vote. Despite the lack of consensus therein registered, the endorsement was let stand through a separate document issued in the name of the OSCE chairman instead of the entire organization.

For Armenia and Karabagh, the announcement was tantamount to a predetermination of the political status of the Nagorno Karabagh Republic (NKR), the core issue as far as Armenians were concerned. Rather than provide impetus, the Lisbon announcement retrenched Armenian foreign policy as Azerbaijan continued its oil diplomacy. The announcement also in part undermined Ter-Petrossian's administration as the one area in which the president had excelled and yielded a stinging defeat. In its wake Ter-Petrossian began to consider between the two packages for a settlement that had been floated by the Minsk Group: one calling for a step-by-step disengagement, and the other calling for a comprehensive settlement. The step-by-step method favored at the time by Western states recommended a staggered process for addressing all the issues and was intended to provide Azerbaijan inducement to negotiate a political settlement on the central questions as Karabagh gradually returned the occupied districts to Azerbaijan. Ter-Petrossian's public endorsement of the step-by-step method in 1997 unraveled his government, and by the following year he and his party, the ANM, were out of power.

President **Robert Kocharian** promoted the alternative approach and announced the primacy of security considerations and the final status of Karabagh in reaching a settlement. A native of Karabagh and one-time president of NKR, he calculated that the step-by-step process presented too many risks with an unreliable opponent and amounted to negotiating away the hard-won advances on the ground that had wrought visible security to the Armenians of Nagorno Karabagh. Expectations that a hard-liner would fail to secure a settlement proved misplaced when Kocharian cautiously entered into direct dialogue with the president of Azerbaijan, Heidar Aliyev. Their meetings created an environment that received its own endorsement at the 1999 Istanbul meeting of the OSCE that commended the bilateral approach in the hope of energizing the Minsk Group process.

In the interval between Lisbon and Istanbul, Azerbaijan had also significantly improved its negotiating position as the country embarked immediately after the 1994 cease-fire upon a strategy to market its oil resources in a manner that secured as many contracts with as many oil-purchasing states as possible. In short order Azerbaijan signed agreements with oil companies based in the United States, Great Britain, Turkey, Russia, and even Iran. Major oil companies were involved in varying degrees, among them Amoco, Exxon, Pennzoil, British Petroleum (BP), and Lukoil of Russia. While the oil fields were one by one auctioned off each to a separate combine, the question of the exportation of the oil also depended on the final resolution of the Karabagh question since the only answer was the laying down of an export pipeline through the unsettled region, an investment estimated in the range of $3 billion, a venture too costly to leave to the mercies of an unresolved dispute. The commercial alignment of Western states with Azerbaijan did not necessarily translate into the stacking of new and impossible odds for Armenia and Karabagh, but it raised the stakes and deadlocked the negotiations. In Armenia it garnered prudence and increased caution as the resolution of the status of NKR was no longer conceived to be divisible from the question of the return of the occupied territories. In Azerbaijan it encouraged intransigence as the government expected to be rewarded for its wholly pro-Western commercial orientation and independence from Russian influence.

Armenia enrolled early in a host of international organizations and multilateral associations, including CIS, OSCE, and the United Nations with its affiliates, UN Education, Scientific and Cultural Organization (UNESCO), and UN Industrial Development Organization (UNIDO). To hasten the process of economic change and obtain support for structural reforms, Armenia also joined EBRD, IMF, World Trade Organization (WTO), and Black Sea Economic Cooperation (BSEC). The latter was a new entity made up of incongruous parts that embraced all the littoral states of the Black Sea and included the Transcaucasian republics and Greece. Given the scarcity of financial resources within the group, BSEC had a slow start. However, the meetings of the new multilateral association provided a framework for Armenian and Turkish officials to come in contact over regional issues. Armenia also joined the International Atomic Energy Agency (IAEA). The compelling need to activate the dormant Metsamor nuclear power plant in Armenia and bring it in line with international safety standards invited the attention of the IAEA whose inspections provided assurances about the proper maintenance and operations of the critical facility.

Armenia also avidly sought to expand its bilateral contacts. By the end of 1999 Armenia had established diplomatic relations with over 50 countries around the world. In over 40 Armenia had permanent representation through embassies or consulates. In many of these countries diaspora communities provided facilities for housing Armenia's diplomatic representation. Fifteen countries opened embassies in Armenia, including China, Egypt, France, Georgia, Germany, Great Britain, Greece, India, Iran, Lebanon, Romania, Russia, Syria, Ukraine, and the United States. Some of Armenia's diplomatic representatives in the early years of independence emanated from the Soviet foreign service. Their experience was an asset for Armenia, but their small number meant that Armenia's foreign service would have to expand with new recruits and a younger team of diplomats. This situation thrust responsibility for Armenia's foreign policy on the shoulders of the Armenian president and prime minister while a new foreign ministry was shaped and a professional team was assembled.

The 21st century began with Armenia still at an impasse on key foreign policy challenges. Azerbaijan remained in a virtual state of war over Nagorno Karabagh. The negotiations for a settlement of the Karabagh question and the future status of the mountainous republic dragged on and were almost derailed by the assassination of **Prime Minister Vazgen Sargsian** whose leadership had come to be regarded as critical for persuading domestic forces to accept a compromise settlement. The blockade of Armenia's transport outlets through Azerbaijan, which previously connected Armenia with Russia, remained in force. But for the road and rail-line connecting Armenia to Tbilisi, Georgia, and the bridge over the **Arax River** to Iran, the encirclement of Armenia with Turkey's borders closed in a gesture of support for Azerbaijan remained unaltered. The blockade continued seriously to impede Armenia's economic recovery. Despite these complications in the immediate region, Armenia's political relations with countries beyond the Caucasus steadily improved. In countries with well-organized diaspora communities those relations were facilitated and even mediated on occasion in favor of Armenia.

– G –

GAREGIN I HOVSEPIANTS (1867–1952). Catholicos. Born in the village of Maghavuz in Karabagh, Hovsepiants received his education at the Gevorgian seminary in **Edjmiadsin** and earned a doctorate in divinity from Leipzig University in 1896. Ordained a celibate priest in 1898, he became a teacher at Edjmiadsin and embarked upon a career of prolific scholarship. In 1918, he participated in the battle of Sardarapat. He was primate of the diocese of Crimea and Nor Nakhichevan in Soviet Russia from 1927 to 1933. He was sent to the United States in 1934 to repair the rift in the **Armenian Apostolic Church** resulting from the assassination of Archbishop Ghevond Turian in 1933. Unsuccessful in that effort, nevertheless he was elected primate of the diocese of North America in 1938. He held the post until 1943 when he was elected catholicos of the Great House of Cilicia, headquartered in Antelias, Lebanon. Anointed in 1945 as Garegin I/Karekin I, he ushered in a period of cooperation between the two rival catholicosates of Edjmiadsin and of Cilicia during a time of serious political divisions and ideological differences in the Armenian **diaspora** during the Cold War.

Throughout his life Garegin I remained an avid researcher and a friend of professional scholars like **Nicholas Adontz**. His publications covered the gamut of Armenian historical scholarship. He published works on Armenian prosopography, epigraphy, ethnography, medieval historiography, art history, and cultural history. He also inaugurated the publication of Armenian colophons as important sources of information on Armenian social and religious history in the late medieval period. He also published some of the earliest studies of Armenian miniature illumination, bringing to public attention one of the most unique forms of Armenian artistic production, as well as studies in medieval Armenian church architecture. *See also* OR-MANIAN, MAGHAKIA; GAREGIN I/KAREKIN II SARKISS-IAN; SRVANTZTIANTS, GAREGIN.

GAREGIN I/KAREKIN II SARKISSIAN (1932–1999). Catholicos. The only clergyman elected to both of the Armenian catholicosates, Garegin I, Supreme Patriarch and Catholicos of All Armenians in April 1995, was formerly Karekin II of the Great House of Cilicia. Born Neshan Sarkissian in the Armenian town of Kesab in Syria, he entered the Antelias seminary at a young age. He was consecrated a celibate priest in 1952 whereupon he took the name Karekin, in honor of **Garegin I Hovsepiants** the scholar-catholicos from Armenia who had presided in Antelias, Lebanon. He continued his education at Oxford University from 1957 to 1959, where he researched and published his work *The Council of Chalcedon and the Armenian Church*, a study on the historical origins of the separation of the **Armenian Apostolic Church** from the Ecumenical Church in Constantinople. After serving as director of the Antelias seminary and chancellor of the catholicosate, he was appointed prelate of the diocese of New Julfa at Isfahan, Iran, in 1971. In 1974 he was elected to the prelacy of North America, the branch of the Armenian Apostolic Church in America that recognized the authority of the Antelias-based catholicosate. In 1977 he was elected catholicos coadjutor during the term of the ailing Catholicos Khoren I. Upon the decease of the latter, in May 1983, he was anointed Catholicos of the Great House of Cilicia.

A proponent of ecumenism within the Christian Church, he was responsible for enlisting the Cilician catholicosate in the World Council of Churches. In response to the December 7, 1988, **Spitak Earthquake,** which devastated parts of Soviet Armenia, he lent moral support to his spiritual brother Vazgen I, Supreme Patriarch and Catholicos of All Armenians in **Edjmiadsin**. A supporter also of the Armenian independence movement, his intellectual stature and moral leadership made him the favored candidate to succeed Vazgen I, who died in 1994. In April 1995 in an election high in symbolic content, held for first time in over 600 years in an independent Armenia, with representation from all dioceses of the Armenian Church worldwide, the catholicos of Cilicia, the leader of the Armenian church in exile, was chosen to head the Holy See of Edjmiadsin in Armenia, in the hope of bringing closer together the various branches of the Armenian Church organization that had existed in separate countries for so many centuries. Thus, Karekin II, Catholicos of the Great House of Cilicia became Garegin I, Catholicos of All Armenians.

Under the trying circumstances of Armenia's post-Communist transition Garegin I's tenure proved too short. Church unity did not materialize due to the polarized relations between the government and the **Armenian Revolutionary Federation** (ARF), which exercised influence over the catholicosate in Antelias. The catholicos inadvertently even created theological friction among his own bishops when he unilaterally agreed to a document announcing the close fraternity of the Roman Catholic and Armenian Apostolic Churches. Despite these internal differences, Garegin I established effective working contact with the papacy, paving the way for John Paul II to make the first papal visit to Armenia in September 2001 to coincide with the Armenian Church's worldwide celebration of the 1,700th anniversary of the introduction of Christianity in Armenia. While he improved the educational and cultural functions of the church to train greater numbers of clergy for the growing church, much as he had done in Antelias, and also encouraged the renovation of church buildings in Armenia, Garegin I's main legacy became his plans for the solemn commemoration of the church's ancient lineage as a means of elevating the role of the church in Armenia and in building more bridges with other Christian churches. It remained to his successor, Garegin II Nersisian, former primate of the diocese of **Ararat** to oversee the programs designed to culminate in the year 2001.

GEOGRAPHY, HISTORICAL. *See* HISTORICAL GEOGRAPHY.

GEOGRAPHY, POLITICAL. *See* POLITICAL GEOGRAPHY.

GHUKASIAN, ARKADY (1957–). President of the **Nagorno Karabagh** Republic (NKR). Born in **Stepanakert**, Ghukasian attended **Yerevan** State University. Graduating from the department of philology in 1979, he spent his early career as a journalist in his hometown, starting as a correspondent and then as deputy editor-in-chief of the Russian-language section of the Karabagh daily newspaper. An activist from the very inception of the **Karabagh Movement** he was placed a number of times under house arrest by Soviet authorities. Detained by Soviet Azerbaijani authorities in 1990, he was sent to prison to Rostov-on-Don, in Russia, for a 30-day sentence. In 1992, at the height of the Azerbaijani military offensive against the Armenians, Ghukasian was appointed political affairs advisor to the chairman of the NKR State Defense Committee, **Robert Kocharian**. Charged with the responsibility of seeking a diplomatic solution to the conflict, Ghukasian emerged as the principal negotiator for the NKR government. In that capacity he participated in the rounds of discussions held in various European capitals sponsored by the Conference for Security and Cooperation in Europe (CSCE) (Organization for Security and Cooperation in Europe, or OSCE, since December 1994), a function he continued to carry out from July 1993 as the first foreign minister of NKR. At the same time he was a member the NKR parliament having been elected in June of the same year. In September 1997 Ghukasian won a majority of votes for a new president in the special elections scheduled upon NKR President Robert Kocharian's acceptance of his nomination as **prime minister** of Armenia. With the cessation of the military conflict, organizing the economic recovery of NKR and reaching a political settlement with Azerbaijan headed his agenda. Delegating responsibility for the economy to the prime ministry, Ghukasian concentrated on diplomatic efforts. He has traveled to Moscow, Paris, and Washington to elevate international attention for the need to reach a settlement.

Three prime ministers have served under Ghukasian, Leonard Petrosian (1994–1998), who had been appointed by Kocharian, Zhirair Poghosian (1998–1999), and Anushavan Danielian (1999–). Poghosian was replaced in what appeared to have been a power struggle between Ghukasian and elements in support of the powerful defense minister, Samvel Babayan. Oleg Yesayian, who was NKR prime minister in the early months of 1992 prior to the formation of the State Defense Committee, was elected chairman of the NKR parliament in 1994 and served during the Kocharian and Ghukasian administration. The Zhirair Poghosian cabinet was composed of the following ministers: Arno Tsaturian, Agriculture; Edvard Sharamanian, Construction; Armen Sargsian, Culture; Samvel Babayan, Defense; Beniamin Babayan, Economic Reform; Hamlet Asiryan, Education and Science; Vladimir Melkumian, Finance; Naira Melkumian, Foreign Affairs; Vladimir Sahakian, Health; Robert Shaferian, Interior; and agency heads: Serge Arushanian, Customs; Ruben Hairapetian, Justice; Davit Ohanian, National Security; Vahe Danielian, Statistics and State Registry; and Garegin Ghazarian, Government staff. The Anushavan Danielian cabinet appointments included: Arno Tsaturian, Agriculture; Vagharshak Palanjanian, Construction; Armen Sargsian, Culture; Seyran Ohanian, Defense; Beniamin Babayan, Economic Reform; Hamlet Grigorian, Education and Science; Spartak Tevosian, Finance; Naira Melkumian, Foreign Affairs; Zoya Lazarian, Health; Bako Sahakian, Interior; Lenston Ghulian, Social Security; and agency heads: Aram Gahramanian, Taxation; Ruben

Hairapetian, Justice; Davit Ohanian, National Security; Vahe Ghukasian, Prosecutor General; and Suren Grigorian, Government Staff.

On March 22, 2000, Ghukasian became the casualty of an assassination attempt in Stepanakert. While he escaped death, he suffered injuries to his legs requiring a period of hospitalization. Occurring mere months after the fatal shooting of Armenian **Prime Minister Vazgen Sargsian** (an incident during which former NKR Prime Minister Leonard Petrosian, then serving in the Sargsian cabinet also died), the attack further shook Armenian society and undermined confidence in the political order of the day. Unlike the assassination of Sargsian, a terrorist act by extremist elements, the armed attack on Ghukasian was described as a coup attempt by his political rival, the former commander of NKR forces and defense minister Samvel Babayan, whom Ghukasian had earlier removed from office. Arrested and tried, Babayan denied responsibility.

GORKY, ARSHILE (1904–1948). American artist. Born Vosdanik Manuk Adoian in the village of Khorkom on the southern shore of **Lake Van**, young Gorky grew up in the city of **Van** where he survived the 1915 atrocities and escaped to **Yerevan** only to see his mother eventually expired from the shock of exile. He reached the United States in 1920 where he pursued a career in art, an interest instilled in him by his mother. Though he attended art schools in Boston and New York, and by 1924 was signing his paintings with his pseudonym, Gorky is regarded mainly as a self-taught artist. He learned the techniques that he ultimately fused into his own original style by replicating the works of the European masters, especially Paul Cézanne and Pablo Picasso, and other modernists. Early in his career he espoused the ideas of cubism. Through repeated effort and experimentation in the 1930s, and exposure to Joan Miró and Roberto Matta, and an early friendship with William de Kooning, Gorky gradually moved beyond the hard formalities of cubism and developed a uniquely fluid linear technique giving birth to a style recognized as abstract expressionism. He began to fill his canvases with biomorphic shapes formed by color and line that articulated the concepts that came to dominate his thematic work. Gorky's signature pieces were produced in the 1940s as he more and more merged his art with the evocation of his birthplace and the recollections associated with life, color, and nature in Armenia. This combination acquired greater creative potency after a summer spent in the northern Virginia countryside in 1943 that revived in him the imagery of his lost homeland. Just as Gorky reached this new pinnacle and attained recognition in the art world for his originality, he suffered a series of personal setbacks ending in his suicide in 1948.

Some of Gorky's most popular works include the *Khorkom* and the *Garden in Sochi* series, fantastical imaginings of wondrous places illuminated with brilliant colors. Critics regard two paintings produced in 1944 as Gorky's breakthrough works: *The Liver Is the Cock's Comb* and *How My Mother's Embroidered Apron Unfolds in My Life*. The full meaning of these and other enigmatic works of organic surrealism, virtually inscrutable at first glance, was realized only after the artist's death as the publication of correspondence with members of his family revealed the extent to which Gorky strove to recreate through art powerfully emotive memories of his homeland and his beloved mother. A much earlier painting, *The Artist and His Mother*, one of his rare representative, and perhaps Gorky's best known, work, of which there are two originals, based on the single photograph of himself as a young boy and his mother, now resides at the center of his life's production as the key to the intensity of his creative search for the medium that might convey the intent of his imagination. Out of that constant fusing of imagination and color-filled memory, Gorky gave form to a new school of art. His paintings now hang in all major museums in the United States.

GREGORY THE ILLUMINATOR. *See* GRIGOR LUSAVORICH.

GRIGOR LUSAVORICH (GREGORY THE ILLUMINATOR) (c. 239–325/326). Evangelizer and patron saint of Armenia. Grigor Lusavorich was the founder of the Christian Church in Armenia. According to the Armenian historical tradition preserved in the work authored by Agatangeghos, Grigor was the son of Anak Partev. An Armenian royal courtier of Parthian descent in the pay of the Sasanid dynasty of Iran, Anak ambushed and assassinated his relative King Khosrov I of Armenia. Rescued as an infant by his nurse from the ensuing massacre of his family by King Khosrov's avenging relatives, Grigor was taken to Caesarea, in the Roman province of Cappadocia, where he was raised a Christian. Returning to Armenia as an adult, he entered the service of King **Trdat IV**, the son of Khosrov, as a palace functionary at **Vagharshapat**, the capital city. With his faith and identity revealed upon his refusal to participate in the pagan cults, he was tortured and thrown in the deep pit of Khor-Virap, the dungeon at **Artashat** for the confinement of those condemned to life imprisonment. Trdat subsequently released him in an act of contrition that resulted in the conversion of the king and his court to Christianity, an event traditionally dated to 301. Thereafter Grigor set about methodically to convert the Armenian population to Christianity, a process accelerated with royal encouragement and patronage.

To formalize his position as head of the new Christian Church in Armenia, Grigor returned to Caesarea to be duly consecrated bishop by the local metropolitan bishop. His ordination, dated at 314, also established close administrative and doctrinal links with the Ecumenical Church in Roman Asia Minor, itself newly accorded formal recognition and religious authority in the state by the Emperor Constantine. Upon his return to Armenia, Grigor is reported to have installed bishops all across the country and to have personally overseen the mass baptism of the population beginning with the feudal aristocracy. As evidence of the degree of official support extended to his missionary activities, the king awarded Grigor large tracts of land as sources of revenue, especially transferring to the Church the feudal domains of the aristocratic families that enjoyed the privilege of overseeing the ancient cults and of maintaining the principal pagan temples dedicated to the Armenian pantheon. Grigor is reported to have overthrown the temples and smashed their idols, to have baptized and recruited many of the pagan priesthood to the new faith, while also waging a military struggle against those feudal principalities that resisted the new religion. In an act of triumph over paganism, Grigor headquartered his bishopric in the central province of Taron at Ashtishat, the holiest and most popular site of worship in ancient Armenia, where he built the monastery of *Surb Karapet*, the shrine of St. John the Precursor [the Baptist], which remained a major center of religious pilgrimage until its destruction in 1915. Besides monasteries, Grigor is also credited with the founding of schools for the training of priests. Toward the end of his life, Grigor retired to the cave of Mane, located in northwestern Armenia, where, it is told, his mortal remains were found and buried at nearby Tordan on the Euphrates River, in Daranaghik, the westernmost province of Trdat's kingdom.

In consonance with the very strong Armenian tradition of feudal dynasticism, King Trdat appointed Grigor's younger of two sons, named Aristakes, to follow his father in the primacy of the **Armenian Apostolic Church**. Aristakes, who was selected for his asceticism, is known to have succeeded to the pontificate by the year 325 as he represented the Armenian Church at the Council of Nicaea, the first universal gathering of bishops convened by the Emperor Constantine to settle matters of Christian dogma. Upon the passing of Aristakes in 333, the pontificate was awarded to his older brother, Vrtanes, who presided until 341. Vrtanes was buried at Tordan, where his brother Aristakes may also have been interred. With the patriarchate of Armenia made hereditary in the family of Grigor Lusavorich, the office passed to Vrtanes's son Husik I, who presided until 347. His episcopate coincides with the reign of King Tiran. Husik was educated at court and was married to a princess of the **Arshakuni** royal dynasty. Like his antecedents on the patriarchal throne he too was consecrated in Caesarea. As the upholder of Orthodoxy, he came into conflict with the court's leanings toward Arianism, a trend in early Christianity emphasizing Christ's human aspect over his divine nature, which subsequently was declared heretical, but was supported by some of the fourth-century emperors in Constantinople. His tragic murder removed Grigor Lusarovich's family from the pontificate as Husik's sons, Atanagines and Pap, were deemed unworthy of the succession. In light of their father's martyrdom, they may have avoided the office and remained in the ranks of the military.

The Grigorian line of succession was restored with the elevation of Nerses I the Great to the patriarchate of Armenia. His reign is dated between 353 and 373. Nerses too began with a military career and served at court before his consecration in Caesarea as the supreme bishop of Armenia. He earned fame for his extensive work in establishing charitable foundations across the country and came to occupy a place of prominence in Armenian ecclesiastical history as the great reorganizer of the Church, whose customs and practices were regulated at the Council of Ashtishat (c. 354), the first major convocation of the religious hierarchy in Armenia and an important occasion for strengthening the institutional integrity of the Church. He went on embassies to Constantinople and through his intervention King Pap was raised to the throne of Armenia. Even so, relations between king and patriarch turned to hostility resulting in Nerses's murder at the instigation of the king. Once again the conflict between Arianism and Orthodoxy, as well as Nerses's Hellenizing ecclesiastical policies, appear to have contributed to the rift with the royal court. His vigorous defense and reform of the Church, and his martyrdom, assured him a place of prominence among the revered saints of Armenia. After another hiatus, one more of Grigor Lusavorich's descendants was raised to the ecclesiastical throne of Armenia in about 387. He was Sahak I the Great, the sponsor and collaborator of **Mesrop Mashtots**, the inventor of the Armenian alphabet. Sahak was the son of Nerses the Great and his episcopate lasted to 428 when he too was deposed along with the last Arshakuni king, though he lived until 439. Direct male descent from Grigor Lusavorich came to an end with Sahak. However, from Sahak's daughter, named Sahakanuysh, was born Armenia's most heroic defender of church and country, Vardan the Brave of the **Mamikonian** family. His martyrdom and canonization meant that, with the exception of Mesrop, virtually all the early and major saints of Armenia sprung from the line of Grigor Lusavorich. *See also* EDJMIADSIN; DVIN.

GRIGOR NAREKATSI (Gregory of Narek) (c. 951–1003). Poet. The paragon of medieval Armenian Christian mysticism, Narekatsi was born into an exceptionally well-educated family. His father Khosrov, the bishop of Antzevatsik, was a scholar of classical learning. His maternal uncle, Anania Narekatsi, a philosopher and theologian, and prior of the monastery of Narek, became his teacher. Grigor joined the monastery at a young age and remained at Narek for his entire life. By the time of his death local folklore ascribed miracles to him and the cloister on the southern shore of **Lake Van** became a place of pilgrimage in the region of Vaspurakan. Narekatsi's literary oeuvre includes a Commentary on Solomon's Song of Songs written in 977 at the behest of Prince Gurgen **Ardsruni** of the royal house of Vaspurakan, panegyrics dedicated to the Holy Cross, the Apostles, and the Mother of God, and the musical composition of over two dozen canticles.

Narekatsi's fame, however, rests on the collection of 95 poems, which run over 10,000 lines in rhymed verse titled the *Book of Lamentations* (*Matian voghbergutian*), which he described as "conversations with God from the depths of the heart." The poetry created by Narekatsi of the human struggle to reach union with God, and the enlightenment therein attained, was achieved with such literary ingenuity and such a profusion of subtle imagery that the *Book of Lamentations* was ranked the unrivaled apex of medieval Armenian literature. Despite its challenging and often obscure text, next to the Bible, the *Book of Lamentations* became the most popular book in Armenian, so much so that it was simply called the "*Narek*," a source of consolation for literate clergy and laymen alike through the difficult centuries of oppressive foreign domination over Armenia. As for the common folk, their reverence was such as they even came to believe that a copy of the *Narek* possessed the power of healing.

GULBENKIAN, CALOUSTE (1869–1955). Oil industry pioneer. Gulbenkian was born in Istanbul to a wealthy family. His father was a banker and oil merchant who had made his fortune importing kerosene from Baku to the Ottoman Empire. He attended King's College in London where he studied mine engineering and wrote a thesis on the technology of the new petroleum industry. He graduated in 1887, at the age of 19, and was quickly sent to Baku by his father to learn the business firsthand. On the basis of his experience there he published a book on the Russian oil industry in 1891 establishing himself as the youngest authority on the subject. He was immediately commissioned by the Ottoman government to investigate the possibility of oil deposits in Mesopotamia. Merely on the basis of geological surveys prepared by others he reported on the potentiality of their existence. With that began his interest in discovering and exploiting the resource.

Before Gulbenkian could embark on any such venture, he fled Istanbul during the 1896 massacre of Armenians and landed in Egypt. There he made the acquaintance of **Nubar** *Pasha*, the Armenian prime minister of the country, who opened doors for him in international finance, and he was soon able to start his own business as a sales representative of Baku oil in London. In 1907 he persuaded the Shell Oil Company in London to open an office in Istanbul under his charge. In addition to his many business interests, Gulbenkian also became a financial adviser to the Turkish government and acquired a 30 percent share in the Turkish National Bank, a British-controlled bank set up in Turkey to advance British interests in the Middle East. From this vantage point, in 1912 Gulbenkian put together the Turkish Petroleum Company by amalgamating the various interests seeking an oil concession in the Ottoman Empire. These included the German Deutsche Bank, The Royal Dutch/Shell combine, and the Turkish National Bank, which in 1914 were joined by another player in the region, the Anglo-Persian Group. By the final terms of the arrangement negotiated by Gulbenkian, the major oil companies agreed to a 5 percent share of the new company for Gulbenkian, hence the origin of the epithet he was known by thereafter, Mr. Five Percent. Just before World War I broke out, the Ottoman government granted the company an exclusive concession in Mesopotamia.

The war saw Gulbenkian once again depart for England. The company he created, however, struck it rich in 1927 when a major oil field was discovered north of Kirkuk in Iraq. The size of the find required renegotiating the partnership in order to bring in additional investors to handle the increased scale of the operations needed to extract, refine, ship, and market the oil. In 1928, Royal Dutch/Shell, Anglo-Persian, Compagnie Française des Petroles, which had acquired the German share after it was seized by the British during the war, and the new Near East Development Company, representing American oil interests, reached the so-called Red Line Agreement, the line drawn by Gulbenkian to demarcate the concession to which the Turkish Petroleum Company still held claim. The agreement became the basis of the renamed Iraq Petroleum Company (IPC) in which Gulbenkian continued to hold 5 percent ownership.

With his increasing wealth, Gulbenkian began to acquire one of the largest art collections assembled by a single individual in the 20th century. He also moved to Paris and took to living at the Ritz Hotel, but found himself fleeing war once again as the Germans entered the city in 1941. He first retreated to Vichy France and from there eventually resettled in Lisbon, Portugal. The British had seized control of his shares in IPC during World War II on grounds that he lived in enemy territory during the conflict. The shares reverted to him after the war and a new Group Agreement was reached in 1948 reflecting the current political and economic realities of the oil business. The new arrangement ended the Red Line Agreement but also translated into even greater revenue for Gulbenkian.

Gulbenkian bequeathed his riches to a foundation in Lisbon bearing his name dedicated to charitable, artistic, educational, and scientific causes. The Fundaçao Calouste Gulbenkian, one of the largest foundations in Europe, maintains the Calouste Gulbenkian Museum that houses the oil baron's fabulous art collection and manages the Gulbenkian Orchestra, the Gulbenkian Choir, and the Ballet Gulbenkian. The foundation is active in a number of countries, including those in the Middle East, the United Kingdom, Brazil, and Portuguese-speaking African countries. The Gulbenkian Foundation also has an Armenian Communities Department that awards financial scholarships to students of Armenian parentage, subvents the publication of academic works of Armenian interest, and supports various Armenian educational institutions and museums.

GYUMRI (also Gumri). Formerly Leninakan, Gyumri is the second largest city in the Republic of Armenia and lies to the east of the Akhurian River, 126 kilometers north of **Yerevan**. Known as Kumayri in Antiquity, and later called Gyumri, the city was renamed Alexandrapol (commonly spelled Alexandropol) by the Russians in 1837 in honor of Czar Nicholas I's wife. In 1924 the Soviets changed it to Leninakan. In 1990 the city recovered its original name. Like most of Armenia's principal towns and cities, Kumayri too has Bronze Age origins dating from the second millennium B.C. and was colonized by the Urartians. Throughout the early centuries, it remained an inconsequential place until the Russians occupied it in 1804, and transformed it into their beachhead on the Armenian plateau. From the vantage point of Tiflis/Tbilisi, the center of Russian administration in the Caucasus, Gyumri sat astride the frontier with the Persian and Ottoman Empires and represented the gateway to the south and the west through the plain of Shirak. A Russian army base was established in 1837 when Nicholas I visited the town. Alexandropol began to grow as Armenians fleeing the Turks from Kars, Erzerum, and other parts of northern Armenia, took refuge in the city beginning in 1829. When it was connected by rail with Tbilisi in 1899, Alexandropol swiftly became the largest city in Russian Armenia. Its strategic location attracted commercial development, and a diverse population included a significant Greek and Russian presence. Starting out with a population of only 3,400 in 1831, by 1914 it had reached 51,000, more than the population of **Yerevan** at the time. Each of the wars along the Russian-Ottoman frontier sent a new wave of Armenian refugees toward Alexandropol, but more Armenians fled to the city during World War I than ever before as the Turks twice seized Kars, in 1918 and conclusively in 1920, and banished its Armenian population.

Ottoman Turkish forces advanced as far as Alexandropol on both occasions but withdrew beyond the Akhurian after Sovietization. Alexander Tamanian drew new foundations for the city along a grid plan in 1924 in order to begin the modernization of the city. Before work was started an earthquake hit Leninakan in 1926 that seriously damaged the city. It was redesigned with wide avenues and open squares with the height of buildings restricted to three or four stories. Its population grew steadily thereafter, reaching 78,000 in 1935, passed 200,000 in the 1970s, and was over 300,000 by the late 1980s. Although Yerevan was eventually connected by rail with Baku through Julfa, and a major portion of the country's trade was conducted over this line, Leninakan continued to function as the principal transport junction of Armenia with its road and rail links to the north. The city also became a textile manufacturing center as well as that of the construction industry in Armenia. Tragically another earthquake, which struck on December 7, 1988, wrecked the city. It inflicted even greater damage to the northern Armenian cities of Kirovakan and Stepanavan, with the town of Spitak as the epicenter. Reconstruction began soon after. However, the scale of the damage and the collapse of the Soviet Union along with its economy, hampered the recovery. Ironically, the city's older structures, constructed to more earthquake resistant specifications fared better than late Soviet-era structures, many of them apartment high-rises, which collapsed upon their residents causing enormous loss of life. The blockade of Armenia since 1991 by neighboring Azerbaijan as a result of the **Nagorno Karabagh** conflict once again made Gyumri the transport hub of the country as the roads and rail connections of Armenia with Georgia to the north became a lifeline. *See also* SPITAK EARTHQUAKE.

– H –

HAMBARTSUMIAN, VIKTOR (also AMBARTSUMIAN) (1908–1996). Astrophysicist. Hambartsumian was born in Tbilisi and received his higher education at Leningrad University, graduating in 1928. Between 1928 and 1931 he studied astronomy at the USSR Academy of Sciences before assuming a teaching post at his alma mater, where he taught until 1943. In 1939 he became the first professor of astrophysics in the USSR at Leningrad University and was regarded as the founder of the science of theoretical astrophysics in the Soviet Union. He developed theories on the origins and evolution of galaxies and methods for measuring their age. His theory that radio waves emitted by certain galaxies are caused by enormous explosions within the galaxies became widely accepted. In 1948 he was elected vice-president of the International Astronomy Association and from 1961 to 1964 was president of the organization. He was also elected an honorary member of the academies of sciences of over a dozen countries around the world.

In 1946 Hambartsumian founded a state-of-the-art observatory at Byurakan on the heights of Mount Aragats, making Armenia one of the world's centers for the study of astrophysics during his lifetime. He exercised enormous influence in the advancement of science in Soviet Armenia and was revered as his country's leading scientist. In 1947 he was elected president of the Armenian Academy of Sciences and served also as the president of the board that developed the *Soviet Armenian Encyclopedia.*

HAMIDIAN MASSACRES. *See* ARMENIAN MASSACRES.

HAROUTIUNIAN, GAGIK (1948–). Vice-President and prime minister of Armenia. Haroutiunian was born in the village of Kotaik in the Geghashen region of Armenia. He received his higher education at **Yerevan** State University where he studied economics. He completed his advanced studies in 1970 and embarked on a career as a lecturer and researcher. In 1973 he was hired as professor of economics at Yerevan State University and subsequently taught at the Yerevan Institute of National Economy. In 1982 he was appointed economic advisor to the Central Committee of the **Communist Party of Armenia**. By 1987 he was heading the economic department of the Central Committee. An advocate of the decentralization and liberalization of the Soviet command economy, in 1990 in the first free elections held in Soviet Armenia, he was elected to the Supreme Soviet and was voted deputy chairman of the parliament. In 1991 **Levon Ter-Petrossian**, the first elected **president** of Armenia, appointed Haroutiunian as his vice-president. His portfolio included multiple domestic and foreign assignments, including the cultivation of relations with the Armenian diaspora. As the leading representative of the *nomenklatura*, the Soviet-era bureaucracy, his nomination to the second highest office in the non-Communist government of Armenia symbolized the peaceful transition of power in the country and the general accommodation reached between the reform-minded elements of the Communist Party and the new liberal forces that gained power in Armenia.

In 1992 Haroutiunian served as acting prime minister for a period of six months. With the approval of the National Assembly, in February 1996 President Ter-Petrossian appointed Gagik Haroutiunian chief justice of the constitutional court, the highest judicial body in Armenia. With his reassignment, the position of vice-president was discontinued according to the terms of the **Constitution** adopted by popular referendum in July 1995. See also HAROUTIUNIAN, GAGIK CABINET.

HAROUTIUNIAN, GAGIK CABINET. The Haroutiunian cabinet served from November 1991 through July 1992.

Prime Minister	**Gagik Haroutiunian**
Agriculture	Gagik Shahbazian
Bread Production	Rafael Shahbazian
Construction	Gagik Martirosian
Culture	Hakob Movses Hakobian
Defense	**Vazgen Sargsian**
Economy	**Hrant Bagratian**
Energy	Sebouh Tashjian
Finance	Janik Janoyan
Foreign Affairs	Raffi Hovannisian
Health	Ara Babloyan
Industry	Ashot Safarian
Internal Affairs	Vano Siradeghian
Justice	Vahe Stepanian
Public Education	Areg Grigorian
Social Security	Ashot Yesayan
Telecommunication	Grigor Poghpatian
Trade	Tigran Grigorian
Transportation	Henrik Kochinian

President **Levon Ter-Petrossian** nominated Gagik Haroutiunian, the vice-president in office, as acting prime minister after **Vazgen**

Manukian's resignation. As the first government of newly independent Armenia, the Haroutiunian cabinet more properly reflected the direction Ter-Petrossian intended to give the republic. In this respect it was staffed with a new crew of ministers most of whom were associates of the **Armenian National Movement** (ANM).

With the Haroutiunian cabinet, some of the figures that would play key roles in the early years of the Republic of Armenia assumed ministerial positions. Leading the reformers, Hrant Bagratian began his rapid rise as minister of economy. Vazgen Sargsian embarked on his long career as minister of defense. Domestic security was the concern of Vano Siradeghian, minister of internal affairs, who also dealt with the issue of the subordination of the former KGB to the new authorities. The Haroutiunian cabinet continued to rely upon the services of some Soviet-era managers in the technical sectors, such as bread production, construction, and transportation, however, its makeup reflected a complete steering away from the socialist system toward a market economy and a Western political orientation. This redirection was most pronounced in the ministries of energy and foreign affairs, which were headed by individuals holding American citizenship.

The blockade of Armenia and the cutoff of gas supplies to the country imposed a reliance on atomic energy, which, however, had been discontinued in the early zest over environmental concerns. The appointment of an American nuclear physicist as minister of energy underscored the energy policy the new Armenian government was perforce required to pursue. Sebouh Tashjian's main assignment became the reactivation of the Medsamor nuclear power plant by refurbishing and operating it according to Western standards of safety. The appointment of Raffi Hovannisian, another **diaspora** Armenian from the United States, signaled another message about Armenia's openness toward the West and its expectations from the United States as the bulwark of democracy. As for Gagik Haroutiunian, he played the valuable role of bridging the Soviet and post-Soviet eras, thereby helping to project a strong sense of national solidarity as Armenians forged a new republic, sought to introduce vast political, economic, and social changes in their country, and coped with military crises on their borders. Though Haroutiunian presided over the cabinet, it was widely understood that the government was largely the responsibility of Levon Ter-Petrossian who had emerged as the dominant figure in Armenian political life in the immediate post-Soviet era.

HARUTIUNIAN, KHOSROV. Prime minister of Armenia. Born in **Yerevan** in 1948, Harutiunian graduated as an engineer from the Yerevan Polytechnic Institute. He was thereupon employed in a number of technical posts. From 1972 to 1977 he worked at the optical-mechanical plant at Byurakan. From 1977 to 1984 he was at the Academy of Sciences first heading the special design office for radio-physics and electronics and later the special design office for radio-physical measurements. In 1984 he moved to management positions in industry, first heading the production and control department at the ArmAuto plant, then as director of cloth manufacturing factories in Ashtarak and Charentsavan.

Harutiunian's involvement in politics began in 1987 with his chairmanship of the executive committee of the Charentsavan Soviet of People's Deputies, effectively the town council. He was elected to the Supreme Soviet in 1990 where he served until 1992 eventually chairing the standing committee on local self-government. In July 1992 President **Levon Ter-Petrossian** appointed him prime minister of Armenia. He served through January 1993 at a time of growing economic and political crises as Armenia went through its first year of independence. A parliamentary deputy from 1993 to 1996, he served as secretary of the standing committee on finance, credit, budgetary, and economic issues and was a member of the committee on state and legal issues. From 1996 to 1998 he held the post of chief advisor to the prime minister, when **Armen Sarkissian** and **Robert Kocharian** held the premiership. Upon the resignation of Babken Ararktsian, a close Ter-Petrossian associate, from the chairmanship of the National Assembly following the president's own resignation, Harutiunian was elected by the deputies on February 4, 1998, to replace the outgoing speaker. He served until June 15, 1999, giving up the post to join the **Vazgen Sargsian** cabinet as minister of regional administration. *See also* HARUTIUNIAN, KHOSROV CABINET.

HARUTIUNIAN, KHOSROV CABINET. Appointed by **President Levon Ter-Petrossian**, the Harutiunian cabinet served from July 30, 1992 to February 11, 1993.

Prime Minister	**Khosrov Harutiunian**
Agriculture	Gagik Shahbazian
Communication	Grigor Poghpatian

Construction	Gagik Martirosian
Culture	Hakob Movses Hakobian
Defense	**Vazgen Manukian**
Economy	**Hrant Bagratian**
Energy and Fuel	Sebouh Tashjian
Environmental Protection	Karine Danielian
Foreign Affairs	Arman Kirakosian
Health	Ara Babloyan
Higher Education and Science	Vardges Gnuni
Industry	Ashot Safarian
Internal Affairs	Vano Siradeghian
Justice	Vahe Stepanian
Labor and Social Security	Ashot Yesayan
Public Education	Areg Grigorian
Transportation	Henrik Kochinian

The Council of Ministers presided over by Khosrov Harutiunian essentially was the same cabinet formed under the acting prime ministry of his predecessor, Vice-President **Gagik Haroutiunian**. The changes of note concerned primarily the external affairs of Armenia. With the growing conflict with Azerbaijan, former defense minister Vazgen Sargsian was reassigned to active duty along Armenia's border as the president's deputy on the ground and subsequently made State Minister of Defense. Vazgen Manukian, the first non-Communist prime minister and a recognized strategist, was assigned the defense ministry in an acting capacity to manage its administration and address logistics, while Sargsian oversaw matters of external security directly in the conflict zone. Arman Kirakosian's appointment, replacing Raffi Hovannisian, signaled a foreign policy somewhat less pronounced in its Western orientation and seeking more balance. It was also a choice predicated on his background and training. His father, John Kirakosian, had long served as titular foreign minister of Soviet Armenia and had played a large role in the ideological redefinition of nationalism in the 1970s and 1980s. During the Harutiunian premiership the device of state ministries as super-coordinating agencies was created to deal with various humanitarian, economic, and military crises that beset the country. Khosrov Harutiunian resigned over budget disagreements with President Ter-Petrossian. *See also* HAROUTIUNIAN, GAGIK CABINET.

HETUM I (1226–1269). King of Cilician Armenia and founder of the **Hetumian** royal dynasty. King **Levon I** did not know at the time of his death in 1219 that the title and dignity Nerses Lambronatsi of the Hetumian family obtained for him from the Holy Roman Emperor one day would pass to Nerses's own family. For if Nerses Lambronatsi was motivated by the larger consideration of the national interest in restoring sovereignty to the Armenians, his Hetumian kinsman Constantine, the lord of Paperon, the king's cousin and closest advisor, made himself master of the situation once regent for the young Queen Zabel, and maneuvered to have his own younger son, Hetum, wedded to her. King Hetum I reigned from 1226 to 1269, first under the tutelage of his long-lived father Constantine the Constable (d. 1263), and later with the aid and council of his older brother, the remarkable Smbat the Constable, who engineered a coup on an order that even exceeded his distinguished antecedent Nerses Lambronatsi's achievement in the annals of diplomacy.

The success of Hetum's reign is to a considerable degree explained by the fact that his father Constantine had snared not just a bride for his son, but engineered his family's monopolization of political power in the Armenian kingdom by securing high office for each of his sons. Smbat, *sparapet* or constable, served as commander-in-chief of the armed forces. Levon, as marshal, was charged with provisioning and equipping the army, and therefore of collecting the revenue. Oshin, as *bailie*, served as chief magistrate of the realm, and as governor of the island fortress of Korikos (Corycus) was responsible for the coastal defense. Barsegh/Basil, the youngest, was the bishop of Sis, the highest-ranking clergyman within the boundaries of the kingdom proper, and as the prior of Drazarg monastery had oversight of the chancellery. The seriousness of the state-building enterprise envisioned by the Hetumians is illustrated by Smbat Sparapet's attention to the introduction of a formal legal system in Cilician Armenia. Reflective of contemporary needs, he prepared an Armenian translation of the Assizes of Antioch, the Latin law code of the Crusader states, while also adapting the Armenian law code compiled by Mekhitar Gosh. He also composed an official history of the Armenian state, as well as authored an account of his continental crossing to Mongolia.

The domestic security and effective management of the state achieved by the Hetumians goes far in explaining the extraordinary and successful diplomacy practiced by the Armenian king when faced with a completely new power on the face of the earth. Mongol dominion over Asia reached beyond anything seen before and it presented as great a threat to the Armenians as to all the other peoples upon whom the steppe horsemen descended. By a stroke of imaginative strategy verging on diplomatic genius, the Hetumians chose to put their negotiating skills to the test rather than admit to a foregone conclusion should they have had to face the might of a Mongol army in battle. Armenia proper was already reduced by conquest and devastation, but the pagan Mongols were also systematically invading the Islamic states of the Middle East, potentially bringing relief to the Christian state of Armenian Cilicia. In 1247 King Hetum sent his brother Smbat Sparapet on an embassy to Karakorum, the capital of Mongolia, to seek an audience at the court of the Great Khan Goyuk, grandson of the empire-builder Jengiz Khan. He returned in 1250 with a promise of protection for the Armenian kingdom. To seal the pledge and forge an alliance, in 1253 King Hetum followed his brother's trail all the way to the court of the Khakan in Karakorum, there being received by Mongke, Goyuk's successor, in the first audience extended to foreign royalty. The impression made by the Armenian king was such that he departed from the Mongol capital having been extended terms vastly improving upon the understanding obtained by Smbat. Boldly Hetum negotiated for more than his kingdom by speaking on behalf of the entire Armenian people. Political relations were established. A mutually supportive military alliance was worked out between the two completely unequal partners. Tax exemptions were granted to Armenian religious establishments across the Mongol Empire. Lastly, laden with gifts, on his way home the king returned through Armenia to bring word to the people of the mother country of the privileges they had been granted by the Great Khan. Thus in 1256, for one brief and last instance, an Armenian monarch, representing his entire people, was in Armenia again.

The moment of glory faded quickly when the Mamluks of Egypt invaded Cilicia in 1266 and devastated the country. The strain proved too great after a lifetime of effort dedicated to bringing the Armenian people peace and security. Hetum I retired to a monastery in 1269 and passed away the following year. His 43-year reign was the longest of any Armenian king, surpassing by three years the reign of **Tigran II the Great**, the monarch who ruled the longest in Armenia proper. *See also* RUBENIAN.

HETUMIAN (HETUMID). Baronial family and royal dynasty of Cilician Armenia. The marriage of **Hetum I** in 1226 to Queen Zabel, the daughter of King **Levon/Leo I** (1199–1219), introduced a new royal dynasty named for the new king. As with virtually all the Armenian royal dynasties, the rise of Hetum to the throne was a family affair, and in his case all the more so, as his coronation marked the sole instance in the history of the Armenians of the transfer of royalty from one dynasty to another through matrimony. In fact the marriage only concluded a century-long process by which two great feudal houses, originally behaving very much in the competitive spirit of the **nakharar** dynasties of Greater Armenia, ultimately fused together and brought to a culmination the consolidation of an Armenian state in Cilicia.

By most measures of medieval polity, the Hetumians began with distinctions greater than that of the Rubenians waging their wars from the Cilician Mountains. As masters of the two mighty fortresses of Lambron and Paperon that guarded the southern approach to the Cilician Gates, the Hetumians defended one of the key strategic points of Asia Minor. Oshin I, the first baron of the Hetumian line who settled in Cilicia in 1073, received his command from Abulgharib **Ardsruni**, the Byzantine governor of western Cilicia in the late 11th century, who held his fief from the Emperor Alexios I Komnenos (1081–1118). Unlike the **Rubenian** family, whose scions seemed endowed with frenetic energy and did not shirk political brinkmanship, for as long as Byzantium conferred legitimacy and protection the Hetumians remained loyal vassals of the emperor. This policy created a serious obstacle to Rubenian ambitions, yet it also guaranteed stable Armenian control over western Cilicia as the Rubenians sorted out relations with the Crusader principality of Antioch to their east. Rivalry might have reached a breaking point between the Rubenian and Hetumian families when in 1152 Toros I overpowered a Byzantine expedition sent against him and took prisoner Oshin II of Lambron. A onetime captive of the Byzantine court himself, Toros knew that the forces he defeated did not represent the Imperial guard and sought to avoid his father's fate who had been taken prisoner by the Emperor John II Komnenos (1118–1143). Before the appearance of the main army under the Emperor Manuel I Komnenos (1143–1180), whose strength he could not match, Toros turned Oshin's captivity into an opportunity to defuse hostility among the two

Armenian families. Toros's daughter was married to Oshin's son Hetum. Toros's brother and right hand man, Stepane, married Oshin's niece, Rita. While the two families continued to jealously guard their domains, and kept each other at arm's length, the turn of events made the offspring of those marriages heirs to a kingdom.

The fortunes of the Hetumians were closely tied to the Komneni ruling in Constantinople. The fall of the Imperial dynasty in 1185, less than 10 years after the Seljuk victory at Myriokephalon in 1176 severed the territorial and political connections between Byzantium and Cilicia. It also spelled the end of Byzantine patronage and redefined the relationship between the Rubenians and the Hetumians, the former constantly given to a policy of aggrandizement and the latter given to the steady and predictable methods of diplomacy and moderation protected by a strong defensive position. When Ruben/Rupen III attempted to force the issue with his brother-in-law in 1183 by besieging Lambron, Hetum checkmated him by arranging for Bohemond III, the Prince of Antioch, to seize him through a ruse. Ruben III's brother, Levon/Leo II (later King Levon I) turned the tables on the wily Hetumians by luring them into a trap. Yet once again, the Rubenians preferred to make peace with their sturdy rivals whom they knew as cousins, but, more importantly, whose talented family they viewed as far more valuable an asset if allied to their cause. Another marriage was arranged and Levon's niece Philippa, was betrothed to Oshin III of Lambron.

Capable warriors to the last, the Hetumians, who finally came to accept Rubenian authority in Cilicia, played an even greater role as Levon's councilors. A number of the Hetumians came with the distinguishing and combined gifts of intellect and political acumen, a characteristic that they shared with their maternal relatives, the Pahlavuni, whose descendants held the Armenian catholicosate at Hromkla, the fortress into which the patriarchs had taken refuge in 1149. Nerses Lambronatsi (Nerses of Lambron) (1153–1198), the youngest son of Oshin II, a poet and a theologian, was also one of the most ecumenical-minded of Armenian clergy and supported religious compromise with the Byzantines. Educated in Constantinople, he was consecrated bishop of Tarsus in 1176 at the age of 23. When the **Catholicos** Grigor *Tgha* (Gregory the Younger) (1172–1189) convened a synod in Hromkla, Nerses Lambronatsi spoke in favor of union. The meetings among Greek and Armenian churchmen did not yield the desired results. Nevertheless, the encounters stood as testament of the extent to which both sides were prepared to revisit the central tenets of their faith and the respective issues that divided them under the leadership of men of learning and forensic skill. This demonstration made Nerses Lambronatsi precisely the person Levon needed to conduct the negotiations and discuss the finer points of ecclesiastical relations in order to deliver on Levon's ultimate goal of winning a royal crown. To do so Lambronatsi headed out to meet Frederick Barbarossa in 1190 as he led the Third Crusade, this time shouldered with the responsibility of finding common ground with the Roman Catholic Church and the German emperor. Neither Frederick nor Nerses lived to see the day, yet the historic decision was taken in favor of the Armenian baron, and Levon in time was crowned king of Armenia.

The Hetumians came into possession of Cilician Armenia when King Levon I died without a male heir, and the regent Constantine arranged for his son Hetum's marriage in 1226 with Levon's daughter already enthroned as Queen Zabel since 1219. King Hetum I proved a skillful strategist. He negotiated a successful alliance with the Mongols, a partnership that markedly improved the security of his country and boosted its economy. By strengthening trade relations, Cilicia became a major hub in the commerce conducted between East and West. This prosperity was reflected in the various spheres of cultural activity. Artistic production reached new heights and achieved greater expression especially in manuscript illumination. The premier exponent of this art form, so widespread among the Armenians throughout the Middle Ages, was the miniaturist Toros Roslin, a man who spent his entire artistic career in Cilician Armenia.

In 1260 the sultan of Egypt, the Mamluk Baybars, who undertook the recovery of Syria for Islam, finally stopped the Mongol advance in the Middle East. In 1266 the Mamluks staged a devastating raid on Cilicia, sacking all the major cities of the country including **Adana**, Ayas, Tarsus, and Sis, the capital, where they plundered the royal treasury of the great wealth accumulated during the reign of the Armenian kings. Smbat Sparapet, joined by royal princes, waged a vigorous and costly defense of the country even though he could not field forces sufficient to stop the Mamluk surge. Prince Toros fell in battle and Prince Levon was taken captive. King Hetum who had gone to appeal personally to the Mongols in Tabriz returned to find his country in ruins. Upon the release of Levon, Hetum abdicated the throne, entrusting his son to his brother Smbat (d. 1276). King Levon II (1269–1289) continued to rely on his father's policy of seeking alliance with the Mongols, but Mongol power was slowly waning as the Mamluks of Egypt prosecuted a campaign to eradicate the Christian states. To forestall further raids, Levon agreed in 1285 to the payment of an annual tribute of a million dirhems. To make up for the shortcoming of manpower, the Armenian state, still deriving significant revenue from commerce, purchased its freedom. The Mamluk advance, however, was not to be stopped. Antioch had been captured in 1268. Acre, the last Crusader city, fell in 1291. Hromkla, the privately held fortress of the Armenian catholicos, was stormed and destroyed in 1292. Then in 1304 the Mongol Ilkhans, who had terminated the Abbasid caliphate in Baghdad in 1258, converted to Islam and restored the faith as the state religion. The options once open to Armenian policy were now closed and the harbinger of things to come occurred in 1307 when a Mongol emir slaughtered King Levon III (1301–1307), his predecessor former King Hetum II (1289–1293, 1294–1297, 1299–1307), and their entire retinue.

The three reigns of Hetum II, interspersed by those of his brothers, Toros (1293–1294), Smbat (1297–1299), Constantine I (1299), and Levon III (joint ruler, 1301–1307) highlighted the growing divisions and policy differences among the Armenian governing classes. The debate between pro-Latin and anti-Latin forces intensified as some argued for accommodation with the existing powers in the region and others hoped to rely upon European support. In the absence of a strong king, these differences became more pronounced and created serious political rifts. The mounting internal tensions also undermined the monarchy as contenders representing opposing factions vied for the throne. These growing differences were underscored by the conversion of Hetum II to Catholicism. It was in this period of dynastic dissensions and external pressures that the two church councils of Sis (1307) and Adana (1316/1317) were convened and a portion of the ecclesiastical and political leadership voted for union with the Catholic Church. The decisions only compounded the divisions in Armenian society. Neither King Oshin (1307–1320) nor his cousin Hetum, called the Historian, author of an account of the Mongols written in French, who traveled to France to appeal in person to Pope Clement V, received tangible promises of relief.

When the Mamluks invaded Cilicia again in 1318 and kept up the campaign for the next four years, the Armenians had only themselves to rely upon. The defense of the country was in the hands of Hetum the Historian's sons, Oshin and Constantine. As the king's brother-in-law, Oshin became regent for the young King Levon/Leo IV (1320–1341), and Constantine held the post of sparapet or constable. Traveling to Cairo in 1323, Oshin negotiated a truce with the Mamluks that for all intents and purposes reversed previous foreign policy. In exchange of half the income of the port of Ayas and a promise by the Armenians to desist from alliances with the West, the Mamluks agreed to the reconstruction of the fortresses damaged or destroyed in the course of their invasions. Reaching adulthood, in 1329 Levon IV ordered the murder of his uncles and once again turned to the West for assistance. It was another costly policy change resulting in the seizure of Ayas by the Mamluks in 1337. The loss of Ayas represented more than a territorial retreat. It spelled the economic decline of Cilician Armenia and its increasing isolation as more and more of its coastline was placed under occupation.

The Armenian barons removed Levon from the throne. Still counting on Western assistance, they turned to nearby Cyprus and asked the Lusignan dynasty ruling the island to send one of its own. Guy de Lusignan, who was crowned by the Armenians as King Constantine II (1342–1344), was hardly given a chance before he was overthrown by one from a junior branch of the Hetumian line opposed to the wholly Latin political alignment of the Levantine Frenchman. The reign of King Constantine III (1344–1363) was denoted by further concessions to the Mamluks to whom he surrendered Tarsus and Adana. Constantine V (1363–1373) seeing the futility of further resistance prepared to surrender the kingdom to the Mamluks when he too was murdered by the barons still unwilling to lay down their arms. They called upon Guy's nephew, Leo de Lusignan, from Cyprus, whom they crowned King Levon V in 1374. It was a desperate gesture as the Mamluks closed on the capital.

The fall of Sis in 1375 marked the end of the kingdom so arduously constructed by the Rubenians and the Hetumians. It also marked the end of statehood for the Armenians, who having emigrated from their conquered homeland, created a second Armenia in Cilicia on the Mediterranean. Thereafter the Armenians lived as subjects of the empires that ruled Armenia and Cilicia. Levon V, the last king of the Armenians, was taken captive to Cairo and ransomed by his relatives in Europe. He died in Paris in 1393 and was given burial in the cathedral of St. Denis, the resting place of French royalty, the only person to bear the crown of Armenia to have a marked grave. As for the defenders of Sis who would not surrender, they took to the fortress of Vahka to make their last stand where nearly three centuries earlier the Rubenian princes had founded the Cilician Armenian state. The defiant survivors of the siege of Vahka retreated farther into the heights of the Taurus range to the town of Hajen (Hadjin) to live in mountaintop isolation.

HISTORICAL GEOGRAPHY. In the long course of its history, Armenia's borders have changed, its political destiny has been divided, and its administrative boundaries have been drawn many times over. Various conventions, therefore, are used in the literature to describe Armenia's historical geography. The Armenian highlands or the Armenian plateau encompasses the entire geographic space defined by the mountains surrounding this part of western Asia that is topographically elevated compared to the surrounding parts. In the ancient and early medieval eras, the political boundaries of the Armenian state extended beyond the highlands.

The first formal state organized in the highlands is called Urartu, which is the Assyrian rendition of the commonly recognized designation of **Ararat**, the name given the country in the Bible. The native Urartians called their land Nairi and Biaini, the latter surviving in the name **Van**. The Persians labeled the country Armena, and the Greeks, and from them the Romans, rendered it Armenia. The Armenians called their country Hayk. In the ancient period there were already two distinct parts to historic Armenia designated Meds Hayk and Pokr Hayk corresponding to Armenia Major and Armenia Minor of the Romans, frequently rendered as Greater Armenia and Lesser Armenia. Armenia Major, or Greater Armenia, incorporated the kingdom in the highlands. Armenia Minor, or Lesser Armenia, rested to the west of the Euphrates River. As evidenced by these designations, the Armenian-speaking population covered a wider area than the plateau. The ancient Armenian state based on the plateau, however, never secured political control of Armenia Minor, and only on brief occasions was Armenia Minor self-governing. The political life of the Armenians remained centered in Armenia Major and its sovereigns went by the title of *Tagavor Hayots Medsats*, King of Greater Armenia. At its height the kingdom of Greater Armenia consisted of 15 provinces: Ayrarat, Turuberan or Taron, Vaspurakan, Siunik, Bartzr Hayk [Upper Armenia] or Karin, Dsopk or Chorrord Hayk [Fourth Armenia], Aghtznik, Mokk, Korjek, Parskahayk [Persarmenia], Paytakaran, Artsakh, Utik, Gugark, and Tayk. The many partitions from the 4th to the 20th century gave rise to other conventions in the historical geography of Armenia. To distinguish the two parts of the country, the labels Eastern Armenia and Western Armenia are used even though there never was a fixed line that demarcated such a division. These divisions were a recurrent pattern and consistently had the characteristics of a line more or less segmenting the Armenian plateau along a north-south axis. At times the line held close to the **Arax River**, along the lowest altitude on the plateau. At other times it followed the highest altitude with the dividing line running from a starting point closer to the city of Karin/Erzerum in northern or Upper Armenia as it was called. The eastern and western parts are also frequently labeled according to the ruling imperial state holding that part of Armenia. Hence over the centuries, Eastern Armenia has been called Persian Armenian, whether in the Sasanid era in the early Middle Ages or the Safavid era in the early modern period. Subsequently the same area was known as Russian Armenia. The western part has been labeled Roman and Byzantine Armenia, and later Ottoman or Turkish Armenia.

The Armenians generally preserved the nomenclature of their historic provinces. Imperial administrative reorganization, however, at times disregarded the topographic reasons for the evolution of the Armenian provinces and introduced new designations. In the early Byzantine era, Armenia Minor and the portion of Western Armenia under Byzantine rule were subjected to Roman systemization, divided into four and numbered accordingly, hence the renaming of the ancient region of Dsopk as Fourth Armenia. In the late Ottoman period, a similar administrative reorganization of the Armenian-inhabited parts yielded what were often called the six Armenian provinces or *vilayets*: Erzerum, Van, Bitlis, Diyarbekir, Mamuret-ul-Aziz or Kharpert/Harput, and Sivas, the latter corresponding closely to ancient Armenia Minor. With the decimation of the Armenians in the Ottoman Empire during World War I, historic Western Armenia ceased to exist as a region populated by Armenians.

In the High Middle Ages, the Armenians created a wholly new state in territory beyond the boundaries of their historic homeland. This was Cilician Armenia, a maritime province of the former Byzantine Empire. The Armenians colonized the region beginning in the 10th and 11th century and converted it into a second homeland. They lived there for nearly a thousand years until the early 1920s when the Nationalist Turks drove out the survivors of the 1915 **Armenian Genocide** through another series of atrocities. *See also* AGHTAMAR; ANI; ARMENIAN KINGDOM; ARTASHAT; DVIN; EDJMIADSIN; GEOGRAPHY, POLITICAL; GYUMRI; MUSA DAGH; NAGORNO KARABAGH; SEVAN, LAKE; SPITAK EARTHQUAKE; STEPANAKERT; TIGRANAKERT; VAGHARSHAPAT; VAN, LAKE; YEREVAN.

HNCHAK, HNCHAKIAN KUSAKTSUTIUN (also Henchak, or Hunchak). *See* SOCIAL DEMOCRATIC HNCHAKIAN PARTY.

HOVHANESS, ALAN (1911–2000). American composer. Hovhaness, nee Chakmakjian, was born in Somerville, and spent his youth in contact with the immigrant Armenian communities of Massachusetts, whence he gained close knowledge of Armenian folk and religious music. His father, Hovhaness Chakmakjian, whose first name Alan later adopted as his own, was a professor of chemistry at Tufts University, and a man of considerable linguistic skills. His *A Comprehensive Dictionary English-Armenian* has been a permanent contribution to Armenian lexicography.

During the 1940s, while an organist at St. James Armenian Church in Watertown, Hovhaness studied the ancient Armenian church music from the priests and deacons who sang the Armenian Mass, and was introduced to the compositions of **Komitas**. He received his formal education at the New England Conservatory of Music and later joined briefly the faculty of the Boston Conservatory of Music. With the performance of his compositions starting in 1941 by the noted orchestra conductor Leopold Stokowski, Hovhaness obtained recognition as a major and original American composer. His interest in Oriental music led him to India in 1959. In subsequent years he traveled to Japan and Korea, where in each country he dedicated himself to the serious study of the native music and continued to absorb elements of each in his compositions, as well as write music incorporating traditional instruments. In 1965 he gave a series of concerts in Armenia.

Despite his interest in Oriental music and the profound influence of Armenian melodic themes detectable across his numerous compositions, Hovhaness's larger works made full use of the symphonic orchestra and are grounded in classical Western harmony and polyphony. He admired Jean Sibelius (1865–1957), whom he went to meet as a young man and with whom he continued to correspond until the Finnish composer's death. Hovhaness emphasized the melodic line. The gracefully ceremonial pace of many of his compositions attests to a refined spirituality that often evokes a sublime and inspired understanding of humanity's quest for communion with nature. His instrument of choice to communicate the loftiness of his pantheistic ideals has been the trumpet. Arguably Hovhaness has composed some of the most beautifully melodic music ever written for a brass instrument. While rhapsodic fanfares bring many of his compositions to a triumphal ending, a serene lyricism is his more frequent signature.

Hovhaness's vast oeuvre numbers more than 500 compositions, with over 60 symphonies. His programmatically Armenian music, or compositions on Armenian themes and subjects constitute only part of his total output and many came chronologically in the earlier decades of his professional life as a composer. Some of the better known are his *Saint Vartan Symphony*, *Symphony Etchmiadzin*, and *Armenian Rhapsodies*. His most popular works are possibly his tone poems, a form of composition for which his gentle and seamless weaving of Eastern and Western motifs appears particularly well suited. With compositions like his *Prayer of Saint Gregory*, *Mysterious Mountain*, and *Fra Angelico*, and his opera *Pericles*, Hovhaness cut across cultures, musical traditions, and schools of philosophy to weld with his genius his own unique language of universality.

– I –

ISAHAKIAN, AVETIK (1875–1957). Poet. Isahakian was born in Alexandropol, now **Gyumri**. He attended local schools and the Gevorgian seminary at **Edjmiadsin**. In 1893 he went to Leipzig University and returned home in 1895. He probably joined the **Armen-**

ian Revolutionary Federation (ARF) at the time as he was arrested for anti-tsarist activities in 1896 and exiled to Odessa. In 1897 he resumed his studies in the history of literature and philosophy at the University of Zurich. Returning in 1902, he was again arrested in 1908 for revolutionary activities and imprisoned. Quitting all political involvement, Isahakian left for Europe in 1911 and lived in France and Germany. He returned to Armenia in 1926, leaving again in 1930. He settled permanently in **Yerevan** only in 1936.

Isahakian's lyric poems, many nostalgic, others in a patriotic vein, enjoyed great popularity in Soviet Armenia. He was revered as 'the master' by younger writers who saw in him a figure of continuity from the prewar and prerevolutionary period of the Armenian cultural renaissance at a time when their own society under Stalin was marked by ideological indoctrination, political conformity, and the persecution of independent thinking intellectuals. From 1944 to 1957 Isahakian served as the permanent president of the Armenian writers' union. His masterpiece, *Abu Lala Mahari*, published in 1909, idealized the search for enlightenment through the symbolism of the worldly traveler's ordeals.

ISAKOV, IVAN (HOVHANNES TER-ISAHAKIAN) (1894–1967). Admiral of the Soviet navy. Isakov was born in the town of Hajikend near Kars. His family moved to Tbilisi where he received his early education. He attended naval school in Petrograd between 1914 and 1917, and served in the Soviet navy from 1918 on. He served in the Baltic fleet against the Germans and in the Caspian fleet against the British. From 1922 to 1927 he was chief of naval operations of the Black Sea fleet, and in 1929 he was appointed chief of the naval section of the supreme staff of the Red Army. In 1937 he was made commander of the Baltic fleet, and from 1938 to 1946 he served as chief of staff of the Soviet navy. During World War II he was responsible for coordinating land and sea operations on the Baltic, North Caucasus, and Black Sea fronts. He was wounded in action in 1942 near Tuapse, Georgia. In 1955 he was promoted to Admiral of the Soviet Navy, thus becoming the highest-ranking officer of Armenian origin to have served in the naval forces of any country. In 1965 Isakov was honored as a Hero of the Soviet Union.

Besides being a superior naval officer, Isakov was also a man of considerable learning who published some 250 works pertaining to naval history and strategy. In 1967 he was made an honorary member of the USSR Academy of Sciences. He served as the president of the editorial board for the preparation of a three-volume Soviet naval atlas, and was editor of the sections pertaining to the navy for the *Great Soviet Encyclopedia. See also* BAGHRAMIAN, IVAN.

– K –

KACHAZNUNI, HOVHANNES (1868–1938). Political leader. Kachaznuni, baptismal name Ruben Ter-Hovannesiants, was born in Akhaltsikhe and educated in Tbilisi. In 1893 he graduated from the St. Petersburg institute of civil engineering and settled in Baku, where he joined the **Armenian Revolutionary Federation** (ARF). In 1908 he moved to **Van** in the Ottoman Empire after the restoration of the Ottoman Constitution. He returned in 1914 to Transcaucasia, where he became a member of the Armenian National Council that was formed in 1917. Elected a member of the Russian Constituent Assembly that was quickly disbanded by the Bolsheviks, Kachaznuni served as the principal spokesman of the ARF in the Transcaucasian Seim formed by the regional members of the Constituent Assembly in February 1918. In this capacity he was appointed a member of the Transcaucasian delegation that opened negotiations with the Ottomans in Trebizond in March. On April 22, 1918, he declared the assent of the ARF, as the principal organization representing the Armenians, to the Seim's declaration of independence from Russia as the Democratic Federative Republic of Transcaucasia. Kachaznuni held the portfolio of minister of welfare in the transitory republic that lasted a month. He was with **Alexander Khatisian** in Batumi negotiating again with the Ottomans, this time on behalf of the Republic of Armenia declared independent on May 28, 1918. He was the third signatory, along with Khatisian and Mikayel Papadjanian, to the Treaty of Batumi, which ended hostilities between the Ottomans and Armenia. Sealed on June 4, the treaty constituted the first international act of the new republic.

Kachaznuni's moderate views made him the most suitable candidate to lead the new country and to invite national reconciliation with the unexpected emergence of an Armenian state. Authorized by the Armenian National Council in Tbilisi to organize the government of the Armenian republic, Kachaznuni became the first president-prime minister of Armenia with his June 30 announcement of the formation of a cabinet. With the end of World War I, Kachaznuni formed a new coalition cabinet on November 4. While seeking greater international recognition for the Armenian republic, Kachaznuni's government grappled with the problem of resolving the multiple border disputes with neighboring states as the Armenian population endured a famine during the first winter of independence. To solicit aid for his country, the premier was prevailed upon to travel to Europe and the United States. After reshuffling his cabinet in March, he embarked on his journey in April 1919. Khatisian was left in charge of the government as acting president-prime minister until he formed his own cabinet on August 10 after the June election in Armenia gave a large majority of seats to the ARF nullifying the need to maintain a coalition cabinet.

After the Sovietization of Armenia in November 1920, Kachaznuni was placed under arrest. He was released from prison during the February 1921 revolt. He left Armenia and settled in Bucharest, Romania, where in 1923 he made a surprise announcement in a pamphlet entitled *Dashnaktsutiunn Ailyevs Anelik Chuni* (The Dashnaktsutiun Has Nothing More to Do) arguing that, having brought into existence an Armenian state, the ARF had fulfilled its mission and ought to disband, and that all Armenians should be supportive of Soviet Armenia. He repatriated to Armenia and resumed his profession. Though he avoided all politics thereafter, it is believed that he was liquidated during the purges. *See also* ARMENIAN REVOLUTIONARY MOVEMENT; VRATZIAN, SIMON.

KAMO (1882–1922). Bolshevik revolutionary. Kamo, given name Simon Ter-Petrosian, was born in Gori, Georgia, and was a boyhood friend of Stalin, who later introduced him to socialism and who also nicknamed him Kamo. Kamo joined the Russian Social Democratic Workers Party (RSDWP) in Tbilisi in 1901. He became famous as an 'expropriator' in the Caucasus for staging dramatic propaganda events and for engaging in daring robberies in order to fund the activities of the Bolshevik wing of the party. He began his career in the underground by hurling seditious leaflets from the balcony of the Tbilisi Armenian theater in February 1903, and calmly leaving before the arrival of the police. He soon took to holding up banks and was apprehended in November 1903, but escaped from prison within a year, ready to resume his exploits during the 1905 revolution. He met Lenin for the first time in St. Petersburg in March 1906 and was sent abroad by the party leader to purchase weapons and smuggle them to Russia.

On June 26, 1907, Kamo undertook the most spectacular expropriation of the period by robbing in daylight in a public square the carriage transporting a large sum from St. Petersburg to the State Bank in Tbilisi. Kamo succeeded in carrying the loot all the way to Berlin where he was finally arrested upon his betrayal by a Russian police spy who had been entrusted with the information by Lenin. The Germans handed Kamo over to the Russian police who placed him in prison in Tbilisi. He escaped in 1911, foiling police searches, and fled to Paris where he linked up with Lenin once again. He returned to Tbilisi in 1912 and was arrested for attempting another holdup in 1913. Condemned to death, his sentence was commuted to 20 years hard labor during the amnesty declared on the 300th anniversary of the Romanov dynasty. Kamo was released from prison in March 1917. During the height of the revolution, he was entrusted by **Stepan Shahumian** to deliver correspondence to Lenin in Petrograd and returned with the communiqué from the Soviet of People's Commissars appointing Shahumian extraordinary commissar for the Transcaucasus. Kamo organized a partisan group that operated near Kursk and Orel. He proceeded to Baku in advance of the Sovietization of the city and returned to Tbilisi after the Sovietization of Georgia. He died there in a car accident. *See also* KASIAN, SARGIS; KARAKHAN, LEV; MIASNIKIAN, ALEXANDER; MIKOYAN, ANASTAS.

KARABAGH MOVEMENT. *See* ARMENIAN NATIONAL MOVEMENT; NAGORNO KARABAGH.

KARAKHAN, LEV (1889–1937). Soviet diplomat. Karakhan, nee Levon Karakhanian, was one of the most prominent diplomats of the early Soviet period. Born in Tbilisi, he studied law at St. Petersburg University. A member of the Russian Social Democratic Workers Party (RSDWP) since 1904, he was arrested for revolutionary activities soon after graduation in 1915 and exiled to Tomsk. After the February 1917 Russian Revolution he was active in organizing the

Irkutsk soviets and was a member of the Petrograd Military Revolutionary Committee under Trotsky that prepared the October Bolshevik coup. In 1917–1918 he served as the secretary of the Soviet delegation headed by Trotsky that negotiated the Treaty of Brest-Litovsk with Germany. In March 1918 he was appointed deputy of the People's Commissariat for Foreign Affairs and conducted negotiations on behalf of the Soviet government with Iran, Afghanistan, Khiva, and Bukhara. He signed with Lenin the SOVNARKOM decree establishing Soviet consulates, as well as the documents establishing diplomatic relations between the Russian Socialist Federated Socialist Republic (RSFSR) and Armenia. In 1919 he participated in the first Communist International and was elected a member of the Executive Committee of the Comintern.

In 1921 Karakhan was appointed RSFSR ambassador to Poland, and from 1923 to 1927 was ambassador to China, having already set the tone for Soviet relations with China with the July 25, 1919, declaration that bears his name renouncing all extra-territorial rights claimed by the tsarist government in that country. The treaty that Karakhan eventually negotiated and signed on May 31, 1924, with the Chinese Republic reestablished Russian power in the East and made Outer Mongolia, over which China claimed sovereignty, into a Soviet protectorate. Karakhan returned to Moscow in 1927 to resume his former position as deputy foreign minister in which capacity he served until 1934. That year he was reassigned as the Soviet ambassador to Turkey until 1937. He was liquidated on trumped-up charges of espionage. *See also* KAMO; KASIAN, SARGIS; MIASNIKIAN, ALEXANDER; MIKOYAN, ANASTAS; SHAHUMIAN, STEPAN.

KARSH, YOUSUF (1908–2002). Canadian photographer. Karsh was born in the town of Mardin, in upper Mesopotamia, where an Arabic-speaking Armenian community had long existed. His family suffered terribly from the persecution of the Armenians during World War I and made their final escape from their birthplace in 1922. While his family struggled to rebuild in Aleppo, Syria, his father sent him to join his maternal uncle, George Nakash, in Canada in 1924. Nakash (1892–1976) was an established photographer himself at the time, having been sponsored by his own maternal uncle, Aziz Setlakwe, one of the earliest Armenian settlers in Canada, and who, for his role as community leader, was known as the patriarch of the Canadian-Armenians. Nakash had arrived in New York in 1913, but after hearing of the killing of his brothers by the Turks, settled permanently in Canada and by about 1918 had opened a studio in the city of Sherbrooke, in Quebec Province. He had learned photography in the studio of a fellow Armenian during a brief stay in Beirut, Lebanon. In 1934 Nakash moved to Montreal where he established a successful career as a portrait photographer of Canadian society.

While attending school in Sherbrooke, Karsh went to work in 1925 for Nakash who soon detected his nephew's talent in photography. He shortly arranged for Karsh to apprentice with his colleague John H. Garo (Garoian). Garo (d. 1939) was the most prominent Armenian photographer in America at time. He originated from Kharpert and had emigrated to the United States after his parents were killed in the 1890s massacres. Garo had made a name for himself photographing the illuminati of Boston society, and was friends with famous personalities of the art world including the likes of orchestra conductors Serge Koussevitzky and Arthur Fiedler, to whom Karsh was introduced at a young age. Garo took Karsh under his wing training him to become a professional in the making of pictures with light and camera.

By 1932 Karsh had moved to Ottawa where in 1936 he was invited to photograph Franklin D. Roosevelt on the occasion of the first official visit of a U.S. president to Canada. That occasion also helped establish a friendship with Canadian Prime Minister Mackenzie King who became a patron and was instrumental in arranging for Karsh to photograph Winston Churchill in 1941 at the height of the Allied struggle against Nazism. The photograph captured the indomitable spirit of the prime minister whose stern look evoked the resolve of the British people at their moment of greatest adversity. The picture became Churchill's emblematic portrait and helped establish Karsh as one of the preeminent photographers of the century. Karsh went on to make portraits of presidents, prime ministers, popes, kings, queens, movie celebrities, and persons of prominence and accomplishment from around the world. A short list includes Dwight Eisenhower, Harry Truman, John F. Kennedy, Gerald Ford, Jimmy Carter, Ronald Reagan, John Paul II, François Mitterand, Nikita Khrushchev, Leonid Brezhnev, Fidel Castro, Eleanor Roosevelt, Margaret Thatcher, Elizabeth II, King Faisal, Ernest Hemingway, Norman Mailer, Vladimir Nabokov, H.G. Wells, George Bernard Shaw, Jean

Cocteau, Albert Camus, Noel Coward, W.H. Auden, Helen Keller, André Malraux, Evelyn Waugh, Thomas Mann, John Steinbeck, Georgia O'Keeffe, Alberto Giacometti, Pablo Picasso, Joan Miro, Ansel Adams, Frank Lloyd Wright, Buckminster Fuller, Albert Schweitzer, Albert Einstein, Carl Jung, Linus Pauling, Paul Robeson, Kurt Weill, Jean Sibelius, Ralph Vaughan Williams, Benjamin Britten, Fritz Kreisler, Eugene Ormandy, Pablo Casals, Ingrid Bergman, Gregory Peck, Clark Gable, Tyrone Power, Boris Karloff, Humphrey Bogart, Audrey Hepburn, Grace Kelly, Sophia Loren, Elizabeth Taylor, and Laurence Olivier.

KASIAN, SARGIS (1876–1937). Bolshevik revolutionary. Kasian, nee Ter-Kasparian, was born in Shushi and received his early education in Baku. He attended Leipzig University where he studied business. Graduating in 1902 he pursed further studies at the University of Berlin until 1904. He joined the Armenian **Social Democratic Hnchakian Party** in 1903. In Baku in 1905 he joined the Russian Social Democratic Workers Party (RSDWP) and organized the publication of a new Armenian and Russian language Bolshevik paper in Tbilisi. Between 1914 and 1917 he was in exile in Astrakhan and Vologda. He resumed his party activities in 1917 and assembled a small underground organization in Armenia. The first attempt to establish Soviet power in Armenia after the May 10, 1920, proclamation by a Revolutionary Committee in Alexandropol (**Gyumri**) failed without the support of the Red Army. The defeat of the Armenian army by the advancing Turkish Kemalist forces in October prompted the Red Army in Sovietized Azerbaijan to move into Armenia. On November 29, as the Armenians were negotiating the transfer of power to the Russian government, Kasian issued the declaration, as president of the Revolutionary Committee (Revkom) of the Soviet Socialist Republic of Armenia, announcing the establishment of Soviet authority in Armenia. The transfer of government from the **Armenian Revolutionary Federation** (ARF) to the Bolsheviks was formalized by treaty on December 2, while the Revkom arrived in Yerevan four days later. Once installed, the Revkom disregarded the terms of the treaty and began wholesale arrests, provoking the February 1921 rebellion that drove the Bolsheviks from **Yerevan**. Ousted from his post by Lenin, Kasian served as rector of the Transcaucasian Communist University from 1924 to 1927 and was on the Central

Committee of the Transcaucasian Communist Party from 1927 to 1931. He was liquidated during the Stalinist purges. *See also* COMMUNIST PARTY OF ARMENIA; MIASNIKIAN, ALEXANDER; VRATZIAN, SIMON.

KASPAROV, GARRY (1963–). World chess champion. Kasparov was born in Baku, Azerbaijan, of Armenian and Jewish parentage. He demonstrated an early aptitude for chess and rapidly rose through the ranks of the Soviet chess circuit. In 1976 he placed first in the USSR youth championship games and in 1980 placed first at the World Youth championship games. In 1985 he won the World Championship match in Moscow against Anatoli Karpov, the title-holder. At age 22 Kasparov was the youngest world champion in the history of the game. He was also the second person of Armenian origin to hold the title after Tbilisi-born Tigran Petrosian (1929–1984) who was world chess champion in the 1960s. In 1996 Kasparov played a set of games against an IBM computer dubbed Deep Blue that was capable of calculating 100 million positions a second. The machine won the first game, but in a demonstration of his prodigious talent, Kasparov won the set in what was characterized as one of the greatest feats of man versus machine. In a rematch in 1998 with an even more sophisticated machine, Kasparov conceded the game, thus symbolically ushering in the era where a man-made device could overwhelm the acknowledged master of man's most sophisticated game of strategy.

KAZANJIAN, VARASTAD (1879–1974). Medical pioneer. Kazanjian was born in the city of Erzinjan in eastern Anatolia to a family of coppersmiths. He journeyed to the United States at the age of 16 and, like many unschooled immigrant Armenians of the time, went to work in the wire mills of Worcester, Massachusetts. By 1905, however, he had graduated from Harvard Dental School. He opened a private practice and took up teaching at Harvard until 1915 when he joined a team of American doctors who went to France to tend to the record number of Allied war casualties two years before the United States entered World War I. In battlefield hospitals, Dr. Kazanjian began to experiment in surgical restoration of the shattered facial bones and muscles of wounded soldiers. The success of his methods was quickly registered in the medical field. He was made an honorary major of the British Royal Army Medical Corps and in 1919 created a

Companion of the Order of St. Michael and St. George by King George V of England. On his return to the United States, Kazanjian went to medical school completing his studies in 1921 and graduating a physician specializing in oral and plastic surgery. He later became a professor at Harvard Medical School and authored the standard book in his specialization, *Surgical Treatment of Facial Injuries*. Dr. Kazanjian is recognized in the medical profession as the founder of reconstructive or plastic surgery.

KERKORIAN, KIRK (1917–). American entrepreneur. Born in Fresno, California, the son of immigrant parents, Kerkorian grew up in Los Angeles. An amateur boxer in his youth, Kerkorian learned to fly in 1939. By the summer of 1943, he was a flight captain for the British Royal Air Force in Canada and spent most of World War II delivering Canadian-built bombers to England in solo transatlantic flights. By earning $1,000 a month for this dangerous job and recycling surplus military planes after the war, Kerkorian used his saving of $50,000 to purchase his first company, Los Angeles Air Service, which ferried travelers from California to the gambling towns of Las Vegas and Reno, Nevada. In 1962 he renamed the company Trans International Airlines and expanded flights to Hawaii. By the time he divested himself of all stocks in his airline company in 1969, he had made $104 million. In the meantime, through his International Leisure Company, Kerkorian had taken ownership of the Flamingo, the first hotel and casino built on the Las Vegas Strip, and built the International Hotel in direct competition with Howard Hughes who owned much of the Strip. Selling his shares in 1971 to Barron Hilton, owner of the Hilton Hotels chain, Kerkorian turned a $16.6 million initial investment into a $180 million sale.

With his new earnings Kerkorian turned to Hollywood in the 1970s where he eventually acquired the MGM studios and United Artists (UA), the studio founded by Charlie Chaplin, Douglas Fairbanks, D.W. Griffith, and Mary Pickford. In 1978 he also acquired 25 percent of Columbia Pictures. While management at Columbia Pictures bought out Kerkorian's stake in the company, turning his $43 million into $134 million, Kerkorian merged the other two movie companies and raised money by selling the MGM film library, which included such classics as *Gone with the Wind*, to Ted Turner, the Atlanta, Georgia-based media entrepreneur and CNN television owner.

In 1990 Kerkorian sold MGM/UA for $1.4 billion. While he still owned MGM, capitalizing on the internationally recognized name, Kerkorian returned to Las Vegas to build the MGM Grand hotel. Like other properties that he owned and companies that he formed, he sold the building only to construct the MGM Grand Hotel and Casino, with 5,000 guest rooms the largest hotel in the world. In the 1990s Kerkorian began acquiring shares in the Chrysler automobile company and bid to purchase the Detroit car manufacturer. When Chrysler later merged with the German automaker Daimler-Benz, Kerkorian more than quadrupled his initial investment of more than $1 billion.

Through the initiative of the Lincy Foundation, named for his daughters Linda and Tracy, Kerkorian also created one of the largest charitable undertakings to assist the newly independent Republic of Armenia. The Lincy Foundation encouraged the formation of the United Armenia Fund (UAF) in 1989, which pooled the resources of Armenian organizations in the United States in response to the December 7, 1988, **Spitak Earthquake** that devastated northern Armenia. The UAF dispatched supplies and equipment necessary for relief and reconstruction. Between the years 1992 and 1995 the UAF played an even more critical role by delivering humanitarian assistance to Armenia when it faced a blockade jointly imposed by Turkey and Azerbaijan. The UAF covered the expenses for flying into Armenia planeloads of emergency food, medicine, and other vital commodities provided by American and Armenian charities. In the winter months when Armenia faced near famine conditions, the dozens of airlifts helped meet the vital needs of the Armenian population. The self-made billionaire whose business acumen had made him one of the wealthiest men in America also became one of greatest benefactors of the newborn Armenian state.

KHACHATURIAN, ARAM (1903–1978). Composer. Khachaturian was born in Tbilisi. He received his musical training in Moscow where he went to study cello and piano in 1922. By the time he completed his studies in composition at the Moscow Conservatory in 1934, Khachaturian had written numerous pieces for piano, mostly dances, waltzes, and marches, and for piano and cello, or violin. With his three symphonies (1934, 1943, 1947), and piano, violin, and cello concertos (1936, 1940, 1946), he quickly established himself as a serious composer. He also produced the music scores for over a dozen Soviet films, including *Pepo*, the first Armenian talking movie made in 1935, and composed music to various plays by Armenian and Russian authors, such as Lermontov's *Masquerade* (1941), which he turned into his popular *Masquerade Suite* (1944) with its beautifully melodic waltz, as well as Shakespeare's plays *Macbeth*, *Othello*, and *King Lear*.

Though reflective of the midcentury Russian style of symphonic orchestration in its tonality, Khachaturian's music stood apart by its distinctive style that bore two characteristic signatures in the finer and more popular compositions he wrote in his mature years. Khachaturian made generous use of traditional Caucasian music and many of his compositions evoke an Armenian melodic line. However, his works markedly differed from the conventional orchestrations of folk themes. They carried the vibrant rhythms and stirring pace of Caucasian dance music, but they were original compositions that reworked that cultural material through new instrumentation and according to European musical canons resulting in a sound unique to the composer.

These attributes lent themselves especially well to the musical form highly cultivated in the Russian theater, the ballet. From melodic waltzes to fiery dances, Khachaturian was able to employ the full rhythmic range of his dance music in this medium. The music for *Spartacus* (1950–1954) and *Gayane* (1941–1942) remain his most successful compositions. The dance suite from *Gayane* is part of the standard performance repertoire of orchestras around the world. As for the "Sabre Dance" from *Gayane*, it has entered the realm of popular music as one of the 20th century's signature pieces.

KHANJIAN, AGHASI (1901–1936). Armenian Communist Party leader. Khanjian was born in **Van**, the son of a teacher and one-time Armenakan party leader whose family took refuge from the 1915 massacres in the monastery of **Edjmiadsin**. He received some of his early education at the Edjmiadsin seminary before moving to **Yerevan**, where in 1919 he was among the founders of the Spartak Armenian Communist youth organization. In 1920 the Caucasian bureau of the Russian Communist Party appointed him to the Central Committee of the **Communist Party of Armenia** (CPA). He was twice arrested for subversive activities by the authorities of the independent Republic of

Armenia. After the Sovietization of Armenia, Khanjian went to Russia to attend the Sverdlov Communist University. In 1922 he was already working as a Communist Party member in Leningrad under Zinoviev. In 1925, however, he sided with Stalin against Zinoviev and became a prótegé of the new Leningrad party chairman, Sergei Kirov, when the latter took over in 1926. Gaining the confidence of Stalin, Khanjian was transferred in April 1928 to Armenia where he rapidly rose through the ranks. By May 1930 he was First Secretary of the Central Committee of the Armenian Communist Party.

Khanjian led the Stalin revolution in Armenia. He gradually removed the older Armenian Bolsheviks from office and virtually replaced the cadre, represented by **Sargis Kasian**, that had ruled in Armenia in the 1920s. In the process he gathered his own following preparing the party to take charge of the collectivization measures introduced under the First Five-Year Plan (1928–1932). As in many parts of the Soviet Union, the peasantry resisted collectivization and Russian armed forces intervened to contain the uprisings that spread in the countryside. By 1932 popular opposition had been crushed and by 1936 four-fifth of Armenia's agricultural sector had been collectivized.

In 1931 Khanjian launched a campaign against the intelligentsia on the charge of nationalism. Eminent scholars such as **Hrachia Ajarian**, Hakob Manandian, and Manuk Abeghian were censored. Accusations were brought against old **Dashnak**s like **Hovhannes Kachaznuni**, and the poet **Yeghishe Charents** found himself caught in the middle of the party debates over chauvinism and the ideological content of socialist culture. Nineteenth century nationalist writers, including such prominent figures as **Raffi**, Rafayel **Patkanian,** and Yervand Shahaziz were condemned and their works banned.

Despite the revolutionary measures implemented in Soviet Armenia by the Communist Party under his leadership, Khanjian was personally well regarded. A gifted speaker also, he was able to secure his position in Armenia by eliminating all opposition forces within the party. No other Communist Party leader in Armenia enjoyed Khanjian's popularity during the 70 years of Soviet rule. It is reported that he promoted the repatriation to Soviet Armenia of the displaced population of Western Armenia, that he worked for the retrocession of **Nagorno Karabagh** and Nakhichevan to the Armenian Soviet Socialist Republic (ASSR) (which from 1922 until 1936 was part of the Transcaucasian Soviet Federated Socialist Republic with its center in

Tbilisi), and sought to improve Armenia's transportation network despite political opposition from party leaders in Transcaucasia.

Indeed Khanjian's growing strength became his undoing. Lavrenti Beria, first secretary of the Georgian Communist Party, and until 1936 the first secretary of the Transcaucasian party committee, another Stalin protégé, plotted his way to exercising a complete monopoly of power over Transcaucasia. The July 9, 1936, announcement that Khanjian had committed suicide in Tbilisi, where he had gone to meet with Beria, marked the beginning of the Great Purges in Armenia. The entire Armenian Communist Party was nearly destroyed. The leaders of both the old Bolsheviks, men of Sargis Kasian's generation, and the new cadre who had risen to office under Khanjian, were executed. Others, such as party ideologue Ashot Hovhannisian, were exiled. As the ranks of the CPA were thinned, ethnic Russians were sent to assume both party and administrative posts in Yerevan. Aghasi Khanjian's six years as Communist Party leader marked a turning point in Armenia's development. The economic reorganization wrought by the Stalin revolution began the transformation of a country with mainly an agrarian economy into a modern industrialized society. *See also* MIASNIKIAN, ALEXANDER.

KHATISIAN, ALEXANDER (1876–1945). Political leader, mayor of Tbilisi, **prime minister** of Armenia 1919–1920. Khatisian was born in Tbilisi to a family associated with the Russian administrative apparatus in the Caucasus. After completing his education at the state school in Tbilisi, he studied medicine in Moscow, Kharkov, and Germany. Upon his return to the Caucasus, however, Khatisian turned to politics, and after serving in various posts in the city administration, Khatisian became mayor of Tbilisi, serving from 1909 to 1917. In his political beliefs, he was aligned with the Russian Constitutional Democrats (Kadets), and only in 1917 joined the **Armenian Revolutionary Federation** (ARF).

From 1915 to 1917, Khatisian was President of the Armenian National Council that guided Armenian political life in the Caucasus during World War I. In 1917 he moved to Alexandropol (**Gyumri**), in **Yerevan** province, where he was elected city mayor. The breakup of the Russian Empire thrust Khatisian, who by then had gained renown as a skillful politician, into the center of national politics. During the very short-lived Democratic Federative Republic of Transcaucasia, declared independent on April 22, 1918, he was named minister of finance. He had earlier participated in the Transcaucasian delegation that negotiated in Trebizond for an end of the war with the Ottomans after the Bolsheviks pulled Russia out of the conflict by signing the Treaty of Brest-Litovsk. Submitting to all Ottoman demands, the delegation signed the Treaty of Batumi on June 4, by which time the Transcaucasian Federation had broken up into Georgia, Armenia, and Azerbaijan.

Khatisian served in the Armenian government for almost the entire period of the existence of the independent Republic of Armenia. He was minister of foreign affairs in the first Armenian cabinet and traveled to Istanbul with **Avetis Aharonian** to reach final settlement with the Ottomans on the status and the borders of Armenia. Khatisian also served briefly as minister of welfare, minister of the interior, and acting prime minister. After national elections were held in Armenia in June 1919, and the ARF swept the majority of seats in parliament, Khatisian was called upon in August to form a new cabinet wherein he held the twin portfolio of prime minister and minister of foreign affairs. He served through May 1920. Khatisian's final service to the independent republic was as chief negotiator with the Nationalist Turks who, by imposing the Treaty of Alexandropol, as Soviet troops occupied Armenia, sealed the fate of the republic in late November 1920. Khatisian spent his remaining years in Paris, France, where he wrote his memoirs, one of the main sources on the history of the era, *Hayastani Hanrapetutian Dsagumn u Zargatsume* (The Origin and Development of the Republic of Armenia). *See also* AGHBALIAN, NIKOL; KACHAZNUNI; HOVHANNES; VRATZIAN, SIMON.

KHRIMIAN, MKRTICH (KHRIMIAN HAYRIK). *See* MKRTICH KHRIMIAN.

KOCHARIAN, ROBERT (1954–). President of **Nagorno Karabagh** and **president** of Armenia. Born in **Stepanakert**, the capital of the Nagorno Karabagh Autonomous Oblast (NKAO) in Soviet Azerbaijan, Kocharian attended local schools. Upon graduating from high school he was drafted into the Soviet army and served for two years. He studied engineering at the **Yerevan** State Polytechnic Institute in Armenia completing his degree in 1982. He returned to Stepanakert and worked in engineering and public administration until 1988.

In 1988 he was instrumental in establishing the Karabagh Committee in Stepanakert that took up the banner of the reform programs of glasnost and perestroika announced by Soviet President Mikhail Gorbachev. The committee mobilized an indigenous popular movement calling for unification with Soviet Armenia. Begun as a petition drive in Stepanakert, the movement spread rapidly and galvanized the masses in Armenia who demonstrated by the tens of thousands in support of their ethnic kin in NKAO.

With the breakup of the Soviet Union, NKAO seceded from Azerbaijan and declared itself an independent republic on January 6, 1992. Tensions between the Nagorno Karabagh Republic (NKR) and the Azeri government led to a virtual state of war in and around Karabagh necessitating the formation of a State Defense Committee in Stepanakert. Already a political activist for more than four years and a leader in organizing for the defense of the Armenian population, which since 1991 had been subjected to a policy of deportation from their native villagers by Soviet interior ministry troops and Azeri armed forces, Kocharian was elected chairman of the defense committee. Entrusted with the leadership of the new country and empowered to organize an army for its protection under conditions amounting to low intensity warfare, Kocharian and the State Defense Committee created a force that reversed the military gains of the forces under the command of the Azeri government. On May 14, 1994, a cease-fire declared by the parties to the conflict brought open hostilities to an end.

With a cease-fire in place, Karabagh Armenians returned to building their ravaged country. On December 22, 1994, parliament appointed Robert Kocharian the first president of the Nagorno Karabagh Republic. With the State Defense Committee dissolved and the state of emergency ended, a cabinet was appointed with Leonard Petrosian as prime minister. On April 30, 1995, the people of Karabagh elected a 33-seat parliament, chaired by Oleg Yesayan, thereby completing the formation of a civilian government.

The end of the fighting cast Kocharian in a new role as the principal negotiator for a settlement. Along with Foreign Minister **Arkady Ghukasian**, Kocharian pressed at international meetings convened to discuss a resolution of the Karabagh conflict for recognition of his country and for a secure peace for the Armenians of Karabagh. The absence of any formal agreements providing assurances that the cease-fire would not be violated by Azerbaijan required the government to keep Karabagh under martial law and its male population up to the age of 45 conscripted into the army, while at the same time repairing its heavily damaged infrastructure and restoring its economy. In a surprise announcement intended to restore credibility to his tarnished administration after the contested 1996 presidential elections, **Levon Ter-Petrossian** appointed Kocharian **prime minister** of Armenia in March 1997. Just months earlier, on November 24, 1996, in the first presidential **elections**, Kocharian had been reconfirmed president of NKR by popular vote. A year later he was president of Armenia, having won a special election in March 1998 upon Ter-Petrossian's resignation under pressure from his own cabinet. While he focused on economic issues as prime minister, as president Kocharian charted a new course in Armenia's foreign policy. He assumed direct responsibility for negotiating a settlement of the Karabagh conflict personally meeting with Azeri President Heidar Aliyev in the search for a compromise resolution. He also pursued policies openly critical of Turkey while embracing closer relations with the Armenian diaspora in an effort to draw investment and broader support for his administration. His role was measurably constrained after the 1999 parliamentary elections that raised **Vazgen Sargsian** and **Karen Demirchian** to the premiership and the chairmanship of the National Assembly respectively with a significant popular mandate. The October 27, 1999, assassination of both political rivals placed Kocharian again at center stage when he personally took charge of defusing the ensuing crisis, but the consequences of the loss of the critical figures of the country's leadership created much uncertainty about his capacity to govern effectively in an environment increasingly defined by strong factional interests. Despite the heightened tensions and rampant suspicions, Kocharian emerged again as a stabilizing factor in Armenia's domestic politics, and as a determined negotiator on the international scene seeking a permanent resolution of differences with Armenia's hostile neighbors. Picking up where his predecessor left off, he resumed meetings with heads of states, including Heidar Aliyev of Azerbaijan, in search of a regional solution. *See also* ARMENIAN NATIONAL MOVEMENT.

KOCHARIAN, ROBERT CABINET. Appointed by **President Levon Ter-Petrossian** on March 20, 1997, the Kocharian cabinet served until April 8, 1998, with Robert Kocharian holding office as acting president from February 3, 1998, when Ter-Petrossian resigned the presidency.

Prime Minister	**Robert Kocharian**
Agriculture	Vladimir Movsisian
Communication	Grigor Poghpatian
Culture, Youth Affairs and Sports	Armen Smbatian
Defense	**Vazgen Sargsian**
Economy and Finance	**Armen Darbinian**
Education and Science	Artashes Petrosian
Energy	Gagik Martirosian
Environmental Protection	Sargis Shahazizian
Foreign Affairs	Alexander Arzoumanian
Health	Gagik Stambuldian
Industry and Trade	Garnik Nanagoulian
Internal Affairs and National Security	Serge Sargsian
Justice	Marat Alexanian
Social Security, Employment, Immigration and Refugee Affairs	Hranush Hakobian
Transportation	Henrik Kochinian
Urban Planning	Felix Pirumian

Arriving from **Stepanakert** without a popular mandate in Armenia other than his stature as president of the **Nagorno Karabagh** Republic (NKR) and the Armenian president's backing, Kocharian made few personnel changes to the short-lived cabinet of Prime Minister **Armen Sarkissian**, assuring continuity while introducing a new style of leadership. With the hope of turning around the economy, which registered modest improvements, he combined the ministries of economy and finance under Armen Darbinian, a market reformer. He also combined the ministries of trade and industry under Garnik Nanagoulian, to augment the role of the department in the privatization process of larger enterprises.

The Kocharian cabinet seriously split with President Ter-Petrossian over the solution to the Karabagh stalemate proposed by the Organization for Security and Cooperation in Europe (OSCE) in October 1996, which called for a step-by-step resolution of the issues separating the two sides. As the president promoted this graduated solution based on a land for peace formula, Kocharian, other ministers, and the NKR government became increasingly concerned with the apparent lack of security guarantees in the first steps of the proposed solution that included the return of occupied buffer territories. By January 1998 the prime minister openly rejected the plan when the defense and national security ministers joined him in a move that divided the cabinet. As the rift spread to parliament, and political factions previously aligned with the government moved to the opposition, the influence of the **Armenian National Movement** (ANM) as a political force completely crumbled. The evident absence of confidence in the foreign policy of the country made the president's position untenable. Anticipating Ter-Petrossian's fall from power as the major power brokers withdrew their support, between February 1 and February 4, 1998, Foreign Minister Alexander Arzoumanian, Yerevan mayor Vano Siradeghian, Central Bank Chairman Bagrat Asatrian, Chairman of Parliament Babken Ararktsian, and Deputy Chairman Ara Sahakian, the top brass of the ANM, tendered their resignations, opening the way for Kocharian to make key new appointments. Deputy Foreign Minister Vartan Oskanian was quickly promoted. Suren Abrahamian, a Vazgen Sargsian protégé at the defense ministry with the rank of general, was sworn in as the mayor of **Yerevan**. **Khosrov Harutiunian**, formerly with the ANM, but of late outside its inner circle, was voted by the National Assembly as its new chairman. When Kocharian won the March 30,1998, special presidential election, the shaping of a new government was already in process for nearly two months. *See also* SARGSIAN, VAZGEN CABINET.

KOMITAS (1869–1935). Composer and ethnomusicologist. Komitas, given name Soghomon Soghomonian, was born in the town of Kutahia in central Anatolia. Orphaned at the age of 11, he was placed at the **Edjmiadsin** seminary in 1881 to receive training because of his native musical talents. Upon completion of his education in 1893, he was appointed choirmaster in the cathedral church of Edjmiadsin. Joining the clergy, Soghomon was ordained a celibate priest, and was known thereafter as Komitas *Vardapet*. Komitas continued his musical education in Berlin from 1896 to 1899 where he studied composition and conducting. In Europe he was befriended by a circle of German and French musicologists who became exposed to Armenian folk music through Komitas.

Though he composed works for the piano, the string quartet, and *a capella* church music, Komitas's principal contribution to Armenian music, and music in general, came from his lifelong devotion to collecting and transcribing Armenian folksongs. He was the first person to do so, and he gathered more than three thousand songs. Seeking to bring appreciation of Armenian music to a wider audience, in 1910 Komitas settled in Istanbul. There he trained a group of students in Armenian melody, and formed a choir that toured the Armenian communities and gave performances of the folk compositions that Komitas had arranged for four-part choir. Besides collecting popular songs, Komitas developed the scholarship that identified the ethnomusical characteristics specific to Armenian folk composition. Thereby, he also identified features of the music of other peoples in the region. Komitas presented his findings at European ethnomusicological symposia. He won recognition as the principal author of Armenian national composition, which also earned him membership in the International Musical Society.

Komitas gathered Armenia's musical heritage in the nick of time. He was among the two hundred prominent figures of the Armenian community of Istanbul arrested on the night of April 24, 1915, which marked the beginning of the deportations and massacres of the Armenians in the Ottoman Empire. Spared execution, Komitas was rescued through the appeals of the International Musical Society. Witness to the decimation of the people through whose towns and villages he had wandered over the years recording their music, by the time he was returned to Istanbul, Komitas' mind had become unhinged. He was taken to Paris in 1919 and spent the rest of his life in a sanitarium. In 1937 his remains were buried in Armenia.

– L –

LAKE SEVAN. Largest lake in the Republic of Armenia. Lake Sevan, or *Geghama Dsov* of the medieval Armenians, is the smallest of the three large lakes of historic Armenia (**Van**, Sevan, and Urmia). With a surface area of approximately 1,400 square kilometers, it covers nearly 5 percent of the superficies of the republic. The lake nearly fills a large triangular basin in Eastern Armenia formed by the Gegham range on the west, the Vardenis range to the south, and the

Sevan Range that continues into the Arguni and Pambak ranges running southeast to northwest. Two facing peninsulas divide the lake into two basins, with the smaller part in the north being the deeper half at 98 meters. The lake is 75 kilometers (45 miles) long and 37 kilometers (23 miles) wide. At an elevation of 1,914 meters (6,280 feet), the lake holds 39,000 million cubic meters of water, making it both a critical source of fresh water for irrigation and hydropower generation in Armenia. Lake Sevan is fed by 28 streams from the surrounding mountains and is drained by a single river, the Hrazdan (Zangi) that empties into the **Arax River** soon after passing through a final gorge in the middle of **Yerevan**. Because its inflow exceeded the outflow, the level of the lake was steadily rising until the 20th century.

Six hydroelectric stations were built between 1930 and 1962 at the points where the Hrazdan cascaded from its embouchure down to Yerevan, and the outflow was increased to meet the growing demand for electrical power. As a result the level of the lake has dropped by more than 18 meters, exposing some of the earliest human habitations in the Armenian highlands. Neolithic settlements dating as far back as the third millennium B.C. have yielded valuable archeological information. The rocky island in the lake that once stood 63 meters above the surface is now attached to the shore by a peninsula. Used as a refuge by the princes of Siunik, the island was embellished as a center of Armenian religious life when Princess Mariam, daughter of King **Ashot I Bagratuni** (884–890), and wife of the **Siuni** prince Vasak Gabur, commissioned the building of two churches in 874. The Sevan basin is dotted by small towns mostly engaged in agriculture and mining. Fishing, however, remains a major industry. While many species of fresh water fish are found in the lake, the most favored is the trout known as *ishkhan* (prince), which is noted for its fine flavor.

LAKE VAN. Largest lake is historic Armenia. The basin of Lake Van was the cradle of Armenian civilization. Towns and cities ringed the lake. The city of **Van**, near its eastern shore, was the first great urban settlement in Armenia dating back to the ninth century B.C. By the early Middle Ages, Berkri, Arjesh, Khlat, along with many smaller towns, lined its northern shore, and Datvan stood at the westernmost point of the lake.

Lake Van is 125 kilometers (80 miles) long and 51 kilometers (31 miles) wide and 145 meters (475 feet) deep. At an altitude of 1,700 meters (5,400 feet), it covers an area 3,760 square kilometers (1,450 sq. miles), making it nearly 2.5 times the size of **Lake Sevan**. Its alkaline water makes it unsuitable for irrigation. The lake sits at the bottom of a vast basin, surrounded by mountains with the Anti-Taurus Range to its south, and fed by multiple streams. Without an outlet, the level of the lake has steadily risen over the centuries, and of the seven islands known to the Armenians, only four remain, Lim, Arter, Ktuts, and **Aghtamar**, each of which held monastic retreats, with the last being famous as the royal residence of the **Ardsruni** dynasty.

The kingdom of Vaspurakan, as well as the ancient province of the same name, encompassed most of the basin, while the province of Taron, once ruled by the **Mamikonian** and then the **Bagratuni**, lay to the west. The Van basin was one of the most densely populated regions of the Armenian plateau. The abundance of Urartian and Armenian monuments attest to the wealth of the region. There is also a greater concentration of Islamic monuments in the area than anywhere else in historic Armenia. The Arabs established a number of emirates along the northern bank of the lake in the ninth century. Although the Arabs eventually withdrew from Armenia, Turkic and Kurdish chiefs established new principalities in the Van basin after the 11th century. During the period of Ottoman rule after 1514, Kurdish tribes penetrated the region and began to settle all around the lake. The conflict between Armenian farmers and Kurdish tribesmen became endemic and the cause of much violence, most frequently to the detriment of the agriculturist. Despite the gradual change in the ethnic composition of the region, in the early 20th century the Van basin still had the highest concentration of Armenians of the six so-called Armenian provinces of the Ottoman Empire. When in April 1915 the Young Turk regime began implementing the **Armenian Genocide**, the Van region witnessed some of the largest-scale massacres of Armenians. With the exception of those in the city of Van, the rest of the population was annihilated. Lake Van is now in southeastern Turkey and the majority of the people living around it are Kurds.

LEVON I (LEO I) (1199–1219). King of Cilician Armenia and founder of the **Rubenian** royal family. Prince Levon's patient and persistent policy of collaboration with the Crusaders was rewarded when Frederick Barbarossa's son, the Holy Roman Emperor Henry VI, gave his consent and directed his emissary to preside at the coronation of the Rubenian baron as the sovereign of the Armenians. In 1199 in the cathedral of Tarsus, in the presence of the great Armenian lords of Cilicia, dignitaries of the various eastern churches, representatives of the Crusader states, the papal legate Conrad, Archbishop of Mainz, and the Imperial chancellor, Conrad of Hildesheim, the Armenian **catholicos** Grigor VI Abirad anointed Levon king of Armenia. The Rubenians, who, in a period of political instability and ethnic migration had forged a state, and having raised themselves to the rank of royalty at a time coinciding with the reign of some of the greatest kings of medieval Europe, had restored sovereignty to the Armenians. The Byzantine emperor, Alexios III Angelos (1195–1203), too recognized the independence of this new Armenia by sending a crown of his own to Levon.

By creating this monarchy, now Levon I, who reigned as king from 1199 until 1219, brought his people into a new Mediterranean community linked by commerce and a shared ruling class. The Venetians and Genoese plied the sealanes with their ships that anchored at Ayas (Lajazzo), the main entrepot of Cilicia for the overland trade to the East, the very same seaport where Marco Polo started his journey to China. Armenians, Greeks, and Latins uneasily discussed ecclesiastical communion. As for Levon, to further bind his dynasty with European royalty, he took as his second wife, Sibyl de Lusignan, daughter of Aimery, King of Cyprus, to whose brother, Guy de Lusignan, the last king of Jerusalem, Richard the Lionhearted had ceded the island. From this marriage was born Levon's successor, his daughter Zabel/Isabel, who reigned from 1219 to 1252. Lastly, he brought organization to his kingdom in a pattern closely imitative of western European feudal monarchy. Readapting Armenian **nakharar** customs, he restructured the conventional and theoretical equality among the Armenian chieftains into a more graded system as practiced by the Crusader states. Western political terminology and practices were absorbed, and the plethora of exchanges, encounters, and intermarriages engendered a cultural revival and a cosmopolitan outlook among the elite and merchant classes.

Levon I hoped to bring the Crusader principality of Antioch under his dominion also. The contest proved as fruitless as it was protracted. He had greater success in bringing under his wing all the Armenian lords of Cilicia, including the **Hetumians**. As a matter of fact the Hetumians played a critical role in negotiating the elevation of Levon to kingship. Their internal support was important. Their role in conducting the external affairs of Levon's principality as the leading Armenians of the era maneuvered to secure his nomination to royalty was no less valuable. Just as importantly, the Hetumians defended Zabel's succession to the throne, the singular instance in the history of the Armenians when the transfer of political legitimacy was permitted through an heiress, interestingly enough soon after another woman famously reigned in the Caucasus, Queen Tamar (1184–1212) of the Georgian **Bagratuni** dynasty.

Levon I's 33-year reign, first as prince from 1186 to 1199 and then as king, culminated in the legitimation of a new Armenian state. The success of his policies secured Cilicia as a new homeland for the Armenians and as a viable political and economic enterprise. It also transformed an originally Caucasian population into a Mediterranean people whose outlook and interests became closely linked to the West. *See also* HETUM I.

LORIS-MELIKOV, MIKAYEL (1825–1888). Russian general and minister of the interior. Loris-Melikov was born in Tbilisi to an Armenian merchant family of noble lineage. He received his early education at the Lazarian Institute in Moscow. He continued his education at the Guards Cadet Institute in St. Petersburg. Upon graduation he joined a Hussar regiment and in 1847 was stationed in the Caucasus where he partook in the campaigns against Shamil. The writer Leo Tolstoy, who as a young man at the time also tasted battle against the Caucasian tribes, included a fictionalized portrait of the dashing Loris-Melikov in his short story *Hadji Murat*. By 1851 he had risen to the rank of captain and aide-de-camp to Prince Michael Vorontsov, the viceroy of the Caucasus. During the Crimean War (1853–1856), he distinguished himself as a cavalry officer under the command of General Muraviev during the siege of Kars. He was appointed commandant of the fortress upon its surrender. While in the Caucasus Loris-Melikov married Princess Nina Argutinsky-Dolgorukov, whose family also carried Armenian noble lineage and was related to Georgian royalty.

In 1865 Loris-Melikov was promoted to the rank of adjutant general and aide-de-camp to the emperor, as well as ataman of the Cossacks of the Terek, in which capacity he governed in Daghestan. After a decade of service in this capacity working to bring the region under civilian rule, he retired from active duty with the rank of general of the cavalry. As Russia prepared for war against Turkey in 1876, Loris-Melikov was recalled and given charge of preparations in the Caucasus. Under the overall command of the front by Grand Duke Michael, Loris-Melikov led the charge against Ardahan, which he captured in May 1877. Repulsed by Mukhtar Pasha, the Ottoman commander, Loris-Melikov regrouped the Russian forces and resumed the offensive in August. On November 19, 1877, his troops entered Kars and pursued the Ottomans to Erzerum. The 1856 Treaty of Paris that had ended the Crimean War had returned the city of Kars to Ottoman rule. By the 1878 Treaty of Berlin, Kars was now annexed to the Russian Empire. In recognition of his military triumphs, in April 1878 Loris-Melikov was given the title of count.

Thrust upon the national stage, Count Loris-Melikov soon emerged as one of the great statesmen to serve Tsar Alexander II in his reform efforts. When plague broke out on the lower Volga River in January 1879, Loris-Melikov was appointed temporary governor of the provinces of Astrakhan, Saratov, and Samara. In three months he had the epidemic contained. When martial law was declared after an attempt on the life of the tsar in April 1879, Loris-Melikov was appointed governor-general of Kharkov, whose previous governor had fallen victim to an act of revolutionary terrorism. His competent administration of the province quickly restored civil order, won public confidence for the government, and even stimulated the economy to the cheers of the merchant class. His success in combating revolutionary anarchism and popular nihilism through legal remedies did not go unnoticed either by the state or the revolutionaries who feared his ability to win over the liberals.

On February 17, 1880, a workman blew up the Imperial dining room in the Winter Palace. The tsar once again escaped death, but the absence of popular sympathy in the face of the dauntless terrorism of the group calling itself "Will of the People" persuaded him that the moment required the restoration of public confidence in the government. On February 27 Alexander II issued an edict establishing the Supreme Executive Commission for the Preservation of National Order and Public Tranquility and named Count Loris-Melikov chief of the commission with unconditional powers. While suppressing terrorism, Loris-Melikov quickly set about reforming the imperial administration. He abolished the Third Department of His Majesty's Own Chancery, the secret police, and placed the police under the direct control of the minister of the interior. He also replaced the reactionary minister of education and minister of finance with more liberal-minded candidates. He gave the press more freedom, resorted to legal measures to contain revolutionary activity, and proposed introducing economic reforms to strike at the root cause of the social unrest besetting Russia. In a gesture that gained him even greater popularity, in August 1880 Loris-Melikov proposed to the emperor disbanding the commission as a signal of the end of the emergency. Thereupon the emperor appointed him minister of the interior charged with the responsibility of drawing up a new set of reforms for the country.

In February 1881 Loris-Melikov presented Alexander II his reform project that proposed expanding representation in the Council of State from the *zemtsvos*, the local governing councils, and forming commissions to reorganize the administration and the national finances. Alexander II signed the reform manifesto on March 13. That same day he was killed by a terrorist bomb. The assassination delayed the promulgation of the reforms until the new tsar, Alexander III decided on a course of action. On May 11, 1881, he issued his own manifesto proclaiming the virtues of autocracy and calling an end to the reforms. It marked the beginning of the decades of reaction and counter-reforms that set Russia irreversibly on the course of revolution. Loris-Melikov was relieved of his post as minister of the interior. He was permitted to retain his place as a member of the Council of State, but chose to depart from St. Petersburg, first returning to his homeland and subsequently moving to Nice for health reasons. He died in France. His remains were interred in the Armenian monastery of St. Stephen in Tbilisi. *See also* ARGHUTIANTS, HOVSEP.

– M –

MAMIKONIAN. Princely family in early medieval Armenia. Of all the great aristocratic families associated with the **Arshakuni** dynasty, none excelled the Mamikonian in its importance to the Armenian state. As holders of the hereditary office of *sparapet*, or grand marshal, of the **Armenian kingdom**, the Mamikonian lords occupied the top echelon of the military hierarchy that buttressed the monarchy. Their rank in the **nakharar system** placed them at the apex of Armenian feudal society, second only to the kings, and when the monarchy was abolished, they became contenders for the governorship of Armenia. As commanders-in-chief of the Armenian military, in time of war they were responsible for organizing the defense of the country, marshaling its forces, and leading into battle the full contingent of troops, cavalry and infantry, supplied by the great houses of Armenia. Under such circumstances the scope of their command was virtually comprehensive, and the other great lords of the land made their appearance at the head of the contingent their families were obligated to supply and placed themselves at the disposal of the sparapet. It was in times of crises especially, therefore, that the Mamikonians exercised their greatest influence. As the Armenian state was buffeted from all quarters and the monarchy increasingly ceded its authority in the face of unyielding imperial powers, particularly the Sasanid Iranians, the Mamikonians began to displace the Arshakuni in the importance and influence wielded by their respective institutions. As regents during the late Arshakuni period, Mushegh Mamikonian and Manuel Mamikonian were rulers in Armenia in all but name.

Like that of many other great landowning families, the origins of the Mamikonians may be traced as far back as the time of King **Tigran II the Great**, during whose reign the indigenous nobility was given a more formalized organization. The domicile of the Mamikonians was the northern province of Tayk in the borderland between Armenia and Iberia, modern-day Georgia, where their fearless martial customs were honed. Their rise to prominence was directly linked to the expansion of their territorial holdings and they were rewarded for their service with ownership of the large province of Taron in southwestern Armenia, of which they had gained possession by the fourth century. From their lands the Mamikonian raised a cavalry force of 3,000 knights, fully armed, trained for warfare, and ready for service. Their capacity to deliver such a significant force made the Mamikonians among the major figures of the Armenian domestic political scene. As the warlords of Armenia, they also exercised preponderant influence in the foreign policy of the country and therefore played a critical role in the external affairs of the state.

The Mamikonians matched their might with skill, audacity, and near reckless bravery. The family probably exercised its moment of greatest power and influence in the fifth century. The abolition of the Armenian monarchy placed them in a position of peculiar advantage, and exceptional risk too. By 439 Hamazasp Mamikonian emerged as the greatest territorial prince in Armenia by his marriage to Sahakanuysh, daughter of **Catholicos** Sahak, when the latter's death made the Mamikonian family owners of vast properties previously in the possession of the house of **Grigor Lusavorich**. More importantly, Hamazasp's and Sahakanyush's offspring, Vardan, thereby became heir to the two most important feudal and ecclesiastical houses of Armenia. His defiance of Yazdegerd II and the Sasanid king's policy of imposing Mazdaism on Armenia made him the leader around whom rallied the forces of resistance. His ardent defense of Armenia's choice of religion inspired popular courage in the face of an imperial army, and his death in 451 in the Battle of Avarayr was recounted as the act of supreme valor and of martyrdom in the name of religious freedom. The legend of *Kachn Vardan*, Vardan the Brave, was created by the most articulate of medieval Armenian narrators. The historian Yeghishe's *Vasn Vardana yev Hayots Paterazmi* (About Vardan and the War of the Armenians) survived as the unsurpassed panegyric written in the Armenian language in which compelling imagery and a style of eloquent laudation made of it a textbook for the depiction of unrivaled heroism. Of all the warriors who laid down their lives throughout the centuries of ceaseless struggle, Vardan Mamikonian continues to command unparalleled respect in the imagination of the Armenian people.

The Sasanids eventually relented and the Armenians were permitted the practice of Christianity. Vardan's nephew, Vahan Mamikonian, with whom the Iranians reached agreement to honor both the Armenian political system as represented by the nakharars and the **Armenian Apostolic Church**, was bestowed the Mazpanate of Armenia in 485. Thus the Mamikonians secured Armenia's internal autonomy within the Persian Empire, and the Sasanids even conceded the post of *marzpan*, or governor-general, to leading Armenian princes. Because of their strong anti-Iranian policies, the Mamikonians also enjoyed Byzantine patronage, and the title of Prince of Armenia was variously bestowed on the dynasty's leading representatives.

The Mamikonian house survived into the Arab period when again it raised the banner of revolt. The reverses suffered in the second half of the eighth century, however, thoroughly undermined its position. The Abbasids imposed Arab rule with a vengeance after Grigor Mamikonian sought to restore Armenia's autonomy by taking advantage of the internecine struggle for the succession to the Umayyads, the first Arab dynasty. The rebellion of the 770s led by Mushegh and Samuel Mamikonian was a worse disaster. The Arabs patronized other nakharar houses, mainly the **Bagratuni**, to compete with the Mamikonians and further isolated Armenia by colonizing the regions toward Byzantium. The Mamikonian domains of Tayk and Taron eventually passed to the Bagratuni and the *sparapetutiun*, the office of the grand marshal, slipped from their hands in the absence of royal and imperial patronage. The vigor of their actions, so long associated in Armenia with fervent patriotism, made the Mamikonians inflexible and less adept at coping with the more complicated politics of the Muslim Arabs. Junior branches of the Mamikonian house survived in the region of Sasun in southern Armenia, and members of the family distinguished themselves in the service of Byzantium. By the end of the eighth century, however, Mamikonian power and prestige was completely eroded and their position at the national level displaced by other great nakharar houses such as the **Ardsruni** and Bagratuni. *See also* SIUNI.

MAMOULIAN, ROUBEN (1897–1987). Hollywood movie director. Mamoulian was born in Tbilisi, Georgia, but spent part of his youth in Paris. He finished high school in Tbilisi and went to the University of Moscow to study law. He inherited his interest in the arts from his mother, who was a successful stage actress in the Armenian Theater of Tbilisi. He joined the so-called Students Drama Studio of the Moscow Art Theater where he learned the Stanislavski method of acting and staging under the direction of his Vladikavkas-born Armenian compatriot Evgeni Vakhtangov (1883–1922), for whom the studio was later renamed after becoming a major training ground for Russian actors.

Mamoulian began his professional career in the dramatic arts as a director in London in 1922. He was soon, however, in the United States where he was hired to direct George Eastman's American Opera Company in Rochester, New York. In 1927 he directed his first production in New York City where he staged *Porgy* for the Theater Guild. The two-and-a-half-year run of the play established Mamoulian as a successful stage director.

In 1929 Mamoulian made his film directing debut with *Applause*, which was shot for Paramount in the Astoria Studios in Long Island City, starring Helen Morgan, the famed star of the musical *Show Boat*. The artistic and commercial success of the film brought him to Hollywood, where, from 1930 to 1957, he made 16 movies, featuring many of the major Hollywood screen actors who achieved stardom through his movies. His best known films included: *City Streets* (1931), the Academy-winning *Dr. Jekyll and Mr. Hyde* (1931) starring Spencer Tracy; *Love Me Tonight* (1932), starring the American soprano Jeanette McDonald and the French singer Maurice Chevalier, that told a story in a modern setting based on an Armenian folktale Mamoulian had heard from his grandmother; *Queen Christina* (1933), starring Greta Garbo, that also included an appearance by the Baku-born Armenian thespian Akim Tamiroff (Hovakim Tamirian) (1899–1972) who enjoyed a long career in Hollywood as a character actor; *Becky Sharp* (1935); *The Gay Desperado* (1936); *Blood and Sand* (1941), starring Tyrone Power and Rita Hayworth; and the two musicals *Summer Holiday* (1948) and *Silk Stockings* (1957).

Mamoulian's films were noted for their cinematic innovations that earned him a place of honor among the new medium's early pioneers. Embarking on his screen directing career soon after sound was introduced, Mamoulian introduced many new technical changes that opened film-making to the possibilities of improved dramatization, which earlier camera use had not allowed because taping sound synchronized with film action initially required making the camera stationary. With *Applause* Mamoulian got the cameras moving again allowing it to pan freely, thereby restoring film as primarily a visual medium capable of capturing dynamic action. He also demonstrated that separately registered sound effects recorded in background or foreground could be mixed later into a single sound track to great effect in *City Streets*. The free movement of the camera in order to film long shots and especially close-ups were put to greatest effect in the closing scene of *Queen Christina* culminating with the clasp on the Garbo profile that helped establish the lasting mystique of the Swedish actress. Possibly Mamoulian's most significant contribution to movie-making came with *Becky Sharp*, the first full-length feature filmed in Technicolor. Mamoulian's highly stylized films, notable for their rhythm, movement, and sensuous color, betrayed his love of the theater. His cinematic directing continually sought to integrate dialogue and action, song, dance and music, and even the dramatic use of color all resulting in his distinctly sophisticated and elegant presentations.

True to his art, Mamoulian returned to New York where he directed in the 1930s and 1940s five hits in a row for the Broadway stage, including such famous American musicals as George Gershwin's *Porgy and Bess* (1935) and Richard Rodgers and Oscar Hammerstein's *Oklahoma!* (1943) and *Carousel* (1945), thus also earning himself a very important place in the history of the American musical theater. Mamoulian continued to direct stage productions until 1966.

MANOOGIAN, ALEX (1901–1996). American industrialist. Alex Manoogian was born in Izmir and immigrated to the United States in 1920. He became a machinist in Detroit where he had moved in 1924 and where in 1929, with two other partners, he founded Masco Screw Products Company, which supplied parts to automobile manufacturers. While the Depression meant that the company would grow slowly, nevertheless by 1936 Masco had gone public on the Detroit Stock Exchange. The real growth phase of the company came after 1954 when Manoogian acquired the right to manufacture the single handle faucet. Upon the improvement of the original device, annual sales of the new faucet exceeded $1,000,000, and Masco was on its way to becoming a major American corporation. In 1972 Manoogian handed management of the company over to his son. Richard Manoogian built the Masco Corporation into a conglomerate of over 30 companies with revenues passing the billion-dollar mark, companies involved in the manufacture of plumbing equipment, power transmission shafts, oil drilling tools, and other related products in over one hundred facilities with 12,000 employees.

Beyond his imprint as a Detroit industrialist, over the decades Manoogian emerged as the leading philanthropist in the Armenian **diaspora**. In 1953 he was elected president of the **Armenian General Benevolent Union** (AGBU). At the time the AGBU had an endowment of $7,000,000, which over the course of his 30 years of leadership was increased tenfold, with outlays for a variety of educational, cultural, and philanthropic purposes of over $10,000,000. In 1954 he established the Alex and Marie Manoogian Foundation and in 1968 he founded the Alex Manoogian Cultural Fund. His name also appears on institutions across the Armenian diaspora. Alex Manoogian Cultural Centers were built in Paris, Buenos Aires, Toronto, Montevideo, Sydney, Beirut, Sao Paulo, and Montreal. He subsidized the construction of Armenian schools in many countries and those bearing his name are found in Detroit, Montreal, and Montevideo, while those bearing his wife's name, Marie Manoogian, are in Tehran, Buenos Aires, and Los Angeles. He contributed funds for the construction of churches and community halls and established an old age home in Michigan in his parents' name. He has also extended large-scale assistance to Armenia beginning with the construction of the so-called Manoogian Treasury to house the priceless collection of Armenian religious artifacts, manuscripts, and paintings of the Holy See of Armenia at **Edjmiadsin**. *See also* BOGHOS NUBAR PASHA.

MANUKIAN, ARAM (1879–1919). Political and military leader. Manukian, given name Sergei Hovhanessian, was born in the village of Zeiva near Ghapan in the southern district of Zangezur in Russian Armenia. He received his education in Shushi and **Yerevan** and from a young age joined the **Armenian Revolutionary Federation** (ARF). In 1901 he was in Baku organizing Armenian workers and in 1903 was in Elizavetpol organizing Armenian self-defense units at the outbreak of the Armeno-Tatar War. In 1904 he traveled to **Van** in the Ottoman Empire and taught at a school in Ordu on the Black Sea coast after the restoration of the Ottoman Constitution in 1908. He returned to Van in late 1912 and was there in April 1915 to organize the defense of Armenian neighborhoods of the city during its month-long siege by the Ottoman forces after they had been defeated on the Russian front. Upon the arrival of the Russian army in May, Manukian was appointed governor of the region. While Russian units continued to advance along the southern shore of **Lake Van**, Manukian attended to the administration of the area. A counteroffensive by the Ottoman army, however, forced a Russian retreat. The Armenians of Van were ordered to evacuate and abandon the city on July 31.

Manukian was in Tbilisi during the war until the Armenian National Council delegated him the responsibility of organizing the local defense and administration of Yerevan in January 1918. With the advance of the Ottoman forces into Transcaucasia as the Russian state broke apart and its army withered in the aftermath of the Bolshevik Revolution, the crisis in the region deepened and conflict between Armenians and Muslims throughout the province intensified. Recognizing the need for unity and discipline, Armenian military and civil leaders proclaimed "Aram Pasha," as Manukian had become popularly known, "Dictator of Yerevan." Selecting directors for internal affairs, provisions, finance, and defense, Aram Manukian assembled an exclusively Armenian administration for Yerevan, thereby creating the nucleus of an Armenian state in the area for the first time in many centuries. In the succeeding months, the Directorate extended its jurisdiction over much of the Plain of **Ararat** and exercised the prerogatives of a de facto government until the May 28, 1918, declaration of independence by the Armenian National Council in Tbilisi upon the breakup of the short-lived Transcaucasian Federative Republic. Aram remained at the head of the Directorate until July 19 when the Armenian cabinet formed in Tbilisi finally arrived in Yerevan. Manukian was appointed minister of internal affairs in the two cabinets organized by Premier-President **Hovhannes Kachaznuni** in 1918. In charge of law and order in a chaotic and tempestuous time, he advocated strong police measures to restrain banditry and centralized control in the effort to organize a government. Preventing the contagion of epidemic diseases spread by the teaming refugees was one responsibility in which Manukian's ministry was less effective. While medical personnel contained the outbreak of cholera by the end of 1918, the appearance of typhus added to the toll of death and suffering. Among its victims was Manukian himself who succumbed on January 26, 1919.

Along with **Andranik**, Aram was remembered as one of the figures who won popular fame during the trying years of World War I and the period of the independent Republic of Armenia. On August 23, 1990, when the parliament of the Armenian Soviet Socialist Republic (ASSR) adopted the decision to secede from the Soviet Union, in a highly symbolic gesture of reverence and historical recovery, members called upon one of the youngest delegates in the body, who happened to bear the name Aram Manukian, to read publicly for the first time to the assembled legislators the text of Armenia's new "Declaration on Independence." *See also* AHARONIAN, AVETIS.

MANUKIAN, VAZGEN (1946–). Political activist, **prime minister** of Armenia. Manukian was born in **Yerevan**, and received his higher education at Yerevan State University. He studied mechanical mathematics and pursued a degree at Lomonosov University in Moscow. While in Moscow he organized an Armenian cultural club. For demonstrating in front of the Turkish Embassy on April 24, 1966, in a commemorative protest of the **Armenian Genocide**, he was expelled from Moscow. He completed his doctorate in Novosybirsk, and began teaching at his alma mater in Yerevan.

Manukian also returned to political activism in Yerevan, and with like-minded academics he founded the Anania Shirakatsi Club. The group was named for the renowned Armenian scientist-mathematician of the Middle Ages. The club attracted members who later emerged as figures in the **Karabagh Movement**. Manukian's involvement in the Karabagh Movement came through his friendship with Igor Muradian, one of the earliest advocates of the unification of Karabagh and Armenia. In February 1988 Manukian became a member of the so-called Karabagh Committee that led popular rallies in Armenia to press the Soviet government, then under Mikhail Gorbachev, to respond to the appeals of the Armenians of **Nagorno Karabagh**. He was arrested on December 10, 1988, along with other members of the Karabagh Committee. Released in May 1989, he set out to organize the **Armenian National Movement** (ANM) by drafting the program of the ANM. When the ANM formally came into being in November 1989, Manukian was elected a member of its governing council and gained recognition as its principal strategist.

In May 1990 Manukian was elected to the parliament of the Armenian Soviet Socialist Republic (ASSR), which in August of the same year saw a peaceful transfer of power from the **Communist Party of Armenia** (CPA) to the ANM. At that time the Armenian parliament elected Manukian prime minister, thus placing him at the head of the first non-Communist government of Armenia while the country was still nominally part of the Soviet Union. In September 1991 Manukian resigned his post as the first free presidential elections were to be held in Armenia and a rival leading figure of the ANM, **Levon Ter-Petrossian**, won at the polls.

Manukian withdrew from the ANM and established the **National Democratic Union** (NDU) and the Center for Strategic Studies. He was elected chairman of the NDU, from which position he resigned when he was invited in August 1992 to join the Ter-Petrossian administration as state minister of defense and military industry. In a January 1993 cabinet reshuffle at the appointment of **Hrant Bagratian** as prime minister, Manukian was appointed to the Council of Ministers as acting minister of defense and served through August 1993. He returned to private life and teaching at Yerevan State University, while remaining active in the NDU, in the Armenian parliament, and the research center he founded. In the September 1996 presidential **elections** in Armenia, he emerged as the principal contender when a number of opposition parties unified behind his candidacy and presented a serious challenge to the incumbent **president** Levon Ter-Petrossian. Because of the questions surrounding the fairness of the elections, Manukian did not concede defeat and the heated challenge to the announced results precipitated mass demonstrations registering the first instance of serious public unrest in the newly independent republic. While Manukian continued to be regarded as a major political figure, popular support for his party dipped as a consequence of the post-election events, clearing the way for the rise of new figures of political consequence in Armenia. *See also* BAGRATIAN, HRANT FIRST CABINET; HAROUTIUNIAN, GAGIK CABINET.

MANUKIAN, VAZGEN CABINET. Appointed in August 1990 by the parliament of the Armenian Soviet Socialist Republic (ASSR), the Manukian cabinet served until November 1991.

Prime Minister	**Vazgen Manukian**
Automobile Transportation	Henrik Kochinian
Communal Industry	Robert Avoyan
Construction	Gagik Martirosian
Culture	Yuri Melik-Ohandjanian
Domestic Trade	Artak Davtian
Finance	Janik Janoyan
Food Industry	Robert Mehrabian
Foreign Trade Relations	Yesayi Stepanian
Foreign Affairs	Armen Yeghiazarian
Grain Products	Rafael Shahbazian
Higher and Special Education	Simeon Akhumian
Health	Artashes Aznavurian
Internal Affairs	Karlos Kazarian
Justice	Vahe Stepanian
Labor and Social Welfare	Ashot Yesayan
Light Industry	Robert Mkrtchian
Service and Water Supply	Yurik Javadian
Public Education	Misak Davtian
Road Construction and Maintenance	Georgi Melkumian

The Manukian cabinet represented a transitional government in the final year of Soviet rule. Installed in the wake of the 1990 elections to the Supreme Soviet that permitted the candidacy of non-Communists, the Manukian cabinet included a few **Armenian National Movement** (ANM) loyalists, but was still made up of Communist holdovers. Provisional in the true sense, the cabinet was not appointed to office altogether. In a period of divided loyalties in the administrative apparatus of the country, with the ANM ascendant in parliament, the cabinet oversaw the peaceful and gradual transition of executive authority to the democratic forces as political anarchy increasingly gripped other parts of the Soviet Union. Manukian managed affairs up to the September 21, 1991, referendum on independence, by which point his position on Armenia's foreign policy especially vis-à-vis the Karabagh question had come to differ from that of **Levon Ter-Petrossian**, then chairman of the Armenian parliament. With the first free presidential elections scheduled in less than a month (October 16, 1991) Manukian bowed out clearing the way for Ter-Petrossian, the ANM nominee, to win the elections and appoint a new cabinet serving at his discretion. *See also* COMMUNIST PARTY OF ARMENIA; HAROUTIUNIAN, GAGIK CABINET; NAGORNO KARABAGH.

MARGARIAN, ANDRANIK (1951–). Prime Minster of Armenia. Margarian was born in Yerevan. A computer engineer by profession, he graduated from the Technical Cybernetics Department of Yerevan Engineering Institute, and until 1990 was employed in various research institutes in the energy sector, as well as the Computer Center of the Ministry of Trade. A public figure in Armenia since then, Margarian's involvement in national politics predated the fall of Communism. Engaged in dissident activities since 1965, he joined the underground United National Party in Armenia in 1968 and was arrested and sentenced to two-years imprisonment in 1974. From 1992 Margarian served on the governing council of the **Republican Party of Armenia** (RPA) and was elected a deputy to the National Assembly in 1995. By January 1999 he had emerged as the president of the RPA council and kept his seat in the National Assembly in the May 1999 **elections**. By then his party's fortune had markedly improved with **Vazgen Sargsian**'s selection of the RPA as his vehicle to the premiership of Armenia, which also elevated Margarian to the leadership of the parliamentary faction *Miasnutiun* (Unity) forged in alliance with the **Populist Party of Armenia** (PPA) led by **Karen Demirchian**, forming a controlling majority of the legislature. The demise of Vazgen Sargsian, and Karen Demirchian, placed Margarian among the lead candidates for the prime ministry, to which he was appointed on May 12, 2000, by **President Robert Kocharian** to work with the legislature and overcome the profound alienation of the majority faction of the National Assembly upon the tragic loss of their effective leadership.

MARGARIAN, ANDRANIK CABINET. Appointed by **President Robert Kocharian** on May 20, 2000.

Prime Minister	Andranik Margarian
Agriculture	Zaven Gevorgian
Culture, Youth Affairs and Sports	Roland Sharoyan
Defense	Serge Sargsian
Education and Science	Edvard Ghazarian
Energy	Karen Galstian
Environmental Protection	Murat Muratian
Finance and Economy	Levon Barkhudarian
Foreign Affairs	Vartan Oskanian
Government Administration	Andranik Manukian
Health	Ararat Mkrtchian
Industrial Productions Coordination	Davit Zadoyan
Internal Affairs	Haik Harutunian
Justice	Davit Harutunian
National Security	Karlos Petrosian
Regional Administration and Urban Planning	Leonard Akopian
Social Welfare	Razmik Martirosian
State Property	Davit Vardanian
State Revenues	Gagik Poghosian
Trade, Servies, Tourism and Industry	Karen Chshmaritian
Transport and Communications	Edvard Madatian

The Margarian cabinet still reflected the Unity parliamentary alliance forged by the late **Vazgen Sargsian** and Margarian himself had been among the founding members of the **Republican Party of**

Armenia (RPA), which Sargsian led to parliamentary victory in 1999. The Margarian cabinet retained many of the ministers of the previous **Aram Sargsian** cabinet while introducing new members to the government. It also saw the return of two longtime ministerial stalwarts with Serge Sargsian attending to the defense ministry and reformist Levon Barkhudarian resuming oversight of the economy, though he was subsequently replaced by Vardan Khachatrian. This more balanced cabinet, involving a broad coalition of political forces, reflected a new accommodation between the president and the parliament, restoring normalcy after the political upheavals of 1999.

MEKHITAR SEBASTATSI (1676–1749). Clergyman and initiator of the modern Armenian Enlightenment. Mekhitar, baptismal name Manuk Petrosian, was born in the town of Sebastia (Sivas). He received his earliest education in the local Armenian monastery of *Surb Neshan* (Holy Cross), which he attended from 1685 to 1691. Thereafter he journeyed to a number of Armenian monasteries, including **Edjmiadsin**, to further his education, and in 1699 was ordained a celibate priest in the **Armenian Apostolic Church**. With his appeal to establish a new fraternal order in pursuit of learning rejected by the Armenian Patriarchate of Istanbul, Mekhitar and his followers converted to Roman Catholicism and took refuge in Venice where in 1717 the Senate allotted the island of San Lazzaro (Saint Lazarus) as the site of their monastery.

Once settled, Mekhitar produced a series of works that revived learning in the **Armenian language**. *Kerakanutiun grabari lezvi haykazan seri* (Grammar for the classical language of the Armenian race) (1730), *Bargirk haykaznian lezvi* (Lexicon of the Armenian language) (vol. 1, 1749; vol. 2, 1769), and *Durn kerakanutian ashkharhabar lezvi hayots sharadretsial tajkakanav lezvav* (Gateway to the grammar of the vernacular language of the Armenians written in the Turkish language) (1727) became the foundations of Armenian philology and modern scholarship.

Of equal significance to his role as educator and cultivator of the mind was Mekhitar's training of a school of followers who formed the Mekhitarian Order as it became known after his death. With their center in Venice, and a second branch established in Vienna in 1811, the Mekhitarians took the lead in establishing schools, promoting education, and publishing in the Armenian language. Their role in the advancement of Armenian learning and scholarship in all its facets made them defining figures of the 19th century Armenian cultural renaissance. See MEKHITARIAN ORDER.

MEKHITARIAN (also MEKHITARIST) ORDER. Religious fraternity of the Roman **Catholic** persuasion founded by **Mekhitar Sebastatsi** and dedicated to the spiritual and educational edification of the Armenian people. Although religious devotion occupied the center of the individual and collective life of the monastic congregants, from the beginning the Mekhitarian contribution to Armenian civilization was located in the Order's dedication to the cultural emancipation and intellectual enlightenment of the Armenian people. The 25-years-old Mekhitar, who even at that age already had gathered a small following from among younger Armenian clergy, founded the order in Constantinople in 1701. This was an unprecedented occurrence in Armenian history, attributable directly to Mekhitar's vision of national restoration through instruction, a habit that for all intents and purposes had gone out of practice under the oppressive rule of the Ottoman Turks. The pursuit of intellectual activity, discouraged by the political climate of the Islamic societies ruling over the Armenians and the retrenchment of the **Armenian Apostolic Church** into the obscurity of unexamined traditions and customs, is also attributable solely to Mekhitar sui generis as no school of learning was in existence in the Armenian world where he could satisfy his profound curiosity and immense gifts. The medieval institutions of learning had long faded by disuse, if not fallen into ruin.

Mekhitar's encounter with two new realities making their presence felt among Armenians in many parts of the world shaped his modern outlook and became the sources of his religious convictions and intellectual commitments. The first resulted from contact with Catholic missionaries operating in the Ottoman Empire. Mekhitar saw in them the proponents of a vigorous faith. The second stemmed from his appreciation of the power of the printing press. Though by no means the first, he was nevertheless the greatest proponent of bringing the Armenian language to print in order to equip the Armenian people with the full dignity of their unique cultural heritage.

The Mekhitarian Order called itself the "Adoptive Sons of the Blessed Virgin Mary and the Teachers of Penitence." The prejudice and ignorance of leaders of the Armenian Apostolic Church and persecution by political authorities soon compelled the friars to relocate to the western Peloponnesus, or Morea as it was called then under Venetian rule, where they established their first cloister in the town of Modon (Methoni). There in 1711 they received from Pope Clement XI recognition as a distinct order adhering to the Benedictine form of monasticism. When the Ottomans recaptured the town from the Venetians in 1714, Mekhitar and his band took refuge in the city of Venice, where they soon became known as the *Padri Armeni* ("Armenian Fathers" in Italian). Once again Mekhitar's powers of persuasion yielded an unprecedented concession. In 1717, the Republic of Venice granted the Mekhitarian Order perpetual right of occupancy of the island of San Lazzaro in the Venetian lagoon. On September 7 Mekhitar and the Armenian fathers took possession of the vacant outpost that previously had been a lepers' colony, hence its name, St. Lazarus, *Surp Ghazar* of the Armenians. A mere islet at the time of occupancy, San Lazzaro was enlarged thrice, in 1740, 1815, and between 1949 and 1953, when it was given its present size and rectangular shape. The rudimentary structure outlined by Mekhitar over time was expanded to include a church with a neo-Gothic interior, a tall campanile, residential quarters, library, museum, printing plant, and sundry research facilities.

In 1773 a group left Venice and established an autonomous branch in the nearby Adriatic port city of Trieste, which at the time was under Austrian rule. Here too the Mekhitarians were well received and extended license by Empress Maria Theresa to reside in perpetuity within her Hapsburg domains. The French occupation of the Adriatic coast under Napoleon Bonaparte unsettled the arrangements under which the Mekhitarians had been extended residence. Napoleon abolished the Venetian republic and waged war against Austria. The Mekhitarians were forced out of Trieste in 1805 and sought refuge in the capital, Vienna. The Mekhitarians of Venice, however, were given the French emperor's personal protection and remained on their island. By imperial decree, the Vienna Mekhitarians were finally settled in 1811 in a vacant Capuchin monastery in the St. Ulrich suburb of Vienna just outside the city walls at the time, now within sight of the Ringstrasse and the Hofburg Palace. Under the guidance of Abbot Adeodat Babikian (1802–1825), the congregants secured the funds to purchase the property in 1814. The Vienna branch reached full flowering during the abbacy of Aristakes Azarian (1826–1855) who oversaw the construction of a new monastery complex under the sponsorship of Emperor Ferdinand I and Empress Maria Anna who laid the cornerstone of the new edifice on October 18, 1837. Later in the century a beautiful church in the German Renaissance style was added, decorated by some of the finest religious art created by local artists who donated their services for the embellishment of the sanctuary.

The exemplary conduct of the emigrant fathers, their spiritual devotion, intellectual ardor, and sense of national mission, at a time of expanding European interest in the East, invited the amity and hospitality of their hosts. Their local ministry to co-religionists earned them as much respect as their long-distance service to their co-nationals, and in so doing secured patronage for their declared purposes of scholarship and **education**. Their foremost instrument was and remains the published book. It is no exaggeration to say no group of men so successfully revived a captive people from its torpor with such thoroughly peaceable methods as the collection, authorship, publication, and distribution of books alone. There is little to compare with this lofty accomplishment in the annals of other stateless people. In so doing, though they stood apart denominationally from the vast majority of Armenians who remained adherents of their ancient Armenian Apostolic Church, they earned the deepest respect and the profoundest admiration, inviting others by their example to emulate equal commitment and commensurate learning.

In this, once again, at the start stood Mekhitar Sebastatsi, who almost single-handedly moved Armenian culture from the age of manuscripts to the era of print. Mekhitar was an instinctual philologist. Ordained a *vardapet* (master of theology) at the Monastery of Surb Nshan (Holy Cross) in his birthplace of Sebasteia/Sivas, he would have attained a basic education in Scripture, theology, and the Armenian classics. Beyond that Mekhitar was a self-taught linguist. No one since **Mesrop Mashtots** had preoccupied himself with every aspect of the usage of the **Armenian language**. In his view the purity of thought and spiritual devotion required purity of language. The re-editing of the Armenian Bible, the authoring of the first modern grammar book, the compilation of the first true dictionary, all revolved around the singular objective of moral empowerment through the proper use of language, whether it be for worship, education, or commerce. All this also attested to his firm grasp of the significance of the printed word as the primary medium of communication in an emerging new world. Mekhitar's rapid assimilation of the fundaments of European civilization is one of the essential points of departure of the Armenian people from the Middle Ages. By this measure he lifted the Armenians of the immured Islamic Middle East far beyond and much earlier than they might have done of their own volition. The Mekhitarians as a group remained especially sensitive to these possibilities and strove at their utmost to achieve those ends. Once Mekhitar sparked the process, the rest unraveled in what now seems a natural progression. At the time, it was a struggle every inch of the way. As innovators they were held in suspicion by a society unaccustomed to change. As Catholics they were vilified by the Armenian Apostolic Church as proselytizers. Their scholarship, however, remained unassailable.

Studying the Armenian language required obtaining the sources of that language. Mekhitar started by collecting Armenian manuscripts. In so doing he inaugurated one of the greatest cultural rescue operations ever staged. By the time the Armenian communities of the Ottoman Empire were destroyed during World War I, the Mekhitarians had retrieved a major portion of the literary heritage of the Armenians by removing to Venice and Vienna all the manuscripts they could acquire. The monastery in Venice came into the possession of some 5,000 manuscripts; the monastery in Vienna nearly 2,600. Next to the Matenadaran in Armenia and the library of St. James monastery in the Armenian quarter of Old Jerusalem, the holdings in Venice and Vienna now constitute the third and fourth largest repositories of the Armenian textual and artistic heritage. These precious books have served the Mekhitarian philologists as an inexhaustible source of information on Armenian history, language, culture, and literature. The manuscripts that reached their hands also became some of the earliest sources on Armenia to be brought to print.

From this base of knowledge the Mekhitarians have issued a stream of publications. Mekhitar's first publication appeared in 1700. Despite his efforts, one objective he did not reach in his lifetime, that of establishing a printing press at San Lazzaro. He could not, however, have chosen a better location to inaugurate a printing revolution in Armenian as Venice at the time was one of the major centers of European publishing and the Armenian typeface had already been cast. A press was finally installed on the island in 1789. The Vienna congregation, while still in Trieste had already started their own printing operation in 1776. Publishing became one of the principal sources of revenue for the Mekhitarians, and they specialized in the typesetting of quality works for the domestic markets in Italy and Austria. They did so for the business of printing Armenian books was an unprofitable enterprise and required subsidy that they garnered through their own commercial ventures. All that effort was driven by the goal of releasing works of Armenian interest. By the end of the 20th century, the Mekhitarians of Venice had issued 1,600 titles and the Mekhitarians of Vienna nearly 1,000 titles. These included series specifically dedicated to Armenian scholarship. The Venetian group specialized in the publication of primary sources of which over 125 volumes were issued. This was paired by a series of over 150 volumes of philological and historical interest. The Viennese group issued a series of over 230 volumes of scholarly analysis on all aspects of Armenian civilization.

Increasingly the publications of Armenological interest acquired the standards of Western European learning, and in this, through their exposure to German academic scholarship, the Vienna congregation came to excel in the production of Armenian philological and historical works, so much so that the Mekhitarians became the point of reference in the European academic community on the subject of the Armenians, their history, literature, language, and culture. The Mekhitarians made their own efforts to be active in this regard and issued publications in European languages, first beginning with works in Latin translation, the language of the Western church, of works of theological and ecclesiastical interest, some 50 titles, and expanded their inventory in other languages including 80 titles in Italian, 75 in English, 65 in French, and 15 in German. The translation of works from the same languages into Armenian paralleled this course. Some 130 titles were ultimately issued, many the classics of European literature, including Baudelaire, Chateaubriand, Corneille, Dante, Hugo, Lamartine, Racine, Tasso, Voltaire, as well as the ancient Greek and Latin classics, among them Augustine, Cicero, Demosthenes, Euripides, Homer, Julius Caesar, Marcus Aurelius, Plato, Seneca, Sophocles, Tacitus, and Virgil.

These translations became the first sources of introduction to Western civilization for many Armenians living all across the Asian continent. Even so, they did not entirely and conveniently mediate between two vastly different cultures, as the Mekhitarian literary effort originally focused on reviving usage of Classical Armenian, the language of an imagined Golden Age. It was a valiant effort, but ultimately one that surrendered to the realization that mass communication required the usage of the language of the masses. In view of their investment in the revival of Classical Armenian as a responsibility bequeathed to them by Mekhitar, the learned fathers were slow to adjust at first, but having crossed the bridge in the second half of the 19th century, once again they stood at the forefront of refining and crafting out of vernacular Armenian a language of the finest literary quality. The venture toward classicism, which had misfired, had proven a laboratory of inestimable value for identifying the features of the modern Armenian language and for standardizing the vernacular into a coherent literary language governed by rules consistent internally and in relation to its progenitor, the original Armenian of Mesrop Mashtots, a figure of veneration for the Mekhitarians. In a further expression of their desire to popularize knowledge and the usage of purely Armenian literary language, each branch of the Mekhitarians also inaugurated the publication of monthly journals. *Bazmavep* from Venice, started in 1843, and *Handes amsorya* (Monthly review) from Vienna, started in 1887, are the two oldest serials in Armenian still in print. Issued in the popular magazine format of their times, both publications evolved into scholarly journals when Armenian newspapers proliferated and the Armenian readership gained access to multiple sources of information about Europe and the rest of the world.

The increase in literacy followed the rapid growth of the Armenian parochial school systems in the 19th century. There too the Mekhitarians led the way. They opened their first schools among the Armenian communities of the Hapsburg Empire in the middle of the 18th century, and expanded their network to the Ottoman and Russian Empires. Their two boarding schools in Venice and Paris, the Mourad-Raphaelian and the Samuel Mouradian respectively, were the most successful of their educational establishments. In the course of two and a half centuries of teaching as a community service, the Mekhitarians founded some 40 schools in places ranging from Elizabetpol and Varadin in Hungary, to Trieste, Istanbul, Galata, Pera, Trebizond, Smyrna, the Anatolian interior at Kutahia and Malatia, the Armenian heartland at Kharput and Mush, the Caucasus at Akhaltsikh, the Crimea at Simferopol and Karasu Bazar, and eventually to the new Armenian **diaspora** communities of Aleppo, Alexandria, Athens, Beirut, Boston, Buenos Aires, and Los Angeles. In 2001, on the 300th anniversary of the founding of the congregation, the Venice and Vienna branches of the Mekhitarian Order reunited and were welcomed in Armenia by Catholicos Garegin II Nersisian of the Armenian Apostolic Church.

Ultimately though the importance of the Mekhitarian contribution, wide-ranging, long-lasting, enduring, and continuing, is located in their revival of learning and the judicious mission of dignifying the Armenian people through the knowledge of their own civilization. More so than the educational institutions, publications, and sundry other ventures, the Mekhitarian legacy remains in the long list of inspired scholars whose prodigious output forms the basis of modern Armenian culture: Nerses Akinian, **Ghevond Alishan**, Gabriel Avetikian, Harutiun Avgerian, Mkrtich Avgerian, Arsen Aytenian, Arsen Bagratuni, Vrtanes Chalekhian, **Mikayel Chamchian**, Hakovbos Dashian, Hovsep Gaterjian, Khachatur Siurmelian, Garegin Zarbhanalian, Hovhannes Zohrapian, and many others. Their landmark publications, Chamchian's *History of the Armenians* (Venice 1784–6), Zohrapian's edition of the Armenian Bible (Venice, 1805), the Avetikian-Siurmelian-Avgerian *New Lexicon of the Armenian Language* (Venice, 1836–7), Aytenian's *Critical Grammar for the Vernacular or Modern Armenian Language* (Vienna, 1866), to list just a few, lie at the core of that culture.

MESROP MASHTOTS (360/370–439/440). Inventor of the Armenian alphabet. Born of humble origins in the town of Hatsekats in the central province of Taron, Mashtots obtained military rank and served at the Armenian royal court, before joining the church to dedicate his life to missionary work. Not long after his initial foray amongst the people in the region of Goghtn in southeastern Armenia, Mashtots came to the realization that the conversion of the Armenians to Christianity was hampered by the absence of instructional literature in their own language. While the preaching and sermonizing was delivered in the vernacular, the liturgy was available only in Greek and Syriac, the two languages of the early Christian Church, thereby depriving popular access to the sources of the new faith promoted in Armenia by the state. In the wake of the partition of Armenia between Rome and Iran in 387 and the increasing political pressure on Armenia, the state authorities lent active support to Mashtots to realize his idea of introducing an alphabet for the **Armenian language**. Both the Armenian **Arshakuni** King Vramshapuh (392–415) and the presiding bishop of Armenia, the **Catholicos** Sahak the Great (387–428), appreciated the value of the proposition and its potential for shaping cultural and spiritual unity among a people only recently and superficially converted, continuously exposed to diverse religious influences, and now politically divided, but still communicating through a common tongue.

Mashtots at first traveled to Edessa/Urfa, the vibrant metropolis of northern Syria and the closest center of Christian learning, in the hope of locating a script that might be adapted to the Armenian language. A natural phonetician of the keenest skill, he came to the conclusion that the adaptation of existing script to the Armenian language was an unworkable solution and thereupon resolved that a new and distinct alphabet was needed. Moving to Samosata in the western Hellenized edge of Armenia, Mashtots intuitively found the linguistic linkage between Armenian and Greek, and there, with the assistance of the Greek calligrapher Rufinius, he gave shape to 36 new symbols creating a precise phonetic match between the sounds of the Armenian language of the fifth century and its new alphabet. With its invention by Mashtots, traditionally dated to 405, the Armenian alphabet has remained in use since that time, with only two letters added in the Middle Ages to accommodate new sounds introduced through borrowings.

The Armenian symbols follow the alphabetic order of Greek with 15 new phonemes unique to Armenian added to the 21 Greek letters. To facilitate their memorization, Mashtots arranged them into phonetically harmonious triplicates. With the true gifts of the scientist, in all his choices, he tested first with his pupils, applying at all times basic educational principles: ease of acquisition, natural correlation, facility for transcription, and instructional transferability. The rapid spread of the usage of the Armenian alphabet attested to the successful solutions devised by Mashtots. It was immediately welcomed as a unique cultural possession and became one of the central markers of Armenian identity.

With the great intellectual challenge of forming an alphabet addressed, Mashtots returned to the original intent of his invention, the translation of the Christian scriptures into Armenian. He immediately assumed the education of a cadre of translators who set upon rendering into Armenian the patristic texts, the canons of the early church councils, the liturgies, and other historical works, and in so doing, in a single generation, introduced into Armenian culture the works of the early church fathers. Mashtots and Sahak together assumed responsibility for translating the most important source of their faith, the Bible. With a commitment to offering the Armenian people an accurate rendering, they collected copies in Syriac and Greek and obtained an official version from Constantinople, and, with intentional symbolism, started their translation with the first line from the Proverbs of Solomon: "That men may know wisdom and instruction." With their completed translation, Mashtots and Sahak produced a literary masterpiece in its own right. By demonstrating the full richness of the Armenian language, they ushered in a period known as the Classical or Golden Age of Armenian literature, so prolific and lasting was the output. The earliest original writings in Armenian are also attributed to Mashtots, who is believed to have authored a set of homilies and several hymns. The first full-length work authored in Armenian, and a virtual hagiographic biography, written by his pupil Koriun, *Vark Mashtotsi* (The Life of Mashtots), depicts the inventor as the great and first teacher of the Armenian people, and in which he is also credited with the invention of alphabets for the Georgian and Albanian peoples of the Caucasus.

Mashtots died on February 17, 439/440 in **Vagharshapat**. Another of his pupils, the nobleman Vahan Amatuni, carried the remains of Mashtots to the town of Oshakan, where he raised a martyrium over the grave of his teacher. The martyrium became a place of pilgrimage, and Mashtots was soon elevated to the highest pantheon of Armenian saints. In the postclassical age authors began referring to him by the name of Mesrop and in modern times his two names became combined as Mesrop Mashtots. Today, Mesrop Mashtots is the most popularly revered of all the great men of the past whose genius and whose invention is regarded the source of the deepest and most cherished cultural values of the Armenian people expressed through their possession of a heritage articulated by the symbols and sounds of the alphabet he invented.

MIASNIKIAN (MIASNIKOV), ALEXANDER (1886–1925). Bolshevik leader. Miasnikian was born in Nor Nakhichevan, in Russia.

He received his early education at the Lazarian Institute in Moscow and went on to graduate from the law faculty of Moscow University in 1911. He had joined the Russian Social Democratic Workers Party (RSDWP) back in 1906 and sided with its Bolshevik wing. An active revolutionary, he was arrested but managed to escape to Baku before returning to Moscow. He enlisted in the Imperial Army in 1914 and served on the Western front. The Bolshevik Revolution found him in Minsk and put his military experience to use. He was briefly chairman of the Military-Revolutionary Committee in Minsk when Soviet power was declared in Byelorussia and in that capacity also had command of the front against the Germans that ran through the country. In the spring of 1918 he was made commander of the Volga front and then minister of war in Byelorussia in 1919. He was subsequently in Moscow where he became secretary of the party committee in Moscow before he was reassigned by the Central Committee to Armenia with instructions from Lenin to moderate Soviet rule that had provoked popular rebellion in February 1921.

Miasnikian became the principal architect of Soviet power in Armenia by rebuilding state structures virtually from scratch and fostering the growth of the **Communist Party of Armenia** (CPA) at the same time. As Chairman of the Council of People's Commissars he stabilized Soviet rule in Armenia by restoring a more tolerant order. Miasnikian oversaw the introduction of the New Economic Policy (NEP) that helped in the recovery of the devastated Armenian economy after years of warfare and unrest. On January 30, 1922, the First Congress of Soviets in Armenia adopted the Constitution of the Armenian Soviet Socialist Republic (ASSR). On March 12, 1922, Armenia, Georgia, and Azerbaijan were joined into the Federation of Soviet Socialist Republics of Transcaucasia, which on December 10, 1922, was reorganized as the Transcaucasian Socialist Federated Soviet Republic in anticipation of its incorporation into the Union of Soviet Socialist Republics (USSR) when it was formally constituted on December 30, 1922. Attention in Armenia remained focused on the improvement of its agrarian economy in order to feed the population. Irrigation was improved and more land brought under cultivation through the construction of canals. The electrification of the country was started by building hydroelectric plants. Reforms in **education** were introduced to promote greater literacy. Miasnikian also served as secretary of the party committee in Transcaucasia and sat on the Presidium of the USSR Central Committee. He died in a plane crash near Tbilisi. *See also* KASIAN, SARGIS; KHANJIAN, AGHASI.

MIKOYAN (also MIGOYAN), ANASTAS (1895–1978). Soviet leader. Mikoyan was born in Sanahin, in Russian Armenia, to a peasant family. He received his education at the Nersisian academy in Tbilisi and the Gevorgian seminary at **Edjmiadsin**. He joined the Bolshevik party in 1915 and also enlisted in General **Andranik**'s volunteer regiment. He linked up in 1917 with **Stepan Shahumian**, the leading Bolshevik in the Caucasus, and participated in organizing the Baku Commune, which lasted from March through August 1918, as editor of the local Armenian and Russian Communist newspapers, *Sotsial-Demokrat* and *Izvestia Bakinskogo Soveta*. He was responsible for saving the lives of the revolutionary leaders, who had been thrown in prison with the fall of the Commune, when in September 1918 the Ottoman army marched into Baku. Though arrested in Krasnovodsk by the British with the "Twenty-six Commissars," who were subsequently executed, Mikoyan eluded death and reached Lenin in 1919.

A dynamic activist and effective organizer, Mikoyan rose rapidly through the ranks of the Communist Party. In 1920 he was heading the party organization in Nizhni Novgorod, in 1922 he was party secretary in Rostov-on-the-Don, in 1923 he was elected a full member of the Central Committee of the Communist Party, and in 1924 was secretary of the party organization in the North Caucasus. In the struggle for party leadership, he sided with Stalin, who sponsored his candidacy to the Politburo in 1926. He was a full member of the Politburo in 1935 and rose to its Presidium in 1952. He survived attempts by Lavrenti Beria to purge him, making him one of the rare Old Bolsheviks in the party leadership to remain in power. He sided with Nikita Khrushchev upon Stalin's death and was the first high-ranking party official to denounce Stalin's excesses by beginning the process of rehabilitation in Armenia in 1954, thus both testing and preparing the ground for Khrushchev's criticism of Stalin in front of the Twentieth Party Congress in 1956.

It was, however, in his capacity as a state official, a skillful administrator, and, ultimately, as international troubleshooter that Mikoyan achieved greater distinction. In 1926 he was appointed head of the USSR Commissariat of Foreign and Internal Trade. In 1930 he was commissar of supplies and in 1934 commissar of food. From 1938 to 1949 he served as minister of foreign trade and from 1953 to 1955 as minister of trade. During World War II he was a member of the state defense committee, and in 1946 became first deputy chairman of the Council of Ministers, the policy-making body of the Soviet state, making him effectively the vice-premier of the USSR. He also played an important role in Soviet foreign policy, traveling abroad on a number of missions, and in negotiations with U.S. President John F. Kennedy, helping to diffuse the Cuban missile crisis, which threatened nuclear exchange with the United States in the most serious escalation of the Cold War. In 1964 he was elected chairman of the Presidium of the Supreme Soviet. He served as titular head, or president, of the Soviet Union into 1965 and retired from public life the following year. Mikoyan authored his memoirs and a number of works on party history before his passing in Moscow. *See also* COMMUNIST PARTY OF ARMENIA; KAMO; KARAKHAN; LEV.

MIKOYAN, ARTEM (also MIGOYAN, ARTYOM) (1905–1970). Aviation pioneer. The brother of **Anastas Mikoyan**, Artem was born in Sanahin, in Russian Armenia. He graduated from the Zhukov Air Force Engineering Academy in 1936 and became a military aircraft designer. In 1940 he led the team that constructed the high-altitude aerial combat plane that was named the MIG–1 in his honor. The MIG–1 was the principal fighter jet of the Soviet Air Force during World War II. More advanced generations of the Soviet air fleet continued to bear the MIG name.

MKRTICH KHRIMIAN (1820–1907). Religious leader, Armenian Patriarch in Istanbul 1869–73, **Catholicos** 1892–1907. Mkrtich Khrimian is commonly known as Khrimian *Hayrik* (Father). He ranks as the most popular clergyman of modern times, revered for his patriotic fervor and staunch defense of Armenian national interests. Born in the city of **Van** in the easternmost Armenian-inhabited province of the Ottoman Empire, Khrimian joined the church in 1845 after the death of his wife and child and subsequently moved to Istanbul. He was ordained a *vardapet*, celibate priest, in 1854, and embarked upon an active career as educator and publisher. He began issuing the periodical *Ardsvi Vaspurakan* (The Eagle of Vaspurakan) in 1855, and a year later returned to Van as the prior of the monastery of Varak. In 1858 he resumed publication of *Ardsvi Vaspurakan*, making it the first periodical issued in Armenia proper. In 1862 he was made prelate of Taron and prior of the monastery of *Surb Karapet* (Saint John the Precursor [the Baptist]). Khrimian traveled widely to visit Armenian communities across the Middle East and took his pastoral assignments as a charge to better the conditions of the Armenian peasantry living at the mercy of local Turkish and Kurdish lords.

Having been ordained a bishop in 1868, Khrimian was elected Armenian patriarch of Istanbul in 1869. He used his office to create awareness in the Armenian community of the capital city and in the Ottoman government about the plight of the Armenian provincial population. His efforts to document the unlawful exploitation of the Armenian populace and to register official complaints with the Sublime Porte were regarded as too radical and he was forced to resign from office in 1873. Even so, in 1878 he was asked to lead an Armenian delegation that hoped to appeal to the conferring Powers at the Congress of Berlin. Denied representation, Khrimian returned to Istanbul and delivered the homily for which he is most remembered, the so-called *Sermon of the Iron Ladle*, reporting metaphorically that those convened in Berlin took a share of the contents of a great soup bowl each with an iron ladle, whereas he had only a paper petition and could bring nothing back to the Armenian people. It marked a turning point in Armenian political consciousness.

Elected prelate of the Armenians in Van in 1879, Khrimian was back in his homeland focusing his energies on religious and educational improvement. Suspected of association with Armenian resistance groups forming in the region, Khrimian was recalled to Istanbul and in 1890 exiled to Jerusalem, only to be elected in 1892 supreme patriarch and catholicos of all Armenians at **Edjmiadsin**, in Russian Armenia. Denied travel rights in the Ottoman Empire, Khrimian arrived in Edjmiadsin more than a year after his election and was anointed on September 26, 1893. Repression of the Armenians in the Russian Empire showed its face with the imperial edict of 1903 seizing the properties of the **Armenian Apostolic Church**. Refusing to submit to the order, Khrimian's actions galvanized the Armenian communities of Russia to protest the decision, resulting in the eventual rescinding of the edict in an effort to reduce the turmoil created in Transcaucasia in the months leading up to the 1905 Russian Revolution. Khrimian continued writing religious and moralistic treatises throughout most of his years. He passed away at Edjmiadsin having elevated the importance of the Mother See to new stature in Armenian national life. *See also* NERSES V ASHTARAKETSI; ORMANIAN, MAGHAKIA; SERVANTZTIANTS, GAREGIN; VARZHAPETIAN, NERSES.

MOVSES KHORENATSI (Moses of Khoren). Historian, fifth/ninth century. By far the most important historian of ancient Armenia, Movses Khorenatsi was much more than a medieval chronicler. His construction of a complete cycle of the history of the Armenians from their origins to the fifth century earned him a place of great distinction as the father of Armenian history (*patmahayr*). Although local historians began recording the important events in the life of the Armenian people virtually from the time of the invention of the Armenian alphabet, none was so bold as to attempt a comprehensive synthesis of their entire history, or more properly, of their historical memory. Out of the legends, myths, oral traditions, epics, and recorded sources handed down to his time, Khorenatsi devised a coherent and continuous history of the Armenians. By integrating the Armenian stories into biblical and classical chronology he attempted to weave into world history the traditions recalled by the Armenians about their kings and the mythical founders of their nation. Because of its sweep, Khorenatsi's History of the Armenians (*Patumtiun Hayots*) was accepted by later generations as the authoritative account of early Armenian history, earning Khorenatsi a place of reverence in the national pantheon of the intellectual figures credited with shaping the Armenian vision of their civilization.

Preoccupied with the question of origins, he traced the genealogy of Armenian royalty and nobility and shed critical light on the evolution of political institutions in Armenia, including the vital **nakharar system** undergirding the Armenian monarchy. Despite its claims, Khorenatsi's History is also a partisan history to the extent that from among the many princely dynasties whose accounts are told, clearly the **Bagratuni** family was given the most favorable treatment, while the noteworthy **Mamikonian** nakharar dynasty was given less attention. This and other characteristics of the work, including the important question of his sources, have been the cause of much of the modern controversy surrounding Khorenatsi. He has been variously dated from the fifth through the ninth century and many of his assertions subjected to serious scrutiny. Khorenatsi's importance for understanding the early history of the Armenians, however, goes undiminished. From the legendary Hayk, the eponymous ancestor of the Armenians, through their list of kings including **Artashes I**, **Tigran II the Great**, and **Trdat IV**, and down to **Mesrop Mashtots**, the inventor of the Armenian alphabet, **Grigor Lusavorich** and his descendants who held the patriarchal throne of Armenia, and the last of the **Arshakuni** kings, Movses Khorenatsi's History is peopled with the primary figures of ancient Armenia from whose actions, deeds, and words he created a historical narrative for the ages.

MUSA DAGH. (*Musa Ler* in Armenian). Mountainous site of resistance to the 1915 deportation of the Armenians of the Ottoman Empire. Of the hundreds of villages, towns, and cities across the Ottoman Empire whose Armenian population was ordered removed to the Syrian desert, Musa Dagh was one of only four sites where Armenians organized a defense of their community against the deportation edicts issued by the Young Turk regime beginning in April 1915. By the time the Armenians of the six villages at the base of Musa Dagh were to be evicted from their homes, the inhabitants had grown suspicious of the government's ultimate intentions and had chosen instead to retreat up the mountain and to defy the evacuation order. Musa Dagh, or the Mountain of Moses, stood on the Mediterranean Sea south of the port city of Alexandretta and west of ancient Antioch.

With a few hundred rifles and the entire store of provisions from their villages, the Armenians on Musa Dagh put up a fierce resistance against a number of attempts by the regular Turkish army to flush them out. Outnumbered and outgunned, the Armenians had little expectations of surviving the siege of the mountain when food stocks were depleted after a month. Their only hope was a chance rescue by an Allied vessel roaming the coast of the Mediterranean. When a passing French warship sighted two large banners hoisted by the Armenians, swimmers went out to meet it. Eventually five Allied ships moved in to transport the entire population of men, women, and children, more than four thousand in all.

The Armenians of Musa Dagh had endured for 53 days from July 21 to September 12, 1915. They were disembarked at Port Said in

Egypt and remained in Allied refugee camps until the end of World War I when they returned to their homes. As part of the district of Alexandretta, or Hatay, Musa Dagh remained under French Mandate until 1939. The Musa Dagh Armenians abandoned their villages for a second, and final, time when the area was incorporated by the Republic of Turkey.

In the face of the complete decimation of the Armenian communities of the Ottoman Empire, Musa Dagh became a symbol of the Armenian will to survive in the postwar years. Of the three other sites where Armenians defied the deportation orders, Shabin-Karahisar, Urfa, and **Van**, only the Armenians of Van were rescued when an advancing Russian army lifted the siege of their city. The Armenians of Urfa and Shabin-Karahisar were either massacred or deported to face starvation in the Syrian desert much as the rest of the Armenians of the Ottoman Empire. Musa Dagh was also the sole instance where the Western Allies at war with the Ottomans averted the death of an Armenian community. That story inspired the Prague-born Austrian writer, Franz Werfel, to write a novelized version of the events as *The Forty Days of Musa Dagh*. Published in 1933, the book became an instant best seller, but with the rise of Hitler, Werfel himself fled Vienna that same year. *The Forty Days of Musa Dagh* was eventually translated into 18 languages, while Metro-Goldwyn-Mayer (MGM), the Hollywood film production company, bought the rights to the book and announced plans for the production of a movie version of the novel. The Turkish ambassador's protestations to the U.S. Department of State resulted in the intervention of the United States government in the matter. With a veiled threat to ban American-made films from Turkey, MGM studios permanently shelved plans to produce the movie. *See also* ADANA MASSACRES; ARMENIAN GENOCIDE.

– N –

NAGORNO KARABAGH (Mountainous Karabagh). Region of historic Armenia, autonomous district in Soviet Azerbaijan, declared an independent republic in 1991. The easternmost range of the Armenian upland, the region of Karabagh, called Artsakh in Armenian, had been continuously governed by Armenian noble families since the

Middle Ages. Regarded as a marchland of the ancient **Armenian kingdom**, the population of the area was distinguished for its martial traditions. Protected by the rugged terrain, these highland areas remained outside the direct political control of the Muslim states established in the Caucasus region after the breakup of the Caliphate and the introduction of the Turkic tribes in the surrounding lowlands to the east. With their privileges renewed by successive rulers of the area from the Mongol through the Safavid era, the Armenian population, under the immediate governance of its native princes, led a separate existence in the isolation of their mountain fastnesses.

Armenian control of the region began to break down in the early 18th century. By the time the area was annexed by Russia in 1813 according to the Treaty of Gulistan, the Armenian feudal dynasties had lost their hold. Karabagh was made part of the province of Elizavetpol (Ganja), which, along with Baku province, held the great bulk of the Azeri Turk population of the Caucasus. When Azerbaijan was declared an independent republic in 1918, its government laid claim to both provinces and thereby incorporated Karabagh in its borders. While the region was virtually completely Armenian-populated, it was cut off from the Republic of Armenia, which did not succeed in resolving the disputed status of the district. Unrest marked the entire period of the independent republics in the Transcaucasus as the Armenian population of Karabagh resisted Azerbaijani rule, while the Baku government enforced its authority through the use of arms.

The problem remained for the Soviet regime to solve. While Moscow recognized Karabagh as part of Soviet Azerbaijan, the Armenian-populated part, which was mainly upland area, was designated an autonomous *oblast* (district) in 1923, hence the designation of *Nagorno Karabakh* in Russian, signifying Mountainous Karabagh. The Nagorno Karabagh Autonomous Oblast (NKAO) was separated from Soviet Armenia by an eight-kilometer wide corridor. Its Armenian population, while severely repressed for its expressions of nationalism, continued to seek unification with Armenia. In 1988, during the Gorbachev era in the Soviet Union, the Armenians of Karabagh began to press Moscow to respond to their appeals. The 150,000 Armenians, out of a total population of 180,000 in NKAO, invoked the lesson of the disappearance of the Armenians from the Nakhichevan Autonomous Republic, Soviet Azerbaijan's exclave to the west of Armenia, as well as the decline of their own population from 95 percent to 75 percent of the total as another example of Azeri and Soviet attempts to depopulate areas historically inhabited by Armenians incorporated into Soviet Azerbaijan. While Soviet authorities procrastinated, the appeals resounded in Armenia in mass protests that became known as the **Karabagh Movement**. Together they beseeched Moscow to permit the Armenians of Nagorno Karabagh to transfer the jurisdiction of their autonomous district from Soviet Azerbaijan to Soviet Armenia.

The Karabagh Movement proved to be the first of the many nationalist crises faced by the Soviet regime in its final years. In Azerbaijan, the Armenian effort at unification engendered hostility and rejection leading to mob violence in a number of Azeri cities and eventually degenerated into small-scale warring in and around Nagorno Karabagh. With the dissolution of the Soviet Union, as the government of Azerbaijan abolished the separate status of Nagorno Karabagh, the district legislature pronounced the area ceded from Azerbaijan by declaring it a republic on September 2, 1991. On January 6, 1992, its popularly elected parliament proclaimed the region the independent Republic of Mountainous Karabagh, or Nagorno Karabagh Republic (NKR). Its government was led by Prime Minister Oleg Yesayan and chairman of the NKR parliament, Artur Mkrtchian, who was killed in April 1992. Azerbaijan, however, regarded itself at war with NKR and by mid–1992 had escalated hostilities to the point where the Armenians of **Stepanakert** lived under constant shelling from the town of Shushi, which was held by the Azeris and whose Armenian population have been driven out. When civilian rule was suspended and the State Defense Committee formed, half of NKR territory was already occupied by Azeri forces that threatened to overran and expel the rest of the Armenian population. The State Defense Committee consisted of: **Robert Kocharian**, chairman; Serge Sargsian, deputy chairman and commander of the NKR self-defense forces; Samvel Babayan, who succeeded Serge Sargsian as commander when the latter became Armenia's defense minister in 1993; Boris Arushanian, advisor on foreign policy; **Arkady Ghukasian**, advisor on political affairs; Georgi Petrosian, acting chairman of the NKR parliament; and Karen Baburian, who succeeded Petrosian in 1993.

During its existence from August 15, 1992, to December 22, 1994, the State Defense Committee planned and executed the capture of

Shushi, the ancient Armenian capital of Karabagh that lay at a height above **Stepanakert**. With its Armenian population driven out, Shushi had served as the main Azeri base for the shelling of the city of Stepanakert. In the face of incredible odds, in a faultlessly executed assault, Karabagh Armenian forces took the city on May 9, 1992, and moved on to establish a corridor with Armenia through the Lachin pass.

While the corridor provided a lifeline for Karabagh, two more years of increasingly intensive warfare kept the fate of the new republic in the balance. Major reverses in the region of Mardakert during the second half of 1992, however, left the northern half of Karabagh under Azeri occupation and its Armenian population driven out. After months of regrouping, the Karabagh army went on the offensive once again and through most of 1993 gained a series of military victories that resulted in the withdrawal of Azeri forces from nearly all of the territories of Karabagh proper and the occupation of surrounding Azeri districts that the Azeris used to stage attacks on the Armenian settlements of Karabagh. In March 1993 the seizure of the region of Kelbajar joined Karabagh and Armenia along the entire western border of Karabagh allowing for a secure flank to move operations to the east and the south. The Karabagh army then captured the regions of Agdam in July, Fizuli in August, and Zangelan and Kubatli in September and October thereby establishing a common border between Karabagh and Iran on the **Arax River**.

A major counteroffensive staged in December 1993 by the Azeri army after the installment of Heidar Aliyev as president of Azerbaijan marked the height of the warfare as both sides committed thousands of troops and hundreds of pieces of armored equipment. The scale of the Azeri offensive also put Armenia's armed forces on high alert as Karabagh military units were stretched to their limit along the entire front line. After weeks of ferocious fighting and some initial advances, the Azeri offensive stalled. By March 1994 the Karabagh army had regained its previous positions and its line of defense was secured. On May 14, 1994, the commanders of the Karabagh, Azeri, and Armenian armies agreed to a truce that ended the fighting.

By that time the army of the self-declared republic had wrested, with the exception of the northernmost districts, all of NKR proper from Azeri control and placed the surrounding districts of Azerbaijan under military occupation. The armistice was secured when the defense ministers of Armenia and Azerbaijan, the commander of the Karabagh army, and the defense minister of Russia as mediator signed a formal agreement on July 27, 1994. Negotiations for a settlement began under the joint auspices of Russia and the Organization for Security and Cooperation in Europe (OSCE) in December 1994 after a three-year period when both parties presided over separate sets of negotiations. The OSCE efforts were led by the so-called Minsk Group of interested countries. That became the name by which the negotiating teams went by thereafter, though in due course a permanent cochairmanship of three countries, United States, France, and Russia, was agreed upon. The Minsk Group's task was to develop various proposals, which the parties to the conflict could examine, consider, and agree upon. By the year 2000 the main outlines of an agreement accounting for all facets of a settlement had reportedly emerged even as its terms and details remained confidential. Even so, final agreement continued to elude the negotiators and the parties in the region. Simultaneously, the presidents of Armenia, both **Levon Ter-Petrossian** and Robert Kocharian, initiated direct discussion with the president of Azerbaijan, Heidar Aliyev, in efforts to create confidence-building measures to move the two sides closer. *See also* ARMENIAN NATIONAL MOVEMENT.

NAKHARAR SYSTEM. The prevailing sociopolitical order in medieval Armenia characterized by a military aristocracy dominated by a host of powerful territorial princes whose families exhibited striking dynastic continuity. The system was akin to the form of advanced feudalism in Europe to the degree that a hierarchically structured society functioned on the basis of the interrelationship of the territorial princes with one another and their allegiance to the crown. All members of the noble clans shared in nakharar status and privilege, while the clan chieftains exercised real political power within the princely domain and in the administrative structure of the country. The senior male enjoyed the lofty height of *nahapetutiun*, patriarchy, and was the *tanuter*, the lord of the noble house, but the retention of authority was contingent on the ability to render military service, hence leadership constantly shifted to the most capable member of the clan. As the great families held vast estates, not always necessarily contiguous, there tended to be sufficient scope of responsibility to apportion among the key members of a nakharar family. If one branch of the family faltered, another was on the ready to fill the void and retain the rank and title associated with their clan.

Nakharar status was inherited and raising one to that rank, which was rarely performed, was the exclusive right of the sovereign. Banishment from nakharar status, which was even more rare, was also a sovereign's privilege, a legal right exercised only in the most extreme situation. Even so only the lesser nakharar families were exposed to such risk, as the great lords could match the king's army in a fight, and both parties preferred avoiding a pointless clash of the type, therein making the great princes virtually immune from royal authority. Accordingly the system functioned best during the reign of a strong and reliable sovereign whose policies and personality provided reason for national solidarity. In instances where leadership qualities were missing at the center of the state, the system functioned much more loosely and conflict and competition ensued. In the view of the princes, the nakharar estate was considered so stable a unit, that central authority did not necessarily have to reside in a domestic sovereign, and, if honored, the system functioned just as well under foreign administration. The social strength and political reliability of the system made it a dependable form of government for whoever happened to occupy the throne, whether at home or abroad. Equally, the nakharar system furnished Armenian society an indigenous administration fundamentally unaltered by imperial government, therein equipping Armenia with the constant reserve of leadership to seek its own destiny when hegemonic powers weakened.

Essentially, wherever the nakharars ruled the Armenians lived freely. Only in the reverse instance were the Armenians truly a conquered people. Thereby invaders whose objectives included occupation and colonization targeted the system for destruction. Those seeking merely annexation tolerated it. The nakharar system was at its height from the reign of the **Artashesian** sovereigns to the reign of the **Bagratuni** kings, a period of well over a thousand years. Its origins trace back to the tribal era and many of the older nakharar families are believed to have been descended of Urartian royalty and nobility, signifying an extraordinary continuity of local government regardless of the existence and strength of the political superstructure. The visible contours of the system and its regulation dates from the time of **Tigran II the Great**, though doubtless he built upon the legacy bequeathed him by his prodigious forebear, **Artashes I**. During the reign of such commanding figures the rendering of services would have been obligatory, and the capacity of the state to marshal the resources of the system is attested by the strength of the Artashesian polity.

There may have been up to a hundred nakharar families in the **Arshakuni** realm. Real power and influence, however, was always concentrated in about a dozen leading clans, all of them closely linked to the royal dynasty and enjoying exceptional rank at court. Their fortunes fluctuated, but their status was never in question. Among them were the Abeghian, Amatuni, Andzevatsi, Apahuni, **Ardsruni**, Arsharuni, **Bagratuni**, Dimaksian, Gabeghian, Gntuni, Gnuni, Kajberuni, Kamsarakan, Khorkhoruni, **Mamikonian**, Mandakuni, Paluni, Rshtuni, Saharuni, **Siuni**, Vahevuni, and Varazhnuni. In the first period of Byzantine domination and the subsequent period of Arab rule, the number of nakharar houses diminished under the strain of rebellion and reprisal. With the rise of the Bagratuni to royalty, new families appeared on the scene, though virtually all descended from older junior branches of once proud and mighty clans. Among them notably were the Pahlavuni, the military commanders of the royal Bagratuni of Armenia, and later the **Zakarian** and Orbelian, the commanders of the royal Bagratuni of Georgia, not to mention the **Rubenian** and **Hetumian** feudal dynasties of Cilician Armenia who elevated themselves to royalty as well, and organized a state even more alike the contemporary feudal monarchies of Europe.

The nakharar system was seriously weakened by the Byzantines and basically destroyed by the Seljuk Turks. The residue of the system held out in the mountainous regions of Eastern Armenia and even survived Mongol rule, by which time it was seriously circumscribed and confined to alpine territory. Major figures during the royal era, the nakharars completely dominated Armenian life in the absence of Armenian kings. Their collective actions and inaction proved as decisive in shaping Armenian society as the commands of kings and emperors. Their loyalty to the **Armenian Apostolic Church**, for instance, preserved the young institution during its most vulnerable phase. By sponsoring the authorship of their family histories, they shaped the outlines of their nation's history and inspired the basic texts of its literary culture. In their deeds and character, writers found them paragons of virtue or vice. By their recklessness they squandered opportunities and fortunes. By their uncommon courage they kept the torch of freedom burning for Armenians. Without them Armenia fell into servitude and decay, not to recover in the same form again. At any one time the nakharar system exhibited all the advantages and disadvantages of government by an aristocratic elite. The strains of class conflict were constantly present in Armenia revealed by the regular resurgence of heterodox practices in **religion**. The exploited peasantry regularly enlisted in puritanical movements dissenting from the prevailing order and defying church and state authorities. In the longer perspective, given that no other form of political management offered an alternative to meet the demands of the terrain and the constant defense needs of Armenia, the government delivered by the nakharar system proved uniquely functional and rooted in the requirements of the age. *See also* ADONTZ, NICHOLAS; ARMENIAN KINGDOM.

NALBANDIAN, MIKAYEL (1829–1866). Literary and political figure. Nalbandian was born in the Armenian town of Nor Nakhichevan, near Rostov-on-the-Don, in Russia. He received his education at the local school run by Gabriel **Patkanian**, one of the pioneering figures of modern Armenian **education**. He continued his studies at the universities of St. Petersburg and Moscow. He began teaching as an instructor of the **Armenian language** at the Lazarian Institute in Moscow in 1853 and became an associate of Stepanos Nazariants who inaugurated the first Armenian periodical in Russia. The earliest public voice of liberalism among Armenians, *Hyusisapayl* (*Aurora Borealis*) was in print between 1858 and 1864. In 1859, 1860, and 1861 Nalbandian traveled extensively in Europe, Asia, and among the Armenian communities on the two continents as far as India. He met with many leaders of the Armenian cultural revival in Istanbul and Tbilisi and became closely acquainted with the condition of the Armenian people worldwide.

Nalbandian also met in London with the Russian intelligentsia in exile, including advocates of political radicalism such as Alexander Herzen and Mikhail Bakunin. In Paris he met with Ivan Sergeevich Turgenev. There, he also authored the first modern Armenian-language political tract entitled *Agriculture as the Just Way* (1862). It reflected the influence of contemporary socialist thought, and the Russian preoccupation with the land question in the aftermath of the 1861 Emancipation of the serfs, as applied to his concern with the state of the Armenian peasantry. On his return to St. Petersburg he made contact with the populist Nicholas Chernishevsky and became involved with the revolutionary *Zemlya i Volya* (Land and Freedom) movement. Tsarist police arrested him in July 1862. He remained in the Petropavlov fortress prison until 1865 when he was exiled to Kamyshin, in Saratov province, only to die of tuberculosis in less than a year.

Nalbandian's criticism was not confined to Russian tsarism. He was a vocal advocate of anticlericalism, critical of both conservative Apostolic and **Catholic** Armenians. He was inspired by the European national liberation movements, especially the Italian struggle against Austria. His two best-known works of poetry echo those sentiments and introduced in Armenian letters the concept of political liberty. In *Azatutiun* (*Freedom*) (1861) he described the idea as basic to human existence and glorified the struggle for it. *The Italian Girl's Song* (1861) described the role of women in the Garibaldi campaign for Italian liberation and called on Armenian women to demonstrate the same spirit. The poem is better known by the words with which it begins, "Our fatherland." Set to music, it was adapted as the national anthem of the first Republic of Armenia (1918–1920). Banned by Soviet authorities, the parliament of Armenia restored the anthem upon the declaration of its intent in 1990 to seek independence once again.

NAREKATSI, GRIGOR. *See* GRIGOR NAREKATSI.

NATIONAL DEMOCRATIC UNION (NDU) (*Azgayin Zhoghovrdavarakan Miutiun, AzhM***).** Political party. After splitting from the **Armenian National Movement** (ANM), **Vazgen Manukian**, Armenia's first non-Communist **prime minister** in 1990–1991, and Davit Vardanian organized NDU in 1992. While sharing in the liberal economic and democratization program of the ANM, the NDU fundamentally differed in its platform over the issue of a national agenda. The NDU strongly advocated for the formation of a national society and the pursuit of clear nationalist goals. It called for the independence of **Nagorno Karabagh** and for strong relations with the Armenian **diaspora**, including dual citizenship. Five deputies in the 1995 parliament and six in the 1999 parliament represented the NDU. The NDU has played a role in Armenian political life larger than that indicated by this small representation by virtue of the fact that the party leader is a nationally recognized politician. As the NDU candidate Manukian garnered at least 41 percent of the vote in the 1996 presidential **elections**. Charges of fraud by the NDU and other parties, and irregularities that marred the elections, provoked protest. The postelection unrest, however, undermined popular support for the NDU. In the 1998 special presidential elections, the NDU once again presented Manukian as its candidate. He garnered only 12 percent of the vote. *See also* MANUKIAN, VAZGEN CABINET; POLITICAL PARTIES; TER-PETROSSIAN, LEVON.

NERSES V ASHTARAKETSI (1770–1857). Religious leader. Nerses was born in the town of Ashtarak in Eastern Armenia during the period of the Persian khanates. He received his education at the **Edjmiadsin** seminary and entered the ministry at a time when the Russian Empire was expanding into the Caucasus. With his appointment as Armenian prelate of Tbilisi in 1814, he became a leading proponent of Armenian support for Russia. In 1824 he founded the Nersisian school, which, over the course of the century, became the leading educational institution of the Armenian community in Russia, teaching and employing many literary luminaries. The school remained open until 1925. From the time of its founding, the school also operated a press, thus playing an additional role in turning Tbilisi into one of the major centers of publishing in the Armenian **diaspora**.

During the Second Russo-Persian War of 1826–1828, Nerses took an active part in the Russian campaigns at Edjmiadsin, Sardarapat and **Yerevan** by leading bands of Armenian volunteers in a conflict, which he imagined held the portents of the liberation of Armenia. He was even decorated in 1828 with the order of Alexander Nevsky. His more important role, however, was in persuading the Russian authorities to encourage the resettlement of the Armenians of Iran in their historic homeland from which they had been forcibly removed some two hundred years earlier. It marked the beginning of the reconcentration of the dispersed Armenian population into the region around Edjmiadsin and Yerevan. His vocal advocacy for an autonomous Armenia under Russian tutelage, however, resulted in his reassignment as prelate of the remote Russian province of Bessarabia, north of the Black Sea. Elected as **Catholicos** Nerses V, he returned to Edjmiadsin in 1843 at the age of 73 and dedicated the rest of his life to the revitalization of the Holy See and to promoting education. As for his resettlement program, it reversed the 800-year dispersion of the Armenian people and helped form the nucleus of the future Armenian state. *See also* ARGHUTIANTS, HOVSEP; ARMENIAN APOSTOLIC CHURCH; YEREVANTSI, SIMEON.

NERSES LAMBRONATSI. *See* HETUM I; HETUMIAN.

NORADOUNGIAN, GABRIEL (1852–1936). Diplomat, Ottoman minister of foreign affairs. Noradoungian was born in Istanbul to one of the families of the old *amira* class representing the crust of Armenian society once associated with service to the Ottoman dynasty and the palace. After attending local Armenian and French schools, he went to Paris in 1870 to pursue a degree in international law. Returning to Istanbul in 1875, he entered the foreign ministry and served as legal counsel. In a four-volume collection published in Paris between 1897 and 1903, Noradoungian issued his *Recueil d'actes internationaux de l'empire Ottoman*. The collection offered the texts, translated into French, of the principal treaties and agreements reached by the Sublime Porte with neighboring states and European Powers.

Noradoungian filled his first cabinet post as minister of public works after the 1908 Young Turk Revolution and the restoration of the Ottoman Constitution. Whereas this appointment was in line with the promotion of other Ottoman Armenians who had risen to positions of responsibility in the services sector of the government, Noradoungian's second cabinet position under Prime Minister Ghazi Ahmet Mukhtar gave an Armenian Christian the exceptional distinction of being tasked with policymaking as minister of foreign affairs of the Ottoman Empire in 1912. His tenure ended with the outbreak of the Balkan War in 1913.

Noradoungian was active in Armenian affairs for all of his adult life. He participated in the Armenian National Assembly in Istanbul and was elected its chairman in 1894. He represented the conservative elements of Armenian society and opposed programs to involve the Western Powers in the Armenian Question. After World War I Noradoungian joined **Boghos Nubar** *Pasha* as part of the Armenian National Delegation organized to represent the interests of the Western Armenians at the Paris Peace Conference. Though the Armenians were not accorded official representation, Noradoungian remained involved in the efforts to negotiate international recognition for the republic founded in Russian Armenia and for the establishment of a national home for the surviving Armenian population of the Ottoman Empire earlier deported during World War I by the order of the Young Turk regime. Ultimately his efforts came to naught as Turkey refused to accede to any Allied plan to resettle the Armenians in the former Armenian provinces. Noradoungian spent the rest of his years in Paris where he served as the vice-president of the **Armenian General Benevolent Union** (AGBU). Before his passing he dictated his autobiography of which only fragments survived. *See also* DAUD PASHA.

NUBAR *PASHA* (1824–1899). Prime Minister of Egypt. Born in Izmir, Nubar and his brother Arakel came to Egypt with the sponsorship of their uncle **Boghos** *Bey* **Yusufian**, minister of commerce and foreign affairs for Muhammad Ali, the Ottoman *vali*, or governor, of Egypt from 1805 to 1848, who secured the viceregency of the country for his dynasty. Arakel *Bey* Nubar (1826–1859), who became minister of commerce in Egypt, began his career as an interpreter for Ibrahim Pasha, the son of Muhammad Ali. The viceroy Abbas I Hilmi (1848–1854) removed him and his brother from office but later tried to regain their friendship by appointing each as his country's representative to Vienna and Berlin, respectively. The two posts were created for the Nubarian brothers, suggesting that Abbas, while seeking their friendship, did not want them to remain in Egypt. Both brothers returned to Egypt when Said ascended the throne as viceroy (1854–1863). Arakel then accompanied Said to the Sudan, where the viceroy assigned him the governorship of the province.

Nubar arrived in Egypt at age 17. He was sent to Europe in 1844 and studied in Geneva and elsewhere. He returned in 1849 and was promoted to various posts in the railways and commerce departments until his appointment as ambassador to Berlin. In 1865 Nubar became minister of public works. A year later he was minister of foreign affairs, and briefly in 1876 he served as minister of commerce. For seven years, beginning in 1876, he labored for the institution of international courts in Egypt and conducted the negotiations with the European Powers. Under the *khedives* Ismail (1863–1879), Tawfiq (1879–1892) when the British began their occupation of Egypt in 1882, and Abbas II Hilmi (1892–1914), Nubar *Pasha* served three terms as prime minister: August 28, 1878 to September 20, 1879; January 10, 1884 to January 8, 1889; and April 16, 1894 to November 1895.

Much as **Boghos** *Bey* **Yusufian** promoted the career of his Nubarian relatives, so did Nubar *Pasha* for his Abroyan, or d'Abro, relatives, also from Izmir. Arakel Bey d'Abro served as Nubar *Pasha*'s advisor from 1866 to 1873. He went to the Sudan with the Egyptian expedition of the khedive Ismail and was appointed governor of Massawa. Dicran *Pasha* d'Abro began his career in politics as a secretary in 1868 under the tutelage of Nubar *Pasha*. He rose to the post of minister of foreign affairs and served between May 14, 1891 and April 15, 1895. He was married to Nubar *Pasha*'s daughter Ziba and was the last Armenian to hold a ministerial post in the Egyptian government. *See also* ARTIN *PASHA* CHRAKIAN; BOGHOS NUBAR *PASHA*; DAUD *PASHA*; NORADOUNGIAN, GABRIEL.

– O –

ORMANIAN, MAGHAKIA (MALACHIA) (1841–1918). Clergyman and scholar, Armenian patriarch of Istanbul (1896–1908). Ormanian was born in Istanbul where he received his elementary education. Sent to religious school in Rome in 1851, he was ordained a Roman **Catholic** priest and engaged in educational work in Istanbul and Rome. In 1875 Ormanian met Garibaldi in Italy and in 1877 quit Roman Catholicism to join the **Armenian Apostolic Church**. He was ordained a celibate priest in 1879 by **Nerses Varzhapetian**, Armenian patriarch of Istanbul, who relied on his linguistic skills to prepare appeals to embassies and foreign governments about the Armenian Question in the Ottoman Empire. In 1880 Ormanian was elected primate of Erzerum, wherefrom he went on to teach theology at **Edjmiadsin** in Russian Armenia in 1887. Banished by the tsarist government for his political views, in 1889 Ormanian became the dean of the seminary of Armash, near Izmit, which became the principal training ground for the Armenian priesthood in Turkey under his leadership. On Ormanian's shoulders fell the appointment of Armenian patriarch of Istanbul in 1896 just after a series of massacres, attributed to the policies of Sultan Abdul-Hamid (Abdulhamit) II, visited the Armenians of the Turkish Empire. As religious leader of the Armenians in the Ottoman state, Ormanian steered a cautious course during the era of the Hamidian repression. It earned him much animosity from radical elements in the Armenian community opposed to the despotism of the sultan. The 1908 Young Turk Revolution saw his removal from office. Thereafter Ormanian devoted his time to writing one of the great works of Armenian historical scholarship. His *Azgapatum* (National History), issued in three volumes between 1912 and 1927 in Istanbul and Jerusalem, was an exhaustive account of Armenian ecclesiastical history. In 1914 Ormanian moved to the Armenian monastery of St. James in Jerusalem, but was exiled to Damascus in 1917 by the Young Turk regime. A year later he died in Istanbul. *See also* ARMENIAN MASSACRES; ARMENIAN *MILLET*: MKRTICH KHRIMIAN.

– P –

PAPKEN SIUNI (1879–1896). Revolutionary. Papken Siuni, nee Bedros Parian, was born in the town of Akn (Egin) in Turkey. He received his education in Istanbul where he also joined the **Armenian Revolutionary Federation** (ARF) and was expelled from school for political activities. He led what became one of the most controversial revolutionary acts of the ARF, the raid on the Ottoman Bank in Istanbul on August 26, 1896. It was staged to draw European attention to the plight of the Armenians who had been subjected to large-scale massacres the previous two years and to require the sultan, Abdul-Hamid (Abdulhamit) II, to commit to reforms in the Armenian provinces. Despite the name, the bank was a European-owned institution and Western ambassadors negotiated the safe conduct of the band of raiders who were placed on a ship for Europe. Twenty-five Dashnaks participated in the seizure of the bank. Four were killed by guards in the fighting, including Papken Siuni, the youngest in the group at age 17. The capture of the bank lasted half a day. Within hours of the departure of the revolutionaries, armed Turkish mobs rampaged through the Armenian neighborhoods of Istanbul. In two days of killings, five to six thousand Armenians were killed. *See also* ARMENIAN MASSACRES; ARMENIAN REVOLUTIONARY MOVEMENT; PASDERMADJIAN, GAREGIN.

PARADJANOV, SERGEI (1924–1990). Cinematographer. Paradjanov was born in Tbilisi, Georgia, to parents who were frequent targets of Stalinist repression. He studied music in Tbilisi. With his interest in the arts, he enrolled in the Institute of Cinematography in Moscow. Upon graduation in 1952, he went to work in Kiev. During the brief Khrushchev period of comparative cultural freedom, he was in the Ukraine where the cinematographer Andrei Tarkovsky filmed a heroic rendition of the life of the great medieval artist *Andrei Rublev*. Focusing on the artist's personal struggle, the film achieved a level of dramatic effect that soon caused the Soviet film bureaucracy in Moscow to censor it. Influenced by this new experimentation in Soviet filmmaking, Paradjanov himself embarked on a difficult career of making artistic films that put him in constant conflict with the authorities. His first individualistic production, *Shadows of Our Forgotten Ancestors*, made in 1964, tapped the regional culture of Moldova, as his later films would rely upon the folklore, mythology, and visual vocabulary of Georgia, Azerbaijan, and Armenia.

Paradjanov began to experiment with the idea of film as more of a visual medium than a theatrical production and began increasingly to depict his subjects in a highly stylized, ritualized, and sensual iconography of images resulting in eloquent series of slow moving tableaux utilizing the minimum of speech and action. His 1969 film called *Nran Guyne*, the *Color of Pomegranate*, immediately established him as the foremost Armenian interpreter of culture on film. In an extraordinary representation of the life of the greatest Armenian minstrel, Sayat Nova, Paradjanov achieved a quality of filmmaking that integrated the entire artistic heritage of Armenia into a singular national concept dramatized through the trials of the bard traveling across country, across social classes, and across life. Paradjanov's own struggle with the authorities as they edited the film against his wishes, and his outspoken defense of other harassed, exiled, or imprisoned artists landed him in jail in 1974. It was 1984 before he was free to make another film. He completed only two more. *The Fortress of Suram*, was based on a Georgian folk tale, and *Ashugh Gharib* was his homage to Azerbaijani culture, thus completing a Caucasian trilogy.

Despite the mere handful of films made by Paradjanov, they were awarded numerous prizes in Europe where they were well received by critics and filmmakers alike who petitioned the Soviet authorities to release him from prison. He enjoyed a brief period of celebrity toward the end of his life as glasnost allowed both artists and audiences to commune more freely. He looked forward to making films in Armenia, but all he could bequeath his homeland was the collection of his fantastic collages now housed in a museum named for him in **Yerevan**.

PASDERMADJIAN, GAREGIN (ARMEN GARO) (1873–1924). Revolutionary and political leader. Pasdermadjian was born in Erzerum and attended the Sanasarian academy, the local Armenian high school, and continued his education in France. He joined the **Armenian Revolutionary Federation** (ARF) in 1895 and assumed the alias Armen Garo. In 1896 Pasdermadjian participated in one of the more daring and notorious acts of the Armenian revolutionaries. He was among the 25 Dashnaks under the leadership of **Papken Suni** who seized the Ottoman Bank in Istanbul on August 26. Despite its name, the bank was European-owned, and the takeover was staged to draw European public attention to the series of massacres of Armenians unleashed during the reign of Sultan Abdul-Hamid (Abdulhamit) II over the course of the previous two years since 1894. European representatives negotiated a pardon for the revolutionaries and removed them from the bank the following day. That night, however, Istanbul became the site of the massacre of some five to six thousand Armenians.

Pasdermadjian remained abroad until 1908. Between 1903 and 1905 he was active in the Caucasus where the Armenians of Russia were in revolutionary ferment prior to the outbreak in St. Petersburg on Bloody Sunday. Pasdermadjian returned to Erzerum with the restoration of the Ottoman Constitution and was elected a deputy to the Ottoman parliament. Anxious over the Young Turk government's war policy and its designs against the Armenians, he joined Russian-Armenian volunteers in the campaign against the Ottomans when war broke out in 1914.

With the founding of the Republic of Armenia on former Russian territory after World War I, Pasdermadjian was sent to Washington to serve as Armenia's unofficial envoy. He also participated in the Armenian delegation sent to the Paris Peace Conference, and worked to obtain United States support for independent Armenia until it was Sovietized by the Red Army. Pasdermadjian is also reported to have had a role in organizing *Nemesis*, the secret group formed by the ARF to hunt down the Young Turk Committee conspirators who had organ-

ized the genocide of the Armenians during World War I. *See also* AR-
MENIAN GENOCIDE; ARMENIAN MASSACRES.

PATKANIAN. Family of writers and educators. Three generations of
Patkanians as activist educators played a major role in the establishment and expansion of a network of schools in the Russian-Armenian
diaspora. Serovpe Patkanian (1769–1836) was born in Istanbul and
educated by the **Mekhitarians** in Venice. He opened one of the first
Armenian schools in the Ottoman Empire in 1792, in the Pera suburb
of Istanbul, where, besides the teaching of the **Armenian language**,
he had introduced music lessons. Denounced for his activities and innovations, he fled the following year to the court of the Georgian
King Irakli II in Tbilisi where he founded the first Armenian school
in the city. In 1793 he also opened a school in Nor Nakhichevan
(New Nakhichevan), in southern Russia, and between 1810 and 1822
taught at the Aghababian school that he founded in Astrakhan. He
passed away in Nor Nakhichevan.

Serovpe's older son, Gabriel Patkanian (1802–1889) was born in
Tbilisi and joined the clergy. He had received his schooling at the
Aghababian school in Astrakhan, where in 1827 he was appointed
head of the city's Armenian seminary. In 1836 he opened his own
school in Nor Nakhichevan. Among his students was **Mikayel Nalbandian**. In 1847 he moved to Tbilisi at the invitation of **Catholicos
Nerses V Ashtaraketsi** to assume the abbacy of the church of No-
rashen and in 1850 was given the rectorate of the Nersisian school.
Accused in 1852 of involvement in political intrigue, he was imprisoned for seven years and then exiled. He was eventually freed and
settled in St. Petersburg where he continued teaching. He was a prolific author who extensively tapped the Armenian historical literature
and popularized the heroes and heroines of the past. His younger
brother, Mikayel Patkanian (1814–1895), was born in Astrakhan and
educated at the Lazarian academy in Moscow, and became a teacher
at the Nersisian school. He also was a writer and active in the development of the Armenian theater in Tbilisi.

Rafayel Patkanian (1830–1892), born in Nor Nakhichevan, was
Gabriel Patkanian's son. He received his elementary education in his
father's school in Nor Nakhichevan and continued at the Lazarian
academy. While at Moscow University he founded, along with two
other colleagues, the literary circle by the name of Kamar Katiba.

Patkanian subsequently signed Kamar Katiba as his pen name. Propounding vernacularism, the group's first collective publication issued in 1855 was titled *Write as You Speak, Speak as You Write.* Patkanian was active in the nascent journalism of the time and became a strong proponent of Armenian emancipation, an idea whose fortunes he wrote about by addressing political developments in the Armenian homeland and on the international scene. In 1880 through his efforts an artisanal school was opened in Nor Nakhichevan for the care and education of destitute Armenian children. Until the end of his days, he remained the principal of the school.

Rafayel Patkanian is also remembered for his patriotic verse. The most popular of his poems, *Araksi Artasuke* (*The Tears of Arax*), written in 1856, is an elegy mourning the fate of Armenia by evoking its past glories with a walk through history. Opening with the line "Along the shores of Mother Arax," namely the great **Arax River** that flows through the length of Armenia watering the central Plain of **Ararat**, he created verbal imagery that was subsequently rendered visually by Armenian artists into an emblematic portrait of Armenia as a forlorn woman sitting among the ruins along the banks of the Arax River. The symbolism endures in the gallery of the sentimental images of the Armenian national consciousness.

POLITICAL GEOGRAPHY. The 1918–1920 independent Republic of Armenia was created out of Russian Armenia. Soviet Armenia was drawn in 1921 to include the portions of the republic under Red Army control and Soviet Russia ceded those parts under Turkish Nationalist control to Turkey. The new Republic of Armenia, independent since 1991, reproduces the territory of Soviet Armenia.

Soviet Armenia was divided into 38 administrative districts (*raion* in Russian). From south to north, these were: Meghri, Ghapan, Goris, Sisian, Vayk, Yegheknatzor, **Ararat**, Martuni, Vardenis, **Artashat**, Baghramian, **Armavir**, **Edjmiadsin**, Masis, **Yerevan**, **Abovian**, Gavar, Talin, Ashtarak, Nairi, **Ani**, Artik, Aragats, Aparan, Hrazdan, **Sevan**, Karmir, Akhurian, **Spitak**, Gugark, Ijevan, Tavush, Amasia, Ashotsk, Stepanavan, Tashir, Tumanian, and Noyemberian.

In 1995 these districts were consolidated into 11 provinces (*marz* in Armenian): Siunik, Vayots Tzor, Ararat, Armavir, Yerevan, Aragatsotn, Kotayk, Gegharkunik, Shirak, Lori, and Tavush, with their respective centers in the towns of Ghapan, Yegheknatzor, Artashat,

Armavir, Yerevan, Ashtarak, Hrazdan, Gavar, **Gyumri**, Vanatzor, and Ijevan.

The ancient Armenian province of Artsakh became known as the Karabagh region during the late Persian period. The Soviets in 1921 designated the upland part of Karabagh that was almost entirely Armenian-populated as an autonomous district with the name of **Nagorno Karabagh** (Mountainous Karabagh). In 1991 its Armenian inhabitants declared the district a republic and in 1992 declared the republic independent. There are five districts in the Republic of Mountainous Karabagh, or Nagorno Karabagh Republic (NKR): Hadrut, Martuni, Shushi, Askeran, and Mardakert. The district of Shahumian to the north of Mountainous Karabagh, once inhabited by Armenians, and claimed by the republic, was depopulated in 1991 and is under the control of neighboring Azerbaijan. On October 3, 2000, the NKR government announced the restoration of the historic Armenian names of the districts: Hadrut became Dizak; Martuni became Varanda; Askeran became Khacheran; Mardakert became Jraberd; Shahumian became Giulistan-Shahumian; Shushi remained unchanged.

POLITICAL PARTIES. Armenians first organized political associations in the 1880s. The **Armenakan** association was formed in 1885 in **Van**. The **Social Democratic** *Hnchakian* **Party** was formed in 1887 in Geneva. The **Armenian Revolutionary Federation** (ARF) (*Hay Heghapokhakan Dashnaktsutiun*, or Dashnak Party) was formed in 1890 in Tbilisi. All three were nationalist organizations. The last two espoused socialism. The Armenakan association remained largely a local group. Though originally formed by Russian Armenians, the Hnchakian party operated a network primarily in the Ottoman Empire. Also founded by Russian Armenians, the ARF too functioned in the Ottoman Empire, but exercised predominant influence over the political life of Armenians in the Russian Caucasus. The membership of the Hnchakian party split over the issue of socialism and a purely nationalist wing was formed as the *Verakazmial*, or Reformed, Hnchakian party in 1896. In 1902 the Union of Armenian Social Democrats (*Hay Sotsial Demokratneri Miutiun*) was formed in Tbilisi, which associated with the Russian Social Democratic Workers Party (RSDWP), but maintained a separate Armenian identity and program earning it the label of Specifist. In 1917 the Armenian Populist Party

(*Hay Zhoghovrdakan Kusaktsutiun*) was organized by former members of the Russian Constitutional Democratic Party, Kadet for short, as the voice of the liberals. While most of these groups functioned in the independent Republic of Armenia during its brief existence from 1918 to 1920 and enjoyed some representations in its parliament and various organs of government, the ARF remained the preeminent political party enjoying a popular mandate.

Sovietization swiftly ended their existence in Armenia and from 1921 only the **Communist Party of Armenia** (CPA), as an integral branch of the Russian Communist Party formed out of the Bolshevik wing of the RSDWP, functioned in Soviet Armenia. The banning of political organizations spelled the end of the smaller groups and the exile of the ARF. In 1921 various liberal groups among Western Armenians including the Constitutional Democratic Party (*Sahmanadir Ramkavar Kusaktsutiun*), the Liberal Party (*Azatakan Kusaktsutiun*) of the Reformed Hnchaks, and the Armenian Populist Party (*Hay Zhoghovrdakan Kusaktsutiun*) formed the **Democratic Liberal Party** (DLP) (*Ramkavar Azatakan Kusaktsutiun*) in Istanbul. After 1922 Armenian political organizations ceased to function in Turkey as well.

The Hnchak, Dashnak, and Ramkavar parties became the political organizations of the Armenian diaspora each espousing a different combination of ideology and national program. Avowing socialism in its platform, nonetheless the ARF became the locus of anti-Communist persuasion and activity. Rejecting the legitimacy of the Armenian Soviet Socialist Republic (ASSR) and regrouping as the torchbearers of a strident nationalism, over the decades the ARF became completely removed from its once-Russian–Armenian origins. The Hnchakian party, as an old-line socialist organization recognized the legitimacy of the Soviet Armenia. Its membership remained small. The Ramkavar party emerged as the liberal alternative to the ARF. As the voice of moderate nationalism, despite its liberal platform, it too recognized the legitimacy of Soviet Armenia. While providing vital leadership in the widely dispersed Armenian diaspora, the 70 years of exclusion from Armenia distanced these parties from the internal political dynamic of Soviet Armenian society. The monopoly of the CPA, however, did not equip it either to play a significant role in the post-Soviet era. Little more than the instrument of the authorities in Moscow, as a body it was probably always slightly more liberal compared to the hard-line party members dominating the central party apparatus. On the whole, however, it remained a mere reflector of the policies of the Central Committee of the Communist Party in Moscow and proved incapable of independent action when democratic reforms reduced the power of the organization in the final years of the Soviet Union. Between 1988 and 1991 popular front forces led by the **Armenian National Movement** (ANM) rapidly displaced the CPA. The end of communism reintroduced political pluralism in Armenia. A host of political organizations articulating widely divergent agendas soon emerged. Even the so-called traditional parties of the diaspora returned to Armenia. The ANM, which exercised a leading role through most of the 1990s, rapidly declined in popularity. This created a highly dynamic and fluid political environment in Armenia where the tendency to organize more political groupings rather than to consolidate into larger organizations prevailed. Personal alliances and parliamentary blocs, more so than parties, became the source of political influence in the late 1990s.

In the 1995 parliamentary **elections**, the first in the newly independent state, the following parties entered the race:

Agrarian Democratic Party (*Hoghayin Zhoghovrdapetakan Kusaktsutiun*)

Communist Party of Armenia (*Hayastani Hamaynavar Kusaktsutiun*)

Democratic Party of Armenia (*Hayastani Zhoghovrdapetakan Kusaktsutiun*)

Liberal Democratic (*Ramkavar*) Party (*Ramkavar Azatakan Kusaktsutiun*)

Mission (*Arakelutiun*)

National Democratic Union (NDU) (*Azkayin Zhoghovrdapetakan Miuntiun*)

National State (*Azkayin Petutiun*)

Populist Organization (*Zhghovrdayin Kazmakerputiun*)

Scientific and Industrial Civil Union (*Gitakan yev Ashkhadankayin Kaghakayin Miutiun*)

Shamiram (*Shamiram* [Semiramis women's party])

Union for National Self-Determination (*Azkayin Inknavarutian Miutiun*)

Will Union and Armenian Federation Party (*Kamk Miutiun yev Hayastani Dashnaktsakan Kusaktsutiun*);

and the Republic (*Hanrapetutiun*) Bloc composed of:

Armenian National Movement (*Hayots Hamazgayin Sharzhum*)
Christian Democratic Union (*Krisdoniya Zhoghovrtapetakan Miutiun*)
Intellectual Armenia (*Mtavorakan Hayastan*)
Liberal Democratic Party (*Ramkavar Azatakan Kusaktsutiun*)
Republican Party (*Hanrapetakan Kusaktsutiun*)
Social Democratic (*Hnchak*) Party (*Sotsial Demokrat Hnchakian Kusaktsutiun*)

Only five of the political organizations met the minimum 5 percent of the vote to qualify for seats in the 1995 parliament: the Republic Bloc, National Democratic Union, Union for National Self-Determination, Shamiram, and the Communist Party. The Liberal Democratic Party of the Republic Bloc was an indigenous spin-off of the mainline Ramkavar Party. The Will Union and Armenian Federation Party was also a spin-off of the mainline Dashnak Party that at the time was suspended from political activity. As for Shamiram, it was a women's party created by the ANM.

In the 1999 parliamentary elections the following parties fielded candidates:

Armenian National Movement (*Hayots Hamazgayin Sharzhum*)
Armenian Revolutionary Federation (*Hay Heghapokhakan Dashnaktsutiun*)
Communist Party of Armenia (*Hayastani Hamaynavar Kusaktsutiun*)
Conservative Democratic Party (*Pahpanoghakan Zhoghovrdapetakan Kusaktsutiun*)
Conservative Party (*Pahpanoghakan Kusaktsutiun*)
Country of Law (*Orinats Yerkir*)
Democratic Homeland (*Zhoghovrdapetakan Hayrenik*)
Democratic Liberal Party of Armenia (*Hayastani Ramkavar Azatakan Kusaktsutiun*)
Democratic Party of Armenia (*Hayastani Zhoghovrdapetakan Kusaktsutiun*)
Free Armenia Mission (*Azat Hayk Arakelutiun*)
Freedom (*Azatutiun*)
Intellectual Armenia (*Mtavorakan Hayastan*)
Kaissa (*Kaissa*)

Mission (*Arakelutiun*)

Motherland Diaspora Union (*Mayrenik Spiurk Miutiun*)

National Democratic Union (*Azgayin Zhovovrdapetakan Miutiun*)

National State (*Azgayin Petutiun*)

Populist Party of Armenia (PPA) (*Hayastani Zhoghovrdakan Kusaktsutiun*)

Republican Party of Armenia (RPA) (*Hayastani Hanrapetakan Kusasktsutiun*)

Social Democratic Party of Armenia (*Hayastani Sotsial Demokrat Kusaktsutiun*)

United Progressive Communist Party of Armenia (*Hayastani Miatsial Arajdimakan Hamaynavar Kusaktsutiun*)

Union of Constitutional Rights (*Sahmanadrakan Iravunkneri Miutiun*)

Union of Intellectuals (*Mtavorakanneri Miutiun*)

Union of Self-Determination (USD) (*Inknavarutian Miutiun*)

Worthy Future (*Arzhani Apaga*)

Women of the Armenian Land (*Hayots Yerkri Ganayk*)

Social Democratic Hnchakian Party (*Sotsial Demokrat Hnchakian Kusaktsutiun*)

Many of these parties, however, joined into blocs to improve their chances of winning seats in the proportional voting requiring the 5 percent minimum qualification. The Unity (*Miasnutiun*) alliance or Unity bloc consisting of the Republican Party of Armenia and the Populist Party of Armenia represented the most significant coalition. The Law and Accord bloc was formed by a number of small groups led by the Union of Constitutional Rights. Voters sent to parliament the following political organizations: Unity Alliance; Communist Party; Law and Accord; Armenian Revolutionary Federation; Country of Law; and the National Democratic Union. With 62 seats in the 131-member parliament, the Unity Alliance emerged as the strongest political coalition. Registering only 10 seats as the second largest delegation was the Communist Party. The ARF garnered eight seats; Law and Accord bloc six seats; Country of Law six seats; and the National Democratic Union six seats. ANM, the once dominant party, sent a single delegate to the National Assembly.

The constantly shifting political fortunes of the political parties in Armenia reflected an absence of partisan adherence to any one organization among voters. As political organizations go, they all remained small, with few resources, and a limited base of popular support. They were yet to take root in the political aspirations of the electorate. They also fell into five distinct categories. One category consisted of organizations led by charismatic leaders. A second category represented the many mutations of the former membership of the Armenian Communist Party. A third category included the traditional parties returning to political life in the homeland. A fourth category involved the electioneering organizations created by power brokers in the country. A fifth category encompassed a myriad band of politically active individuals striving for a regulated society by emphasizing one or another aspect of the continuing reforms needed in a period of transition, change, economic distress, and national predicaments. This diversity and the absence of strong political organizations were also reflected in the large number of unaffiliated delegates in the National Assembly. In the 1999 elections, 29 independents were elected, almost a quarter of the legislature. *See also* ARMENIAN REVOLUTIONARY MOVEMENT.

POPULIST PARTY OF ARMENIA (also People's Party of Armenia, PPA) (*Hayastani Zhoghovrdakan Kusaktsutiun, HZhK*). Political party. Founded in May 1998, the PPA was formed after the respectable showing of **Karen Demirchian** in the March 1998 special presidential **elections**. Though he lost out to **Robert Kocharian**, Demirchian garnered 40 percent of the popular vote. With this mandate Demirchian and his cohorts formed the PPA. The party platform formalized the program on which Demirchian had run his presidential campaign calling for what was described as a socially oriented market economy. The centerpiece of the platform was a reaction to the liberal market economics and the rapid and stringent reforms promoted by the **Armenian National Movement** (ANM) in accordance with World Bank and International Monetary Fund (IMF) stipulations for the extension of loan guarantees. The PPA successfully tapped into the mass discontent and popular resentment of the strata of society whose living standards had rapidly eroded in the post-Soviet economic environment. They held the ANM, its policies on developing a market economy, and the class of newly rich who had acquired their wealth by capitalizing on the legal and illegal opportunities offered by privatization, responsible for their dire straits. The PPA elevated its political standing when Defense Minister **Vazgen**

Sargsian chose to enter the electoral arena as head of the **Republican Party of Armenia** (RPA) and negotiated an alliance with the PPA for the May 1999 parliamentary elections. The so-called Unity (*Miasnutiun*) alliance won a plurality of seats. This victory propelled Demirchian to the chairmanship of the National Assembly and catapulted the PPA as a midsized political association into the government. Armen Khachatrian of the PPA succeeded Demirchian as chairman upon the latter's demise.

PRESIDENT. Only three persons in the 20th century held the title of president of Armenia. During the first independent Republic of Armenia (1918–1920), **Hovhannes Kachaznuni**, its first **prime minister**, was also titular president in 1918. The office did not exist in the Soviet period. Its symbolic equivalent was the president of the Supreme Soviet, or more properly the chairman of the Presidium of the Supreme Soviet, the rubberstamp legislature of the Armenian Soviet Socialist Republic (ASSR), who acted as honorary head of state. In June 1991, the Armenian parliament enacted legislation creating the office of president and thereupon voted to hold **elections**. The first presidential election was held on October 16, 1991, and **Levon Ter-Petrossian** won the post. The Armenian **Constitution**, adopted on July 5, 1995, provided for a presidential system of government, established the term of five years for the head of state, and entrusted the office the responsibility for the independence, territorial integrity, and security of the republic. Ter-Petrossian was reelected on September 22, 1996. He resigned on February 3, 1998, making Prime Minister **Robert Kocharian** acting president. Failing to clear the 50 percent mark required by the constitution in the first round of the special presidential elections held on March 16, 1998, Kocharian was elected to the office on March 30, 1998, in a second round of voting. *See also* POLITICAL PARTIES.

PRIME MINISTER. Since the founding of the state in 1918 and through all its various phases, the government of Armenia has been headed by a prime minister. **Hovhannes Kachaznuni**, **Alexander Khatisian**, Hamazasp Ohandjanian, and **Simon Vratzian** served as the four prime ministers during the 1918–1920 independent Republic of Armenia. During the Soviet era, the president of the Council of Ministers, the nominal premier or prime minister, was a less important figure than the first secretary of the **Communist Party of Armenia** (CPA) who actually led the government. The prime ministers of the Armenian Soviet Socialist Republic (ASSR) tended to be persons of technocratic background, with experience both in technical fields and in bureaucratic management, the so-called apparatchiks. At least two in the second half of the 20th century achieved prominence. Anton Kochinian, before rising to the post of CPA first secretary, served in this capacity from 1952 to 1966. The most accomplished prime minister in the Soviet period was Fadey Sargsian (b. 1923, Yerevan), who held the post from 1976 to 1989. With a doctorate in technology from the University of Leningrad, he worked in the Soviet defense ministry from 1946 to 1963. He returned to Yerevan in 1963 eventually to lead the country's computer institute. Armenia's notable achievements in developing an industrial and educational base in advanced technologies, and its concomitant economic benefits in the late Soviet period, were registered under his guidance. He succeeded **Viktor Hambartsumian** as president of Armenia's National Academy of Sciences in 1996. The last person to lead the Council of Ministers while the Soviet Union was still in existence was **Vazgen Manukian**. A non-Communist and nationalist installed by the **Armenian National Movement** (ANM), his premiership marked the end of Communist power in a country already declared in August 1990 simply as the Republic of Armenia. In the final decade of the 20th century, eight persons held the post of prime minister of Armenia: **Gagik Haroutiunian**, **Khosrov Harutiunian**, **Hrant Bagratian**, **Armen Sarkissian**, **Robert Kocharian**, **Armen Darbinian**, **Vazgen Sargsian**, and **Aram Sargsian**. **Andranik Margarian** became the first prime minister in the 21st century.

According to the Armenian **Constitution**, the **president** appoints the prime minister whom he is obligated to select from the leading political party elected to the National Assembly. This formula created an elastic political arrangement allowing for the fluctuation of power between the president and the prime minister. Even though the constitution gives the president extensive authority as head of state, it also creates conditions for the appointment of a government led by a prime minister heading a competing political party. When the ANM held the majority of seats in the legislature, power was concentrated in the presidency since **Levon Ter-Petrossian** led the party. When the **Republican Party of Armenia** (RPA) became the lead party in

1999, influence shifted to the prime ministry of Vazgen Sargsian, which explains the depth of the political turmoil created in Armenia upon his assassination and the potentially dangerous vacuum of authority resulting therefrom.

In May 2000 **Andranik Margarian** became prime minister introducing a low-key style of management conducive to restabilizing the political environment in Armenia and returning the cabinet to the business of running the country. *See also* POLITICAL PARTIES.

PROTESTANT CHURCH, ARMENIAN. Protestantism reached Armenians and Armenia in the early 19th century through the evangelization of American missionaries sent to the Ottoman Empire for the purpose of bringing Christianity to a presumed heathen country. The organization promoting this endeavor was the American Board of Commissioners for Foreign Missions (ABCFM) based in Boston, Massachusetts, an association of Presbyterians and Congregationalists formed in the wake of a religious movement in the United States known as the Second Revival. With the discovery of the American missionaries that conversion from Islam to a different **religion** was punishable by death in Turkey, the missionaries redirected their attention to proselytizing the Eastern Orthodox and began preaching among Greek and Arab Christians. However, they located their most receptive audience among the Armenians who identified in the Americans the deliverers of a personalized interpretation of the Bible emphasizing spiritual values and a literal understanding of the Scriptures. For Armenians accustomed to a communitarian church steeped in ritual and tradition headed by a controlling priesthood, Protestantism offered a contrast. The alternative appealed to those alienated by the standards and practices of the **Armenian Apostolic Church**, a captive institution strictly conforming to the limitations imposed by the Ottoman government through the **Armenian *Millet*** system and discouraging change and innovation.

Much like Catholicism, Protestantism created a new channel for moral expression and individual participation, which the conservative Armenian Church was in no position to provide. Unlike joining the Armenian **Catholic Church**, which required a redirection of allegiance and submission to Rome and papal authority, both externally located and entangled with European politics, adherence to Protestantism did not obligate similar readjustment. Hence, in the beginning the American missionaries were well received by members of the Armenian Church who viewed them as the exponents of renewal. If on the one hand a blind conservatism defined a good portion of the Armenian clergy, another much lesser current in the Armenian Church already reflected Western influences seeping into the Ottoman Empire, primarily registered in efforts to promote education. Early forays by reformist church leaders focused on improving the morals of a semiliterate clergy whose standards of conduct were one of the sources of disaffection with the Armenian Church. Thus in the 1820s the missionaries actually found their earliest contacts among religious-minded Armenians seeking improvement within the existing structure of the Armenian Church. The incapacity of the Armenian Church to satisfy its internal demand and a more determined campaign of proselytization by the missionaries created the breach that resulted in the emergence of a distinct and new religious grouping among Armenians known more properly as the Armenian Evangelical Church.

The first mission expressly established to reach Armenians was started by the Reverend William Goddell in Istanbul in 1831. Among the first converts were reform-minded clergymen right out of the academy of the Armenian Patriarchate of Istanbul. Under the principalship of Krikor Peshtimaljian since 1829, the patriarchal academy had become a center for educational innovation not all of whose graduates were satisfied with the state of affairs in the church. From this and other examples, the missionaries from the beginning realized that their objective of evangelization would progress with the least degree of friction through education, something for which a stratum of Armenian society was thirsting. Even more perceptively, they realized that Armenians no longer enjoyed access to the Scriptures, which had become frozen and obscured in the **Armenian language** of the fifth century. Continuing the very innovation introduced by Martin Luther of delivering the Bible to the common people in their vernacular, in 1842 Goddell and Harrison Dwight, with the help of native speakers, laymen and clergymen, translated the two Testaments into Armeno-Turkish, the dialect spoken by Armenians in many parts of Asia Minor, a mixture of Armenian and Turkish written in Armenian characters. When in 1853 Elias Riggs delivered the entire Bible for publication in modern Armenian, the whole nature of the debate over church reform, religious revival, and conversion changed. Now every literate Armenian could have access to the Bible, and hereafter, with the missionary press making it readily available, a once scarce item could be distributed to every household.

The Armenian Church had earlier reacted to this type of popularization, which undermined the authority of the Armenian ecclesiastical hierarchy and its monopoly on theological doctrine. Already reeling from the headway made by the Catholic Church, after attempts made to persuade the converts to recant, in 1844 Armenian Patriarch of Istanbul Madteos Chukhadjian resorted to anathema and excommunication, thereby severing the evangelicals from the apostolic church and leaving them little choice but to contemplate a separate course of action. Although the patriarch exercised his legitimate authority in civil and religious matters afforded him by the Ottoman government, the expulsion had no effect in arresting the spread of Protestantism. Without institutional status within the Ottoman system, the Protestants were bereft of formal protection and sought the mediation of foreign diplomats, of whom British Ambassador Stafford Canning obliged and negotiated with the Sublime Porte the grant in 1850 of *millet* status to the Protestant community issued by an imperial *firman* (edict) in the name of Sultan Abdul-Mejid (Abdulmejit). The political formalization of the separate civil and religious character of the Protestant community extended to the evangelical Armenians the privilege of conducting their own affairs under the guidance of their chosen leadership. Stepan Seropian, the brother of former Patriarch Hakobos, was elected the first *azkapet*, or national leader, of the Protestant Armenians.

With Bible in hand in their own language, Armenian Protestants turned to the matter of organizing the growing community of converts. In the case of the Armenian Protestant Church, there is a precise founding date for its first formal congregation, which occurred on July 1, 1846, in the Pera district of Istanbul at the residence of Harrison Dwight. Apisoghom Utudjian served as the first pastor of the church, and another early convert who became a pastor, Hovhannes Der-Sahakian, moved out to found churches in the nearby towns at Adabazar, Bardizag, Hasskeuy, and Nicomedia. Before Der-Sahakian died in 1865, American missionaries and Armenian preachers had spread Protestantism far beyond the immediate vicinity of Istanbul, with churches opened in Trebizond in 1846, Bursa in 1847, Aintab in 1848, Sivas in 1851, Rodosto/Tekirdagh, Merzifon/Marsovan and

Adana in 1852, Smyrna/Izmir and Diyarbekir in 1853, Talas and Marash in 1854, Harput in 1855, and Tarsus in 1859. There were so many missions established all across Armenia and Anatolia that in 1860 the ABCFM divided the mission field into three regions: Eastern, Central, and Western Turkey. Following this example, the Armenian evangelical churches also formed regional organizations: Eastern, Central, Cilicia, and Bithynia (for the west) Unions. By 1883 the Protestant Church had achieved enough self-sufficiency that when the Armenian evangelical leadership and American missionaries convened a conference to clarify matters of jurisdiction, the parties agreed that while the missions would manage the funds they received from ABCFM, the native churches would administer the contributions raised locally at their own discretion.

On the eve of World War I in 1914, 137 churches serviced the Armenian Protestant community headed by preachers and evangelists of whom 82 were ordained ministers. The *Badveli* (Reverend) represented a genuine leader of a community, a figure of greater importance to the flock than the parish priest who stood at the lowest end of the ecclesiastical totem pole of the Armenian Apostolic Church. Many derived their qualities of leadership from the fact that they were highly educated individuals who had acquired the skills of articulate persuasion and preaching and who elevated a people chafing under a repressive government with their example of moral fortitude. In this regard they were some of the finest products of the vast educational system created by the American missionary effort in Ottoman Turkey.

In tandem with the founding of places of worship, the missionaries established schools and created opportunities for attendance to whole strata of Armenian society that otherwise would never have received instruction for the lack of means, teachers, and educational institutions. By 1914, in one form or another the ABCFM was responsible for the founding of 369 elementary schools with an attendance of 19,361 students, these in addition to 46 high schools with 4,090 students, 10 colleges with 1,748 students, 3 theological seminaries with 24 students, 8 industrial schools, 2 schools for the blind and 1 for the deaf and dumb. Also, 5 nurses training schools prepared medical professionals for the 10 hospitals and the dispensaries set up by the ABCFM. The majority of students in these institutions were Armenians.

Medical education was just one of the innovations introduced by the American missionary movement. Another was education for girls. As a matter of fact some of the first schools founded by the missionaries in the 1860s were expressly for girls, the gender whose education was neglected by the larger Armenian community. As for higher education, initially the missionaries planned only to train clergy and had founded their first seminary in the district of Bebek in Istanbul in 1840, and a second in Armenia proper at Harput in 1854. In 1863, however, with the founding of Robert College by Cyrus Hamlin, a new momentum toward higher education was introduced. Anatolia College in Marsovan founded in 1865, Central Turkey College in Aintab opened in 1876, and Euphrates College in Harput also opened in 1876, among others, became major centers for the education of new generations of Armenians who became infused with religious, ethical, as well as political ideals imparted by American educators, missionaries, and medical professionals.

The atrocities associated with the **Hamidian Massacres** of the 1890s and the 1909 **Adana Massacre** presented a new and difficult challenge to the Protestant community. Many fell victim, including the leaders of the Cilician churches who happened to be meeting in Adana in April 1909. With the support of the ABCFM, the Protestant community responded to the crying need of those terrifying days by organizing orphanages to care for the many children left without parent or guardian. But these horrors paled in comparison to the atrocities that devastated the Protestant community during the **Armenian Genocide** of 1915. Of the 51,000 Armenian Protestants living in Turkey at the start of World War I, a mere 14,000 survived at the end of it. Many of the institutions of the hinterland beyond Istanbul were ruined. Of a once shining corps of ministers, only 25 survived, the rest succumbing to the policy of extermination and some, like the Reverend Krikor Der-Boghosian of Aintab, choosing martyrdom in the desert in order to remain to the last with their deported flocks.

The plight of the Armenians resonated in America and the response organized by the American evangelical community proved critical for the survival of the Armenian people, Protestant and non-Protestant alike. At the urging of American Ambassador to Turkey, Henry Morgenthau, to prevent the complete destruction of the Armenian population, the U.S. government took a number of steps. Among them was the effort to send humanitarian relief. The Department of State quietly turned to the ABCFM to begin an emergency drive for the collection of funds. Under the leadership of James L. Barton and Cleveland H. Dodge, the American Committee for Armenian and Syrian Relief was founded in 1915. The Committee enjoyed the ardent support of President Woodrow Wilson. Through public rallies, church collections, and with the assistance of charitable organizations and foundations, the Committee raised millions in its campaigns to save "the starving Armenians." The Committee was able to deliver funds through the American Embassy in Constantinople, which relied upon the missionaries and its consuls to distribute the aid. While the U.S. entry into war against Germany and Turkey in April 1917 disrupted this critical lifeline, the Committee widened its scope of activities at the end of the war also to include Russian Armenia where hundreds of thousands had taken refuge. Renamed the American Committee for Relief in the Near East in 1918, it was incorporated by an act of Congress in 1919 as Near East Relief (NER). Between 1915 and 1930, when it ended operations, NER administered $116,000,000 of assistance. It delivered food, clothing, and materials for shelter by the shipload from America. It set up refugee camps, clinics, hospitals, orphanages, and centers for vocational training. NER is credited with having cared for 132,000 Armenian orphans scattered across the region from Tbilisi and Yerevan to Constantinople, Beirut, Damascus, and Jerusalem.

The expulsion of the Armenians and the founding of the Turkish republic in 1923 confronted the missionaries with a serious predicament: to continue ministering to the Armenian people now in exile, or protecting their investments in Turkey. In the main they tended toward the latter. At that critical moment a new organization formed in America arrived to the rescue of the Armenian Protestant Church. The repression and massacres in the Ottoman Empire had driven many Armenians from their home even before 1915. With the assistance and guidance of missionaries, Protestant Armenians had begun migrating across the Atlantic, and as early as 1881 had founded in the United States the first Armenian church of any denomination in the industrial town of Worcester in central Massachusetts. To assist the survivors of the genocide, the Armenian Evangelical community formed in 1918 in Worcester, at the Armenian Congregational Church of the Martyrs, the Armenian Missionary Association of America (AMAA).

As the missionary influence waned, the AMAA became the primary conduit for the delivery of aid to the Protestant Armenian community now dispersed and resettled mainly in Syria and Lebanon. With Armenian-American support churches were established all across the Middle East and slowly but surely the ABCFM was replaced by the AMAA as the American backbone of the Armenian Protestant Church. By 1936 the missionary oversight of the church had passed and the Armenian Evangelical community was running its own affairs. In time the church resumed its role in education and with resources made available by American benefactors, namely the Mehagian and Philibosian families, in 1955 the AMAA even established the Haigazian College in Beirut, Lebanon, the only institution of higher learning maintained in the Armenian **diaspora**. The college was designated a university in December 1996 by the Lebanese ministry of higher education. By the start of the 21st century the Armenian Protestant Church had founded parishes on every continent and returned to Armenia to revive the moribund community of evangelicals suppressed during the Soviet era. The Ottoman-era institution of azkapet did not survive the Armenian Genocide and the Protestant community no longer has a single figure as its leader. Instead a number of regional unions in the Near East, France, and the United States provide a coordinating umbrella structure to local churches. In the absence of a central authority, the AMAA with its resource base in the United States came to fill the void. Under the stewardship of the Reverend Giragos Chopourian from 1969 to 1987, the organization whose assets were valued at $1.5 million grew to $40 million, and to $100 million by the end of the century, thereby positioned the AMAA as the critical buttress of the Armenian Evangelical Church. The worldwide Armenian Protestant community is estimated at 150,000 members.

– R –

RAFFI (1835–1888). Writer, principal novelist of the 19th century. Raffi was the pen name of Hakob Melik-Hakobian who was born in the village of Payak, in the Salmas district of northwest Iran. He received his elementary education locally and continued high school in Tbilisi at the Russian *gymnasium*. He first settled in his hometown, but the impoverishment of his family led him to seek employment as an educator in Tabriz and Akulis between 1875 and 1879, when he quit to turn to writing full-time and earned his keep as a contributor to the liberal Armenian paper *Mshak* (Laborer). *Mshak* was issued in Tbilisi, where Raffi lived for the rest of his life.

Raffi had started writing at an early age and remained a prolific author for all his years. Influenced by the European romantic novel, Raffi himself became the greatest epic novelist in the **Armenian language** by tackling the literary themes of the age: emancipation, social injustice, political inequality, and national identity. Himself born to a patriarchal clan whose declined stature and lost wealth typified the wrenching transition from a feudal to a modern economy and society, Raffi became a student of Armenian traditional society whose virtues and limitations he eloquently transcribed into fine literature.

The Russo-Turkish War of 1877–1878 turned his attention to the question of political emancipation and national liberation, themes that he developed in his best and mature works. *Khente* (The Fool) issued in 1881 and *Kaydser* (Sparks) in two volumes in 1883 and 1887 explored the subject in a contemporary setting, while his novels *Davit Bek* (1882) revived the memory of the Armenian liberation struggle of the early 18th century and *Samuel* (1886) relocated the struggle for Armenian freedom and identity into the fourth-century setting of the contest between Byzantium and Persia over Armenia.

Raffi is regarded a major figure in the Armenian cultural renaissance of the 19th century and in the creation of modern Armenian literature. His immense output recorded and analyzed the social and political issues of the era. His skill in crafting popular literature in Armenian was matched by his influence in drawing the attention of an increasingly literate audience to the broader issues facing the Armenians as a people. He epitomized the entry of romanticism in Armenian thinking, manifest in the historicizing of values and beliefs in a national culture. The companion volume of *Davit Bek* that Raffi also issued in 1882 best exemplifies this revived interest in the past. In *Khamsayi Melikutiunnere* (The Five Melikdoms [of Karabagh]) he published the historical evidence on which he had based his novel. *See also* DAVIT BEK; NAGORNO KARABAGH.

RAMKAVAR, RAMKAVAR KUSAKTSUTIUN. *See* DEMO-CRATIC LIBERAL PARTY (DLP).

RELIGION. Religion played a decisive role in the history of the Armenians. Their choice of religion defined their country's long-term cultural orientation. Even more fundamentally, it determined their political fate and status as a people. While Christianity was the final choice of religion, a choice made comparatively early in their history, spiritual life in Armenia was always more diverse than the guardians of the faith were necessarily prepared to admit. The periodic struggle against sectarianism attested to a variety of sources of religious persuasion. In constant contact with many faiths, and always under pressure to reconsider their religious loyalties, Armenians were influenced by, absorbed, reflected upon, and inevitably integrated elements of faith and religious practice from surrounding peoples and regions.

Folk beliefs never retreated into the background in Armenia. They endured across the country and much of it was absorbed into the calendar, practices, and festivals of the **Armenian Apostolic Church**. Many of these beliefs were held in common by peoples elsewhere in the world: the early worship of a mother goddess; a celestial pantheon associated with the powers of nature beyond human control; the habitation of spirits among the natural wonders of the land. There were also specific aspects to the folk religion of the Armenians. Most were in one form or another associated with the landscape of Armenia. The abundance of mountain ranges made for plenty of dwelling places for the gods, but these were surpassed by the great size of Mount **Ararat**, *Meds Masis* (Great Masis) of the Armenians, an object of veneration since the first inhabitants of the highlands beheld its mighty presence. They sensed in its immensity a point of majestic solemnity and serene eternity against the course of life and historical experience etched by hardship and transience. For as long as the Armenians lived within sight of them, they spoke and sang to their mountains. One simple and sublime melody began: *Alakiaz batser sar e* (Alagyaz/Aragats is a high mountain).

If the mountains were distant symbols defining a psychological perimeter, the land was strewn with fragments of the volcanic cones. Many villages boasted a sacred stone famed in its immediate vicinity for its powers of fertility. These local cults were the special preserve of womenfolk, much like the sacred trees where wishes were made. If some ancient arbors were festooned with knotted ribbons, or mountains were the haunt of spirits, and fairies and nymphs inhabited the waters, the cult of the magical stones predominated, so much so that a whole mass of so-called *vishapakar*, dragon-stones, were planted across the country. What probably started as simple menhirs were carved into large cigar-shaped monuments with fish heads and serpents etched on them. Some seemingly took the dimensions of obelisks. Watchful guardians of the country and likely tribal totems, they were probably installed to ward off evil spirits, the beasts of the wild, and the snakes in the fields. In Armenian folk belief the power of the watchful eye was the most penetrating and the most threatening as evidenced by the plethora of expressions invoking the attributes of the eye. The evil eye (*char achke*), to fall from grace or disappoint (*achke iynal*, literally "to fall from the eye"), greed (*achketsakutiun*, literally "having a hole in the eye"), but also an alert person who was "open eyed" (*achke pats*), one worthy or noticeable (*achk zarnogh*, "eye striking"), to impress (*achke mednel* or "enter the eye"), and so forth, testify to ancient beliefs and ocular superstitions that have entered as very common expressions in Armenian speech.

The formation of tribal confederations and subsequently more structured political organization in the first millennium B.C invited the rise of official cults and pantheons. The conflict between tribal allegiance based on kinship and state power based on political relations became imbedded in the primary myth of origins of the Armenian nation. The titanic struggle between freedom and slavery, between good and evil, was symbolized in the mythological contest of Hayk and Bel, with Hayk the eponymous patriarch of the Hay, as the Armenians called themselves, and Bel representing formal and arbitrary authority and a personified echo of Urartu, the most ancient state forged on the Armenian highlands. The Urartian religion imitated or resembled the Mesopotamian royal tradition with a hierarchical order to the governing power of heavenly deities. Male gods, as reflected in the surviving art of the period, in royal garb or military armor, dominated in a clear association with the earthly power of the kings of Urartu. The god Khaldi held court over this pantheon. Symbols like the griffin, the lion, and the bull were borrowings from Assyria, the imperial hegemon of the era when Urartians prevailed in the highlands. Armenian mythology absorbed elements of the Urartian cults, and in one of the earliest stories surrounding the search for immortality grew the legend of Ara the Beautiful the unattainable beloved of Semiramis

(Shamiram) struck down by the jealous queen who vainly sought to revive the handsome youth by keeping his flesh from corruption.

Religion as a formal affair ascribed an institutional role in society dates from the Urartians who built stone temples across the country and utilized some as treasuries. Even so, their most sacred site remained associated with the great Rock of **Van**, a natural outcrop whose summit served as a vast fortress and within which, out of the stone, were carved the necropolis of the Urartian kings and places for the worship of their protecting divinities. The faded memory of these rock-hewn sanctuaries in turn became assimilated with the myths associated with the cult of Mher, the Armenian version of the Iranian Mithras, favored by soldiers and warriors. As the Armenian folk epic of the "Daredevils of Sasun" recounted, the royal residence of the immortal Mher was inside a great rock, too. Locals pointed to a large Urartian slab, illegible to them, as Mheri Dur, the Gate of Mher, the entrance to the interior chamber wherein he resides with his stallion waiting for the day to bring justice to the world. The potency of the myth was such that it was transferred even to the non-Armenians who came to live beneath the Urartian acropolises.

Another series of syncretisms occurred during the period of Persian predominance under the Achaemenids and later the **Arshakuni**, or Arsacids. While new features entered the Armenian pantheon from Iran, the process rather made some deities more pronounced than others and did not entirely replicate the Persian gods. Aramazd (Ahuramazda of the Persians) regained his paternal role in line with the Indo-European belief system in a male hierarchy. Astghik, however, the Astarte of the Mesopotamians, retained her stellar role as goddess of heaven and of life-giving water. Astghik was also the goddess of love and fertility and was celebrated in the most popular festival of the Armenian pagan calendar known as Vartevar; a celebration whose customs unchanged was absorbed by the Armenian Church as the Feast of the Transfiguration of Christ, in another of the practical steps taken by its founder to expedite the spread and acceptance of Christianity in Armenia. Right down to the second decade of the 20th century Armenians celebrated Vartevar as they always had as a joyous occasion for feasting, games playing, sporting contests, animal sacrifices at local shrines, the bearing of fruits, flowers, and grain to the associated ceremonies, the release of doves, and the parading of the sacrificial sheep with lighted candles on their horns. The happiest moment of the festival coincided with the excitement created with the free throwing of water on one and all in an annual washing away of the burdens weighing down on young and old. It is believed that Vartevar means the "flaming of the rose" very likely indicating the delivery of roses at an alter of fire, much as rose petals were strewn in acts of worship into the rivers and wreathes of roses worn as crowns of joy. The word *astgh* still means "star" in Armenian. The gender balance in the Armenian pantheon hints at the popular origins of the worship of the main deities. The onomastic association of Anahita of the Iranians with the mother goddess of the Armenians also took hold, but the cult of female and earthly fertility and its popularity was rooted in the country and probably flourished greatly as more and more of the land was brought under the plow.

The Armenians appear to have had a special attachment to the mother goddess Anahit and the newer god of fire and valor, the youthful Vahagn, who was celebrated in glowing verse, clearly a favorite of poets and bards who sang of his cosmic birth and shining features. In the surviving fragment of his epic, Vahagn is conceived from the labors of heaven, and earth, and the crimson sea, with flaming hair and eyes shining like suns. So radiant a figure was also the favorite of the class of men who exercised an increasingly greater role in society, the mounted warriors or feudal cavalry of ancient Armenia, ever ready to wield the sword and take to the field of battle. The military class carved out a large presence in Armenian society and the cults they favored spread with their influence. A dynamic and energetic individual, or the fearless and undaunted, is still described in Armenian as someone who is *krak u pots* (fire and flame).

One other form of worship closely linked with Iran also flourished in Armenia. Many ancient faiths maintained a sacred fire or temples dedicated to its worship. The Iranians elevated fire to the highest echelons of sacredness. The appreciation of fire in a country with cold winters like Armenia, where warmth meant the difference between life and frozen death, had indigenous origins, and it seems to have become associated particularly with Vahagn in whose worship fire, flame, and sun all merged into a powerful solar deity. The importance of the hearth is manifest in the expression preserved to this day and uttered unknowingly in the most serious consequence with which one Armenian can threaten another. *Mukhe marel*, literally "to put out the smoke" of someone, implied more than dousing another's fire. It meant their vengeful destruction, so essential was the smoking fire to sustaining life. When the Iranian Sasanids established their dominion, the strong ideological component of their rule was basically reflected by their promotion of Zoroastrianism whose two most identifiable features were its dualism, the belief in the competing powers of good and evil, and the emphasis on fire worship as a distinct cult. Both spread across Armenia. Over those two issues the Armenians and Iranians eventually clashed in one of the fiercest contests for the freedom of worship waged between two peoples of unequal power. The historical triumph of the Armenians on this issue constitutes one of the central events of their national culture.

The reason was elemental. The Armenians had converted to Christianity in the fourth century. By the middle of the fifth century, when the Sasanids promulgated a policy of religious conformity, designed to uproot Christianity in Armenia and impose Zoroastrianism, they encountered resistance of the kind heretofore unknown. Religious persecution previously was a practice associated with pagan Roman policy toward the early Christians. Mass resistance of a national character over religion was unheard of, with the exception of the special case of the Jews in Israel. It was precisely those chapters of the Bible, which recorded the saga of Jewish resistance that became the source of the Armenian polemic defense of their faith, and the parallels became the sources of inspired historical narratives that as a consequence further fused Christianity with Armenian identity.

The voluntary and conscious choice of the Armenians to adopt Christianity had much to do with their strong sense of affinity to the new faith. The political necessity of defense in the name of their faith and its high cost in human life instilled an even closer bond. The experience under the Persians prepared the Armenians for spiritual resistance against the next great monotheistic religion to appear in the Middle East. From the midseventh century onward Armenians would face Islam as the faith of their rulers and of the gravest challengers of their religion. In view of the fact that Islam would prevail in establishing itself as the dominant and permanent faith of most of the peoples of the Middle East, and of virtually all the ruling powers of the region, meant that Armenian Christianity has existed in a state of perpetual conflict with one of the world's great religions. Other historical cases of a people in a permanent state of conflict with its neighbors and rulers over the matter of their faith are extremely rare. These are exhausting struggles when the dominant faith is maintained in a mode of hostility toward the subordinated religion. Islam imposed long periods of isolation, brutal repression, and soul-searching episodes in the lives of countless Armenians who faced a choice frequently cast as life and death decisions.

The conflict with Islam reinforced a process of cultural readjustment that had begun almost a thousand years earlier, but which had gained strength with Christianization. Until the time of the Romans, who arrived in Armenia in the first century B.C., Armenia had drawn upon its southern neighbors for religious ideas. Assyria and Iran had been the great inheritors and mediators of the Semitic cultures of Mesopotamia, while Iran with its Indo-European religious system had aligned more closely with native Armenian beliefs, also of Indo-European origin. That pantheon had further been syncretized during the Hellenistic era from the third century B.C. onward when the Greek gods were paired with their Armenian kin. This fusion received its greatest expression in the funerary monuments at Nemrud (Nimrut) Dagh where a branch of the **Yervanduni** (Orontid) royal line ruling over the westernmost reaches of Armenia created a spectacular necropolis presided over by colossal sculptures carved in the Armenian Hellenistic mode, an amalgam of Greek, Persian, and Armenian motifs.

Armenia's exposure to the Hellenistic world came primarily with its interaction with Seleucid Syria to the south. The formal adoption of Christianity in 301 strengthened this relationship with the main urban centers of the region, especially those in northern Syria, Antioch and Edessa (Urfa), and further to the south, Jerusalem and Alexandria in Egypt. The early Syriac mediation of Christianity into Armenia, however, was overtaken by political considerations and the necessity of the legitimation of the Armenian Church's role in relation to the Imperial Church, once Constantine extended in 313 official tolerance of Christianity across Roman territory. The strongest vector of cultural proclivity in Armenia inclined westward even more when the emperor founded in 330 the city of Constantinople on the Bosphorus. This new orientation was symbolized by the consecration of **Grigor Lusavorich** (Gregory the Illuminator) as the first bishop of Armenia in the city of Caesarea (Kayseri) in Roman Cappadocia. This act, repeated by his successors to the episcopate of Armenia, culminated the 180 degree redirecting of Armenian religious and cultural values that had slowly proceeded over the course of the preceding centuries, but which also increasingly alienated Armenia from its eastern neighbors, first Iran, then Islam.

Islam also exposed the two strands of Christianity in Armenia: the simple form of Christianity introduced possibly as early as the first century A.D. directly from the original centers of the new religion in Palestine and Syria; and the official form of Christianity imposed by the state authorities of Armenia that tapped the more developed tradition of the Greek-speaking church where debate and dispute had encouraged the elaboration of a systematic theology. One was based on the teachings of Christ as recorded in the New Testament. The other was based on the fullness of the Biblical tradition with all its implications for the social and political order in Armenia. The early form of Christianity that passed down through unofficial circles, and whose continuity speaks of a rootedness among the populace, emphasized a communitarian and egalitarian faith that rejected the hierarchy and practices of the formal church. Its appeal to the lower classes, among the laboring peasantry, and a population based in the countryside in rural settlements requiring self-sufficiency and preserving ancient modes of democracy, was manifest in the simplicity of its customs, its rudimentary beliefs, absence of an ecclesiastical establishment, and connections with social unrest and resistance against the feudal order. By weakening the church, Islam created conditions for this strand of Armenian Christianity to emerge as a visible movement appealing to parts of the population pushed to the margins by the double burden of bearing the costs of the **nakharar system**, the distinct form of Armenian feudalism, and of the tax collected by the Muslim overlords. In times and places of economic distress, the flight to, or refuge in, elementary modes of belief in salvation rejecting and defying the given systems and realities exercised their influence. In a country under as much strain as Armenia, contested by Arabs, Byzantines, and Armenian lords, the hardships borne by the general populace were extreme.

Under these circumstances, egalitarian Christianity became the fountainhead of two popular movements that were severely condemned as heresies, inviting upon its adherents persecution by outlawing their existence. These were the Paulician (*Pavghikian*) and the Tondrakian (*Tondraketsi*) movements, the first being better known for its surprising strength and organized resistance to Byzantine rule.

The Tondrakian sect remained a localized movement and was suppressed in the 11th century by the state and church authorities of the time. The Paulician movement, however, assumed much wider ramifications. By the middle of the ninth century, Paulicianism had become implanted in the frontier zone between Western Armenia and Byzantium where the Arabs once dominated and waged their yearly raids against the Christian world. In this environment of martial habits, constant warfare, and absence of regular government, the social and political order thoroughly loosened and the established church was nowhere to be seen. In a society so clearly leveled, the older form of Christianity that already had a presence in Armenia filled the void. That many of its elements, such as the absence of organized clergy and the rejection of elaborate ritual and egalitarian principles paralleled features of Islam that would have been even more characteristic of a frontier zone where militancy and religiosity combined, gives reason to think that the spread of Paulicianism was a response to the crisis induced by the destabilization of Armenian society by Islam and might be viewed as a good barometer of the depth of the crisis.

In a curious twist, as the forces of Islam retreated from Western Armenia under Byzantine military pressure, the Paulicians filled the political void and formed their own state centered on the town of Tephrike (Divrik) where from they waged a decades-long war of resistance until Basil I the Macedonian, the Byzantine emperor himself of Armenian origin, ordered in 873 a full-scale military campaign to eradicate the heresy and the frontier state in which it flourished. While their political role may have become eclipsed, the defeated Paulicians, who were dispersed and resettled on the Bulgarian frontier of the Byzantine Empire, appear to have held onto their beliefs and practices, and in turn influenced the so-called Bogomil movement, a Balkan heresy that spread from Bulgaria to Bosnia. Some scholars speculate, because of the chronological sequence of the spread of popular antiestablishment religious movements, that even the Albigensian heresy in southern France was stimulated by the spread of the elementary Christology traced to the Armenian Paulicians. It is noteworthy that Basil I opted to make use of the military skills of the Paulicians by assigning them frontier duty as many preceding emperors had done with the manpower recruited or conscripted from Armenia over the centuries.

The Paulicians were an important indicator of the course of religion and the influence of new religions on the Armenians. As once their predecessors might have been the harbingers of early Christianity in Armenia, they also became the measure of the impact of Islam in Armenia. Those Paulicians who remained within the Christian fold ultimately faded from sight, yet the Armenian Church retrieved the main source on the theology of the movement, the book known as the *Key of Truth*, from private hands only in the 19th century. Other movements banned as heresy by the Armenian Church also appear to have registered survivals, including the so-called *Arevorti* (Children of the Sun), worshipper of the sun as their appellation implies. Chalcedonian, Catholic, and Protestant Christianity also gained adherents from among Armenians, whether these be for political or economic reasons, or for purely religious reasons, as sometimes among defecting clergy. In spite of the Armenian Church's efforts to contain the spread of heterodoxy, throughout the course of the centuries the Armenian people remained open to other forms of religious belief. In the absence of a state enforcing conformity, this was inevitable, and yet despite the absence of a sponsoring state, the Armenian Church retained the loyalties of the majority of Armenians in all parts of the world as an institution defining the distinct national character of their people.

Armenian Christianity in part survived because of the tolerance of Islam of the religions of the book, as the Koran labeled Christians and Jews whose faith was based upon the Bible. Religious tolerance of the so-called *dhimmi*, however, was more a matter of political expediency, and as such varied from administration to administration. In times of strength the Islamic states tended toward greater tolerance and tapped the skills of Christians and Jews as productive members of society. In times of weakness or internal conflict, intolerance became the trend, and persecution and exploitation of non-Muslims increased. As pressure, persuasion, and other causes led to the Islamification of the Middle East under the Arabs, Armenia was reduced to a Christian pocket. When the Turks swept Byzantium in the 11th century, Armenia was left behind an island, and Armenians were reduced to minority status once the Iranian Safavid and the Turkish Ottoman Empires introduced policies in the 17th century designed to alter the demographic balance of the various religious groups in Armenia. The Muslim presence in Armenia grew as Turks, Kurds, Persians, and others settled in the country or expanded their areas of settlement, while the Armenians as Christians diminished in numbers both in relative and absolute terms.

The fracture in Armenian Christianity symbolized by the later strength of the Paulician movement also pointed to another process, one that occurred regularly, but whose divisive consequences were so traumatic that it has remained a subject little studied to this day, the spread of Islam among Armenians. The condemnation of apostasy by the Armenian Church could not halt the introduction of Islam as the multitude of Islamic powers that came to rule over the Armenians encouraged the growth of their religion and applied the benefits of cooptation to enlist Armenians into their ranks. From the very beginning Armenians appeared among the Muslim armies as they spread out from Arabia. One flag-bearer of Amr ibn al-As, the Muslim conqueror of Egypt, who may have the honor of being the first Armenian Muslim on record as Wardan al-Armani, Vardan the Armenian, distinguished himself in the military service of the newly emerged world power. Similarly, having stepped beyond the pale of the official church, the Paulicians too would have been predisposed toward gradual Islamification once their political power was broken. The most prominent Muslim Armenian of the 11th century, who tapped into the military manpower of Armenia as it went through another period of political and religious anarchy during the Seljuk Turkish invasions, was Badr al-Jamali of Egypt. As guardian of the Fatimid throne in Cairo, he gained complete mastery of the country, and secured dynastic succession for his immediate descendants in the office of commander-in-chief and prime minister (wazir). His cohorts included Christian and Muslim Armenians.

The intensification of religious persecution during the Ottoman period resulted in numerous instances of conversion. In one case of mass conversion, unlike prior experiences of the eventual loss of linguistic and ethnic identity, the Armenians of Hamshen maintained their communal distinctness. While practicing Islam, and becoming isolated from the rest of their Christian kin as a result, the *Hamshentsi* continued to speak a dialect of Armenian all their own. Retreating as a group into the mountain recesses of the Pontic region south of the Black Sea, they survived as a group and continue to inhabit a region of northeastern Turkey. The conversion of the Hamshentsi occurred in the 18th century. Conversions of groups or individuals during the era of the massacres in the Ottoman Empire in the late 19th and early 20th century were the choice of persons in desperate straits facing imminent death. It proved another means of extinguishing the Armenian community of the late Ottoman Empire. The brutality associated with the final persecution and decimation of the Armenians in Turkey marked the Armenians with bitterness toward Islam and a profound suspicion of Muslims in general. Even so, that did not remain the sole picture of Islam among Christian Armenians, who as refugees coexisted in the Arab part of the Middle East and in Iran, and where tolerance, more so than persecution, defined the relationship between Muslims and Christians.

Religion in Armenia contributed to the consolidation of a distinct ethnic identity deeply attached to a national church. Christianization marked one of the pivotal moments in the history of ancient Armenia. The Armenians as a people thereafter saw themselves as part of a larger community defined by the Christian religion. That proved a costly choice, however, when Islam prevailed. The conflict with a world religion with the strength of Islam deeply alienated the Armenian people from their surroundings. For long periods of time it condemned them to existence as second class citizens merely tolerated as contemptible *giavur* ("infidel" in Turkish) at the price of onerous taxes, which sapped their viability as a separate community. Despite the enormity of the social hardship, political disadvantage, and psychological strain endured under those conditions, Armenians also negotiated a difficult peace with their neighbors, themselves, and the God they worshipped, in order to survive and endure. All those arrangements came under close scrutiny when the Christian world underwent a period of rapid expansion in the 19th century and Armenians everywhere reconnected with Christendom in Europe and America. By then, however, the prevailing currents of Western civilization tended toward secularism that challenged the role of religion and limited its influence in society.

Rational secularism turned out to be the least problem for organized religion in Armenia. The decimation of the clergy during the **Armenian Genocide** seriously undermined the capacity of religion as a social institution. Its already weakened structure was completely swept away with the imposition of official atheism that accompanied the Sovietization of Armenia. The eradication of religion constituted part and parcel of Bolshevik revolutionary dogma and the program to stamp out church and religion were among some of the more successful ideological campaigns waged under the Soviet system. With the guidelines of ethical conduct derived from Communist Party authority and revolutionary justification, objective materialism eliminated room for spirituality. Through indoctrination and denial of access to religion, an atheistic society was formed in Soviet Armenia.

The consequences of the deprivation of a population of a value system based on moral principles became all the more evident with the collapse of Communism. If ideology had substituted for religion in the Soviet era and had provided, at least for Communist Party cadres, notional principles, the psychological brutality of the system had only alienated the masses from any sense of ethical norms. With the removal of the controlling role of ideology only a moral vacuum remained. The need to fill the void redefined the relationship of state and religion in the post-Soviet republic. On the one hand the **Constitution** of the Republic of Armenia guarantees freedom of worship and the separation of church and state. On the other hand, legislation regulating religious organizations favors the Armenian Apostolic Church and the government treats it as the national church of Armenia. There is little interference by the state with the churches, which it regards as social assets addressing needs of the populace that the government is not equipped to meet. Forces enjoying the protection of the government, however, also oppose the spread of religious groups, labeled sects, outside the mainstream of the three main branches of Christianity. Religious issues do not factor in Armenia's domestic politics. Religion continues to factor in Armenia's foreign relations to the degree that the conflict over **Nagorno Karabagh** pits a predominantly Christian Armenia against a mainly Muslim Azerbaijan. Even in the beginning of the 21st century the context of regional and international tensions has repositioned religion as a contributive determinant of Armenia's cultural and political reorientation. *See also* CATHOLIC CHURCH, ARMENIAN; PROTESTANT CHURCH, ARMENIAN.

REPUBLICAN PARTY OF ARMENIA (RPA) (*Hayastani Hanrapetakan Kusaktsutiun, HHK*). Political party. Founded in 1990 under the leadership of Ashot Navasardian and Andranik Margarian, the RPA advocated for strong national statehood. This fundamentally differed from the type of civil society that the **Armenian National**

Movement (ANM) wanted introduced in Armenia. In the 1995 parliamentary elections and the 1996 presidential elections, the RPA joined the Republic Bloc led by the ANM in support of **Levon Ter-Petrossian**. The RPA emerged as an important center of opposition to the government in 1998 when deep political fissures appeared on the Armenian political landscape in reaction to Ter-Petrossian's proposed compromise settlement of the **Nagorno Karabagh** issue. The so-called *Yekrapah* faction in the National Assembly withdrew its support of the **president** and joined ranks with the RPA. The *Yekrapah Kamavorakanneri Miutiun* (Union of Volunteer Defenders of the Land), representing the Karabagh war veterans association, had become an important group in the 1995 parliament and the core nationalist organization in the country. With the resignation of Ter-Petrossian in February 1988, Defense Minister **Vazgen Sargsian** moved the *Yekrapah* and the RPA together to form a political organization with broader appeal. When the so-called Unity (*Miasnutiun*) alliance consisting of the RPA and the **Populist Party of Armenia** (PPA) won the majority of seats in the May 1999 parliamentary elections, President **Robert Kocharian** invited Vazgen Sargsian to form a cabinet as the new **prime minister** of Armenia. Effectively, the RPA displaced the ANM as the leading political party in the country. While this registered a shift to the right of the spectrum from the centrist position of the ANM, the change was obtained as a result of an alliance with a new moderate left party.

RUBENIAN/RUPENIAN (RUBENID/RUPENID). Baronial and royal dynasty of Cilician Armenia. Armenian settlement on the Mediterranean coast began with the Byzantine reconquest of Cilicia in the 10th century and accelerated with the Seljuk occupation of Armenia in the mid-11th century. In the process the Byzantines appointed Armenian noblemen as governors of various fortresses and districts in the region. Following the breakup of the empire in the aftermath of the Battle of Manzikert in 1071, these local barons created a number of autonomous statelets. Pilardos Varazhnuni, or Philaretus of Melitene, governed over an area encompassing Edessa/Urfa and Antioch. Abulgharib **Ardsruni** governed Tarsus and its environs on the behalf of the emperor. One of his officers named Oshin, whose family became known as the **Hetumian**/Hetumid, was responsible for the defense of Lambron, a fortress guarding the Cilician Gates, the passage to the interior of Asia Minor.

The family around which the Armenians in Cilicia ultimately rallied, however, started with more modest means and from a more remote location. In contrast to the other Armenian warriors who sought legitimacy under the mantle of the Byzantine emperor, Ruben/Rupen and his descendants instead claimed the banner of the deposed **Bagratuni** dynasty. An associate of the last king of Armenia, Ruben (d. 1093/1095) sought refuge in Gobidara in the heart of the Taurus Range after Gagik II's assassination in 1079. Ruben's son Constantine I (1093/1095–1100/1102) took the nearby fortress of Vahka in 1091, thereby planting the foundations of a new Armenian state. Constantine's son Toros I (1100/1102–1129), enlarging his domain by seizing the fortresses of Bartsrberd and Anazarba, secured the Armenian hold over the mountains.

As the Rubenian barons fortified their castles and eyed the plain of Cilicia and its cities, the Crusaders arrived in the East. On their way to Jerusalem, which they took in 1099, the Crusaders also captured the principal cities of the eastern Mediterranean including Antioch and as far inland as Edessa/Urfa, which was still held by the Armenians at the time. Fighting the Seljuk Turks, the Crusaders brought a measure of relief to the besieged Armenians who welcomed their arrival. At the same time they planted themselves as the new Latin lords of the region. Baldwin of Boulogne established the County of Edessa in 1098, while his brother Godfrey of Bouillon captured Palestine. To encourage cooperation among the Franks and the Armenians, Baldwin set an example by marrying the niece of Constantine of Vahka named Arda, and when Godfrey passed away in 1100, Baldwin succeeded as King of Jerusalem, along with Arda as queen. The Crusaders lost Edessa to the Muslims in 1144 and Jerusalem in 1187. The Principality of Antioch lasted longer. Founded by Bohemond in 1099, it was overtaken in 1268. The Rubenians thus found their small independent barony sandwiched between the Latins to the east, the Byzantines to the west, and the Seljuk Sultanate of Iconium/Konia to the north. Militarily this combination presented an especially complicated challenge. Politically and culturally it offered possibilities, which the Rubenians utilized to their advantage as they persisted with their ambition to create a viable Armenian state in Cilicia.

Toros I treaded carefully, especially where the unpredictable and tempestuous Frankish knights were concerned. His brother **Levon/Leo I** (1129–1138/1140) moved swiftly against the local

Byzantine vassals. Between 1132 and 1135 he took Mamistra (Mop-suestia), **Adana**, and Tarsus. Such daring precipitated intervention by the emperor himself. In 1137–1138 John II Komnenos (1118–1143) marched into Cilicia, retook the occupied cities, and having given the chase to Levon into the mountains, seized both him and two of his sons, Ruben and Toros. Levon died in captivity in Constantinople, and Ruben, his heir, was killed, seemingly putting an end to Armenian hopes of carving a self-ruling haven out of the Byzantine frontierland. The younger Toros who was kept hostage at court, however, escaped. Toros II (1144/1145–1168) made his way to Cilicia in secret. By 1148 he had retaken Anazarba and Vahka and began a vigorous restoration of the Armenian state. When in 1152 he defeated a Byzantine force under the command of Andronikos Komnenos, cousin of the Emperor Manuel I (1143–1180), he also captured the emperor's Armenian vassals who controlled the western portions of Cilicia. Toros used the opportunity to repair relations between the opposing camps among the Armenians in Cilicia by encouraging matrimonial alliances. He released Oshin II of Lambron and married one of his daughters to Oshin's son Hetum, whom he kept as hostage. Toros's brother Stepane/Stephen married Rita, the daughter of Smbat of Paperon, Oshin's brother, who had fallen in battle. From this marriage were born the future rulers of Cilician Armenia, the brothers Ruben/Rupen III and Levon/Leo II.

To restrain the Armenians, the Emperor Manuel resorted to intrigue with the Seljuk sultan of Iconium and the Latin prince of Antioch, but Toros and Stepane checked their incursions, until Manuel arrived in person in 1158 and obtained a voluntary submission. Cilicia did not long remain in vassalage to Byzantium as the Armenians continued to press the Greeks. With Manuel's defeat by Kilij Arslan II (1156–1192), the sultan of Iconium, at the Battle of Myriokephalon in 1176, Byzantine influence over Asia Minor collapsed, just as the Zangids were restoring Muslim unity in Syria. The latter sponsored the turbulent reign of Mleh (1170–1175), Toros's renegade brother, who made Sis the capital city, and who had his young nephew, Ruben/Rupen II (1169–1170) dispatched. After almost a hundred years of struggle, Armenian society had taken firm root in the soil of Cilicia and a class of noblemen in the service of the Rubenian princes governed its cities, defended its fortresses, and manned its forces. They rid themselves of Mleh once his patron Nur-ad-Din of Aleppo passed away and raised Ruben/Rupen III (1175–1186/1187) to the throne. He consolidated Armenian rule over Cilicia by forging alliances with the principality of Antioch to the east, with Kilij Arslan in the north, and as Byzantine suzerainty faded and imperial intervention no longer presented a threat, by moving upon the Hetumians.

It was left to Ruben's younger brother Levon/Leo II (1186/1187–1199) to complete the unification of Cilician Armenia just as Saladin, the Ayyubid sultan of Egypt, routed the Franks and by retaking Jerusalem reduced the Crusader presence in the eastern Mediterranean to a series of coastal towns. With its population base, fertile plain, prosperous cities, and defensive ring of fortresses guarding the passes in the surrounding Taurus and Amanus Ranges, Cilician Armenia under the control of the Rubenians emerged as the strongest Christian state in the East. Levon saw his opportunity of lawfully joining the rank of royalty when the Third Crusade promised the arrival of the Holy Roman Emperor Frederick Barbarossa. Having traveled all the way from Germany, the emperor accidentally drowned in 1190 when fording a river in Cilicia. The promise of a crown received in the presence of the mightiest warlord of Europe slipped away. Even so, Levon persisted by promoting a strong pro-Latin policy. He encouraged negotiations between the **Armenian Apostolic Church** and Rome and sent embassies to the papacy to enlist its endorsement. In 1191 he sent troops to support the king of France, Philip Augustus, in the siege of Acre and joined Richard I the Lionhearted, king of England, in the conquest of Cyprus from the Byzantines. With the consent of Henry VI, Frederick Barbarossa's son, Levon was finally crowned in 1199. The titles and privileges of monarchy once again were restored to the Armenians and a new era ushered in with the enthronement of a dynasty. As dynasties go, however, Levon left his daughter Zabel as his heir in 1219. Zabel's marriage, therefore, was a matter of the highest political importance for the Armenian grandees of Cilicia as her husband once crowned as king would legally exercise lordship over them. At first the Armenian barons endorsed her wedding to Philip, the son of Bohemond IV of Antioch, in a gesture designed to bring an end to the conflict between the two states. Philip, however, treated his marriage as occasion to appoint Latins to high posts in government, while reneging on his promise to follow Armenian Church ritual. In three short years he only won the animosity of the Armenian nobility who deposed and killed him. That strategy for strengthening Armenian-Latin relations having dismally failed, for her second husband, the Armenian lords chose one of their own. The marriage of Zabel in 1226 to **Hetum**, the son of the regent Constantine the Constable, sealed the union of the two great founding dynasties of Cilician Armenia.

– S –

SARGSIAN, ARAM (1961–). Prime Minister of Armenia, November 1999–May 2000. Aram Sargsian was nominated by the Armenian parliament to succeed his brother Prime Minister **Vazgen Sargsian** upon the latter's assassination on October 27, 1999. Born in the town of **Ararat**, Sargsian graduated in 1989 from **Yerevan** Polytechnic Institute with an engineering degree. He was employed by construction companies in his native district and had risen to the executive directorship of the state-run Araratcement firm by 1998. A member of the **Republican Party of Armenia** (RPA) and of the *Yekrapah Kamavorakanneri Miutiun* (Union of Volunteer Defenders of the Land), the Karabagh war veterans association, both led by his brother who had made his reputation as the forceful defense minister of Armenia, Aram Sargsian, otherwise, had little political exposure at the national level. His appointment on November 3, 1999, by President **Robert Kocharian** was designed to fill the vacuum of leadership as quickly and smoothly as feasible in the aftermath of the crisis created by the terrorist attack on the Armenian parliament and to prevent tension with the RPA, the leading party in the National Assembly and the Unity (*Miasnutiun*) parliamentary alliance that had elevated Vazgen Sargsian to the premiership. Lacking his brother's experience and presence, Aram Sargsian, however, proved a transitional figure who nevertheless bridged a difficult period. Friction with Kocharian and the intensity of the recriminations hampered his ability to manage the government. His short tenure in public life ended by May 2000. *See also* SARGSIAN, ARAM CABINET; SARGSIAN, VAZGEN CABINET.

SARGSIAN, ARAM CABINET. Appointed by **President Robert Kocharian** on November 13, 1999, the Sargsian cabinet served until May 2, 2000.

Prime Minister	**Aram Sargsian**
Agriculture	Gagik Shahbazian
Culture, Youth Affairs and Sports	Roland Sharoyan
Defense	Vagharshak Harutunian
Economy	**Armen Darbinian**
Education and Science	Edvard Ghazarian
Energy	Davit Zadoyan
Environmental Protection	Gevorg Vardanian
Finance	Levon Barkhudarian
Foreign Affairs	Vartan Oskanian
Government Administration	Shahen Karamanukian
Health	Haik Nikoghosian
Industrial Productions Coordination	Vahan Shirkhanian
Internal Affairs	Haik Harutunian
Justice	Davit Harutunian
National Security	Karlos Petrosian
Post and Communications	Ruben Tonoyan
Privatization	Pavel Ghaltakhchian
Regional Administration	**Khosrov Harutiunian**
Social Welfare	Razmik Martirosian
State Revenues	Smbat Aivazian
Statistics, State Register and Analysis	Stepan Mnatsakanian
Trade and Industry	Karen Cheshmaritian
Transport	Yervand Zakharian
Urban Planning	Hrair Hovhanisian

Keeping to the promise of continuing his brother's policies, the Council of Ministers formed by Aram Sargsian virtually reproduced the cabinet assembled by Prime Minister **Vazgen Sargsian**. New appointments were made at the ministries of internal affairs and national security, both of which bore the brunt of the responsibility for failing to provide adequate security to cabinet members and the National Assembly. Longtime Minister of National Security Serge Sargsian (no relation to the prime ministers) resigned in the wake of the October 27 assassinations. So did Minister of Internal Affairs

Suren Abrahamian, both ironically allies of Vazgen Sargsian. The ministry of government operations was abolished. It was headed by Leonard Petrosian, formerly prime minister in **Nagorno Karabagh Republic (NKR)**, another victim of the October 27 terrorist action in the National Assembly. The only other change in personnel occurred at the ministry of trade and industry.

The Aram Sargsian government proved a temporary device to diffuse the politically charged atmosphere of the postassassination months. Lacking a commanding figure of Vazgen Sargsian's stature, the cabinet functioned uneasily as President Kocharian emerged the singular political figure capable of holding together the state while appeasing critics and contenders. *See also* SARGSIAN, VAZGEN CABINET.

SARGSIAN, FADEY. *See* PRIME MINISTER.

SARGSIAN, VAZGEN (1959–1999). Prime Minister of Armenia, June–October 1999. Born in the village of **Ararat** in Armenia, Sargsian graduated from **Yerevan** State Institute for Physical Education in 1979. While employed in the Komsomol, the Communist youth organization in his native district, in the 1980s Sargsian turned to the field of journalism and worked for the *Garun* (Spring) literary magazine. An ardent nationalist, he joined the Karabagh Movement from the beginning in 1988 and by 1990 was leading the armed volunteers associated with the **Armenian National Movement** (ANM) engaged in the defense of the Armenian population facing expulsion in **Nagorno Karabagh**. He was elected to parliament in 1990 and appointed Armenia's first minister of defense by **President Levon Ter-Petrossian** in 1991. In that capacity he was responsible for the organization of an Armenian army where none existed before by bringing together the volunteer armed units that had sprung up as a result of the Karabagh crisis. This involved integrating independently formed contingents, the strongest of which was actually the so-called Armenian National Army (ANA) commanded by Razmik Vasilian. Sargsian succeeded in forging an effective military loyal to the Armenian government at a time when the country was under blockade, the sole source of military supplies was Russia, and the defense forces of Karabagh were engaged in a struggle for survival and required all the logistical support they could get from Armenia. In charge of the state ministry of defense from 1993 to 1995, the super-ministry created to address the critical military challenge faced by Armenia and Karabagh as Azerbaijan waged a full-scale war, Sargsian oversaw the turnaround of the situation in the field of battle until such time as a cease-fire was agreed to by all the warring parties. Sargsian initialed the May 12, 1994, armistice on behalf of Armenia.

The state ministry of defense was reduced to a regular cabinet level ministry in 1995. Sargsian remained in charge and turned his attention to strengthening the air defense systems of Armenia and developing institutions for military training. As chairman of the *Yekrapah Kamavorakanneri Miutiun* (Union of Volunteer Defenders of the Land) that increasingly became an influential voice in the Armenian parliament with the 1995 **elections**, Sargsian also devoted more attention to political matters. If his endorsement of President Ter-Petrossian's surprise March 1997 nomination of **Robert Kocharian**, then president of the Nagorno Karabagh Republic (NKR), as prime minister of Armenia was important, his support was critical for the rise of Kocharian to the presidency of Armenia when Ter-Petrossian resigned in February 1998. Sargsian returned to electoral politics in 1999 in anticipation of the May balloting for the National Assembly by assuming leadership of the **Republican Party of Armenia** (RPA) and forming a coalition with the **Populist Party of Armenia** (PPA) of **Karen Demirchian**. With the coalition's victory at the polls, President Kocharian invited Sargsian to form a government as Armenia's new prime minister. Sargsian was gunned down on October 27, 1999, in the chamber of the National Assembly, where his cabinet was gathered to report to the legislature. He was the only leading Armenian political figure of the 20th century to suffer such a fate. *See also* SARGSIAN, VAZGEN CABINET.

SARGSIAN, VAZGEN CABINET. Appointed by **President Robert Kocharian** on June 15, 1999, the Sargsian cabinet formally served only until October 27, 1999.

Prime Minister	**Vazgen Sargsian**
Agriculture	Gagik Shahbazian
Culture, Youth Affairs and Sports	Roland Sharoyan
Defense	Vagharshak Harutunian
Economy	**Armen Darbinian**

Education and Science	Edvard Ghazarian
Energy	Davit Zadoyan
Environmental Protection	Gevorg Vardanian
Finance	Levon Barkhudarian
Foreign Affairs	Vartan Oskanian
Government Administration	Shahen Karamanukian
Government Operations	Leonard Petrosian
Health	Haik Nikoghosian
Industrial Productions Coordination	Vahan Shirkhanian
Internal Affairs	Suren Abrahamian
Justice	Davit Harutunian
National Security	Serge Sargsian
Post and Communications	Ruben Tonoyan
Privatization	Pavel Ghaltakhchian
Regional Administration	**Khosrov Harutiunian**
Social Welfare	Razmik Martirosian
State Revenues	Smbat Aivazian
Statistics, State Register and Analysis	Stepan Mnatsakanian
Trade and Industry	Haik Gevorgian
Transport	Yervand Zakharian
Urban Planning	Hrair Hovhanisian

The Council of Ministers formed by Vazgen Sargsian represented as much change as continuity with the retention of 10 previous ministers at their posts: Roland Sharoyan, Gevorg Vardanian, Vartan Oskanian, Haik Nikoghosian, Davit Harutunian, Serge Sargsian, Pavel Ghaltakhchian, Haik Gevorgian, Smbat Aivazian, and Yervand Zakharian. Many other key figures in the cabinet were prominent politicians many of whom had served in the government. Gagik Shahbazian, an experienced Soviet-era technocrat, returned to the ministry of agriculture. Armen Darbinian, the outgoing prime minister, returned to the ministry of economy. Levon Barkhudarian, like Darbinian another young and central figure in the economic policy sector, resumed charge of the ministry of finance. Shahen Karamanukian, long the chief of staff of President **Levon Ter-Petrossian**, also resumed his previous functions at the ministry level office of government administrator. Leonard Petrosian, the minister of government operations, was former prime minister in NKR. Suren Abrahamian, Vazgen Sargsian's chief of staff at the defense ministry, and of late mayor of

Yerevan, assumed leadership of the ministry of internal affairs, a department separated out from the joint ministry held by Serge Sargsian. Khosrov Harutiunian, previously chairman of the National Assembly and a former prime minister, assumed charge of the ministry for regional administration. The elevation of General Vagharshak Harutiunian, a military man by profession, to minister of defense, was the most notable new face in the government

These appointments and reappointments underscored a number of trends in the formation of Armenian cabinets. The endurance of figures like Darbinian and Barkhudarian as the principal formulators of economic policy meant the continuance of the program for liberalization and privatization that all successive Armenian governments since independence promoted despite the enormous hardships incurred, and the privations and loss of income endured by the population. The retention of the American-trained foreign minister, Vartan Oskanian, signaled the standing adherence to a **foreign policy** that sought to maintain a balance in Armenia's East-West relations. The appointments of Shahbazian, Petrosian, Karamanukian, and Khosrov Harutiunian testified to an increasing reliance on administrators with a proven record of performance. Lastly, the continuing role of Serge Sargsian and Suren Abrahamian pointed to the importance of their services and the control exercised over those departments by the country's power brokers.

The October 27, 1999, assassination of the prime minister effectively spelled the tragic end of the Sargsian cabinet. Leonard Petrosian was another fatality of the terrorist attack in the National Assembly chamber where the cabinet was gathered to respond to questions in a public meeting of the full government. Serge Sargsian and Suren Abrahamian tendered their resignation taking responsibility for the calamitous failure of domestic security. To preserve a semblance of continuity, the National Assembly swiftly promoted the candidacy of Vazgen Sargsian's brother, **Aram Sargsian**, as prime minister. *See also* DARBINIAN, ARMEN CABINET.

SARKISSIAN (SARGSIAN), ARMEN (1953–). Prime Minister of Armenia, November 1996–March 1997. Born in **Yerevan**, Sarkissian attended Yerevan State University, graduating from the department of physics in 1976. He completed doctoral studies in 1979 with a degree as Candidate of Sciences in Physics, the equivalent of a Ph.D., with a specialization in astrophysics, and started to teach at Yerevan State University where he lectured on statistical mechanics and differential geometry. In 1984 and 1985 he concentrated on research at Cambridge University in England, and returned to his alma mater as an associate professor in the department of theoretical physics where in 1990 he assumed charge of the university's program in mathematical modeling of complex systems. He was back in England in 1991 teaching as a professor at the University of London. A recognized authority in his field with publications to his name, Sarkissian's career in science that had led him to recognition among British colleagues prompted President **Levon Ter-Petrossian** to call upon him to assume charge of opening the Armenian embassy in London in 1992, first as chargé d'affaires and by 1993 as a full-fledged ambassador to the United Kingdom of Great Britain and Northern Ireland. The scientist's talents in diplomacy resulted in the expansion of his portfolio. By 1996 he held Armenia's ambassadorship to the European Union, Belgium, the Netherlands, Luxembourg, and the Holy See in Rome. He played a critical role in opening relations between Armenia and western Europe and in paving the way for important state visits by Ter-Petrossian to Britain and the Vatican.

Stationed overseas for this entire period, Sarkissian was untainted by the controversies surrounding Ter-Petrossian's 1996 reelection. Facing the challenge of remaking his government such as to regain a semblance of leverage and order following the unrest that marred the postelection week, Ter-Petrossian called upon Sarkissian to assume the prime ministry of Armenia. Sarkissian quickly embarked on overseas diplomatic missions in an effort to restore Armenia's standing in the West as a country undergoing a promising transition to democracy and market economics. A bout with cancer cut short his stay as head of the Armenian government. Already enjoying popular respect and despite requests that he remain at his post during treatment, the seriousness of his condition necessitated his resignation. After a year of incapacitation, Sarkissian resumed his prior duties as Armenia's ambassador to Great Britain. *See also* BAGRATIAN, HRANT; SARKISSIAN, ARMEN CABINET.

SARKISSIAN, ARMEN CABINET. Appointed by **President Levon Ter-Petrossian** on November 4, 1996, the Sarkissian cabinet served until March 20, 1997. **Prime Minister Armen Sarkissian** resigned because of illness. Most of the ministers remained at their posts under the succeeding premiership of **Robert Kocharian**.

Prime Minister	**Armen Sarkissian**
Agriculture	Vladimir Movsisian
Communication	Grigor Poghpatian
Culture, Youth Affairs and Sports	Armen Smbatian
Defense	**Vazgen Sargsian**
Economy	Vahram Avanesian
Education and Science	Artashes Petrosian
Energy	Gagik Martirosian
Environmental Protection	Suren Avetisian
Finance	Levon Barkhudarian
Foreign Affairs	Alexander Arzoumanian
Health	Ara Babloyan
Industry	Ashot Safarian
Information	Hrachia Tamrazian
Internal Affairs and National Security	Serge Sargsian
Justice	Marat Alexanian
Social Security, Employment, Immigration, Refugee Affairs and Welfare	Hranush Hakobian
Trade, Services and Tourism	Garnik Nanagoulian
Transportation	Henrik Kochinian
Urban Planning	Felix Pirumian

The Sarkissian cabinet represented a combination that sought to accommodate the given political reality in Armenia while seeking to project a foreign and economic policy even more open to the West than previously. It included managerial stalwarts such as Vladimir Movsisian and Gagik Martirosian, perhaps the two most prominent of Soviet-era administrators upon whom succeeding governments had called to assume charge of various ministries or agencies. Grigor Poghpatian, Levon Barkhudarian, Ashot Safarian, and Henrik Kochinian were held over from the preceding cabinet headed by **Hrant Bagratian**. Defense and security remained in the hands of Vazgen Sargsian and Serge Sargsian, the two veterans of the Karabagh war. On the other hand, Vano Siradeghian, the controversial minister of internal affairs, was not reappointed, but was assigned mayor of **Yerevan** by the president. The new appointees reflecting the prime minister's own policy orientation most closely were the two former ambassadors whom he elevated to ministerial posts. Alexander Arzoumanian, who started as chargé d'affaires in Washington, Armenia's first emissary to the United States, and subsequently assigned as the permanent representative to the United Nations, became foreign minister. Garnik Nanagoulian, a professional out of the Soviet diplomatic corps, and the second chargé d'affaires in the United States, and later Armenia's first ambassador to Canada, became the trade and tourism minister with a portfolio to build up Armenia's economic relations beyond its immediate neighborhood. *See also* KOCHARIAN, ROBERT CABINET.

SAROYAN, WILLIAM (1908–1981). American writer. Saroyan was one of the most popular 20th-century American writers. He was born in Fresno, California, to immigrant parents. He did not finish high school and was a self-taught author. He won fame as a short-story writer, novelist, and playwright known for his sentimental and rhapsodic style. The optimism of his writings sharply parted company from the literature born of the Great Depression of the 1930s and was received as a new genre of American writing. His first works of poetry were published in 1932 in the Armenian-community journal *Hairenik*. His first short story "The Daring Young Man on the Flying Trapeze" appeared in 1934 and was quickly issued as the title of his first collection of stories. It was rated a masterpiece and was an immediate critical and commercial success. In 1936 he published *Inhale and Exhale* and went to work in Hollywood as a scriptwriter. His first theatrical work, *My Heart's in the Highlands*, opened in 1939 to enthusiastic reviews, and *The Time of Your Life* won the Critics Circle Award and the Pulitzer Prize in 1940. That same year he published his very popular suite of short stories, *My Name Is Aram*, fictionalizing his boyhood growing up in a community of doleful immigrant Armenians struggling to create a new life in a foreign country. In 1943 Saroyan published the novelized version of his screenplay for the movie *The Human Comedy*, which had been made by Metro-Goldwyn-Mayer (MGM), starring Mickey Rooney. Regarded his finest work, it captured the poignancy and tragedy of war on the home front. Saroyan served in the U.S. Army during World War II.

Saroyan continued to publish regularly until his final years but his later works did not surpass his earlier writings. In 1951 he published

The Assyrian and Other Stories, *Rock Wagram*, and coauthored with his cousin Ross Baghdasarian the lyrics of the song "Come On-a My House," an adaptation of an old Armenian folksong. Released by Columbia Records with Rosemary Clooney singing, it sold 900,000 copies and reached the top of the Hit Parade that summer. Baghdasarian who went on to a career in the entertainment industry as a commercial songwriter was the creator of the animated characters *Alvin and the Chipmunks*, a long-running children's cartoon television program.

Saroyan issued *The Bicycle Rider in Beverly Hills* in 1952, *The Laughing Matter* in 1953, *Mama, I Love You* in 1956, *Papa, You're Crazy* in 1957. That year he also saw the staging of his new play *The Cave Dwellers*. In 1959 Saroyan moved to Europe and kept homes in Paris and Fresno. His later works also became more autobiographical and some were written as memoirs. *Here Comes There Goes You Know Who* was printed in 1962, *Short Drive, Sweet Chariot* in 1966, *I Used to Believe I Had Forever, Now I'm Not So Sure* in 1968, *Places Where I've Done Time* in 1972, *Sons Come and Go, Mothers Hang in Forever* in 1976, *Obituaries* in 1979, and *Births* posthumously in 1983. In all he published over 50 books and left a large collection of unpublished material.

The hardships of immigrant life were deeply imprinted in Saroyan's mind. His father had died young. Saroyan, along with his siblings, was placed in an orphanage at the age of three while his mother went to work to earn a living. He spent his youth in Fresno, a community settled by Armenians mostly engaged in farming. He drew on the colorful characters of this community and of his own extended clan. Saroyan displayed no political interests during his life, but with his first success he traveled all the way to Armenia in 1935 to see his homeland where he returned a number of times. He was a friend of Armenian writers everywhere. His works were the first major artistic productions to place Armenians in the American landscape. His books were widely translated and well received in other countries also. In 1964 Saroyan traveled to Turkey to visit the town of Bitlis, his father's birthplace. According to his will, Saroyan's remains were buried in the writers' pantheon in Armenia.

SEVAN, LAKE. *See* LAKE SEVAN.

SHAHUMIAN, STEPAN (1878–1918). Bolshevik leader. Born and educated in Tbilisi, Shahumian founded the first Marxist circle in Armenia in 1899 and joined the Russian Social Democratic Workers Party (RSDWP) in 1900. He enrolled in the University of Berlin in 1902 and graduated from its department of philosophy in 1905. He returned to Tbilisi that same year to join the ferment sweeping Russia, and was especially active as a journalist, literary critic, and translator into Armenian of works by Karl Marx, Friedrich Engels, and Vladimir Lenin. He was an early Armenian adherent to the Bolshevik wing of the RSDWP. Engaged in revolutionary activity across the Caucasus, Shahumian demonstrated his organizational skills in Baku where a large working class employed in the highly volatile oil industry presented a proletarian element predisposed toward socialism. By 1914 Shahumian was leading the Bolshevik organization in Baku and when the Communists seized power in Russia, the Council of People's Commissars chaired by Lenin appointed Shahumian extraordinary commissar for Caucasian affairs. Effectively given responsibility for leading the revolution in the Caucasus, Shahumian organized the Baku Commune in March 1918 and placed the city under Bolshevik control. Rejected by the Azeri population, who joined forces with the advancing Ottoman army, the commune collapsed in September. With the assistance of **Anastas Mikoyan**, a young cohort at the time, Shahumian fled Baku only to be arrested by British interventionist troops in Central Asia. Among the 26 commissars executed upon capture, Shahumian was hailed an early hero of the revolution, one who recognized the distinct needs of each nationality while encouraging international socialism. His intellectual gifts earned him the respect of Armenian nationalists and his death deprived the Armenian Bolsheviks of the leadership skills that had distinguished him among the Caucasian revolutionaries. Towns and districts in Soviet Armenia and Soviet Azerbaijan were named after him, including **Stepanakert**, the capital city of **Nagorno Karabagh**. *See also* KAMO; KARAKHAN, LEV.

SIAMANTO (1878–1915). Poet. Siamanto, nee Atom Yarjanian, was born in Akn and grew up in Istanbul. As a result of the **Hamidian Massacres** he left for Europe, where he continued his education and began publishing poetry. He returned to Istanbul after the 1908 Young Turk Revolution and was active in Armenian political life. He traveled to the United States in 1910 and was the editor of the **Armenian Revolutionary Federation** (ARF) paper *Hairenik* for a year. He wrote powerful romantic and nationalistic poetry and emerged as the loudest voice of pained outrage against the abuses suffered by the Armenian people under Turkish rule. Through a series of poems like *The Thirst*, *Starvation*, *From the Fate of Orphans*, *Torches of Despair and Hope*, *Bloody News from My Friend*, the last in response to the 1909 **Adana Massacre**, he created haunting imagery of torment and injustice. His best-known verse was packed with emotions. It ranged from the shame and humiliation of the hideous brutalization of Armenian women as described in *The Dance* to the hopelessness and despair from the ruin of Armenia tearfully told in *A Handful of Ash, Native Home* (*Ap me Mokhir, Hayreni Tun*) (1907). Siamanto also invoked the ancient glories of Armenia. He sang of a vibrant and vigorous golden age in antiquity that inspired him to write in the form of incantation poems entitled *A Navasardian Prayer to the Goddess Anahit* (1911) and *Saint Mesrop*. The latter, published in 1912, culminated his oratorical style in phraseology that has since gripped the Armenian imagination. It also marked the apogee of Western Armenian literature. Siamanto was arrested on the night of April 24, 1915, deported and executed. *See also* ARMENIAN GENOCIDE.

SIMEON YEREVANTSI (Simon of Yerevan) (1710–1780). Ecclesiastical leader, **catholicos** (1763–1780). Simeon was born in **Yerevan** when it was the seat of a Persian khanate. Educated at the Holy See of **Edjmiadsin**, where he later taught, Simeon was one of the most learned figures of the **Armenian Apostolic Church**. A wide-ranging intellectual, he wrote works on the theology, history, and administrative status of the church and on the catholicosate at Edjmiadsin. He traveled as a legate of the Holy See to Istanbul and to Madras, an important center of Armenian intellectual activity at the time.

Simeon Yerevantsi was elected catholicos at Edjmiadsin in 1763 and his pontificate marked a turning point in the importance of Edjmiadsin for the Armenians. While the Armenian patriarchate of Istanbul had become the most influential office in the Armenian Apostolic Church, the remoteness of Edjmiadsin in a frontier province of Iran left it isolated. He labored to expand the role of the Holy See. In 1771 he established a printing press at the catholicosate, the first on the territory of historic Armenia. He organized against the spread of Catholicism in Eastern Armenia. He improved the school at the monastery preparing the ground for when it would become a major center of learning in the 19th century with the establishment of the full-fledged academy in 1874 under Catholicos Gevorg IV (1866–1885).

Simeon Yerevantsi also codified the possessions and rights of the church by gathering and recording the evidence documenting the privileges of the Edjmiadsin catholicosate. Lastly, he secured from Catherine the Great formal acknowledgment of his jurisdictional authority over the Armenian community and church in Russia. With Iran and India already within his administrative competence, he made Edjmiadsin a focal point of the Armenian Apostolic Church rivaling the Armenian Patriarchate in Istanbul. With the Russian conquests of the Yerevan khanate in 1828, and the absorption of Edjmiadsin into a Christian state, the ascendancy of Edjmiadsin in Armenian ecclesiastical affairs became assured. In the 20th century, with the founding of an Armenian state, the spiritual supremacy of the Holy See at Edjmiadsin was secured in the eyes of the Armenian people around the world.

SINAN (1490–1588). Ottoman architect. Regarded as the greatest of Ottoman architects and royal architect to Sultan Suleyman I, the Magnificent (1520–1566), and his successors Selim II (1566–1574) and Murat (1574–1595), Sinan was born to an Armenian family in the environs of Kayseri. He was taken to Istanbul as a *devshirme*, the levy of boys taken from Christian families to be raised as slaves of the sultan and servants of the state. He was trained in the Janissary corps, the elite slave army, and rose through its ranks and earned his reputation as a military engineer before his official appointment in 1539 as Architect of the Abode of Felicity. He spent the next 50 years of his long life constructing many of the greatest architectural monuments of the Ottoman Empire. He was originally commissioned by Suleyman's wife, Roxelana, to expand the Topkapi into a royal residence. The death of her son and the heir apparent prompted Sultan Suleyman to commission the first great mosque built by Sinan, the Shehzade Jamii or Prince's Mosque, in Istanbul. Thereafter Sinan went on to oversee the construction of a reported 360 structures across the empire including large and small mosques, *medreses* or religious schools, mausoleums, hospitals, bridges, caravansarais, baths, and palaces. Of these buildings, 120 were to be found in Istanbul alone. The planting of these impressive symbols of Ottoman might through the tremendous financial resources placed at Sinan's disposal for raising all these structures was part of Suleyman's program of political consolidation of the vast lands of the newly created empire. It was for the imperial capital also that Suleyman commissioned the massive complex that bears his name. Considered the architectural masterpiece of Ottoman Istanbul, the Suleymaniye covers an entire hill overlooking the Golden Horn. Construction began in 1550 and took seven years to complete. With its theological colleges, hospices, and eventually the sultan's tomb, all surrounding a colossal central mosque, the Suleymaniye was designed to project the global power exercised by the sultan and the Ottomans and was intended to overshadow architecturally the great monument of Byzantium and Christianity by outdoing for Islam the church of Hagia Sophia. Raised to a height of 53 meters (174 feet) with a diameter of 26 meters (85 feet), buttressed by half domes on two sides of the four great arches supporting it, the central dome encloses an immense space and is lighted by 130 windows in the tympanums and the semidomes. The Suleymaniye was intended to give definition to Ottoman imperial grandeur. If the interior tile decorations of the Suleymaniye were applied with restraint, the brilliantly colorful Iznik tile work was generously applied for the Rustem Pasha mosque commissioned by one of Suleyman's grand viziers.

Suleyman's last grand vizier, Sokullu Mehmet Pasha, sponsored an equally grand edifice. Mihrimah, Suleyman's daughter and wife of Grand Vizier Rustem Pasha, commissioned two mosques from Sinan, one in Uskudar across the Bosphorus and one in Istanbul, both featuring a central dome raised high over a square and the supports significantly reduced, especially with the second one, and so pronounced as to represent a new and original model for a compact style at variance with the numerous cascading domes and semidomes covering the roofs of the larger rectangular mosques. The trend toward vertical expression in Sinan's artistry reached its apex in the structure universally regarded his masterpiece, the Selimiye mosque complex in Edirne. This time Sinan placed the 31-meters-wide (103 feet) dome up to the height of 45 meters (148 feet) over an octagon stacked upward in four layers of arches, semidomes, and buttresses altogether displaying an exceptional conceptual cohesiveness lending toward the illusion of a spherical enclosure within. With 80-meters-high (262 feet) minarets at the four corners, the whole of the Selimiye is a soaring edifice. Started in 1569 for Selim II, construction was completed in 1575 when Sinan had reached the age of 85, quite evidently still in full command of his artistic vision and of his extraordinary skills in planning and managing all aspects of erecting such a vast structure from the hue of the stone, the decorative paneling in Iznik tile, and the armies of masons and artisans required to assemble such a tremendously complex and finely crafted monument. Sinan remained active until the end of his life and did not neglect to design a mausoleum for himself in Istanbul adjacent to his residence in a triangular walled garden with a stone fountain at its corner. By the time Sinan laid down his draftsman's pen for the last time he had single-handedly stamped upon the Ottoman Empire an architectural heritage that became its greatest symbol of cultural achievement.

SIUNI. Princely family in medieval Armenia. One of the most important and durable princely families of medieval Armenia, the Siuni dynasty ruled over the homonymous province of Siunik, one of the 15 historic provinces of Armenia Major. Encompassing the basin of **Lake Sevan** and the mountainous regions to the south, Siunik was one of the most remote and rugged areas of ancient Armenia. Lacking cities of any size, it was dotted with fortresses and monasteries, a haven for a fiercely independent people and for churchmen seeking isolation. Like so many of the important Armenian **nakharar** families, the Siunis too originated as indigenous nobility that by the time of the **Arshakuni** royal dynasty were fully integrated into the feudal aristocracy of the country. Because of the location of Siunik, the region was highly exposed and its ruling family faced challenges requiring discretion in its relations with neighboring powers. As the easternmost province of Armenia in the late Arshakuni period, the Siuni bore responsibility for the defense of the border in that part. Its exposure and isolation at the same time encouraged a strong separatist tendency under the constant pressure of Sasanid Iran. Capable of fielding up to 19,000 horsemen, the military resources of the Siuni were such as to equip them with the capacity to manage their affairs as a virtually autonomous principality.

Once the Armenian monarchy was abolished in 428, the proximity of Siunik to Iran and the direct vassalage of its ruling family to the

Great King placed the Siuni in an exceptionally advantageous position. Yazdegerd II (439–457) appointed the lord of the province, Vasak Siuni, as the first Armenian *marzpan*, or viceroy, of Persian Armenia governing from the city of **Dvin**. Yazdegerd's religious policy of imposing Mazdaism, however, divided and polarized Armenian society and undermined the marzpan's authority among the Armenians. The great rebellion of 451 led by Vardan **Mamikonian** that culminated in the Battle of Avarayr against Yazadegerd's army further isolated the viceroy, leading him and his successors to prefer charting their own destiny by requesting the separation of their province from the Marzpanate of Armenia. In so doing the Siunis secured their rule over their domain and maintained it for many centuries. During the Arab period, Siunik formed part of the vast province of Arminiya, and the Siuni even succeeded in expanding their holdings eastward to the region of Artsakh, present-day **Nagorno Karabagh**.

With the weakening of Arab rule in Armenia, and the rise of the **Bagratuni** and **Ardsruni** houses to royal status, the Siunis too hoped to shed Arab suzerainty. With the Arab viceroys and the succeeding local tribal chieftains still holding the city of Dvin and its surrounding regions, and thus maintaining a strong Islamic presence in eastern Armenia, aspirations were delayed until about 970 when Prince Smbat II declared sovereignty by styling himself the king of Siunik. The importance of this gesture was underscored when his successor, Vasak VI Siuni (ca. 998–1019), gave his daughter and only child, Katranide, in marriage to Gagik I Bagratuni, king of Armenia (989–1020). Queen Katranide was a great patroness of the arts in the capital city of **Ani**, and she probably financed her projects from her dowry that was given the Bagratuni king in the form of the northern half of the kingdom of Siunik. This political marriage amplified the Bagratuni domains and for a time reunified Siunik with the Armenian heartland. This unification also marked the termination of the senior line of the Siuni family. A junior line continued to govern as the princes of Ghapan, the alpine district lying to the south of Lake Sevan down to the **Arax River**.

The Bagratunis of Ani succumbed to the Byzantines in 1045 and central Armenia soon after was overrun by the Seljuk Turks. The Siunis in Ghapan held title to their fiefdom until about 1170, when under Turkish pressure they retreated into Khachen, the central district of their principality. The Armenian social structure in the area was still sufficiently intact such that, when the Georgians during the reign of Queen Tamar (1184–1212) conquered Siunik, two new Armenian feudal houses in her service, the Haghbakian and the Orbelian, succeeded in setting roots in Siunik and in outlasting even Mongol rule, which in a blow devastated the Armeno-Georgian kingdom forged during the reign of Queen Tamar. The descendants of the Haghbakian, Orbelian, and Siuni maintained a presence in their mountain redoubts and exercised autonomous lordship at the pleasure of the sovereigns of Iran right down to the early 18th century.

SOCIAL DEMOCRATIC HNCHAKIAN PARTY (SDHP), *Sotsial Demokratakan Hnchakian Kusaktsutiun* (*SDHK*). Political party. Founded in 1887 in Geneva, Switzerland, by seven Russian Armenians, the organization started as the Hnchakian Revolutionary Party. The original members were Avetis Nazarbekian, Mariam Vardanian (better known as Maro Nazarbekian, the other half of the husband and wife team), Gevorg Gharadjian, Ruben Khan-Azat, Kristapor Ohanian, Gabriel Kafian, and Levon Stepanian. Influenced by the Narodnik revolutionary movement in Russia and especially by Alexander Herzen, in imitation of the latter's publication *Kolokol* (Bell), the Armenian activists called their publication *Hnchak* (Clarion). From the onset the Hnchaks, as they became known, advocated a revolutionary path and adhered to the socialist ideal. Despite their geographic origin, the focus of their attention was Western Armenia and the plight of the Armenian people under Ottoman rule. Urging the people to organize and rely upon its own resources instead of waiting for European intervention, the Hnchakian organization proposed the outright liberation of Western Armenia.

The Hnchakian party's most active phase lasted only six years. Its public demands and confrontational tactics proved too provocative in the Ottoman Empire. The organization's first significant action was the 1890 Kum Kapi demonstration in Istanbul. This was followed by the 1895 Bab Ali demonstration. The first was staged at the Armenian Patriarchate, the second at the gate of the Ottoman government. In both instances a list of demands for reforms topped by the call for an end to arbitrary rule in Armenia were presented. The choice of location for the second demonstration was prompted by the Turkish reprisals against the Armenians of Sasun, in the interior, who had risen in rebellion against the unlawful exactions of the Kurds in 1894.

Hnchaks had a role in leading this uprising, much as they organized the rebellion in Zeitun in 1895–1896. The Hnchaks hoped to mobilize the rest of the Armenian people from these centers of resistance, however, both Sasun and Zeitun were remote pockets inhabited by hardy and defiant people accustomed to the small measure of autonomy still left to their isolated communities in the Armenian mountains. The atrocities eventually prompted the European Powers in May 1895 to pressure the sultan, Abdul-Hamid (Abdulhamit) II, into agreeing to a reform program for the Armenian provinces to satisfy part of the demands presented by the Hnchaks. Once issued, however, the Great Powers turned their attention to other matters. The May reform program became a dead letter and the September 1895 demonstration at Bab Ali was violently suppressed.

The struggle had been costly and the party membership split over what many regarded as the radical aspects of the Hnchakian organization, its revolutionary and socialist rhetoric, which was blamed as the cause for the reluctance of the European Powers to introduce real reforms in Western Armenia. In 1896 at the London party congress, the antisocialists split and formed the Reformed (*Verakazmial*) Hnchakian organization. The turmoil in the Caucasus from 1903 and the 1905 revolution in Russia required that the party face the need of responding to the crisis in Eastern Armenia. In the context of the ideological struggle waged over the first Russian revolution, in 1909 the party was officially renamed the *Sotsial Demokratakan Hnchakian Kusaktsutiun*. The Hnchakian party never took root in Russia. Armenians of a strong socialist persuasion preferred joining Russian revolutionary societies, and Armenians supportive of a nationalist agenda joined the ranks of the **Armenian Revolutionary Federation** (ARF). The Hnchaks had greater success in creating an underground organization in Cilicia and made efforts to defend Armenian neighborhoods during the 1909 **Adana Massacre**. They waged their last armed struggle defending the Armenians of Hajen (Hadjin) in 1920 against the Kemalist forces besieging the town.

Although represented by small groupings all across the diaspora, the Hnchakian party lacked the membership to make a measurable impact anywhere other than in the large Armenian community of Lebanon made up of refugees from Cilicia. The party remains headquartered in Beirut. For both nationalistic and ideological reasons the Hnchaks recognized the legitimacy of the Armenian Soviet Socialist

Republic (ASSR) but lacked the resources to extend other than polemic support. Since independence, the SDHP has sought to create an organization in Armenia. It aligned with the **Levon Ter-Petrossian** administration but did not participate in electoral politics in the 1990s. *See also* ARMENIAN REVOLUTIONARY MOVEMENT; POLITICAL PARTIES.

SPITAK EARTHQUAKE. The greatest natural disaster to occur in Armenia in modern times. The town of Spitak in northern Armenia was the epicenter of an earthquake that shook the entire region on December 7, 1988. A tremor measured at 6.9 on the Richter scale struck at 11:41 a.m. followed by a second tremor registered at 5.8 at 11:45 a.m. All the major cities in northern Armenia were effected. Spitak with a population of 27,000 was leveled. The larger urban centers of Kirovakan (population 170,000) and Stepanavan (population 40,000) suffered extensive damage, and nearly half of Leninakan (now **Gyumri**), the second largest city in Armenia with a population of 300,000, was in ruins. The true proportions of the human disaster were never established as it proved impossible to extricate all the dead from countless structures turned into great heaps of rubble. The official death toll was placed at 25,000, though estimates have run as high as 100,000. The injured were counted at 12,000, the majority suffering crushed limbs. Over 500,000 were left homeless. In a country of 3.5 million people, the percentages in terms of casualties, urban devastation, economic ruin, and damage to industry and infrastructure were staggering.

A country prone to seismic tremors, late Soviet-era construction, architecture, and urban planning had flouted the basic principles of building earthquake-resistant structures. Poor quality cement, minimal usage of steel reenforcement and prefabricated blocks made a deadly combination. High-rises flattened like pancakes, crumbled, or toppled over. These conditions made rescue incredibly difficult. With the transport system obstructed, the health care network demolished, and communications disrupted, the state of emergency provoked a crisis exposing all the flaws of the Soviet state, which proved incapable of responding to or relieving the plight of the survivors. The political consequences of the Spitak earthquake were far-reaching and its effect on Armenian economy and society long lasting. Ironically, the Spitak earthquake opened the once tightly closed Soviet

Union to Western aid. The reliance on such assistance, however, undermined Soviet authority, as the vaunted achievements of socialism were graphically shown to have been catastrophically defective. The occurrence of the earthquake at the end of a year of political ferment across Armenia over the **Nagorno Karabagh** issue triggered reverberations across the entire Armenian political landscape. Reacting negatively to mounting public pressure to remedy quickly both the political and humanitarian crisis, USSR Communist party chairman Mikhail Gorbachev instead resorted to arresting the Karabagh Committee in the hope of focusing attention on the emergency. This had the opposite effect in Armenia but alienated the authorities in Moscow as central control over the periphery and the nationalities was clearly slipping from their hands. All this occurred in the glare of international media attention that helped to draw assistance from many countries around the world. The United States alone within a month of the disaster delivered over $100 million in emergency aid to Armenia transported by American military aircraft. The horror of the scenes of devastation broadcast everywhere also galvanized the Armenian **diaspora** and communities on all continents hastened to organize relief efforts.

The unraveling of the Soviet Union and the precipitous decline of the Armenian economy soon after prevented the recovery of northern Armenia. A new term entered the geography of the country and the belt along the Spitak fault line became known as the "disaster zone" or the "earthquake zone" creating a permanent condition of privation, absence of basic amenities, and cramped temporary shelters. Ten years after the earthquake at best only half of the homeless population had been resettled in more permanent housing.

The Spitak earthquake was a reminder that the entire Armenian plateau is seismically active. It prompted authorities to retrofit critical structures with special attention paid to the Medsamor nuclear power plant that was deemed vulnerable. Numerous tremors are recorded in Armenian history. The greatest frequency of earthquakes is actually tabulated for the city of Erzinjan in historic Western Armenia. Chronicles mention the wholesale destruction of cities and their effect on the fate of the Armenian people. Armenia, however, was never more densely populated than in the second half of the 20th century, and the Spitak earthquake may well have been the worst natural catastrophe to visit the Armenian highlands. *See* KARABAGH MOVEMENT.

SRVANTZTIANTS, GAREGIN (1840–1892). Ecclesiastical leader, ethnographer, folklorist. Srvantztiants was born in **Van** and received his education in local parochial schools. He became a teacher and was ordained a celibate priest in 1867. Whilst assigned ecclesiastical responsibilities in Van, Erzerum, Bitlis, and Kharpert, he organized a number of schools, and was the assistant prior of the Armenian monastery of *Surp Karapet* (Saint John the Precursor), one of the most hallowed sites of Armenian religious pilgrimage, at Mush. After his investiture as bishop in 1886, he also was appointed prior of *Surp Karapet*. A fervent preacher and exponent of Armenian emancipation, he was removed from office and placed under surveillance in Istanbul.

Well before his confinement to the Ottoman capital, Srvantztiants already had published what in the aggregate was the most important ethnographic data on the Armenians yet gathered at the time. As an associate of **Mkrtich Khrimian**, he had traveled with the later **catholicos** through the Armenian provinces in 1860 and 1861. Recognized much like his mentor for the kinship he felt with his own people, Srvantztiants was instructed by the Armenian Patriarch of Istanbul, **Nerses Varzhapetian**, to investigate and report on the condition of the Armenian communities in eastern Anatolia after the Russo-Turkish War of 1877–1878, while Khrimian prepared to plead the Armenian case at the Congress of Berlin.

During these trips, and at all other opportunities, Srvantztiants tirelessly recorded the folklore of the Armenian rustic population. He released the results of his expeditions in a series of works issued in the 1870s and 1880s. In *Grots u brots* (The Written and the Spoken) (1874) he published popular Armenian folk stories and traditions. In *Hnots yev norots* (From the Old and the New) (1874), he published Armenian stories from manuscript records. *Manana* (Manna) (1876) included proverbs, riddles, songs, and epigraphic data from the Van region. In *Hamov-hotov* (The Flavorful and the Colorful) (1884) he described the topography, climate, and monuments of Armenia.

The most significant of his discoveries was the first cycle of what was hence recognized as the Armenian national folk epic *Sasna dserer* (The Daredevils of Sasun), more popularly known by the name of its main hero. Srvantztiants recorded that section of the epic bearing the heading of *Sasuntsi Davit kam Meheri tur* (David of Sasun or the Gate of Meher), later augmented by discoveries of additional portions of the cycle. Srvantztiants also published important studies on the subjects he recorded and was elected honorary member of the Imperial Academy of Antiquities in St. Petersburg. He passed away in Istanbul.

STEPANAKERT. Capital of **Nagorno Karabagh** Republic. Originally Vararakn, renamed Khankend in 1847 during the Russian period, the town was renamed again in 1923 during the Soviet period for **Stepan Shahumian**, the Bolshevik leader in the Caucasus in 1917–1918. From 1923 to 1991, Stepanakert was the capital city of the Nagorno Karabagh Autonomous Oblast (District) of Soviet Azerbaijan Situated below the great height of Shushi, Stepanakert acquired its Armenian population after the Azeris torched the Armenian quarters of the city of Shushi in March 1920. In 1926 Alexander Tamanian, the architect of **Yerevan**, designed a new radial plan for the city, which over the decades was considerably expanded to accommodate a population of 50,000 by 1983. In 1988 Stepanakert became a hotbed of political activity as the Armenians organized a movement calling for the unification of Nagorno Karabagh with Armenia. When the district declared itself severed from Azerbaijan in 1991, Azeri forces in Shushi and the nearby town of Khojalu started the shelling of Stepanakert inflicting extensive damage. The siege of the city was lifted only in May 1992 after nearly a year of artillery bombardment when Karabagh Armenian forces captured the heights of Shushi and silenced the guns. That same month Karabagh forces broke through the Lachin corridor separating Nagorno Karabagh from Armenia and de facto joined the two Armenian states.

SURMELIAN, LEON Z. (1905–1995). Author and educator. Born in Trebizond, Turkey, Surmelian was orphaned in 1915. He received his primary education in Armenian institutions in Turkey at the Agricultural School in Armash and the Istanbul Central School. He continued his higher education in the United States where he remained for the rest of his life. He first attended Kansas State College of Agriculture. He also attended the University of Nebraska and the University of Southern California, where he eventually received appointment as professor of English and literature.

The poet **Vahan Tekeyan** who took an interest in young Surmelian published his earliest writings in Paris. The slim volume of poetry was to remain his sole contribution in the Armenian language.

Though he published thereafter in English, all his works recalled the world of his childhood. In the process he became one of the principal transmitters of Armenian folk literature into English. *I Ask You, Ladies and Gentlemen*, an autobiographical novel, appeared in 1945 and became an international bestseller. In 1964 he issued *Daredevils of Sassoun*, a prose translation of the Armenian national epic, which was followed in 1968 with *Apples of Immortality*, a collection of folktales from Armenia. The Union of Writers in Armenia bestowed on Surmelian in 1983 the **Khachatur Abovian** Award, the highest honor awarded an Armenian author. *See* SRVANTZTIANTS, GAREGIN.

– T –

TEKEYAN, VAHAN (1878–1945). Poet. Tekeyan was born in the Ortakoy district of Istanbul and educated in the local Armenian schools. He quit school to go to work in 1894. He was variously employed as a clerk, editor, and teacher in sundry Armenian commercial, educational, and political institutions for the rest of his life, which saw him holding positions in Liverpool, Marseilles, Hamburg, Cairo, and Cyprus. He was briefly with the Reformed Hnchaks before joining the Ramkavar Sahmanadrakan, or Democratic Constitutional Party, in 1909. He remained an active participant in the affairs of the liberal organization for the rest of his life and in 1920 played a leading role in unifying the Reformed Hnchak and the Liberal Constitutional groups into the *Ramkavar Azatakan Kusaktsutiun*, or **Democratic Liberal Party** (DLP). In 1919 he traveled to the Republic of Armenia as a representative of **Boghos Nubar** *Pasha* to conduct negotiations between the Armenian National Delegation, led by the latter, which was based in Paris, and the newly formed Armenian government.

Tekeyan was one of the handful of Armenian men of letters to survive the **Armenian Genocide**. Like many other intellectuals and political figures, he had returned to Istanbul after the restoration of the Ottoman Constitution in 1908, but by luck happened to be out of the country on a business assignment when the war broke out and thus escaped the fate of his generation that had spawned a group of poets who had won acclaim in Armenian literary life as the exponents of the worship of beauty. They were authors of verse with exceptional polish and introduced a level of sensitivity through the emotive power of their words. This new esthetic resulted in a highly personal poetry laying bare the immense anguish of the solitariness of the individual. It also happened to be an especially powerful genre to record the punishing fate of the Armenian people. Tekeyan published six volumes of poetry in his lifetime. *Hogere* (Cares) appeared in 1901 in Paris; *Hrashali Harutiun* (Miraculous Resurrection) with 107 poems in 1914 in Istanbul; *Kes Gisheren Minchev Arshaluys* (From Midnight to Dawn) in 1918 in Paris; *Ser* (Love) in 1933; *Hayerkutiun* (Armeniansong) in 1943; and *Tagharan* (Lyrics) in 1945. Of his best-loved poems, *K'antzreve Deghas* (It Is Raining, My Child) (1901) is pure sentimentality. His popular elegy *Yekeghetsin Haykakan* (The Armenian Church) (1924) evokes the historical solemnity of faith, ritual, and hymn. As for *Piti Esenk Astudso* (We Shall Say to God) (1917), it is the most bitter poem penned in the Armenian language railing against God for the hell endured on earth by the Armenian people.

TER-PETROSSIAN, LEVON (1945–). President of Armenia 1991–1998. Ter-Petrossian was born in Aleppo, Syria. His family, which originated from **Musa Dagh**, emigrated to Soviet Armenia in 1946. A graduate in Oriental studies from the department of philology at **Yerevan** State University, Ter-Petrossian continued his education at the Leningrad Institute of Oriental Studies. He received his master's degree in 1971 with specializations in Armenian and Syriac philology. From 1972 to 1978 he worked as a junior scholar at the Institute of Literature of the Academy of Sciences of Armenia, and from 1978 to 1985 was the academic secretary at the Matenadaran, the repository of ancient manuscripts, in Yerevan. He was promoted to senior scholar at the Matenadaran in 1985 and was awarded his doctorate in philology from Leningrad University in 1987.

That same year, with the era of glasnost and perestroika in the Soviet Union declared by Mikhail Gorbachev, Armenian political activists raised the issue of the unification with Armenia of the Armenian-populated enclave of **Nagorno Karabagh** in Soviet Azerbaijan. By early 1988 these activities resulted in a mass movement led by a group called the Karabagh Committee. Ter-Petrossian's natural skills in oratory and persuasion earned him a place on the committee and he soon emerged as one of its most respected figures. His arrest after the December 7, 1988, **Spitak Earthquake** in Armenia, along with the rest of the Karabagh Committee, drew the attention of human rights organizations in the West that protested his imprisonment in Moscow. He was released on May 31, 1989, and in August of that year he was elected a deputy to the Supreme Soviet, or parliament, in Armenia in an open **election**.

When in November 1989 the **Armenian National Movement** (ANM) was formally organized to lead the popular movement for democracy and independence, Ter-Petrossian assumed the presidency of the ANM, and the Supreme Soviet in Armenia voted him a member of its presidium. He was reelected in May 1990 to the Supreme Soviet of Armenia, while by August of the year in a series of nationwide free elections, the ANM wrested control of the legislature away from the **Communist Party of Armenia** (CPA). On August 4, 1990, by an overwhelming majority vote the deputies elected Ter-Petrossian president of the Armenian parliament. On August 23 the same parliament adopted a declaration on independence charting for Armenia a new course as envisioned in the ANM program: popular democracy, free market system, political pluralism, and a legal society guaranteeing basic freedoms. It also changed the name of the country proclaiming it the Republic of Armenia.

Under the leadership of Ter-Petrossian the Armenian parliament wasted no time in introducing laws on privatization. Its first most sweeping enactment legalized the private ownership of farms and in a year's time most of the agricultural land in Armenia was denationalized. Proceeding with the program of the August 1990 declaration, parliament scheduled a national referendum for September 21, 1991, which saw the Armenian people in a near-unison vote for independence from the Soviet Union. A month later, on October 16, by popular vote in an open election Levon Ter-Petrossian became the first president of newly independent Armenia.

The first years of independence were trying ones and daily presented new challenges to the president. The conflict over Nagorno Karabagh resulted in the blockade of the landlocked country by neighboring Azerbaijan, joined in subsequently by Turkey. The economic impact of the blockade was devastating, especially in view of the serious reduction of energy supplies reaching Armenia. Ter-Petrossian's government came under criticism from domestic opposition groups, but no **political party** garnered the support necessary to challenge the ANM. Ter-Petrossian earned high marks for conducting a **foreign**

policy promoting moderation and compromise in a zone rife with conflict, and built good relations with countries as diverse as Russia, Iran, France, and the United States. His domestic program, especially the policies on structural reform, disaffected growing sectors of the Armenian population seriously impacted by the energy crisis, the economic downslide, and the resulting shortages. Despite calls for halting the process of denationalization until such time as peace was established in the region, Ter-Petrossian maintained the course of the privatization of the economy. In contrast to many of the other post-Soviet republics, and despite its economic woes, Armenia proceeded the furthest in the program to introduce free market reforms.

The effects of the reforms, however, were eroded by the costs of prosecuting the Karabagh war that drained Armenia of resources, subjected it to continuing blockade by Azerbaijan and Turkey, and threatened to isolate Armenia as Azerbaijan slowly improved relations with the West by touting the availability of its oil reserves for investment and development. The emergency of the open conflict that endangered the very existence of the Armenians of Karabagh restrained the expression of public grievances with the deteriorating conditions in the country. The May 14, 1994, cease-fire that finally brought an end to the hostilities around Karabagh, while registering the military success of Armenian forces in the battlefield, also took the lid off the mounting domestic problems plaguing the Ter-Petrossian administration by that time. The powerbrokers in Armenia who relied on the armed forces of the country responded with measures designed to repress dissent and to consolidate their political influence, as well as dominance in the economy.

The growing political conflict between the progovernment factions led by the ANM and opposition groups was primarily waged over the nature of the constitution being drafted in the legislature, itself controlled by the ANM. The ANM promoted a **constitution** extending considerable powers to the executive branch, while the opposition asked for a parliamentary system. The heated debate delayed the adoption of the constitution until the date for a referendum was set for July 5, 1995. The parliamentary election was also scheduled for the same day. Before the final date was selected and the electorate went to cast their ballots, the assassination in December 1994 of the former mayor of Yerevan, Hambartsum Galstian, a onetime close ally of Ter-Petrossian, precipitated a political crisis. The killing occurred at a time of mounting government accusations of conspiracy by the **Armenian Revolutionary Federation** (ARF), whose activities were suspended by the president. While the two events were unconnected, they nonetheless exposed the deep fissures running through Armenian society and more and more put Ter-Petrossian on the defensive. The July 5 election further aggravated conditions when charges of widespread fraud were leveled as the ANM claimed control of the new National Assembly.

The September 22, 1996, presidential election provided one more occasion to reignite domestic tensions. Although Ter-Petrossian was declared the winner, the ensuing public protest in the capital city that culminated with angry demonstrators storming the parliament building required the stationing of armed troops to calm the situation. By that point the legitimacy of Ter-Petrossian's administration and re-election was seriously undermined and the president grew more dependent on the support of the ministers controlling the internal and external security forces of the country to keep him in power.

Armenia's internal problems did not go unnoticed and Ter-Petrossian suffered further embarrassment when he failed to prevent the Organization for Security and Cooperation in Europe (OSCE) from releasing a statement issued on the occasion of its December 1996 meeting in Lisbon, Portugal, that appeared to predetermine the status of Nagorno Karabagh while difficult negotiations were still in process. It was a serious reversal for a person whose domestic policies had always been questioned but whose diplomacy in the international arena was regarded as skillful and even daring.

Efforts to salvage the situation eventually led Ter-Petrossian to invite **Robert Kocharian**, president of the Nagorno Karabagh Republic (NKR), to assume the prime ministry of Armenia in March 1997. It proved a temporary measure as his willingness to consider the step-by-step settlement of the Karabagh question promoted by the OSCE now divided his own government. When toward the end of the year he publicly announced Armenia's endorsement of the OSCE proposals, his political base fractured. As the powerbrokers realigned their support, ANM loyalists resigned from office leaving Ter-Petrossian with the options of surrendering his policy-making functions or resigning. On February 3, 1998, Ter-Petrossian stepped down from the presidency and entered private life. *See also* BAGRATIAN, HRANT FIRST CABINET; BAGRATIAN, HRANT SECOND CABINET;

HAROUTIUNIAN, GAGIK CABINET; HARUTIUNIAN, KHOS-ROV CABINET; KOCHARIAN, ROBERT CABINET; MANUKIAN, VAZGEN CABINET.

TIGRAN II THE GREAT (TIGRANES II) (95–55 B.C.). King of Armenia. Tigran's reign began with his annexation of the Kingdom of Dsopk/Sophene in 94 B.C. and the unification of Armenia under the rule of a single sovereign. With all of Greater Armenia at his feet, Tigran embarked upon a series of foreign adventures manifestly showing imperial ambitions. In this he found an ally in King Mithridates Eupator of Pontus, himself a restless and aspiring warrior. Together they seized and divided Cappadocia, only to invite Roman intervention on behalf of its deposed ruler. While Mithridates of Pontus continued to challenge Roman expansion into Asia Minor, Tigran turned his attention to Parthia and in 87 B.C. descended upon Ecbatana, the summer residence of the Persian court and burned it down. With his path cleared, he annexed all the minor kingdoms and principalities to the south of Armenia, from east to west Atropatene, Adiabene, Gordyene, Osrhoene, and Upper Mesopotamia. In 83 B.C. he overthrew the Seleucids in Syria, taking along Commagene, Cilicia, and Phoenicia. Thereby he created an empire stretching from the Caspian Sea to the Mediterranean. Having subjugated Armenia's neighboring kings, all of whom he left to reign as his vassals, Tigran deemed himself king of kings, a title first assumed by his former Arsacid captor, Mithridates II (123–87 B.C.), from whom he had exacted retribution.

Tigran's empire began to unravel with the arrival of the Romans. In pursuit of Mithridates of Pontus, who, defeated by the Romans, had taken refuge in Armenia, the Roman general Licinius Lucullus used the pretext to invade Syria and advance upon **Tigranakert** (Tigranocerta), the new southern capital of the **Armenian kingdom**. In 69 B.C., in front of the gates of the city, Lucullus handily defeated Tigran's forces and captured his treasury. Tigran beat a retreat into Armenia proper as Lucullus followed in his train, but the rough terrain, the great distances crossed, and the regular harassment by Armenian forces fighting on their native soil persuaded the Romans to give up the chase. It took a larger force and more disciplined legions under the command of Pompey, who was charged by the Senate to settle Roman affairs in the East, to compel Tigran to come to terms with the growing might of the Romans in the eastern Mediterranean. In 66 B.C. Pompey marched his troops all the way to **Artashat** (Artaxata). However, both parties avoided a showdown. Pompey stopped short of the Armenian capital and the 74-year-old Tigran, in full regalia, proceeded to the Roman camp to negotiate a peaceful resolution of the conflict. Preserving the integrity of his kingdom, he surrendered his western acquisitions and agreed to friendship with Rome.

Besides the construction of his capital city of Tigranakert at a point central to his empire, Tigran's ambitions and vision for his state were also revealed by the coinage he minted. He may not have been the first sovereign in Armenia to issue his own coin. He certainly was the sovereign who issued the most coin, in gold, silver, and bronze. The coinage was intended for use as the new standard of exchange in his realm. In the custom of the time, he struck his visage on them. In so doing he became the first Armenian in history whose visage is known and whose regal profile is easily discernible crowned by the distinct tiara of the **Artashesian** monarchs.

Tigran remained on the Armenian throne until 55 B.C., when he died at the ripe old age of 85, having lived longer, reigned longer, and ruled over a larger state than any other king of Greater Armenia before or after. In the long history of the Armenians, for him alone is reserved the ultimate recognition of royal majesty and the constant honor of being remembered as Tigran the Great. *See also* AR-TASHES I; YERVANDUNI.

TIGRANAKERT. Capital of Tigran the Great's empire. The incorporation of Seleucid Syria in 83 B.C. into the kingdom of **Tigran II the Great** (95–55 B.C.), who expanded the Armenian state southward toward Parthia, Mesopotamia, and the Mediterranean Sea, placed the historic capital of Artashat in a remote corner of the new empire. To govern his vast kingdom from a more central location, and to be close to the wealthy province of Syria, Tigran founded a new city in his name in southernmost Armenia. Tigranakert, or Tigranacerta, whose construction began soon after Tigran moved into Syria, was built as a multinational capital on the model of the Hellenistic city. Tigran's rule over Syria lasted only from 83 B.C. to 68 B.C. as the Romans pressed their expansion into the eastern Mediterranean. Because of its exposed position, located midway between northern Syria and

Parthia, Tigranakert was both vulnerable to attack and not easily defended from the Armenian heartland. While it initially withstood a siege even after Tigran was defeated in front of its gates at the hands of the Roman general Licinius Lucullus, Tigranakert eventually fell in 69 B.C. and was plundered of its wealth and royal treasury. Tigran retreated into Armenia, and although Tigranakert remained within his kingdom, the surrender of Syria to the Romans eliminated any reason for maintaining it as a capital city. Even so, Tigranakert became a permanent settlement and remained an important place. During the conflict between Rome and Parthia over Armenia during the mid-first century A.D., the Roman general Corbulo occupied Tigranakert in 59 A.D. The Romans raised their candidate, King Tigran VI (60–61 A.D.), to the Armenian throne in Tigranakert. In the struggle to secure his brother **Trdat I**'s claim to the Armenian throne, the Parthian King Vologases I (51–75 A.D.) attempted to dislodge Tigran, but the city was strong enough to withstand the siege.

With the partition of Armenia between Rome and Sasanid Persia in 387, Tigranakert came under direct Roman administration and was renamed Martyropolis. With the redivisioning of the Armenian districts of the Roman Empire into four provinces by Justinian I in 536, Martyropolis was made the administrative center of Armenia IV. The city was one of the first captured by the Arabs in Armenia in 640 and they renamed it Mayarfarkin. The concentration of Arab tribesmen in the region of Tigranakert and neighboring Diyar-el-Bakr (later Diyarbekir) began to change the ethnic composition of southern Armenia, until Kurdish chieftains drove out the Arab population of Mayarfarkin in 995–996 and consequently restored the city to its Armenian population. Seljuk rule after 1071 lasted until Salah-al-Din (Saladin) (1175–1194) restored Arab dominion under the Ayyubids, which lasted until 1260 when Hulagu, the Mongol khan, captured the city. Thereafter Tigranakert/Mayarfarkin was reduced to a secondary town in sight of the great walls once erected by Tigran the Great at the founding of the city. The Armenians of Tigranakert were deported in 1915. *See also* ARTASHAT.

TRDAT I (TIRIDATES I) (63–88). King of ancient Armenia and founder of the Armenian **Arshakuni** dynasty. Trdat was assigned the Armenian crown in 52 A.D. by his brother the great king of Iran, Vologases I (51–80 A.D.). At first a king in name only, Trdat marshaled sufficient forces by 54 A.D. to enter Armenia. His arrival, which co-incided with the coronation of Nero (54–68) as emperor, precipitated a 10-year conflict with Rome culminating in the ferocious campaign in Armenia of general Corbulo who laid waste to **Artashat** and **Tigranakert**. Roman fortunes, however, were reversed in 63 A.D. when a joint Armenian-Parthian force defeated the Romans at Rhandia and Corbulo returned a second time, on this occasion as a negotiator, and initialed the Treaty of Rhandia by which a formula for the succession to the Armenian throne was found acceptable to all three parties, Rome, Parthia, and Armenia. To Parthia was assigned the right of nomination and to Rome the right of investiture, the two great empires sharing equal and undivided suzerainty over Armenia. As for the Armenians, in Trdat they had a king of their liking, a sovereign who had earned their loyalty and respect by tirelessly waging the long struggle against the Romans.

Trdat's coronation fills a special chapter in the annals of Antiquity. In a unique and exceptional display of cordiality between the two great powers of the western half of the known world, in 66 A.D. Trdat, the victorious scion of the Arshakuni family, and his royal retinue of Parthian guards and courtiers, with great pomp and ceremony, traveled by land all the way to Rome, there to receive the diadem directly from the emperor. To the Romans, the journey of the Oriental king offered a spectacle the likes of which they had not seen, and Trdat's public submission to investiture by Nero marked a rare occasion to display the near-global reach of Roman prestige.

With its security guaranteed, Armenia enjoyed a half-century of comparative peace. During the long reign of King Trdat I, the prosperity of the country was restored and the state coffers generated revenue sufficient for the building of the fortress of Garni as the summer residence of the court. Surrounded by strong walls constructed of finished blocks of white limestone, with comfortable quarters, heated baths decorated with mosaics, courtyards, garden terraces, and a private Roman temple for worship, Garni bears the stamp of the Classical world like no other place in Armenia. *See also* ARTASHESIAN.

TRDAT IV (TIRIDATES IV) (298–330). First Christian king of Armenia. The full cycle of the life of King Trdat IV, at least in its legendary form, is well known. The reason is that his reign was pivotal in the history of the Armenian people. There are two phases to his life and the first is related to the story of his childhood flight from Armenia to the Roman Empire upon the assassination of his father King Khosrov I. An accomplished athlete in his youth, Tradat is acclaimed in the Armenian tradition as a man of both physical and intellectual attributes. The beginning of his reign coincides with that of Emperor Diocletian (284–305) who reconsolidated Roman authority internally and externally. With the signing of the Peace of Nisibis in 298 between Rome and Iran, and with the consent of the Sasanids, Diocletian raised Trdat to the Armenian throne as king of an Armenia reunified into a single monarchy once again. If the political destiny of King Trdat IV was tied to the policies of Emperor Diocletian, the historic role for which he is remembered by posterity is more closely linked to the religious policy of Emperor Constantine I (306–337) who in 313 legalized Christianity in the Roman Empire. Trdat IV shares with Constantine the common stage of contemporary monarchs who made Christianity the faith associated with the crown and the state.

Armenian church chronography dates the conversion of King Trdat IV to Christianity in the year 301. Historical research has proposed other possible dates, while the latest scholarship favors the year 314. By either calculation, in the truest sense, Armenia became the first formally Christian nation as a result of King Trdat's decision to adopt Christianity not just as a personal confession of faith but as a state religion. Whatever his political calculations might have been, there is little debate that the decision was voluntary. Whether **Grigor Lusavorich** (Gregory the Illuminator) was the actual force of persuasion, or was merely Trdat's effective ally and instrument in the introduction of a new policy on the choice of religion, and thereby much else in terms of political strategy, cultural proclivity, and social responsibility, the fact remains that their collaboration was active and not just symbolic, and that the conversion of Armenia to Christianity was given the financial and military support of the crown.

Trdat IV sought to counterbalance the aristocracy by sponsoring the rapid growth of the **Armenian Apostolic Church**, an institution upon which considerable administrative responsibilities were thrust. The church's own bureaucratic and centralizing tendency paralleled the type of administrative practices a central government prefers. Yet once the church was established it became the locus of influence resented by later kings who were prepared to follow the lead of the emperors in Constantinople on theological, ergo ideological, policies, while the church increasingly assumed the character of an institution defending orthodoxy on the basis of national identity. It was not long either before the more permanent political institution in Armenia, the **nakharar system**, determined the organizational aspect of the church, resulting in the feudalization of Armenia's religious institution and aligning it closely with aristocratic, as much as monarchist, interests. (Note: Recent historical scholarship has renumerated the Arshakuni kings of Armenia. Trdat IV in earlier histories was commonly identified as Trdat III with different regnal dates.) *See also* ARSHAKUNI; DVIN; EDJMIADSIN.

TURIAN, BEDROS (1851–1872). Poet. Turian was born in the district of Scutari in Istanbul. Although he wrote only 39 poems, and his life was cut short by tuberculosis, his verses epitomize the Romantic movement in Armenian literature. Most were woven around the singular theme of idealized love whose objects included his homeland, woman, nature, and God. With titles like *Little Lakes* (*Ljak*), *Plaints* (*Trtunjk*), *Repentance* (*Zghdjum*), *New Dark Days* (*Nor Sev Orer*), *The Sorrows of the Armenian* (*Vishdk Hayun*), and *To Love* (*Sirel*), they are touched by sentiment. The most melancholic of his poems is the one called *My Death* (*Im Mahe*), a contemplation upon mortality and the tragedy of his life.

Bedros's brother, Yeghishe Turian (1860–1930), was Armenian Patriarch of Istanbul between 1909 and 1910. He was elected Armenian Patriarch of Jerusalem in 1921 and served until his death. He authored works on Armenian literature and on religious subjects.

– U –

UNION FOR SELF-DETERMINATION (USD), *Inknoroshman Miavorum* **(IM).** Political party. Founded as the Union for National Self-Determination (UNSD) in September 1987, the USD started as a strongly anti-Communist and nationalist organization advocating for rapid devolution from the Soviet Union. In the post-Soviet era the USD became the main, if not the leading, party defending the principle of individual rights and equality and the rule of law. In the mid–1990s in an effort to promote a moral society, the USD made the enhancement of Christian values part of its platform. From the beginning Paruyr Hayrikian was the guiding figure of the USD. A Soviet-era dissident born in **Yerevan** in 1949, by the age of 20 Hayrikian was under arrest for anti-Soviet activities. Among the charges leveled against him was membership in the United National Party of Armenia, a small organization of nationalists that was broken up almost as soon as it had been formed. He spent his years in prison bravely defying the system and defending the rights of inmates. By the time he was released when Mikhail Gorbachev began dismantling the gulag camps after 1985, he had won respect as a dissident unbent by the prison experience. First sent abroad, after a stay in the United States, Hayrikian returned to Armenia as soon as the **Karabagh Movement** picked up momentum. Hayrikian made a number of attempts for the presidency of Armenia, but the USD did not register significant growth after independence. With a small representation in parliament inclusive of Hayrikian, the USD was a vocal opposition party until the 1999 **elections** when it failed to muster any seats in the National Assembly. *See also* POLITICAL PARTIES.

– V –

VAGHARSHAPAT. Capital of ancient Armenia. Vagharshapat served as the capital of Armenia during the reign of the **Arshakuni** dynasty. It lies 20 kilometers west of modern-day **Yerevan.** The city was founded by King Vagharsh I (117–140) who assumed the throne upon the withdrawal of the Romans from Armenia. Emperor Trajan's brief annexation of Armenia (114–117) was reversed by his successor, Emperor Hadrian (117–138), after revolts broke out in the country. An armistice signed by the Roman governor of Armenia, Lucius Catilius Severus, restored the throne of Armenia according to the terms of the Treaty of Rhandia of 63 A.D. Vagharsh established a new royal residence in the town of Vardgesavan, which he embellished, fortified with a surrounding wall, and renamed after himself. **Artashat**, however, remained the most important city in the country until the year 163, when the Romans attempted their third annexation of Armenia. The Roman governor, Statius Priscus, reduced Artashat and garrisoned his troops in Vagharshapat, which he renamed Kainepolis, or New City. Although Artashat was rebuilt three years later, Vagharshapat remained the political center of the **Armenian kingdom**. It too suffered serious damage in 368–369 when the Sasanid Persians destroyed the great cities of Armenia. As an urban settlement, Vagharshapat never attained the size and luster of Artashat, and it was eventually overshadowed by the new capital of **Dvin**. Vagharshapat's long-term significance, however, exceeded that of any other capital of Armenia, as it continues to exist today as the city of **Edjmiadsin**.

Vagharshapat's transformation from a royal capital into the religious center of Armenia is intimately connected with the reign of King **Trdat IV** (298–330). The confrontation between the monarch and his crypto-Christian courtier, **Grigor Lusavorich** (Gregory the Illuminator) the later evangelizer of Armenia, occurred at the palace in Vagharshapat. The martyrdom of early Armenian converts to Christianity also occurred in Vagharshapat. The conversion of the king in 301 and of his court at his command, as well as Trdat's strong support of Grigor in his activities to spread Christianity throughout Armenia, made Vagharshapat the nerve center of the campaign to transform the Armenian people's polytheistic and Zoroastrian-influenced systems of belief into a monotheistic faith. This process also linked the institutionalization of the Christian faith in Armenia with the city of Vagharshapat, where too some of the earlier churches in Armenia were soon constructed. Lastly, in the second half of the fourth century, with the patriarchate of Armenia moved from Ashtishat in Taron, where Grigor had his headquarters, Vagharshapat became the seat of the **Armenian Apostolic Church**.

The fast-growing influence and wealth of the church had become a source of tension with the monarchy after the reign of Trdat and later fourth century kings struggled to keep the patriarchs under their watch. The renewed alliance between Vramshapuh, the last important Arshakuni king, and Sahak I the Great, the last male descendant of Grigor to sit upon the pontifical throne of Armenia, strengthened the church's association with the state while securing its autonomy in religious affairs. The building by Sahak of a stone edifice worthy of the supreme patriarch, later designated Catholicos of All Armenia, ensconced the Armenian Church in the city of Vagharshapat. From here then Sahak and Vramshapuh sponsored the critically important cultural activities of **Mesrop Mashtots**, first with the invention of the Armenian alphabet, and second with the spread of education on the basis of the new native script. When in 428 the Arshakuni dynasty was deposed and the institution of the monarchy allowed to lapse, the royal aura of Vagharshapat fell upon the Armenian Catholicosate, the sole royal institution from the time of the original monarchy of Armenia to survive to modern times.

VAN, LAKE. *See* **LAKE VAN**.

VAN. Capital of the Urartian state and the **Ardsruni** kingdom. Van is the oldest city on the Armenian Plateau continuously inhabited since its founding. It is located on the eastern shore of the lake by the same name. Van began as the city of Tushpa and as the royal capital of Biaini, better known as Urartu. In time the names of Tushpa and Biaini were transposed and by the Armenian period the region was called Tosp (from Tushpa) and the city Van (from Biaini).

King Sarduri I (c. 835–825 B.C.) established Tushpa as the capital of his newly forged kingdom of Urartu, or Ararat. Lying on a coastal plain the city was dominated by the Rock of Van, a massive limestone promontory on the shore of the lake. At its highest ridge, which rises to about 115 meters, Sarduri built his stronghold. The fortress of Van marked only the beginning of an energetic building program to match the vigorous expansion of the Urartian state. While other royal residences were established further north in the Plain of **Ararat** at Erebuni and at Argishtihinili by King Argishti I (c. 785–760 B.C.), and at Teishebaini by King Rusa II (c. 685–645 B.C.), Van remained at the center of the Urartian kingdom as testified by the multiple cuneiform inscriptions left upon the Rock by succeeding monarchs. Besides the citadel, the Rock held the royal necropolis in the form of tomb chambers carved into the mount, and an open-air shrine with its walls hewn smooth.

The importance of the Urartian legacy of urban development is attested by the irrigation works constructed during this period. King Menua (c. 810–785 B.C.), more than anyone else in history, secured the permanence of Van by building an 80-kilometers-long canal to bring fresh water to the city from the Artos range in the east. From that day the Armenians called the place a garden city for the constant abundance of orchards and vineyards in and around Van. Armenian popular tradition retained memories of the time of the construction of the water conduit by calling it the "Shamiram channel," which attributed it to King Menua's legendary contemporary, Queen Semiramis of Assyria.

After the fall of the Urartian kingdom, Van passed to the Persians, and the Achaemenid satrap, the governor of the region, continued to reside in Van. Proclaiming his dominion over Armenia, the Persian King Xerxes (486–465 B.C.) added his own triplicate inscription on the Rock, in Ancient Persian, Elamite, and Babylonian, the official languages of the Achaemenid Empire. Van receded from center stage when the **Yervanduni** selected **Armavir** as the new capital of Armenia after the fall of Persia to the Greeks in the late fourth century B.C. **Tigran II the Great** enlarged the city in the first century B.C., and as Armenia's economy was increasingly integrated with the expanding commerce conducted between East and West, Van, like other cities in Armenia, acquired an international population. In the **Arshakuni** period a large Jewish population resided in Van. Their entire community, along with the Armenian inhabitants of Van, was deported to Persia by the Sasanid King Shapur II during the course of his devastation of the Armenian cities in 368–369.

The Rshtuni *nakharar* family, who were likely descended from Urartian royalty, held Van during the time of the Arshakuni dynasty, and a scion of their house, Theodoros Rshtuni, Byzantine governor of Armenia in the early seventh century, negotiated the submission of Armenia to the Arabs on favorable terms. The Rshtuni, however, were soon displaced by another nakharar family, the Ardsruni, who gradually acquired possession of the entire region of Van. By the early 10th century their might was a match to the **Bagratuni** family that held the territories of northern Armenia. When the Arabs extended a royal crown to the Ardsruni prince Gagik in 908, Van was restored to its ancient glory as a capital city. Though the royal residence was eventually moved to the island of **Aghtamar** once the palace complex was constructed, the period of Ardsruni sponsorship transformed Van into a major center of Armenian cultural activity.

Van retained its importance as a center of the arts even after the Byzantine occupation in the early 11th century and the succeeding period of Seljuk Turk domination, until Tamerlane laid waste the city in 1387. Van did not recover until well after the Ottomans had secured control over the region in the 17th century, and even then not without suffering a major earthquake in 1648. Van resumed its place as a center of Armenian culture in the 19th century. The effort to establish educational institutions, however, contributed only to the growing tensions with Ottoman authorities who treated all efforts at organization by Armenians with high suspicion. The harsh rule of the Ottomans and their local Kurdish surrogates made Van a place rife with political agitation. In 1862 the Armenian population, joined by the Kurdish peasantry, rose up in revolt against arbitrary and increasing taxation. Such open acts of rebellion were brutally crushed. Constant surveillance and restrictions on assembly induced Armenians increasingly inclined to resist Ottoman repression to resort to forming clandestine organizations.

The first such Armenian association dedicated to the purpose of promoting the principle of self-protection against the lawlessness prevailing in the remote corners of the Ottoman Empire was organized in Van. In 1872 the Union of Salvation (*Miutiun i Perkutiun*) was secretly formed and sought to mobilize the Armenian population to defend themselves. In 1878 the Black Cross Society (*Sev Khach Kazmakerputiun*) was formed by a group of young Armenians in Van who proposed actively responding to the unchecked violence and extortion of the population. Finally, in 1885 the first Armenian revolutionary organization emerged in Van known as the **Armenakan** Party. In view of the unhindered abuses of the government, its mistreatment of the Christian population, and the continuing indulgence of the Ottoman regime by the European Powers despite treaty obligations, the Armenakan Party put forth the concept of self-rule for the Armenian people.

Tight surveillance by the Ottoman police during the reign of Abdul-Hamid (Abdulhamit) II (1876–1909) prevented the Armenakans from spreading their organization beyond the region of Van. The results of their decade-long effort to educate the populace about the need for self-reliance became evident when the Armenakans, joined by members of other revolutionary outfits, averted a wholesale massacre during the height of the Hamidian atrocities when they prepared a defense of the city in 1896. This rare success equipped the Armenians of Van with the confidence and foresight to organize a second time in April 1915 when the Young Turk regime began the implementation of their policy of genocide. Besieged in their neighborhoods packed with refugees from outlying areas, and despite the cannon fire applied against them, the Armenians manned the barricades long enough to be rescued by an advancing Russian force. By then the old city was in ruins and the Armenians abandoned Van when the Russian army retreated in July 1915. Though the Russians regained

Van in 1916 and held it through 1917, the hardships of World War I left little chance of rebuilding the city. With the final retreat of the Russian forces in early 1918, the last of the Armenians bid their ancient city farewell. *See also* ARMENIAN GENOCIDE; ARMENIAN MASSACRES; MANUKIAN, ARAM; MKRTICH I KHRIMIAN, GRIGOR NAREKATSI; SRVANTZTIANTS, GAREGIN.

VARDAN MAMIKONIAN. *See* MAMIKONIAN.

VARUZHAN, TANIEL (also Varoujan, Daniel) (1884–1915). Poet. Varuzhan, nee Taniel Chpugkiarian, was born in Brgnik, a village in Sivas province. He was sent to Istanbul for schooling in 1896 and continued his education with the **Mekhitarians** of Venice at the Mourad-Raphaelian school, which he attended from 1902 to 1905. He proceeded to the University of Ghent, in Belgium, from where he graduated in 1909. Returning to Turkey, he was employed as an educator in Armenian schools at Sivas and Tokat and subsequently was the headmaster of the Armenian **Catholic** institution, the *Lusavorchian* (Illuminator) school from 1912 to 1915. Varuzhan published his first collection of poetry in 1906 under the tile of Shivers (*Sarsurner*). His second collection published in 1909 as The Heart of the Nation (*Tseghin Sirde*) articulated a nationalism reacting to a period marked by atrocities and established him as a major poet. While some of the poems angrily lamented the destruction of Armenia, through other patriotic verse Varuzhan also constructed a vision for a future invigorated by the memory of an era predating lachrymose Christianity. The poem *Vahakn* addressed the ancient god of war and manly courage and anticipated his next collection published in 1912 called *Pagan Songs* (*Hetanos Yerker*). Like other Armenian poets who reanimated this sense of a physical vitality, Varuzhan also penned verse of exquisite sensuality. His poem *Oriental Bath*, considered his best, was a departure from the modesty with which women were addressed in Armenian literature and introduced a vividly sexual depiction of the female figure. His last collection of poems, *The Song of Bread* (*Hatsin Yerke*), was published posthumously in 1921. Varuzhan was arrested on the night of April 24, 1915, deported and killed.

VARZHAPETIAN, NERSES (1837–1884). Armenian patriarch of Istanbul (1873–1884). Born in Istanbul, Varzhapetian spent his entire life in or near the Ottoman capital. Though deprived of a formal education, at the age of 15 after the death of his father, Varzhapetian became a teacher and joined the clergy in the **Armenian Apostolic Church**. Anointed a celibate priest in 1858, he was a bishop by 1862. Active in the administrative affairs of the **Armenian *Millet***, he had a hand in drafting of the so-called Armenian national constitution by which the Armenian Church and *Millet* were regulated in the Ottoman Empire. In 1873, at age 37, he was elected Armenian patriarch of Istanbul.

The Russo-Turkish War of 1877–1878, partly waged over the Armenian-populated provinces of eastern Anatolia, brought the question of the Armenians to the fore of the diplomatic contest for influence in the Ottoman Empire. When the extent of the Kurdish predations over the Armenian communities became known, Varzhapetian, who had issued an encyclical supporting the Ottoman war effort, was authorized by the Armenian National Assembly to appeal to Grand Duke Nicholas at San Stefano for consideration of local self-government in the areas of Armenian concentration. In the formal treaty of San Stefano, signed on March 3, 1878, by the Ottomans and Russians, Article 16 provided for reforms and security under Russian trusteeship in the so-called Armenian provinces.

While Russian withdrawal from these areas was made conditional to the implementation of the reforms, the Congress of Berlin revised the terms of the treaty. The Armenian delegation led by **Mkrtich Khrimian**, which Varzhapetian sent to Berlin, received no hearing, and Article 61 of the Treaty of Berlin, signed on July 13, 1878, provided only for reforms as those territories were to revert to the Ottomans. Still Armenians had expectations that an international treaty would prove more binding on the Ottomans than mere promises. The failure of the European Powers to require Sultan Abdul-Hamid (Abdulhamit) II to proceed with reforms became the source of disillusionment. By the time of Varzhapetian's death in Istanbul, small groups of provincial Armenians had begun to resort to self-defense in response to the continuing insecurity. *See also* ORMANIAN, MAGHAKIA.

VRATZIAN, SIMON (1882–1969). Political leader. Vratzian was born at Great Sala, near Nor Nakhichevan, in southern Russia. He received his primary education locally at Russian and Armenian schools and graduated from the Gevorgian academy at **Edjmiadsin** in Russian Armenia. He joined the **Armenian Revolutionary Federation** (ARF) in 1898 and remained one of its most active figures for the rest of his life. Regarded a leader of the left wing of the party, he was a delegate at the 1907 Vienna congress of the ARF when the party formally adopted socialism in its program. Fleeing Russia during the Stolypin reaction, he went to Erzerum, where before the outbreak of World War I he was involved in the discussions initiated by the Young Turk government for ARF support in the impending war and the intended invasion of Russian Transcaucasia. Elected to the party's governing Bureau, instead he escaped to Russia and became a member of the Armenian National Council in 1917.

With the establishment of the independent Republic of Armenia in 1918, Vratzian was sent to negotiate for military support from the Volunteer Army in Russia. In 1919 he was elected to the Armenian parliament and reelected to the ARF Bureau. In 1920 he was appointed minister of labor and agriculture. With the fall of the Armenian government in the prelude to Sovietization, Vratzian briefly held the office of prime minister from November 24 to December 2, 1920, and handed power over to the Red Army.

Going into hiding, he reemerged at the head of the Committee for the Salvation of the Fatherland when an uprising against the Bolsheviks broke out in Armenia in February 1921. He fled through Iran, spent the years 1927 to 1933 in Paris as editor of *Droshak*, the ARF party organ, and there wrote the primary historical narrative on the short-lived independent Armenian state, *Hayastani Hanrapetutiun* (Republic of Armenia) (Paris, 1928; revised edition, Beirut, 1958). He eventually settled in Beirut, Lebanon, where he passed away after many years as the principal of Neshan Palanjian Academy, the premier educational institution in the Armenian **diaspora** at the time.

– Y –

YEREVAN. Capital of the Republic of Armenia. Founded in 782 B.C. by King Argishti I, Yerevan started as the royal Urartian fortress of Erebuni commanding the Plain of **Ararat** and a view of Mount Ararat. From its strategic location Erebuni controlled the north-south corridor of the **Arax River** valley in Eastern Armenia and its cyclopean walls attest to a massive structure containing barracks, a temple, a palace, craftsmen's quarters, and storage facilities well stocked with provisions from the nearby fertile lands. With the growth of cities in the Plain of Ararat, Yerevan was sidelined, and throughout Antiquity and the Middle Ages it was little more than a rural town.

Yerevan recovered its political significance in the 16th century as the Ottomans of Turkey and the Safavids of Iran contested Armenia and sought to divide the country along the Arax River. In 1582/3 the Ottomans raised a new fortress on the top of the bluff overlooking the Hrazdan (Zangi) River directly north of the promontory of Erebuni. The Safavids captured it in 1604 and designated it the administrative center of the border province. Yerevan changed hands 17 times with the last major Ottoman invasion occurring in the 1720s. Throughout this period Yerevan was primarily a market town whose economy was largely based on servicing the surrounding farmlands and some caravan trade.

The growth of Yerevan dates from the 18th century. By the early 19th century, the town had a population of about 15,000. The Russians occupied Yerevan in 1827 and the ethnic composition of the city began to change with the departure of the Muslims, mostly Persians and Turks, but the city as a whole did not register major growth. While other cities of the Caucasus underwent rapid expansion in the course of the 19th century, Yerevan remained a backwater even though it continued to serve as the administrative center of Erevan/Yerevan Province under the Russians. The Armenian urban population inhabited cities such as Tbilisi and Baku where trade and industry flourished, and even Alexandropol (later Leninakan, now **Gyumri**), the first city in Eastern Armenia connected by rail to Tbilisi, underwent faster modernization than Yerevan. At the end of the century the population of the city stood at about 30,000 and winemaking was its principal source of revenue.

The modernization of Yerevan is attributable to political, more so than to economic, reasons. It was connected by rail to Alexandropol in 1902, but still it remained a remote outpost undistinguished otherwise, until 1918, when the breakup of the Russian Empire precipitated the formation of an independent Armenian state in May. The Armenian political leadership, which functioned out of Tbilisi, designated Yerevan the capital of Armenia because of its central location and because it was the only urban center of any consequence in the former Russian province not under Turkish military control or facing imminent occupation. The independent Republic of Armenia lasted only two and half years, but Yerevan was spared the ruin of warfare that visited virtually every other part of the country. As a consequence, at times the city bulged as a vast refugee camp and the winter of 1918–1919 took a terrible toll. When Soviet power was declared in Armenia in late 1920, the appearance of the city had changed very little, but Yerevan remained the capital of the newly declared Armenian Soviet Socialist Republic (ASSR).

The transformation of Yerevan into a metropolis occurred under Soviet rule and thereby bears all the markings of Soviet urban planning. With its modest size and provincial rusticity, Yerevan had none of the makings of a capital city. A master plan to develop Yerevan into a city that met its stature as a capital was commissioned by the Soviet authorities in the mid–1920s from the architect Alexander Tamanian. Built around a concentric plan with broad projecting avenues, open spaces, and locations for major institutions, Tamanian created one of the more eminently workable models of the urban socialist utopia. Filled with buildings designed in a grand style combining European classical architecture supported by an abundance of Armenian artistic detail, Yerevan was slowly transformed. Because of the seismicity of the region, structures were raised only to four or five stories all surfaced with the native tufa stone in its many hues. By the 1950s and 1960s Yerevan was a city with its own character and unique architecture all harmonized by Tamanian's vision. An oval piazza circumscribed by four quadricircular official buildings created a vast ceremonial space in the heart of the city and an outer ring anchored by the university, a stately opera house, and a neoclassical parliament building gave Yerevan all the accoutrements of a modern city. Although early Soviet in its chronological origin, Yerevan was given the ambiance of the idealized 19th-century urban setting. That unifying character was seriously marred from the mid-1960s onward as a cruder Soviet modernism and greater allowable height to buildings, not to mention sloppy construction techniques, markedly modified the appearance of the city.

That transformation was driven by rapid population expansion, itself a product of Soviet planning that sought to create vast urban concentrations to support rapid industrialization in the post-World War II era. When the modernization of Yerevan was begun in 1926, the population of the city was 65,000. By 1939 it had reached 200,000. The rate of expansion accelerated after the war. In 1959 the population had reached half a million, by 1970 three quarters of a million, and by mid-1980s it was at a million, at which point Yerevan contained about a third of the entire population of the country. This growth is explained by the rapid industrialization of Soviet Armenia and the concentration of most of the new industrial plants in and around Yerevan. The leading industries included metalworking and machine building. These in turn supported computer and other precision instrument manufacturing. Chemical and petrochemical production, largely based in a single huge complex known as the Nayirit rubber plant, was another branch of industry. Electrical power generation, capped by the construction of the Medsamor nuclear station, supplied the energy to the proliferating industrial base. Lastly, the brandy distillery topped the list of the more profitable industries in Armenia.

The industrialization of the economy of Yerevan was matched by a rapidly expanded **education** system that included technical universities, institutes, and centers for advanced scientific research. The Academy of Sciences was a major employer. Other institutions of higher learning included music conservatories, medical schools, and pedagogical centers. The intellectual attainment of Yerevan was symbolized by the Matenadaran, the repository of manuscripts, which became a major center for study of Armenian culture, and which was housed in an imposing building on a hillside overlooking the city. This and other cultural institutions, as well as an atmosphere slightly less restrictive than in Russia proper, contributed to making Yerevan a thriving center of culture and cultural exchange as diaspora Armenians and foreigners began to visit the city in the post-Stalin era.

If these connections had given reason for the Soviet authorities to make Yerevan into a showcase, they also contributed to a political ferment that took on the characteristics of a mass movement in the final years of the Soviet Union. Unlike Tbilisi, Baku, or even Batumi, Yerevan lacked a revolutionary history. Only once in the Soviet period had the city witnessed unauthorized demonstrations in April 1965 coinciding with the 50th commemoration of the **Armenian Genocide**. In the Gorbachev era, however, the **Karabagh Movement** that began in February 1988 saw the masses take to the streets in peaceful demonstration over the course of the year. This kind of sustained and unscripted public activity with a distinct political agenda was unprecedented in the Soviet Union as the Armenians of Yerevan put into practice the promise of glasnost, or openness. It was far from the minds of the demonstrators or the authorities in 1988 that Soviet authority could be challenged or that the USSR could unravel. Yet such was the final outcome as other Soviet nationalities, taking the example of Yerevan, first separately and ultimately together undermined the Soviet state.

The political ferment in Yerevan between the years 1988 and 1991 was more intense and grew increasingly more liberal ideologically with every passing year, such that when the Soviet Union disbanded, Armenia plunged ahead with economic and political liberalization at a rapid pace. That effort, however, did not spare the city all the vicissitudes of the transformation introduced by the new authorities. While the entire country was effected, because of the vulnerabilities of a large urban metropolis, Yerevan was especially hard hit economically as Armenia's industries were shuttered because of an energy crisis in 1992 and 1993. The urban population declined as plants were permanently closed and workers began to emigrate. The gradual turnaround since 1994 has introduced profound structural changes as commerce, light industry, and services have come to replace heavy industry as the basis of the urban economy.

Yerevan is also a city studded with monuments. No major figure from the Armenian past was overlooked and each was honored with a statue or a bust in a public space. The Armenian Genocide memorial complex covers the entire hilltop of Tsitsernakaberd. The statue of Stalin that once stood at the highest point of the cityscape was removed soon after de-Stalinization was introduced and replaced with a statue of Mother Armenia upon the same pedestal. The statue of Lenin that watched over the central piazza is also gone, along with every trace of its once lofty pedestal, and the place has been renamed Republic Square where the Armenian armed forces now hold parades. And as the architect Tamanian once intended, embassies presently line the street leading to parliament house.

YERVANDUNI (ORONTID). Royal dynasty of ancient Armenia. The origins of the Yervanduni family may be traced back to the legendary king Yervand Sakavakiats (c. 570–560 B.C.). The fall of Urartu in 590

B.C., precipitated by the Scythian invasions from the north, had opened the way for the Median occupation of the Armenian plateau and ushered in a period of rapid political change in Armenia. Median rule was followed by Persian suzerainty when the Achaemenids of Iran under Cyrus II (550–529 B.C.) established their empire over the region. Achaemenid rule stabilized government in Armenia. The Persians divided the plateau into eastern and western provinces. In the eastern half of Armenia a succession of satraps by the name of Yervand (Orontes), claiming royal rights according to the Armenian epic tradition, governed on behalf of the Achaemenids.

The Yervanduni, however, were more than provincial administrators. The country was prosperous and important enough for the Achaemenids to have paid close attention to it. When Darius I (522–485 B.C.) contested the Achaemenid throne, the Armenians took advantage of the occasion to secede from Iranian control, and a reoccupation of the country was organized by the Persians. It is in relation to this event that the first mention of the whole country by the name of Armenia, or Armena in Old Persian, is recorded on the royal inscription dated at about 520 B.C. found at Behistun in Persia wherein Darius's achievements are described. When the Greek general Xenophon retreated through Armenia in 401 B.C., the reigning Yervanduni, as the son-in-law of the Great King Artaxerxes I (464–424 B.C.), enjoyed patronage to the point of being married into the imperial family. As for Darius III Codomannus (336–330 B.C.), the last of the Achaemenids, when still heir apparent, he governed in Armenia prior to his accession to the Persian throne.

The close association of the two dynasties is explained by the significance of the military contributions delivered by the Armenians. Horse breeding was a major economic activity at the time, and the tribute from Armenia was in part paid by an annual delivery of 20,000 colts. Armenians also provided fully armed contingents in time of war and they were expedited as far as Egypt. In the first major battle waged by the Persians against Alexander at Issus in 333 B.C., the Armenian contingent is reported to have numbered 40,000 infantry and 7,000 cavalry. At the fateful battle of Gaugamela, or Arbela, in 331 B.C., where the Macedonians dealt their crushing defeat upon Darius, another Yervand/Orontes was present performing his duty to his sovereign. He survived the battle and appears to have secured his family's title to the Armenian throne. While in theory Armenia also was inherited by the Macedonians with the capture of the Iranian empire by Alexander, the latter's drive to India relieved Armenia of direct pressure by the new claimants, and an understanding to perpetuate the previous arrangement of local dynastic rule with the recognition of imperial sovereignty appears to have contributed to the establishment of good relations for a stretch of time.

The sources for this remote period of Armenian history are scarce and the reconstruction of the Yervanduni dynasty remains provisional. Even so, the period of their governorship of Armenia is marked by a critical set of cultural transformations that they appear to have consciously accommodated. While the evidence indicates that as titular royalty they aspired to increase the sovereignty of Armenia as opportunities arose, the Yervanduni also appear to have maintained a policy of cultural openness. Their obligations to the Achaemenids may have limited their freedom of action, but their association with the Persian imperial dynasty could have only elevated their stature and legitimacy both nationally and regionally at a time when royal institutions in Armenia were only in their formative stages. In a society still dominated by tribal allegiances and local practices, the Yervanduni period is notable also for maintaining a continuity as cultural norms evolved under the influence of major neighboring powers. The early Yervanduni located their capital in **Van**, the great city of the Urartians, and their restoration of the Urartian city of Argishtihinili as the new capital of **Armavir** farther north appears to have been linked with their renewed attempt to consolidate their rule in Armenia in the post-Achaemenid era. Nevertheless, the Yervanduni period is notable for the degree to which Iranian culture, language, and political practices penetrated Armenia.

Iranian influence in Western Armenia was no less strong than in the eastern parts over which the main line of the Yervanduni family ruled. Situated along the royal highway that led from the capital of Persepolis to the town of Sardis, the center of Persian rule in Asia Minor, Western Armenia soon was exposed to cultural influences flowing from both directions. A line of royal dynasts related to the Yervanduni ruled as vassals of the Seleucids, heirs to Alexander's empire, and embellished their part of Armenia, called Sophene, or Dsopk in Armenian. King Samos (c. 260–240 B.C.) unified Sophene and Commagene, on the two sides of the Euphrates, into a single monarchy and founded the city of Shamshat, better known by its

Greek appellation of Samosata. His successor, King Arsham/Arsames (240–220 B.C.), founded Arshamshat/Arsamosata. More interesting, however, is the other location associated with Arsham's name, Arsameia on Nymphaios, where his descendant, Antiochus I (69–34 B.C.) left behind a striking syncretistic monument depicting himself clean-shaven, yet in Oriental garb, with a recognizable five-pointed Armenian royal tiara, shaking hands with the naked god Mithra-Helios, a deity combining Persian and Greek elements. Hellenistic monumentality is given its highest expression in this part of the world at another nearby site associated with the tumulus in which Antiochus is buried, Nemrut Dagh, where colossal statues of Iranian and Hellenistic deities stand together in a joint Olympian pantheon literally at the top of the highest mountain in the kingdom.

Yervanduni rule in Armenia was a period of political consolidation by native dynasties that secured their hold in the country and established lasting monarchies. Under the influence of the Achaemenids, the upper echelons of Armenian society absorbed and adapted the royal, administrative, and scribal customs of the Persians. In so doing they became integrated into the international ruling class taking form under Iranian tutelage. A similarly pronounced political and cultural influence, but perhaps more unequally distributed across Armenia, was imprinted by Hellenism. The near complete Hellenization of the Commagene dynasty is the most extreme manifestation of this influence. Their possible Yervanduni descent, claim to Achaemenid origins, and Seleucid relations, reflected an amalgam that also spoke of the continuing integration of distant and mountainous Armenia with the cosmopolitan cultures rising all along its periphery. The rarefied world of Hellenistic monarchy is exemplified by the last representative of the Commagene house, Gaius Julius Antiochus, whose name reflects the newest wave of political dominance and cultural influence to descend upon ancient Armenia in the form of the Romans. Known as Philopappos (Grandfather-Loving), he was a Roman consul and lived in Athens in the time of Emperor Hadrian (117–138), and is famous for having built his mausoleum on the Hill of the Muses, the rise facing the Acropolis whence the spectator enjoys the best view of the Parthenon, the greatest monument of Antiquity.

As for the Yervanduni dynasty in Armenia, it expired with Yervand the Last (220–201 B.C.). His reign is associated mainly with the founding of another city and a new royal capital, Yervandashat, named after himself in the Hellenistic practice of the time, and meaning "Yervand's Joy." The rise of Shamshat and Arshamshat in the west, and of Armavir, Yervandashat, and soon to be followed by **Artashat**, in the east, anchored Armenia to viable urban centers associated with both government and commerce. The Yervanduni era ended with the economic integration of Armenia into the international trade patterns of the ancient world, and with royal authority secured by its new imitation of Hellenistic monarchialism, itself hoisted upon native customs already heavily laden with Iranian practices. *See also* ARTASHES I.

– Z –

ZAKARIAN. *See* ANI; BAGRATUNI.

ZOHRAB, KRIKOR (1861–1915). Writer and deputy in the Ottoman parliament. Zohrab was born in Istanbul. He received his education in his birthplace and was practicing law by 1883. He distinguished himself as an attorney who defended cases against the government until he was deprived of his license in 1905 and went abroad to France and Egypt. With the end of the Hamidian autocracy and the restoration of the Ottoman Constitution, Zohrab returned to Istanbul. From 1908 to 1915 he was a member of the Armenian National Assembly. He was also elected a deputy to the Ottoman parliament where he defended the cause of universal social justice and gained recognition as an orator of distinction. Shocked by the 1909 **Adana Massacre** of Armenians, he published his findings in Paris under a pseudonym as Marcel Leart, *La question arménienne a la lumière des documents* (1913).

Zohrab also earned fame as an author excelling in short stories and novellas written in the realist style. The subjects of social inequality, injustice, and prejudice preoccupied him. His more important works include *Anhetatsads serunt me* (A Vanished Generation) (1887), *Khghjmdanki Tzayner* (Voices of Conscience) (1909), *Kyanke inchpes vor e* (Life As It Is) (1911), and *Lur Tsaver* (Silent Sorrows) (1911). He also published essays on literature, politics, and the Armenian community. Before his own demise, he protested to Talaat, the Young Turk minister of the interior, the summary arrests on the night of April 24, 1915, and subsequent execution of the Istanbul Armenian community leaders. His own immunity as a parliamentary deputy did not spare him from being arrested on June 3, deported, and killed near Diyarbekir. *See also* ARMENIAN GENOCIDE; KOMITAS; SIAMANTO; VARUZHAN, TANIEL.

Bibliography

CONTENTS

INTRODUCTION

The literature about Armenia is vast and the literature produced by Armenians in considerable. Most of it, of course, is in the Armenian language. A bibliography on Armenia in a Western language, therefore, will be partial, incomplete, and reflect more on the topics addressed in that language than on the total historical experience of the Armenians. While Armenians look back from the threshold of the 21st century to 1,600 years of literature in their native tongue, Western scholarship about Armenia begins only in about the middle of the 19th century and did not appear in any volume to inform the West until the 20th century. Much of that literature is in French, or Russian, and some of it in German and Italian.

Literature about Armenia in the English language in any measurable quantity began to appear only in the 1960s. As such, virtually all of the scholarship and writing on Armenia in English is the product of just two generations of authors. Considering the range of books and articles published on Armenia, the work of these two generations of specialists has been prodigious. Additionally, the scholarship has been of the highest quality thus making up for the earlier deficit of a library on Armenia. They were successful in so doing as they generously benefited from the profusion of scholarly publications produced in Armenia.

An additional characteristic of the English-language bibliography on Armenia is its publication primarily in the United States. That fact is explained by the expanding interest of the Armenian-American community, the largest in the Armenian diaspora, and its support of scholarly endeavors. In view of this background, the English-language literature reflects disproportional interest in modern and contemporary history, and does not reproduce a fair quantity on earlier periods about which there is much published in Armenian. Moreover, as a diaspora community born out of the flight from genocide, the American literature on Armenia captures the emphasis on those topics most meaningful to, or demanding explanation from, the viewpoint of this specific community. To compensate for these imbalances, and to introduce the reader to the principal sources on Armenia, some of the main references in other Western languages have been included in the bibliography. Only the most vital references in Armenian have been included, works regarded as central to the existing knowledge and scholarly examination of Armenian civilization.

There is a shortcut through the bibliography that merits advising readers about. The works of the premier experts in the field of Armenian studies are the most reliable guide to the rest of the literature. These experts are prolific to a degree where certain specializations or topics in history are entirely defined by their individual output. For those interested in Armenian art, the list begins with Sirarpie Der Nersesian. For ancient and medieval history, the place to begin is Nicholas Adontz and Hakob Manandian, whose critical works are now available in English thanks to Nina Garsoian, who herself may be counted the equal of her eminent predecessors. For Armenian culture, Robert Thomson and Avedis Sanjian will access readers many facets of the literary basis of that civilization. For the modern period Richard Hovannisian and George Bournoutian between them cover the era. As for the tragedy of the Armenian Genocide, Vahakn Dadrian is the recognized authority. Other scholars whose works should be consulted as starting points include Levon Avdoyan, Kevork Bardakjian, Peter Cowe, Robert Hewsen, Dickran Kouymjian, Krikor Maksoudian, James Russell, Ronald Grigor Suny, and Michael Stone, all scholars in the United States with the exception of the last who is based in Israel. For the Francophone reader, Anahide Ter Minassian, Claire Mouradian, and Raymond Kevorkian are the principal guides. As for the polyglot reader, Boghos Levon Zekiyan in Italy is the finest authority. For insight into the broader Caucasian context Cyril Toumanoff and Ronald Suny, for the medieval and modern periods respectively, should be consulted. As for the larger framework of Western civilization, Sirarpie Der Nersesian's works still provide the best overview.

The bibliography is limited to books. The periodical literature on Armenia can be found naturally in the journals listed in the bibliography. The periodicals published in the West include numerous articles in English and should be consulted by anyone interested in locating more detailed information about the topics covered in the bibliography. *Bazmavep*, *Handes Amsorya*, and *Revue des Etudes Arméniennes*, all published in Europe, contain a wealth of information in a range of languages for the premodern period. The *Armenian Review* and the *Journal of the Society for Armenian Studies*, both issued in the United States, have published articles covering many facets of Armenian history, all of them in English. For a more comprehensive bibliography on the literature about Armenia, Vrej Nersessian's catalogues should be consulted. For a general history of Armenia, Bournoutian's *A History of the Armenian People* is introductory, and Hovannisian's *The Armenian People from Ancient to Modern Times* is more advanced. For the modern period, Christopher Walker's *Armenia: Survival of a Nation* remains the standard.

GENERAL

Albums

Agoudjian, Antoine. *Fragile Dreams: Armenia*. Nantes: Actes Sud, 1999.

Ermakov, D. I., Herman Vahramian, and Mario Verdone. *Ermakov, Armenia 1910*. Venice: Armena, 1982.

Goltz, Hermann, and Klaus E. Göltz, eds. *Rescued Armenian Treasures from Cilicia: Sacred Art of the Kilikia Museum, Antelias, Lebanon*. Wiesbaden: Ludwig Reichert Verlag, 2000.

Haratunian, Jirair. Foreword to *Armenians in America: Celebrating the First Century*. Washington, D.C.: Armenian Assembly of America, 1987.

Hasratian, Morous. Introduction to *Monuments of Armenia: From the Prehistoric Era to the 17th Century A.D.* Beirut, Lebanon: Vahan Tekeyan Cultural Association, 1975.

Iguitian, Henrik. Preface to *Gallery Noah's Ark*. Yerevan: Modern Art Museum of Armenia, 1995.

Keheyan, Garo, ed. *Stream of Fire: New Art from Armenia*. Nicosia, Cyprus: Pharos Publishers, 1995.

Keshishian, James Mark. *Inscribed Armenian Rugs of Yesteryear*. Sterling, Va.: James Mark Keshishian, 1994.

Khachaturian, Shahen. Introduction to *Armenian Artists 19th–20th Centuries*. New York: National Gallery of Armenia, 1993.

Khatcherian, Hrair Hawk. *Artsakh: A Photographic Journey*. Montreal: AAA Publishing House, 1997.

Khazaryan, Mania. Preface to *Alex and Marie Manoogian Museum*. Helsinki: Editions Erebouni, 1984.

Kurkjian, Robert, and Matthew Karanian. *Out of Stone: Armenia Artsakh.* Washington, D.C.: Stone Garden Productions, 1999.

Mazmanian, N. Preface to *The Art Gallery of Armenia.* Leningrad: Aurora Art Publishers, 1975.

Olivetti Manoukian, Franca, Agopik Manoukian, Herminè Avakian, Bryan Fleming, and Daniel Dutard. *Hishatak 1865–1930: Pictures and Memories from Armenian Family Albums between the 19th and 20th Centuries.* Milan: Oemme, 1990.

Tcholakian, Arthur. *Armenia: State, People, Life.* New York: Paradon, 1975.

Thomasian, Ruth. *Treasured Images: Armenians through the Camera's Eye.* Watertown, Mass.: Project Save, 1989.

Atlases

Baghdasaryan, A. B. *Haykakan Sovetakan Sotsialistakan Respublikayi Atlas* [Atlas of the Armenian Soviet Socialist Republic]. Yerevan: ASSR Academy of Sciences, 1961.

Chaliand, Gérard, and Jean-Pierre Rageau. *The Penguin Atlas of Diasporas.* New York: Viking, 1995.

Hewsen, Robert H. *Armenia: A Historical Atlas.* Chicago: University of Chicago Press, 2001.

Yeremian, Suren T. *Hayastane est Ashkharhatsuytsi* [Armenia According to the Ashkharhatsuyts] Yerevan: ASSR Academy of Sciences, 1963.

Bibliographies

Adalian, Rouben Paul, ed. *Armenian Genocide Resource Guide.* Washington, D.C.: Armenian Assembly of America, 1988.

Anasian, Hakob. *Armyanskii Vopros i Genotsid Armyan v Turtsii* [The Armenian Question and the Genocide of the Armenians in Turkey]. Los Angeles: American Armenian International College, 1983.

———. *Haykakan Matenagitutiun 5–15 dd.* [Armenian Bibliology 5th–15th Centuries] 3 vols. Yerevan: ASSR Academy of Sciences, 1959, 1976.

Avakian, Anne M. *Armenia and the Armenians in Academic Dissertations: A Bibliography.* Berkeley, Calif.: Professional Press, 1987.

———. *Armenian Folklore Bibliography.* Berkeley: University of California Press, 1994.

Bardakjian, Kevork B. *A Reference Guide to Modern Armenian Literature, 1500–1920, with an Introductory History.* Detroit, Mich.: Wayne State University Press, 1999.

Charny, Israel W. *Genocide: A Critical Bibliographic Review.* New York: Facts on File, 1988.

Dobkowski, Michael N., and Isidor Wallimann. *Genocide in Our Time: An Annotated Bibliography with Analytical Introductions*. Ann Arbor, Mich.: Pierian Press, 1992.

Hovannisian, Richard G. *The Armenian Holocaust: A Bibliography Relating to the Deportations, Massacres, and Dispersion of the Armenian People, 1915–1923*. Cambridge, Mass.: Armenian Heritage Press, 1980.

Miansarov, Mikhail Misropovich. *Bibliographia Caucasica et Transcaucasica*. Amsterdam: Meridian, 1967, reprint.

Nersessian, Vrej Nerses. *Armenia*. World Bibliographic Series, Vol. 163. Santa Barbara, Calif.: ABC-Clio Press, 1993

———. *A Bibliography of Articles on Armenian Studies in Western Journals, 1869–1995*. Richmond, Surrey, U.K.: Curzon in association with the British Library, 1997.

Salmaslian, Armenag. *Bibliographie de l'Arménie*. Paris: 1946.

Thomson, Robert W. *A Bibliography of Classical Armenian Literature to 1500 AD*. Turnhout, Belgium: Brepols, 1995.

Uluhogian, Gabriella. *Bibliography of Armenian Dictionaries*. Bologna: Patron Editore, 1987.

Vassilian, Hamo B. *The Armenian Genocide: A Comprehensive Bibliography and Library Resource Guide*. Glendale, Calif.: Armenian Reference Books, 1992.

———. *Armenians and Iran: A Comprehensive Bibliographic Guide to Books Published in the Armenian, Persian, English and Russian Languages (romanized form)*. Glendale, Calif.: Armenian Reference Books, 1994.

Zarbhanalian, Geregin. *Matenadaran Haykakan Targmanuteants Nakhneats (dar 4–13)* [Bibliography of Early Translated Armenian Literature, 4th–13th Centuries]. Venice: Mekhitarist Press, 1889.

Dictionaries

Acharian, Hrachia. *Hayeren Armatakan Bararan* [Armenian Etymological Dictionary]. 4 vols. Yerevan: Yerevan University Press, 1971–1979.

Aghayan, Edvard. *Ardi Hayereni Batsatrakan Bararan* [Explanatory Dictionary of Modern Armenian]. 2 vols. Yerevan: Hayastan, 1972.

Avetikian, Gabriel, Khachatur Siurmelian, and Mkrtich Avgerian. *Nor Bargirk Haykakan Lezvi* [New Lexicon of the Armenian Language]. 2 vols. Venice: Mekhitarist Press. 1836–1837.

Bedrosian, Madatia. *New Dictionary Armenian-English*. Venice: S. Lazarus Armenian Academy, 1875.

Chakmakjian, Haroutioun Hovanes. *A Comprehensive Dictionary, English-Armeniam*. Boston, Mass.: E. A. Yeran, 1922.

Hannessian, Ohannes. *Shirak's English-Armenian Dictionary with Transliteration*. Los Angeles: Shirak, 1999.

Kouyoumdjian, Mesrob G. *A Comprehensive Dictionary, Armenian-English*. Cairo: Sahag-Mesrob Press, 1950.

Malkhasian, Stepanos. *Hayeren Batsatrakan Bararan* [Armenian Explicatory Dictionary]. 4 vols. Yerevan: ASSR State Publishers, 1944–1945.

Samuelian, Thomas J. *Armenian Dictionary in Transliteration, Western Pronunciation: Armenian-English, English-Armenian*. New York: Armenian National Education Committee, 1992.

Weitenberg, Joseph Johannes Sicco, and Paul Jungmann. *A Reverse Analytical Dictionary of Classical Armenian*. Berlin: Mouton de Gruyter, 1993.

Encyclopedias and References

Asher, R. E., ed. *The Encyclopedia of Language and Linguistics*. Oxford: Pergamon Press, 1994.

Bright, William. *International Encyclopedia of Linguistics*. Oxford: Oxford University Press, 1992.

Campbell, George L. *Compendium of the World's Languages*. London: Routledge, 1991.

Charny, Israel, editor-in-chief, Rouben Paul Adalian, Steven L. Jacobs, Eric Markusen, and Samuel Totten, associate editors. *Encyclopedia of Genocide*. Santa Barbara, Calif.: ABC-Clio, 1999.

Di Bernardino, Angelo, ed. *Encyclopedia of the Early Church*. Adrian Walford, trans. 2 vols. New York: Oxford University Press, 1992.

Elide, Mircea, ed. *The Encyclopedia of Religion*. London: Macmillan, 1987.

Friedrich, Paul and Norma Diamond, eds. *Encyclopedia of World Cultures: Volume VI, Russia and Eurasia/China*. Boston: G.K. Hall, 1994.

Gibb, Hamilton, ed. *Encyclopedia of Islam*. 2nd ed. Leiden: E.J. Brill, 1954.

Great Soviet Encyclopedia: A Translation of the Third Edition. 31 vols. London: Macmillan, 1973–1983.

Hambartsumian, Viktor, ed. *Haykakan Sovetakan Hanragitaran* [Soviet Armenian Encyclopedia]. 12 vols. Yerevan: ASSR Academy of Sciences, 1974–1987.

Karasik, Theordore W. *Russia and Eurasia: Facts and Figures Annual*. Vols. 18, 19, 20. Gulf Breeze, Fla.: Academic International Press, 1993, 1994, 1995.

Kazhdan, Alexander P., ed. *The Oxford Dictionary of Byzantium*. 3 vols. New York: Oxford University Press, 1991.

Pysent, Robert B., ed. *The Everyman Companion to East European Literature*. London: J.M. Dent, 1993.

Rhyne, George N., ed. *The Supplement to the Modern Encyclopedia of Russian, Soviet and Eurasian History*. Gulf Breeze, Fla.: Academic International Press, 1995.

Schultz-Torge, Ulrich-Joachim, ed. *Who Was Who in the Soviet Union: A Biographical Dictionary of More Than 4,600 Leading Officials from the Central Apparatus and the Republics to 1991.* Munich: K.G. Saur, 1992.

Simon, Reeva S., Phillip Matter, and Richard W. Bulliet. *Encyclopedia of the Modern Middle East.* 4 vols. New York: Macmillan Reference, 1996.

Strayer, Joseph R. *Dictionary of the Middle Ages.* 12 vols. New York: Charles Scribner's Sons, 1982.

Weber, Harry B., ed. *The Modern Encyclopedia of Russian and Soviet Literature.* Gulf Breeze, Fla.: Academic International Press, 1977.

Wieczyncki, Joseph L. *The Modern Encyclopedia of Russian and Soviet History.* 54 vols. Gulf Breeze, Fla.: Academic International Press, 1976–1990.

Yarshater, Ehsan, ed. *Encyclopedia Iranica.* London: Routledge and Kegan Paul, 1985.

Guide Books

Ananikian, R. G. *Yerevan: A Guide.* Moscow: Progress, 1982.

Asratian, Grigorii Oganesovich, and R. Mazelov. *Yerevan and Its Environs.* Leningrad: Aurora Art, 1973.

Darke, Diana. *Discovery Guide to Eastern Turkey and the Black Sea Coast.* London: Haag, 1990.

Karanian, Matthew, and Robert Kurkjian. *Edge of Time: Traveling in Armenia and Karabagh.* Washington, D.C.: Stone Garden Productions, 2001.

Mazelev, R. A., and G. Hasratyan. *Yerevan and Its Environs.* Leningrad: Aurora Art, 1973.

Mehling, Marianne, ed. *Turkey: A Phaidon Cultural Guide.* Oxford: Phaidon, 1989.

Oganesian, G. A. *The Museums of Yerevan.* Yerevan: Hayastan, 1986.

Shakhkian, Garnik S. *Architectural Monuments in Soviet Armenia: Guidebook.* Yerevan: Parberakan, 1989.

Periodicals

AIM: Armenian International Magazine. Glendale, Calif.: AIM, 1991–.

Annual of Armenian Linguistics. Cleveland, Ohio: Cleveland State University, 1980–.

Ararat: A Quarterly. New York: Armenian General Benevolent Union, 1960–.

Armenian Forum: A Journal of Contemporary Affairs. Princeton, N.J.: Gomidas Institute, 1998–.

The Armenian Review. Boston, Mass.: Hairenik Association, Armenian Research Foundation, and Armenian Review, 1948–1992.

Banber Matenadarani [Review of the Matenadaran]. Yerevan: Matenadaran, 1956–.

Bazmavep: Hayagitakan-banasirakan-grakan Handes [Bazmavep: Armenological-philological-literary Journal]. Venice: Mekhitarist Press, 1843–.

Diaspora: A Journal of Transnational Studies. Oxford University Press; University of Toronto Press; and Zoryan Institute for Contemporary Armenian Research and Documentation, 1991–.

Hairenik Monthly. Vol. 1–45. Boston: Hairenik Association.

Handes Amsorya: Zeitschrift für armenische Philologie [Journal of Armenian Philology]. Vienna: Mechitharisten-kongregation, 1887–.

Haykazian Hayagitakan Handes [Haigazian Armenological Review]. Beirut: Haigazian College, 1970–.

Journal of Armenian Studies. Cambridge, Mass.: National Association for Armenian Studies and Research, 1975–.

Journal of the Society for Armenian Studies. Los Angeles: University of California, 1984–.

Lraber Hasarakakan Gitutiunneri/Vestnik Obshestvennikh Nauk [Journal of Social Sciences]. Yerevan: Armenian Academy of Sciences, 1940–.

Monthly Digest of News from Armenia. Washington, D.C.: Armenian Assembly of America, 1993–1994.

Patma-banasirakan Handes [Historico-philological Journal]. Yerevan: Armenian Academy of Sciences, 1958–.

Raft: Journal of Armenian Poetry and Criticism. Cleveland, Ohio: Cleveland State University, 1987–.

Revue des études arméniennes. Paris: Association de la revue des études arméniennes. Old Series, 1920–1933; Société des études armeniennes and Fundação Calouste Gulbenkian, New Series, 1964–.

Revue d'histoire arménienne contemporaine. Paris: Bibliothèque Nubar de l'Union Générale Arménienne de Bienfaisance, 1995–.

HISTORICAL

General

Bournoutian, George A. *A History of the Armenian People*. 2 vols. Costa Mesa, Calif.: Mazda, 1994.

Brosset, Marie-Félicité. *Collection d'historiens arméniens*. St. Petersburg: Imprimerie de l'Académie imperiale des sciences, 1874.

Chamchian, Michael. *History of Armenia, by Father Michael Chamich, from B.C. 2247 to the year of Christ 1780, or 1229 of the Armenian era, tr. from the original Armenian, by Johannes Avdall*. Calcutta: Bishop's College Press by H. Townsend, 1827.

Dédéyan, Gérard. *Histoire des Arméniens*. Toulouse: Editions Privat, 1982.

Grousset, René. *Histoire de l'Arménie: des origines à 1071, Le Regard de l'histoire*. Paris: Payot, 1973, reprint.

Hovannisian, Richard G., ed. *The Armenian People from Ancient to Modern Times*. 2 vols. New York: St. Martin's Press, 1997.

Institute of History. *Hay Zhoghovrdi Patmutiun* [History of the Armenian People] 8 vols. Yerevan: ASSR Academy of Sciences, 1967–1981.

Kévorkian, Raymond H. *Arménie, entre Orient et Occident: trois mille ans de civilisation*. Paris: Bibliothèque nationale de France, 1996.

Manandian, Hakob. *Knnakan Tesutiun Hay Zhghovrdi Patmutian* [Critical History of the Armenian People], 4 vols. Yerevan: Haypethrat, 1945–1957.

Morgan, Jacques Jean Marie de. *Histoire du peuple arménien depuis les temps les plus reculés de ses annales jusqu'à nos jours*. Paris: Berger-Levrault, 1919.

———. *The History of the Armenian People from the Remotest Times to the Present Day*. Boston: Hairenik Press, 1965.

Pasdermadjian, Hrant. *Histoire de L'Arménie, depuis les origines jusqu'au traité de Lausanne*. Paris: H. Samuelian, 1949.

Redgate, Anne Elizabeth. *The Armenians: The Peoples of Europe*. Oxford: Blackwell, 1997.

Tournebize, Henri François. *Histoire politique et religieuse de l'Arménie*. Paris: A. Picard et fils, 1910.

Ancient (Origins to 4th century)

Adonts, Nicolas. *Histoire d'Arménie, les origines du Xè siècle au VIè (av. J.C.)*. Paris: Melkonian Fond, 1946.

Armen, Herant K. *Tigranes the Great: A Biography*. Detroit, Mich.: Avondale, 1940.

Aslan, Kevork, and Frédéric Macler. *Études historiques sur le peuple arménien*. New edition. Paris: P. Geuthner, 1928.

Burney, Charles Allen, and David Marshall Lang. *The Peoples of the Hills: Ancient Ararat and Caucasus*. London: Weidenfeld and Nicolson, 1971.

Chahin, M. *The Kingdom of Armenia*. London: Croom Helm, 1987.

Diakonoff, I. M. *The Prehistory of the Armenian People*. Lori Jennings, trans. Delmar, N.Y.: Caravan Books, 1984.

Manandian, Hagop. *A Brief Survey of the History of Ancient Armenia*. New York: Diocese of the Armenian Church of America, 1975.

———. *Tigrane II and Rome: nouveaux éclaircissements à la lumière des sources originales*. H. Thorossian, trans. Lisbon: Imprensa Nacional, 1963.

———. *The Trade and Cities of Armenia in Relation to Ancient World Trade*. Nina Garsoian, trans. Lisbon: Livraria Bertrand, 1965.

Piotrovskii, B. B. *The Ancient Civilization of Urartu*. New York: Cowles, 1969.

Salvini, Mirjo. *Geschichte und Kultur der Urartäer*. Darmstadt: Wissenschaftliche Buchgesellschaft, 1995.

———. *Nairi e Ur(u)atri: Contributo alla storia della formazione del regno di Urartu*. Rome: Edizioni dell'Ateneo, 1967.

Wartke, Ralf-B. *Urartu, das Reich am Ararat, Kulturgeschichte der antiken Welt, Bd. 59*. Mainz am Rhein: P. von Zabern, 1993.

Zimansky, Paul E. *Ancient Ararat: A Handbook of Urartian Studies*. Delmar, N.Y.: Caravan Books, 1998.

———. *Ecology and Empire: The Structure of the Urartian State*. Chicago: The Oriental Institute, 1985.

Medieval (5th through 17th century)

Adonts, Nicolas. *Études arméno-byzantines*. Lisbon: Livraria Bertrand, 1965.

Adontz, Nicholas. *Armenia in the Period of Justinian: The Political Conditions Based on the Naxarar System*. Nina G. Garsoian, trans. Louvain: Imprimerie Orientaliste, 1970.

Agatangeghos. *History of the Armenians*. Robert W. Thomson trans. Albany: State University of New York Press, 1976.

Ahrweiler, Hélène, and Angeliki E. Laiou. *Studies on the Internal Diaspora of the Byzantine Empire*. Washington, D.C. and Cambridge, Mass.: Dumbarton Oaks and Harvard University Press, 1998.

Anania Sirakaci. *The Geography of Ananias of Sirak: (Asxarhacoyc): The Long and the Short Recensions*, Robert H. Hewsen, trans. Wiesbaden: Reichert, 1992.

Arzoumanian, Zaven. *History of Lewond, the Eminent Vardapet of the Armenians*. Wynnewood, Pa.: St. Sahag and St. Mesrob Armenian Church, 1982.

Avdoyan, Levon. *Pseudo-Yovhannes Mamikonean, The History of Taron (Patmutiwn Taronoy): Historical Investigation, Critical Translation, and Historical and Textual Commentaries*. Atlanta, Ga.: Scholars Press, 1993.

Boase, T. S. R. *The Cilician Kingdom of Armenia*. Edinburgh: Scottish Academic Press, 1978.

Dédéyan, Gérard. *La chronique attribuée au connétable Smbat*. Documents relatifs à l'histoire des croisades. Paris: R. Guenther, 1980.

Dostourian, Ara Edmond. *Armenia and the Crusades, Tenth to Twelfth Centuries: The Chronicle of Matthew of Edessa*. Lanham, Md.: University Press of America, 1993.

Eghishe. *History of Vardan and the Armenian War*. Robert W. Thomson, trans. Cambridge, Mass.: Harvard University Press, 1982.

Garsoian, Nina G. *Armenia between Byzantium and the Sasanians*. London: Variorum Reprints, 1985.

———. *East of Byzantium: Syria and Armenia in the Formative Period*. Garison, Nina G., Thomas F. Mathews, and Robert W. Thomson, eds. Washington, D.C.: Dumbarton Oaks, 1982.

Ghazarian, Vatche. *Armenians in the Ottoman Empire: An Anthology of Transformation, 13th–19th centuries*. Waltham, Mass.: Mayreni, 1998.

Ghougassian, Vazken, S. *The Emergence of the Armenian Diocese of New Julfa in the Seventeenth Century*. Atlanta, Ga.: Scholars Press, 1998.

Grigor of Akanc. *History of the Nation of the Archers [Mongols]*. Robert P. Blake, trans. Cambridge, Mass.: Harvard University Press, 1954.

Holt, P. M. *Early Mamluk Diplomacy, 1260–1290: Treaties of Baybars and Qalawun with Christian Rulers, Islamic History and Civilization*. Leiden and New York: E.J. Brill, 1995.

Kaegi, Walter Emil. *Byzantium and the Early Islamic Conquests*. Cambridge: Cambridge University Press, 1992.

Kouymjian, Dickran, ed. *Armenian Studies: Etudes arméniennes in memoriam Haig Berbérian*. Lisbon: Imprensa de Coimbra, 1986.

Lazar, Parpeci. *The History of Lazar Parpeci*. Robert W. Thomson, trans. New York: Scholars Press, 1991.

Lewond. *History of Lewond the Eminent Vardapet of the Armenians*. Zaven Arzoumanian, trans. Philadelphia: Rosekeer, 1982.

Mahé, G., Jean-Pierre, and Robert W. Thomson. *From Byzantium to Iran: Armenian Studies in Honour of Nina G. Garsoian*. Atlanta, Ga.: Scholars Press, 1997.

McCabe, Ina Baghdiantz. *The Shah's Silk for Europe's Silver: The Eurasian Trade of the Julfa Armenians in Safavid Iran and India (1530–1750)*. Atlanta, Ga.: Scholars Press, 1999.

Movses Dasxuranci. *The History of the Caucasian Albanians*. C. J. F. Dowsett, trans. London: Oxford University Press, 1961.

Movses Khorenatsi. *History of the Armenians*. Robert W. Thomson, trans. Cambridge, Mass.: Harvard University Press, 1978.

Mutafian, Claude, Catherine Otten-Froux, Lilit Zakarian, and Krikor Chahinian. *Le royaume arménien de Cilicie, XIIe–XIVe siècle*. Paris: CNRS éditions, 1993.

Papazian, Kapriel Serope, and P. M. Manuelian. *Merchants from Ararat: A Brief Survey of Armenian Trade through the Ages*. New York: Ararat Press, 1979.

Pawstos Buzand. *The Epic Histories Attributed to Pawstos Buzand: (Buzandaran Patmutiwnk)*, Nina G. Garsoian, trans. Cambridge, Mass.: Harvard University Press, 1989.

Rudt-Collenberg, W. H. *The Rupenides, Hethumides and Lusignans: The Structure of the Armeno-Cilician Dynasties*. Paris: Klincksieck, 1963.

Sanjian, Avedis Krikor. *A Catalogue of Medieval Armenian Manuscripts in the United States*. Berkeley: University of California Press, 1976.

———. *Colophons of Armenian Manuscripts, 1301–1480: A Source for Middle Eastern History*. Cambridge, Mass.: Harvard University Press, 1969.

———. *Medieval Armenian Manuscripts at the University of California, Los Angeles*. Berkeley: University of California Press, 1999.

Savvides Alexes, G. K. *Byzantium in the Near East: Its Relations with the Seljuk Sultanate of Rum in Asia Minor, the Armenians of Cilicia and the Mongols, A.D. c. 1192–1237*. Thessaloniki: Center of Byzantine Studies, 1981.

Setton, K. M. *A History of the Crusades*. 4 vols. Madison: University of Wisconsin Press, 1969–1977.

Ter-Ghewondyan, Aram. *The Arab Emirates in Bagratid Armenia*. Nina G. Garsoian, trans. Lisbon: Livraria Bertrand, 1976.

Tovma Artsruni. *History of the House of the Artsrunik*. Robert W. Thomson, trans. Detroit, Mass.: Wayne State University Press, 1985.

Thomson, Robert W., Nina G. Garsoian, and Thomas F. Mathews. *East of Byzantium: Syria and Armenia in the Formative Period*. Washington, D.C.: Dumbarton Oaks, 1982.

Toumanoff, Cyril. *Studies in Christian Caucasian History*. Wetteren, Belgium: Georgetown University Press, 1963.

Toynbee, Arnold. *Constantine Porphyrogenitus and His World*. London: Oxford University Press, 1973.

Ukhtanes of Sebastia. *History of Armenia. Part II, History of the Severance of the Georgians from the Armenians*. Zaven Arzoumanian, trans. Fort Lauderdale, Fla.: 1985.

———. *History of the Patriarchs and Kings of Armenia*. Zaven Arzoumanian, trans. Fort Lauderdale, Fla.: 1988.

Vahram. *Vahram's Chronicle of the Armenian Kingdom of Cilicia, During the Time of the Crusades*. Charles F. Neumann, trans. London: Oriental Translation Fund, 1831.

Vardan Arewelci. *The Historical Compilation of Vardan Arewelci*. Robert W. Thomson, trans. Washington, D.C.: Dumbarton Oaks, 1989.

Yovhannes Drasxanakertci. *History of Armenia*. Krikor H. Maksoudian, trans. Atlanta, Ga.: Scholars Press, 1985.

Modern (18th through 20th century)

Adontz, Nicolas. *Towards the Solution of the Armenian Question*. London: Eyre & Spottiswoode, 1920.

Aftandilian, Gregory L. *Armenia, Vision of a Republic: The Independence Lobby in America, 1918–1927*. Charlestown, Mass.: Charles River Books, 1981.

Alexander, Edward. *A Crime of Vengeance: An Armenian Struggle for Justice*. New York: Free Press, 1991.

———. *The Serpent and the Bees: A KGB Chronicle*. Lanham, Md.: University Press of America, 1990.

Allen, W. E., and Paul Muratoff. *Caucasian Battlefields: A History of the Wars on the Turco-Caucasian Border 1828–1921*. Cambridge: Cambridge University Press, 1953.

Artinian, Vartan. *The Armenian Constitutional System in the Ottoman Empire 1839–1863: A Study of Its Historical Development*. Istanbul: Brandeis Univesity, 1988.

Atamian, Sarkis. *The Armenian Community: The Historical Development of a Social and Ideological Conflict*. New York: Philosophical Library, 1955.

Bliss, Edwin Munsell, Cyrus Hamlin, and Frances Elizabeth Willard. *Turkey and the Armenian Atrocities*. Philadelphia: Hubbard, 1896.

Bournoutian, George A. *Abraham of Erevan: History of the Wars 1721–1738*. Costa Mesa, Calif.: Mazda, 1999.

———. *Armenians and Russia, 1626–1796: A Documentary Record*. Costa Mesa, Calif.: Mazda, 2001.

———. *The Chronicle of Abraham of Crete: Patmutiwn of Katoghikos Abraham Kretatsi*. Costa Mesa, Calif.: Mazda, 1999.

———. *A History of Qarabagh: An Annotated Translation of Mirza Jamal Javanshir Qarabaghi's Tarikh-e Qarabagh*. Costa Mesa, Calif.: Mazda, 1994.

———. *The Khanate of Erevan under Qajar Rule, 1795–1828*. Costa Mesa, Calif.: Mazda, 1992.

———. *Russia and the Armenians of Transcaucasia, 1797–1889: A Documentary Record*. Costa Mesa, Calif.: Mazda, 1998.

Chalabian, Antranig. *General Andranik and the Armenian Revolutionary Movement*. Detroit: 1988.

Chambers, William Nesbitt. *Yoljuluk: Random Thoughts on a Life in Imperial Turkey*. Paramus, N.J.: Armenian Missionary Association of America, 1988.

Dasnabedian, Hrach. *History of the Armenian Revolutionary Federation, Dashnaktsutiun, 1890–1924*. Milan: Oemme Edizioni, 1990.

Demirchian, Karen Seropovich. *Soviet Armenia*. Moscow: Progress, 1984.

Ghazarian, Vatche. *Boghos Nubar's Papers and the Armenian Question, 1915–1918: Documents*. Waltham, Mass.: Mayreni, 1996

Gidney, James B. *A Mandate for Armenia*. Kent, Ohio: Kent State University Press, 1967.

Greene, Frederick Davis, and Henry Davenport Northrop. *Armenian Massacres, or, The Sword of Mohammed*. Philadelphia: International, 1896.

Hewsen, Robert H. *Russian-Armenian Relations, 1700–1828*. Cambridge, Mass.: Society for Armenian Studies, 1984.

Hovannisian, Richard G. *Armenia on the Road to Independence, 1918*. Berkeley: University of California Press, 1967.

———. *The Republic of Armenia*. 4 vols. Berkeley: University of California Press, 1971–1996.

Kasharian-Bricout, Béatrice. *La société arménienne au XIXe siècle*. Paris: Pensée universelle, 1981.

Kayaloff, Jacques. *The Battle of Sardarabad*. The Hague: Mouton, 1973.

Kazanjian, Paren. *The Cilician Armenian Ordeal*. Boston: Hye Intentions, 1989.

Kerr, Stanley E. *The Lions of Marash: Personal Experiences with American Near East Relief, 1919–1922*. Albany: State University of New York Press, 1973.

Kévorkian, Raymond H., and Paul B. Paboudjian. *Les Arméniens dans l'Empire Ottoman à la veille du génocide*. Paris: Editions d'art et d'histoire, 1992.

Krikorian, Mesrop G. *Armenians in the Service of the Ottoman Empire, 1860–1908*. London: Routledge and Kegan Paul, 1977.

Lambert, Rose. *Hadjin and the Armenian Massacres*. New York: Revell, 1911.

Lepsius, Johannes. *Armenia and Europe: An Indictment*. London: Hodder and Stoughton, 1897.

Mandelstam, Andre Nikolaevich. *La Société des nations et les puissances devant le problème arménien*. Paris: A. Pedone, 1925.

Matossian, Mary Allerton Kilbourne. *The Impact of Soviet Policies in Armenia*. Leiden: E.J. Brill, 1962.

Mikoyan, Anastas. *Memoirs of Anastas Mikoyan. Volume I: The Path of Struggle*. Boston: Sphinx Press, 1988.

Minassian, Caro Owen. *The Chronicle of Petros di Sarkis Gilanentz: Concerning the Afghan Invasion of Persia in 1722, the Siege of Isfahan and the Repercussions in Northern Persia, Russia and Turkey*. Lisbon: Imprimerie Nacional, 1959.

Mouradian, Claire. *De Staline à Gorbatchev: histoire d'une république soviétique, l'Arménie*. Paris: Editions Ramsay, 1990.

Mukhitarian, Onnig, and Haig Gossoian. *The Defense of Van*. N.p.: Society of Vasbouragan, 1980.

Nalbandian, Louise. *The Armenian Revolutionary Movement: The Development of Armenian Political Parties through the Nineteenth Century*. Berkeley: University of California Press, 1963.

Nansen, Fridtjof. *Armenia and the Near East*. New York: Duffield, 1928.

Nassibian, Akaby. *Britain and the Armenian Question, 1915–1923*. New York: St. Martin's Press, 1984.

Norman, Charles Boswell. *Armenia, and the Campaign of 1877*. London: Cassell Petter & Galpin, 1878.

Sachar, Howard M. *The Emergence of the Middle East: 1914–1924*. New York: Alfred A. Knopf, 1969.

Sarkissian, Arshag Ohan. *History of the Armenian Question to 1885*. Urbana: University of Illinios Press, 1938.

Sarkisyanz, Emanuel. *A Modern History of Transcaucasian Armenia: Social, Cultural, and Political*. Leiden: E.J. Brill, 1975.

Schwarz, Gerard, Hinako Fujihara, Scott Goff, Martin Berkofsky, Chris Butler, and James H. Tashjian. *The Armenian American in World War II: With an appendix on the part played in the Korean War*. Boston: Hairenik Association, 1952.

Shaginian, Marietta Sergeevna. *Journey through Soviet Armenia*. Moscow: Foreign Languages Publishing House, 1954.

Somakian, Manoug Joseph. *Empires in Conflict: Armenia and the Great Powers, 1895–1920*. London: Tauris Academic Studies, 1995.

Suny, Ronald Grigor. *The Baku Commune 1917–1918: Class and Nationality in the Russian Revolution*. Princeton, N.J.: Princeton University Press, 1972.

———. *Looking toward Ararat: Armenia in Modern History*. Bloomington: Indiana University Press, 1993.

———. *The Revenge of the Past: Nationalism and Revolution, and the Collapse of the Soviet Union*. Stanford, Calif.: Stanford University Press, 1993.

———. ed. *Transcaucasia, Nationalism, and Social Change: Essays in the History of Armenia, Azerbaijan, and Georgia*. Revised edition. Ann Arbor: University of Michigan Press, 1996.

Ter Minasian, Rouben. *Armenian Freedom Fighters: The Memoirs of Rouben Der Minasian*. James G. Mandalian, trans. Boston: Hairenik Associates, 1963.

Ter Minassian, Anahide. *Nationalism and Socialism in the Armenian Revolutionary Movement (1887–1912)*. Cambridge, Mass.: Zoryan Institute, 1984.

———. *La question arménienne*. Roquevaire, France: Parenthèses, 1983.

———. *La République d'Arménie: 1918–1920*. Brussels: Editions Complexe, 1989.

Ter Minassian, Anahide, and Pierre Vidal-Naquet. *Histoires croisées: diaspora, Arménie, Transcaucasie, 1880–1990*. Marseille: Parenthèses, 1997.

Ternon, Yves, and Jean-Claude Kebabdjian. *Arménie 1900*. Paris: Editions Astrid, 1980.

Troukhtanova, Nadejda *De l'histoire des liens historiques entre l'Arménie et la Russie aux XVIIe-XVIIIe siècles*. Yerevan: Academy of Sciences of the Armenian S.S.R. Institute of Arts, 1978.

United States. American Military Mission to Armenia, and James G. Harbord. *Conditions in the Near East. Report of the American Military Mission to Armenia*. Washington, D.C.: Government Printing Office, 1920.

United States. Congress. Senate. Committee on Foreign Relations. *Maintenance of Peace in Armenia. Hearings before the United States Senate Committee on Foreign Relations, Subcommittee on S.J. Res. 106, Sixty-Sixth Congress, first session, on Sept. 27, 30, Oct. 2, 10, 1919*. Washington, D.C.: U.S. Government Printing Office, 1919.

Villa, Susie Hoogasian, and Mary Kilbourne Matossian. *Armenian Village Life Before 1914*. Detroit, Mich.: Wayne State University Press, 1982.

Villari, Luigi. *Fire and Sword in the Caucasus*. London: T. F. Unwin, 1906.
Walker, Christopher J. *Armenia: The Survival of a Nation*. London: Croom Helm, 1980.

Armenian Genocide

Adalian, Rouben Paul, ed. *The Armenian Genocide in the U.S. Archives, 1915–1918*. Alexandria, Va.: Chadwick-Healey, 1991–1993. (microfiche)
———. ed. *Guide to the Armenian Genocide in the U.S. Archives, 1915–1918*. Alexandria, Va.: Chadwick-Healey, 1994.
Akçam, Taner. *Armenien und der Völkermord: die Istanbuler Prozesse und die türkische Nationalbewegung*. Hamburg: Hamburger Editionen, 1996.
Andreopoulos, George J. *Genocide: Conceptual and Historical Dimensions*. Philadelphia: University of Pennsylvania Press, 1994.
Baghdjian, Kévork K. *La confiscation, par le gouvernement turc, des biens arméniens . . . dits "abandonnés."* Montréal: K. K. Baghdjian, 1987.
Baliozian, Ara. *The Armenian Genocide and the West*. Kitchener, Ontario: Impressions, 1985.
Bardakjian, Kevork B. *Hitler and the Armenian Genocide*. Cambridge, Mass.: Zoryan Institute, 1985.
Barton, James L. *Turkish Atrocities: Statements of American Missionaries on the Destruction of Christian Communities in Ottoman Turkey, 1915–1917*. Ann Arbor, Mich.: Gomidas Institute, 1998.
Beylerian, Arthur. *Les Grandes Puissances, l'Empire Ottoman et les Arméniens dans les archives Françaises (1914–1918)*. Paris: Sorbonne, 1983.
Carzou, Jean Marie. *Un génocide exemplaire: Arménie 1915*. Paris: Flammarion, 1975.
Dadrian, Vahakn N. *Documentation of the Armenian Genocide in German and Austrian Sources*. New Brunswick, N.J.: Transaction Books, 1994.
———. *Genocide as a Problem of National and International Law: The World War I Armenian Case and its Contemporary Legal Ramifications*. New Haven, Conn.: Yale Journal of International Law, 1989.
———. *German Responsibility in the Armenian Genocide: A Review of the Historical Evidence of German Complicity*. Watertown, Mass.: Blue Crane Books, 1996.
———. *The History of the Armenian Genocide: Ethnic Conflict from the Balkans to Anatolia to the Caucasus*. Providence, R.I.: Berghahn Books, 1995.
———. *The Naim-Andonian Documents on the World War I Destruction of Ottoman Armenians: The Anatomy of a Genocide*. International Journal of Middle East Studies, v. 18, no. 3. Cambridge University Press, 1986.
———. *Warrant for Genocide: Key Elements of Turko–Armenian Conflict*. New Brunswick, N.J.: Transaction Books, 1999.

Davis, Leslie A. *The Slaughterhouse Province: An American Diplomat's Report on the Armenian Genocide, 1915–1917*. Susan Blair, ed. New Rochelle, New York: A.D. Caratzas, 1989.

Derogy, Jacques. *Resistance and Revenge: The Armenian Assassination of the Turkish Leaders Responsible for the 1915 Massacres and Deportations*. New Brunswick, N.J.: Transaction Books, 1990.

Dobkin, Marjorie Housepian. *Smyrna 1922: The Destruction of a City*. London: Faber, 1972.

Graber, G. S. *Caravans to Oblivion: The Armenian Genocide, 1915*. New York: J. Wiley, 1996.

Great Britain. Foreign Office. *The Treatment of Armenians in the Ottoman Empire, 1915–1916: Documents Presented to Viscount Grey of Fallodon, Secretary of State for Foreign Affairs, by Viscount Bryce,* Command Paper, Cd 8325. London: Stationery Office, 1916.

Gust, Wolfgang. *Der Völkermord an den Armeniern: die Tragödie des ältesten Christenvolkes der Welt*. Munich: Carl Hanser, 1993.

Hovannisian, Richard G., ed. *The Armenian Genocide: History, Politics, Ethics*. London: Macmillan, 1991.

———. ed. *The Armenian Genocide in Perspective*. New Brunswick, N.J.: Transaction Books, 1986.

Institut für Armenische Fragen. *The Armenian Genocide: Documentation*. 2 vols. Munich: Institut für Armenische Fragen, 1987, 1988.

Kloian, Richard Diran, ed. *The Armenian Genocide: News Accounts from the American Press, (1915–1922)*. 3rd ed. Richmond, Calif.: ACC Books, 1985.

Knapp, Grace H., Grisell Mand McLaren, and Myrtle O. Shane. *The Tragedy of Bitlis*. New York: Fleming H. Revell, 1919.

Lepsius, Johannes. *Deutschland und Armenien, 1914–1918: Sammlung Diplomatischer Aktenstücke*. Potsdam: Der Tempelverlag, 1919.

———. *Rapport secret sur les massacres d'Arménie*. Paris: Payot, 1987, Reprint.

Libaridian, Gerard J., ed. *A Crime of Silence: The Armenian Genocide*. London: Zed Books, 1985.

———. ed. *Genocide, Crime against Humanity: Essays and Documents. Armenian Review, v. 37, no. 1*. Boston, Mass.: Armenian Review, 1984.

Loti, Pierre. *Les massacres d'Arménie*. Paris: Calmann-Lévy, 1918.

Maleville, Georges de. *La tragédie arménienne de 1915*. Paris: Editions Lanore, 1988.

Mazian, Florence. *Why genocide? The Armenian and Jewish Experiences in Perspective*. Ames: Iowa State University Press, 1990.

Mécérian, Jean. *Le génocide du peuple arménien; le sort de la population arménienne de l'Empire ottoman, de la Constitution ottomane au Traité de Lausanne, 1908–1923*. Beirut: Imprimerie Catholique, 1965.

Melson, Robert. *Revolution and Genocide: On the Origins of the Armenian Genocide and the Holocaust*. Chicago: University of Chicago Press, 1992.

Miller, Donald E., and Lorna Touryan Miller. *Survivors: An Oral History of the Armenian Genocide*. Berkeley: University of California Press, 1993.

Morgenthau, Henry. *Ambassador Morgenthau's Story*. Garden City, N.Y.: Doubleday Page, 1918.

Nersisian, Mkrtich G., and Ruben G. Sahakyan. *Genotsid armian v Osmanskoi imperii; sbornik dokumentov i materialov* [The Genocide of Armenians in the Ottoman Empire: Collections of Documents and Materials]. Yerevan: ASSR Academy of Sciences, 1966.

Niepage, Martin. *The Horrors of Aleppo: Seen by a German Eyewitness*. London: Fisher Unwin, 1916.

Ohandjanian, Artem. *Armenien: der verschwiegene Völkermord*. Vienna: Böhlau, 1989.

Riggs, Henry H. *Days of Tragedy in Armenia: Personal Experiences in Harpoot, 1915–1917*. Ann Arbor, Michigan: Gomidas Institute, 1997.

Sarafian, Ara, ed. *United States Official Documents on the Armenian Genocide*. 3 vols. Watertown, Mass.: Armenian Review, 1993–1995.

Simpson, Christopher. *The Splendid Blond Beast: Money, Law, and Genocide in the Twentieth Century*. New York: Grove Press, 1993.

Tamcke, Martin. *Armin T. Wegner und die Armenier: Anspruch und Wirklichkeit eines Augenzeugen*. Gottingen: Cuvillier, 1993.

Ternon, Yves. *The Armenians: History of a Genocide*. Delmar, N.Y.: Caravan Books, 1981.

Totten, Samuel, William S. Parsons, and Israel W. Charny. *Century of Genocide: Eyewitness Accounts and Critical Views*. New York: Garland, 1997.

Toynbee, Arnold Joseph, and James Bryce. *Armenian Atrocities: The Murder of a Nation*. London: Hodder & Stoughton, 1915.

Trumpener, Ulrich. *Germany and the Ottoman Empire, 1914–1918*. Princeton, N.J.: Princeton University Press, 1968.

United States. Congress. House. Committee on Foreign Affairs. *Relief of Armenians Hearings before the United States House Committee on Foreign Affairs, Sixty-Fourth Congress, first session, on June 21, 1916*. Washington, D.C.: U.S. Government Printing Office, 1916.

Ussher, Clarence Douglas, and Grace H. Knapp. *An American Physician in Turkey, a Narrative of Adventures in Peace and War*. Boston: Houghton Mifflin, 1917.

Winter, J. M., and Blaine Baggett. *The Great War and the Shaping of the Twentieth Century*. New York: Penguin Books, 1996.

Yeghiayan, Vartkes. *The Case of Soghomon Tehlirian*. Cambridge, Mass.: Zoryan Institute, 1985.

Zarewand. *United and Independent Turania: Aims and Designs of the Turks*. Vahakn N. Dadrian, trans. Leiden Netherlands: E.J. Brill, 1971.

Contemporary (1965–2001)

Croissant, Michael P. *The Armenia-Azerbaijan Conflict: Causes and Implications*. Westport, Conn.: Praeger, 1998.

Goldenberg, Suzanne. *Pride of Small Nations: The Caucasus and Post-Soviet Disorder*. London: Zed, 1994.

Herzig, Edmund. *The Armenians: A Handbook*. New York: St. Martin's Press, 1998.

———. *The New Caucasus: Armenia, Azerbaijan and Georgia*. London: Pinter, 1998.

Hunter, Shireen. *The Transcaucasus in Transition: Nation-building and Conflict*. Washington, D.C.: Center for Strategic and International Studies, 1994.

Malkasian, Mark. *Gha-ra-bagh! The Emergence of the National Democratic Movement in Armenia*. Detroit, Mich.: Wayne State University Press, 1996.

O'Ballance, Edgar. *Wars in the Caucasus, 1990–1995*. New York: New York University Press, 1997.

Saroyan, Mark, and Edward W. Walker. *Minorities, Mullahs, and Modernity: Reshaping Community in the Late Soviet Union*. Berkeley: University of California, 1997.

Schwartz, Donald V., and Razmik Panossian. *Nationalism and History: The Politics of Nation Building in Post-Soviet Armenia, Azerbaijan and Georgia*. Toronto: University of Toronto Centre for Russian and East European Studies, 1994.

Shahmuratian, Samvel. *The Sumgait Tragedy: Pogroms against Armenians in Soviet Azerbaijan*. New Rochelle, N.Y.: Aristide D. Caratzas and Zoryan Institute, 1990.

Verluise, Pierre, and Levon Chorbajian. *Armenia in Crisis: The 1988 Earthquake*. Detroit, Mich.: Wayne State University Press, 1995.

Wright, John F. R., Suzanne Goldenberg, and Richard N. Schofield. *Transcaucasian Boundaries*. New York: St. Martin's Press, 1996.

CULTURAL

General

Adalian, Rouben Paul. *From Humanism to Rationalism: Armenian Scholarship in the Nineteenth Century*. Atlanta, Ga.: Scholars Press, 1992.

Alpago Novello, Adriano, et al. *The Armenians*. New York: Rizzoli, 1986.

Baliozian, Ara. *The Armenians: Their History and Culture.* New York: Ararat Press, 1980.

Bauer, Elisabeth. *Armenia, Past and Present.* Lucerne: Reich Verlag, 1981.

Boettiger, Louis A. *Armenian Legends and Festivals.* Minneapolis: University of Minnesota, 1920.

Der Nersessian, Sirarpie. *The Armenians.* Ancient peoples and places, no. 68. New York: Praeger, 1970.

———. *Études byzantines et arméniennes. Byzantine and Armenian Studies.* Louvain: Imprimerie Orientaliste, 1973.

Hovannisian, Richard, G. *Armenian Van/Vaspurakan.* Costa Mesa, Calif.: Mazda, 2000.

Samuelian, Thomas J. *Classical Armenian Culture: Influences and Creativity.* Chico, Calif.: Scholars Press, 1982.

Samuelian, Thomas J., and Michael E. Stone. *Medieval Armenian Culture.* Chico, Calif.: Scholars Press, 1984.

Sarafian, Kevork Avedis. *History of Education in Armenia.* La Verne, Calif.: Press of the La Verne Leader, 1930.

Tahmizyan, Nikoghos. *Position and Signification of Music in the System of Professional Arts in Medieval Armenia (V–XV centuries).* Yerevan: ASSR Academy of Sciences Institute of Arts, 1978.

Archeology

Alekseev, V. P. *Contributions to the Archaeology of Armenia.* Henry Field, trans. Cambridge, Mass.: Peabody Museum, Harvard University, 1968.

Azarpay, Guitty. *Urartian Art and Artifacts. A Chronological Study.* Berkeley and Los Angeles: University of California Press, 1968.

Bedoukian, Paul Z. *Coinage of Cilician Armenia.* Danbury, Conn.: Bedoukian, 1979.

———. *Coinage of the Artaxiads of Armenia.* London: Royal Numismatic Society, 1978.

Brosset, Marie-Félicité. *Les ruines d'Ani, capitale de l'Arménie sous les rois Bagratides, aux xe et xie s; histoire et description.* St. Petersburg: Académie impériale des sciences, 1860.

Loon, Maurits Nanning van. *Urartian Art: Its Distinctive Traits in the Light of New Excavations.* Istanbul: Nederlands Historisch-Archaeologisch Instituut, 1966.

Podvigina, Natali. *The Preservation and Restoration of Cultural Monuments in Soviet Armenia—1920–1930.* Yerevan: ASSR Academy of Sciences Institute of Arts, 1978.

Stone, Michael E. *Armenian Inscriptions from Sinai: Intermediate Report with Notes on Georgian and Nabatean Inscriptions.* Sydney: Maitland Publications, 1979.

Thierry, Jean-Michel. *Le couvent arménien d'Horomos, Matériaux pour l'archéologie arménienne*. Louvain, Belgium: Peeters, 1980.

——. *Monuments arméniens du Vaspurakan, Bibliothèque archéologique et historique, 129*. Paris: Librairie orientaliste Paul Geuthner, 1989.

Tiratsyan, Gevorg Artashesi. *Urartu und Armenien (zur frage der Kontinuität der Materiellen Kultur)*. Yerevan: ASSR Academy of Sciences Institute of Arts, 1978.

Architecture

Alpago Novello, Adriano, and Manoukian A. *Armenian Architecture: IVth–XVIIIth Centuries*. Milan: Facoltá di architettura del Politecnics di Milano, 1981.

Ayvazyan, Argam. *The Historical Monuments of Nakhichevan*. Detroit, Mich.: Wayne State University Press, 1990.

Carswell, John. *New Julfa: The Armenian Churches and Other Buildings*. Oxford: Clarendon Press, 1968.

Davies, J. G. *Medieval Armenian Art and Architecture: The Church of the Holy Cross, Aghtamar.* London: Pindar Press, 1991.

Der Nersessian, Sirarpie. *Aghtamar: Church of the Holy Cross*. Cambridge, Mass.: Harvard University Press, 1965.

Edwards, R. W. *The Fortifications of Armenian Cilicia*. Washington, D.C.: Dumbarton Oaks, 1987.

Karapetian, Karapet. *Isfahan, New Julfa: The Houses of the Armenians*. Rome: Istituto Italiano per il Medio, 1974.

Mnatsakanyan, S. Kh. *Pre-Ani Stage in the Development of Armenian Architecture*. Yerevan: ASSR Academy of Sciences Institute of Arts, 1978.

Mnatsakanyan, S. Kh, and Rainer K. Lampinen. *Aghtamar*. Los Angeles: Editions Erebouni, 1986.

Mnatsakanyan, Suren. *Memorial Symbolism in Medieval Armenian Art and Architecture*. Yerevan: ASSR Academy of Sciences Institute of Arts, 1978.

Sinclair, Thomas A. *Eastern Turkey: An Architectural and Archaeological Survey*. 4 vols. London: Pindar, 1987.

Strzygowski, Josef, Thoros Thoramanian, Heinrich Glück, and Leon Lissitzian. *Die Baukunst der Armenier und Europa*. Vienna: A. Schroll, 1918.

Thierry, Jean-Michel. *La Cathédrale des Saints-Apôtres de Kars: 930–943*. Louvain: Peeters, 1978.

——. *La décoration sculptée de la Cathédrale des Saints-Apôtres de Kars*. Yerevan: ASSR Academy of Sciences Institute of Arts, 1978.

——. *Répertoire des monastères arméniens*. Turnhout: Brepols, 1993.

Thierry, Jean-Michel, Patrik Donabedían, and Nicole Thierry. *Armenian Art*. New York: H.N. Abrams, 1989.

Thierry, Jean-Michel, Patrik Donabedían, and Nicole Thierry. *Les arts arméniens, L'Art et les grandes civilisations, 17*. Paris: Mazenod, 1987.

Thierry, Nicole. *Les peintures de l'église de la Sainte-Croix d'Aghtamar (915–921)*. Yerevan: ASSR Academy of Sciences Institute of Arts, 1978.

Tokarskij, Nikolaj M., and Adriano Alpago-Novello. *Amberd*. 2nd ed. *Documenti di architettura armena/Documents of Armenian architecture, 5*. Milan: Ares, 1978.

Tuglaci, Pars. *The Role of the Balian Family in Ottoman Architecture*. Istanbul: Yeni Cigir Bookstore, 1990.

Utudjian, Edouard. *Armenian Architecture, 4th to 17th century*. Paris: Editions A. Morancé, 1968.

Vahramian, Herman, and Sirarpie Der Nersessian. *Aghtamar. Documenti di architettura armena, 8*. Milan: Ares, 1974.

Arts

Abramian, Jackie. *Conversations with Contemporary Armenian Artists*. Brattleboro, Vt.: Amana, 1990.

Abrahamian, Levon, and Nancy Sweezy, eds. *Armenian Folk Arts, Culture, and Identity*. Bloomington: Indiana University Press, 2001.

Basmadjian, Garig. *A Century of French-Armenian Painting (1879–1979)*. Paris: 1979.

Buschhausen, Heide, Helmut Buschhausen, and Eva Zimmermann. *The Illuminated Armenian Manuscripts of the Mekhitarist Congregation in Vienna*. Vienna: Mekhitarist Press, 1977.

Carswell, John, and C. J. F. Dowsett. *Kütahya Tiles and Pottery from the Armenian Cathedral of St. James, Jerusalem*. Oxford: Clarendon Press, 1972.

Chanashian, Mesrop. *Armenian Miniature Paintings of the Monastic Library at San Lazzaro*. Venice: Casa editrice armena, 1966.

Der Manuelian, Lucy. *Weavers, Merchants, and Kings: The Inscribed Rugs of Armenia*. Fort Worth, Tex.: Kimbell Art Museum, 1984.

Der Nersessian, Sirarpie. *Armenia and the Byzantine Empire: A Brief Study of Armenian Art and Civilization*. Cambridge, Mass.: Harvard University Press, 1945.

———. *Armenian Art*. London: Thames and Hudson, 1978.

———. *Armenian Manuscripts in the Freer Gallery of Art*. Washington, D.C.: The Freer Gallery, 1963.

———. *Armenian Manuscripts in the Walters Art Gallery*. Baltimore: The Trustees, 1973.

———. *The Chester Beatty Library: A Catalogue of the Armenian Manuscripts with an Introduction on the History of Armenian Art*. Dublin: Hodges Figgis, 1958.

————. *An Introduction to Armenian Manuscript Illumination: Selections from the Collection in the Walters Art Gallery.* Baltimore: The Gallery, 1974.

————. *Manuscrits arméniens illustrés des XIIe, XIIIe, et XIVe siècles de la Bibliothèque des pères Mekhitharistes de Venise.* Paris: E. de Boccard, 1936.

Der Nersessian, Sirarpie, and Sylvia Agémian. *Miniature Painting in the Armenian Kingdom of Cilicia from the Twelfth to the Fourteenth century.* Washington, D.C.: Dumbarton Oaks Research Library and Collection, 1993.

Der Nersessian, Sirarpie, and Arpag Mekhitarian. *Armenian Miniatures from Isfahan.* Brussels: Les Editeurs d'Art Associés Armenian Catholicosate of Cilicia, 1986.

Ghazarian, Manya, and Vazgen Boghossian. *Treasures of Etchmiadzin.* Helsinki: Editions Erebouni, 1984.

Haykents, M. *Simon Samsonian: His World through Paintings.* New York: Armenian General Benevolent Union, 1978.

Karsh, Yousuf. *Karsh: A Fifty Year Retrospective.* Boston: Little, Brown, 1985.

Keusseyan, Krikor. *Carzou, Painter of a Magic World.* Southfield, Michigan: Armenian General Benevolent Union Alex Manoogian Cultural Fund, 1982.

Mathews, Thomas F. *Art and Architecture in Byzantium and Armenia: Liturgical and Exegetical Approaches.* Brookfield, Vt.: Variorum, 1995.

Mathews, Thomas F., and Avedis Krikor Sanjian. *Armenian Gospel Iconography: The Tradition of the Glajor Gospel.* Washington, D.C.: Dumbarton Oaks, 1991.

Mathews, Thomas F., and Roger S. Wieck. *Treasures in Heaven: Armenian Art, Religion, and Society.* New York: Pierpont Morgan Library, 1997.

Mathews, Thomas F., and Roger S. Wieck. *Treasures in Heaven: Armenian Illuminated Manuscripts.* New York: Pierpont Morgan Library; 1994.

Matossian, Nouritza. *Black Angel: A Life of Arshile Gorky.* London: Chatto & Windus, 1998.

Mazmanian, Nazeli Mikaelovna. *The Art Gallery of Armenia.* Leningrad: Aurora Art, 1975.

Mekhitarian, Arpag. *Treasures of the Armenian Patriarchate of Jerusalem.* Jerusalem: Armenian Patriarchate, 1969.

Museum Bochum and Stiftung für Armenische Studien. *Armenien: 5000 Jahre Kunst und Kultur.* Tübingen: E. Wasmuth, 1995.

Narkiss, Bezalel, Michael E. Stone, and Avedis K. Sanjian. *Armenian Art Treasures of Jerusalem.* Jerusalem: Massada Press, 1979.

Nersessian, Vrej Nerses. *Armenian Illuminated Gospel-books.* London: British Library, 1987.

Nersessian, Vrej, and Institute of Armenian Music (London, England). *Essays on Armenian Music.* London: Kahn & Averill, 1978.

Parsegian, Vazken L., Armenian Educational Council, and Inter Documentation Company. *Cumulative index and guide to the Armenian architecture micro-*

form collection, books I–VII: A documented photo-archival collection on microfiche with 42,000 photographs for the study of early- and late-medieval Christian architectural arts of Transcaucasia and the Middle East. Leiden, Netherlands: Inter Documentation, 1990.

Pilikian, Hovhanness I. *Armenian Cinema: A Source Book*. London: Counter-Point, 1981.

Santrot, Jacques, and Rouben S. Badalian. *Arménie: trésors de l'Arménie ancienne: des origines au IVe siècle*. Paris: Somogy and Musée Dobrée, 1996.

Spender, Matthew. *From a High Place: A Life of Arshile Gorky*. New York: Alfred A. Knopf, 1999.

Stepanian, N., and Arutiun Surenovich Chakmakchian. *L'art décoratif de l'Arménie médiévale*. Leningrad: Aurore, 1971.

Stone, Nira. *The Kaffa Lives of the Desert Fathers: A Study in Armenian Manuscript Illumination*. Louvain, Belgium: Peeters, 1997.

Taylor, Alice. *Book Arts of Isfahan: Diversity and Identity in Seventeenth-century Persia*. Malibu, Calif.: J. Paul Getty Museum, 1995.

Thierry, Jean Michel, Patrick Donabédian, and Nicole Thierry. *Les arts arméniens*. Paris: Mazenod, 1987.

Thierry, Nicole. *Les peintures de l'église de la Sainte-Croix d'Aghtamar (915–921)*. Yerevan: ASSR Academy of Sciences Institute of Arts, 1978.

Zekiyan, Levon, Centro studi e documentazione della cultura armena (Milan Italy), Università degli studi di Venezia, and Haykakan SSH Gitutyunneri Akademia. *Atti del Quinto Simposio internazionale di arte armena: Venezia, Milano, Bologna, Firenze: 1988, 28 maggio-5 giugno*. Venice: Tipo-litografia armena, 1991.

Literature

Alishan, Leonardo P. *Essays on Nationalism and Asian Literatures*. Austin: University of Texas, 1987.

Antreassian, Jack Arthur. *Ararat: A Decade of Armenian-American Writing*. New York: Armenian General Benevolent Union of America, 1969.

Baliozian, Ara. *Zohrab: An Introduction*. Kitchener, Ontario: Impressions, 1985.

Bedrosian, Margaret. *The Magical Pine Ring: Culture and the Imagination in Armenian/American Literature*. Detroit, Mich.: Wayne State University Press, 1991.

Callisthenes, Pseudo-. *The Romance of Alexander the Great: An English translation of an Armenian version of The Life of Alexander of Macedon*. Albert Mugrdich Wolohojian, trans. New York: Columbia University Press, 1969.

Downing, Charles. *Armenian Folk-tales and Fables*. London: Oxford University Press, 1972.

Dowsett, Charles. *Sayat-Nova, an 18th-century Troubadour: A Biographical and Literary Study*. Louvain, Belgium: Peeters, 1997.

Etmekjian, James. *The French Influence on the Western Armenian Renaissance, 1843–1915*. New York: Twayne, 1964.

———. *History of Armenian Literature: Fifth to Thirteenth Centuries*. New York: St. Vartan Press, 1985.

Greppin, John A. C. *Studies in Classical Armenian Literature*. Delmar, N.Y.: Caravan Books, 1994.

Hamalian, Leo. *As Others See Us: The Armenian Image in Literature*. New York: Ararat Press, 1980.

Hayrapetean, S. P., and Barlow Der Mugrdechian. *A History of Armenian Literature: From Ancient Times to the Nineteenth Century*. Delmar, N.Y.: Caravan Books, 1995.

Hoogasian-Villa, Susie. *100 Armenian Tales and Their Folkloristic Relevance*. Detroit, Mich.: Wayne State University Press, 1966.

Hovannisian, Richard G. *The Armenian Image in History and Literature*. Malibu, Calif.: Undena Publications, 1981.

Kendall, Bridget, and Robert W. Thomson. *David the Invincible: Definitions and Divisions of Philosophy*. Chico, Calif.: Scholars Press, 1983.

Kherdian, David. *The Road from Home: The Story of an Armenian Girl*. New York: Greenwillow Books, 1979.

Kudian, Mischa. *Three Apples Fell from Heaven: A Collection of Armenian Folk and Fairy Tales*. London: Hart-Davis, 1969.

Oshagan, Vahé. *Armenia*. Review of national literatures, v. 13. New York: Council on National Literatures by Griffon House, 1984.

———. *The English Influence on West Armenian Literature in the Nineteenth Century*. Delmar, N.Y.: Caravan Press, 1982.

Peroomian, Rubina. *Literary Responses to Catastrophe: A Comparison of the Armenian and the Jewish Experience*. Atlanta, Ga.: Scholars Press, 1993.

Russell, James R. *Yovhannes Tlkurantci and the Mediaeval Armenian Lyric Tradition*. Atlanta, Ga.: Scholars Press, 1987.

Sakayan, Dora. *Armenian Proverbs: A Paremiological Study with an Anthology of 2,500 Armenian Folk Sayings*. Delmar, N.Y.: Caravan Books, 1994.

Sanjian, Avedis K. *David Anhaght the "Invincible Philosopher."* Atlanta, Ga.: Scholars Press, 1986.

Sanjian, Avedis K., and Andreas Tietze. *Eremya Chelebi Kömürjian's Armeno-Turkish Poem "The Jewish Bride."* Wiesbaden: Otto Harrassowitz, 1981.

Saroyan, William. *An Armenian Trilogy*. Dickran Kouymjian, ed. Fresno: California State University Press, 1986.

———. *The Daring Young Man on the Flying Trapeze, and Other Stories*. New York: New Directions, 1997.

———. *My Name Is Aram*. New York: Harcourt Brace, 1937.

Shalian, Artin K. *David of Sassoun: The Armenian Folk Epic in Four Cycles*. Athens: Ohio University Press, 1964.

Shirinian, Lorne. *Armenian-North American Literature, A Critical Introduction: Genocide, Diaspora, and Symbols*. Lewiston, N.Y.: E. Mellen Press, 1990.

———. *Armenian-North American Poets: An Anthology*. St. Jean, Quebec: Manna, 1974.

———. *The Republic of Armenia and the Rethinking of the North-American Diaspora in Literature*. Lewiston, N.Y.: E. Mellen Press, 1992.

Surmelian, Leon Z. *Apples of Immortality: Folktales of Armenia*. London: Allen & Unwin, 1968.

———. *I Ask You, Ladies and Gentlemen*. New York: E. P. Dutton, 1945.

———. *Daredevils of Sassoun: The Armenian National Epic*. Denver, Colo.: A. Swallow, 1964.

Tashjian, Virginia A., and Nonny Hogrogian. *Three Apples Fell from Heaven; Armenian Tales Retold*. Boston: Little Brown, 1971.

Terian, Abraham. *Philonis Alexandrini de animalibus: The Armenian text with an introduction, translation, and commentary*. Chico, Calif.: Scholars Press, 1981.

———. *Quaestiones et solutiones in Exodum I et II: e versione armeniaca et fragmenta graeca, edited by Philo*. Paris: Editions du Cerf, 1992.

Ter-Petrossian, Levon. *Ancient Armenian Translations*. New York: St. Vartan Press, 1992.

Ter-Petrossian, Levon, and Bernard Outtier. *Textes arméniens relatifs à S. Ephrem*. Louvain, Belgium: Peeters, 1985.

Thomson, Robert W. *The Armenian Version of the Works Attributed to Dionysius the Areopagite*. Louvain, Belgium: Peeters, 1987.

———. *Indices to the Armenian Version of Pseudo-Dionysius the Areopagite: Greek-Armenian and Armenian-Greek*. Amsterdam: Rodopi, 1997.

———. *Rewriting Caucasian History: The Medieval Armenian Adaptation of the Georgian Chronicles, the Original Georgian Texts and the Armenian Adaptation*. Oxford: Clarendon Press, 1996.

———. *Studies in Armenian Literature and Christianity*. Aldershot, Hampshire, England: Variorum, 1994.

Thomson, Robert W., and Bridget Kendall. *David the Invincible. Definitions and Divisions of Philosophy*. Chico, Calif.: Scholars Press, 1983.

Tolegian, Aram. *David of Sassoun: Armenian Folk Epic*. New York: Bookman Associates, 1961.

Verneuil, Henri. *Mayrik*. New York: Armenian Apostolic Church of America, 1987.

Villa, Susie Hoogasian. *100 Armenian Tales and their Folkloristic Relevance*. Detroit, Mich.: Wayne State University Press, 1966.

Weitenberg, Joseph Johannes Sicco. *Parallel Aligned Text and Bilingual Concordance of the Armenian and Greek Versions of the Book of Jonah*. Atlanta and Amsterdam: Rodopi, 1992.

Weitenberg, Joseph Johannes Sicco, and Henning J. Lehmann. *Armenian Texts: Tasks and Tools*. Aarhus, Denmark: Aarhus University Press, 1993.

Weitenberg, Joseph Johannes Sicco, and Andrea de Leeuw van Weenen. *Lemmatized Index of the Armenian Version of Deuteronomy*. Atlanta, Ga.: Scholars Press, 1990.

Werfel, Franz. *The Forty Days of Musa Dagh*. New York: Viking, 1967.

Literature in Translation

Alishan, Ghevond M. *Armenian Popular Songs*. Venice: S. Lazarus, 1852.

Baronian, Hagop. *The Honorable Beggars: A Comedy in Two Acts*. Jack Antreassian, trans. New York: Ashod Press, 1980.

———. *Honourable Beggars: A Satire*. Mischa Kudian, trans. London: BCM-Mashtots Press, 1978.

Basmadjian, Garig. *Armenian-American Poets: A Bilingual Anthology*. Detroit: Alex Manoogian Cultural Fund of the Armenian General Benevolent Union, 1976.

Blackwell, Alice Stone. *Armenian Poems, Rendered into English Verse*. Delmar, N.Y.: Caravan Books, 1978.

Boyajian, Zabelle C. *Armenian Legends and Poems*. New York: Columbia University Press, 1959.

Der Hovanessian, Diana, trans. *Come Sit Beside Me and Listen to Kouchag: Medieval Armenian Poems of Nahabed Kouchag*. New York: Ashod Press, 1984.

Der Hovanessian, Diana, and Marzbed Margossian. *Anthology of Armenian Poetry*. New York: Columbia University Press, 1978.

Gregory of Narek. *Lamentations of Narek: Mystic Soliloquies with God*. London: Mashtots Press, 1977.

Kudian, Mischa. *The Muse of Sheerak: Selected Works of Avetik Issahakian*. London: Mashtots Press, 1975.

———. *Soviet Armenian Poetry*. London: Mashtots Press, 1974.

Margossian, Marzbed, and Diana Der Hovanessian. *Anthology of Armenian Poetry*. New York: Columbia University Press, 1978.

Shahnour, Shahan. *Retreat without Song*. Mischa Kudian, trans. London: Mashtots Press, 1982.

Shirvanzade. *Evil Spirit, A Play: The Armenian Theater*. New York: St. Vartan Press, 1980.

Tashjian, Virginia A. *Hovhannes Tumanyan. Once There Was and Was Not: Armenian Tales Retold*. Boston: Little Brown, 1966.

Tolegian, Aram. *Armenian Poetry Old and New: A Bilingual Anthology*. Detroit, Mich.: Wayne State University Press, 1979.

Totovents, Vahan. *Jonathan Son of Jeremiah*. Mischa Kudian, trans. London: Mashtots Press, 1985.

———. *The Pigeon Fancier; and, Was It Love?* Mischa Kudian, trans. London: Mashtots Press, 1994.

———. *Scenes from an Armenian Childhood*. London: Oxford University Press, 1962.

———. *Tell Me, Bella: A Selection of Stories*. London: Mashtots Press, 1972.

Toumanian, Hovannes [Tumanyan, Hovhannes]. *Anoush, Gikor and Others: Selected Works of Hovannes Toumanian*. Mischa Kudian, trans. London: Mashtots Press, 1994.

———. *The Bard of Loree: Selected Works of Hovannes Toumanian*. Mischa Kudian, trans. London: Mashtots Press, 1970.

———. *The Hunter's Tale*. Alexander Grigorian, trans. Yerevan: Sovetakan Grogh, 1983.

———. *The Master and the Laborer, Nazar the Brave*. Brian Bean and Mihran Sosoyan, trans. Moscow: Sovetakan Grogh, 1979.

———. *A Selection of Stories, Lyrics, and Epic Poems*. New York, T & T Publishing, 1971.

Tsarukian, Andranik. *Men without Childhood*. New York: Ashod Press, 1985.

Zarian, Gostan. *Bancoop and the Bones of the Mammoth*. New York: Ashod Press, 1982.

———. *The Traveller and His Road*. New York: Ashod Press, 1981.

Zohrab, Krikor. *Voice of Conscience: The Stories of Krikor Zohrab*. New York: St. Vartan Press, 1983.

Language and Linguistics

Adjarian, Herachyah H. *Classification des dialectes arméniens*. Paris: H. Champion, 1909.

Adontz, Nicolas. *Denys de Thrace et ses commentateurs arméniens*. René Hotterbeex, trans. Louvain, Belgium: Imprimerie Orientaliste, 1970.

Bardakjian, Kevok B., and Robert W. Thomson. *Textbook of Modern Western Armenian*. New York: Caravan Books, 1985.

Godel, Robert. *Introduction to the Study of Classical Armenian*. Wiesbaden: Dr. L. Reichert, 1975.

———. *Linguistique arménienne: études diachroniques*. Vaduz, Liechtenstein: Librairie H. Samuel, 1982.

Greppin, John A. C., and Amalya A. Khachaturian. *A Handbook of Armenian Dialectology*. Delmar, N.Y.: Caravan Books, 1986.

Hübschmann, Heinrich. *Armenische Grammatik*. Hildesheim: Georg Olms Verlag, 1972. Reprint.

———. *Die Altarmenischen Ortsnamen. Mit Beiträgen zur historischen Topographie Armeniens*. Amsterdam: Oriental Press, 1969.

Law, Vivien, and I. Sluiter. *Dionysius Thrax and the Techne Grammatike*. Münster, Germany: Nodus Publikationen, 1995.

Leroy, Maurice, and Francine Mawet. *La place de l'arménien dans les langues indo-européennes*. Louvain, Belgium: Peeters, 1986.

Mann, Stuart E. *Armenian and Indo-European: Historical Phonology*. London: Luzac, 1963.

Meillet, Antoine. *Esquisse d'une grammaire comparée de l'arménien classique*. 2nd ed. Vienne: Imprimerie des Pères Mékhitharistes, 1936.

———. *Études de linguistique et de philologie arméniennes*. Lisbon: Imprensa Nacional de Lisboa, 1962.

Riggs, Elias. *A Grammar of the Modern Armenian Language as Spoken in Constantinople and Asia Minor*. 2nd ed. Constantinople: A.B. Churchill, 1856.

———. *Outline of a Grammar of the Turkish Language as Written in the Armenian Character*. Constantinople: A.B. Churchill, 1856.

Samuelian, Thomas J. *A Course in Modern Western Armenian: Exercises and Commentary*. New York: Armenian National Education Committee, 1989.

Thomson, Robert W. *An Introduction to Classical Armenian*. Delmar, N.Y.: Caravan Books, 1975.

Tryjarski, Edward. *Dictionnaire arméno-kiptchak d'après trois manuscrits des collections viennoises*. Warsaw: Pantstwowe Wydawn Naukowe, 1968.

Publishing

Bardakjian, Kevork B. *The Mekhitarist Contributions to Armenian Culture and Scholarship: Notes to Accompany an Exhibit of Armenian Printed Books in the Widener Library, Displayed on the 300th anniversary of Mekhitar of Sebastia, 1676–1976*. Cambridge, Mass.: Harvard College Library, 1976.

Nersessian, Vrej Nerses. *Catalogue of Early Armenian Books, 1512–1850*. London: British Library Department of Oriental Manuscripts and Printed Books and Bodleian Library, 1980.

Kévorkian, Raymond H. *Catalogue des "incunables" arméniens (1511–1695): ou chronique de l'imprimerie arménienne*. Geneva: P. Cramer, 1986.

———. *Les imprimés arméniens des XVIe et XVIIe siècles*. Paris: Bibliotheque nationale, 1987.

———. *Les imprimés arméniens: 1701–1850*. Paris: Bibliothèque nationale, 1989.

SOCIETAL

Church and Religion

Agatangeghos. *The Teaching of Saint Gregory: An Early Armenian Catechism*. Robert W. Thomson, trans. Cambridge, Mass.: Harvard University Press, 1970.

Burchard, Christoph, ed. *Armenia and the Bible: Papers Presented to the International Symposium Held at Heidelberg, July 16–19, 1990*. Atlanta, Ga.: Scholars Press, 1993.

Chopourian, Giragos H. *The Armenian Evangelical Reformation: Causes and Effects*. New York: Armenian Missionary Association of America, 1972.

Conybeare, Frederick Cornwallis. *The Armenian Church Heritage and Identity*. Nerses Vrej Nersessian, comp. New York: St. Vartan Press, 2001.

———. *The Key of Truth: A Manual of the Paulician Church of Armenia*. The Armenian Text Edited and Translated with Illustrative Documents and Introduction by F. C. Conybeare. Oxford: Clarendon Press, 1898.

Cowe, S. Peter. *Mxitar Sasneci's Theological Discourses*. Louvain, Belgium: Peeters, 1993.

Dowsett, Charles J. F. *The Penitential of David of Ganjak*. Louvain, Belgium: Corpus Scriptorum Christianorum Orientalium.

Eznik of Kolb. *A Treatise on God Written in Armenian by Eznik of Kolb (floruit c.430–c.450): An English Translation, with Introduction and Notes*. Monica J. Blanchard and Robin Darling Young, trans. Louvain, Belgium: Peeters, 1998.

Garsoïan, Nina G. *Church and Culture in Early Medieval Armenia*. Variorum collected studies series. Brookfield, Vt.: Ashgate, 1999.

———. *The Paulician Heresy. A Study of the Origin and Development of Paulicianism in Armenia and the Eastern Provinces of the Byzantine Empire*. The Hague: Mouton, 1967.

Ghazarian, Vatche, ed. *The Life and Work of Coadjutor Catholicos Papken Guleserian*. Waltham, Mass.: Mayreni, 2000.

Maksoudian, Krikor H. *Chosen of God: The Election of the Catholicos of All Armenians from the Fourth Century to the Present*. New York: St. Vartan Press, 1995.

Mécérian, Jean. *Histoire et institutions de l'église arménienne; évolution nationale et doctrinale, spiritualité, monachisme*. Beirut: Imprimerie Catholique, 1965.

Megerdichian, Robert. *The Armenian Churches in North America, Apostolic, Protestant and Catholic: A Geographical and Historical Survey*. Cambridge, Mass.: Society for Armenian Studies, 1983.

Nersessian, Vrej. *The Tondrakian Movement: Religious Movements in the Armenian Church from the Fourth to the Tenth Centuries*. London: Kahn & Averill, 1987.

Ormanian, Malachia. *The Church of Armenia: Her History, Doctrine, Rule, Discipline, Liturgy, Literature, and Existing Condition*. G. Marcar Gregory, trans. Derenig Poladian, ed. 2nd ed. London: A.R. Mowbray, 1955.

———. *A Dictionary of the Armenian Church*. Bedros Norehad, trans. New York: St. Vartan Press, 1984.

Petrowicz, Gregorio. *L'unione degli Armeni di Polonia con la Santa Sede (1626–1686)*. Rome: Pontificium Institutum Orientalium Studiorum, 1950.

Runciman, Steven. *The Medieval Manichee: A Study of the Christian Dualist Heresy*. New York: Viking, 1961.

Russell, James R. *Zoroastrianism in Armenia*. Cambridge, Mass.: Harvard University Department of Near Eastern Languages and Civilizations, 1987.

Sarkissian, Karekin. *A Brief Introduction to Armenian Christian Literature*. London: Faith Press, 1960.

———. *The Council of Chalcedon and the Armenian Church*. London: S.P.C.K, 1965.

Stone, Michael E. *Armenian and Biblical Studies*. Jerusalem: St. James Press, 1976.

———. *Armenian Apocrypha Relating to the Patriarchs and Prophets*. Jerusalem: Israel Academy of Sciences and Humanities, 1982.

———. *The Armenian Version of IV Ezra*. Missoula, Mont.: Scholars Press, 1979.

———. *The Armenian Version of the Testament of Joseph: Introduction, Critical Edition, and Translation*. Missoula, Mont.: Scholars Press for the Society of Biblical Literature, 1975.

———. *The Penitence of Adam*. Louvain, Belgium: Peeters, 1981.

———. *Selected Studies in Pseudepigrapha and Apocrypha with Special Reference to the Armenian Tradition*. Leiden: E.J. Brill, 1990.

———. *The Testament of Levi: A First Study of the Armenian MSS. of the Testaments of the XII Patriarchs in the Convent of St. James, Jerusalem*. Jerusalem: St. James Press, 1969.

———. *Texts and Concordances of the Armenian Adam Literature*. Atlanta, Ga.: Scholars Press, 1996.

Taft, Robert F. *The Armenian Christian Tradition: Scholarly Symposium in Honor of the Visit to the Pontifical Oriental Institute, Rome, of His Holiness Karekin I, Supreme Patriarch and Catholicos of all Armenians, December 12, 1996*. Rome: Pontificium Institutum Orientalium Studiorum, 1997.

Tekeyan, Pascal. *Controverses christologiques en Arméno-Cilicie dans la seconde moitié XIIe siècle (1165–1198)*. Rome: Pontificium Institutum Orientalium Studiorum, 1939.

Tekeyan, Vartan. *Le patriarcat Arménien Catholique de Cilicie: au temps de Grégoire Pierre VI (1812–1840)*. Beirut: Imprimerie Catholique, 1954.

Tootikian, Vahan H. *The Armenian Evangelical Church*. Detroit, Mich.: American Heritage Committee, 1982.

Winkler, Gabriele. *Studies in Early Christian Liturgy and its Context: Byzantium, Syria, Armenia*. Aldershot, Hampshire, England: Ashgate, 1997.

Diaspora

Abu Salih. *The Churches and Monasteries of Egypt and Some Neighbouring Countries Attributed to Abû Sâlih, the Armenian*. B. T. A. Evetts, trans. 1st ed., 1895. Oxford: Clarendon Press, 1969.

Arlen, Michael J. *Passage to Ararat*. New York: Farrar Straus & Giroux, 1975.

Avakian, Arra S. *The Armenians in America*. Minneapolis, Minn.: Lerner, 1977.

Azarya, Victor. *The Armenian Quarter of Jerusalem: Urban Life Behind Monastery Walls*. Berkeley, Calif.: University of California Press, 1984.

Bakalian, Anny P. *Armenian-Americans: From Being to Feeling Armenian*. New Brunswick, N.J.: Transaction Books, 1992.

Baladouni, Vahé, and Margaret Makepeace. *Armenian Merchants of the Seventeenth and Early Eighteenth Centuries: English East India Company Sources*. Transactions of the American Philosophical Society, v 88, pt 5. Philadelphia: American Philosophical Society, 1998.

Balakian, Peter. *Black Dog of Fate: A Memoir*. New York: Basic Books, 1997.

Baliozian, Ara. *Fragmented Dreams: Armenians in Diaspora*. Kitchener, Ontario: Impressions, 1987.

Basil, Anne. *Armenian Settlements in India, from the Earliest Times to the Present Day*. Calcutta: Armenian College, 1969.

Bozorgmehr, Mehdi. *Internal Ethnicity: Armenian, Bahai, Jewish, and Muslim Iranians in Los Angeles*. Ann Arbor, Mich.: Diss. UMI, 1994.

Chaquèri, Cosroe. *The Armenians of Iran: The Paradoxical Role of a Minority in a Dominant Culture: Articles and Documents*. Cambridge, Mass.: Harvard University Press, 1998.

Charanis, Peter. *The Armenians in the Byzantine Empire*: Lisbon: Livraria Bertrand, 1963.

Dadoyan, Seta B. *The Fatimid Armenians: Cultural and Political Interaction in the Near East, Islamic History and Civilization*. New York: E.J. Brill, 1997.

Davidian, Nectar. "The Seropians: First Armenian Settlers in Fresno County, California: Recollections of George Seropian (1868–1947)," as related to Nectar Davidian during two interviews on April 23 and May 2, 1945, at his residence in San Francisco, 1965.

Der-Karabetian, Aghop, Armine Proudian Der-Karabetian. *California Armenians: 1981 Survey*. The Armenian Assembly, California Council and Resource Center. La Verne, Calif.: University of La Verne, 1981.

Hamalian, Arpi. *The Armenians: Intermediaries for the European Trading Companies*. Winnipeg: University of Manitoba Department of Anthropology, 1976.

Herzig, Edmund M. *The Armenian Merchants of New Julfa Isfahan: A Study in Pre-modern Asian Trade*. Oxford: University of Oxford, 1991.

Hewins, Ralph. *Mr. Five Per Cent: The Biography of Calouste Gulbenkian*. London: Hutchinson, 1957.

Hintlian, Kevork. *History of the Armenians in the Holy Land*. Jerusalem: St. James Press, 1976.

Hovannisian, Richard G., and David N. Myers, eds. *Enlightenment and Diaspora: The Armenian and Jewish Cases*. Atlanta, Ga.: Scholars Press, 1999.

Lang, David Marshall. *The Armenians: A People in Exile*. London: Unwin Hyman, 1988.

Melkon Rose, John H. *Armenians of Jerusalem: Memories of Life in Palestine*. London: Radcliffe Press, 1993.

Milne, Tom. *Rouben Mamoulian*. Bloomington: Indiana University Press, 1970.

Mirak, Robert. *Torn between Two Lands: Armenians in America, 1890 to World War I*. Cambridge, Mass.: Harvard University Press, 1983.

Oles, Marian. *The Armenian Law in the Polish Kingdom (1356–1519): A Juridical and Historical Study*. Rome: Edizioni Hosianum, 1966.

Pankhurst, Richard. *The History of Ethiopian–Armenian Relations*. Paris: Librairie C. Klincksieck, 1977.

Pattie, Susan Paul. *Faith in History: Armenians Rebuilding Community*. Washington, D.C.: Smithsonian Institution Press, 1997.

Philips, Jenny K. *Symbol, Myth, and Rhetoric: The Politics of Culture in an Armenian American Population*. New York: AMS Press, 1988.

Pilibosian, Khachadoor, and Helene Pilibosian. *They Called Me Mustafa: Memoir of an Immigrant*. Watertown, Mass.: Ohan Press, 1992.

Sabbagh, Rachel. *Armenians in London: A Case-study of the Library Needs of a Small and Scattered Community*. London: Polytechnic of North London School of Librarianship, 1980.

Sanijan, Avedis Krikor. *The Armenian Communities in Syria under Ottoman Dominion*. Cambridge, Mass.: Harvard University Press, 1965.

Schütz, E. *An Armeno-Kipchak Chronicle on the Polish-Turkish Wars in 1620–1621*. Budapest: Akademiai Kiado, 1968.

Stone, Michael E. *The Manuscript Library of the Armenian Patriarchate in Jerusalem*. Jerusalem: St. James Press, 1969.

Tabakian, Eva. *Los armenios en la Argentina*. Buenos Aires: Editorial Contrapunto, 1988.

Talai, Vered Amit. *Armenians in London: The Management of Social Boundaries*. Manchester: Manchester University Press, 1989.

Tekeyan, Harowtiwn. *Controverses christologiques en Arméno-Cilicie dans la seconde moitié du XIIe siècle (1165–1198)*. Rome: Pontificium Institutum Orientalium Studiorum, 1939.

Tioupitch, A., and G. Hotune. *Les édifices arméniens de Kaménets-Podolsk*. Yerevan: ASSR Academy of Sciences Institute of Arts, 1978.

United States. Congress. Senate. Committee on the Judiciary. *Amendment to Refugee Relief Act of 1953. Hearing before the subcommittee, Eighty-fourth Congress, second session, on S. 2248, a bill to amend the Refugee Relief Act of 1953, so as to permit the issuance of visas to 20,000 persons of an Armenian ethnic origin. January 18, 1956*. Washington, D.C.: U.S. Government Printing Office, 1956.

Waldstreicher, David. *The Armenian Americans, Peoples of North America*. New York: Chelsea House, 1989.

Waterfield, Robin Everard. *Christians in Persia: Assyrians, Armenians, Roman Catholics and Protestants*. London: Allen and Unwin, 1973.

Wertsman, Vladimir. *The Armenians in America, 1618–1976: A Chronology and Fact Book*. Dobbs Ferry, N.Y.: Oceana Publications, 1978.

Yartemian, Tachat. *San Lazzaro Island: The Monastic Headquarters of the Mekhitarian Order (Venice)*. Venice: Mekhitarian Publishing House, 1990.

Survivor Accounts

Bedoukian, Kerop. *Some of Us Survived: The Story of an Armenian Boy*. New York: Farrar Straus Giroux, 1979.

Darpasian, Hrach. *Erzurum (Garin), Its Armenian History and Traditions*. New York: Garin Compatriotic Union of the United States, 1975.

Davidson, Khoren K. *Odyssey of an Armenian of Zeitoun*. New York: Vantage Press, 1985.

Dzeron, Manoog B., and Arra S. Avakian. *Village of Parchanj: General History (1600–1937)*. Fresno, Calif.: Panorama West Books, 1984.

Ghazarian, Vatche. *A Village Remembered: The Armenians of Habousi*. Waltham, Mass.: Mayreni, 1997.

Hartunian, Abraham H. *Neither to Laugh nor to Weep: A Memoir of the Armenian Genocide*. Boston: Beacon Press, 1968.

Highgas, Dirouhi Kouymjian. *Refugee Girl*. Watertown, Mass.: Baikar Publications, 1985.

Jernazian, Ephraim K. *Judgment unto Truth: Witnessing the Armenian Genocide*. New Brunswick, N.J.: Transaction Books, 1990.

Ketchian, Bertha Nakshian, and Sonia Ketchian. *In the Shadow of the Fortress: The Genocide Remembered*. Cambridge, Mass.: Zoryan Institute, 1988.

Mardiganian, Aurora, and H. C. Gates. *Ravished Armenia; or, "The auction of souls": The story of Aurora Mardiganian, the Christian Girl Who Survived the Great Massacres*. New York: Kingsfield Press, 1919.

Mardiganian, Aurora, and Anthony Slide. *Ravished Armenia and the Story of Aurora Mardiganian*. Filmmakers series, no. 57. Lanham, Md.: Scarecrow Press, 1997.

Martin, Ramela. *Out of Darkness*. Cambridge, Mass.: Zoryan Institute, 1989.

Minassian, John. *Many Hills Yet to Climb: Memoirs of an Armenian Deportee*. Santa Barbara, Calif.: J. Cook, 1986.

Mugerditchian, Esther. *From Turkish Toils: The Narrative of an Armenian Family's Escape*. New York: G. H. Doran, 1917.

Sakayan, Dora, and Garabed Hatcherian. *An Armenian Doctor in Turkey, Garabed Hatcherian: My Smyrna Ordeal of 1922*. Montreal: Arod Books, 1997.

Shipley, Alice Muggerditchian. *We Walked, Then Ran.* Phoenix, Ariz.: A.M. Shipley, 1983.

Taft, Elise Hagopian. *Rebirth: The Story of an Armenian Girl Who Survived the Genocide and Found Rebirth in America.* Plandome, N.Y.: New Age Publishers, 1981.

Toomajan, Harry J. *Exit from Inferno: The Odyssey of an Armenian American.* Waukegan, Ill.: Trustees of the H. J. Toomajan Estate, 1955.

Topalian, Naomi. *Dust to Destiny.* Watertown, Mass.: Baikar Publications, 1986.

Yervant, John. *Needle, Thread and Button.* Cambridge, Mass.: Zoryan Institute, 1988.

Yessaian, Harry. *Out of Turkey: The Life Story of Donik "Haji Bey" Yessaian.* Dearborn: University of Michigan, The Armenian Research Center, 1994.

Travel Accounts

Baliozian, Ara. *Armenia Observed.* New York: Ararat Press, 1979.

Bryce, James. *Transcaucasia and Ararat: Being Notes of a Vacation Tour in the Autumn of 1876.* London: Macmillan, 1877.

Lynch, H. F. B. *Armenia, Travels and Studies.* London: Longmans Green and Co., 1901.

Marsden, Philip. *The Crossing Place: A Journey among the Armenians.* London: HarperCollins, 1993.

Svajian, Stephen G. *A Trip through Historic Armenia.* New York: Green Hill, 1977.

Walker, Christopher J. *Visions of Ararat: Writings on Armenia.* London and New York: I.B. Tauris, 1997.

POLITICAL

Government

Adalian, Rouben Paul, ed. *Armenia and Karabagh Factbook.* Washington, D.C.: Armenian Assembly of America, 1996.

———. ed. *Armenia Factbook.* Washington, D.C.: Armenian Assembly of America, 1994.

Danopoulos, Constantine P., and Daniel Zirker. *Civil-Military Relations in the Soviet and Yugoslav Successor States.* Boulder, Colo.: Westview Press, 1996.

United States. Congress. Commission on Security and Cooperation in Europe. *Presidential elections and independence referendums in the Baltic States, the Soviet Union and successor states: A compendium of reports, 1991–1992.* Washington, D.C.: The Commission, 1992.

———. Congress. Commission on Security and Cooperation in Europe. *Report of the Helsinki Commission on the U.S. Congressional Delegation visit to Vienna, Latvia, Estonia, Lithuania, Georgia, Armenia, and Moscow (Codel Hoyer)*. Washington, D.C.: Commission on Security and Cooperation in Europe, 1991.

———. Congress. Commission on Security and Cooperation in Europe. *Report on Armenia's parliamentary election and constitutional referendum: July 5, 1995, Yerevan, Armenia*. Washington, D.C.: The Commission, 1995.

———. Congress. Commission on Security and Cooperation in Europe. *Report on Armenia's presidential election March 16 and 30, 1998*. Washington, D.C.: The Commission, 1998.

———. Congress. Commission on Security and Cooperation in Europe. *Report on Armenia's presidential election of September 22, 1996, Yerevan*. Washington, DC: The Commission, 1996.

———. Congress. Commission on Security and Cooperation in Europe. *Report on the Armenian presidential elections, October 16, 1991: Yerevan and Kamo*. Washington, D.C.: Commission on Security and Cooperation in Europe, 1991.

———. Congress. Commission on Security and Cooperation in Europe. *Report on the Helsinki Commission visit to Armenia, Azerbaijan, Tajikistan, Uzbekistan, Kazakhstan, and Ukraine: (Codel DeConcini) April 10–18, 1992*. Washington, D.C.: Commission on Security and Cooperation in Europe, 1992.

Institutions

Bremmer, Ian A., and Ray Taras, eds. *Nation and Politics in the Soviet Successor States*. Cambridge, U.K.: Cambridge University Press, 1993.

Curtis, Glenn E. *Armenia, Azerbaijan, and Georgia, Country Studies*. Area handbook series. Washington, D.C.: Federal Research Division, Library of Congress, 1995.

Dekmejian, R. Hrair, and Angelos Themelis. *Ethnic Lobbies in U.S. Foreign Policy: A Comparative Analysis of the Jewish, Greek, Armenian and Turkish Lobbies*. Athens, Greece: Institute of International Relations, Panteion University of Social and Political Sciences, 1997.

Libaridian, Gerard J. *Armenia at the Crossroads: Democracy and Nationhood in the Post-Soviet Era*. Watertown, Mass.: Blue Crane Books, 1991.

———. *The Challenge of Statehood: Armenian Political Thinking since Independence*. Watertown, Mass.: Blue Crane Books, 1999.

Masih, Joseph R., and Robert O. Krikorian. *Armenia at the Crossroads*: Post-Communist States and Nations, 2. Amsterdam: Harwood Academic Publishers, 1999.

Parrott, Bruce. *State Building and Military Power in Russia and the New States of Eurasia*. Armonk, New York: M.E. Sharpe, 1995.

Issues

Aharonian, Kersam. *A Historical Survey of the Armenian Case*. Watertown, Mass.: Baikar Publications, 1989.

Armenian Center for National and International Studies and Armenian Assembly of America. *Nagorno Karabagh: A White Paper*. Yerevan and Washington, D.C.: Armenian Center for National and International Studies and Armenian Assembly of America, 1997.

Attarian, Varoujan. *Le génocide des Arméniens devant l'ONU, Interventions*. Brussels: Edition Complexe, 1997.

Boyajian, Dickran H. *Armenia: The Case for a Forgotten Genocide*. Westwood, N.J.: Educational Book Crafters, 1972.

Burdett, Anita L. P. *Armenia, Political and Ethnic Boundaries, 1878–1948*. Slough, U.K.: Archive Editions, 1998.

Chaliand, Gérard, and Yves Ternon. *The Armenians, from Genocide to Resistance*. London: Zed Press, 1983.

Chorbajian, Levon, and George Shirinian. *Studies in Comparative Genocide*. New York: St. Martin's Press, 1999.

Dawisha, A. I., and Karen Dawisha. *The Making of Foreign Policy in Russia and the New States of Eurasia: The International Politics of Eurasia*. Armonk, N.Y.: M.E. Sharpe, 1995.

Dawisha, Karen, and Bruce Parrott. *Conflict, Cleavage, and Change in Central Asia and the Caucasus: Democratization and Authoritarianism in Postcommunist Societies*. Cambridge, U.K.: Cambridge University Press, 1997.

Gunter, Michael. *"Pursuing the Just Cause of Their People": A Study of Contemporary Armenian Terrorism*. New York: Greenwood, 1986.

Hovannisian, Richard G. *Remembrance and Denial: The Case of the Armenian Genocide*. Detroit, Mich.: Wayne State University Press, 1998.

Kurz, Anat, and Ariel Merari. *ASALA, Irrational Terror or Political Tool*. Jerusalem and Boulder, Colo: Jaffee Center for Strategic Studies by the Jerusalem Post and Westview Press, 1985.

Libaridian, Gerard J., ed. *The Karabagh File: Documents and Facts on the Region of Mountainous Karabagh, 1918–1988*. Cambridge, Mass.: Zoryan Institute, 1988.

Marashlian, Levon. *Politics and Demography: Armenians, Turks, and Kurds in the Ottoman Empire*. Cambridge, Mass.: Zoryan Institute, 1991.

Melkonian, Monte, and Markar Melkonian. *The Right to Struggle: Selected Writings by Monte Melkonian on the Armenian National Question*. 2nd ed. San Francisco: Sardarabad Collective, 1993.

Minority Rights Group. *The Armenians*. London: Minority Rights Group, 1982.

National Association for Armenian Studies and Research. *Genocide and Human Rights: Lessons from the Armenian Experience*. Belmont, Mass.: Armenian Heritage Press, 1993.

Panico, Christopher. *Azerbaijan: Seven Years of Conflict in Nagorno-Karabakh*. New York: Human Rights Watch, 1994.

Sarkisian, Ervand Kazarovich, Ruben G. Sahakian, and Elisha B. Chrakian. *Vital Issues in Modern Armenian History: A Documented Expose of Misrepresentations in Turkish Historiography*. Watertown, Mass.: Armenian Studies, 1965.

Ternon, Yves. *The Armenian Cause*. Delmar, N.Y.: Caravan Books, 1985.

————. *L'Etat criminel: les génocides au XXe siècle*. Paris: Ed. du Seuil, 1995.

Toloyan, Khachig, ed. *"What Is to Be Asked?"* 2nd ed. Cambridge, Mass.: Zoryan Institute for Contemporary Armenian Research and Documentation, 1986.

Toriguian, Shavarsh. *The Armenian Question and International Law*. 2nd ed. La Verne, Calif.: University of La Verne Press, 1988.

United States. Congress. House. Select Committee on Hunger. *Humanitarian crisis in Armenia: A round table discussion: informal hearing before the Select Committee on Hunger, House of Representatives, One Hundred Third Congress, first session, hearing held in Washington, DC, March 11, 1993*. Washington, D.C.: U.S. Government Printing Office, 1993.

United States. Congress. Senate. Committee on Foreign Relations. *Commemorating the Armenian genocide: report together with additional views (to accompany S. Res. 241)*. Edited by States United, Congress and Senate, *Report/98th Congress, 2d session, Senate; 98–642*. Washington, D.C.: U.S. Government Printing Office, 1984.

United States. Congress. House. Committee on International Relations. *The history of the Armenian genocide: Hearing before the Committee on International Relations, House of Representatives, One Hundred Fourth Congress, second session, May 15, 1996*. Washington, D.C.: U.S. Government Printing Office, 1996.

United States. Congress. House. Committee on Post Office and Civil Service. *National Day of Remembrance of the Armenian genocide of 1915–1923 report together with minority and additional views (to accompany H.J. Res. 132), Report; 100–232*. Washington, D.C.: U.S. Government Printing Office, 1987.

United States Institute of Peace. *Armenia, Azerbaijan and Nagorno Karabakh: State Sovereignty vs. Self-determination*. Washington, D.C.: U.S. Institute of Peace, 1992.

Walker, Christopher J. *Armenia and Karabagh: The Struggle for Unity*. London: Minority Rights Group, 1991.

Zoryan Institute. *Problems of Genocide: Proceedings of the International Conference on "Problems of Genocide," April 21–23, 1995, National Academy of Sciences, Yerevan, Republic of Armenia.* Toronto: Zoryan Institute of Canada, 1997.

ECONOMIC

Gazarian, K., V. Karapetian, and M. Barseghian. *Forest and Forest Products Country Profile: Republic of Armenia.* New York: United Nations Food and Agriculture Organization and Economic Commission for Europe, 1995.

Pastor, Gonzalo C., and Amer Bisat. *Armenia: Reform and Growth in Agriculture.* Washington, D.C.: International Monetary Fund, 1993.

Ter Sabonis-Chafee, Theresa. *Power Politics: National Energy Strategies of the Nuclear Newly Independent States of Armenia, Lithuania and Ukraine.* Atlanta: Emory University, Department of Political Science, 1999.

Ulbricht, Carl. *Armenian Commercial Law: Foreign Investor's Handbook.* Yerevan: C. Ulbricht, 1995.

United States. Congress. House. Committee on International Relations. *Effectiveness of U.S. Assistance Programs in Russia, Ukraine, Armenia, and the Other Newly Independent States Hearing before the Committee, One Hundred Fourth Congress, Second Session, June 13, 1996.* Washington, D.C.: U.S. Government Printing Office, 1996.

Valdivieso, Luis. *Republic of Armenia, Recent Economic Developments.* Washington, D.C.: International Monetary Fund, 1998.

Vodopivec, Milan, and Wayne Vroman. *The Armenian Labor Market in Transition: Issues and Options.* Washington, D.C.: World Bank, Transition and Macro-Adjustment Division Policy Research Department, 1993.

World Bank, and Csaba Csáki. *Armenia: The Challenge of Reform in the Agricultural Sector.* Washington, D.C.: World Bank, 1995.

World Bank. Europe and Central Asia Region. Country Dept. IV. Infrastructure Operations Division. *Armenia, Earthquake Reconstruction Project.* Washington, D.C.: World Bank, 1994.

World Bank. Europe and Central Asia Region. Rural Development and Environment Sector Unit. *Armenia, Title Registration Project.* Washington, D.C.: World Bank, 1998.

About the Author

Rouben Paul Adalian holds a Ph.D. in history from the University of California, Los Angeles, and is a specialist on Armenia and the Caucasus. He is the director of the Armenian National Institute in Washington, D.C., and, among other places, he has taught at George Washington University, Elliott School of International Affairs; Georgetown University, School of Foreign Service; and at Johns Hopkins University, School of Advanced International Studies. He has published numerous works on Armenian intellectual history, the Armenian Diaspora, Armenian foreign policy, and the Armenian Genocide. He is the author of *Armenia and Karabagh Factbook* and associate editor of *Encyclopedia of Genocide*.